Algorithmics
The Spirit of Computing

Algorithmics

The Spirit of Computing

THIRD EDITION

David Harel
The Weizmann Institute

with

Yishai Feldman
The Interdisciplinary Center, Herzliya

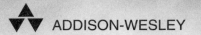
ADDISON-WESLEY

An imprint of **Pearson Education**

Harlow, England • London • New York • Boston • San Francisco • Toronto • Sydney • Singapore • Hong Kong
Tokyo • Seoul • Taipei • New Delhi • Cape Town • Madrid • Mexico City • Amsterdam • Munich • Paris • Milan

Pearson Education Limited
Edinburgh Gate
Harlow
Essex CM20 2JE
England

and Associated Companies throughout the world

Visit us on the World Wide Web at:
www.pearsoned.co.uk

First published 1987
Second edition 1992
Third edition published 2004

ISBN 0 321 11784 0

British Library Cataloguing-in-Publication Data
A catalogue record for this book is available from the British Library.

Library of Congress Cataloging-in-Publication Data
Harel, David, 1950–
     Algorithmics : the spirit of computing / David Harel, with Yishai Feldman.–3rd ed.
          p. cm.
     Includes bibliographical references and index.
     ISBN 0-321-11784-0
     1. Computer algorithms.   I. Feldman, Yishai A., 1958–   II. Title.

     QA76.9.A43H37   2004
     005.1–dc22   2004041063

10 9 8 7 6 5 4 3 2 1
08 07 06 05 04

Typeset by 59 in 10/12pt Times
Printed and bound in Great Britain by Biddles Ltd., Guildford and King's Lynn

For my dear mother, Joyce Fisch
And in memory of my dear father, Harold Fisch
Beloved parents and gifted teachers both

(D.H.)

To the memory of my dear parents,
Hadassa and Moshe Feldman
For their unfailing love and support

(Y.F.)

Tell me, I pray thee,
in what thy great strength lies

Judges 16: 6

Behold, this I have found . . .
counting one thing to another, to find out the sum

Ecclesiastes 7: 27

Contents

*Declare the things
that are to come
hereafter*

Isaiah 41: 23

Preface

Read this, I pray thee

Isaiah 29: 12

(written for the First Edition)

This book tells a story. The story concerns the concepts, ideas, methods, and results fundamental to computer science. It is not specifically about computer technology, nor is it about computer programming, though obviously it is heavily influenced by both.

The book is intended to fill a rather disturbing gap in the literature related to the computer revolution. Scores of excellent books can be found on computers themselves, with details of their structure, workings, and operation. There are also numerous books about the act of writing programs for computers in any of a growing number of languages. These books come at a wide range of levels, some aimed at people with no computer-related background at all, and some aimed at the most computer-literate professionals. In addition, there are many books on subjects peripheral to the technology, such as the social and legal aspects of the revolution, as well as books describing the relevance of computers to a variety of application areas. All this comes as no surprise. People are curious about computers, and want to learn how to put them to use. They are typically interested in specific kinds of computers, and often for specific purposes, too.

Then there are textbooks. Indeed, computer science is a fast-growing academic discipline, with ever-larger numbers of potential students knocking at the doors of admission offices. Well-established academic disciplines have a habit of yielding excellent textbooks, and computer science is no exception. Over the years many comprehensive and clearly written textbooks have appeared, containing detailed technical accounts of the subjects deemed appropriate to students of computer science. However, despite the dizzying speed with which some of the *technological* innovations become obsolete and are replaced by new ones, the fundamentals of the *science* of computation, and hence many of the basic concepts that are considered important in a computer science curriculum, change slowly, if at all. Of course, new technologies and new languages require revisions in scientific emphasis, which are eventually reflected in the scientific literature. However, by and large, there is almost universal agreement on a core of fundamental topics that computer science students should be taught.

It would appear that anyone associated with computers ought to be aware of these topics, and not only those who have decided to spend three or four years getting a particular kind of academic diploma. Moreover, given that a revolution is indeed taking place before our very eyes, many of these topics, and the special ways of thinking that go with them, ought to be available to the enquiring person even if that person is not directly associated with a computer at all.

Books concerned primarily with computers or programming are intended to fulfill quite different needs. Computers are made of bits and bytes, and programming is carried out using languages with rigid rules of grammar and punctuation. Consequently, computer books often suffer from the "bit/byte syndrome" and programming books from the "semicolon syndrome." In other words, the reader becomes predominantly involved in the principles of a particular computer or the syntactic rules of a particular programming language (or both). It would seem that things cannot be explained without first describing, in detail, either a machine or a medium for communicating with one (or both).

Many advanced textbooks *do* treat the fundamentals, but by their very nature they concentrate on specific topics, and do so at an advanced technical level that is usually unsuitable for the general reader. Even professional programmers and systems analysts might lack the background or motivation required to get through books aimed at full-time computer science students.

Curiously, there appears to be very little written material devoted to the *science* of computing and aimed at the technically-oriented general reader as well as the computer professional. This fact is doubly curious in view of the abundance of precisely this kind of literature in most other scientific areas, such as physics, biology, chemistry, and mathematics, not to mention humanities and the arts. There appears to be an acute need for a technically-detailed, expository account of the fundamentals of computer science; one that suffers as little as possible from the bit/byte or semicolon syndromes and their derivatives, one that transcends the technological and linguistic whirlpool of specifics, and one that is useful both to a sophisticated layperson and to a computer expert. It seems that we have all been too busy with the revolution to be bothered with satisfying such a need.

This book is an attempt in this direction. Its objective is to present a readable account of some of the most important and basic topics of computer science, stressing the fundamental and robust nature of the science in a form that is virtually independent of the details of specific computers, languages, and formalisms.

This book grew out of a series of lectures given by the first author on "Galei Zahal," one of Israel's national radio channels, between October 1984 and January 1985. It is about what shall be called **algorithmics** in this book, that is, the study of algorithms. An algorithm is an abstract recipe, prescribing a process that might be carried out by a human, by a computer, or by other means. It thus represents a very general concept, with numerous applications. Its principal interest and use, however, is in those areas where the process is to be carried out by a computer.

The book could be used as the basis of a one-semester introductory course in computer science or a general computer science literacy course in science and engineering schools. Moreover, it can be used as supplementary reading in many kinds of computer-related educational activities, from basic programming courses to advanced graduate or undergraduate degree programs in computer science. The material covered herein, while not directly aimed at producing better programmers or system analysts, can aid people who work with computers by providing an overall picture of some of the most fundamental issues relevant to their work.

The preliminary chapters discuss the concept of an **algorithmic problem** and the **algorithm** that solves it, followed by cursory discussions of the **structure** of algorithms, the **data** they manipulate, and the **languages** in which they are programmed. With the stage thus set, Part Two of the book turns to some general **methods** and paradigms for algorithmic design. This is followed by two chapters on the **analysis** of algorithms, treating, respectively, their **correctness** and **efficiency** (mainly time efficiency), including techniques for establishing the former and estimating the latter. Part Three of the book is devoted to the **inherent limitations** of effectively executable algorithms, and hence of the computers that implement them. Certain precisely defined problems, including important and practical ones, are shown to be *provably* not solvable by any computers of reasonable size in any reasonable amount of time (say, the lifetime of a person), and never will be. Worse still, it is shown that some problems are provably not solvable by computers at all, even with unlimited time! In Part Four of the book[1] the requirements are relaxed, for example, by employing **concurrent** activities or **coin tossing**, in order to overcome some of these difficulties. These chapters also discuss reactive and distributed systems, and cryptography. Finally, the relationship of computers to **human intelligence** is discussed, emphasizing the "soft" heuristic, or intuitive, nature of the latter, and the problems involved in relating it to the "hard" scientific subject of algorithmics.

The book is intended to be read or studied sequentially, not to be used as a reference. It is organized so that each chapter depends on the previous ones, but with smooth readability in mind. Most of the material in the preliminary Part One should be familiar to people with a background in programming. Thus, Chapters 1 and 2 and parts of Chapter 3 can be browsed through by such readers.

Certain sections contain relatively technical material and can be skipped by the reader without too much loss of continuity. They are indented, set in smaller type and are prefixed by a small square. It is recommended, however, that even those sections be skimmed, at least to get a superficial idea of their contents.

Whenever appropriate, brief discussions of the research topics that are of current interest to computer scientists are included. The text is followed by a section of detailed bibliographic notes for each chapter, with "backward" pointers connecting the discussions in the text with the relevant literature.

---

[1] See the section below, "New to the third edition," as there is now a fifth Part and the division is somewhat different.

It is hoped that this book will facilitate communication between the various groups of people who are actively involved in the computer revolution, and between that group, and those who, for the time being, are observers only.

David Harel
Pittsburgh, Pennsylvania   February, 1987

New to the Second Edition

See, this is new; but it has already been
ECCLESIASTES 1: 10

The first edition of this book was intended to be read from beginning to end, and could be used as supplementary reading in a number of courses. Teaching a course based exclusively on it was possible, but would have required the instructor to prepare exercises and add examples and more detail in certain places. The present edition contains numerous exercises, as well as solutions to about a third of them. The solved exercises can thus be used to supplement the text. Three chapters have not been supplied with exercises. Chapter 1 is an introduction, the bulk of Chapter 3 is really just a brief survey of several programming languages, and Chapter 12 is a nontechnical account of some topics in artificial intelligence.[2] In a sense, the three are not integral parts of the topic of the book—algorithmics—and hence in teaching a course based on the book these should probably be assigned as homework reading.

The text itself remains largely without change, except for a new section in Chapter 11 describing the recent topics of interactive proofs and zero-knowledge. The reader may wonder why a more extensive revision of the text was not called for. Have computer scientists been idle during the five years since the first edition was written? Rather than taking this as a criticism of the field, I think that it shows that the topics selected for inclusion in the book are really of fundamental nature, so that no significant changes had to be made. The issues discussed herein are thus probably basic and lasting. Maybe the term "classical" is most fitting.

David Harel
Rehovot, Israel   May, 1991

New to the Third Edition

they three were of one measure
EZEKIEL 40: 10

This time around, a significant revision was carried out. There are several important changes in this edition of the book, compared to the first and second editions, including two brand new chapters, new sections, and more.

---

[2] Again, see the section below, "New to the third edition," as some of these chapter numbers have changed.

The first noticeable difference is that for this revision I needed real help..., and was fortunately joined by Yishai Feldman. He has taken part in all aspects of the revision, but most significantly took upon himself the thorough revision of the material on programming languages and the writing of the new chapter on software engineering.

The main changes are as follows:

The book now has five Parts, rather than four. In Part I (**Preliminaries**) Chapter 3 has been completely rewritten, and is now titled "Programming Languages and Paradigms." The list of languages discussed has been revised and is organized into paradigms, thus giving a more informative and updated exposition of the media we use when we program computers. Discussions of some languages (e.g., APL and SNOBOL) have been dropped altogether and those of others (e.g., C, C++ and JAVA) have been added.

Part II (**Methods and Analysis**) and Part III (**Limitations and Robustness**), i.e., Chapters 4 through 9, required no sweeping changes. This can again be attributed to the "classical" nature of the topics chosen for these, as mentioned in the "New to the second edition" section above.

The first chapter of Part IV (**Relaxing the Rules**) was previously titled "Parallelism and Concurrency" and is now called "Parallelism, Concurrency, and Alternative Models." It incorporates new sections on quantum computing, including Shor's factoring algorithm, and a discussion of molecular computing. These topics may be considered to be additional forms of parallelism, albeit more radical ones. The remaining two chapters of Part IV were constructed by separating out the material on probabilistic algorithms (Chapter 11) from that on cryptography (now Chapter 12)—presented together in a single chapter in the previous editions—and extending both by discussions of some of the new developments in these fields.

Part V (**The Bigger Picture**) ends with the closing chapter of the previous editions, "Algorithmics and Intelligence," which is now Chapter 15. However, this is now preceded by two new chapters: Chapter 13, "Software Engineering," and Chapter 14, "Reactive Systems." The first of these is an attempt to provide a general introduction to the issues and problems arising in the development of large software systems. The second new chapter zeros in on the particular difficulties arising in the special case of reactive systems, as a result of their complex behavior over time.

Besides these more noticeable changes, the entire text has been brought up to date in many less subtle and more subtle ways. There are discussions on abstract data types, on the nonapproximability of certain NP-complete problems, on probabilistically checkable proofs, and on the brand new AKS polynomial-time algorithm for primality. The final chapter has been modified in many places too, e.g., with a discussion added on the Chinese room argument.

While we have left the exercises and solutions essentially as they were in the second edition, the bibliographic notes were a completely different story. Twelve years in Computer Science is almost an eternity... The format of the notes is the same as in the previous editions; i.e., a general section at the start of each chapter, which lists relevant books and periodicals, followed by detailed notes that progress with the text of the chapter itself and point back to its page numbers. In revising them, we had to prepare new notes for the large amount of newly added material, of course, but we also had to painstakingly reconsider and thoroughly revise the entire set of existing notes. Hopefully, the result of all of this will turn out to be a useful and up-to-date tool linking the text of this expository book with the accepted archival scientific literature.

Now that the revision is done, if hard-pressed to give my list of the most significant developments in pure, "classical" algorithmics (i.e., excluding software and systems engineering) in the last dozen or so years, it would probably contain three: the non-approximability results for NP-complete problems, Shor's quantum polynomial time factoring algorithm, and the AKS polynomial-time primality test. And all I can say about these is this: wouldn't it be wonderful if the bulk of the work on the next edition of this book—if and when, of course—will be spent on results of similar caliber and importance.

David Harel
Rehovot, Israel   August, 2003

a threefold cord is not quickly broken

ECCLESIASTES 4: 12

Write the vision, and make it plain upon tablets,
that he who reads it may run

HABAKKUK 2: 2

Acknowledgments

Therefore will I give thanks to thee

PSALM 18: 50

First thanks go to my home institution, the Weizmann Institute of Science, for providing the ideal supportive and encouraging environment for this kind of endeavor.

My deepest gratitude goes to Yishai Feldman (who was my very first PhD student many years ago, and) who graciously agreed to join me in the preparation of this, the third, edition. I am grateful for the time, energy, and talent he put into this project. There is absolutely no way the revision would have been carried out without him.

Parts of the original edition of the book were written while I was visiting Digital Equipment Corporation's Systems Research Center in Palo Alto, California, in the summer of 1985 and Carnegie-Mellon University's Computer Science Department for the 1986/7 academic year. I would like to express my deepest gratitude for these opportunities to work on the book undisturbed. Later visits to Cornell University, Bell Labs, NASA, and Lucent Technologies provided time to work on some of the revisions for the second and third editions.

The late T. Yuval, Managing Editor of the Broadcast University programs on the Israeli radio channel "Galei Zahal," deserves special thanks for convincing me to prepare the 1983–4 lecture series out of which the original version of this book later grew.

I am indebted to my colleagues at the Weizmann Institute, A. Pnueli, A. Shamir, and S. Ullman, for discussions related to the material appearing herein. It is amazing how one's whole approach can benefit from being surrounded by researchers of such caliber.

A very special thanks goes to R. Rosner, who co-authored the exercises and solutions, which first appeared as part of the second edition, and to Eyal Mashiah for his help in preparing the index for the present edition.

I am grateful to the many people who read parts of the original 1987 manuscript or later editions, identified errors, made bibliographic suggestions, or provided helpful and insightful feedback. They include: S. Banerjee, M. Ben-Ari, H. Berliner, S. D. Brookes, A. K. Chandra, N. Dershowitz, R. Fagin, A. Fiat, J. Gal-Ezer, A. Heydon, C. A. R. Hoare, L. Kari, D. E. Knuth, Q. Limmois, W. Pollock, R. Raz, Z. Reisel, E. Roberts, R. Rosner, S. Safra, J. Seiferas, D. Sherman, R. Sherman, B. Simons, D. Sleator, R. Topor, D. Tygar, M. Vardi, P. Wegner, and L. Zuck.

D.H.

PART I

Preliminaries

Now, these are the foundations

II CHRONICLES 3: 3

C H A P T E R   1

Introduction and Historical Review

or, What's It All About?

Computers are amazing machines. They seem to be able to do anything. They fly aircraft and spaceships, and control power stations and hazardous chemical plants. Companies can no longer be run without them, and a growing number of sophisticated medical procedures cannot be performed in their absence. They serve lawyers and judges who seek judicial precedents in scores of documented trials, and help scientists in performing immensely complicated and involved mathematical computations. They route and control millions of telephone calls in networks that span continents. They execute tasks with enormous precision—from map reading and typesetting to graphical picture processing and integrated circuit design. They can relieve us of many boring chores, such as keeping a meticulous track of home expenses, and at the same time provide us with diverse entertainment such as computer games or computerized music. Moreover, the computers of today are hard at work helping design the even more powerful computers of tomorrow.

It is all the more remarkable, therefore, that the digital computer—even the most modern and complex one—can be thought of as merely a large collection of switches. These switches, or **bits** as they are called, are not "flipped" by the user, but are special, internal switches that are "flipped" by the computer itself. Each bit can be in one of two positions, or, to put it another way, can take on one of two **values**, 0 or 1. Typically, the value of a bit is determined by some electronic characteristic, such as whether a certain point has a positive or a negative charge.

A computer can directly execute only a small number of extremely trivial operations, like flipping, zeroing, or testing a bit. Flipping changes the bit's value, zeroing makes sure that the bit ends up in the 0 position, and testing does one thing if the bit is already in the 0 position, and another if it is not (see Figure 1.1).

Computers may differ in size (according to the number of available bits), in the types of elementary operations they can perform, in the speed in which these operations are performed, in the physical media that embody the bits and their internal organization, and, significantly, in their external environment. This last item means that two computers, which are otherwise similar in function, might seem very

Figure 1.1

Operations on bits.

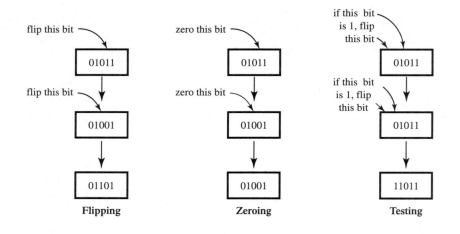

<table>
<tr><td>flip this bit ⟶</td><td>zero this bit ⟶</td><td>if this bit is 1, flip this bit ⟶</td></tr>
</table>

Flipping   Zeroing   Testing

different to an observer: one might resemble a television set with a keyboard, while the other might be buried under the dials and knobs of an automatic knitting machine. However, the outward appearance is of peripheral importance when compared to the bits and their internal arrangement. It is the bits that "sense" the external stimuli arriving from the outside world via buttons, levers, keys on a keyboard, electronic communication lines, and even microphones and cameras. It is the bits that "decide" how to react to these stimuli and respond accordingly by directing other stimuli to the outside via displays, screens, printers, loudspeakers, beepers, levers, and cranks.

How do the computers do it? What is it that transforms such trivial operations on bits into the incredible feats we see computers perform? The answer lies in the central concepts of this book: the **process**, and the **algorithm** that prescribes it and causes it to take place.

Some Gastronomy

Imagine a kitchen, containing a supply of ingredients, an array of baking utensils, an oven, and a (human) baker. Baking a delicious raisin cake is a process that is carried out from the ingredients, by the baker, with the aid of the oven, and, most significantly, according to the recipe. The ingredients are the **inputs** to the process, the cake is its **output**, and the recipe is the **algorithm**. In other words, the algorithm prescribes the activities that constitute the process. The recipes, or algorithms, relevant to a set of processes under discussion are generally called **software**, whereas utensils and oven represent what is generally known as **hardware**. The baker, in this case, can be considered a part of the hardware (see Figure 1.2).

As in the case of bit operations, the baker/oven/utensils constellation has very limited direct abilities. This cake-baking hardware can pour, mix, spread, drip, light the oven, open the oven door, measure time, or measure quantities but cannot directly bake cakes. It is the recipes—those magical prescriptions that convert the limited abilities of kitchen hardware into cakes—and not ovens or bakers, that are the subject of this book.

Figure 1.2

Baking a cake.

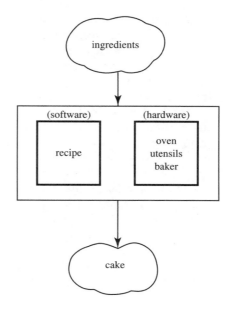

Recipes, as just mentioned, are called algorithms here, while the area of human study, knowledge, and expertise that concerns algorithms will be termed **algorithmics** in this book. The analogy drawn here has been made as exact as possible: the recipe, which is in a sense an abstract entity, is the algorithm; the formal written version of the recipe, such as the one found in a cookbook, is analogous to a computer **program**. Software actually refers more to programs—precise representations of algorithms written in special computer-readable languages—than to the algorithms themselves. However, until we discuss programming languages in Chapter 3, this distinction is quite immaterial.

We confront algorithms wherever we go. Many everyday processes are governed by algorithms: changing a flat tire, constructing a do-it-yourself cabinet, knitting a sweater, dividing numbers, looking up a telephone number, updating a list of expenses, or filling out an income tax form. Some of these (division, for example) might be more immediately related in our minds to computers, than others (cabinet construction, for example), but this is of less concern to us here. Although computers are fundamental to the topic of this book, we shall not concentrate on their physical aspects at all, except implicitly in parts of Chapters 3 and 9. It is with their spirit that we are concerned; with the recipes that make them tick—with their algorithms.

Algorithmics vs. Computer Science

Algorithmics is more than a branch of computer science. It is the core of computer science, and, in all fairness, can be said to be relevant to most of science, business, and technology. The very nature of algorithmics renders it particularly applicable to those disciplines that benefit from the use of computers, and these are fast becoming an overwhelming majority.

People have been known to ask: "What really *is* computer science? Why don't we have submarine science, dishwasher science, or telephone science?" Telephones and dishwashers, it might be argued, are as important to modern life as computers are; perhaps more so. A slightly more focussed question is whether computer science is subsumed by such classical disciplines as mathematics, physics, neuro-science, electrical engineering, linguistics, logic, and philosophy.

This book does not attempt to answer these questions. It is hoped, however, that the book will implicitly convey something of the uniqueness and universality of algorithmics, and hence something of the importance of computer science as an autonomous—albeit, young—field of study. Since computers could conceivably restrict the generality of algorithmics, some people view the unavoidable link between the two as unfortunate. In fact, terming the field "computer science," someone once said, is like referring to surgery as "knife science." Be that as it may, it is clear that algorithmics would never have developed the way it has without that link. However, it is generally agreed that the term "computer science" is misleading, and that something like "information science," "process science," or "the science of the discrete" might be better. Again, we only claim that our subject matter, algorithmics, forms the underpinnings of computer science, not that it replaces it.

Some of the topics we discuss in the sequel, such as the existence of problems that computers *cannot* solve, have philosophical implications, not only on the limits of the wonderful machines we are able to build, but also on our own limits as mortals with finite mass and a finite life span. The profound nature of such implications notwithstanding, the emphasis in this book is on the more pragmatic goal of acquiring a deep understanding of the fundamentals of machine-executable processes, and the recipes, or algorithms, that govern them.

■ ■

■ Some History

Let us now review several important milestones in the development of computers and computer science, mainly to illustrate that as an orderly scientific discipline the field is extremely young.

Somewhere between 400 and 300 B.C., the great Greek mathematician Euclid invented an algorithm for finding the greatest common divisor (gcd) of two positive integers. The gcd of X and Y is the largest integer that exactly divides both X and Y. For example, the gcd of 80 and 32 is 16. The details of the algorithm itself are of no concern here, but the **Euclidian algorithm**, as it is called, is considered to be the first non-trivial algorithm ever devised.

The word *algorithm* is derived from the name of the Persian mathematician Mohammed al-Khowârizmî, who lived during the ninth century, and who is credited with providing the step-by-step rules for adding, subtracting, multiplying, and dividing ordinary decimal numbers. When written in Latin, the name became Algorismus, from which *algorithm* is but a small step. Clearly, Euclid and al-Khowârizmî were algorithmicians *par excellence*.

Turning from software to hardware, one of the earliest machines to carry out a process controlled by what might be called an algorithm was a weaving loom invented in 1801 by a Frenchman, Joseph Jacquard. The pattern woven was determined by cards with holes punched at various locations. These holes, which were sensed by a special mechanism, controlled the selection of threads and other actions of the machine. It is interesting that Jacquard's loom had nothing to do with the narrow numerical connotation of the term "computation."

One of the most important and colorful figures in the history of computer science was Charles Babbage. This English mathematician, after having partially built a machine in 1833, called "the difference engine," for evaluating certain mathematical formulas, conceived and planned a remarkable machine that he called "the analytical engine." In contrast to the difference engine, which was designed to carry out a specific task, the analytical engine was to have been capable of executing algorithms, or programs, encoded by the user as holes punched in cards. Had the analytical engine been built, it would have been the mathematical analogue of Jacquard's loom, which was in fact its inspiration. Needless to say, Babbage's machine was mechanical in nature, based on levers, cogs, and gears, rather than on electronics and silicon. Nevertheless, the ideas present in his design of the analytical engine form the basis of the internal structure and workings of today's computers. Babbage is generally considered to have lived well ahead of his time, and his ideas were not really appreciated until much later.

Ada Byron, Countess of Lovelace, was Babbage's programmer. She is one of the most interesting figures in the history of computing, and is credited with laying the foundations for programming, more than a hundred years before the first working computer was available.

An American engineer by the name of Herman Hollerith invented a machine, also based on punched cards, that was used by the American Census Bureau to help tabulate the 1890 national census. However, the first general-purpose computers were built only in the 1940s, partly as a response to the computational needs of physicists and astronomers, and partly as a natural outgrowth of the availability of the appropriate electromechanical and electronic devices. Ironically, the Second World War, with its bomb-building and code-cracking activities, also helped. Some of the key figures in this crucial and exciting period were the Englishman Alan Turing, the Americans Howard Aiken, John Mauchly, J. Presper Eckert, and Herman Goldstine, and the famous German/American mathematician John von Neumann.

Returning to software and algorithmics, the mid-1930s witnessed some of the most fundamental work on the theory of algorithms, yielding results that concern the capabilities and limitations of machine-executable algorithms. It is remarkable that this work, parts of which will be described later in the book, predated the actual materialization of the computer. Nevertheless, it is of universal and lasting importance. Some of the key figures here, all mathematicians, are, again, Alan Turing, the German Kurt Gödel, the Russian Andreĭ A. Markov, and the Americans Alonzo Church, Emil Post, and Stephen Kleene.

The 1950s and 1960s witnessed far-reaching and rapid technological advancements in computer design and construction. This can be attributed to the arrival of the era of nuclear research and space exploration on the one hand, and to the boom in large businesses and banks, and diverse government activity on the other. Precise prediction of various nuclear phenomena required very heavy computing power, as did the planning and simulation of space missions. Space exploration also required advances in computer-supported communication, facilitating reliable analysis and filtering, and even improvement of data that was communicated to and from satellites and spaceships. Business, banking, and government activity required computers to help in the storage, manipulation, and retrieval of information concerning very large numbers of people, inventory items, fiscal details, and so on.

Interesting evidence of the importance of the technological machine-oriented developments during that period can be found in the names of the world's largest computer company, IBM, and one of the world's largest computer-related professional organizations, the ACM. The former name was coined around 1920 and the latter around the late 1940s. In both cases the "M" comes from the word "machine": International Business Machines, and the Association for Computing Machinery. (IBM evolved from a company formed in 1896 by the aforementioned Herman Hollerith to produce his tabulating machines.)

The recognition of computer science as an independent academic discipline occurred around the mid-1960s, when several universities formed computer science departments. In 1968, the ACM published a widely acclaimed recommendation for a curriculum of courses in computer science, which forms the basis of most current computer science programs of study at the undergraduate level. This curriculum is revised periodically. Today, almost every academic institution has a department of computer science, or a computer science group within its mathematics or electrical engineering departments. The 1960s showed a renewed interest in the 1930s work on algorithmics, and the field has been the subject of extensive and far-reaching research ever since.

We shall not dwell any further on the present technological situation: computers are simply everywhere. We use them to surf the internet, which means that we use them to receive and deliver information, to read, to hear, and to see, and, of course, to browse and buy. There are desktop, laptop, and palm-sized computers, so we need never be without one, and the fast-closing gap between cellular phones and computers is heralding the age of wearable computers. Almost every modern appliance is controlled by a computer, and a single modern car, for example, contains dozens of them. Children request, and get, personal computers for their birthdays; students of computer science in most universities are required to have their own computers for homework assignments; and there is no industrial, scientific, or commercial activity that is not crucially assisted by computers.

▓ A Strange Dichotomy

Despite all of this (or possibly as a result of it) the general public is strangely divided when it comes to computer literacy. There are still those who know absolutely nothing about computers, and then there are the members of the ever-growing class of computer literates. Starting with the 10-year-old owners of personal computers, this expanding group of people who use computers on a day-to-day basis includes managers, engineers, bankers, technicians, and, of course, professional programmers, system analysts, and members of the computer industry itself.

Why is this strange? Well, here is a science about which some people know nothing, but about which a rapidly increasing number of people apparently know everything! As it happens, however, the really unusual phenomenon is that large and important parts of the *science* of computing are not sufficiently known, not only to members of the first group, but to members of the second group as well.

It is one of the purposes of this book to try to illuminate an important facet of the computer revolution by presenting some of the fundamental concepts, results, and trends underlying the *science* of computation. It is aimed at both the novice and the expert. A reader with no knowledge of computers will (it is hoped) learn about their "spirit" here, and the kind of thinking that goes into making them work while seeking elsewhere material concerning their "flesh." The computer-knowledgeable reader, who might find the first couple of chapters rather slow going, will (it is hoped) be able to learn much from the later ones.

Some Limitations of Computers

Before embarking on our tour, let us contrast the opening paragraph of this chapter with some feats that current computers are as yet incapable of performing. We shall return to these contrasts in the final chapter of the book, which deals with the relationship between computers and human intelligence.

Currently, computers are capable of on-the-spot analysis of an enormous quantity of data resulting from many X-ray pictures of a human patient's brain, taken from gradually increasing angles. The analyzed data is then used by the computer to generate a cross-cut picture of the brain, providing information about the brain's tissue structure, thus enabling precise location of such irregularities as tumors or excess fluids. In striking contrast, no currently available computer can analyze a single, ordinary picture of the very same patient's face and determine the patient's age with an error margin of, say, five years. However, most 12-year-old kids can! Even more striking is the ability of a one-year-old baby to recognize its mother's face in a photograph it has never before seen, a feat computers are nowhere near imitating (and this is not merely because they have no mothers . . .).

Computers are capable of controlling, in the most precise and efficient way imaginable, extremely sophisticated industrial robots used to construct complex pieces of machinery consisting of hundreds of components. In contrast, today's most advanced computers are incapable of directing a robot to construct a bird's nest from a pile of twigs, a feat any 12-month-old bird can perform!

Today's computers can play chess on the level of an international grand-master, and hence can beat the vast majority of human players. However, on changing the rules of the game very slightly (for example, by allowing a knight two moves at a time, or by limiting the queen's moves to five squares), the best of these computers will not be able to adapt without being reprogrammed or reconstructed by humans. In contrast, a 12-year-old amateur chess player will be able to play a reasonably good game with the new rules in a very short time, and will become better and better with experience.

As mentioned, these dissimilarities are related to the difference between human and computerized intelligence. We shall be in a better position to discuss these matters further in Chapter 15, after having learnt more about algorithms and their properties.

■ A Recipe

Here is a recipe for chocolate mousse, taken from Sinclair and Malinowski's *French Cooking* (Weathervane Books, 1978, p. 73). The ingredients—that is, the inputs—include 8 ounces of semisweet chocolate pieces, 2 tablespoons of water, a $\frac{1}{4}$ cup of powdered sugar, 6 separated eggs, and so on. The outputs are six to eight servings of delicious *mousseline au chocolat*. Here is the recipe, or the algorithm for it.

> *Melt chocolate and 2 tablespoons water in double boiler. When melted, stir in powdered sugar; add butter bit by bit. Set aside. Beat egg yolks until thick and lemon-colored, about 5 minutes. Gently fold in chocolate. Reheat slightly to melt chocolate, if necessary. Stir in rum and vanilla. Beat egg whites until foamy. Beat in 2 tablespoons sugar; beat until stiff peaks form. Gently fold whites into chocolate-yolk mixture. Pour into individual serving dishes. Chill at least 4 hours. Serve with whipped cream, if desired. Makes 6 to 8 servings.*

This is the "software" relevant to the preparation of the mousse; this is the algorithm that controls the process of producing mousse from the ingredients. The process itself is carried out by the "hardware," in this case the person preparing the mousse, together with the various utensils: the double boiler, the heating apparatus, beater, spoons, timer, and so on.

■ Levels of Detail

Let us take a closer look at the most elementary instructions present in this recipe. Consider the instruction "stir in powdered sugar." Why does the recipe not say "take a little powdered sugar, pour it into the melted chocolate, stir it in, take a little more, pour, stir, . . .?" Even more specifically, why does it not say "take 2365 grains of powdered sugar, pour them into the melted chocolate, pick up a spoon and use circular movements to stir it in, . . .?" Or, to be even more precise, why not "move your arm towards the ingredients at an angle of 14°, at an approximate velocity of 18 inches per second, . . .?" The answer, of course, is obvious. The hardware knows how to stir powdered sugar into melted chocolate, and does not need further details. Well, how about turning things around and asking whether it is possible that the hardware knows how to prepare sugared and buttered chocolate mixture? In such a case, the entire first part of the recipe could be replaced by the simple instruction "prepare chocolate mixture." Taking this to the extreme, maybe the hardware knows how to prepare chocolate mousse. This would make it possible to replace the entire recipe by "prepare chocolate mousse." Given such a level of hardware expertise, a single line of instruction is a perfect recipe for obtaining *mousseline au chocolat*; this short recipe is clear, it contains no mistakes, and is guaranteed to produce the desired outputs.

Such thought experiments make it clear that the level of detail is very important when it comes to an algorithm's elementary instructions. It must be tailored to fit the hardware's particular capabilities, and should also be appropriate for the comprehension level of a potential reader or user of the algorithm.

Consider another example learnt early in our lives, and which is somewhat closer to computation—the orderly multiplication of numbers. Suppose we are asked to multiply 528 by 46. We know exactly what to do. We multiply the 8 by the 6, yielding 48, write down the units digit of the result, 8, and remember the tens digit, 4; we then multiply the 2 by the 6 and add the 4, yielding 16; we write down the units digit 6 to the left of the 8 and remember the tens digit 1; and so on.

Here, the very same questions can be asked. Why "multiply the 8 by the 6?" Why not "look up the entry appearing in the eighth row and sixth column of a multiplication table," or "add 6 to itself 8 times"? Similarly, why can't we solve the entire problem in one stroke by the simple and satisfactory algorithm "multiply the two numbers?" This last question is rather subtle: why are we allowed to multiply 8 by 6 directly, but not 528 by 46? Again, it is clear that the level of detail is a crucial feature of our acceptance of the multiplication algorithm. We assume that the relevant hardware (in this case, we ourselves) is capable of carrying out 8 times 6 but not 528 times 46, and that we can do so in our heads, or at least we know of some other way of doing it, so that we do not have to be told how to look up the result in a table.

These examples show the need for agreeing right at the start on the basic actions that an algorithm is considered to be capable of prescribing. Without doing so there is no point in trying to find algorithms for anything. Furthermore, different problems are naturally associated with different kinds of basic actions. Recipes entail stirring, mixing, pouring, and heating; multiplying numbers entails addition, digit multiplication, and, significantly, remembering a digit; looking up a telephone number might entail turning a page, moving a finger down a list, and comparing a given name to the one being pointed at.

In the precise kinds of algorithms we shall be discussing, these basic instructions must be stated clearly and precisely. We cannot accept things like "beat egg whites until foamy," since one person's idea of foam might be quite unlike another's! Instructions must be adequately distinguishable from non-instructions such as "makes 6 to 8 servings." Fuzzy phrases, such as "about 5 minutes," have no place in an algorithm suited for computer execution, as is the case with ambiguities like "serve with whipped cream, if desired." (Is it the actual serving, or the addition of whipped cream, that depends on the person's desires?) Recipes for mousse, in contrast with the algorithms that will be of interest to us, take too many things for granted, the most notable of which is the fact that a human being is part of the hardware. We cannot depend on that kind of luxury, and hence have to be far more demanding. The overall quality of an algorithm depends crucially on the selection of allowed basic actions and their appropriateness to the matter at hand.

Abstraction

Earlier it was stated that real computers can only carry out extremely simple operations on extremely simple objects. This might seem to contrast with the present discussion, which recommends that different algorithms be designed using basic actions of varying levels of detail. However, the analogy is still valid. An apprentice chef may need to be given the chocolate mousse recipe, but after a few years of making mousse the instruction "prepare chocolate mousse" will be sufficient. We say that concepts like "chocolate mousse," "lemon meringue," and "Bavaria cream" are on a higher abstraction level than operations like "mix," "stir," and "pour" used in the recipes for making them. In the same way, by appropriate programming, a computer can be made to recognize higher-level abstractions such as numbers, text, and pictures.

As in cooking, there are many levels of abstraction in the computer, each appropriate for describing different kinds of algorithms. For example, the same computer is viewed differently by a 12-year-old playing a computer game, by his sister who is surfing the internet, by his father who is using a spreadsheet program to compute his students' grades, and by his mother who is writing a program for the management of an efficacy trial of a new vaccine. None of them knows or even cares about the bits that really make up the computational process they are using.

This process of abstracting away from the details in order to see common patterns in the remainder is at the heart of almost every human endeavor. For example, reading this book has an effect on your brain, which consists of several distinct regions, each of which is composed of neurons and other cells. These cells are built out of complex molecules, which are built out of atoms, which, in turn, are made of more elementary particles. All these different levels of abstraction are relevant to what happens in your brain, but they can't all be considered together. In fact, they belong to different fields of study: particle physics, chemistry, molecular biology, neurobiology, and psychology. A psychologist performing experiments on short-term memory retention will only be distracted by thinking about the relationships between atoms and molecules in the brain.

The same is true in computer science. If we were forced to think at the bit level at all times, the computer would hardly be useful. Instead, we can, for example, think of a group of bits (typically eight bits, or a "byte") as denoting a character. We can now consider sequences of bytes to denote English words, sequences of words and punctuation to denote sentences, and so on to paragraphs, chapters, and books. There are algorithms appropriate for each of these levels. For example, spell-checking applies to words but not to characters, left-justification applies to paragraphs, and creating a table of contents applies to books. In each case, we can describe the algorithm while completely ignoring the bits that make up the words, the paragraphs, or the entire books. As this book unfolds, and especially in Chapters 3 and 9, we will be discussing the technical means that allow us to make such abstractions. Meanwhile, we shall describe each algorithm on the level of abstraction appropriate for it.

◼ Short Algorithms for Long Processes

Suppose we are given a list of personnel records, one for each employee in a certain company, each containing the employee's name, personal details, and salary. We are interested in the total sum of all salaries of all employees. Here is an algorithm for carrying out this task:

(1) make a note of the number 0;

(2) proceed through the list, adding each employee's salary to the noted number;

(3) having reached the end of the list, produce the noted number as output.

Figure 1.3

Summing salaries.

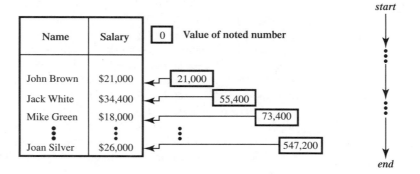

Before proceeding, we should first convince ourselves that this simple algorithm does the job. The "noted" number, which can be thought of as being memorized or written down on a piece of paper, starts out as having the value zero. After carrying out the addition in clause (2) for the first employee, this number actually takes on the value of that employee's salary. After the second employee, its value is the sum of the salaries of the first two employees. At the end, its value is clearly the sum of all salaries (see Figure 1.3).

It is interesting that the *text* of this algorithm is short and fixed in length, but the *process* it describes and controls varies with the length of the employee list and can be very, very long. Two companies, the first with one employee and the second with a million, can both feed their employee list into the same algorithm, and the salary summation problem will be solved equally well for each. Of course, the process will not take long for the first company, whereas for the second it will be quite lengthy. The algorithm, however, is fixed.

Not only is the text of the algorithm short and of fixed size, but both the small and large company require only a single noted number in order to do the job, so that the quantity of "utensils" here is also small and fixed.

Of course, the potential *value* of the noted number will presumably have to be greater for larger companies, but there will be only one number all along.

The Algorithmic Problem

And so, we have a fixed algorithm prescribing many processes of varying lengths, the precise duration and nature of the process depending on the inputs to the algorithm. Indeed, even the simple example of salary summation shows a variety of possible inputs: one-person companies, companies with a million people, companies in which some of the salaries are zero, or ones in which all salaries are equal. At times an algorithm must also work with bizarre inputs, such as companies with no employees at all, or those that employ people receiving negative salaries (that is, employees who pay the company for the pleasure of working for it).

Actually, the salary algorithm is supposed to perform satisfactorily for an *infinite* number of inputs. There is an infinite number of perfectly acceptable lists of employees, and the algorithm should be able to sum the salaries in any one of them when given as an input.

This issue of infinitely many potential inputs does not quite fit the recipe analogy, since although a recipe should work perfectly no matter how many times it is used, its ingredients are usually described as being fixed in quantity, and hence in essence the recipe has only one potential input (at least as quantities go; clearly the molecules and atoms will be different each time). However, the chocolate mousse recipe could have been made generic; that is, its list of ingredients could have read something like "X ounces of chocolate pieces, $X/4$ tablespoons of water, $X/32$ cups of powdered sugar, etc.," and its final line could have been "makes $3X/4$ to X servings." This would be more in line with the real notion of an algorithm. In its present form, the recipe is an algorithm of somewhat trivial nature, as it is tailored for one specific set of ingredients. It might be carried out (or, in algorithmic terminology, it might be **run** or **executed**) several times, but with essentially the same input, since one cup of flour is considered exactly the same as any other.

The input itself has to be *legal*, relative to the purpose of the algorithm. This means, for example, that the *New York Times* list of bestsellers would not be acceptable as input to the salary summation algorithm, any more than peanut butter and jelly would be accepted as ingredients for the mousse recipe. This entails some kind of *specification* of the allowed inputs. Someone must specify precisely which employee lists are legal and which are not; where exactly in the list the salary occurs; whether it is given in longhand (for example, $32,000) or perhaps in some abbreviated form (for example, $32K); where an employee record ends and another begins, and so on.

To put it in the most general terms, recipes, or algorithms, are solutions to certain kinds of problems, called **computational** or **algorithmic problems**. In the salary example, the problem may be specified in the form of a request for a number that represents the sum of the salaries of a list of employees of an organization. This list may vary in length but must be organized in a particular fashion. Such a problem can be viewed as the search for the contents of a "black box," which is specified by a precise definition of the legal inputs and a precise definition of the required outputs as a function of those inputs; that is, the way in which each output depends on the input (see Figure 1.4). An algorithmic problem has been solved when an appropriate algorithm has been found. The black box has then actually been provided with contents; it "works" according to that algorithm. In other words, the black box can produce the appropriate output from any legal input by executing the process that is prescribed and governed by that algorithm. The word "any" in the previous sentence is very important. We are not interested in solutions that do not work for all specified inputs. A solution that works well for only some of the legal inputs is easy to come by. As an extreme example, the trivial algorithm:

(1) produce 0 as output.

works extremely well for several interesting lists of employees: those with no employees at all, those in which everyone earns $0.00 (or multiples thereof), as well as those with a payroll that reflects a perfect balance between positive and negative salaries.

Figure 1.4

The algorithmic problem and its solution.

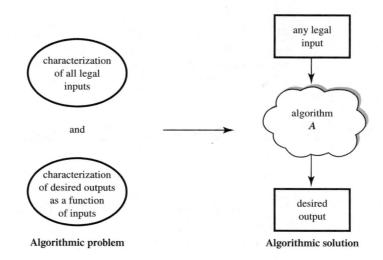

Algorithmic problem   Algorithmic solution

Later we shall address such issues as the efficiency and practicality of algorithms. Here we claim the minimal requirement that an algorithm does, in fact, solve the problem, even though it might do so inefficiently. Of course, the problem itself can specify the required behavior of a potential algorithm on undesirable inputs, but then these inputs, although undesirable, are still legal. For example, the salary summation problem could conceivably contain the requirement that for an employee whose record does not show a number in the salary area but, say, a question mark, or some other nonsensical data the algorithm should add that employee's name to a special list, which will be forwarded to the payroll office for further action. Such an unorthodox list of employees is nevertheless legal; it just is not dealt with in the standard way, but is given some special treatment that befits its abnormal nature. Thus, keeping *illegal* inputs separate is the responsibility of the algorithmic problem, while treating special classes of unusual or *undesirable* inputs is the responsibility of the algorithm itself.

Bounds on Basic Actions

There is one other important matter that we need to address at this point concerning the execution of the basic actions, or operations, prescribed by an algorithm. It is obvious that each of these actions must be carried out in a finite amount of time, otherwise, of course, the algorithm will never reach an end. Thus, infinitely long actions are bad. Actions that can take infinitesimally small amounts of time are outlawed too, a fact that needs little justification. It is unthinkable that a machine will ever be able to perform actions in diminishing amounts of time. The speed of light, for one, would always serve as a limit on the speed of any machine. Similar limits on the resources (that is, utensils) used in performing basic actions have to be enforced too, but we shall not discuss the reasons here.

Clearly, these assumptions about basic actions indeed hold for real computers. The basic bit-manipulation actions, for example, are precise and unambiguous, and take bounded amounts of time and resources. Thus, as promised, the theory of algorithmics described herein will be directly applicable to problems intended for computer-based solution.

■ The Problem and Its Solution: Summary

To summarize, an algorithmic problem consists of:

1. a characterization of a legal, possibly infinite, collection of potential input sets, and
2. a specification of the desired outputs as a function of the inputs.

It is assumed that either a description of the allowed basic actions or a hardware configuration together with its built-in basic actions are also provided in advance. A solution to an algorithmic problem consists of an algorithm, composed of elementary instructions prescribing actions from the agreed-on set. This algorithm, when executed for any legal input set, solves the problem, producing the output as required. Starting in Chapter 10 we shall be generalizing these notions, but until then the present definition will suffice.

It is important to recognize the considerable difficulty involved in solving algorithmic problems satisfactorily. By starting out with a mousse recipe and then giving a simple summation algorithm, a certain amount of injustice has been done, as it might appear that things are easy. Nothing is further from the truth. Algorithmic problems, in practice, can be incredibly complex, and can take years of work to solve successfully. Worse still, as we shall see in later chapters, many problems do not admit satisfactory solutions, while others do not admit any solutions at all. For many problems the status, as far as good algorithmic solutions are concerned, is as yet unknown, despite extensive work by many talented people.

Obviously, we shall not be able to illustrate the issues treated in this book with overly lengthy and complex examples, but we can get a feel for the difficulty in designing algorithms by thinking about the following (informally described) algorithmic problems. In the first problem the input is a legal chess position (that is, a description of the situation reached at some point during a chess game), while the output is the best move for White (that is, the description of a move that maximizes White's chances of winning the game). The second problem concerns newspaper distribution. Suppose 20,000 papers are to be distributed to 1000 locations in 100 towns using 50 trucks. The input contains the road distances between the towns and between the locations within each town, the number of papers required at each location, the present location of each truck, each truck's newspaper-carrying ability, as well as its gasoline capacity and miles-per-gallon performance, and details of available drivers, including their present whereabouts. The output is to be a list, matching drivers to trucks, and containing detailed itineraries for each of the trucks so that the total number of miles driven is minimized. Actually, the problem calls for an algorithm that works for any number of newspapers, locations, towns, and trucks, so that the numbers of these also vary and form part of the inputs.

Before we can discuss issues of correctness and efficiency, or deeper questions concerning the nature or very existence of solutions to certain algorithmic problems, we have to learn more about the structure of algorithms, and the structure of the objects they manipulate.

I have declared the former things from the beginning

ISAIAH 48: 3

CHAPTER 2

Algorithms and Data

*And this is the
fashion of which
thou shalt make it*

GENESIS 6: 15

or, Getting It Done

We already know that algorithms contain carefully selected elementary instructions that prescribe the basic actions to be performed. We have not yet discussed the arrangement of these instructions in the algorithm that enables a human or a computer to figure out the precise order of the actions to be performed. Nor have we discussed the objects manipulated by these actions.

An algorithm can be thought of as being executed by a little robot, or a **processor** (who might appropriately be named Runaround). The processor receives orders to run around doing this and that, where the "this and thats" are the basic actions of the algorithm. In the salary summation algorithm of the previous chapter, little Runaround is told to make a note of 0 and then to start working its way through the employee list, finding salaries and adding them to the noted number. It should be quite obvious that the order in which the basic actions are carried out is crucial. It is of paramount importance not only that the elementary instructions of the algorithm be clear and unambiguous, but that the same should apply to the mechanism that controls the sequence in which those instructions are carried out. The algorithm must therefore contain control instructions to "push" the processor in this or that direction, telling it what to do at each step and when to stop and say "I'm done."

◾ Control Structures

Sequence control is usually carried out with the aid of various combinations of instructions called **control-flow structures**, or simply **control structures**. Even the chocolate mousse recipe contains several typical ones, such as the following:

- **Direct sequencing**, of the form "do *A* followed by *B*," or "do *A* and then *B*." (Every semicolon or period in the recipe hides an implicit "and then" phrase, for example, "gently fold in chocolate; [and then] reheat slightly . . .")

■ **Conditional branching**, of the form "if Q then do A otherwise do B," or just "if Q then do A," where Q is some condition. (For example, in the recipe "reheat slightly to melt chocolate, if necessary," or "serve with whipped cream, if desired.")

As it happens, these two control constructs, sequencing and branching, do not explain how an algorithm of fixed—maybe even short—length can describe processes that can grow increasingly long, depending on the particular input. An algorithm containing only sequencing and branching can prescribe processes of some bounded length only, since no part of such an algorithm is ever executed more than once. Control constructs that are responsible for prescribing ever-longer processes are indeed hidden even in the mousse recipe, but they are far more explicit in algorithms that deal with many inputs of different sizes, such as the salary summation algorithm. They are generically called **iterations**, or **looping constructs**, and come in many flavors. Here are two:

■ **Bounded iteration**, of the general form "do A exactly N times," where N is a number.
■ **Conditional iteration**, sometimes called **unbounded iteration**, of the form "repeat A until Q," or "while Q do A," where Q is a condition. (For example, in the recipe "beat egg whites until foamy.")

When describing the salary summation algorithm in Chapter 1, we were quite vague about the way the main part of the algorithm was to be carried out; we said "proceed through the list, adding each employee's salary to the noted number," and then "having reached the end of the list, produce the noted number as output." We should really have used an iteration construct, that not only makes precise the task of the processor proceeding through the list, but also signals the end of the list. Let us assume then that the input to the problem includes not only the list of employees, but also its length; that is, the total number of employees, designated by the letter N. It is now possible to use a bounded iteration construct, yielding the following algorithm:

(1) make a note of 0; point to the first salary on the list;
(2) do the following $N - 1$ times:
    (2.1) add the salary pointed at to the noted number;
    (2.2) point to the next salary;
(3) add the salary pointed at to the noted number;
(4) produce the noted number as output.

The phrase "the following" in clause (2) refers to the segment consisting of subclauses (2.1) and (2.2). This convention, coupled with textual indentation to emphasize the "nested" nature of (2.1) and (2.2), will be used freely in the sequel.

You are encouraged to seek the reason for using $N - 1$ and adding the final salary separately, rather than simply using N and then producing the output and halting. Notice that the algorithm fails if the list is empty (that is, if N is 0), since the second part of clause (1) makes no sense.

If the input does not include N, the total number of employees, we must use a conditional iteration that requires us to provide a way by which the algorithm can sense when it has reached the end of the list. The resulting algorithm would look very much like the version given, but would use the form "repeat the following until end of list reached" in clause (2). You should try writing down the full algorithm for this case.

Notice how iteration constructs make it possible for a short portion of an algorithm's text to prescribe very long processes, the length being dictated by the size of the inputs—in this case the length of the employee list. Iteration, therefore, is the key to the seeming paradox of a single, fixed algorithm performing tasks of ever-longer duration.

Combining Control Structures

An algorithm can contain many control-flow constructs in nontrivial combinations. Sequencing, branching, and iteration can be interleaved and nested within each other. For example, algorithms can contain **nested** iterations, more commonly called **nested loops**. A loop inside a loop can take on the form "do A exactly N times," where A itself is, say, of the form "repeat B until C." The processor executing such a segment has to work quite hard; each of the N times it carries out A—that is, each time the *outer loop* is traversed—the *inner loop* must be traversed repeatedly until C becomes true. Here the outer loop is bounded and the inner one conditional, but other combinations are possible too. The A part of the outer loop can contain many further segments, each of which can, in turn, employ additional sequencing, branching, and iteration constructs, and the same goes for the inner loop. Thus, there is no limit to the potential intricacy of algorithms.

Let us consider a simple example of the power of nested iterations. Suppose that the problem was to sum salaries, but not of *all* employees, only of those who earn more than their direct managers. Of course it is assumed that (except for the true "boss") an employee's record contains the name of that employee's manager. An algorithm that solves this problem might be constructed so that an outer loop runs down the list as before, but for each employee "pointed at" an inner loop searches the list for the record of that employee's direct manager. When the manager has finally been found, a conditional construct is used to determine whether or not the employee's salary should be accumulated in the "noted number," a decision that requires comparing the two salaries. Upon completing this "internal" activity, the outer loop resumes control and proceeds to the next employee, whose manager is then sought for, until the end of the list is reached. (See Figure 2.4 for a diagrammatic version of this algorithm.)

Bubblesort: An Example

To further illustrate control structures, let us examine a sorting algorithm. **Sorting** is one of the most interesting topics in algorithmics, and many important developments are connected with it in one way or another. The input to a sorting problem is an *unordered* list of elements, say numbers. Our task is to produce the list sorted in

Figure 2.1

Two bubblesort traversals on five elements. (Arrows indicate elements exchanged, not elements compared.)

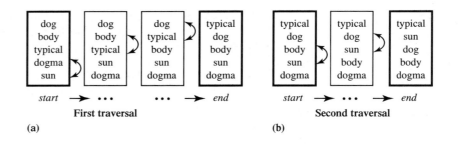

(a) First traversal

(b) Second traversal

ascending order. The problem can be phrased more generally by substituting, say, lists of words for lists of numbers, with the intention that they be sorted by their lexicographic ordering (that is, as in a dictionary or telephone book). It is assumed that the list of elements is preceded by its length, N, and that the only way to obtain information concerning the magnitude of these elements is to perform binary comparisons; that is, to compare two elements and act according to the outcome of the comparison.[1]

One of the many known sorting algorithms is called **bubblesort**. Actually, bubblesort is considered to be a bad sorting algorithm, for reasons explained in Chapter 6. It is used here only to illustrate control structures.

The bubblesort algorithm is based on the following observation. If the jumbled list is traversed in sequence, one element at a time, and whenever two adjacent elements are found to be in the wrong order (that is, the first is larger than the second) they are exchanged, then on completion of the traversal, the largest element is in its rightful place; namely, at the end of the list.

Figure 2.1(a) illustrates such a traversal for a simple five-element list. (The list has been drawn from bottom to top: the first element is the lowest in the picture. The arrows show only the elements exchanged, not those compared.) Clearly, the traversal might correct other incorrect orderings besides placing the maximal element in its final position. However, Figure 2.1(a) shows that one traversal does not necessarily sort the list. Now, a second traversal will bring the second largest element to its proper resting point, the penultimate position in the list, as can be seen in Figure 2.1(b). This leads to an algorithm that carries out $N - 1$ such traversals (why not N?), resulting in the sorted list. The name "bubblesort" stems from the way in which large elements "bubble up" to the top of the list as the algorithm proceeds, exchanging places with smaller elements that are pushed lower down.

Before writing down the algorithm in more detail, it should be pointed out that the second traversal need not extend to the last element, since by the time the second traversal starts, the last position in the list already contains its rightful tenant—the largest element in the list. Similarly, the third traversal need not go any further than the first $N - 2$ elements. This means that a more efficient algorithm would traverse only the first N elements in its first traversal, the first $N - 1$ in its second, $N - 2$ in its third, and so on. We shall return to the bubblesort algorithm and this improvement

---

[1] There is some subtlety to this. If we knew in advance, for example, that the input list consisted precisely of half of the integers between 1 and N jumbled in some unknown way, a trivial sorting algorithm could be written that simply prepared a new list of length N, initially containing blanks in all locations, then directly inserted each number encountered in the input list into its proper place in the new list, and finally simply reading out the contents of the non-blank places from beginning to end.

Figure 2.2

The main stages in bubblesort of eight elements. (The first element of each list is at the bottom; arrows indicate elements changing places.)

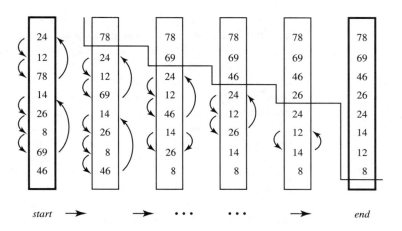

start → → ⋯ ⋯ → end

in Chapter 6, but for now the unimproved version will suffice. The algorithm reads as follows:

(1) do the following $N - 1$ times:
    (1.1) point to the first element;
    (1.2) do the following $N - 1$ times:
        (1.2.1) compare the element pointed to with the next element;
        (1.2.2) if the compared elements are in the wrong order, exchange them;
        (1.2.3) point to the next element.

Notice how two-level indentation is used here. The first "following," on line (1), involves all lines starting with 1, and the second, on line (1.2), involves those starting with 1.2. In this way, the nested nature of the looping constructs is clearly visible.

The main steps taken by the algorithm on an eight-item list are illustrated in Figure 2.2, where the situation is depicted just before each execution of clause (1.2). The elements appearing above the line are in their final positions. Notice that in this particular example the last two traversals (not shown) are redundant; the list becomes sorted after five, not seven, traversals. However, observe that if, for example, the smallest element happens to be last in the original list (that is, at the top in our illustrations), then all $N - 1$ traversals are in fact necessary, since elements that are to be "bubbled down" (elbbubed? . . .) cause more trouble than those that "bubble up."

The "Goto" Statement

There is another important control instruction that is generally called the **goto** statement. It has the general form "goto G," where G marks some point in the text of the algorithm. In our examples we could write, say, "goto (1.2)," an instruction that causes the processor Runaround to literally go to line (1.2) of the algorithm and resume execution from there. This construct is controversial for a number of reasons, the most obvious of which is pragmatic in nature. An algorithm that contains many "goto" statements directing control backwards and forwards in a tangled fashion quickly becomes very difficult to understand. Clarity, as we shall argue later, is a very important consideration in algorithmic design.

Besides potentially reducing our ability to understand an algorithm, "goto" statements can also introduce technical difficulties. What happens if a "goto" statement directs the processor into the midst of a loop? Inserting the instruction "goto (1.2.1)" between (1.1) and (1.2) in the bubblesort algorithm is an example of this. Is the processor to execute (1.2.1) through (1.2.3) and then halt, or should these be executed $N - 1$ times? What if the same instruction appears within the (1.2.1)–(1.2.3) sequence? This kind of problem is rooted in the ambiguity resulting from an attempt to match the text of an algorithm with the process it prescribes. Clearly, there is such a match, but since fixed algorithms can prescribe processes of varying length, a single point in the text of the algorithm can be associated with many points in the execution of the corresponding process. Consequently, "goto" statements are in a sense inherently ambiguous creatures, and many researchers are opposed to using them freely in algorithms.

■ Diagrams for Algorithms

Visual, diagrammatic techniques are one way of presenting the control flow of an algorithm in a clear and readable fashion. There are various ways of "drawing" algorithms, as opposed to writing them down. One of the best known of these involves writing the elementary instructions in rectangular boxes and the tests in diamond-shaped ones, and using arrows to describe how the processor Runaround runs around executing the algorithm. The resulting objects are called **flowcharts**. Figure 2.3 shows a flowchart of the regular salary summation algorithm, and Figure 2.4 shows

Figure 2.3

Flowchart for salary summation.

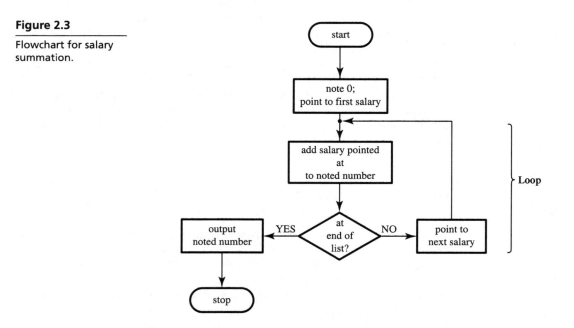

Figure 2.4

Flowchart for
sophisticated salary
summation.

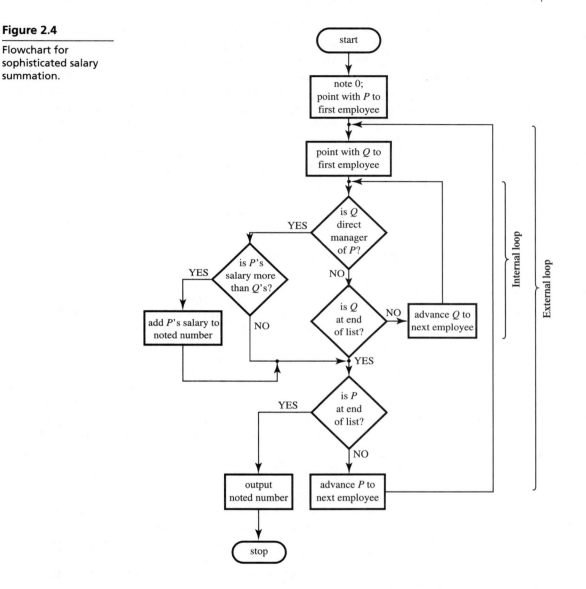

one for the more sophisticated version that involves only employees earning more
than their direct managers.

Notice the way an iteration shows up visually as a cycle of boxes, diamonds,
and arrows, and nested iterations show up as cycles within cycles. This explains
the use of the term "looping." The flowcharts in Figures 2.3 and 2.4 also illustrate
the appropriateness of the term "branching" that was associated with conditional
instructions.

Flowcharts also have disadvantages. One of these is rooted in the fact that it is
more difficult to encourage people to adhere to a small number of "well-formed"
control structures. When using flowcharts it is easy to succumb to the temptation to
employ many "goto's," since these are depicted simply as arrows just like those that

would represent "while" loops or conditional statements. Thus, this abuse of the medium of flowcharts has also caused many researchers to recommend that they be used with caution. Another concern is the fact that many kinds of algorithms simply do not lend themselves naturally to graphical, diagrammatic rendition offered by the likes of flowcharts. The resulting artifacts will often be spaghetti-like, decreasing, rather than increasing, a viewer's ability to understand what is really going on.

The above discussion notwithstanding, we shall see in Chapter 14 that there are diagrammatic languages (we shall call them visual formalisms) that are very successful, mainly in the context of specifying the behavior of large and complex systems. The problem there is not describing computations, as algorithms do, but specifying reactive and interactive behavior over time.

Subroutines, or Procedures

Suppose we are given a lengthy text and we are interested in finding out how avaricious its author is by counting the number of sentences that contain the word "money." In such instances, we are not interested in the number of times the word "money" occurs, but in the number of sentences in which it occurs. An algorithm can be designed to run through the text looking for "money." Upon finding such an occurrence, it proceeds to run ahead looking for the end of a sentence, which for our purposes is assumed to be a period followed by a space; that is, the ". " combination. When the end of a sentence is found, the algorithm adds 1 to a **counter** (that is, a "noted number," as in the salary summation algorithm), which was initialized to 0 at the start. It then resumes its search for "money" from the beginning of the next sentence; that is, from the letter following the combination. Of course, the algorithm must keep looking out for the end of the text, so that it can output the value of the counter when it is reached.

The algorithm takes the form of an external loop whose duty it is to count the relevant sentences. Within this loop there are two searches, one for "money" and one for the ". " combination, each constituting a loop in itself (see the schematic flowchart of Figure 2.5). The point is that the two internal loops are very similar; in fact, they both do exactly the same thing—they search for a sequence of symbols in a text. Having both loops appear explicitly in the algorithm clearly works, but we can do better.

The idea is to write the searching loop only *once*, with a **parameter** that is assumed to contain the particular combination of symbols searched for. This algorithmic segment is called a **subroutine** or a **procedure** and it is activated (or **invoked**, or **called**) twice in the main algorithm, once with "money" as its parameter, and once with the ". " combination. The text of the subroutine is provided separately, and it refers to the varying parameter by a name, say X. The subroutine assumes that we are pointing to some place in the input text, and it might look as follows:

subroutine **search-for** X:

(1) do the following until either the combination X is being pointed at, or the end of the text is reached:

    (1.1) advance the pointer one symbol in the text;

(2) if the end of the text is reached, output the counter's value and stop;

(3) otherwise return to the main algorithm.

The main part of the algorithm will utilize the search subroutine twice, by instructions of the form "call **search-for** 'money' " and "call **search-for** '. ' " Contrast Figure 2.5 with Figure 2.6, in which the version with the subroutine is shown schematically.

The processor that runs around doing things will now have to be slightly more sophisticated. When told to "call" a subroutine, it will stop whatever it has been doing, remember where it was, pick up the parameter(s), so to speak, and move

Figure 2.5

Schematic flowchart for sentences with "money."

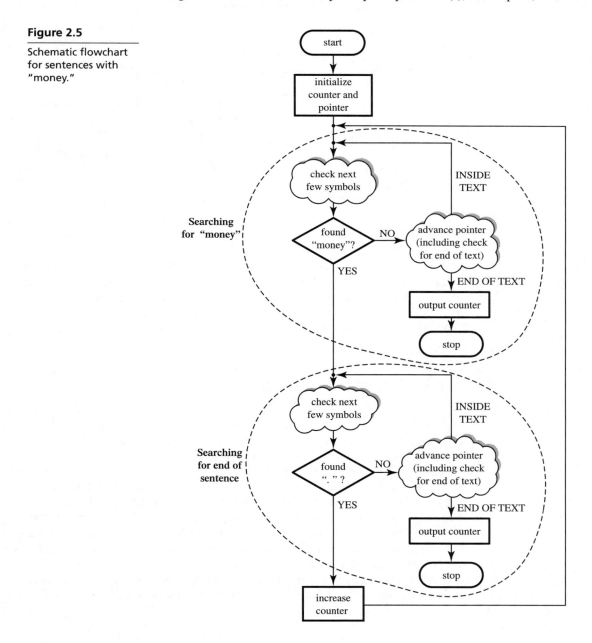

Figure 2.6

Sentences with "money" using a subroutine.

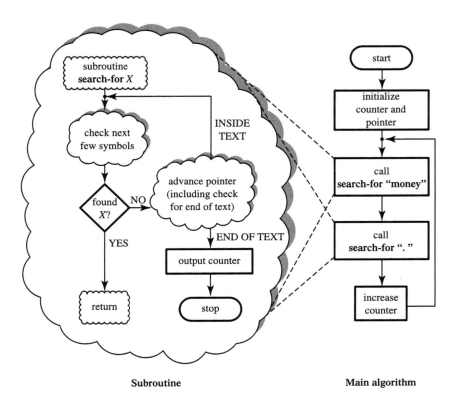

Subroutine   Main algorithm

over to the text of the subroutine. It will then do whatever the subroutine tells it to do, using the current value of a parameter wherever the subroutine refers to that parameter by its internal name (X, in our example). If and when the subroutine tells it to return, it will do just that; namely, it will return to the point following the "call" that led it to the subroutine in the first place, and will resume its duties from there.

The Virtues of Subroutines

Obviously, subroutines can be very economical as far as the size of an algorithm is concerned. Even in this simple example, the searching loop is written once but is used twice, whereas without it, of course, the algorithm would have had to include two detailed versions of that loop. This economy becomes considerably more significant for complex algorithms with many subroutines that are called from various places. Also, an algorithm can contain subroutines that call other subroutines, and so on. Thus, algorithmic structure is given a new dimension; there are not only nested loops but nested subroutines. Moreover, loops, conditional statements, sequential constructs, "goto" statements, and now subroutines, can all be interleaved, yielding algorithms of increasing structural complexity.

Economy, however, is not the only advantage of subroutines. A subroutine can be viewed as a "chunk" of algorithmic material, some kind of building block, which, once formed, can be used in another algorithmic chunk by a single instruction. This is just like saying that we have extended our repertoire of allowed elementary instructions. In the "money" counting example, once the search routine is there (and even beforehand, as long as it has been decided that such a routine will eventually be written) the instruction "call **search-for** 'abc' " is, for every practical purpose, a new elementary instruction. Thus, subroutines are one way in which we can create our own abstractions, as is appropriate for the specific problem we are trying to solve. This is a very powerful idea, as it not only shortens algorithms but also makes them clear and well structured. Clarity and structure, as is repeatedly emphasized, are of the utmost importance in algorithmics, and many an effort is devoted to finding ways of imposing them on algorithm designers.

In the same way that a user of a computer program typically knows nothing about the algorithms that it uses, a subroutine can be used as a "black box," without knowing how it is implemented. All that the user of the subroutine has to know is *what* it does, but not *how* it does it. This greatly simplifies the problem, by reducing the amount of detail that needs to be kept in mind.

Using subroutines, it is possible to develop a complex algorithm gradually, step by step. A typical algorithmic problem calls for a fully detailed solution that utilizes the allowed elementary actions only. The designer can work towards that goal gradually, by first devising a **high-level algorithm**, which uses "elementary" instructions that are not in the book. These are actually calls to subroutines that the designer has in mind, which are written later (or, perhaps, earlier). These subroutines, in turn, might use other instructions, which, not being elementary enough, are again regarded as calls to subroutines that are eventually written. At some point, all elementary instructions are at a sufficiently low level to be among those explicitly allowed. It is then that the gradual development process ends. This approach gives rise either to a "top-down" design, which, as just described, goes from the general to the specific, or to a "bottom-up" design, whereby one prepares the subroutines that will be needed, and then designs the more general routines that call them, thus working from the detailed to the general. There is no universal agreement as to which of these is the better approach to algorithmic design. The common feeling is that some kind of mixture should be used. We discuss this question further in Chapter 13.

Returning for a moment to gastronomy, preparing a "chocolate mixture" might be a good candidate for a subroutine within the chocolate mousse recipe of Chapter 1. This would enable us to describe the recipe in the following way, where each of the four instructions is treated as a call to a subroutine (or should we say, a sub-recipe) whose text would then be written separately:

(1) prepare chocolate mixture;

(2) mix to produce chocolate-yolk mixture;

(3) prepare foam of egg whites;

(4) mix both to produce the mousse.

It is worth pointing out that the book from which the mousse recipe was taken employs subroutines quite extensively. For example, pages 72–77 therein describe a number of recipes whose ingredients contain items such as Sweet Pastry Dough, Croissants, or Puff Pastry, for which the user is referred to previously given recipes dedicated to these very items.

It is fair to say that the power and flexibility provided by subroutines cannot be overestimated.

Recursion

One of the most useful aspects of subroutines, which to many people is also one of the most confusing, is **recursion**. By this we mean simply the ability of a subroutine, or procedure, to call itself. Now, this might sound absurd, since how on earth does our processor come any closer to solving a problem by being told, in the midst of trying to solve that problem, to leave everything and start solving the same problem all over again?

The following example should aid us in resolving this paradox, and it might help if we say at the start that the resolution is based on the very same property of algorithms mentioned earlier: the same text (in this case, that of the recursive subroutine) can correspond to many portions of the process described by it. Iterative constructs are one way of mapping lengthy processes on to short texts; recursive subroutines are another.

The example is based on a rather ancient puzzle known as the Towers of Hanoi, originating with Hindu priests in the great temple of Benares. Suppose we are given three towers, or to be more humble, three pegs, A, B, and C. On the first peg, A, there are three rings piled in descending order of magnitude, while the others are empty (see Figure 2.7). We are interested in moving the rings from A to B, perhaps using C in the process. By the rules of the game, rings are to be moved one at a time, and at no instant may a larger ring be placed atop a smaller one. This simple puzzle can be solved as follows:

> move A to B;
> move A to C;
> move B to C;
> move A to B;
> move C to A;
> move C to B;
> move A to B.

Before proceeding, we should first convince ourselves that these seven actions really do the job, and we should then try the same puzzle with four rather than three rings on peg A (the number of pegs does not change). A moderate amount of work should suffice for you to discover a sequence of 15 "move X to Y" actions that solve the four-ring version.

Such puzzles are intellectually challenging, and those who enjoy puzzles may like to consider the original Hindu version which involves the same three pegs,

Figure 2.7

The Towers of Hanoi with three rings.

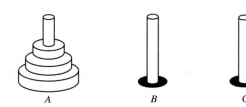

but with no fewer than 64 rings on A. As we shall see in Chapter 7, the inventors of the puzzle were not completely detached from reality when they stated that the world will end when all 64 rings are correctly piled on peg B. However, we are not dealing with puzzles here but with algorithmics, and consequently we are more interested in the general algorithmic problem associated with the Towers of Hanoi than with this or that particular instance of it. The input is a positive integer N, and the desired output is a list of "move X to Y" actions, which, if followed, solve the puzzle involving N rings. Clearly, a solution to this problem must be an algorithm that works for every N, producing a list of actions that satisfy the constraints; in particular, following them never causes a larger ring to be placed atop a smaller one.

This is the problem we should really be trying to solve, since once an algorithm is available, every instance of the puzzle, be it the three-, four-, or 3078-ring version, can be solved simply by running the algorithm with the desired number of rings as input. Well, how is it done? The answer is simple: by the magic of recursion.

A Solution to the Towers of Hanoi

The algorithm presented here accomplishes the task of moving N rings from A to B via C in the following way. It first checks to see whether N is 1, in which case it simply moves the one ring it was asked to deal with to its destination (or, more precisely, it outputs a description of the one move that will do the job), and then returns immediately. If N is greater than 1, it first moves the top $N - 1$ rings from A to the "accessory" peg C using the same routine recursively; it then picks up the only ring left on A, which has to be the largest ring (why?), and transfers it to its final destination, B; it then, recursively again, moves the $N - 1$ rings it had previously "stored" on C to their final destination, B. That this algorithm abides by the rules of the game is a little difficult to see, but on the assumption that the two processes involving the $N - 1$ rings contain only legal moves, it is fairly easy to see that so does the overall process of moving the N rings.

Here then is the algorithm. It is written as a recursive routine whose title and parameters (there are four of them) speak for themselves:

subroutine **move** N **from** X **to** Y **using** Z:

(1) if N is 1 then output "move X to Y";

(2) otherwise (i.e., if N is greater than 1) do the following:
    (2.1) call **move** $N - 1$ **from** X **to** Z **using** Y;
    (2.2) output "move X to Y";
    (2.3) call **move** $N - 1$ **from** Z **to** Y **using** X;

(3) return.

To illustrate the workings of this routine, which might look rather ridiculous at first sight, we could try running it when N is 3; that is, simulating the processor's work when there are three rings. This should be done by executing a "main algorithm" consisting of the single instruction:

call **move** 3 **from** A **to** B **using** C

Figure 2.8

Structured run of the recursive solution to the Towers of Hanoi.

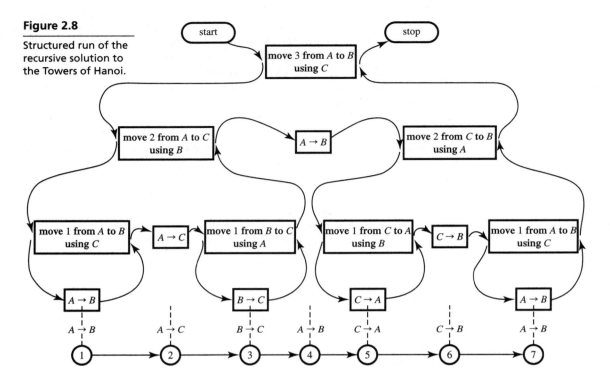

The simulation should be carried out carefully, since the parameter names X, Y, and Z start out innocently enough as being A, B, and C, but change each time the processor re-enters the routine. As if to make things more confusing, they resume their old values when the "call" is over and the processor returns to where it came from. Figure 2.8 helps illustrate the sequence of actions for this case. Notice that the processor (and we too, if indeed we are trying to simulate the routine) now has to remember not only where it came from in order to return to the right place, but also what the values of the parameter names were prior to its new errand, in order to resume its work properly. Figure 2.8 is organized to reflect the **depth of recursion** and the corresponding way the parameters change values. The arrows represent the processor's trips: downward arrows correspond to calls, upward arrows to returns, and horizontal arrows to simple sequencing. As if by magic, the final sequence of actions is found to be identical to the one arrived at earlier by trial and error.

As it turns out, the Towers of Hanoi problem admits another algorithmic solution, which employs a simple iteration and no subroutine calls at all, and can be carried out by a small child! This algorithm will be presented in Chapter 5.

■ The Expressive Power of Control Structures

Can we do with only a few simple control structures? The answer is yes. Various **minimal sets** of control structures have been identified, meaning that in certain technical senses other control structures can be replaced by appropriate combinations of those in the minimal set, so that in practice these are the only ones needed. A well-known minimal set consists of sequencing (and-then), conditional branching (if-then), and some kind of unbounded loop construct (for example, while-do). It is not too difficult, for example, to show that an instruction of the form "repeat A until Q is true," can be replaced by "do A, and then while Q is false do A," so that in the presence of "while-do" constructs one can do without "repeat-until" constructs. In a similar vein, it is possible to completely eliminate "goto" statements from any algorithm, albeit at the expense of expanding the algorithm somewhat and changing its original structure.

Similarly, there is a precise sense, in which anything that can be done with subroutines and recursion can be done using only simple loops. However, using this result to rid a given algorithm of its subroutines involves adding considerable "machinery" (in the form of new elementary instructions) to the algorithm. It is possible to show that if such machinery is not allowed, then recursive subroutines are more powerful than iteration, so that certain things can be done with the former only. These topics are touched upon here only in the most superficial way in order to give you some feel for the relevant questions of interest.[2]

Data Types and Data Structures

So we now know what an algorithm looks like and how, given inputs, the processor runs around executing the process the algorithm describes. However, we have been quite vague as to the objects manipulated by an algorithm. We had lists, words, and texts, as well as funny things like "noted numbers" that increased, and "pointers" that made progress. If we wish to go to extremes, we can also say we had flour, sugar, cakes, and chocolate mousse, as well as towers, pegs, and rings. These objects constituted not only the algorithm's inputs and outputs, but also intermediate accessories that were constructed and used during its lifetime, such as the counters ("noted numbers") and the pointers. For all of these we use the generic term **data**.[3]

Data elements come in various flavors, or can be of various types. Some of the most common **data types** present in algorithms that are executed by computers are **numbers** of various kinds (integers, decimals, binary numbers, and so on), and **words** written in various alphabets. Actually, numbers can be construed as words too; *decimal integers*, for example, are "words" over an alphabet consisting of the digits 0, 1, 2, . . . , 9, and *binary numbers* use the alphabet consisting of 0 and 1 only. It is beneficial, however, to keep such types separate, not only for clarity and good order, but also because each type admits its own special set of allowed operations, or actions. It makes no more sense to list the vowels in a number than it does to

---

[2] To better appreciate the subtlety induced by the self-referential nature of recursion, the following book is heartily recommended, together with those of its references that are heartily recommended therein: D. Harel, with Y. A. Feldman, *Algorithmics: The Spirit of Computing* (3rd edn), Addison-Wesley, Harlow, 2004.

[3] The singular form is **datum**, but we shall mostly use the terms **data item** and **data element** here.

multiply two words! And so, our algorithms will have to be told what objects they can manipulate and precisely which manipulations are allowed. Manipulation includes not only carrying out operations but also asking questions, such as testing whether a number is even or whether two words start with the same letter.

These observations seem quite natural in view of our discussion of elementary operations in Chapter 1, and are reminiscent of the facts about the bit-manipulation capabilities of computers. Here we take basic data types and the operations and tests associated with them for granted. What we are interested in are the ways algorithms can organize, remember, change, and access collections of data. While control structures serve to tell the processor where it should be going, data structures, and the operations upon them, organize the data items in ways that enable it to do whatever it should do when it gets there.

The world of data structures is just as rich in abstraction levels as the world of control structures. In fact, a useful mental trick, which is the basis for the object-oriented programming paradigm, shows that we can switch between them! This will be discussed further in Chapter 3.

Variables, or Little Boxes

The first objects of interest are **variables**. In the salary summation algorithm, for example, we used a "noted number," which was first initialized to 0 and was then used to accumulate the sum of the employees' salaries. We were actually using a variable. A variable is not a number, a word, or some other item of data. Rather, it can be viewed as a small box, or cell, in which a single item can be kept. We can give the variable a name, say X, and then use instructions like "put 0 in X," or "increase the contents of X by 1." We can also ask questions about the contents of X, such as "does X contain an even number?" Variables are very much like hotel rooms; different people can occupy a room at different times, and the person in the room can be referred to by the phrase "the occupant of room 326." The term "326" is the name of the room, just as X is the name of the variable.

This use of the word "variable" to denote a cell that can contain different values at different times is unlike the meaning of a variable in mathematics, where it denotes a single (usually unknown) value. In Chapter 3 we shall be discussing the functional programming paradigm, which does not deal with cells, but with the values directly, like in mathematics.

Algorithms typically utilize many variables with different names, and for very different purposes. In the bubblesort algorithm, for example, a detailed version might use one variable to count the number of times the outer loop is performed, another for the inner loop, and a third to help in exchanging two elements in the list. To perform the exchange, one element is "put in the box" for a moment, the other is put in its place, and the "boxed" element is then put in the second element's original place. Without using the variable, there would appear to be no way to keep the first element around without losing it. This illustrates the use of variables as **memory** or **storage** in an algorithm. Of course, the fact that elements are exchanged many times in one run of bubblesort does not mean that we need many variables—the same "box" can be used each time. This is a result of the fact that all exchanges in the bubblesort algorithm are disjoint; no exchange starts before the previous one has ended. Variables can thus be reused.

When variables are used in practice the phrase "contents of" is usually omitted, and we write things like $X \leftarrow 0$ (read "X gets 0" or "set X to 0") to set the initial **value** of (that is, contents of) X to 0, and $X \leftarrow X + 1$ (read "X gets $X + 1$") to increase the value of X by 1. This last instruction, for example, tells the processor to "read" the number found in X, increase it by one, and replace it with the result. More about such instructions and the way to formally write them down can be found in Chapter 3.

■ Vectors, or Lists

Let us take a closer look at our employee list. Such a list might be viewed simply as a multitude of data elements, which we might decide to keep, or **store**, in a multitude of variables, say $X, Y, Z, \ldots$ This clearly would not enable an algorithm of fixed size to "run" through the list, whose length can vary, since each element in the list would have to be referred to in the algorithm by a unique name. Lengthier lists would require more variable names and hence longer algorithms. What we need is a way of referring to many elements in a *uniform* manner. We need **lists** of variables that can be "run through," or accessed in some other way, but without the need to name each of their elements explicitly. We want to be able to "point" to elements in these lists, to refer to the "next" element or the "previous" one, and so on. For these purposes we use **vectors**, also called **one-dimensional arrays**.

If a variable is like a hotel room, then a vector can be thought of as an entire corridor, or floor, in the hotel. Rooms $301, 302, \ldots, 346$ might be the individual "variables"; each can be referred to separately, but in contrast to a simple collection of variables, the entire corridor or floor also has a name (say "floor 3"), and the rooms therein can be accessed by their index. The 15th room along that corridor is 315, and the Xth room is $3X$. This means that we can use a variable to **index** the vector. Changing the value of X can be used to refer to the contents of different elements in the vector. The notation used in practice separates the name of the vector from its index by parentheses; we write $V[6]$ for the sixth element of vector V, and similarly $V[X]$ for the element of V whose index is the current value of the variable X. We might even write $V[X + 1]$, which refers to the element following $V[X]$ in the list. (Notice that $V[X + 1]$ and $V[X] + 1$ denote two completely different things!)

In the bubblesort algorithm, for example, we can use a variable X to control the inner loop, and at the very same time it can double as a pointer to the vector V of elements being sorted. Here is what the resulting (more concise, and also more precise) version of the algorithm might look like, with "$<$" standing for "is smaller than":

(1) do the following $N - 1$ times:
    (1.1) $X \leftarrow 1$;
    (1.2) while $X < N$ do the following:
        (1.2.1) if $V[X + 1] < V[X]$ then exchange them;
        (1.2.2) $X \leftarrow X + 1$.

You are encouraged to modify this algorithm, incorporating the observation mentioned earlier, to the effect that with each traversal of the outer loop the number of elements inspected in the inner loop can be decreased by 1.

Vectors that represent lists of elements have numerous applications. A telephone book is a list, and so are dictionaries, personnel files, inventory descriptions, course requirements, and so on.

In a way, a vector as a **data structure** is closely related to a loop as a control structure. Traversing a vector (for the purpose of inspection, search, summation, etc.) is typically carried out with a single iterative construct. Just as the loop is a control structure for describing lengthy processes, so is a vector a data structure for representing lengthy lists of data items.[4]

There are also special "indexed" versions of iterative control constructs, tailored towards vector traversal. For example, we can write:

> for X going from 1 to 100 do the following

which is similar to:

> do the following 100 times

except that with the former we can refer directly to the Xth element in a vector within the repeated segment, whereas with the latter we cannot.

◼ Arrays, or Tables

In many cases it is convenient to arrange the data not in a simple, one-dimensional list, but in a **table**. The corresponding algorithmic data structure is called a **matrix**, or a **two-dimensional array**, or simply an **array** for short. Here too, applications are plentiful. The standard second-grade multiplication table is a 10 by 10 array in which the data item at each point is the product of the row and column indices; a list of students plotted against a list of courses can be thought of as an array, where the data items are the student's grade in the course; the earth's latitude/longitude grid can be the basis of an array giving the altitudes at each intersection point, and so on.

Referring to an array element is typically achieved using *two* indices, *row* and *column*. We write $A[5, 3]$ for the element located at row 5 and column 3, so that, for example, if A is the multiplication table, then the value of $A[5, 3]$ is 15. As before, we may write $A[X, Y]$, as well as $A[X + 4, 17 - Y]$, and the like.

If a variable is like a hotel room and a vector is like a hotel corridor/floor, then a matrix, or an array, is like an entire hotel. Its "rows" are the various floors, and its "columns" represent the locations along the corridor/floor. If a vector as a data structure corresponds to a loop as a control structure, then an array corresponds to nested loops (see Figure 2.9). Running through the entire array of students' grades can be achieved by an outer loop running through all students and an inner one running through all of a particular student's grades, or vice versa.

---

[4] Despite this close relationship between vectors and loops, we should emphasize that loops are used for many other purposes, and that other control structures are also used with vectors.

Figure 2.9

Data structures,
control structures, and
hotels.

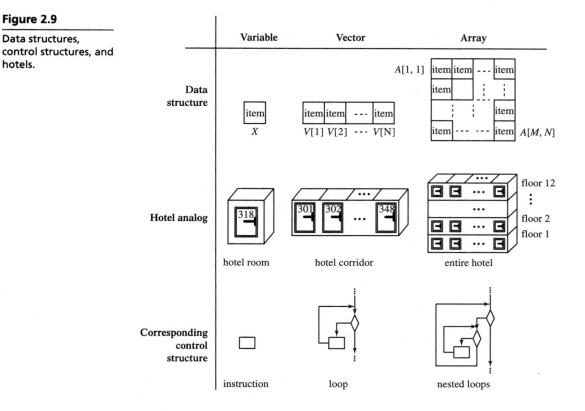

It is not always the case that data can be arranged in a precise rectangular format. Take the students and courses example; different students might be associated not only with different courses, but also with a different *number* of them. We might still use an array (wide enough to contain the maximal number of possible courses), but leaving parts of it empty, wherever the student in question has not taken the course in question. Alternatively, we can use a new data structure, consisting of a vector whose elements themselves point to vectors of varying length. The difference is illustrated in Figure 2.10.

Algorithms can use more elaborate arrays, such as ones with higher dimensionality. A three-dimensional array is like a cube, with three indices needed to point

Figure 2.10

An array vs. a vector
of vectors.

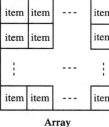
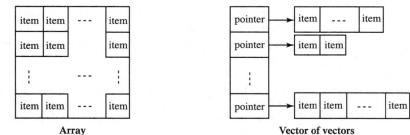

Figure 2.11

A queue and a stack.

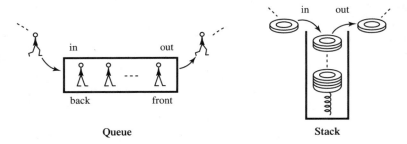

Queue   Stack

to an element.[5] If so desired, we can utilize only special portions of arrays, such as the upper triangular portion of a two-dimensional array, obtained by restricting the indices in $A[X, Y]$ so that X is smaller than Y.

Queues and Stacks

An interesting variation on the vector/array theme follows from the observation that in many applications of vectors and arrays, we do not need the full power provided by indices. Sometimes a list is used just to model a **queue**, in which case all the algorithm needs in way of interaction with the list is the ability to add elements to its "back" and remove them from its "front." Other times the list is to model a **stack**, like those used in a restaurant for storing plates. Here the algorithm needs adding and removing abilities only at one end of the list, its "top." A queue is sometimes referred to as a FIFO list (First-In-First-Out), and a stack as a LIFO list (Last-In-First-Out). Elements are pushed on to a stack, the topmost element being the only one exposed for inspection, and then the stack can be *popped*, meaning that the topmost element is removed (see Figure 2.11). The point in these special cases is that it is worthwhile, at least for reasons of algorithmic clarity, to think of queues and stacks as being in themselves data structures, rather than being merely special kinds of lists. We can then use specially devised elementary instructions such as "add X to queue A," or "push X on stack S," rather than obscure formulations that explicitly involve indices.

■ When discussing recursion earlier, we implicitly came across the need for a vector that is really used only as a stack. The details will not be presented here, but you are invited to think about the way the processor goes about remembering where it really is when executing a recursive algorithm. Remembering its whereabouts in the *text* of the algorithm does not pose a problem. What does require some bookkeeping is managing the list of recursive calls that have not yet been completed, and figuring out where to return to when each call is completed. It is not too difficult to see—and we can use the Towers of Hanoi algorithm to illustrate this—that we actually need a stack. Whenever it is asked to re-enter the routine by a recursive call, the processor "pushes" its return "address" and the current values of the parameters on to the stack. (In the Towers example there is a choice of two such possible addresses, corresponding to the locations of the two call instructions

---

[5] Stretching the hotel metaphor becomes difficult here. Is a three-dimensional array not a single hotel but a whole resort area?

in the algorithm.) When it completes an execution of the recursive routine, it reads the "pushed" information from the top of the stack, restores the old values to the parameters, and returns to the specified address in the algorithm's text. In the process, it also "pops" that information off the top of the stack and discards it.

Another example of the use of stacks involves traversing a labyrinth by exhausting all possibilities. Such a traversal requires that we keep a list of crossroads already visited, adding new ones to the stack as they are reached, and deleting the ones whose paths have all been traversed. In this way, the stack can be seen to contain at all times a path from the start to the presently visited point in the labyrinth.

Trees, or Hierarchies

One of the most important and prominent data structures in existence is the **tree**. This is not a tree in the botanic sense of the word, but one of more abstract nature. We have all seen such trees used to describe family connections. The two most common kinds of family trees are the "ancestor tree," which starts at an individual and works back through parents, grandparents, and so on, and the "descendant tree," which works forward through children, grandchildren, and so on.

A tree is essentially a hierarchical arrangement of data. One item resides in a special place called the **root**, and the others are organized as the root's **descendants**. In computer science, trees are usually visualized "upside down"—the root at the top, and the rest of the tree spread out below. The terminology used is a strange mixture of terms from mathematics, botany, and mono-parental family life. We talk about the root, about a tree's **nodes** (points in the tree), its **offspring** (immediate descendants), its **leaves** (nodes at the "bottom" of the tree, having no offspring), its **paths**, or **branches** (sequences of nodes corresponding to downward traversals in the direction from the root to a leaf), as well as about parents, ancestors, descendants, and siblings (two nodes are siblings if they have the same parent). Figure 2.12

Figure 2.12

A tree.

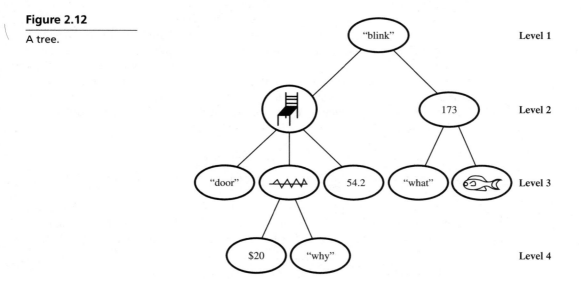

shows a tree, deliberately constructed with no particular explanation in mind for its contents or arrangement. Nevertheless, the word "blink" is its root, or to use different terminology, it is a node on level 1 of the tree; the chair and the number 173 are the root's offspring, or, equivalently, they are the nodes on level 2 of the tree, and so on. An example of trees familiar to computer users is the hierarchical organization of files in directories, which may themselves be contained in other directories.

Trees are to be found elsewhere in everyday life. The organizational charts of most companies are trees, as are schematic descriptions of the breakup of complex machines. Even algorithms themselves can often be described in a tree structure; roughly speaking, the levels of the tree correspond to the levels represented by the sequences of numbers we use in this book for labeling instructions.

Another important example concerns **game trees**. The root of a chess tree, for example, contains a description of the opening board configuration in chess. The root's offspring represent the 20 possible board configurations resulting from White making a first move, and the offspring of each of them would represent the results of all possible responses on Black's part, and so on. Most two-person game trees, like that of chess, have a number of interesting properties. Odd-numbered levels correspond to the first player's turn to move, whereas even-numbered ones correspond to the other player's turn. Paths correspond to actual games, and any possible game appears as a path in the tree. Finally, leaves represent game endings (for example, in chess by checkmate or a threefold repetition). We shall have occasion to return to game trees later on in the book.

Trees are used in numerous diverse applications, and more than any other structural method for combining parts into a whole they can be said to represent the special kind of structuring that abounds in algorithmics.

■ Treesort: An Example

To give some kind of feel for the usefulness of trees, let us now consider another sorting routine, based on binary trees. A **binary tree** is one in which each node has at most two offspring. (The ancestor family tree, for example, is binary.) A binary tree can also be defined as a tree whose **outdegree** is bounded by 2. The advantage of the latter term is in its generality; we can talk about trees with outdegree 17 or 938, or even of those with infinite outdegree.[6] Returning to binary trees, since the outdegree at each node is at most 2, it is convenient to distinguish between the two offspring, referring to them as the left-hand and right-hand ones, respectively.

Treesort, as we shall call it, consists of two main steps:

(1) transform the input list into a binary search tree T;

(2) traverse T in a left-first fashion, and output each element on the second visit.

An explanation is in order here. To sort a list of elements (say numbers), the algorithm first organizes the elements into a special kind of binary tree, called a **binary search tree**. Every node of this tree enjoys the following property: all of its

---

[6] Notice that a tree with outdegree 1 is simply a list, or a vector.

Figure 2.13

A list and its resulting binary search tree.

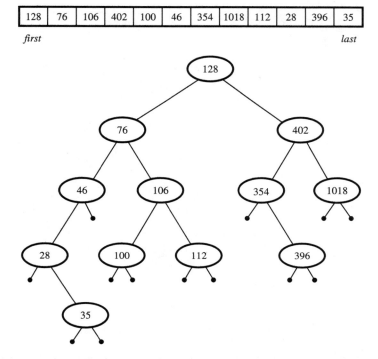

| 128 | 76 | 106 | 402 | 100 | 46 | 354 | 1018 | 112 | 28 | 396 | 35 |

first   *last*

"left descendants" (that is, all elements in its entire left-hand subtree, not only its immediate left-hand offspring) are smaller in value than the value of the node itself, and all of its right descendants are larger than it. Figure 2.13 shows an example of such a binary search tree. This tree can be constructed as follows: The first element in the list is taken to be the root, and then each element is considered in turn, and is attached to the growing tree as a new leaf, possibly "unleafing" previously inserted leaves in the process. Finding a new element's rightful place as a leaf in the tree is done by comparing it repeatedly with the nodes arrived at, turning left or right according to the outcome of the comparison. If the new element is smaller than the element at the node we are looking at we go left (since it then belongs to the left of that node); otherwise we go right. You should use Figure 2.13 to become acquainted with this procedure, and should then try writing down the subroutine representing step (1).

Now comes the interesting part. Having constructed the binary search tree, the second stage of treesort calls for traversing it in the following manner. The processor starts at the root and moves downwards, always keeping to the left.[7] Whenever it tries to move left but cannot (for example, when there is no left-hand offspring) it reluctantly moves right. Having exhausted both left and right, either because it finds no offspring, or because it has already visited those offspring, it **backtracks**; that is, it moves upwards to the current node's parent. If this upward move completes the trip from the parent node to its *left* offspring, the processor turns right and plunges downwards once more; but if it has just returned from the *right*ward trip, it has

---

[7] Note that we are using the directions from the point of view of an observer looking at the tree as pictured. The processor itself, if viewed, say, as driving a vehicle, sees our left as its right.

Figure 2.14

Left-first traversal of a binary search tree.

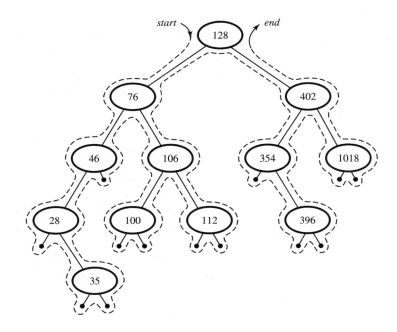

actually exhausted both possibilities of the parent node, and so it moves up to *its* parent. This process continues until both downwards directions of the tree's root have been exhausted, having thus traversed the entire tree. Figure 2.14 shows the left-first traversal of the tree of Figure 2.13.

Why do we carry out this strange traversal? Well, first observe that if we consider the absence of an offspring to cause a short "stump," or "dead end," to be present, which also has to be traversed, then each node in the tree is "visited" precisely three times. Now, if, when traversing the tree in this fashion, we consistently output the data element found at a node when visiting it precisely for the *second* time, the list will eventually be sent to the output in its entirety, sorted in ascending order! This might sound like magic, but it can be easily illustrated by following the twisted traversal arrows in Figure 2.14, jotting down the numbers as they are visited, and then marking the second appearance of each in the resulting list. These marks form the sorted list (see Figure 2.15).

Both stages of the treesort algorithm can be described rather easily as recursive subroutines. Here is a routine for the second stage, where we use "*left(T)*" to denote the left-hand subtree of T, and similarly for "*right(T)*." By our convention regarding the presence of stumps when offspring do not exist, "*left(T)*," for a tree that has no left subtree, will be the special **empty tree**; that is, the tree containing nothing, not even a root.

Figure 2.15

Second-visit marking in the left-first traversal of Figure 2.14.

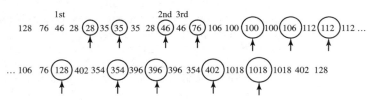

subroutine **second-visit-traversal-of** T:

(1) if T is empty then return;

(2) otherwise (i.e., if T is not empty) do the following:

    (2.1) call **second-visit-traversal-of** *left*(T);

    (2.2) output the data element found at the root of T;

    (2.3) call **second-visit-traversal-of** *right*(T);

(3) return.

In constructing this routine we have exploited the fact that the second time a node is visited will always be just after completing the traversal of its entire left-hand subtree, and just before starting that of its right-hand subtree. Thus, we first call the subroutine recursively in order to complete the entire traversal for the left-hand subtree, and when that call has terminated (that is, the traversal of that subtree has been completed), we output the element at the root, since it is now visited for the second time (the first time being when we proceeded downwards to its left-hand subtree). We then proceed recursively downwards to the right to carry out the right-hand traversal.

The "left-first" nature of this special traversal becomes quite apparent from the structure of the recursive formulation, since for every subtree (that is, for every recursive call) the routine can easily be seen to go first to the left and then to the right. Incidentally, it is interesting to see what happens in terms of the output list when we turn this around, going consistently first to the right and then to the left. (What does happen, and how do we change the subroutine accordingly?)

The structure of this routine is reminiscent of the **move** routine for the Towers of Hanoi. In fact, if we apply this routine to a sample tree and then draw the picture of the processor's toils, as was done in Figure 2.8, the picture will precisely reflect the shape of the sample tree. Figure 2.8 itself forms a tree which, being of uniform depth (or height, depending on our point of view), is sometimes called a **full** tree.

We can, then, conclude that if vectors and arrays as data structures correspond to loops and nested loops as control structures, then trees correspond to recursive routines. A tree is an inherently recursive object, consisting of nothing (that is, an empty tree, as explained earlier), or of a root attached (recursively) to some number of trees. This explains why tree traversals, such as the one just considered, are relatively easy to describe recursively.

There are some interesting ways to introduce flexibility into existing data structures. A good example is the concept of **self-adjustment**. By this we mean that each time an element is inserted or deleted from a data structure, the structure executes an adjustment routine that makes simple changes, intended to retain certain "nice" properties. For example, in many applications of trees it is possible that, due to some sequence of insertions/deletions, the tree becomes thin and long, whereas for reasons of efficiency (see Chapter 6) it might be desirable that it be wide and short. It is possible—though we shall not get into the details—to make small local changes to a tree whenever an operation is performed on it, which will guarantee the property of being wide and short.

■ Databases and Knowledge Bases

For many computer applications data structures are not enough. It is not always a question of merely pondering an algorithmic problem and finding, or defining, nice and useful data structures for its solution. At times there is a need for a very large "pool" of data, which many algorithms treat as part of their inputs, and which must therefore be of fixed structure, and readily available for retrieval and manipulation. Examples include the financial and personnel data of a company, the reservations and flight information of an airline, and the indexing data of a library. Such masses of data are called **databases**.

Typically, databases are very large, and contain many different kinds of data, ranging from names and addresses to obscure codes and symbols, and in some cases even free text. They are usually subjected to numerous kinds of insertion, deletion, and retrieval procedures, utilized for different purposes and by different people. While the addition of a new student to a university database, or the removal of an old one, are relatively easy tasks, when it comes to **querying** a database, with the purpose of retrieving information from it, intricacy seems to have no bounds. Just for perspective, here are a few queries that might be addressed to the database of a flight reservation system:

- list all passengers confirmed on flight 123;
- list all seats on flight 123 occupied by passengers with no checked baggage;
- find the number of passengers who have reserved seats on two identically numbered flights scheduled for consecutive days in March of this year;
- list the names and seat numbers of all first-class passengers on tomorrow's Paris-bound flights, who have ordered vegetarian food, and who have intercontinental continuation flights upon which economy-class service does not provide special meals, and whose stopover points are either Zurich or Rome.

These examples illustrate the importance of a "good" organization of the database. If continuation flights are listed in the database in some obscure place, and if there is no easy way to gather the information concerning a given passenger's itinerary, then writing an algorithm to solve the last-listed retrieval problem will become a difficult task indeed. As with data structures, good database design is important not only for reasons of clarity and ease in writing; it can be of the utmost importance when it comes to questions of efficiency, and to the feasibility of constructing a database system that can respond to such queries in a reasonable amount of time.

Various general **models** for database organization have been proposed and are used in real databases. These models are designed to maintain large quantities of data, while capturing, faithfully and efficiently, the relationships between the data items. One of the most popular database models, the **relational** model, caters for the arrangement of the data in large tables, which are reminiscent of the array data structure. Others call for certain kinds of tree-like, or network-like arrangements such as the **hierarchical** model, which organizes data in multiple-layer tree-like form (like that of Figure 3.3). There does not seem to be a sweeping consensus as to the preferable models for particular applications, and many methods and languages have been developed for manipulating and querying databases constructed in each of these models. However, there is a significant movement towards the relational model, and the more recent **object-oriented databases** are waiting off-stage for their turn.

Databases are often used to support operational systems that keep track of changes in the myriad details necessary for the functioning of a large organization. As such, they must support efficient modifications of the data as well as queries thereof, but they are less concerned with keeping information that is of historical value only. However, the large amounts of data stored in databases can also be used for analytical purposes, such as discovering trends or improving processes. For example, a bank might wish to discover correlations between loan defaulting and other account-holder properties, in order to develop better predictive tools. This can be done by applying statistical analysis methods to the large amount of old data available in the bank's own databases. The science of discovering such useful nuggets of information from huge sources of data is called **data mining**, and it deals mostly with historical data that does not change. Typically, the amount of historical data is much greater than what is needed for operational purposes; often hundreds of times larger. In recent years, biology offers particularly tantalizing kinds of databases, resulting from the genome project and its spinoffs, and these are beginning to require the development of powerful new kinds of data-mining techniques.

A new kind of database, called the **data warehouse**, has been developed in order to support huge amounts of data that changes slowly, or in which only very small portions change at all. Some data warehouses appear to be similar to other databases to their users; however, the internal organization may use a completely different set of algorithms to achieve its goals efficiently.

Certain kinds of data are better viewed as fragments of knowledge, rather than just as numbers, names, or codes. In addition to a large database describing the inventory of a manufacturing company, we might want to have a large **knowledge base** containing information relevant to the running of that company. Its **knowledge items** might have to somehow encode information such as "Changes in salaries are personnel issues," "Mr Smith is a better manager than Ms Brown when it comes to personnel problems, but not when technical issues are concerned," or "If the price of oil goes up we shall have to lower all salaries within the following month."

Unlike a database, which stores data for later retrieval, a knowledge base uses its knowledge in more sophisticated ways. For example, we might want to infer from the rules given above and the fact that oil prices have gone up, that Mr Smith should handle the salary changes. It is obvious that such inference capabilities require more complex organization than data items of more or less fixed format, especially if we are interested in efficient retrieval. Knowledge bases are thus becoming the natural next step after databases, and they provide a rich source of interesting questions regarding representation, organization, and algorithmic retrieval. We shall have more to say about knowledge in Chapter 15.

Exercises

2.1. The algorithm for summing the salaries of N employees presented in the text performs a loop that consists of adding one salary to the total and advancing a pointer on the employee list $N - 1$ times. The last salary is added separately. What is the reason for this? Why don't we perform the loop N times?

2.2. Consider the bubblesort algorithm presented in the text.

(a) Explain why the outer loop is performed only $N - 1$ times.
(b) Improve the algorithm so that on every repeated execution of the outer loop, the inner loop checks one element less.

2.3. Prepare flowcharts for the bubblesort algorithm presented in the text and for the improved version you were asked to design in Exercise 2.2.

2.4. Write algorithms that, given an integer N and a list L of N integers, produce in S and P the sum of the even numbers appearing in L and the product of the odd ones, respectively.

(a) Using bounded iteration.
(b) Using "goto" statements.

2.5. Show how to perform the following simulations of some control constructs by others. The sequencing construct "and-then" is implicitly available for all the simulations. You may introduce and use new variables and labels if necessary.

(a) Simulate a "for-do" loop by a "while-do" loop.
(b) Simulate the "if-then" and "if-then-else" statements by "while-do" loops.
(c) Simulate a "while-do" loop by "if-then" and "goto" statements.
(d) Simulate a "while-do" loop by a "repeat-until" loop and "if-then" statements.

2.6. Write down the sequence of moves resolving the Towers of Hanoi problem for five rings.

The *factorial* of a non-negative integer N is the product of all positive integers smaller than or equal to N. More formally, the expression N *factorial*, denoted by $N!$, is recursively defined by $0! = 1$ and $(N + 1)! = N! \times (N + 1)$. For example, $1! = 1$ and $4! = 3! \times 4 = \ldots = 1 \times 2 \times 3 \times 4 = 24$.

2.7. Write algorithms that compute $N!$, given a non-negative integer N.

(a) Using iteration statements.
(b) Using recursion.

2.8. Show how to simulate a "while-do" loop by conditional statements and a recursive procedure.

For a positive integer N, denote by A_N the set of integers 1 through N. A *permutation* of the set A_N is an ordered sequence $(a_1, a_2, \ldots, a_N)$ in which each integer from the set A_N appears exactly once. For example, $(2, 3, 1)$ and $(1, 2, 3)$ are two different permutations of the set A_3.

2.9. Prove that the number of permutations of A_N is $N!$.

2.10. A permutation $(a_1, \ldots, a_N)$ can be represented by a vector P of length N with $P[I] = a_I$. Design an algorithm which, given an integer N and a vector of integers P of length N, checks whether P represents any permutation of A_N.

2.11. Design an algorithm which, given a positive integer N, produces all the permutations of A_N.

We say that a permutation $\sigma = (a_1, \ldots, a_N)$ can be obtained by a stack, if it is possible to start from the input sequence $(1, 2, \ldots, N)$ and an empty stack S, and produce the output σ using only the following types of operations:

read(X): Read an integer from the input into variable X.
print(X): Print the integer currently stored in variable X on the output.
push(X, S): Push the integer currently stored in variable X on to the stack S.

pop(X, S): Pop the integer from the top of the stack S into variable X. (This operation is illegal if S is empty.)

For example, the permutation (2, 1) can be obtained by a stack, since the following series of operations

read(X), **push**(X, S), **read**(X), **print**(X), **pop**(X, S), **print**(X)

applied to the input sequence (1, 2) produces the output sequence (2, 1).

A permutation can be obtained by a queue, if it can be similarly obtained from the input $(1, 2, \ldots, N)$, using an initially empty queue Q, and the operations **read**(X), **print**(X), and

add(X, Q): Add the integer currently stored in X to the rear of Q.
remove(X, Q): Remove the integer from the front of Q into X. (This operation is illegal if Q is empty.)

We can similarly speak of a permutation obtained by two stacks, if we permit the **push** and **pop** operations on two stacks S and S'.

2.12. (a) Show that the following permutations can be obtained by a stack:
    i. (3, 2, 1).
    ii. (3, 4, 2, 1).
    iii. (3, 5, 7, 6, 8, 4, 9, 2, 10, 1).
 (b) Prove that the following permutations cannot be obtained by a stack:
    i. (3, 1, 2).
    ii. (4, 5, 3, 7, 2, 1, 6).
 (c) How many permutations of A_4 *cannot* be obtained by a stack?

2.13. Design an algorithm that checks whether a given permutation can be obtained by a stack. In case the answer is yes, the algorithm should also print the appropriate series of operations. In your algorithm, in addition to **read**, **print**, **push**, and **pop**, you may use the test **is-empty**(S) for testing the emptiness of the stack S.

2.14. (a) Give series of operations that show that each of the permutations given in Exercise 2.12(b) can be obtained by a queue and also by two stacks.
 (b) Prove that every permutation can be obtained by a queue.
 (c) Prove that every permutation can be obtained by two stacks.

2.15. Extend the algorithm you were asked to design in Exercise 2.13, so that if the given permutation cannot be obtained by a stack, the algorithm will print the series of operations on two stacks that will generate it.

2.16. Consider the treesort algorithm described in the text.

 (a) Construct an algorithm that transforms a given list of integers into a binary search tree.
 (b) What would the output of treesort look like if we were to reverse the order in which the subroutine **second-visit-traversal** calls itself recursively? In other words, we consistently visit the right offspring of a node before we visit the left one.

And thou shalt make loops

EXODUS 26: 4

And he spoke of trees

I KINGS 5: 13

CHAPTER 3

Programming Languages and Paradigms

Come, let us go down, and there confound their language, that they may not understand one another's speech

GENESIS 11: 7

or, Getting It Done by Computer

Thinking about algorithmic problems and their solutions is fine, and in fact, as should be obvious by now, it is beneficial not only in computer-related problem solving, but also in the realms of cake baking, tire changing, cabinet making, and telephone book lookup. However, clearly our main concern is with algorithms that are intended for computer execution, and hence before we continue with our account of the scientific aspects of algorithmics, we should spend some time relating algorithms to real computers.

As mentioned in Chapter 1, even the most sophisticated computer is really only a large, well-organized volume of bits, and moreover it can normally carry out only a small number of extremely simple operations on them, such as zeroing, flipping, and testing (see Figure 1.1). How do we present an algorithm to a real computer and get it to carry out the corresponding process as intended? Let us put it more bluntly. How do we get a dumb machine, capable of so little, to impressively perform our subtle and carefully worked-out algorithms? Of course, this question becomes all the more pressing when we look around and see computers carrying out not only our toy examples of salary summation and word searching, but incredibly complex feats such as automatic flight control, graphical simulation of chemical reactions, or the orderly maintenance of communication networks with millions of subscribers.

The first observation is that our algorithms must be written in an unambiguous and formal fashion. Before trying to understand how playing around with bits can be made to accomplish even a simple task such as "proceed through the list, adding each salary to the noted number," that task itself has to be precisely specified: Where does the computer find the list? How does it proceed through it? Where does it find the salary and the "noted number"? and so on. "Beat egg whites until foamy" is not much worse in terms of precision and unambiguity than "proceed through a list."

To describe an algorithm for a computer's benefit, rather than just for human comprehension, we use a **programming language**, in which we write **programs**. A program is an official and formal rendition of the algorithm, suitable for computer execution. A programming language consists of the notation and rules by which one writes programs, and the person writing the program is called a **programmer**. (This person need not be the one who devised the algorithm upon which the program is based.)

Of course, the "raw" computer doesn't directly understand any of these programming languages, but only programs written in **machine language**, which consists of bit-manipulation instructions, themselves coded as series of bits. As mentioned in Chapter 1, it is the use of abstraction that allows us to act as if the computer in fact understands the **high-level** programming languages we are discussing here. Later on we will see some of the mechanics of this abstraction.

Programs Require Precise Syntax

A programming language is typically associated with a rigid **syntax**, allowing the use of only special combinations of selected symbols and keywords. Any attempt at stretching this syntax might turn out to be disastrous; for example, if **input** X is written in a language whose input commands are of the form **read** X, the chances are that the result will be a blunt "*SYNTAX ERROR E4514 ON LINE 108*." This, of course, precludes even such polite but imprecise requests such as "please read a value for X from the input," or "how about getting me a value for X." These might result in a long string of obscure error messages. It is true that nice, talkative instructions are more pleasant and perhaps less ambiguous than their terse and impersonal equivalents for a human reader. It also true that we would like computers to be as "user friendly" as possible. However, these facts should be contrasted with the current inability of computers to understand freely spoken (or freely typed) natural languages like English (see Chapter 15). A formal, concise, and rigid set of syntactic rules is therefore essential.

The formal syntax of a typical programming language includes orderly versions of several control structures, orderly ways of defining various data structures, and orderly formats for the basic instructions supported by the language. The difference is that now our imaginary little robot Runaround is less imaginary, since the computer is doing the work, and it will not carry out any instruction, however clear and unambiguous, if that instruction is not among those allowed by the programming language.

An algorithm for summing the numbers from 1 to N might be written in a typical (hypothetical) programming language PL as follows:

```
input N;
X:=0;
for Y from 1 to N do
        X:=X + Y
end;
output X.
```

Here $X:=0$ is the **assignment** statement that sets variable X to initial value 0 (in our algorithms we write $X \leftarrow 0$ for this). Notice the boldface keywords; they are part of the syntax of PL, meaning that the formal definition of that syntax most

Figure 3.1

Syntax diagrams for programming language definition.

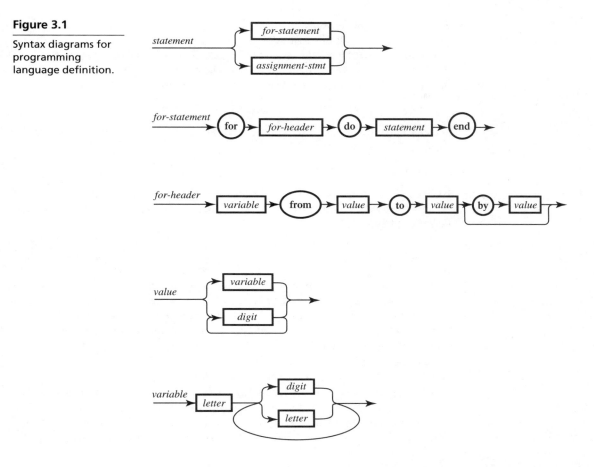

probably contains a clause to the effect that one of the legal kinds of **statements** in the language is a *for-statement*, whose general format consists of the keyword **for**, followed by a legal *for-header*, followed by **do**, followed by a legal statement, followed by **end**.[1] Syntax definitions can be written symbolically, in a form termed BNF (standing for Backus-Naur Form, after its inventors), as follows, where "|" denotes "or":

⟨statement⟩ is: ⟨for-statement⟩ | ⟨assignment-stmt⟩ | · · ·
⟨for-statement⟩ is: **for**⟨for-header⟩ **do** ⟨statement⟩ **end**

The description of the header clause might read:

⟨for-header⟩ is: ⟨variable⟩ **from** ⟨value⟩ **to** ⟨value⟩

The ⟨value⟩ might then be specified to be a variable, an explicit number, or some other object. Figure 3.1 shows a diagrammatic way of presenting such syntax rules.

---

[1] Notice that this definition is recursive. Statements are defined in terms of themselves! To resolve this apparent cyclicity there must be an "escape clause," whereby certain statements, such as assignments, do not recursively refer to statements in their definition, only, say, to values and variables.

The example shows how the language enforces a special format for a particular kind of bounded-loop control construct.

Formats for defining data structures are similarly enforced. For example, a two-dimensional array *AR* of size 50 by 100, whose values can be integers, might be defined in the hypothetical language PL by the statement:

> **define** *AR* **array** [1..50, 8..107] **of integers**

and the language might allow reference to elements of *AR* by expressions of the form:

> *AR(value, value)*

Notice how we have not only specified the dimensions of *AR*, but also its subscript values; its rows are numbered 1, 2, ..., 50, but its columns are (for some reason) numbered 8, 9, ..., 107.

Actually, the syntax prescribes much more than the available control and data structures and the allowed elementary operations. Usually a language has rigid rules even for such petty issues as the legal strings of symbols that may be used to name variables or data structures, and the maximal number of digits allowed in numeric values. Some languages restrict variable names to be at most, say, eight symbols long, the first being alphabetical. Here *punctuation* does not get overlooked either; it is not atypical for a programming language to require that a semicolon is to follow some kinds of statements, that a space is to follow others, that comments are to be enclosed in special brackets, and so on, all with penalties for violators. This is the reason for our use of the term "semicolon syndrome" in the preface to this book. In order to make readers knowledgeable enough to bend computers to their will, some computer books start out with a meticulous description of the syntax of a specific programming language, semicolon rules and all, with these tedious details of the syntax being the dominant elements a student is required to remember.

Programs Require Precise Semantics

Providing the language with a precise syntax is only part of a programming language designer's job. Without a formal and unambiguous **semantics**—that is, without a *meaning* for each syntactically allowed phrase—the syntax is all but worthless. If meanings for instructions in the language have not been provided, the program segment:

> **for** *Y* **from** 1 **to** *N* **do**

in the hypothetical language PL might, for all we know, mean "subtract *Y* from 1 and store the result in *N*." Worse still, who says that the keywords **from**, **to**, **do**, and so on, have anything at all to do with their meaning in conventional English? Maybe the very same program segment means "erase all of the computer's memory, change the values of all variables to 0, output 'TO HELL WITH PROGRAMMING LANGUAGES,' and stop!" Who says that ":=" stands for "assign to" and "+" stands for "plus?" Who says that instructions are carried out in their written order? Maybe ";" means "after doing the following" rather than "and then do the following."

Of course, we might be able to guess what is meant, since the designer of PL probably chose keywords and special symbols intending that their meaning be as similar to the accepted norm as possible. But a computer cannot be made to act on such assumptions. Even if it could somehow reason about the conventional meaning of English words and of symbols like "+," how, without being told explicitly, would it know what to do with the loop header:

for Y **from** 1 **to** N **do**

when the value of N is, say, -314.1592? Is the body of the loop to be carried out 316 times, with Y working its way through the values $1, 0, -1, -2, \ldots, -313$, and -314? Maybe it is carried out 317 times, including the case -315; or 633 times, running through $1, \frac{1}{2}, 0, -\frac{1}{2}, -1, \ldots, -315$? Maybe it is not carried out at all, the rationale being that N's value is smaller than 1, and **for** loops must *in*crease their built-in counters, not *de*crease them. Maybe arriving at the **for** statement with such a bizarre value in N should be treated as *"LOOP INDEX ERROR Z3088 ON LINE 365."*

It seems clear, therefore, that a programming language requires not only rigid rules for defining the form of a legal program, but also rules, just as rigid, for defining its meaning.

It might come as a surprise to some people that for many modern programming languages a satisfactory semantics has not been worked out at all. And we don't mean an implementation. Some people think that since a language has been implemented and its programs actually run (for example, it has a compiler, a term we shall explain later in the chapter), that is good enough a semantics. The fact is that we need a rigorous, machine-independent definition of the meaning of each program in the language; one that can be employed to give unambiguous answers to every possible question regarding what a program will do under any set of circumstances, whether what it will do is what we intend it to do, and so on. (See Chapter 5 for more on this gap between programs and our expectations from them.) Wherever adequate semantic definitions exist, they were usually prepared, not by the language designer or the computer manufacturer, but by independent researchers interested in the semantical problems raised by specific languages and their powerful features.

Designers and manufacturers do supply detailed **documentation** to go along with the language—volumes of it. These **language manuals**, as they are sometimes called, contain a wealth of information concerning both syntax and semantics, but the semantical information is usually not sufficient for the user to figure out exactly what will happen in each and every syntactically legal program. The problem is a real one, and evidence for this can be found in the deep and intricate work of programming language semanticists. It is very tempting to add a new and powerful feature to a language, and to specify how to deal with it in a natural context. However, it is the unpredictability of the interaction of such a feature with all others supported by the language that can cause things to get out of hand.

Routines as Parameters: An Example

Let us assume that a language supporting recursive routines is to allow, not only variables whose values are numbers or words (= symbol strings), but also special variables whose values are the very names of routines. Once such features are allowed, it should also be possible to use routine variables as parameters to other routines. In this way if a routine P is defined as:

>subroutine P-**with-parameter-**V

where V is a routine variable, and somewhere inside P there is an instruction of the form:

>call V

then if P is invoked with the value of V being the routine Q, this instruction will effect a call to Q inside P, whereas if P is invoked with V being some other routine R, it will effect a call to R inside P. This is quite a powerful feature, enabling external control over the routines that P calls, simply by changing V's value. However, serious semantical problems arise. What if V is also a routine whose parameter is a routine variable?

▨ To sharpen the question, here is an example of such a P:

>subroutine P-**with-parameter-**V
>(1) call V-**with-parameter-**V, placing returned value in X:
>(2) if $X = 1$ then return with 0; else return with 1.

But what will our confused processor do when asked to carry out the following initial call to P:

>call P-**with-parameter-**P

Syntactically, everything is fine; the routines are all called with the right syntax and the right kinds of parameters. Nevertheless, there is a paradox embodied in the very question. It is impossible that the call returns 0, because by the definition of the body of P, the value returned is 0 if a call to V-**with-parameter-**V (which is now really a call to P-**with-parameter-**P) returns 1. So, the call can return 0 only if it returns 1, which is ridiculous! A similar argument shows that the P-**with-parameter-**P call cannot return 1 either, but by the text of P it cannot return anything *other* than 0 or 1. So what *does* it do? Does this strange call entail an endless seesaw process? Is it simply forbidden by the language? Neither of these suggestions sounds quite right. With the first we might want to see the infinite nature of the execution reflected more explicitly in the text. The second is even worse, since it is not clear how to characterize the forbidden programs syntactically. Obviously, a formal semantics to such a language must imply precise and unambiguous answers to such questions.

From High-Level Languages to Bit Manipulation

So here we are, with a high-level programming language PL, syntax, semantics, and all, and we have just finished devising an algorithm A for the solution of some algorithmic problem. We now proceed to program the algorithm in the language PL, an action sometimes referred to as the **coding** of A into PL, and we would like to present the resulting program, called A_P, to our computer. What happens next? The answer is that basically there are two possibilities, depending on the language and computer used. Here is the first.

The program A_P is entered into the computer's memory, by typing it in from a keyboard, reading it in from a recording device such as a magnetic disk, receiving it along an electronic communication channel from another computer, or by some other means. While these physical media and their use are of no concern here, what happens next is of importance to us. The program A_P goes through a number of **transformations**, which gradually bring it "down" to a level the computer can deal with. The final product of these transformations is a program A_M on the **machine level** (it is also said to be written in **machine language**), meaning that its basic operations are those which the computer "understands," such as bit-manipulation instructions. The number of such downward transformations varies from language to language and from one machine to another, but is typically between two and four. The intermediate objects are usually legal programs in increasingly more primitive programming languages. Their repertoire of control and data structures—and hence the basic instructions—gradually becomes more humble, until finally only the most elementary bit capabilities remain. It is after this final transformation stage that the computer can really *run*, or execute, the original program, or at least can give the user the impression that it is doing just that, by asking for a set of legal inputs and running the transformed version A_M (see Figure 3.2).

The downward transformations are somewhat reminiscent of replacing subroutines by their bodies. An instruction in a high-level language can be thought of as a call to a routine, or as a basic instruction that is not basic enough for the computer. As a consequence, it has to be refined and brought down to the computer's level of competence.

Compilation and Assembly Languages

Let us talk about the first transformation, called **compilation**, in which the high-level program A_P is translated into a program A_S in a lower-level language, called **assembly language**. Assembly languages differ from machine to machine, but, as a rule, they employ rather simple control structures, that resemble **goto** statements and **if-then** constructs, and they deal not only with bits but also with integers and strings of symbols. They can refer directly to locations in the computer's **memory**—that large area containing acres upon acres of bits—they can **read** from those locations whatever numbers and strings they encode, and they can **store** encodings of numbers and strings therein.

A typical high-level loop construct such as:

```
for Y from 1 to N do
      ⟨body-of-loop⟩
end
```

Figure 3.2

Transforming a
high-level program
into machine code.

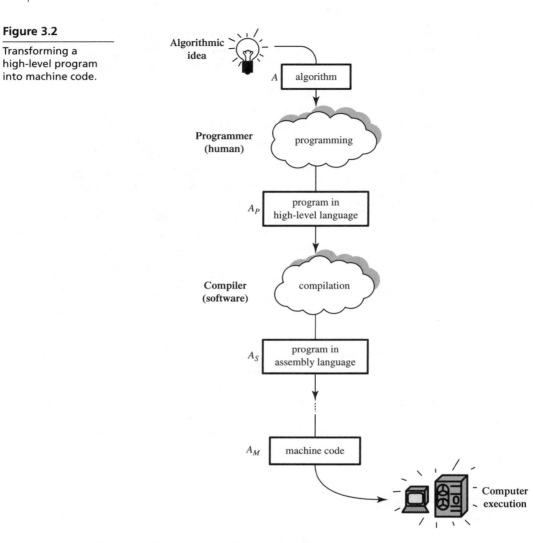

might be translated into an assembly language equivalent looking like this (the parenthesized explanations are not part of the program):

$$
\begin{array}{lll}
& \textbf{MVC}\ 0,\ Y & \text{(move constant 0 to location } Y) \\
\text{LOOP:} & \textbf{CMP}\ N,\ Y & \text{(compare values at locations } N \text{ and } Y) \\
& \textbf{JEQ}\ \ \text{REST} & \text{(if equal jump to statement labelled ``REST'')} \\
& \textbf{ADC}\ \ 1,\ Y & \text{(add constant 1 to value at location } Y) \\
\end{array}
$$

⟨translated-body-of-loop⟩

$$
\begin{array}{lll}
& \textbf{JMP}\ \ \text{LOOP} & \text{(jump back to statement labeled ``LOOP'')} \\
\text{REST:} & & \text{(rest of program)} \\
\end{array}
$$

Prior to (or following) the assembly program itself there would appear additional instructions to associate the symbols Y and N with certain fixed memory locations, but we shall not get into these matters here.

Now comes the interesting point. The compilation process that translates high-level computer programs into assembly language is itself carried out by a computer program. This lengthy and complex piece of software, called a **compiler**, is usually supplied by the computer manufacturer together with the hardware. Figure 3.2 illustrates the downward transformation process, of which compilation is the first and most intricate part. The remaining steps translate assembly language into machine language. They are somewhat more straightforward than compilation and hence we shall not deal with them here.

As an aside, it is worth pointing out that compilers for the various high-level languages are but one kind of a large number of manufacturer-supplied programs, sometimes generically called **system software**. Their general role is to facilitate a variety of high-level modes of operation of the computer, while subtly insulating the user from many of the low-level details involved. Running user-written programs is one of these modes, communicating with other computers and interfacing with special external equipment is another.

Interpreters and Immediate Execution

There is another way computers can execute the programs they are presented with, which does not involve translating the entire program into a lower-level language. Rather, each of the program's high-level statements is translated into machine-level instructions immediately on being encountered, and these in turn are promptly executed. In a sense, the computer is playing the role of the robot or processor directly, running around and actually carrying out the high-level instructions one by one precisely as given. The mechanism responsible for this local-translation-and-immediate-execution is also a piece of system software, usually called an **interpreter**.

The interpreter approach has certain obvious advantages, among which are:

- it is usually easier to write a "quick-and-dirty," but reasonably useful, interpreter, than it is to write a reasonable compiler;
- interpreter-driven execution yields a more traceable account of what is happening, especially when working interactively with the computer through a terminal with a display screen.

There are, however, several disadvantages of interpretation over compilation, which will be briefly touched upon in later chapters.

Whether a particular computer will compile or interpret a given program depends on the computer at hand, the programming language, and the particular package of system software in use. Nevertheless, while some programming languages lend themselves to interpretation more easily than others, all languages can, in principle, be compiled.

◼ Why Not an Algorithmic Esperanto?

Since the time high-level programming languages started to appear in the 1950s, hundreds have been designed, and compilers and/or interpreters have been written for them. Many are extinct, and probably many more should be, but there are still scores of languages in common day-to-day use. These languages are, for the most part, quite diverse in nature, both in looks and in substance. Moreover, new ones pop up like mushrooms after rain.

Why? Would it not have been better to have a single universal language, some kind of algorithmic Esperanto, in which all algorithms are written, and which anyone can easily learn to use? Why the multitude of languages? What makes them different from one another? Who uses which languages, and for what purposes?

To answer this question, we must go back to the essential purpose of high-level programming languages, which is to provide new abstractions for programmers. There are basically two forces that drive the need for new kinds of abstractions: new technological developments in hardware, and new and diverse application areas. A good example of the first is the development of **parallel** computers. These are machines that employ many distinct but interconnected "single-track" computers. One of the consequences of these technological developments is the considerable effort devoted to the development of so-called **concurrent** programming languages, which, very briefly, cater for many processors carrying things out simultaneously. Chapter 10 is devoted to the subject of concurrency, hence we shall not dwell on it any further here.

As the power of computers is harnessed in more and more application areas, programmers encounter more and more types of abstractions: from words to pictures, to video, and to virtual reality environments; from strings of characters to DNA, to protein folding, and even to entire biochemical processes; and from syntax of natural languages to story understanding, to commonsense reasoning, and to artificial intelligence. Each application area has its own set of concepts that need to be incorporated into computer programs. This can be done in many ways, one of which is the creation of a variety of special-purpose programming languages, which embody the concepts of specific areas.

◼ Programming Paradigms

The multitude of existing programming languages can be organized into several families, based on their organizing principles, or **paradigms**. A programming paradigm is a way of thinking about the computer, around which other abstractions are built. The first, and most prevalent paradigm, is called **imperative programming**, and its view of the computer (the "von Neumann model") is closest to the bare machine. In this paradigm, which we have used in all the examples up to this point, we think of the computer as a collection of memory cells, organized into many types of data structures, such as arrays, lists, and stacks. Programs in this approach are concerned with building, traversing, and modifying these data structures, by reading and modifying the values stored in memory.

While this paradigm is close to the real architecture of the computer, it is quite far from its mathematical origins. As mentioned in Chapter 2, a mathematical variable denotes a single value. It is only a variable in that we conceive of different instances of the same problem (or different calls of the same function), in which it can take on different values. But while the value of a mathematical variable doesn't change in mid-problem, this is exactly what happens in an imperative computer program! Suppose you see an assignment $X \leftarrow 3$ somewhere in a program. It would be wrong to assume that when you encounter X again a few lines later, it will have the value 3, although our mathematical training encourages us to make that assumption. Even if there is no other assignment to X in the intervening lines, they may contain a subroutine call that changes the value of X. In general, careful and tedious reasoning is required in order to ascertain the value of each variable at each point in the program, and this is one of the causes of complexity in programming and the resulting plethora of problems, or "bugs." More about this in Chapter 5.

A different paradigm, called **functional programming**, looks at the computer at a higher level of abstraction, as a mathematical model. In this view, programs define mathematical functions, and have no concept of modifiable memory. Instead of cells, these programs deal only with immutable values. The details of where these values are actually stored in the computer are hidden by the functional abstraction. Programmers used to imperative thinking often find themselves hampered by this abstraction and the lack of control they have over memory. However, with use, many find it to be liberating, since they have less to worry about. Furthermore, the fact that functional programming deals with mathematics as we are used to it, makes it possible to apply an array of standard mathematical tools to the synthesis and analysis of functional programs and to reasoning about them. From the theoretical point of view, it is interesting to note that the concept of a mathematical function is sufficient to generate all possible kinds of computations (in a sense to be explained in Chapter 9).

Taking its model from logic rather than mathematics, the **logic programming** paradigm views the computer as a logical inference device. A logic program is stated as a set of rules, or simple logical statements of the form *if A, B, ... then X*. When a query is put to the computer, it searches this set of rules for a possible proof (which can also supply information missing from the original query). Such a proof provides an answer to the query; if no proof is found, the query is considered to have no possible answer. Like functional programs, logic programs do not refer explicitly to the computer's memory. It is interesting to note that the functional and logic paradigms have been greatly favored by researchers working in artificial intelligence.

An important offshoot of imperative programming is the well-known **object-oriented programming** paradigm. The major ingredients in an imperative program are the functions (or subroutines) that build and modify data structures; the functions are active, and the data structures are passive. The object-oriented paradigm, in contrast, turns the picture on its side. It views the computer's memory as being composed of many **objects**, corresponding to the data structures of the imperative view. Each object has an associated set of operations it can carry out, and the execution of the program consists of objects sending messages that request operations from one another, getting responses, and further processing the results to satisfy their own callers. In this view, objects are active, and the functions from the imperative view have been reduced to passive messages.

This mental trick is a powerful structuring mechanism. For example, while an imperative program may be organized as a set of subroutines that operate on various data structures, an object-oriented program is constructed around the data types, usually called **classes**. One class might represent a queue, and provide operations to add to it a new element, to remove its first element, to find out whether it is empty, and so on. Another class might represent a bank account, with operations such as withdraw, deposit, obtain current balance, etc. And the bank-account class can use the queue class to keep track of incoming transactions.

The utility of this way of organizing programs is based on the fact that in many (although by no means all) cases it is a natural way to think about the world we are trying to model inside the computer. For example, we could have two objects that represent bank accounts exchanging messages to model a fund transfer operation. Similarly, an object that represents a car being assembled may exchange messages with objects corresponding to the various processing stages it has to go through and the information in the original order that specifies the accessories it needs. It should come as no surprise that the object-oriented paradigm has developed out of languages for the simulation of real-world processes.

The rest of this chapter briefly describes a number of programming languages, touching upon each of these paradigms. It should be noted that no attempt is made to teach any of the languages, nor is the treatment claimed to come anywhere near being a survey of them. Rather, the aim is to present a small sample of the essential features and to give you some idea of what the programs look like and wherein their power lies. Many other important languages deserve to be mentioned too, but diversity in form and applications is preferred to extensive coverage.

Imperative Programming: The Pioneers

Since the view of the imperative paradigm is closest to the "bare" machine, it is no wonder that the first high-level languages were imperative. Three of the earliest (whose pedigrees can be traced as far back as the late 1950s) are FORTRAN, COBOL, and ALGOL. The first two are still in use today, having successfully evolved to meet new developments in hardware and software, while the third, though defunct, has been perhaps the most influential of all.

FORTRAN (FORmula TRANslator) was the result of an acute need for numerical computations in scientific and engineering applications, such as the simulation of the effects of a nuclear reaction. It was designed with efficient compilation in mind, rather than clarity or readability. As a result, the basic version of the language does not support many features for enhancing good program structure, which are considered important in a high-level language. The 1977 extension of the language, FORTRAN 77, remedies this situation to some extent. FORTRAN supports vectors and multi-dimensional arrays, but virtually no other data structures. As to its numerical capabilities, these are quite powerful and extensive. The popularity of the language in the scientific and engineering community has resulted in numerous complex mathematical functions that have been preprogrammed as fixed subroutines, and which are cataloged in various **function libraries**. Such functions, although not an original part of the FORTRAN language, are made available simply by the same kind of subroutine calling that one would normally use in the language. This can significantly extend the programmer's repertoire of elementary operations, and the availability of these function libraries has played a large part in the continuing vitality of the language.

COBOL (COmmon Business Oriented Language) is antithetical to FORTRAN in almost every aspect. It was designed in response to the acute need for a language appropriate to the voluminous data-processing requirements of banks, government agencies, and large corporations. Thus, while it is quite natural to write programs for personnel management in COBOL, a typical FORTRAN application, like the numerical simulation of a nuclear reaction, is hopelessly difficult.

COBOL was designed with readability and certain kinds of clarity in mind, and to that end programs look less like terse and cryptic mathematics, and more like human exchanges. This has its disadvantages, of course; programs are much longer and "watered down" in COBOL, and therefore rather tedious to write, and it can be quite difficult at times to comprehend a program's basic structure.

Unlike its commercially-successful cousins, which were developed for specific applications, with efficiency the paramount design criterion, ALGOL (ALGOrithmic Language) was designed based on pure algorithmic principles, and included many ideas that were decades ahead of their time. The large family of languages collectively called ALGOL *descendants* includes such famous ones as PASCAL and C.

PL/I: A General-Purpose Language

In 1964, IBM announced its own language, called PL/I (an ambitious acronym for Programming Language ONE). In the spirit of the "bigger-is-better" school, PL/I collected all the best features of FORTRAN, COBOL, and ALGOL, into one huge language. In contrast with FORTRAN and COBOL, the designers of PL/I emphasized ease of programming, at the expense of the complexity of the implementation of the language itself. As a result, PL/I was only available on the largest computers of the time, IBM mainframes. (Today there are implementations of PL/I available for PCs, which are much stronger than the mainframes of the 1960s and 1970s.)

Here is the bubblesort algorithm, coded in PL/I:[2]

```
bubblesort: procedure(a);
    declare a(*) binary fixed;
    declare i, j, temp binary fixed;
    do i = lbound(a) + 1 to hbound(a);
        do j = lbound(a) to i - 1;
            if a(j + 1) < a(j) then
            begin
                temp = a(j + 1)
                a(j + 1) = a(j);
                a(j) = temp;
            end;
        end;
    end;
end;
```

---

[2] In this book and elsewhere, programs are often shown adhering to certain typographic conventions, such as the use of special fonts and indentation. These conventions are not part of the program syntax, and are ignored by the compiler.

■ This notation is quite similar to the one used earlier in our hypothetical language PL. Note the unfortunate use of the equals sign for assignment, instead of the more appropriate left arrow (typographically represented as ":=" in many programming languages, because of the lack of an arrow on most keyboards). This leads to potentially confusing statements such as $x = x + 1$, which means "increment x by 1," but looks like a mathematical equation that has no solutions. Also, in PL/I arrays are referred to using parentheses rather than square brackets.

The control construct we wrote earlier as

for Y **from** 1 **to** N **do**

would be written in PL/I as

do $Y = 1$ **to** N;

Here is a PL/I program that first reads n, the number of elements in the list, then allocates a vector of the appropriate length and reads the list into it, then sorts it using the bubblesort subroutine, and finally prints out the sorted result:

```
sort: procedure options(main);
        declare n binary fixed;
        get list(n);
        begin
            declare a(n) binary fixed;
            declare i binary fixed;
            get list ((a(i), do i = 1 to n));
            call bubblesort(a);
            put list ((a(i), do i = 1 to n));
        end;
    end;
```

The data-processing part of PL/I takes after COBOL. The major innovation in the design of COBOL is the facility for defining a **file structure**, whereby objects resembling arrays crossed with trees are possible. Here is a PL/I definition of a simple university file containing information relevant to student performance and university courses. The structure of the file is illustrated in Figure 3.3. The **picture** parts appearing in the textual definition specify the format of data items: an "A" stands for an alphabetic character, and a "9" for a digit. Thus, for example, "(5)A" means five letters and "AAAA999" means four letters followed by three digits.

```
declare 1 UNIVERSITY_FILE,
            2 STUDENT(100),
                3 STUDENT_NAME picture '(15)A',
                3 COURSE(30),
                    4 COURSE_CODE picture 'AAAA999',
                    4 SCORE picture '99',
                3 STUDENT_ID picture '99999',
            2 DEPARTMENT(20),
                3 DEPT_NAME picture '(10)A',
                3 COURSE(80),
                    4 COURSE_CODE picture 'AAAA999',
                    4 TEACHER picture '(10)A';
```

Figure 3.3

Structure of a PL/I
university file.

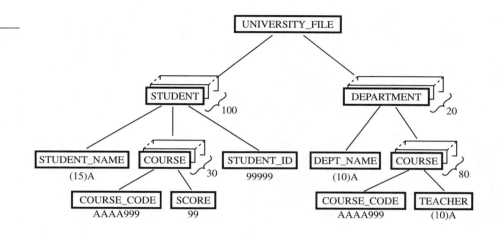

Slimming Down

PASCAL, which first appeared in 1970, was in part a reaction to the sheer size of PL/I. PASCAL was designed as a language for teaching programming, and it is characterized by elegance and simplicity rather than extensive features. In this, PASCAL was hugely successful, and it was used for many years as the major language in the computer-science curriculum in many colleges and universities. Inevitably, this success led to extensive use of PASCAL in commercial applications, where its shortcomings, such as its meagre facilities for memory management, became apparent. This in turn led to the development of various dialects of PASCAL that extend the basic language with the features necessary for large-scale applications.

In the late 1970s, the C language came out of AT&T Labs and took the programming world by storm. Here is the bubblesort algorithm, this time in C:

```
void bubblesort(int *a, int n)
{
    int i, j, temp;
    for (i = 1; i < n; i++)
        for (j = 0; j < i; j++)
            if (a[j + 1] < a[j])
            {
                temp = a[j + 1];
                a[j + 1] = a[j];
                a[j] = temp;
            }
}
```

It is instructive to compare this program with the corresponding implementation of the same algorithm in PL/I shown earlier. Of course, the syntactic differences are apparent, but we shall ignore those, and focus on deeper issues. While the PL/I procedure needed a single parameter, the array to be sorted, the C function needs to receive the size of the array (n) as well. Arrays in PL/I are objects that contain, beside the cells that store the array's contents (the "hotel rooms"), information about the legal range of indexes (the "room numbers"); these are available using the functions lbound and hbound. However, in C an array is just a pointer to the first cell, and contains no other information. The first array cell in C always has the number zero, but there is no way to tell how many cells the array contains. Since this information is unavailable to the compiler, the machine code it generates for the expression $a[j]$ just takes the address of a (that is, the first cell of the array), adds j to it, and retrieves the value stored in that address. (In fact, the same expression can also be written in C as $*(a + j)$, which more closely reflects its implementation.) In contrast, when the PL/I compiler encounters the corresponding expression, it will also generate code to check that the index is indeed within the legal bounds.

If the caller of the C bubblesort function gives an erroneous value for n, one that is greater than the correct value, the function will blithely access and modify the value stored in the indicated address, although it is not part of the array. With high likelihood, it is part of some other data structure, which will be wrongly modified. This could cause the computer to fail in mysterious ways later on. The same thing will happen if the bubblesort function itself tries to access a cell outside the array (for example, if the test $i < n$ is mistakenly replaced by $i <= n$).

In PL/I the first kind of error is impossible, since the caller does not provide the size argument at all. The second kind of error is obviously possible; however, it will be caught much earlier, and the error message will point the programmer to the bubblesort procedure that contains the error rather than to some other innocent procedure.

The reason for this behavior of the C language is that it was originally meant to be used for systems programming; that is, writing the most basic programs without which the computer is just a bit-manipulator. These include the operating system, through which users interact with the computer; device drivers that operate peripheral devices such as keyboards, displays, and printers; and compilers. In particular, C was used for writing the immensely-successful Unix operating system.

System programs often need explicit control of the computer's resources, which are usually hidden from high-level languages (and for good reason!). C provides such low-level control, while bypassing many of the sanity checks incorporated into high-level languages. This allows it to produce efficient code, which is often necessary for system programs that run very often. However, it also allows, and even encourages, the creation of subtle errors of the kind we saw before. Worse yet, such "buffer overrun" bugs in C programs have been used by hackers to subvert computer operating systems and exploit them to propagate viruses and other malicious software over the internet. While it is certainly possible to write high-quality programs in C, it takes more effort than in some other languages.

Like PASCAL, C has become very popular and is used for almost every kind of application, way beyond its originally intended purpose. Unfortunately, this has contributed to the plethora of low-quality software we often encounter.

Nowadays, imperative programming languages have mostly merged into the newer object-oriented paradigm, which we discuss later.

Functional Programming

One of the first high-level languages, dating back to 1958, is LISP (LISt Processing). Unlike its contemporaries, which were concerned primarily with numerical calculations, LISP was meant to be used for **symbolic computation**. Very early in the history of computer science, people were interested in the capabilities of the computer as a reasoning device, and not only as a calculating one. Reasoning is naturally carried out by means of symbols rather than numbers, and LISP was intended to provide easy means of operating on symbols. Its basic data structure is the list, written as a sequence of elements in parentheses; for example, (Computers are more than 0 and 1). One of the early and most famous LISP programs was ELIZA (also called Doctor), which mimicked a psychiatrist having a dialog with a patient. ELIZA is further discussed in Chapter 15.

Here is an example of our first algorithm, the salary-summing one. This example is written in SCHEME, one of the many dialects of LISP:

```
(define (sum-salaries employees)
  (if (null? employees)
      0
      (+ (salary (first employees))
         (sum-salaries (rest employees)))))
```

This code defines a function called `sum-salaries` with a parameter `employees`. One of the peculiarities of LISP is immediately apparent even in this small example, and that is its use of parentheses as the major syntactic feature. Instead of writing expressions such as $a + b$, LISP programmers write (+ a b). While this takes some getting used to, it makes the syntax particularly straightforward, by virtue of its simplicity and uniformity: everything is written in the same way, and there are no problems such as which arguments go with which function, in what order do functions get evaluated, and so on.

We are assuming that the employees' records are given as a list; each element of the list contains the employee's name (itself as a list) and salary, and possibly other personal details. Here is a short example of such a list:

```
(((John A. Doe) 85000 (Senior Accountant) Accounting)
 ((Jane B. Smith) 97000 Manager (Web Services))
 ((Michael Brown) 70000 Programmer (Systems Support)))
```

The function `first` returns the first element of the list it is given, while `rest` returns the **tail** of the list, that is, a list of all elements except the first. The function `null?` checks for the end of a list. It is now easy to see that the `sum-salaries` function goes over the list, element by element, extracting the salary of the current employee, and adding it to the sum it accumulates.

Another way of looking at the above program is as a definition. It actually *defines* the value of the function (sum-salaries employees) for a given list of employees, to be 0 if the list is empty, and otherwise to be the salary of the first employee on the list added to the sum of the salaries of all the other employees on the list. Unlike the formulation of this algorithm in Chapter 1, this definition is recursive. And, in fact, recursion is the central and most natural control structure in LISP.

Interestingly, since the salary is the second element of the employee record, we can define it as the `first` element of the `rest` of the list (which is reminiscent of the aphorism stating that today is the first day of the rest of your life . . .):

```
(define (salary employee)
  (first (rest employee)))
```

Now, it is quite likely that we will want to sum many types of things, not just employee records. In a functional language, it is natural to generalize the `sum-salaries` function to `sum-records`, which can be used to compute the sum of any given field in a list of records:

```
(define (sum-records records selector)
  (if (null? records)
      0
      (+ (selector (first records))
         (sum-records (rest records)))))
```

The structure of `sum-records` is exactly the same as that of `sum-salaries`, except that it takes another parameter, `selector`, which is itself a function. This function selects the field of the record we want to add to the sum. Given this definition, `sum-salaries` can now be defined more simply as:

```
(define (sum-salaries employees)
  (sum-records employees salary))
```

In fact, we can generalize the accumulation operation as well; in addition to computing sums of elements, we may want to compute products, maximum elements, and so on. An accumulation operation is specified by the function that accumulates a new value into the running total: addition for sums, multiplication for products, and so on. We need to know the "unit element" of the operation, that is, the value to be used when we reach the end of the list; this would be 0 for sums and 1 for products. This generalization, and the new definition of `sum-salaries`, are written in SCHEME as follows:

```
(define (accumulate-records records selector accum unit)
  (if (null? records)
      unit
      (accum (selector (first records))
             (accumulate-records records selector accum
                                 unit))))
```

```
(define (sum-salaries employees)
  (accumulate-records employees salary + 0))
```

Similarly, if we have a list of student grades called cs101, we could compute the maximum grade (assuming they are non-negative) using the following expression (where the max function computes the maximum of its two arguments):

```
(accumulate-records cs101 final-grade max 0)
```

As these examples demonstrate, functional languages treat functions like any other type of data, and, in particular, they allow passing functions as arguments to other functions and returning them as the results of computations. This feature, which is either unavailable in a typical imperative language or is very inconvenient, gives functional languages great expressive power, and allows them to describe many algorithms very concisely. It is interesting to note that this treatment of functions and the computational power it carries date back to the **lambda calculus**, further discussed in Chapter 9, which is a mathematical formalism invented in the 1930s, before general-purpose electronic computers existed.

It is also clear from the examples that the LISP programs themselves look very similar to the basic LISP data structure—the list. In fact, LISP programs are *exactly* lists, which means that they themselves can be easily treated as data. It is therefore convenient and natural to write LISP programs that process and/or generate other programs. In particular, it is quite easy to write interpreters for LISP in LISP. This, together with the fact that many of the people who use LISP also have a strong interest in programming-language design, has caused the proliferation of many different LISP dialects. In the early 1980s, the LISP community reached a decision that a single unified language is necessary, and the result was a new language, COMMON LISP. Like PL/I, COMMON LISP comes from the "bigger-is-better" school, and contains most of the good ideas from the various LISP dialects that preceded it.

SCHEME, the language used in the examples above, can be viewed as the reaction of the "small-and-elegant" school to COMMON LISP. (SCHEME is also nicknamed "UnCommon Lisp.") Like PASCAL, it was originally intended as an educational tool, and is therefore designed to contain a few strong and elegant features rather than everything that could potentially be useful in practice.

Although LISP and SCHEME are based on the functional paradigm, and can be used as functional languages, they also contain imperative programming constructs. In contrast, there are also some purely functional languages, such as HASKELL and MIRANDA. These languages do not contain any constructs for modifying memory; the program creates new data elements instead of modifying existing ones. Of course, the computer's memory is limited, and will eventually be used up by all these new data elements. One part of the running environment provided by purely functional languages for their programs is a **garbage collector**, which is responsible for automatically identifying data elements that are no longer in use and reclaiming the memory they occupy. As a result, a new data element can occupy the same physical memory previously used for something else. However, this reuse of memory occurs below the level of abstraction provided by the language; the programmer is free to think in terms of data elements that never change.

As a result of this abstraction, the semantics of purely functional programming languages is relatively easy to specify formally. In practical terms, this means that programmers can use familiar mathematical tools for reasoning about their programs. For example, the most basic mathematical techniques of substitution of equals, which is not valid in imperative languages (see Chapter 2), works as we expect in purely functional languages, and it considerably simplifies the task of writing correct programs.

Logic Programming

All logic programming languages are variants of the first and best-known one, called PROLOG (PROgrammation en LOGique), which was developed in the early 1970s. A logic program consists of a set of logical axioms, called *rules*, that define various properties relevant to the problem to be solved. For example, a chess-playing program might define a predicate legal_move(P, X, Y), which is true when board-configuration Y is the result of a legal move for player P in configuration X. It could also use the predicate value(P, X, N) that is true when the value of the board-configuration X to player P is N. (Providing a good definition for the value of a game position is one of the secrets of a good chess-playing program; see Chapter 15.)

As a much simpler example, consider the predicate member(X, S), which is true when X is an element of the list S. The following assertions should all be true (PROLOG lists are denoted by square brackets):

member(1, [1, 2, 3])
member(b, [a, b, c])
member($apples$, [$oranges$, $apples$])

However, member(2, [a, b, c]) is false. Here is the definition of this predicate as a PROLOG program:

member(X, [$X|Xs$]).
member(X, [$Y|Ys$]) ← member(X, Ys).

This program consists of two rules. The first states that X is a member of every list whose first element is X. The second states that X is a member of a list whose first element is Y and whose tail is the list Ys if X is a member of the tail Ys. (The direction of the arrow is very important: this rule does *not* mean that in order for X to be a member of the list it must be a member of the tail; only that this is one possible way in which X can belong to the list.)

Given this program, a PROLOG interpreter can easily prove that the first set of examples above are all true, while member(2, [a, b, c]) is false. However, it can do more than that; for example, given the query member(X, [a, b, c]), the interpreter will say that this assertion can be true (only) if X is one of a, b, or c. (PROLOG treats names starting with an uppercase letter as variables, and other names as constants.)

The first rule of the "member" program is unconditional; it states that its goal member(X, [$X|Xs$]) is always true. The second rule is conditional; it says that one way of proving its goal, member(X, [$Y|Ys$]), is to try to prove member(X, Ys). Faced with the query member(X, [a, b, c]), we could try either rule to prove it. The first would yield one solution: $X = a$. The second would reduce the problem to proving member(X, [b, c]). This new problem can be solved using the first rule to yield $X = b$, or can be reduced to the problem of proving member(X, [c]) using the second rule. This, in turn, will yield the third solution, $X = c$, or reduce the problem to member(X, []). However, here we stop, since this last problem cannot be solved using either of the rules, both of which require a non-empty list. Thus, there are no further solutions.

The PROLOG interpreter works in the way sketched above. It keeps a set of goals it is trying to prove, and tries to prove each in turn by using the rules that constitute the program. An unconditional rule can prove the goal directly, in which case it is removed from the list of goals to be proved. A conditional rule can be used to reduce the problem to other ones, by replacing the goal with one or more subgoals, which are then added to the to-be-proved list. A solution to the original query is found when all outstanding goals have been proved (that is, the list is empty). If some goal cannot be proved by any of the rules, there is no solution to the original problem, which is like saying that the program cannot be run to completion.

Here is a more complex PROLOG program, solving the Towers of Hanoi problem of Chapter 2. The predicate hanoi(N, A, B, C, *Moves*) is true when *Moves* is a list of moves that solves the problem of moving N rings from A to B using C.

```
hanoi(0, A, B, C, [ ]).
hanoi(N, A, B, C, Moves) ←
    N > 0, N1 is N − 1,
    hanoi(N1, A, C, B, M1),
    hanoi(N1, C, B, A, M2),
    append(M1, [move(A, B)|M2], Moves).
```

The first rule is unconditional, and states that an empty list of moves solves the problem of moving zero rings. The second rule says that *Moves* is a set of moves that will legally transfer a positive number N of rings from A to B using C, if it can be decomposed into three parts: the initial portion, *M1*, is a set of moves that will legally transfer $N − 1$ rings from A to C using B; then the single move that takes the top ring off A and moves it to B; and then *M2*, a set of moves that will legally transfer $N − 1$ rings from C to B using A. This is very similar to our original formulation of this algorithm in Chapter 2.

Given the query hanoi(3, a, b, c, M), PROLOG will respond with:

M = [move(a, b), move(a, c), move(b, c), move(a, b),

move(c, a), move(c, b), move(a, b)].

A PROLOG program is a set of logical axioms and rules, but these do not have a computational meaning by themselves. There are many ways of using the rules to prove a given goal, and the PROLOG interpreter chooses one of them (its strategy is to try the rules in the order they are given, and also check conditions in rules in the original order). Suppose we have a database of facts about the employees of a certain company. The database contains, among other information, facts of the form supervises(X, Y), meaning that X is the direct supervisor of Y. We can use these facts to define the relationship outranks(X, Y), which means that X supervises Y, directly or through a chain of middle managers. This could be written in PROLOG as follows:

```
outranks(X, Y) ← supervises(X, Y).
outranks(X, Y) ← outranks(X, Z), supervises(Z, Y).
```

For simplicity, suppose that the company has just three employees: Huey, the general manager, supervises Dewey, who in turn manages Louie. The PROLOG interpreter will easily prove that Huey outranks Louie. However, if we change the order of the rules, they will still have the same logical meaning, but the interpreter will be in trouble when asked to prove the fact outranks(huey, louie).[3] It will first try to find some Z that is outranked by Huey; this can be done by the second rule (which is now first) if we can first find some Z' that is outranked by Z. This may be done by finding Z'' that is outranked by Z', and the search continues indefinitely in this way without ever producing useful results. In fact, even the original program will fail in the same way when given the goal outranks(louie, huey), instead of stopping and saying that this is false. (Can you see why?) The solution is to rewrite the second rule to first test for supervisors, then for outranking employees:

$$\text{outranks}(X, Y) \leftarrow \text{supervises}(X, Z), \text{outranks}(Z, Y).$$

This dependency of the computation on the behavior of the interpreter is unfortunate, since it means that it is not enough that the rules themselves are correct, and PROLOG programmers also have to worry about the manner in which the interpreter tries the rules. This they can do by various means, including carefully arranging the order of rules and conditions. However, the need to address these issues is a weakness in a language that tries to specify *what* should be done rather than *how* to do it.

PROLOG was given a large boost by the announcement of the Japanese Fifth-Generation Project in 1981. This ambitious project was considered to have the potential of producing a significant boost to the state-of-the-art research in computer science, using parallel computers as the hardware platform and PROLOG as the main programming language. Unfortunately, while it started with a bang, the project ended with something of a whimper, and PROLOG is now in use only for some specialized applications.

Object-Oriented Programming

Object-oriented languages trace their beginnings to SIMULA, which was developed in the early 1960s as a special-purpose language for simulation (although SIMULA actually became a general-purpose programming language). The original goal of SIMULA's designers was to create a language that would allow easy programming of discrete-event simulations, that is, computerized models of real-world events that are not continuous, like physical phenomena, but happen at distinct points in time. For example, the simulation of checkout queues in a supermarket may provide useful information that can be used to manage the number of active checkout counters at different times of the day, minimizing idle counters and unacceptably long queues.

It is natural to specify such a program by describing the behavior of each object participating in the simulation (these are sometimes called *agents*) separately. In this example, there are three types of agents: customers, checkout queues, and cashiers. Customers will be generated by the simulation program with a frequency

---

[3] We cannot capitalize the names here, since they should be considered constants rather than variables.

that depends on the time of day. Each customer object then decides on the number of items it has, according to statistics gathered from the real supermarket being modeled. It then chooses a queue to enter; for example, if it has fewer than 10 items, it will choose the express queue, and otherwise it will choose the shortest queue. (In the simulation, the customer object figures out which queue is shortest by sending messages to the queues, asking how many customers they contain, and comparing the answers.) The customer object then sends a message to the object representing the chosen queue, asking to join that queue. When the queue object determines that the customer object has reached the front of the queue, and after getting a message from the cashier object saying that it is ready for the next customer, the queue notifies the customer that it can approach the cashier. The customer then informs the cashier of the number of items it has. The nature of the simulation is such that the cashier object doesn't actually do any real work, but simply decides how much time to wait (making believe, so to speak, that it is ringing up the customer's items) based on the number of items the customer has, and after that amount of (simulated) time has passed, it notifies the queue that it is ready for a new customer.

Such a description of a real-world system in terms of the objects it contains and the messages they exchange is very natural not just for discrete-event simulations, but also for many other kinds of computerized models (and, as it turns out, even for more abstract concepts that have no direct correspondence in the real world). This view is the first basis for the object-oriented paradigm, in which what happens (the actions) is subordinate to what makes it happen, and who it happens to (the objects), and should be contrasted with the imperative view of programming, in which the routines are dominant, operating on passive data structures. This paradigm leads to a programming style in which the basic unit, called a **class**, is a description of a certain type of object, together with its associated operations (or, equivalently, the messages they can handle). When the program actually runs, each class is instantiated by possibly many instance objects.

The second basis of the object-oriented paradigm is called **inheritance**, and denotes the ability of the programmer to define inclusion relationships between classes. For example, the class of cows is a **subclass** of the class of mammals, which, in turn, is a subclass of the class of all animals. Or, to remain somewhat closer to mathematics and computation, the class of squares is a subclass of the class of rectangles, which is a subclass of all parallelograms, which is a subclass of all quadrilaterals, and so on. This means that squares have all the properties of rectangles: all their angles are straight, and opposite sides are equal. Squares also have properties that are not shared by all rectangles: all their sides are equal. From the point of view of the programmer, squares can handle all messages defined for rectangles, such as requests to compute the perimeter or area. In addition, squares may support messages of their own, not shared by rectangles, such as a request to return the length of the side of the square, which is not uniquely defined for rectangles. Thus, the class of squares *inherits* all the operations from the rectangle class, including the code that implements them.

This leads to an important style of programming, in which some classes have only partial code, or even no code at all. Such classes are called **abstract**, and, of course, they do not completely describe the behavior of their objects. However, they are very useful as the high levels of the inheritance hierarchy. For example, it is possible to define an abstract class that describes queues (see Chapter 2). Such a class describes *what* a queue can do, but not *how* it does it. What is nice about this distinction is that the "what" is exactly the information that other classes need in order to use queues; they don't really need the "how." There are many ways to implement queues, and these differ in the data representation and the algorithms used. All such implementations can be defined as subclasses of the abstract queue class, which guarantees that they support all the necessary operations. In this way, the programs that use the queue class and the programs that implement it have a well-defined and narrow interface, which is that embodied in the abstract queue class. This independence allows separate development of the relevant classes, a property that is crucial for the development of large programs, as we discuss in Chapter 13.

The first truly object-oriented programming language was SMALLTALK, developed in the 1970s. Since then many other object-oriented languages have been developed, the best-known of which are C++ and JAVA. C++ is based on C, with object-oriented features added to it. As such, it suffers from the aforementioned problems of C (but is very popular nevertheless). JAVA is also based on the C/C++ tradition, but it not an extension of either; many of the problematic features of these languages have been removed from JAVA (as well as some of the more useful ones . . .). Here is the Queue class in JAVA (an "interface" is JAVA's term for an abstract class that lacks an implementation).

```java
public interface Queue
{
    boolean empty();
    Object front();
    void add(Object x);
    void remove();
}
```

This class defines four operations (called **methods** in the common object-oriented terminology): *empty*, which returns a boolean value (true or false) according to whether the queue is empty or not; *front*, which returns the object at the front of the queue (the class Object is the top of the inheritance hierarchy, and denotes all objects in the language); *add*, which takes an object x and inserts it at the back of the queue; and *remove*, which removes the object at the front of the queue. This definition contains all the information about queues needed by the writer of the Customer class, which represents the customers in our supermarket simulation example.

Of course, in order to perform the simulation, it is necessary to have some implementation of the Queue class. In order to implement it, we will use a linked list to hold its elements; the list will be implemented using the class Linkable, which describes a single link therein.

```java
public class Linkable
{
    private Object _item;
    private Linkable _next;

    public Linkable(Object x)
    {
        _item = x;
        _next = null;
    }
}
```

```
    public Object item()
    {
        return _item;
    }

    public Linkable next()
    {
        return _next;
    }

    public void set_next(Linkable next)
    {
        _next = next;
    }
}
```

This is a simple class that only stores data, and in that sense it is similar to a data structure in an imperative program. Object-oriented programs typically feature classes with more complex operations. The definition of the Linkable class consists of two **fields** that hold the state of the object, a **constructor** (whose name in JAVA is the same as the name of the class), used to create new objects of this class, and three methods.

The object held by the linkable cell is stored in the variable named _item, and the reference to the next cell is in the variable named _next. These variables are declared to be private, which means that other classes may not read or modify them. All outside access to these variables must be routed through the other methods of the Linkable class. (This is an example of the principle of **information hiding**, which we discuss in Chapter 13.) The variable _item is set in the constructor; clients can only read its value (using the *item* method) but cannot modify it. The variable _next is initialized to **null** in the constructor, and can be read and modified by clients (using the *next* and *set_next* methods).

Here is the definition of the class LinkedQueue, which uses the Linkable class in order to implement the Queue interface.

```
public class LinkedQueue implements Queue
{
    private Linkable _front = null, _back = null;

    public boolean empty()
    {
        return _front == null;
    }

    public Object front()
    {
        return _front.item();
    }
```

```
public void add(Object x)
{
    Linkable new_back = new Linkable(x);
    if (_front == null)
    {
        _front = new_back;
        _back = new_back;
    }
    else
    {
        _back.set_next(new_back);
        _back = new_back;
    }
}

public void remove()
{
    _front = _front.next();
}
}
```

This class has two fields: one points to the front of the queue (which is the first element of the linked list), and the other points to its back (the last element of the list). The queue is considered to be empty when the front pointer is null (meaning that it doesn't point to any object). Operations that modify the queue need to maintain the correct relationship between these pointers. Removing the front element is easy, requiring only that the front pointer move to the next element. Addition is more complicated, and needs to consider two cases. If the queue is initially empty, adding an element to it will create a list of one element, so both the front and back pointers should point to that single element. If the queue is non-empty, the addition of a new element only affects the back pointer, which moves to point to the newly added element at the end of the list.

Figure 3.4 illustrates this program in action. Part (a) shows the initial state of an object that can be generated by the expression **new** LinkedQueue(). If we insert the values 1, 2, and 3 (using the method *add*) and then remove the front element (using the method *remove*), we obtain the series of changes shown in parts (b)–(e).

There can be many other ways to implement an interface such as that of the Queue (not just the way we did it with the LinkedQueue class). A client need not be aware of which particular implementation is being used; all the information clients need is available in the abstract interface. This property, called **modularity**, is an important feature of the object-oriented paradigm, making possible, indeed encouraging, the breaking up of complex problems into relatively independent smaller parts, and is crucial for the development of large-scale systems, as we shall see in Chapter 13.

One of the most interesting object-oriented languages is EIFFEL, which was designed based upon a solid theoretical foundation, while at the same time being practical for large programming projects. In Chapter 5 we will discuss a unique

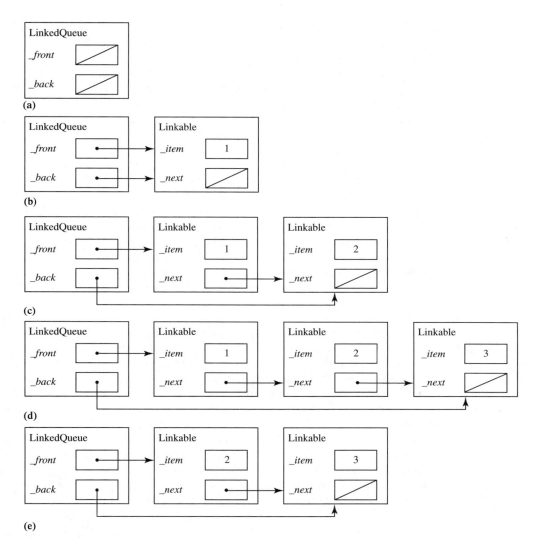

Figure 3.4

Queue in action.

feature of EIFFEL called **design by contract**, which is an attempt to bring the proof methods discussed in that chapter to bear on large-scale programs.

◾ ◾

◾ Research on Programming Languages

Programming languages form an active and widely-addressed research area in computer science, and we have only been able to touch upon a few of the issues involved.

People are interested in general-purpose and special-purpose languages, and in their precise definition and efficient implementation. Sophisticated compilation and translation techniques are developed, new control structures and data structures are proposed, and powerful methods for enabling programmers to define their own are established. Languages that encourage "good" programming style are sought for, and people try to design them to incorporate various recommended ways of thinking about algorithms. **Concurrent programming languages** are a major part of this effort, and some aspects of them will be discussed briefly in Chapters 10 and 14. The same goes for graphical languages, or as they are more accurately called, **visual formalisms**. We shall have more to say about these in Chapter 14.

In terms of paradigms, there is no doubt that object-orientation, in its several guises, receives more attention than any of the others, and it is the subject of a tremendous amount of research and extensive commercialization.

As far as semantics goes, computer scientists are interested in providing tools and methods for producing computer programs with mathematically sound meaning. This is necessary both for manual, human-driven inspection and for computerized verification and analysis, as explained in Chapter 5. Obviously, precise syntax is a prerequisite for precise semantics, and therefore the phrase "semantics of algorithms" is somewhat meaningless. It is only when an algorithm has been programmed in a formal programming language that it can be given a formal and unambiguous meaning.

There are several approaches to semantic definitions. One, called **operational semantics**, describes the meaning of a program by rigorously defining the sequence of steps taken during execution, and the effect of each step on the **program state**. A state is like a snapshot of all that is of relevance in a program at a given instant, and it typically includes the values of all variables, parameters, and data structures, as well as the current location of control (i.e., of the processor) in the program's text.[4] A more abstract approach, called **denotational semantics**, describes the meaning of a program as a pure mathematical object, typically a kind of **function** that captures the transformation from the initial start state to the final end state that a program entails. This approach pays less attention to the actual steps in an execution of the program and more to its overall externally observable effects. Whatever the approach, getting such definitions right is not easy even for simple languages, and for ones including tricky features it can become a formidable task indeed.

We mentioned databases in Chapter 2. Query and data manipulation languages for databases can actually be viewed as special-purpose programming languages. People are interested in developing ones that are powerful, flexible, and efficient, and in this particular case design teams also have to be sensitive to the fact that many database users are not professional programmers, so that the languages should be extra easy to use.

Researchers are interested in developing **programming environments**, namely, user-friendly interactive systems that enable a programmer to write, edit, change, execute, analyze, correct, and simulate programs. Some of these involve visual techniques (made possible by modern graphical computer terminals and workstations), such as the animation of program execution coupled with pictures of the data structures as they change. As mentioned briefly, and further discussed in Chapter 14, there is the more recent direction of visual formalisms, in which these and other

---

[4] The functional programming and logic programming paradigms are different in this respect, and must be given different notions of state and step.

research issues arise in full force, but with additional dimensions, so to speak. (How, for example, is recursion best visualized?)

A final remark here concerns the **universality** of programming languages. In a certain technical sense, all the programming languages discussed here, and for that matter virtually all others too, are *equivalent* in their expressive power. Any algorithmic problem solvable in one language is, in principle, solvable in any other language, too. The differences between languages are pragmatic, and involve appropriateness for certain applications, clarity and structure, efficiency of implementation, and varying algorithmic ways of thinking. Given the significant differences between programming languages this might come as something of a surprise. In actuality, it is one of the most fundamental facts of algorithmics, and will be discussed in detail in Chapter 9.

people of a strange speech and of a hard language
EZEKIEL 3: 5

PART II

Methods and Analysis

Come now, and let us reason together
ISAIAH 1: 18

CHAPTER 4

Algorithmic Methods

*And he strictly raises
it according to the
method prescribed*

ISAIAH 28: 26

or, Getting It Done Methodically

It seems that we can now proceed happily with our algorithmic chores. We know how algorithms are structured and how to arrange the objects they manipulate, and we also know how to write them up for computer execution. We can therefore tell our processor what it should be doing and when. However, this is an overly naive assessment of the situation, and we shall see various reasons for this as we proceed.

One of the problems is rooted in the fact that we have not provided any methods that can be used to *devise* an algorithm. It is all very well talking about the *constructs* that an algorithm may use—that is, the pieces it might be composed of—but we must say something more about the ways of going about using these pieces to make a whole. In this chapter we shall review a number of quite general **algorithmic methods** that a designer can employ in order to find a solution to an algorithmic problem.

It must be noted, however, that there are no good recipes for devising recipes. Each algorithmic problem is a challenge for the algorithm designer. Some problems are straightforward, some are complicated, others are tantalizing; the present chapter shows only that certain algorithms follow certain general paradigms quite nicely. As a moral, the algorithm designer might benefit from looking at these first, trying to see whether they can be used, or adapted for use, in the situation at hand. By and large, however, algorithmic design is a creative activity that may require real ingenuity, but which can definitely benefit from mastery of the available toolbox of techniques and methods.

Searches and Traversals

Many algorithmic problems give rise to the need to **traverse** certain structures. At times, the structure we have to traverse is present explicitly as one of the data structures defined in the algorithm, but at times it is some implicit abstract structure that perhaps cannot be actually "seen," but that exists under the surface. At times, one is looking for something special within the structure ("who is the director of the public relations department?"), and at times some work has to be done at each point ("compute the average grades of all students"). The straightforward salary summation problem of Chapter 1, for example (see Figure 2.3), is readily seen to require a simple traversal of the given list of employees. On the other hand, the problem that involved only employees earning more than their managers (see Figure 2.4) can be thought of as requiring the traversal of an imaginary two-dimensional array, in which employees are plotted against employees, and the search is for certain employee/manager pairs.

In such cases the task is to find the most natural way of traversing the data structure at hand (whether explicit or implicit) and thus devise the algorithm. When vectors or arrays are involved, loops and nested loops typically appear, as explained in Chapter 2 (see Figure 2.9), and in quite the same vein, when trees are involved recursion appears, as indeed was the case in the treesort example. It is true that the idea behind the treesort algorithm is quite subtle and cannot be found by simply figuring out the best control structure for traversing the given data structure. However, once the idea has been hit upon, it is a small thing to realize that the second-visit trip, in which the elements are output in order, is nothing more than a certain traversal of a binary tree, from which it is not too difficult to reach the conclusion that recursion should be used.

The traversal induced by the recursive left-first trip of Figure 2.14 is sometimes called **depth-first** search with backtracking, as the processor "dives" into the tree trying to get as deep down as possible, and when it cannot go any further it backtracks reluctantly, always striving to resume its diving. The only additional feature here is the requirement that diving be performed as much to the left as possible. There are several other ways of traversing trees, one of which, dual to depth-first search, is termed **breadth-first** search. Traversing in a breadth-first manner means that the levels of the tree (see Figure 2.12) are exhausted in order; first the root, then all of its offspring, then *their* offspring, and so on.

Exhaustive Search, or the British Museum Procedure

When you need to find something in a data structure, you could simply examine all its elements one by one until you find what you are looking for. This is what we did when we were looking for employees earning more than their managers. This simple idea is called **exhaustive search**, or, more colorfully, the **British Museum procedure**. The latter term alludes to the way a serious-minded person would inspect each and every exhibit in a museum.

Exhaustive search is sometimes the only way to solve an algorithmic problem. However, often there are far better ways. For example, if you wanted to find a number in a telephone book using exhaustive search, you would have to look through every name in the book until you find the one you are looking for (or discover that it is not there). This could take you a *long* time. Instead, you estimate roughly where to open the book, based on the first letter of the name, then quickly correct your estimate based on the names in the page you open, and find the number you are looking for in

Figure 4.1

Two convex polygons.

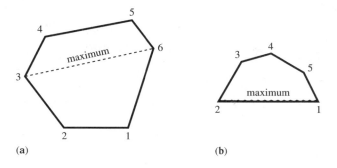

(a)   (b)

less than a minute. This so-called **interpolation search** procedure, which is much more efficient than exhaustive search for this problem, is a human-oriented version of an algorithm we discuss in detail in Chapter 6.

Thus, in many cases, exhaustive search is not the best way to go, to say the least. Still, it is a useful procedure for those cases where there are no other solutions, and it also serves as a baseline against which other solutions can be compared.

Maximal Polygonal Distance: An Example

Many interesting algorithmic problems involve geometric concepts such as points, lines, and distances, and are thus part of the subject known as **computational geometry**. Many of the problems in this area are deceptively easy to "solve" using the human visual system, but are often a real challenge for algorithm designers. Here is a very simple one.

Suppose we are given a simple convex polygon[1] of the kind appearing in Figure 4.1, and suppose we are interested in finding two points of maximal distance on its borderline. The polygon is assumed to be represented by a sequence of the coordinates of the vertices, in clockwise order. As the maximum distance will clearly occur for two of the vertices (why?), there is no need to look at any points along the polygon's edges other than the vertices.

A trivial solution would involve considering *all* pairs of vertices in some order, keeping the current maximum and the pair achieving this maximum in variables. Each new pair considered is subjected to a simple distance computation; the new distance is compared with the current maximum and the variables are updated if the new distance is found to be larger, which means that it is actually a new maximum. If we ponder this solution for a moment, it becomes clear that we are actually traversing an imaginary array in which vertices are plotted against vertices. The imaginary data item at point $\langle I, J \rangle$ of this array is the distance between the vertices I and J. The traversal can then be easily carried out by two nested loops, and you are indeed encouraged to write down the resulting algorithm.

This solution, however, considers far too many potential pairs. Should it not be possible to consider only "opposite" pairs of points, such as $\langle 1, 4 \rangle$, $\langle 2, 5 \rangle$, and

[1] A polygon is termed simple and convex if its borderline does not cross itself and if none of its angles is greater than $180°$.

Figure 4.2

Finding maximal distance by clockwise traversal.

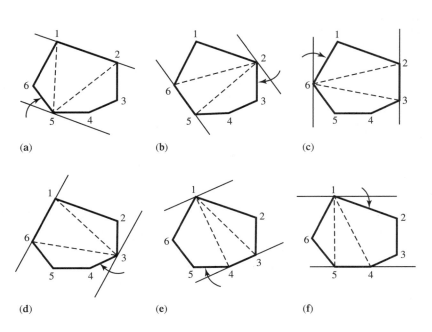

(a)　　　　　　　(b)　　　　　　　(c)

(d)　　　　　　　(e)　　　　　　　(f)

⟨3, 6⟩ in Figure 4.1(a)? This would mean traversing only a vector of "special" pairs, rather than the array of all pairs, clearly resulting in a more efficient algorithm that requires only a single loop. Now, this is not quite as simple as it sounds, since the desired opposite pairs are not necessarily those which have an equal number of vertices on either side; Figure 4.1(b) shows a polygon in which the maximum occurs in *neighboring* vertices, which would have been missed by an algorithm that considered only oppositely numbered ones. The better solution, which indeed employs a single loop and considers only the "right" kind of opposite pairs, is illustrated in Figure 4.2.

■ Let us describe how it works. We shall do so using informal geometric notions, though a detailed description of the algorithm would have to translate these into numerical manipulations using data and control structures, which we shall not carry out here.

First, a line is drawn along the edge between vertex 1 and 2. Next, a line parallel to it is gradually brought towards the polygon from beyond the polygon on the opposite side of the first line, until one of the vertices is hit; see Figure 4.2(a), in which it is clear that vertex 5 is the first one to be thus reached. The initial approximation to the maximum is now taken to be the larger of the distances between that vertex (5 in this case) and vertices 1 and 2. Then, a clockwise movement is started, each step of which involves:

1. rotating one of these two lines until it lies along the next edge of the polygon in clockwise order (in Figure 4.2(b) this can be seen to be the bottom line rotating to fit the edge from 5 to 6); and

2. adjusting the other line to be parallel to it (in Figure 4.2(b) the top line is adjusted).

Exactly which of the lines is rotated and which is adjusted is determined by comparing the efforts needed for rotation: the line with the smaller angle to the next edge is the one rotated (in Figure 4.2(a) the angle between the bottom line and the edge from 5 to 6 is smaller than that between the top line and the edge from 2 to 3). Upon completing a rotation, a new vertex appears on the line just rotated, one that was not there before the rotation. The distance between this new vertex and the one on the adjusted line is computed, and is compared to the current maximum as before. This procedure is carried out in a complete circle around the entire polygon. When the procedure ends, the current maximum is the desired maximal distance.

It can be shown that all the actions required by this algorithm involve simple numerical manipulations of the coordinates of the vertices, which follow from elementary analytic geometry. Figure 4.2 illustrates the sequence of transformations on the lines.

This example was chosen to further illustrate that recognizing the need for a traversal, and figuring out what really is to be traversed, is important and can be of considerable help, but it does not always suffice when it comes to solving tricky algorithmic problems; some insight and a good deal of knowledge of the relevant subject matter can do no harm.

■ Divide-and-Conquer

Often a problem can be solved by reducing it to smaller problems of the same kind and solving them, and then, with some additional work, combining the partial solutions to form a final solution to the original problem. If the smaller problems are precisely the same problem at hand but applied to "smaller" or "simpler" inputs, then clearly recursion can be used in the algorithm. This method is called **divide-and-conquer** for obvious reasons.

Several algorithms in this book embody this "split-and-hit" idea. We have already seen it implicitly in the Towers of Hanoi example: the algorithm solved the problem for N rings by solving two problems for $N-1$ rings in the proper order and with the proper parameters. Other cases appear later. Here are two additional applications of dividing and conquering.

Imagine being given a jumbled telephone book, or, to sound more profound, an unordered list L. We are not interested in sorting L, but merely in finding the largest and smallest elements appearing therein. Clearly we can simply traverse the list once, keeping the current minimum and current maximum in variables, comparing each element to both as we proceed, and updating them if the element considered is smaller than the current minimum or larger than the current maximum. However, the following algorithm utilizes the divide-and-conquer strategy in a simple way, and, as explained in Chapter 6, is actually slightly better. Schematically, it reads:

(1) if L consists of one element, then that element is taken as both the minimum and the maximum; if it consists of two elements, then the smaller is taken as its minimum and the larger as its maximum;

(2) otherwise do the following:
  (2.1) split L into two halves, Lleft and Lright;
  (2.2) find their extremal elements MINleft, MAXleft, MINright, and MAXright;

(2.3) select the smaller of *MIN*left and *MIN*right; it is the minimal element of *L*;

(2.4) select the larger of *MAX*left and *MAX*right; it is the maximal element of *L*.

(Obviously, the splitting in line (2.1) should be defined in such a way as to cover the case of a list *L* of odd length, say, by taking the first half to be longer than the second by one element.)

Now, line (2.2) begs to be carried out recursively, since the problems to be solved there are precisely the **min&max** problem on the smaller lists *L*left and *L*right. This recursion is not quite as simple as it seems, since here, in contrast with the Towers of Hanoi routine, the recursive call has to produce results that are used in the sequel. Somehow, the processor must not only remember its return address and how to restore the environment to the situation prior to embarking on the present recursive endeavor, but it must also be capable of bringing back certain items from its toils. In this case it would be most helpful if the processor could return from a recursive call along with the minimum and maximum it was sent out to compute.[2] The following is the result of extending the notion of a subroutine accordingly, and applying it to the **min&max** problem:

subroutine **find-min&max-of** *L*:

(1) if *L* consists of one element, then set *MIN* and *MAX* to it; if it consists of two elements, then set *MIN* to the smaller of them and *MAX* to the larger;

(2) otherwise do the following:

(2.1) split *L* into two halves, *L*left and *L*right;

(2.2) call **find-min&max-of** *L*left, placing returned values in *MIN*left and *MAX*left;

(2.3) call **find-min&max-of** *L*right, placing returned values in *MIN*right and *MAX*right;

(2.4) set *MIN*to smaller of *MIN*left and *MIN*right;

(2.5) set *MAX* to larger of *MAX*left and *MAX*right;

(3) return with *MIN* and *MAX*.

As mentioned, the reason this algorithm is actually a little better than the naive one will become clear in Chapter 6.

The divide-and-conquer paradigm can be used beneficially in *sorting* a list, not only in finding its extremal elements. Here is how. To sort a list *L* containing at least two elements, we similarly split it into its halves, *L*left and *L*right, and recursively sort them both. The one-element case is treated separately, as in the **min&max** example. To obtain the final sorted version of *L*, we proceed by merging the sorted halves into a single sorted list. To merge two sorted lists, we repeatedly remove and send off to the output the smaller of the two elements currently at the heads of the two lists. The workings of this algorithm, which is called **mergesort**, are illustrated in Figure **??**, and you are urged to write down the algorithm in detail. Mergesort is considerably better than both bubblesort and treesort, a fact we shall have more to say about in Chapter 6.

---

[2] A subroutine or procedure that returns with values is sometimes called simply a **function**.

Figure 4.3

The workings of
mergesort.

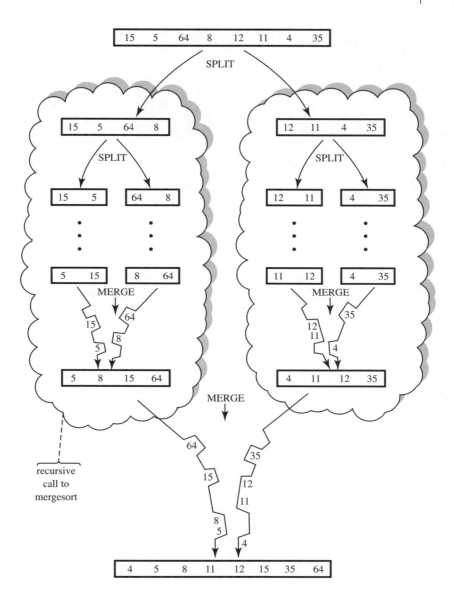

Greedy Algorithms and Railroad Contractors

Many algorithmic problems call for producing some kind of *best* result from an
appropriate set of possibilities. Consider a network of cities, and a lazy railroad
contractor. The contractor was paid to lay out rails so that it would be possible to
reach any city from any other. The contract, however, did not specify any criteria,
such as the need for certain nonstop rail connections, or a maximum number of
allowed cities on the path connecting any two others. Hence our contractor, being
lazy, is interested in laying down the cheapest (that is, the shortest) combination

Figure 4.4

City network and its minimal spanning railroad.

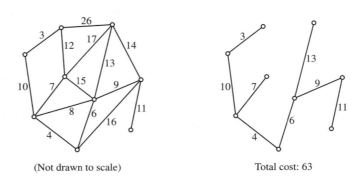

(Not drawn to scale)   Total cost: 63

of rail segments. Assume that not all cities can be connected by direct segments of rail to all others due to objective reasons such as physical obstacles, and that the distances are given only between those pairs of cities that can be connected. We further assume that the cost of directly connecting city *A* with *B* is proportional to the distance between them. Also, we do not allow railroad junctions outside cities.

Such a network is called a **labeled graph**, or simply a **graph** for short. Graphs are similar to trees, except that trees cannot "close on themselves"; that is, they cannot contain cycles, or loops, whereas graphs can. Figure **??** presents an example of a city graph and its minimal railroad. Notice that the contractor is really after what we sometimes call a **minimal spanning tree**. This is a tree that "spans" the graph, in the sense that it reaches each and every one of its nodes (that is, the cities, in our case), and is the cheapest such tree, in the sense that the sum of the labels along the edges (that is, the distances between cities, in our case) is the smallest possible. It is quite easy to see that the desired solution must be a tree (that is, it cannot contain cycles), since if it were to contain some cycle a lazy contractor could have obtained a cheaper railroad, which still connected all cities, by eliminating one of the segments of that cycle.

There is an algorithmic approach to such problems, called the **greedy method**. It recommends constructing the minimal spanning tree edge by edge, choosing as the next edge the cheapest one possible as far as the current situation is concerned. This is really like adopting a kind of "eat and drink as tomorrow we die" attitude: do as much as you can now because otherwise you might be sorry you didn't. Figure **??** illustrates the construction of such a tree. Start out with the degenerate tree consisting of the cheapest edge in the graph, all alone. Now, at each stage extend the tree constructed so far by adding the cheapest edge not yet considered, as long as this results in a connected structure that is actually a tree. In particular, it should not introduce a cycle; if it does, then go on to the next cheapest edge. For example, going from Figure **??**(e) to **??**(f) involves adding the edge labeled 9 instead of the edge labeled 8. The latter would have introduced a cycle in the graph.

It can be shown that this simple strategy actually produces a minimal spanning tree, and you are encouraged to write down the algorithm in detail.

Greedy algorithms exist for a variety of interesting algorithmic problems. They are usually quite easy to come by, and in some cases they are quite intuitive. The difficult part is usually in showing that a greedy strategy indeed gives the best

Figure 4.5

The workings of the greedy spanning tree algorithm.

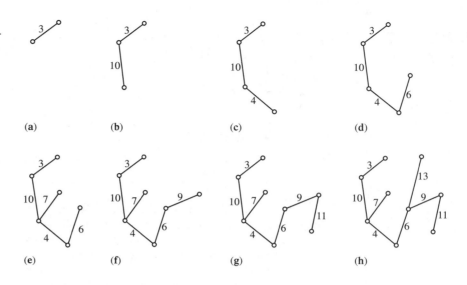

solution, and as the next section shows, there are cases in which greed does not pay at all.

Dynamic Programming and Weary Travelers

Here is a problem that is similar to that of the minimal spanning tree, but this one defies naive greedy solutions. It too involves a city network, but instead of a lazy railroad contractor we have a weary traveler who is interested in traveling from one city to another. Though both have a job to do, and both want to minimize the overall cost of getting it done, there is a crucial difference: whereas the contractor has to connect all cities by a subnetwork of rails, the traveler will usually travel only through *some* of the cities. It is clear, therefore, that the traveler is not after a minimal spanning tree, but a **minimal path**; that is, the cheapest trip leading from the start city to the desired destination.

For ease of exposition, we assume that all lines in the city graph are **directed**, meaning that if two cities are connected by a line in the graph, then that line represents a one-way connection. Also, we assume that the graph is **connected**, meaning that the graph does not consist of separate, disconnected parts. We further assume that the city graph has no cycles, so that a really weary traveler will not be liable to go around in circles, because there will be none to go around in. Such a complex is called a **directed acyclic graph**, or a **DAG** for short.

And so, we are given a DAG, and the traveler is interested in getting from point A to point B. A greedy approach to the problem might cause a path to be constructed by starting at A, and continuously adding to the current incomplete path the cheapest edge leading from the city reached so far to some city not yet visited, until the target city B is reached. Figure **??** shows an example of applying this natural-looking algorithm to a graph whose minimal path from A to B is of length 13. The algorithm finds a path of length 15, which is not as good. Greed does not pay here, as a clever

Figure 4.6

For weary travelers
greed does not pay.

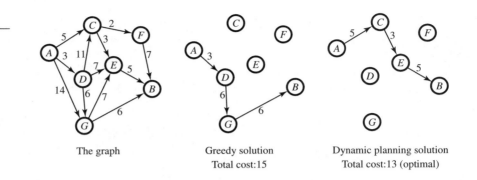

The graph

Greedy solution
Total cost:15

Dynamic planning solution
Total cost:13 (optimal)

algorithm must be devious enough to take the edge of length 5 to C and then that of length 3 to E, even though these are not the locally best-looking choices.

A different, non-greedy algorithmic method, called **dynamic planning**, enables such subtle choices to be made. (Actually, this method is known as **dynamic programming**, not planning, but we have decided to use the latter word, both to better reflect the idea behind the method and to avoid a conflict with the algorithmic use of the term "programming," which refers to the coding of an algorithm for computer execution, as explained in Chapter 3.) Dynamic planning is based on a refinement of the rather coarse criterion of immediate greed, and can be described abstractly as follows.

Suppose the solution to some algorithmic problem is to consist of a sequence of choices that is to lead to some optimal solution. As already shown, it is quite possible that simply picking the best-looking choice from among each local set of possibilities will not lead to an optimal solution. However, it is often the case that the optimum can be obtained by considering all combinations of (a) making a single choice, and (b) finding an optimal solution to the smaller problem represented by the remaining choices. For example, in Figure **??** the length of the shortest path from A to B is the smallest of the three numbers obtained by first selecting one of the cities C, G and D (those directly reachable from A) and then adding its distance from A to the length of the shortest path leading from it to B. Symbolically, denoting the length of the shortest path from X to B by $L(X)$, we can write:

$$L(A) = \text{minimum of: } 5 + L(C), 14 + L(G), 3 + L(D)$$

(See Figure **??**.) In other words, we are finding the shortest path from A to B by finding three "simpler" shortest paths (those from each of C, G and D to B), combining their solutions with the direct edge from A, and then choosing the best of the three results. This means that we can find the optimal solution by first finding the optimum solutions to three "smaller" problems, and then carrying out a few additions and comparisons. This process can then be continued, writing, for example:

$$L(D) = \text{minimum of: } 7 + L(E), 6 + L(G), 11 + L(C)$$

When such derivations yield clauses involving $L(B)$ (that is, the minimal distance from B to itself) no further development is needed, since even an exhausted traveler knows that $L(B)$ is simply 0, by virtue of the fact that the best way to go from B to B is to just stay where you are.

These observations lead to a dynamic planning algorithm for the general weary traveler problem (sometimes called the **shortest-path problem**), which works from the endpoint B backwards to A. In the example of Figure **??**, it first calculates the shortest paths from F and E to B, that is, $L(F)$ and $L(E)$ (these are the only cities that lead nowhere except to B). It then calculates $L(G)$ and $L(C)$ (here G and C are the only cities that lead only to B, F and E, that is, to cities already dealt with), then $L(D)$, and finally $L(A)$. Each calculation is carried out with the help of the results of those already available, so that, for example, $L(G)$ is the minimum of 6 (the direct distance from G to B) and $7 + L(E)$. While carrying out this procedure we also keep track of the backwards path that is gradually constructed from B to A; it is the optimal path sought for.

Dynamic planning can be thought of as divide-and-conquer taken to the limit: *all* subproblems are solved in an order of increasing magnitude, and the results are stored in some data structure to facilitate easy solutions to the larger ones. The method can be applied to many more elaborate problems, which require data structures more complex than mere vectors to store the partial solutions. You might want to try to devise a dynamic planning algorithm for the closely related "traveling salesman" problem described in Chapter 7.

Heaps and Getting Work Done on Time

Many algorithms depend on a clever choice of data structures with properties that are tailored to the needs of the specific algorithm. For example, the treesort algorithm described in Chapter 2 employs binary search trees, which restrict the placing of elements such that smaller elements go to the left and larger elements to the right. There are a great many types of data structures, some with curious names such as "Fibonacci heaps" or "red-black trees," each suitable for a particular algorithmic purpose.

Suppose we want an algorithm that receives elements in some order, and has to be able to provide the smallest one whenever queried. For example, consider the schedule of a printing shop. At any moment, a customer may arrive with some printing job. Each job has its own deadline; some are urgent and others can wait. When a copying machine becomes available, the shop manager needs to find the most urgent job to perform. Here, the elements that the algorithm needs to handle are printing jobs, ordered by their deadlines.

A suitable data structure for this problem is a **heap**, which is a binary tree with the property that the value of each node is smaller than the values of all its offspring.[3] As a result of this property, the smallest element of the heap is always located at the root of the tree, and is immediately accessible. When we indeed access that element, we have to remove it from the heap (as in the printing shop example). But in doing so, we must maintain the heap's characteristic property, by replacing that smallest

---

[3] Note that, unlike the case of binary search trees, there is no requirement distinguishing the left offspring from the right.

element with the smaller of its offspring, which has just become the smallest element of the heap. However, if we simply move this new minimal element up to the root, we create a "hole" in the tree, which must be filled by the smaller of *its* offspring. This is indeed done, and the process is continued downward until we reach a leaf. So much for removing the smallest element. Inserting a new element into the heap is similar, except it starts from one of the leaves and works its way towards the root until its proper place is found (that is, until going any higher would violate the heap's characteristic property).

A clever implementation of heaps uses a vector. A heap containing N elements will occupy cells 1 to N of the vector, with the two offspring of the node residing at cell I being located in cells $2 \cdot I$ and $2 \cdot I + 1$. In this representation, removing the minimum element cannot be done as described above, since that might create a "hole" in the middle of the vector. Instead, the element from the last position in the vector replaces the first element (the one just removed), and it is then "bubbled" downward until it finds its correct place in the heap. This vector representation enjoys certain properties that make heap-manipulation algorithms quite efficient. We discuss these further in Chapter 6.

Nondestructive Algorithms

Another elegant example of the use of data structures comes from the functional programming paradigm, discussed in Chapter 3. This paradigm makes programs easier to understand and reason about, at the price of a higher level of abstraction that uses only nonmodifiable objects. Typically, algorithms are described in an imperative style, using data structures that the algorithm can modify as it goes along. Functional algorithms, on the other hand, must treat their data structures with more respect, since they cannot be modified. In this view, instead of changing data structures, we always create new ones. For example, the operation of adding an element to a stack returns a new stack, containing all the elements of the original stack plus the new element on top. The original stack is not changed, and is available for further computation if necessary.

Since stacks can be accessed only at one end, it is quite easy to implement stacks using linked lists. Adding an element to the stack is just adding an element to the front of the list (or, more accurately, creating another link that points to the original list, which, as mentioned, does not change). Similarly, removing the top element of a stack just means moving along to the next element in the list (see Figure **??**).

In contrast to stacks, queues are harder to implement in a functional language, since they allow access (and therefore require modification) at both ends. Removing an element is easy, and is done just as in a stack. However, adding an element means adding it to the end of the list, as in the JAVA example we saw in Chapter 3. In an imperative language, this is easily done by modifying the "next" pointer of the last link in the list, but this is impossible in a functional language. Of course, we could copy the entire list and add the new element at the end of the new list, but this would be a waste of time and memory. A clever idea allows us to implement functional queues with the same efficiency as in the imperative implementation. The trick is to implement each queue as two stacks. The "front" stack contains the elements in the

Figure 4.7

A functional stack: (a) a stack containing the elements 1, 2, and 3; (b) the result of adding 8 to the previous stack; (c) the result of removing the top element of (b); (d) removing another element.

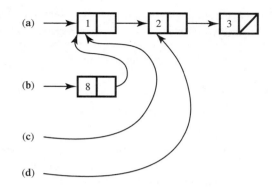

front of the queue, ordered so that the top element of the stack is the front element of the queue, and the "back" stack contains the elements in the back of the queue, in reverse order—the top element of the stack being the last element of the queue (see Figure **??**).

Adding an element to the back of the queue is now easy: it is pushed on the back stack. Removing an element from the queue is just as easy: simply remove the element residing on the top of the front stack. Now, what if the front stack is empty but the back stack is not? In this case, we first turn the back stack into the front stack by moving all of its elements into the front stack in reverse. The back stack now becomes empty, which is fine, because we never need to remove anything from it. (In fact, we never let the front stack become empty while the back stack is non-empty, by performing this reversal when the last element is removed from the front stack.) This serial reversal is indeed an expensive operation, involving moving all the contents of the back stack. However, notice that each element of the queue will pass from the back stack to the front stack at most once. The cost of this operation can therefore be "charged" to the element being moved, so that when summarized

Figure 4.8

A functional queue implemented as two stacks: (a) a queue containing the elements 1, 2, 3, and 4; (b) the result of adding 5 to the previous queue; (c) the result of removing the top element of (b); (d) removing another element.

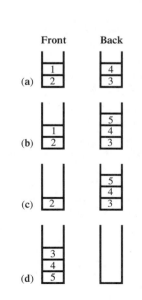

and averaged out over the full execution of the algorithm, each insertion or removal operation takes a fixed amount of time. This accounting method, called **amortized cost**, is an important technique for analyzing the efficiency of algorithms, and will be discussed further in Chapter 6.

On-Line Algorithms

Assume that some parents take their children to a ski resort for the first time in their lives. It is impossible to say how much they will like skiing, and how much of it they will want to do. Skis can be rented or bought. If it turns out that the children will want to ski a lot, it would be cheaper to buy skis once and for all. However, if not, it would be cheaper just to rent skis whenever the fancy takes them. If the parents knew in advance how much skiing the children would want to do, the choice would be obvious. However, this information is unknown, and we are left with adopting some strategy of the general form that calls for starting out by renting skis some number of times to see how things go, and then deciding to actually buy. What would be the parents' best strategy?

Figuring this out is an example of an interesting class of problems whose solution requires what we call **on-line algorithms**. The name comes from the fact that these algorithms must make decisions as they go along, without knowing all the relevant information; specifically, they do not know what requests may be made on them in future.

The first question in analyzing on-line algorithms is how to analyze their cost. The usual method is to compare each algorithm with the omniscient off-line algorithm— the one that can correctly predict the future (in our case, to what extent will the kids enjoy skiing). Of course, no on-line algorithm can do better than this off-line algorithm; the best on-line algorithm is the one that comes closest to that goal.

In our example, it turns out that the best on-line algorithm for the skiing problem is to rent until the cost of renting equals the cost of buying, and then buy. This algorithm is less than twice as bad as the omniscient algorithm. To see this, suppose the cost of buying skis is equal to the cost of M rentals, and consider the number of times the children will eventually want to ski. If they ski fewer than M times, both algorithms will pay the same amount (the off-line omniscient one knows in advance that they will ski fewer than M times, so it will rent, rather than buy). If the children want to ski more than M times, the on-line algorithm will rent $M-1$ times and then buy, for a total cost equal to $2 \cdot M - 1$ rentals. The off-line algorithm, knowing the future, will buy immediately, for a cost of M rentals. In any case, the on-line algorithm never exceeds twice the cost of the off-line algorithm.

It is possible to show that no other strategy will prove to be better, in general.[4] A strategy that will have the parents buy the skis after K rentals, where K is strictly less than $M - 1$, may end up costing $K + M$ rental units while the off-line algorithm pays only $K + 1$. (How many times do the children have to want to ski in order for

---

[4] This is a sort of optimality result, and is stated in a *worst-case* sense, which we shall discuss in detail in Chapter 6.

this to happen?) If K is more than $M - 1$, the on-line algorithm may again cost the parents $K + M$, while the off-line algorithm calls for buying skis immediately, for a cost of only M rentals. In either case, the cost of the on-line algorithm is at least twice the cost of the off-line omniscient algorithm.

■ ■

Research on Algorithmic Methods

There are really very few universally accepted paradigms that are general enough to deserve a special name and the title "algorithmic method," and most of the better-known ones have already been described. Despite this, without particularly aiming at general paradigms, computer scientists are continually searching for better methods to solve increasingly more complex algorithmic problems.

It is somewhat difficult to discuss these attempts further here, since issues of efficiency creep in at a very early stage, and efficiency is treated in detail only in Chapter 6. Moreover, the notions of concurrency and probabilism, discussed in Chapters 10 and 11, are becoming more and more crucial to recent developments in algorithmic design. When treating these topics we shall see some additional ways of coming up with good algorithms.

Exercises

In the following exercises, a tree is given by (a pointer to) its root. A node V of a tree with outdegree N has N offspring, labeled as the first through the Nth, and contains some data item. A leaf is a node without offspring. A binary tree limits the number of offspring of each node to at most two. The depth of a node of a tree is as follows: the depth of the root is 0, and if the depth of V is N then the depth of its offspring is $N + 1$.

For a node V, the available operations include retrieving its contents, testing whether it has an Ith offspring, and if so, assigning a pointer to that offspring.

4.1. Consider the problem of summing the salaries of employees earning more than their direct manager, assuming each employee has a single manager. The employees are labeled 1, 2, etc. Write algorithms that solve the problem for each of the following representations of the input data:

(a) The input is given by an integer N and a two-dimensional array A, where N is the number of employees, $A[I, 1]$ is the salary of the Ith employee and $A[I, 2]$ is the label of his or her manager.

(b) The input is given by a binary tree constructed as follows: The root of the tree represents the first employee. For every node V of the tree representing the Ith employee,
- V contains the salary of the Ith employee;
- the first offspring of V is a leaf containing the label of the manager of the Ith employee; and
- if there are more than I employees, the second offspring of V is the node that represents the $I + 1$th employee.

4.2. (a) Write an algorithm which, given a tree T, calculates the sum of the depths of all the nodes of T.

(b) Write an algorithm which, given a tree T and a positive integer K, calculates the number of nodes in T at depth K.

(c) Write an algorithm which, given a tree T, checks whether it has any leaf at an even depth.

4.3. Write algorithms that solve the following problems by performing breadth-first traversals of the given trees. You may assume the availability of a queue Q. The operations on Q include adding an item to the rear, retrieving and removing an item from the front, and testing Q for emptiness.

(a) Given a tree T whose nodes contain integers, print a list consisting of the sum of contents of nodes at depth 0, the sum of contents of nodes at depth 1, etc.

(b) Given a tree T, find the depth K with the maximal number of nodes in T. If there are several such Ks, return their maximum.

An arithmetic expression formed by non-negative integers and the standard unary operation "$-$" and the binary operations "$+$", "$-$", "$\times$", and "$/$", can be represented by a binary tree as follows:

■ An integer I is represented by a leaf containing I.

■ The expression $-E$, where E is an expression, is represented by a tree whose root contains "$-$" and its single offspring is the root of a subtree representing the expression E.

■ The expression $E * F$, where E and F are expressions and "$*$" is a binary operation, is represented by a tree whose root contains "$*$", its first offspring is the root of a subtree representing the expression E and its second offspring is the root of a subtree representing F.

Note that the symbol "$-$" stands for both unary and binary operations, and the nodes of the tree containing this symbol may have outdegree either 1 or 2.

4.4. Design an algorithm that checks whether a given tree represents an arithmetic expression.

4.5. (a) Design an algorithm that calculates the value of an arithmetic expression, given its tree representation. Note that division by zero is undefined.

(b) Extend your algorithm to first print the expression represented by the input tree, followed by the equality sign "$=$" and its evaluation. The printed expression should be fully parenthesized, i.e., a pair of matching parentheses should embrace every application of a binary operation.

We say that two arithmetic expressions E and F are *isomorphic*, if E can be obtained from F by replacing some non-negative integers by others. For example, the expressions $(2 + 3) \times 6 - (-4)$ and $(7 + 0) \times 6 - (-9)$ are isomorphic, but none of them is isomorphic to any of $(-2 + 3) \times 6 - (-4)$ and $(7 + 0) + 6 - (-9)$.

An expression E is said to be *balanced*, if every binary operation in it is applied to two isomorphic expressions. For example, the expressions -5, $(1 + 2) * (3 + 5)$ and $((-3)/(-4))/((-1)/(-100))$ are balanced, while $12 + (3 + 2)$ and $(-3) * (-3)$ are not.

4.6. Design an algorithm that checks whether two expressions are isomorphic, given their tree representation.

4.7. Design an algorithm that checks whether an expression is balanced, given its tree representation. (Hint: perform breadth-first traversal of the tree.)

4.8. Prove that the maximal distance between any two points on a polygon occurs between two of the vertices.

4.9. Write a program implementing the maximal polygonal distance algorithm.

4.10. Design an algorithm that, given (the vertices of) a not necessarily convex polygon, finds a pair of vertices of *minimal* distance.

4.11. Write algorithms that find the two maximal elements in a given vector of N distinct integers (assume $N > 1$).

   (a) Using an iterative method.
   (b) Using the divide-and-conquer method.

4.12. Write in detail the greedy algorithm described in the text for finding a minimal spanning tree. The **integer-knapsack** problem asks to find a way to fill a knapsack of some given capacity with some elements of a given set of available items of various types in the most profitable way. The input to the problem consists of:

   ■ C, the total weight capacity of the knapsack;
   ■ a positive integer N, the number of item types;
   ■ a vector Q, where $Q[I]$ is the available number of items of type I;
   ■ a vector W, where $W[I]$ is the weight of each item of type I, satisfying $0 < W[I] \leq C$; and
   ■ a vector P, where $P[I]$ is the profit gained by storing an item of type I in the knapsack.

   All input values are non-negative integers. The problem is to fill the knapsack with elements whose total weight does not exceed C, such that the total profit of the knapsack is maximal. The output is a vector F, where $F[I]$ contains the number of items of type I that are put into the knapsack.

   The **knapsack** problem is a variation of the integer-knapsack problem, in which instead of discrete items, there are materials. The difference is that instead of working with integer numbers, we may put into the knapsack any *quantity* of material I which does not exceed the available quantity $Q[I]$. The vectors W and P now contain the weight and profit, respectively, of one quantity unit of material I. All input and output values are now non-negative real numbers, not necessarily integers.

4.13. (a) Design a dynamic planning algorithm for the integer-knapsack problem.
   (b) What is your algorithm's output for the input

   ■ $N = 5$
   ■ $C = 103$
   ■ $Q = [3,1,4,5,1]$
   ■ $W = [10,20,20,8,7]$
   ■ $P = [17,42,35,16,15]$
   and what is the total profit of the knapsack?

4.14. (a) Design a greedy algorithm for the knapsack problem.
   (b) What is your algorithm's output for the input given in Exercise 4.13(b), and what is the total profit of the knapsack now?

4.15. (a) How would you relate the total profits gained for a given *integer* input, when subjected to the knapsack problem and to the integer knapsack problem?
   (b) Consider a modification to the algorithm you have designed in Exercise 4.14(a) that produces in F the integer part of the quantities calculated by the original algorithm. Prove that the modified algorithm does not solve the integer-knapsack problem. That is, give an integer input for which the (modified) greedy algorithm will produce an acceptable integer filling which is not maximally profitable. Find such an input

with N, the number of types, as small as possible. (Hint: correct solutions to the integer-knapsack problem, in contrast to the knapsack problem, might leave available items out of the knapsack, even when it is not full.)

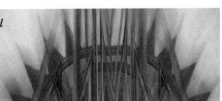

For every matter has its time and method

ECCLESIASTES 8: 6

The Correctness of Algorithms

*Behold, I have …
erred exceedingly*

I SAMUEL 26: 21

*Cause me to
understand wherein
I have erred*

JOB 6: 24

or, Getting It Done Right

- In the early 1960s one of the American spaceships in the Mariner series sent to Venus was lost forever at a cost of millions of dollars, due to a mistake in a flight control computer program.

- In 1981 one of the television stations covering provincial elections in Quebec, Canada, was led by its erroneous computer programs into believing that a small party, originally thought to have no chance at all, was actually leading. This information, and the consequent responses of commentators, were passed on to millions of viewers.

- In a series of incidents between 1985 and 1987, several patients received massive radiation overdoses from Therac-25 radiation-therapy systems; three of them died from resulting complications. The hardware safety interlocks from previous models had been replaced by software safety checks, but all these incidents involved programming mistakes.

- Some years ago, a Danish lady received, around her 107th birthday, a computerized letter from the local school authorities with instructions as to the registration procedure for first grade in elementary school. It turned out that only two digits were allotted for the "age" field in the database.

- At the turn of the millennium, software problems became headline news with the so-called **Year 2000 Problem**, or the **Y2K bug**. The fear was that on January 1, 2000, all hell would break loose, because computers that used two digits for storing years would erroneously assume that a year given as 00 was 1900, when in fact it was 2000. An extremely expensive (and, in retrospect, quite successful) effort to correct these programs had to be taken by software companies worldwide. (We discuss this example further in Chapter 13.)

Figure 5.1

Erroneous version of
the salary summation
flowchart of
Figure 2.4.

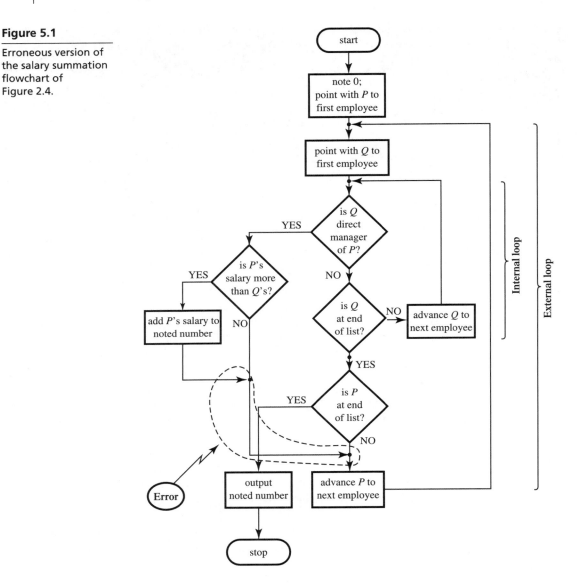

These are just a few of the numerous tales of software errors, many of which have
ended in catastrophes, often with loss of life.[1] The importance of the correctness
issue cannot be overestimated. We have been naively assuming throughout that the
algorithms and programs we write do precisely what we intend them to do. This has
absolutely no justification; in a preliminary manuscript of the first edition of this
book, the flowchart of Figure 2.4, which sums salaries of employees earning more
than their direct managers, contained an embarrassing error that went undetected
for several months. The original version, presented in Figure 5.1, will not always
work as desired. More about this example later.

---

[1] For some other spectacular examples, see Chapter 13.

▪ Language Errors

One of the most frequent kinds of errors occurring in the preparation of computer programs stems from abusing the syntax of the programming language. We met with these in a previous chapter. Writing:

> **for** Y **from** 1 **until** N **do**

instead of:

> **for** Y **from** 1 **to** N **do**

as the language requires, is wrong, but it is not an error in the algorithm. Syntax errors are but a troublesome manifestation of the fact that algorithms carried out by a computer are required to be presented in formal attire.

Compilers and interpreters are made to spot syntax errors, and will notify the programmer, who will typically be able to correct them with little effort. Moreover, and here is where compilers have an edge over interpreters, a clever compiler will attempt to correct certain kinds of syntax errors on its own, making possible the desired translation into machine language (see Chapter 3).

A compiler is not limited, as is an interpreter, to looking at one line or one instruction of the program at a time. It is usually also programmed to spot more subtle errors, which, rather than violating local syntactic rules of the language, cause contradictions between possibly distant parts of the program, typically between a definition and an operational instruction. Examples include arithmetical operations applied to non-numerical variables, references to the 150th element of a vector whose indices were defined to range from 1 to 100, and subroutine calls with the wrong number of parameters.

All of these, however, also represent incorrect use of the language. Whether or not a compiler or interpreter catches such an error in advance, an attempt at running the program will fail when the offensive part is reached; the program will be **aborted**, that is, it will be stopped and an appropriate message will be displayed to the user. In contrast to the errors discussed in the next section, and despite the possibly unpleasant nature of program failure, language errors are not considered to be the most serious. Often they are detected automatically, and they can usually be corrected with relative ease.

▪ Logical Errors

Let us recall the "money"-counting algorithm introduced in Chapter 2. The problem was to count sentences containing occurrences of the word "money." The solution consisted of carrying out a search for "money" followed by a search for the end of the sentence, which, by convention, is always denoted in the input text by the ". " combination, namely, a period followed by a space. Upon succeeding in both searches, the initially zeroed counter is incremented, and the "money" search is resumed from the beginning of the next sentence (see Figures 2.5 and 2.6).

What would have happened had the algorithm used "." (without the space) instead of ". "? Assume for the moment that we are not discussing the algorithm, but its formal version, as a program containing no language errors. It is clear that the new version, which differs from the original only in the absence of the space, contains no language errors either. To an observer, compilers and interpreters included, the new program is perfect. Not only are there no discernible syntax errors, but whenever run on an input text the program dutifully halts and presents a number as the final value of its counter.

Of course, there *is* an error in the new program. It is rooted in the fact that periods can appear *within* sentences. Consider the following:

> *The total amount of money in my bank account is $322.56, a truly remarkable sum, given my talents for making money. I am a rich man.*

When turned loose on this two-sentence text, our modified version will output 2, even though "money" appears only in the first sentence. The program is fooled by the decimal point appearing in $322.56. The new program is correct as far as the language is concerned, and it actually solves an algorithmic problem, but, unfortunately, not exactly the one we set out to solve.

The program contains what we shall be calling a **logical error**, resulting not in a syntactically incorrect or meaningless program, but in a program that does something other than that which it was intended to do.

Logical errors can be notoriously elusive. While it might not be too difficult to notice that a space had been left out of the ". " combination in the "money"-counting program, the following mistake is not as easy to find. Let us assume that different pointers to the text are used for the "money" search and the ". " search. Clearly, once ". " has been found and the counter incremented, the first pointer should be forwarded to the position of the second, prior to resuming the search for "money." Failing to do so constitutes a logical error that would also yield 2 when run on the previous example, but for a different reason; this time the sentence boundaries are correctly detected, but the counter is incremented twice within the first sentence. (Why?)

Such errors do not indicate that something is wrong with the program *per se*, but that something is wrong with the combination of the program and a particular algorithmic problem; the program, which on its own is fine, does not correctly solve that problem.

Logical errors can be caused by a misunderstanding of the semantics of the programming language ("I thought that $X*Y$ denoted X raised to the power of Y, not X times Y," or "I was sure that when a loop of the form **for** Y **from** 1 **to** N is completed the value of Y is N, not $N + 1$"), in which case we might term them **semantic** errors. However, it is far more typical to encounter "real" logical errors; that is, errors in the logical process used by the designer of the algorithm to solve the algorithmic problem. These have nothing to do with the program written later to implement the algorithm. They represent flaws in the algorithm itself, when considered as a proposed solution to the problem. They are **algorithmic** errors, and are the ones we are interested in here. Failing to forward the "money" counter to the next sentence is an algorithmic error. So was the erroneous connection, in the early version of Figure 2.4 presented in Figure 5.1, of one of the exits from "is P's salary more than Q's?" to "advance P to next employee" instead of to "is P at end of list?"

Computers Do Not Err

The analogy between algorithms and recipes fails when it comes to issues of correctness. When a cooking or baking endeavor does not succeed there can be two reasons:

1. the "hardware" is to blame, or
2. the recipe is imprecise and unclear.

For the most part, the first of these is really the reason, especially after having decided, as we indeed have done, that cooks and bakers are part of the hardware. But if there are problems with a recipe, rather than with the baker, oven, or utensils, they usually have to do with its author's assumptions about the competence of its users. "Beat egg whites until foamy" requires some knowledge of egg foam on the part of the baker, without which the result of the baking endeavor might not be a chocolate mousse but a chocolate mess!

In contrast to recipes, algorithms written for computer execution end up in a formal unambiguous programming language, which all but eliminates reason (2). Moreover, reason (1) can also be discarded. By and large, computers do not make mistakes! A hardware error is such a rarity in modern computers that when our bank statement is in error and the banker mumbles something to the effect that the computer made a mistake, we can be sure that it was not the computer that erred—it was probably one of the bank's employees. Either incorrect data was input to one of the programs, or the program itself, written, of course, by a human, contained an error.

An incorrectly working program is not the result of a problem with the computer. If the input data are checked and found to be correct, the problem is with the program and its underlying algorithm.

Testing and Debugging

Algorithmic errors can go undetected for ages. Sometimes they are never detected. It is quite possible that "telltale" inputs for which the error produces an incorrect output just do not occur in the lifetime of the algorithm. Alternatively, such an input might indeed appear, but the incorrect output might never be noticed.

To detect the error in the Figure 5.1 version of Figure 2.4, for example, an input list in which the last employee indeed has a direct manager (and is not, say, the company's president) would be required. (Why?) In a similar vein, you should try to figure out why even the better algorithm of Figure 2.4 works correctly only if employees are required to have no more than one direct manager. Since we never imposed this restriction on input lists explicitly when introducing the problem in Chapter 2, you have really fallen into the little trap; Figure 2.4, strictly speaking, is also incorrect! Only by either explicitly outlawing employees with multiple managers, or by correcting the algorithm itself (how?), can it really be said to be correct.

Some logical errors show up when the processor cannot carry out an instruction for some unanticipated reason. Attempting to divide X by Y, for example, will fail if Y happens to be 0 at the time. Similarly, failure will result from an attempt to move down a tree from a node that happens to be a leaf (that is, there is no place to move down to). These are not language errors, and a compiler will, in general, be unable to spot them in advance. They are called **run-time errors**, and follow from logical flaws in the design of the algorithm. Often the flaw consists simply of forgetting to provide separate treatment for special "borderline" cases such as zeros (in numbers) and leaves (in trees).

A designer might try out an algorithm on several typical and atypical inputs and not find the error. In fact, a programmer will normally test a program on numerous inputs, sometimes called **test sets**, and will gradually rid it of its language errors and most of its logical errors. He cannot be sure, however, that the program (and its underlying algorithm) is totally error free, simply because most algorithmic problems have infinite sets of legal inputs, and hence infinitely many candidate test sets, each of which has the potential of exposing a new error.

Logical errors, someone once said, are like mermaids. The mere fact that you haven't seen one doesn't mean they don't exist.

The process of repeatedly executing an algorithm, or running a program, with the intention of finding and eliminating errors is called **debugging**. The name has an interesting history. One of the first computers to have been built stopped working one day and was later found to have a large insect jammed in some crucial part of its circuitry. Since then, errors, usually logical errors, are affectionately termed **bugs**.

Debugging a program, especially a complex and lengthy one, can be quite a hefty undertaking. Even if the program is observed to produce the wrong outputs on a certain test case, no indication might be available as to the source of the error. However, there are several techniques for narrowing down the possibilities. A version of the program can be run with artificially inserted instructions for intermediate printouts. These show the debugger partial results and values during execution. Alternatively, if the program is interpreted, not compiled, its execution can be followed line by line, making it possible to detect suspicious intermediate values, especially when working with an interactive display. We also mentioned programming environments. These support many kinds of testing and simulation tools to aid the algorithm designer and programmer in getting things to work the way they should.

It is necessary to re-emphasize, however, that none of these methods guarantees bug-free algorithms that produce the right outputs on any legal input. As someone once put it, testing and debugging cannot be used to demonstrate the absence of errors in software, only their presence.

■ Infinite Loops

The incorrectness of an algorithm as a solution to an algorithmic problem can thus manifest itself either in an execution that terminates normally but with incorrect outputs, or in an aborted execution.

As if to make things worse, an algorithm set out to run on one of the problem's legal inputs may not terminate at all! Obviously this represents an error too. Infinite computations, or **infinite loops**, as they are sometimes called, can be of oscillating nature, repeating some number of instructions on the same values over and over again, or of nonoscillating, but diverging nature, resulting in ever-larger or ever-smaller values. An example of an oscillating loop is a search routine in which there is no instruction to forward the appropriate pointer; the algorithm keeps searching in the very same area of the data structure. An example of a divergence is a loop that increments X by 1 on each pass and which is instructed to terminate when X becomes 100. If the loop is erroneously reached with an initial value of 17.6 in X, the loop will "miss" 100 and keep incrementing X forever (see Figure 5.2). Of course, real computers have limited memories and will generally abort programs of the second kind when the value of X exceeds some ultimate maximum, but the *algorithm* on which the program is based admits the infinite loop nevertheless.

Testing and debugging can also help in detecting potential infinite loops. By printing out intermediate values, a debugger may notice suspicious oscillations or an abnormal increase or decrease of values, which, if left untouched, might lead to nontermination. As before, there are always more inputs than we can test, hence no such method is guaranteed to find all potential infinite loops.

In Chapters 10 and 14, we shall discuss algorithms that are not supposed to terminate at all. For these, nontermination is a blessing, and termination indicates

Figure 5.2

An infinitely looping algorithm.

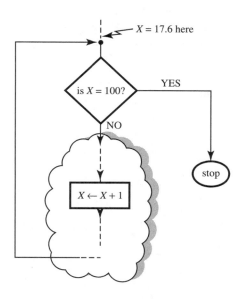

the presence of an error. For now, however, a correct algorithm has to terminate normally on all legal inputs and produce the right outputs each time.

■ Partial and Total Correctness

As discussed in Chapter 1, an algorithmic problem can be concisely divided into two parts:

1. a specification of the set of legal inputs; and
2. the relationship between the inputs and the desired outputs.

For example, each legal input might be required to consist of a list L of words in English. The relationship between the inputs and desired outputs might specify that the output must be a list containing the words in L sorted in ascending lexicographic order. In this way, we have specified the algorithmic problem that asks for an algorithm A, which sorts each legal input list L.

To facilitate precise treatment of the correctness problem for algorithms, researchers distinguish between two kinds of correctness, depending upon whether termination is or is not included. In one case it is assumed *a priori* that the program terminates and in the other it is not. More precisely, it is said that an algorithm A is **partially correct** (with respect to its definition of legal inputs and desired relationship with outputs) if, for every legal input X, if A terminates when run on X then the specified relationship holds between X and the resulting output set. Thus, a partially correct sorting algorithm might not terminate on all legal lists, but whenever it does, a correctly sorted list is the result. We say that A **terminates** if it halts when run on any one of the legal inputs. Both these notions taken together—partial correctness and termination—yield a **totally correct** algorithm, which correctly solves the algorithmic problem for every legal input: the process of running A on any such input X indeed terminates and produces outputs satisfying the desired relationship (see Figure 5.3).

Figure 5.3

Partial and total correctness.

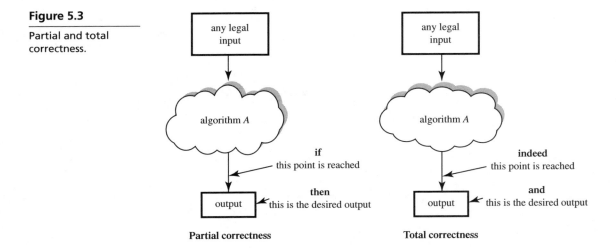

Partial correctness   **Total correctness**

The Need for Proving Correctness

We now know exactly what we would like to establish when confronted with an algorithmic problem and a candidate solution, and we have various testing and debugging techniques to help us in doing so. However, none of these techniques is foolproof, and just like the examples quoted at the beginning of the chapter, computer science folklore is full of stories of catastrophes, some of them fatal, others causing the loss of incredible amounts of money, and all following from algorithmic errors, usually in large and complex software systems.

Claiming that a particular algorithm is correct with respect to an algorithmic problem is perhaps less profound than claiming that mermaids are imaginary, but it can be so crucial as to have many lives or fortunes depend on it. It suffices to think of computer systems that control nuclear weapons or multi-million dollar transactions to appreciate the point.

However, it is not only the many publicized and unpublicized cases of errors that are of concern. It is commonly believed that more than 70% (!) of the effort and cost of developing a complex software system is devoted, in one way or another, to error correcting. This includes delays caused by misconceived specifications (that is, unclear and imprecise definitions of the algorithmic problems), extensive testing and debugging of the algorithms themselves, and, worst of all, changes and rewrites of already working systems (generally termed **maintenance**), as a result of newly-discovered bugs.

Referring to large commercially-used software systems, the situation has been described nicely by saying that software is released for use, not when it is known to be correct, but when the rate of discovering new errors slows down to one that managers consider acceptable.

This situation is clearly bad. We need ways of proving that an algorithm is correct beyond doubt. No one asks whether there might exist some "undiscovered" equilateral triangle having unequal angles. Someone proved once and for all that all equilateral triangles have equal angles, and from then on no doubts remained.

Can anything be done to facilitate such proofs? Can the computer itself help verify the correctness of our algorithms? Actually, what we would like most would be an **automatic verifier**; namely, some sort of super-algorithm that would accept as inputs a description of an algorithmic problem P and an algorithm A that is proposed as a solution, and would determine if indeed A solves P. Perhaps it would also point out the errors if the answer was no (see Figure 5.4). In Chapter 8 we shall see that in general this is but wishful thinking. No such verifier can be constructed.

For now, however, let us ignore the issue of getting a computer to help. Can we *ourselves* prove our algorithms to be correct? Is there any way in which we can use formal, mathematical techniques to realize this objective? Here we have better news.

Invariants and Convergents

There do indeed exist methods for program verification. In fact, in a certain technical sense, any correct algorithm can be rigorously demonstrated to be

Figure 5.4

A hypothetical
algorithmic verifier.

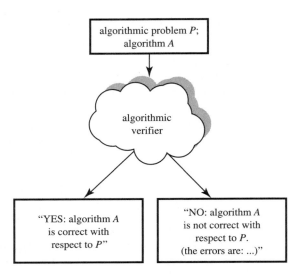

correct![2] Before illustrating with an example, let us say something about the proof methods themselves.

In trying to establish *partial* correctness, we are not interested in showing that certain desirable things *do* happen, but in showing that certain undesirable things *do not*. We do not care whether execution ever reaches the endpoint, but that if it does we will not be in a situation where the outputs differ from the expected ones. Accordingly, we wish to capture the behavior of the algorithm by making careful statements about what it is doing at certain points. To prove partial correctness, we thus attach **intermediate assertions** to various **checkpoints** in the algorithm's text. Attaching an assertion to a checkpoint means that we believe that whenever execution reaches the point in question, in any execution of the algorithm on any legal input, the assertion will be true. This, of course, includes points that are reached many times within a single execution, notably, those within loops. For this reason such assertions are commonly called **invariants**; they remain true no matter how often they are reached.

For example, a sorting algorithm might be such that, at a certain point in its text, exactly half of the input list is sorted, in which case we might attach the assertion "half the list is sorted" to that point. It is more typical, however, that invariants depend on the values of the variables available at the checkpoint. Thus, to some point we might attach the assertion "the partial list from the first location to the Xth is sorted," where X is a variable that increases as more of the list gets sorted.

The initial assertion, namely, the one attached to the starting point of the algorithm, is typically formulated to capture the requirements on legal inputs, and, likewise, the final assertion, the one attached to the ending point, captures the desired relationship of outputs to inputs (see Figure 5.5).

---

[2] This fact notwithstanding, in Chapter 8 we shall see that it is impossible to find such proofs algorithmically. All we are saying here is that if the program is correct there is a proof of that fact. At present, we claim nothing about whether such proofs are easy to come by.

Figure 5.5

Annotating an
algorithm with
invariants.

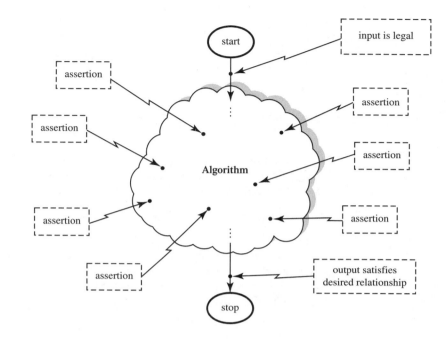

Now, suppose we can establish that all the assertions we have attached are indeed invariants, meaning that they are true whenever reached. Then, in particular, the final assertion is also an invariant. But this means that the algorithm is partially correct. Hence all we have to do is establish the invariance of our assertions. This is done by establishing certain local properties of our assertions, sometimes called **verification conditions**, to the effect that proceeding locally from checkpoint to checkpoint does not bring about any violations of the invariance properties. This approach to proving correctness is sometimes called the **invariant assertion method**, or **Floyd's method**, after one of its inventors.

How do we go about choosing checkpoints and intermediate assertions, and how do we establish the verification conditions? The example given in the next section should shed some light on these questions.

Turning from partial correctness to termination, our main interest is in showing that something good eventually happens (not that bad things do not); namely, that the algorithm indeed reaches its endpoint and terminates successfully. To prove such a statement we use checkpoints as before, but we now find some quantity depending on the algorithm's variables and data structures, and show that it **converges**. By this we mean that the quantity keeps decreasing as execution proceeds from one checkpoint to another, but that it cannot decrease forever—we need to show that there is some bound below which it can never go. Hence there is no way for the algorithm to run forever, since the **convergent**, as it is sometimes called, would then have to decrease forever, contradicting this bound.

In a sorting algorithm, for example, the number of elements not yet in their final positions in the sorted list might be shown to decrease as execution proceeds, but never to be less than 0. When that number reaches 0, the algorithm presumably terminates.

How does one choose such convergents, and how are they shown to converge? Again, an example will help to answer these questions.

Reversing a Symbol String: An Example

A legal input to the following problem is a string S of symbols, say a word or text in English. The goal is to produce the reverse image of S, denoted **reverse**(S), consisting of the symbols of S in reverse order. Thus, for example:

reverse("ajj$dt8") = "8td$jja"

Figure 5.6 shows a simple flowchart of an algorithm A that solves the problem. It uses the unique empty string Λ, which consists of no symbols at all (and which we might denote by the empty quotes ""), and the functions **head**(X) and **tail**(X), which, for any string X, denote, respectively, the first symbol of X and the string X with its head removed. We thus have:

head("ajj$dt8") = "a"

and:

tail("ajj$dt8") = "jj$dt8"

Also, we use the special symbol "·" for string concatenation, or attachment. Thus:

"ajj$dt8" · "tdd9tr" = "ajj$dt8tdd9tr"

Figure 5.6

A flowchart for reversing a symbol string.

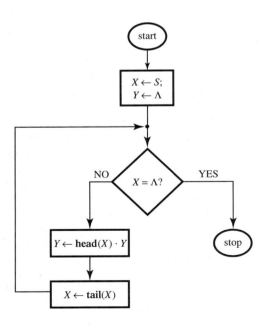

Thus, you will be able to verify easily that attaching the head to the tail of any string yields the string itself. In symbols:

head(S) · **tail**(S) = S

The algorithm for reversing S works by repeatedly "peeling off" the symbols of S one by one, and attaching each in turn to the front of the newly constructed string Y. The new string Y starts out initially as empty. The procedure ends when there is nothing left to peel off S. In order not to destroy S in the process, the peeling off is done in a variable X, which is initialized to the value S.

The claim is that this algorithm correctly produces **reverse**(S) in the variable Y. That is, the algorithm A of Figure 5.6 is **totally correct** with respect to the algorithmic problem that asks for the output Y to be the reverse image of the input string S.

We shall first establish that A is partially correct, using the intermediate assertion method, and then, separately, that it also terminates. We therefore first show that if A happens to terminate on an input string S, then it produces **reverse**(S) in Y.

To this end, consider Figure 5.7, in which three checkpoints have been identified. As already explained, Assertion 1 captures the requirements on the input set, and Assertion 3 embodies the desired relationship between the input string S and the output Y, namely that Y is to be equal to **reverse**(S).

The significance of Figure 5.7, however, is in Assertion 2, which is supposed to capture the situation just prior to either going around the loop once again, or terminating. Assertion 2 states that at checkpoint (2) the current values of X and Y together make up the original string S, in the sense that Y contains some initial portion of S in reverse, and X contains the rest of S unreversed, which is exactly the same as saying that concatenating **reverse**(Y) with X yields S.

Figure 5.7

An annotated flowchart for reversing a symbol string.

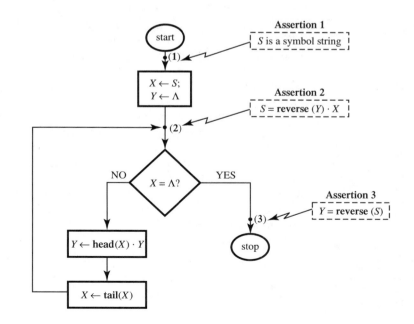

Figure 5.8

The three paths
through the reverse
algorithm.

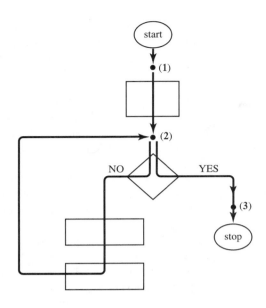

We want to show that all three assertions are invariants, meaning that in each execution of A on any legal input they are true whenever reached. The trick is to consider all possible "hops" from checkpoint to checkpoint that the processor might take in executing the algorithm. In this case, given the form of this particular flowchart, there are three possible hops: point (1) to point (2), point (2) to point (3), and point (2) back to point (2) (see Figure 5.8). The first of these is traversed exactly once in any execution of A; the second is traversed at most once, since at its end the algorithm terminates; the third can be traversed many times (how many?). Notice that the algorithmic segments corresponding to these paths are **loop free**. They consist of simple sequences of elementary instructions and tests, and contain no iterations. As we shall see, this implies that they can be dealt with quite easily.

We now have to show that, for each of these simple segments, if we assume that the assertion attached to its start point is true, and that the segment is actually traversed, then the assertion attached to its endpoint will also be true when reached. The claim is that this is all it takes to establish partial correctness, since the invariance of all three assertions will follow.

Why? Well, the reason is rooted in the fact that any legal execution of A consists of a sequence of segments separated by checkpoints (see Figure 5.9). In this way, if the truth of the start assertion of each of these segments implies the truth of the end assertion, and if the first assertion of the entire sequence is the one corresponding to the input being legal, and is hence assumed to be true to begin with, then truth of assertions propagates along the entire sequence, making all assertions true as execution proceeds. In particular, as explained, the final Assertion 3 will be true upon termination, establishing A's partial correctness.

Figure 5.9

A typical execution
sequence of the
reverse algorithm.

$$(1) \longrightarrow (2) \longrightarrow (2) \longrightarrow (2) \longrightarrow \cdots \longrightarrow (2) \longrightarrow (3)$$
start   *stop*

To summarize, we have to show now that truth of assertions indeed propagates forward along the simple paths between checkpoints.

The details of these proofs will not be presented here, but you are urged to try to fill them in. It helps, however, to make careful note, in symbols, not words, of what exactly has to be proved. Consulting Figures 5.7 and 5.8, and recalling the three possible "hops" between checkpoints, we find that there are three statements to prove:

$(1 \rightarrow 2)$: for any string S, after carrying out the two instructions $X \leftarrow S; Y \leftarrow \Lambda$, the equality $S = \mathbf{reverse}(Y) \cdot X$ will hold.

$(2 \rightarrow 3)$: if $S = \mathbf{reverse}(Y) \cdot X$, and $X = \Lambda$, then $Y = \mathbf{reverse}(S)$.

$(2 \rightarrow 2)$: if $S = \mathbf{reverse}(Y) \cdot X$, and $X \neq \Lambda$, then after carrying out the instructions $Y \leftarrow \mathbf{head}(X) \cdot Y; X \leftarrow \mathbf{tail}(X)$, the same equality, namely $S = \mathbf{reverse}(Y) \cdot X$, will hold for the new values of X and Y.

Formally establishing that these three statements are true concludes the proof that the algorithm is partially correct.

We now have to show that the algorithm terminates for any input string S. To that end, let us consider checkpoint (2) again. The only way an execution of the algorithm might not terminate is by passing through point (2) infinitely often. That is shown to be impossible by exhibiting a convergent (that is, a quantity that depends on the current values of the variables) which, on the one hand, decreases each time checkpoint (2) is revisited, but, on the other hand, cannot become ever smaller.

The convergent that works in our case is simply the length of the string X. Each time the loop is traversed, X is made shorter by precisely one symbol, since it becomes the tail of its previous value. However, its length cannot be less than 0 because when X is of length 0 (that is, it becomes the empty string) the loop is not traversed further and the algorithm terminates.

This concludes the proof that the **reverse** algorithm is totally correct. It might occur to you that this proof is not worth the trouble, since the correctness of the program seems obvious enough, and the proof appears to be tediously technical. There is some truth to this here, and the example was chosen to illustrate the proof technique itself, not so much the need for it in this particular example. Nevertheless, it is not too difficult to imagine a version of the same algorithm with some subtle bug in one of the extremal cases, or a more complicated version where, say, the even-numbered positions are to be reversed and the odd-numbered ones not. In these cases, verifying the program by just looking at it is dangerously inadequate and formal proofs are a necessity.

As an aside, we need not work with flowcharts when verifying correctness. Although the visual nature of a flowchart can at times be helpful in choosing checkpoints and reasoning about the dynamics of the algorithm, there are straightforward ways of attaching intermediate assertions to points in standard textual formats of an algorithm.

Even in this small example, the problematic nature of imperative programming is apparent. The statements to be proved were all phrased in terms of different times, distinguishing between the "new" and "original" values of the variables. Writing this algorithm in a functional programming language is straightforward, and the statements to be proved would be simpler. For example, the last one becomes:

$(2 \rightarrow 2)$: if $S = \textbf{reverse}(Y) \cdot X$, and $X \neq \Lambda$, then
$S = \textbf{reverse}(\textbf{head}(X) \cdot Y) \cdot \textbf{tail}(X)$.

This does not solve the essential problem of proving correctness, but it removes the somewhat cumbersome element of dealing explicitly with the changes of values over time, which does not always mesh naturally with our mathematical expectations regarding variables.

What's in a Proof?

The correctness proof outlined in the last section is one of the simplest of its kind, without being completely trivial. This is rather discouraging, to say the least.

Let us discuss its constituents. A basic element in both the partial correctness and termination proofs is the selection of checkpoints in the text of the algorithm. These, in general, consist of the start and stop points and sufficiently many intermediate locations, so that every loop of the algorithm's text contains at least one such location.

Having chosen checkpoints, we must attach intermediate assertions to them, whose invariance has to be established by proving the local verification conditions. These involve only loop-free algorithmic segments because we were careful to "break open" all of the loops with checkpoints. We also have to exhibit a convergent and show that it actually converges. Which of these activities can be automated algorithmically? In other words, for which can we expect to get considerable help from a computer?

Finding a set of checkpoints to cover each of the loops, even some kind of minimal set, can be fully automated. Moreover, under certain technical conditions, much of the local checking of verification conditions, as well as the local decrease in the value of a convergent, can be automated too. However, the heart of such proofs is to be found elsewhere. It lies in the *choice* of the appropriate invariants and convergents. Here it can be shown that there is no general algorithm that can automatically find invariants and convergents that "work," meaning that they satisfy the local conditions needed for producing the proof (this issue is taken up in more detail in Chapter 8). The right choice of an invariant is a delicate and subtle art, and can demand more ingenuity than that involved in designing the algorithm in the first place. Indeed, the algorithm designer may possess the right kind of intuition required to produce a good algorithm, but might be at a loss when asked to formulate precisely "what is going on" at a certain point therein.

Paradoxically, adequate invariants and convergents always exist, so that, as mentioned earlier, a correct algorithm can, in principle, always be proved correct. This seems to contradict our statements to the effect that the verification process cannot be automated, and that an algorithm designer might not be able to prove correctness. It does not. And the key is the phrase "in principle." Although proofs exist, they cannot always be found by a computer, and humans are often also at a loss. For large and complex software systems, **after-the-fact** verification is often impossible, simply because of the unmanageable magnitude and intricacy of the task. When presented with a large piece of software that has been endlessly changed, corrected, patched, and updated, providing formal and precise assertions that completely characterize its behavior at various points is essentially out of the question.

In such cases, an alternative method, called **as-you-go** verification, to be discussed later, has to be adopted.

The Towers of Hanoi: An Example

The foregoing discussion notwithstanding, verification is at times somewhat easier than anticipated. It might appear that the subtle nature of recursion would render the verification of recursive subroutines more difficult than that of mere iterative algorithms. This is not always so.

Recall the Towers of Hanoi problem and the following recursive solution, presented in Chapter 2:

subroutine **move** N **from** X **to** Y **using** Z:

(1) if N is 1 then output "move X to Y";

(2) otherwise (that is, if N is greater than 1) do the following:

    (2.1) call **move** $N - 1$ **from** X **to** Z **using** Y;

    (2.2) output "move X to Y";

    (2.3) call **move** $N - 1$ **from** Z **to** Y **using** X;

(3) return.

That this routine terminates for every N (where the values of X, Y, and Z are A, B, and C in some order) seems quite easy to see: the only kind of infinite computation at all possible is obtained by performing an infinitely deep cascade of recursive calls. However, on observing that the depth of the tree of recursive calls (see Figure 2.8) cannot be greater than N, since the only things that happen to N during execution are a decrease by 1 whenever a lower-level recursive call is executed, we find that N must "hit" the value 1 at some point. But when N is exactly 1 the **escape clause** of the recursion is reached, causing not another, deeper recursive call, but a simple instruction followed by a **return**, which entails *ascending* the tree. Consequently, the tree of recursive calls is finite and execution must terminate.

Notice that this termination proof does not require any "understanding" of the workings of the routine; we only used superficial observations about the behavior of N and the presence of an appropriate escape clause. However, the proof is not entirely correct! If the initial value of N is zero or less, it is possible to decrease it an infinite number of times without hitting 1, and the routine will indeed not terminate if given such a value for N. What we must do here is to add to this routine a specification of the legal inputs that precludes non-positive values of N. (Interestingly, a comparison of this algorithm with the version given in PROLOG in Chapter 3, shows that the PROLOG version will in fact handle the case of $N = 0$ correctly.)

To prove partial correctness, we use a variant of the intermediate assertion method that befits the non-iterative nature of recursive algorithms. Rather than trying to formulate the local situation at a given point, we try to formulate our expectations of the entire recursive routine just prior to entering it. This is then used in a cyclic-looking, but perfectly sound, fashion to support itself! Here is a possible formulation for the **move** routine.

For any N, the following statement, call it (S), holds true:

> *Assume that the peg names A, B, and C are associated, in some order, with the variables X, Y, and Z. Then, a terminating execution of the call **move** N **from** X **to** Y **using** Z lists a sequence of ring-moving instructions, which, if started (and followed faithfully) in any legal configuration of the rings and pegs in which at least the N smallest rings are on peg X, correctly moves those N rings from X to Y, possibly using Z as temporary storage. Moreover, the sequence adheres to the rules of the Towers of Hanoi problem, and it leaves all other rings untouched.*

If we can now show that (S) is true for all N, we will have established the partial correctness of our solution, since we are interested particularly in a call to **move** N **from** A **to** B **using** C, where A holds N rings and B and C are empty. In this case, (S) is but a rephrasing of the requirements of the problem, as you can verify.

Statement (S) can be established by the classical method of **mathematical induction**. This means that we first show directly that the statement is true when N is 1 and then show that under the assumption that it is true for some given $N - 1$ (where $N - 1$ is at least 1, so that N is at least 2), it must also be true for N itself. It follows, therefore, that (S) must be true for all N, since the separately proven truth for the case $N = 1$ implies truth for $N = 2$ which, in turn, implies truth for $N = 3$, and so on, *ad infinitum*.

■ Let us now carefully go through the details of the proof. That (S) holds when N is 1 is trivial: asserting (S) in this case is simply asserting that when the subroutine is called with N being 1 a sequence is produced, which correctly moves the topmost ring from X to Y. This is immediately seen to be accomplished by the first line of the subroutine.

Assume now that the statement (S) holds for some arbitrary $N - 1$. We now have to show that it holds also for N. Accordingly, let us assume that a call to the move routine has just been made with the number N and some association of pegs A, B, and C with the variables X, Y, and Z. The three pegs contain some legal arrangement of rings, with peg X containing at least the N smallest rings (see Figure 5.10(a)). Now, since the value of N is not 1, the first thing the routine does is to call itself recursively on line (2.1) with parameter $N - 1$. By the **inductive hypothesis**, that is, by our assumption that (S) holds for calls to the routine with $N - 1$, that call, if completed successfully, will correctly and legally move the topmost $N - 1$ rings from X to Z, leaving everything else unchanged (see Figure 5.10(b)). However, since X was guaranteed to contain at least N rings to begin with, there is still at least one ring left on X after the call on line (2.1) is completed, and the instruction on line (2.2) moves that ring directly to Y (see Figure 5.10(c)). Since

Figure 5.10

Partial correctness of
the Towers of Hanoi:
proving *N* from *N*−1.

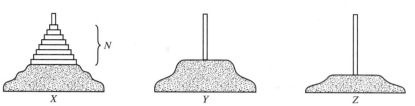

(a) **Initial configuration:** *X* contains (at least) *N* smallest rings; others are scattered.

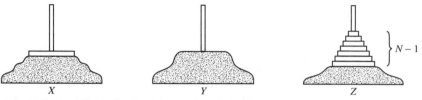

(b) **Inductive hypothesis:** *N* − 1 top rings on *X* are correctly moved to *Z*.

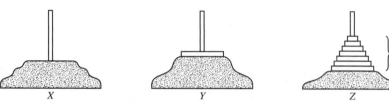

(c) **Direct move:** 1 ring on *X* is moved directly to *Y*.

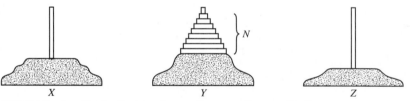

(d) **Inductive hypothesis:** *N* − 1 top rings on *Z* are correctly moved to *Y*.

all the rings on *Y* before this move (if any) must have been larger than the *N*th ring being moved, this move is legal. The same assumption about *N* − 1, but now applied to the next call, on line (2.3) of the subroutine, can be seen to complete the picture by moving the *N* − 1 rings from *Z* to *Y*, right on top of the single ring that was moved separately (see Figure 5.10(d)).

You should go through this proof carefully, noticing why the legality of all moves is also guaranteed throughout the process, not only the final outcome. Also, it is possible to show (using the same inductive hypothesis for the two calls) that no rings other than the top *N* ones on peg *X* are touched by this procedure, so that (*S*) has been established in full for this call with *N*, assuming it for calls with *N* − 1. As mentioned, this establishes that the statement (*S*) holds for all *N*.

The partial correctness of the recursive Towers of Hanoi algorithm is thus proven, and since we have already proved termination, the algorithm is totally correct.

More on the Towers of Hanoi: A Simple Iterative Solution

In Chapter 2 we promised to exhibit an extremely simple-to-execute iterative algorithm for the Towers of Hanoi problem. The reason for discussing it here, rather than in Chapter 2, is rooted in the fact that it is not quite clear why it works and the fact that it does requires proof. Indeed, we shall not present a proof of its correctness here, and you are invited to try to construct a proof, by showing that the iterative and recursive algorithms are really equivalent. This can be done by induction on N.

To describe the algorithm, let us assume that the three pegs are arranged in a circle, and that all N rings are piled on one of them (the names of the pegs are unimportant). Here is the algorithm:

(1) do the following repeatedly, until, prior to step (1.2), all rings are correctly piled on some other peg:
  (1.1) move the smallest ring from its current peg to the next peg in clockwise order;
  (1.2) make the only move possible that does not involve the smallest ring.

It should be clear that step (1.2) is well defined and unambiguous, since one of the pegs has to have the smallest ring on top, and of the two remaining pegs one has a smaller ring on top than the other; hence the only move not involving the smallest ring is transferring that smaller ring to the other peg.

This algorithm can be executed easily by a small child, even if many rings are involved. Notice, in passing, that if N is odd the rings will end up on the next peg in clockwise order, and if N is even they will end up on the next one in *counter-clockwise* order.

After-the-Fact vs. As-You-Go Verification

The alternative to proving correctness of an already-completed algorithm is to develop the algorithm and proof hand in hand. The idea is to match the disciplined, gradual, step-by-step construction of the algorithm or software system with the gradual construction of proof segments, which will ultimately accumulate to form a complete proof of the entire system.

Clearly, this is easier said than done. However, an obvious mechanism that encourages such practice is the subroutine. As explained in Chapter 2, a complex program can be built carefully out of many routines, some nested inside others, resulting in a well-structured and stratified piece of software. Good design practice dictates that each routine be carefully analyzed in terms of its overall purpose, and then verified as a separate entity. In principle, once this has been done, the entire system will also have been verified. The reason is that what has been proved about a given routine can be used to prove things about other routines that call it. If, for example, we verify that the **search-for** routine of Chapter 2 (cf. Figure 2.6) correctly finds X in an input text and outputs the counter if it reaches the end of the text, then that proof could be used to verify the "money"-finding algorithm.

Here, too, there are many possible pitfalls. It is far from easy to correctly identify the **interface** of a routine and its intended behavior under all circumstances, but good algorithmic design recommends that we do not construct a subroutine unless we can do so. Of course, a *recursive* routine requires a cyclic-looking verification process, which involves assuming it to be correct for its self-calls, as was done for the Towers of Hanoi. Obviously, this process is not always as straightforward as it sounds either.

In short, good stepwise algorithmic design, coupled with informative and precise documentation of design decisions, can form the basis of the construction of verified software, by breaking up the overall proof into pieces that reflect the breakup of the software itself. When **concurrency** and **reactivity** are introduced into algorithms, as is done in Chapters 10 and 14, things become more difficult, and even a small and innocent-looking algorithm can cause formidable problems when it comes to verification. We shall discuss that bridge, but not quite cross it, when we reach it.

Design by Contract

The object-oriented paradigm carries this idea of as-you-go verification a step forward, in the form of a methodology called **design by contract**. As mentioned in Chapter 3, each class in an object-oriented program describes some abstract set of objects with their associated behaviors, or methods. Such a description may include instructions on how to carry out each method, but it doesn't have to. In fact, it is often very useful to have completely abstract classes that only specify *what* is to be done, but not *how*. The JAVA incarnation of the Queue class is such an example, in that it does not specify the behavior of each method, only how it is to be called. Moreover, by replacing the word "Queue" with "Stack" we would get a perfectly legal description of stacks instead of queues. What is missing is the *meaning* of each method: how it affects the state of the object and what (if anything) it returns. In the design-by-contract approach, this specification is called a **contract**, and it consists of three kinds of assertions: **class invariants**, **method preconditions**, and **method postconditions**.

Class invariants state conditions that must be true for every object of the class before and after the execution of each operation. Method preconditions specify the legal inputs to each method (or, in other words, what has to hold prior to the execution of the method), and method postconditions specify what must hold after the execution of the method. In terms of the previous discussions in this chapter, method preconditions and postconditions are really just the assertions at the start and end of routines, and class invariants are analogous to loop invariants.

For example, in the Queue class, the precondition for the *front* method would be that the queue is not empty. The postcondition for add(X) is that *front* will return X if the queue was empty before calling *add*, and otherwise it will return the same value it would have returned prior to this operation. In contrast, the postcondition for the corresponding method in the Stack class would say that after calling the method add(X), *front* will return X, regardless of the previous state of the object. This captures the essential difference between stacks and queues.

The design-by-contract methodology calls for specifying the contract before writing the implementing program, and for carefully modifying the contract as the specification changes. From here, it is but a short step to the verification of the program, and tools are emerging to help in this endeavor.

Design by contract is an integral feature of the programming language EIFFEL, which also supports loop invariants and convergents. While not yet part of the official JAVA language, there are a number of tools that add this capability to JAVA too. They allow the compiler to generate code that actually checks the assertions while the program is running, alerting the programmer to violations as they are encountered. However, while such tools are useful for testing programs, the major contribution of the design-by-contract method is the attention given to the correctness of the program as it is being written and modified. As such, it can be practiced even by programmers using object-oriented languages that do not yet have tool support for checking assertions at run-time.

Specifying the behavior of functions or subroutines by preconditions and postconditions is possible in every programming language. There are essentially two reasons why design by contract is especially appropriate for the object-oriented paradigm. First, the division of the program into classes and methods and the possibility of abstract classes provide natural points for placing the assertions. Second, the object-oriented style provides a real promise of the possibility of **code reuse**, which is the ability to use the same class—implementing code and all—in many different applications. However, in order for this to work, a clear specification of what classes and methods are intended to mean is essential. Lacking this, a programmer trying to reuse somebody else's class might make such mistakes as confusing a queue for a stack. A spectacular example of this is the loss of the first Ariane 5 launch[3] in 1996. The failure of the navigation module has been traced to the practice of reusing programs from Ariane 4 without understanding the assumptions on which the original programs were based; these assumptions were no longer true for the Ariane 5, but were not documented in the code. (Some details about this incident appear in Chapter 13.)

Interactive Verification and Proof Checking

Despite the fact that, in general, automatic algorithmic verification is out of the question, there is much that can be done with a computer's aid. We shall only examine a number of issues briefly here since most of them are too technical to be discussed here in detail.

A computer can be programmed to help in after-the-fact verification. A possible scenario involves an interactive program that attempts to verify a given algorithm with respect to a formal description of the algorithmic problem. Every now and then

---

[3] The Ariane series of rockets are part of the European Union's space program.

it asks the human user to supply it with, say, a candidate invariant (recall that this is the kind of task it cannot, in general, do on its own). It then goes ahead and tries to establish the relevant verification conditions, then moves on to additional points in the algorithm if it succeeds, or backtracks to previous decisions if it fails.

Since the entire procedure is interactive, the human user can stop it whenever it seems to be going off in wrong directions, and attempt to put it back on track. The computer is being used here as a fast and meticulous apprentice, checking the details of local logical conditions, keeping track of past invariants, assertions, and comments, and never tiring of trying out another possibility.

Such a process can also lead to the discovery of hidden bugs or missing assumptions. For example, a computerized verifier will not accept the erroneous proof given earlier for the termination of the Towers of Hanoi program. Examination of why the proof is rejected would lead the programmer to the realization that an appropriate precondition was missing.

This idea can also be used to aid in as-you-go verification efforts. Here, previously established proofs of portions of the algorithm (say, subroutines) can be kept track of by the automatic apprentice, and used in algorithmic attempts to verify larger portions (say, calling routines). Such an interactive system can be part of the entire programming environment, which might include the editing, debugging, and testing tools too. A user might be interested in verifying some of the smaller and better identified algorithms in the software system under development, and leave the less manageable parts to be debugged and tested conventionally.

Another possibility for computer-aided verification is in **proof checking**. Here, a human produces what seems to be a proof—invariants, convergents, and all—and a computer is programmed to generate and verify the lengthy sequences of logical and symbolic manipulations that constitute the fully-fledged proof. Considerable work has been, and still is, devoted to these topics, and several systems exist that can aid in the design and verification of nontrivial programs.

As we discuss in Chapters 10 and 14, powerful methods (many of them based on a technique called **model checking**) have been developed for verifying even complex software and hardware systems. Under certain reasonable assumptions, such as a finite number of states of system behavior and simple, well-defined properties to verify, these work pretty well in practice. So there are encouraging signs. Still, many problems remain, and the use of smooth and widely applicable verification aids will still take a while to become common practice.

Research on Algorithmic Correctness

Besides the topics discussed in the previous section, researchers are interested in developing new and useful methods for verification, and the invariant and convergent methods are examples of only the most basic of these. Different language constructs trigger different methods, as will become apparent with the introduction of concurrency and probabilism in Chapters 10 and 11.

One issue we have not treated at all is that of **specification languages**, sometimes called **assertion languages**. How do we specify the algorithmic problem formally? How do we write down the intermediate assertions so that they are unambiguous and lend themselves to algorithmic manipulation? The alternatives differ not only in pragmatics, but also in the underlying mathematics. For some kinds of assertion languages, establishing the local verification conditions of loop-free segments between checkpoints is algorithmically feasible, whereas for others the problem can be shown to be as hard as the global verification problem itself, and hence not solvable algorithmically. In both cases, people are interested in developing **theorem-proving** techniques that form the basis of condition-checking algorithms.

Many research topics are relevant both to verification and debugging, and to efficient and informative compilation. A good example is **data-flow analysis**, whereby methods are developed to symbolically follow the flow of data in an algorithm. This means that the possible changes a variable can undergo during execution are analyzed without actually running the algorithm. Such analysis can reveal potential errors, such as out-of-bounds indexes for arrays, possible zero values for divisors in arithmetic operations, and so on.

Researchers are also interested in more complex properties of algorithms. At times it may be important to know whether two algorithms are *equivalent*. One reason for this might be the availability of a simple but inefficient algorithm, and a designer's candidate for a more efficient but more intricate algorithm. The desire here is to prove that both algorithms will terminate on the same class of inputs and produce identical results.

One of the approaches to the investigation of such richer classes of algorithmic properties is to formulate **logics of programs**, or algorithmic logics, which are analogous to classical systems of mathematical logic, but which enable us to reason about algorithms and their effects. Whereas classical systems are sometimes called static, algorithmic logics are **dynamic** in nature; the truth of statements made in these formalisms depends not only on the present state of the world (as in the statement "it is raining"), but on the relationship between the present state and other possible ones.

As an example, consider the basic construct of such dynamic logics:

after(A, F)

which means that after executing algorithm A, the assertion F will necessarily be true. The assertion F might state that the list L is sorted, in which case the statement can be used to formalize the partial correctness of a sorting routine. The power of such a construct, however, is in the possibility of using it more than once in a statement and combining it with other logical objects. Consider the following, where "$\rightarrow$" stands for "implies":

if $F1 \rightarrow$ **after** $(A, F2)$ and $F2 \rightarrow$ **after** $(B, F3)$
then $F1 \rightarrow$ **after** $(A; B, F3)$

This statement asserts that if (1) whenever $F1$ is true $F2$ is true after executing A, and if also (2) whenever $F2$ is true $F3$ is true after executing B, then we can conclude (3) whenever $F1$ is true $F3$ is true after executing $A; B$ (that is, A followed immediately by B). This statement might seem obvious, but it is quite subtle. It actually forms the mathematical justification for inserting intermediate assertions into an algorithm. $F2$ can be thought of as an intermediate assertion attached to the point separating A from B, and the statement says that establishing the local conditions on A and B separately amounts to establishing the more global condition on $A; B$.

More complicated statements can be made (and proved) in such logics, concerning the equivalence and termination of programs, and other properties of interest. Logics of programs thus help place the theory of algorithmic verification on a sound mathematical basis. Moreover, they enable us to investigate questions concerning the feasibility of automating proof methods for termination, correctness, equivalence, and the like. One of the most successful methods for verification, called **model checking**, can be used to check a program against a logical formula, but here too there are inherent limitations to any such effort, which will be further discussed in Chapters 7 and 8. Also, Chapter 10 discusses the verification of concurrent systems, and Chapter 12 discusses the addition of interaction to mathematical proofs in general, as well as proofs that are both interactive and probabilistically checkable. Chapters 13 and 14, which discuss large and complex systems, also touch upon some issues of correctness.

Another promising line of research is concerned with automatic or semiautomatic algorithmic **synthesis**. Here the interest is in synthesizing a working algorithm or program from a specification of the algorithmic problem. As with verification, the general synthesis problem is algorithmically unsolvable, but parts of the process can be aided by a computer.

One of the issues relevant to both synthesis and equivalence proofs is that of **program transformations**, in which parts of an algorithm or program are transformed in ways that preserve equivalence. For example, we might be interested in such transformations in order to make an algorithm comply with the rules of some programming language (for example, replacing recursion by iteration when the language does not allow recursion) or for efficiency purposes, as illustrated in Chapter 6.

Research in the fields of correctness and logics of algorithms blends nicely with research on the semantics of programming languages. It is impossible to prove anything about a program without a rigorous and unambiguous meaning for that program. The more complex the languages we use, the more difficult it is to provide them with semantics, and the more difficult it is to devise methods of proof and to investigate them using algorithmic logics. This is another reason why functional languages are more amenable to proofs of correctness than imperative languages.

■ The Four-Color Theorem

It seems appropriate to close this chapter with a story of some philosophical interest. The **four-color problem** was formulated in 1852, and for about 120 years was considered to be one of the most interesting open problems in all of mathematics. It involves maps, of the kind found in an atlas: diagrams consisting of partitions of a finite portion of the plane by closed regions signifying countries.

Let us assume we want to color such a map, associating a color with each country, but in such a way that no two countries that share part of a border will be colored

Figure 5.11

Coloring a map.

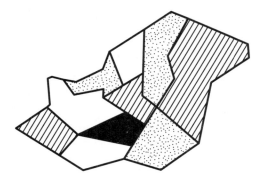

with the same color. (Figure 5.11 shows a legal coloring of a sample map; notice that two countries sharing only a point may have the same color.) How many colors are necessary to color any map?

At first sight it seems that we can construct increasingly intricate maps that require ever-larger numbers of colors. When we play with some examples, however, it turns out that four colors always suffice. The four-color problem asks whether this is always true. On the one hand, no one could prove that four colors were sufficient to color any map, but, on the other hand, no one was able to exhibit a map requiring five.

Over the years many people worked on the problem, and many deep and beautiful results emerged in the branch of mathematics called **topology**. A couple of "proofs" that four colors suffice were published, but were later shown to contain subtle errors. Then, in 1976, the problem was finally solved by two mathematicians. They proved what is now known as the **four-color theorem**, which asserts that four colors do indeed suffice.

What has this got to do with us? Well, the 1976 proof was achieved with the aid of a computer. The proof can be viewed as consisting, very roughly, of two parts. In the first, the two researchers used several previously established results, with some additional mathematical reasoning, to prove that the general problem could be reduced to showing that a finite number of special cases could be colored with four colors. Computer programs were then written to meticulously generate all such cases (there turned out to be about 1700 of them) and to go through them all in order to find a four-coloring. The theorem was established when the programs terminated, answering the question positively: all 1700 cases were found to be four-colorable.

Can we put the traditional Q.E.D. (standing for *quod erat demonstrandum*, freely translated as "that which was to be proved") at the end of the proof? The problem is that no one has ever verified the programs used in the proof. It is possible that the algorithms constructed to carry out the subtle case generation were flawed. Not only that, no one has ever verified the correctness of the compiler used to translate the programs into machine-executable code. No one has verified any of the other relevant system programs that could influence the correct running of the programs, and for that matter (though this is not our concern here) no one has verified that the hardware was working the way it should.

In actuality, the mathematics community has accepted the theorem. Possibly relevant to this is the fact that since 1976 a number of additional proofs have appeared, all of which use a computer, but some of which need to check only a smaller and more manageable set of cases and use shorter and clearer programs. The philosophical question, however, remains: will absolute mathematical truth, as opposed to practical computer applications, be allowed to depend on the somewhat doubtful performance of unverified software?

■ Exercises

5.1. Consider the problem of sorting lists of mutually distinct integers, each of which is between 1 and 12. Let us assume that you have a candidate algorithm for solving this problem, which is known to terminate on every input.

   (a) Could you prove the partial correctness of this algorithm (if it is indeed correct) by employing testing only?
   (b) Would your answer to (a) change if the algorithm was designed to lexicographically sort lists of mutually distinct words in English?
   (c) How would you generalize your answers to these two questions?
   (d) When would you recommend performing such testing in practice?

5.2. Consider the following suggestion for the construction of an automated verifier for algorithms operating on finite sets of inputs. The verifier accepts three inputs:

   ■ an algorithm;
   ■ the finite set of legal inputs to this algorithm;
   ■ a specification of the input/output requirements from the algorithm.

   Upon receiving these inputs, the verifier proceeds to "run" the given algorithm on the first legal input, then on the second, etc. If all these runs yield outputs that satisfy the given specification, the verifier declares the algorithm to be partially correct. Otherwise, it declares it to be incorrect.

   What is wrong with this suggestion, and how may it be remedied by adding an assumption about the algorithms? Can this assumption be similarly tested?

5.3. Construct an employee list that generates an error if subjected to the algorithm in Figure 5.1, but produces the correct answer if subjected to the algorithm of Figure 2.4.

5.4. (a) Modify Figure 2.4, so that if an employee has several direct managers then the employee's salary is added to the accumulated sum if it is higher than that of at least one of those direct managers. Call the new algorithm CA.
   (b) Prove the total correctness of algorithm CA with respect to this new specification.
   (c) Assuming that each employee has at most one manager, is algorithm CA correct with respect to the original specification given for Figure 2.4?
   (d) Assuming that each employee has at most one manager, is the algorithm of Figure 2.4 correct with respect to the new specification for algorithm CA?

5.5. Suppose your algorithm CA is used as a subroutine in a large salary accounting system, and that on some occasion a salary report is found to be erroneous.

   (a) What are the possible sources of the error? What potential source of error can you eliminate with confidence?
   (b) What can you say in general about the correctness of a system, some part of which has been proven to be partially correct? Totally correct?
   (c) Suppose you are required to design and manage the production of a large software system. Your team includes someone who is capable of verifying programs, but who, obviously, is unable to verify all of the software you intend to produce. Is there any point in asking that person to work on verification (assuming that he or she could otherwise be utilized as a programmer)? If your answer is "yes," how would you characterize the kinds of programs you would ask the person to verify?

5.6. We have seen in the correctness demonstration for the **reverse** algorithm that only three (well-placed) invariants are sufficient for the proof.

(a) How would you generalize the above claim to any algorithm whose structure (i.e., the structure of its flowchart) is similar to **reverse**?

(b) What kind of flowchart enables a partial correctness proof of the corresponding algorithm with only two invariants, attached to the **start** and **stop** points?

(c) How many well-attached invariants are sufficient for proving the partial correctness of an algorithm whose flowchart contains two loops?

(d) For any flowchart with two loops, how many invariants are necessary for proving partial correctness in the method given in the text? How would you classify the sufficient number of assertions according to the structure of a two-loop flowchart? (Hint: consider connectedness, nesting.)

5.7. Prove the three verification conditions for the reverse algorithm presented in the text.

For Exercises 5.8–5.14 you are given the following three new operations on strings:

- **last**(X): yields the last symbol of string X;
- **all-but-last**(X): yields the string X with its last symbol removed;
- **eq**(s, t): is applicable to symbols only, and is true if s and t are identical symbols.

For example, **last**("town") = "n", **all-but-last**("town") = "tow", and **eq**("a", "a") is true, but **eq**("a", "b") is false.

Also, by convention, **head**(Λ) = **last**(Λ) = **tail**(Λ) = **all-but-last**(Λ) = Λ.

5.8. Construct a function **rev**(X) that reverses the string X, using only the operations **last**, **all-but-last**, **eq**, and "·" (concatenation), in addition to testing the emptiness of a string. Prove the total correctness of your algorithm.

5.9. Construct a function **equal**(X, Y) that tests whether the strings X and Y are equal. It should return true or false accordingly. You may use the operations mentioned in the text and those defined above. (Note, however, that there is no way of comparing arbitrarily long strings in a single operation.) Prove the total correctness of your algorithm.

5.10. A palindrome is a string that is the same when read forwards and backwards. Consider the following algorithm *Pal1* for checking whether a string is a palindrome. The algorithm returns true or false, according to whether the input string S is a palindrome or not.

$Y \leftarrow$ **rev**(S);
return **equal**(S, Y).

(a) Prove the total correctness of *Pal1*.

(b) The termination of *Pal1* can be easily proved by relying on the termination of the functions **rev** and **equal**. Can you generalize this type of reasoning to a similar composition of any two programs?

5.11. Algorithm *Pal1* is not very efficient, as it always reverses entire strings. Often, a string can be shown not to be a palindrome with far fewer applications of the allowed basic operations.

(a) Give an example of such a string.

(b) How many operations would suffice to determine whether your string is a palindrome?

5.12. Here is another algorithm, *Pal2*, designed to perform the same task as *Pal1*, but more efficiently:

$X \leftarrow S$;

$E \leftarrow$ true;
while $X \neq \Lambda$ do the following:
   if **eq**(**head**(X), **last**(X)) then $X \leftarrow$ **all-but-last**(**tail**(X));
   otherwise $E \leftarrow$ false.
return E.

Unfortunately, *Pal2* is not totally correct. Prove or disprove:

(a) *Pal2* is partially correct.
(b) *Pal2* terminates on every input string S.

5.13. The following algorithm, *Pal3*, is another attempt to improve *Pal1*:

$X \leftarrow S$;
$E \leftarrow$ true;
while $X \neq \Lambda$ and E is true do the following:
   $Y \leftarrow$ **tail**(X);
   if **eq**(**head**(X), **last**(Y)) then $X \leftarrow$ **all-but-last**(Y);
   otherwise $E \leftarrow$ false.
return E.

Pal3 is not totally correct either. Prove or disprove:

(a) *Pal3* is partially correct.
(b) *Pal3* terminates on every input string S.

5.14. (a) Construct a correct solution to the problem of checking efficiently whether a string is a palindrome, following the general ideas of *Pal2* and *Pal3*. Call your algorithm *Pal4*.
(b) Prove the total correctness of *Pal4*.
(c) Explain why the string you gave in Exercise 5.11 to exhibit the inefficiency of *Pal1* is no longer a "bad" example for the efficiency of *Pal4*.

For any two positive integer numbers m and n, denote by m^n the number m raised to the power of n. For example, $2^3 = 2 \times 2 \times 2 = 8$, and $3^2 = 3 \times 3 = 9$. Also, $m^1 = m$ and $1^n = 1$, for every positive m and n. In addition, for $n = 0$, we define $m^0 = 1$ for every positive integer m.

5.15. Each of the following algorithms, *Pwr1*, *Pwr2*, *Pwr3*, and *Pwr4*, computes the value of m^n and produces the result in the variable PW. It is assumed that m is a positive integer and that n is a natural number (i.e., either 0 or a positive integer). Prove the total correctness of all four algorithms.

i. Algorithm *Pwr1*:

$PW \leftarrow 1$;
do the following n times:
   $PW \leftarrow PW \times m$.

ii. Algorithm *Pwr2*:

call **compute-power-of** m and n.

The subroutine **compute-power** is defined as:

subroutine **compute-power-of** B and E:
   if $E = 0$ then $PW \leftarrow 1$;
   otherwise (i.e., if E is positive) do the following:
      call **compute-power-of** B and $E - 1$;
      $PW \leftarrow B \times PW$;
   return.

iii. Algorithm *Pwr3*:

$PW \leftarrow 1$;
$B \leftarrow m$;
$E \leftarrow n$;
while $E \neq 0$ do the following:
   if E is an even number then do the following:
      $B \leftarrow B \times B$;
      $E \leftarrow E/2$;
   otherwise (i.e., if E is an odd number) do the following:
      $PW \leftarrow PW \times B$;
      $E \leftarrow E - 1$.

iv. Algorithm *Pwr4*:

call **times-power-of** 1, m, **and** n.

The subroutine **times-power** is defined by:

subroutine **times-power-of** Q, B, **and** E:
  if $E = 0$ then $PW \leftarrow Q$;
  otherwise, if E is an even number then
    call **times-power-of** Q, $B \times B$, **and** $E/2$;
  otherwise (i.e., if E is an odd number)
    call **times-power-of** $Q \times B$, B, **and** $E - 1$;
  return.

5.16. (a) Prove total correctness of the algorithm for testing whether a given vector represents a permutation you were asked to design in Exercise 2.10.
   (b) Prove total correctness of the algorithm for generating all permutations of A_N you were asked to design in Exercise 2.11.

5.17. Prove total correctness of the algorithms you were asked to design in Exercise 4.3.

5.18. Prove total correctness of the algorithm for testing tree isomorphism you were asked to design in Exercise 4.6.

5.19. Algorithms *Pwr1* and *Pwr2* can be said to be equivalent, in the sense that for every positive number m and natural number n, they both terminate and produce m^n in the variable PW. Therefore, a proof of the total correctness of both these algorithms serves as a proof of their equivalence.

   (a) How would you define the equivalence of programs that do *not* necessarily terminate on all legal inputs?
   (b) Does a proof of the partial correctness of two given algorithms serve as a proof of equivalence in the sense you gave in (a)? If not, can you re-answer (a) so that a partial correctness proof is sufficient?
   (c) Is there any sense in defining the equivalence of programs for which we do not have a correctness specification at all?

let thy word be verified

II CHRONICLES 6: 17

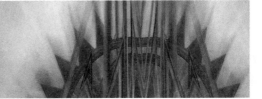

CHAPTER 6

The Efficiency of Algorithms

I would declare to him the number of my steps

Job 31: 37

answer me speedily

Psalm 69: 18

or, Getting It Done Cheaply

When asked to construct a bridge over a river, it is easy to construct an "incorrect" one. The bridge might not be wide enough for the required lanes, it might not be strong enough to carry rush-hour traffic, or it might not reach the other side at all! However, even if it is "correct," in the sense that it fully satisfies the operational requirements, not every candidate design for the bridge will be acceptable. It is possible that the design calls for too much manpower, or too many materials or components. It might also require far too much time to bring to completion. In other words, although it will result in a good bridge, a design might be too *expensive*.

The field of algorithmics is susceptible to similar problems. An algorithm might be too expensive, and hence unacceptable. And so, while Chapter 5 was devoted to proving that *incorrect* algorithms are bad, and that methods are needed for establishing algorithmic correctness, this chapter argues that even a *correct* algorithm might leave much to be desired.

Since manpower and other related costs are not relevant here, we are left with two criteria for measuring economy—materials and time. In computer science these are termed the **complexity measures** of **memory space** (or simply **space**) and **time**. The first of these is measured by several things, including the number of variables, and the number and sizes of the data structures used in executing the algorithm. The other is measured by the number of elementary actions carried out by the processor in such an execution.

Both the space and the time required by an algorithm typically differ from input to input, and, accordingly, the performance of an algorithm reflects the way these resources are consumed as the inputs vary. It is clear that the salary summation algorithm takes longer on bigger lists. This does not mean that we cannot formulate its time performance precisely; all it means is that the formulation will have to account for the fact that the algorithm's running time depends on, or *is a function of*, the length of the input list. The same applies to memory space. In the dynamic planning solution to the weary traveler problem of Chapter 4, we calculated many optimal partial trips, and had to store them in a vector since they were used in the calculation of others. Their number, and hence the amount of memory the algorithm uses, depends directly on the number of nodes in the input city graph.

Although we concentrate on the time measure in this chapter, it should be remarked that issues quite analogous to the ones raised here apply to the space measure too.

Improvements Are Needed

It is only proper to start our discussion of time efficiency in algorithmics with a downright rejection of the myth concerning the computer's speed. Some people think that computers are so incredibly fast that there is no real problem of time. Well, this opinion is groundless.

Here are two brief examples, about which we shall have more to say in later chapters. Assume we are interested in finding the shortest route for a traveler who wishes to visit each of, say, 200 cities. As of now, there is no computer that can find the route in fewer than *millions of years* of computing time! Similarly, no computer is capable of factoring (that is, finding the prime numbers that divide) large integers, say, 300 digits long, in fewer than millions of years. The status of both of these problems may change, but as of now no one knows of any reasonable solutions for them. A more detailed discussion of the actual time a modern computer would take to solve these problems appears in Chapter 7.

Time is a crucial factor in almost every use of computers. Even in day-to-day applications, such as weather prediction programs, inventory management systems, and library lookup programs, there is vast room for improvement. Time is money, and computer time is no exception. Moreover, where computers are concerned, time can actually be the critical factor. Certain kinds of computerized systems, such as flight control, missile guidance, and navigation programs, are termed **real-time systems**. They have to respond to external stimuli, such as pressing buttons, in "real" time; that is, almost instantaneously. Failing to do so could prove to be fatal. See more on these in Chapter 14.

After-the-Fact Improvements

There are many standard ways of improving the running time of a given algorithm. Some are incorporated into compilers, turning them into **optimizing** compilers, which actually make amends for certain kinds of poor decisions on the part of the programmer.

Many chores of an optimizing compiler can be thought of as carrying out certain kinds of **program transformations** (see Chapter 5). One of the most widely applicable of these is modifying a program or an algorithm by transferring instructions from the inside to the outside of loops. Sometimes this is straightforward, as in the following example. Assume that a teacher, in the interest of getting a class to register reasonably good results in an exam, wants to normalize the list of grades, by giving the student who scored best in the exam 100 points and upgrading the rest accordingly. A high-level description of the algorithm might look like this:

(1) compute the maximum score in *MAX*;

(2) multiply each score by 100 and divide it by *MAX*.

(We must assume that there is at least one nonzero grade, for the division to be well defined.)

If the list is given in a vector $L(1), \ldots, L(N)$, both parts can be executed by simple loops running through the vector. The first searches for the maximum in some standard way, and the second might be written:

(2) **for** I **from** 1 **to** N **do**:
    (2.1) $L(I) \leftarrow L(I) \times 100/MAX$

Notice that for each grade $L(I)$ the algorithm carries out one multiplication and one division within the loop. However, neither 100 nor the value of *MAX* actually changes within the loop. Hence, the time for executing this second loop can be cut almost in two (!) by calculating the ratio $100/MAX$ before the loop starts. This is done by simply inserting the statement:

FACTOR $\leftarrow 100/MAX$

between steps (1) and (2), and multiplying $L(I)$ by *FACTOR* within the loop. The resulting algorithm is:

(1) compute the maximum score in *MAX*;

(2) *FACTOR* $\leftarrow 100/MAX$;

(3) **for** I **from** 1 **to** N **do**:
    (3.1) $L(I) \leftarrow L(I) \times FACTOR$.

The reason for the near 50% improvement is that the body of the second loop, which originally consisted of two arithmetical operations, now consists of only one. Of course, not in all implementations of such an algorithm will the time be dominated by the arithmetical instructions; it is possible that updating the value of $L(I)$ is more time consuming than numerical division. Even so, there is a significant improvement in the running time, and clearly the longer the list the more time is gained by this change.

As mentioned, modifications such as this are quite straightforward, and many compilers are able to carry them out automatically. However, even simple instruction removal sometimes requires a sly trick or two. Let us look at another example.

Linear Search: An Example

Suppose that we are searching for an element X in an unordered list (say for a telephone number in a jumbled telephone book). The standard algorithm calls for a simple loop, within which two tests are carried out: (1) "have we found X?" and (2) "have we reached the end of the list?" A positive answer to any one of these questions causes the algorithm to terminate—successfully in the first case and unsuccessfully in the second. Again, we may assume that these tests dominate the time performance of the searching algorithm.

The second test can be taken outside of the loop using the following trick. Prior to commencing the search, the required element X is added fictitiously to the *end* of the list. Then the search loop is carried out, but without testing for the end of the list; within the loop we only test whether X has been found. This also reduces the time of the entire algorithm by a factor of about 50%. Now, since we have added X to the list, X will *always* be found, even if it did not appear in the original list. However, in this case we will find ourselves at the end of the new list when confronting X for the first time, whereas we will end up somewhere *within* it if X did appear in the original list. Consequently, upon reaching X, a test for being at the end of the list is carried out *once*, and the algorithm reports success or failure depending on the outcome. (Incidentally, a common error can occur here if we forget to remove the fictitious X from the end of the list before terminating.) This time we had to be a little more creative to save the 50%.

Order-of-Magnitude Improvements

A 50% decrease in the running time of an algorithm is quite impressive. However, as it happens, we can do much better on many occasions. When we say "better" we do not mean just fixed-rate decreases of 50%, 60%, or even 90%, but decreases whose *rate* gets increasingly better as the size of the input increases.

One of the best-known examples involves searching for an element in an ordered, or sorted list (for example, looking up a telephone number in a normal telephone book). To be more precise, assume that the input consists of a name Y and a list L of names and their telephone numbers. The list, which is of length N, is assumed to be sorted in alphabetic order by the names.

A naive algorithm that searches for Y's telephone number is the one previously described for an unsorted list: work through the list L one name at a time, checking Y against the current name at each step, and either checking for the end of the list at the same time, or applying the trick described in the previous section and checking for it only once, when Y is found. Even if the trick is employed to cut the running time by 50%, there still might be a case in which fully N comparisons are necessary; namely, when Y does not appear in L at all, or when it appears in the last position. We say that the algorithm, call it A, has a **worst-case** running time which is **linear** in N, or, to use an equivalent term, it is **on the order of** N. This is described more concisely by saying that A runs in time $O(N)$ in the worst case, with the big-O standing for "order of."

The $O(N)$ notation is quite subtle. Notice that we said "A runs in time $O(N)$." We did not particularize the statement to refer only to the number of *comparisons*, although comparisons between Y and the names in L were the only type of instruction we were counting. The reason for this will be explained later. For now, it suffices to say that when using the **big-O notation**, as it is sometimes called, we do not care whether the algorithm takes time N (that is, it executes N elementary instructions), time $3N$ (that is, it takes threefold that number of elementary instructions), or $10N$, or even $100N$. Furthermore, even if it takes only a *fraction* of N, say $N/6$, we still say that it runs in time $O(N)$. The only thing that matters is that the running time grows **linearly** with N. This means that there is some constant number K, such that the algorithm runs in time that is no more than $K \times N$ in the worst case. Indeed, the version that checks for the end of the list each time runs roughly in time $2N$, and the tricky version cuts that down to roughly N. Both, however, have running time directly proportional to N. They are thus linear-time algorithms, having a worst-case running time of $O(N)$.

The term "worst-case" means that the algorithm could presumably run for much less on certain inputs, perhaps on *most* inputs. All we are saying is that the algorithm never runs for more than $K \times N$ time, and that this is true for any N and for any input of length N, even the worst ones. Clearly, if we try to improve the linear-time search algorithm by starting the comparisons from the *end* of the list, there would still be equally bad cases—Y not appearing at all, or Y appearing as the first name on the list. Actually, if an exhaustive search throughout the list is called for by the algorithm, the order in which names are compared to Y is of no importance. Such an algorithm will still have an $O(N)$ worst-case running time.

Despite this, we *can* do better in searching an ordered list, not only in terms of the constant factor "hidden inside" the big-O, but in terms of the $O(N)$ estimate itself. This is an **order-of-magnitude improvement**, and we shall now see how it can be achieved.

Binary Search: An Example

For concreteness, let us assume that the telephone book contains a million names, that is, N is 1,000,000, and let us call them $X_1, X_2, \ldots, X_{1,000,000}$.

The first comparison carried out by the new algorithm is not between Y and the first or last name in L, but between Y and the *middle* name (or, if the list is of even length, then the last name in the first half of the list), namely $X_{500,000}$. Assuming that the compared names turn out to be unequal, meaning that we are not done yet, there are two possibilities: (1) Y precedes $X_{500,000}$ in alphabetic order, and (2) $X_{500,000}$ precedes Y. Since the list is sorted alphabetically, if (1) is the case we know that if Y appears in the list at all it has to be in the first half, and if (2) is the case it must appear in the second half. Hence, we can restrict our successive search to the appropriate half of the list.

Accordingly, the next comparison will be between Y and the middle element of that half: $X_{250,000}$ in case (1) and $X_{750,000}$ in case (2). And again, the result of this comparison will be to narrow the possibilities down to half of this new, shorter, list; that is, to a list whose length is a *quarter* of the original. This process continues, reducing the length of the list, or in more general terms, the **size of the problem**,

Figure 6.1

Schematic flowchart
for binary search.

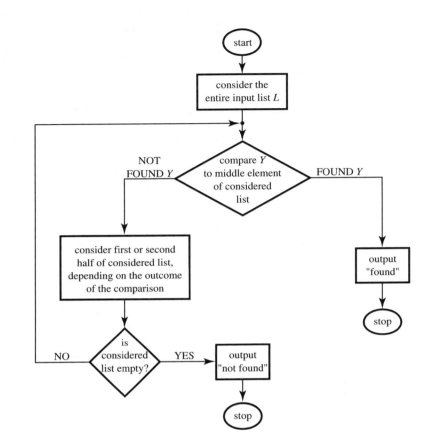

by half at each step, until either Y is found, in which case the procedure terminates, reporting success, or the trivial empty list is reached, in which case it terminates, reporting failure (see Figures 6.1 and 6.2).

This procedure is called **binary search**, and it is really an application of the divide-and-conquer paradigm discussed in Chapter 4. The difference between this example and the ones introduced therein (**min&max** search and **mergesort**) is that here after dividing we need only conquer *one* of the parts, not both. Figure 6.1 contains a schematic iterative version of binary search, but it is actually possible to write down a simple recursive version too. You are encouraged to do so.

What is the time complexity of binary search? To answer this, let us first count comparisons. It is quite instructive to try to guess how many comparisons the binary search algorithm will require in the worst case on our one-million-name telephone book. Recall that the naive search would require a million comparisons.

Well, in the very worst case (what is an example of one? how many worst cases are there?) the algorithm will require only 20 comparisons! Moreover, the larger N becomes, the more impressive the improvement. An international telephone book containing, say, a billion names, would require at most 30 comparisons, instead of a billion!

Figure 6.2

Binary search applied
to a small telephone
book (numbers
omitted).

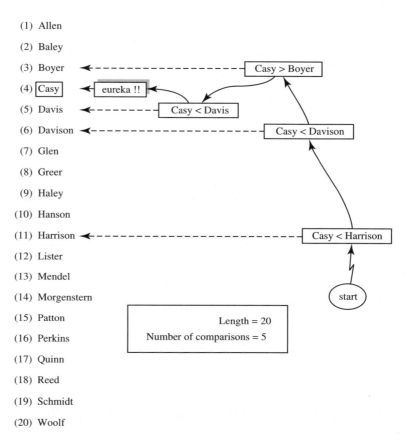

(1) Allen
(2) Baley
(3) Boyer
(4) Casy
(5) Davis
(6) Davison
(7) Glen
(8) Greer
(9) Haley
(10) Hanson
(11) Harrison
(12) Lister
(13) Mendel
(14) Morgenstern
(15) Patton
(16) Perkins
(17) Quinn
(18) Reed
(19) Schmidt
(20) Woolf

Recall that each comparison reduces the length of the input list L by half, and that the process terminates when, or before, the list becomes empty. Hence, the worst-case number of comparisons is obtained by figuring out how many times a number N can be repeatedly divided by 2 before it is reduced to 0. (The rules of the game are to ignore fractions.) This number is termed the **base-2 logarithm**[1] of N, and is denoted by $\log_2 N$. Actually, $\log_2 N$ counts the number required to reduce N to 1, not 0, so the number we are really after is $1 + \log_2 N$.[2] In any event, we can safely say the algorithm takes $O(\log N)$ comparisons in the worst case.

We can get a feel for the kind of improvement binary search offers by studying the following table, which plots several values of N against the number of comparisons required by binary search in the worst case:

---

[1] The similarity between the words "algorithm" and "logarithm" is purely coincidental.
[2] We are abusing the term slightly by using the **integer part** of $1 + \log N$. Our logarithms can thus be thought of as always yielding integers.

N	$1 + \log_2 N$
10	4
100	7
1000	10
a million	20
a billion	30
a billion billions	60

It is noteworthy that we ourselves use a variant of binary search when we search for a number in a telephone book. The difference is that we do not necessarily compare the name at hand with the one occurring precisely at the middle of the book and then with that at the $\frac{1}{4}$ or $\frac{3}{4}$ position, and so on. Rather, we make use of additional knowledge we possess, concerning the expected **distribution** of names in the book. This technique is often called **interpolation search**. If we are searching for "Mary D. Ramsey," for example, we would open the book roughly at the two-thirds point. Obviously this is far from being precise, and we work with rough, intuitive rules of thumb, to be discussed under the term **heuristics** in Chapter 15. Nevertheless, there are precise formulations of search algorithms that proceed in a skewed fashion, dictated by the nature and distribution of the elements. In general, while being considerably more economical on the average, these variations also exhibit a similar worst-case behavior of $O(\log_2 N)$ comparisons.

Why Is It Enough to Count Comparisons?

To complete our complexity analysis of binary search, we now show that if we are happy with a big-O estimate, it suffices to count comparisons only. Why? Clearly, in binary search there are considerably more instructions executed than just comparisons. Refocussing on the correct half of the list and preparing it for the next time around the loop would presumably involve some testing and changing of indices. And then there is the test for an empty list, and so on.

As it turns out, the checkpoints used in the previous chapter for correctness proofs turn out to be helpful here too. Figure 6.3 shows the schematic flowchart of Figure 6.1 with checkpoints included, and it illustrates the possible local paths, or "hops," between them. Notice that here too the checkpoints cut all loops—there is only one in this case—so that the four local paths are loop free, as in the example given in Chapter 5. Whereas this fact was important for correctness proofs because it gave rise to manageable verification conditions, here it is important because loop-free and subroutine-free segments take at most *fixed* amounts of time. It is true that the presence of conditional statements in such a segment might yield several different ways of traversing it. However, the absence of loops (and of recursive routines) guarantees that there is a bound on this number, and hence that the total number of instructions carried out in any single execution of such a segment is no greater than some constant. As we shall now see, this often facilitates easy calculation of the time taken by the algorithm.

Figure 6.3

Binary search with
checkpoints and local
time bounds.

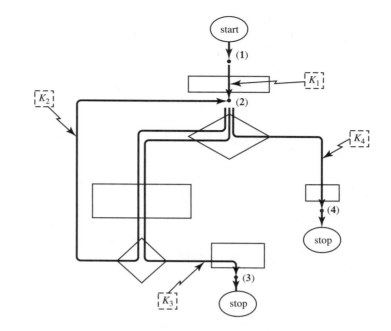

■ In Figure 6.3 we have associated the constants K_1 through K_4 with the four possible local paths. For example, this means that any single execution of the local path from checkpoint (2) back to itself is assumed to involve no more than K_2 instructions. (By convention, this is taken to include the comparison made at the beginning of the segment, but not the one made at its end.) Now consider a typical execution of binary search (see Figure 6.4). Since checkpoint (2) is the only place in the text of the algorithm involving a comparison, it is reached (in the worst case) precisely $1 + \log_2 N$ times, since, as discussed above, this is the total number of comparisons made. Now, all but the last of these comparisons result in the processor going around the loop again, hence executing at most another K instructions. This means that the total time cost of all these $\log_2 N$ traversals of the $(2) \rightarrow (2)$ segment is $K_2 \times \log_2 N$.

To complete the analysis, notice that the total number of all instructions carried out, which are not part of $(2) \rightarrow (2)$ segments, is either $K_1 + K_3$ or $K_1 + K_4$, depending on whether the algorithm halts at checkpoint (3) or (4) (see Figure 6.4); in both cases we have a constant that does not depend on N. If we denote by K the maximum of these two sums, we can conclude that the total number of instructions carried out by the binary search algorithm on a list of length N is bounded by:

$$K + (K_2 \times \log_2 N)$$

Figure 6.4

A typical worst-case
execution of binary
search.

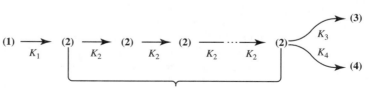

Hence, since we are using the order-of-magnitude notation, the constants K and K_2 can be "buried" beneath the big-O, and we may conclude simply that binary search runs in time $O(\log_2 N)$ in the worst case. This is called a **logarithmic-time** algorithm.

The Robustness of the Big-O Notation

As explained, big-Os hide constant factors. Hence, in the worst-case analysis of binary search there was no need for us to be more specific about the details of the particular instructions that make up the algorithm. It was sufficient to analyze the algorithm's loop structure and to convince ourselves that between any two comparisons there is only a constant number of instructions in the worst case.

Somehow this does not sound quite right. Surely the time complexity of binary search *does* depend on the elementary instructions allowed. If we were to allow the instruction:

search list L for item Y

the algorithm would consist simply of a single instruction, and hence its time complexity would be $O(1)$, that is, a constant number not depending on N at all. So how can we say that the details of the instructions are unimportant?

Well, the time complexity of an algorithm is indeed a *relative* concept, and it makes sense only in conjunction with an agreed-on set of elementary instructions. Nevertheless, standard kinds of problems are usually thought of in the context of standard kinds of elementary instructions. For example, searching and sorting problems usually involve comparisons, index updates, and end-of-list tests, so that complexity analysis is carried out with respect to these. Moreover, if a particular programming language is fixed in advance, then a particular set of elementary instructions has also been fixed, for better or for worse. What makes these observations significant is the fact that for most standard kinds of elementary instructions we can afford to be quite vague when it comes to order-of-magnitude complexity. Writing an algorithm in a particular programming language, or using a particular compiler, can obviously make a difference in the final running time. However, if the algorithm uses conventional basic instructions, these differences will consist of only a constant factor per basic instruction, and this means that the big-O complexity is *invariant* under such implementational fluctuations.

In other words, as long as the basic set of allowed elementary instructions is agreed on, and as long as any shortcuts taken in high-level descriptions (such as that of Figure 6.1) do not hide unbounded iterations of such instructions, but merely represent finite clusters of them, big-O time estimates are *robust*.

Actually, for the benefit of readers who feel at home with logarithms, it should be added that the logarithmic base is of no importance either. For any fixed K, the number $\log_2 N$ and $\log_K N$ differ only by a constant factor, and hence this difference can also be hidden under the big-O notation. Consequently, we shall refer to logarithmic-time performance simply as $O(\log N)$, not $O(\log_2 N)$.

The robustness of the big-O notation constitutes both its strength and its weakness. When someone exhibits a logarithmic-time algorithm A, whereas someone else's algorithm B runs in linear time, it might very well be found that B runs faster on sample inputs than A! The reason is in the hidden constants. Let us say that we have painstakingly taken into account the constant number of elementary instructions between checkpoints, the programming language in which the algorithm is coded, the compiler which translates it downwards, the basic machine instructions used by the computer running the machine code, and the very speed of that computer. Having done so, we might find that algorithm A performs in time bounded by $K \times \log_2 N$ nanoseconds, and B performs within $J \times N$ nanoseconds, but with K being 1000 and J being 10. This means, as you can verify, that for every input of length less than a thousand (actually, the precise number is 996), algorithm B is superior to A. Only when inputs of size 1000 or more are reached does the difference between N and $\log_2 N$ become apparent, and, as already hinted, when the difference starts paying off, it does so very handsomely: by the time inputs of size a million are reached, algorithm A becomes upwards of 500 times more efficient than algorithm B, and for inputs of size a billion the improvement is over 330,000-fold!

Thus, a user who is interested only in inputs of length less than a thousand should definitely adopt algorithm B, despite A's order-of-magnitude superiority. In most cases, however, the constant factors are not quite as far apart as 10 and 1000, hence big-O estimates are usually far more realistic than in this contrived example.

The moral of the story is to first search for a good and efficient algorithm, stressing big-O performance, and then to try improving it by tricks of the kind used earlier to decrease the constant factors involved. In any event, since big-O efficiency can be misleading, candidate algorithms should be run experimentally and their time performances for various typically occurring kinds of inputs should be tabulated.

The robustness of big-O estimates, coupled with the fact that in the majority of cases algorithms that are better in the big-O sense are also better in practice, renders the study of order-of-magnitude time complexity the most interesting to computer scientists. Accordingly, in the name of science and robustness, we shall concentrate in the sequel mainly on big-O estimates and similar notions, although they may hide issues of possible practical importance, such as constant factors.

Time Analysis of Nested Loops

Obviously, complicated algorithms, which involve many intertwined control structures and contain possibly recursive subroutines, can become quite difficult to analyze. Let us briefly discuss the time complexity of some of the algorithms appearing in previous chapters.

The bubblesort algorithm of Chapter 2 consisted of two loops nested as follows:

(1) do the following $N - 1$ times:

    ...

    (1.2) do the following $N - 1$ times:

        ...

The inner loop is executed $N - 1$ times for each of the $N - 1$ times the outer loop is executed. As before, everything else is constant; hence the total time performance of bubblesort is on the order of $(N - 1) \times (N - 1)$, which is $N^2 - 2N + 1$. In this case, the N^2 is called the **dominant term** of the expression, meaning that the other parts, namely, the $-2N$ and the $+1$, get "swallowed" by the N^2 when the big-O notation is used. Consequently, bubblesort is an $O(N^2)$, or **quadratic-time**, algorithm.

Recall our discussion of the improved bubblesort version, which allowed for traversing smaller and smaller portions of the input list. The first traversal is of $N - 1$ elements, the next is of $N - 2$ elements, and so on. The time analysis, therefore, results in the sum:

$$(N - 1) + (N - 2) + (N - 3) + \cdots + 3 + 2 + 1$$

which can be shown to evaluate to $(N^2 - N)/2$. This is less than the $N^2 - 2N + 1$ of the naive version, but is still quadratic, since the dominant factor is $N^2/2$, and the constant factor of $\frac{1}{2}$ gets lost too. We thus have a 50% reduction in time, but not a big-O improvement.

The simple salary summation algorithm (Figure 2.3) is easily seen to be linear, that is, $O(N)$, but the one for the more sophisticated version, which entailed a nested loop to search for direct managers (Figure 2.4), is **quadratic**. (Why?)

The "money"-searching algorithm, with or without the use of a routine (Figures 2.5 and 2.6) can be seen to be linear, a fact that you should carefully check; although there might be two pointers advancing separately, the text is traversed only once, in linear fashion.

With the knowledge acquired in the present chapter, it should be quite straightforward to figure out the reason we tried to improve the algorithm for maximal polygonal distance in Chapter 4. The naive algorithm, which runs through all pairs of vertices, is quadratic (where N is taken to be the number of vertices), whereas the improved algorithm cycles around the polygon only once, and can be shown to be linear.

Time Analysis of Recursion

Let us now consider the **min&max** problem of Chapter 4, which called for finding the extremal elements in a list L. The naive algorithm runs through the list iteratively, updating two variables that hold the current extremal elements. It is clearly linear. Here is the recursive routine, which was claimed in Chapter 4 to be better:

subroutine **find-min&max-of** L:

(1) if L consists of one element, then set *MIN* and *MAX* to it; if it consists of two elements, then set *MIN* to the smaller of them and *MAX* to the larger;

(2) otherwise do the following:

    (2.1) split L into two halves, Lleft and Lright;

    (2.2) call **find-min&max-of** Lleft, placing returned values in *MIN*left and *MAX*left;

    (2.3) call **find-min&max-of** Lright, placing returned values in *MIN*right and *MAX*right;

(2.4) set *MIN* to smaller of *MIN*left and *MIN*right;

(2.5) set *MAX* to larger of *MAX*left and *MAX*right;

(3) return with *MIN* and *MAX*.

It will turn out that this recursive routine runs in linear time too. (In fact, as we argue later, no algorithm for the **min&max** problem can possibly be sublinear, say, logarithmic.) However, the recursive routine has a smaller constant under the big-O.

To see why, a more refined complexity analysis is called for. The iterative algorithm operates by carrying out two comparisons for each element in the list, one with the current maximum and one with the current minimum. Hence it yields a total comparison count of $2N$. The interesting part is the way one counts time for a *recursive* routine. Since we do not know offhand how many comparisons the routine requires, we use a specially tailored abstract notation: let $C(N)$ denote the (worst-case) number of comparisons required by the recursive **min&max** routine on lists of length N.

Now, although we do not know the explicit value of $C(N)$ as a function of N, we do know two things:

1. If N is 2, precisely one comparison is carried out—the one implied by line (1) of the routine; if N is 3, three comparisons are carried out, as you can verify.

2. If N is greater than 3, the comparisons carried out consist precisely of two sets of comparisons for lists of length $N/2$, since there are two recursive calls, and two additional comparisons—those appearing on lines (2.4) and (2.5). (If N is odd, the lists are of length $(N + 1)/2$ and $(N - 1)/2$.)

We can therefore write down the following equations, sometimes called **recurrence relations**, which capture, respectively, the two observations just made:

i. $C(2) = 1$

ii. $C(N) = 2 \times C(N/2) + 2$

(This is for the case where N is a power of 2. The general case is a little more complicated.) We would like to find a function $C(N)$ satisfying these constraints. And indeed, methods do exist for solving such recurrence equations, and in this case, as can be readily checked, the solution turns out to be:

$$C(N) = 3N/2 - 2$$

That is, $C(N)$ is less than $1.5N$. Even in the general case, for numbers that are not powers of 2, the recursive routine requires fewer than $1.7N$ comparisons for lists of length N, which is better than the $2N$ required by the iterative solution. As mentioned, this is still $O(N)$, but it is nevertheless an improvement, especially if comparisons are highly time consuming in the desired application.

The recursive **min&max** routine was presented here to give an example of the time analysis of a recursive algorithm. However, it is noteworthy that we can actually achieve a better behavior, using only $1.5N$ comparisons for the general case of

Figure 6.5

A list and its long and thin binary search tree (compare with Figure 2.13).

28	1018	402	396	35	46	354	76	128	112	106	100

first   *last*

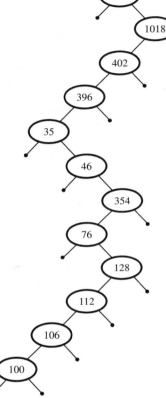

finding the minimum and maximum in a list by a (different) iterative algorithm as follows. First arrange the N elements into pairs, then compare the two elements within each pair, marking the larger of the two. This costs $N/2$ comparisons. Then go through the $N/2$ larger elements, keeping track of the current maximum, and similarly through the $N/2$ smaller elements, keeping track of the minimum. This costs twice more $N/2$ comparisons, yielding a total of $1.5N$.

In Chapters 2 and 4 two additional sorting algorithms were briefly described, **treesort** and **mergesort**. We shall not embark on a detailed time analysis here, except to make the following remarks: Treesort, if implemented naively, is a quadratic algorithm. The reason stems from the possibility that certain sequences of elements result in very long and narrow binary search trees, such as the one in Figure 6.5. Although traversing such a tree in left-first traversal is a linear-time procedure, *constructing* the tree from the input sequence can be shown to be quadratic. However, it is possible to employ a **self-adjustment** scheme, of the kind hinted at in Chapter 2, and keep the tree wide and short. Incorporating such a scheme into the construction phase of treesort will result in an order-of-magnitude improvement, yielding an algorithm that uses time on the order of the product of N and the logarithm of N (rather than N); in symbols, then, it is an $O(N \times \log N)$ algorithm. The following table should give an idea of the savings this improvement provides, though its effect on the constant factors does not show up.

N	N^2	$N \times \log_2 N$
10	100	33
100	10,000	665
1000	a million	9966
a million	a thousand billions	20 million
a billion	a billion billions	30 billion

Turning to mergesort, you are left with the interesting exercise of showing that this algorithm is in itself $O(N \times \log N)$. Mergesort is really one of several time-efficient sorting algorithms, and is definitely the easiest to describe from among the $O(N \times \log N)$ ones. It should be remarked, however, that it uses a new list to store partial results, and hence it requires an additional linear amount of space, which is a disadvantage when compared to some of the other sorting methods.

Thus, mergesort is one of the most time-efficient sorting routines and also one of the easiest to describe. We would like to credit recursion with both virtues: it makes the algorithm easy to describe, and it also provides a clean mechanism for splitting the problem into two smaller problems of half the size, which is the root of the algorithm's $O(N \times \log N)$ time performance.

A different approach uses a heap (described in Chapter 4) instead of a binary search tree as in treesort. The **heapsort** algorithm first inserts all the elements of the input list into the heap, and then repeatedly extracts the minimum element to form the sorted list. The representation of a heap as a vector (see Chapter 4) ensures that the heap is always balanced, and therefore each insertion and extract-minimum operation takes logarithmic time, yielding a total running time of $O(N \times \log N)$.

Average-Case Complexity

The worst-case nature of our time analyses can be construed as a disadvantage. It is true that one cannot guarantee, say, linear-time performance of an algorithm unless the time bound applies to *all* legal inputs. However, it might be the case that an algorithm is very fast for *most* of the standard kinds of inputs, and the ones that cause its worst-case performance to soar are a minority that we are willing to ignore.

Accordingly, there are other useful estimates of an algorithm's time performance, such as its **average-case** behavior. Here we are interested in the time required by the algorithm on the average, taking the entire set of inputs and their probability of occurring into consideration. We shall not get into the technical details here, except to remark that average-case analysis is considerably more difficult to carry out than worst-case analysis. The mathematics required is usually far more sophisticated, and many algorithms exist for which researchers have not been able to obtain average-case estimates at all.

Despite the fundamental difference, many algorithms have the same big-O time bound for both worst-case and average-case behavior. For example, simple salary summation behaves in a fixed fashion, always running to the very end of the list, and is hence linear in the worst, best, and average cases. The version that goes looking for direct managers, which is quadratic in the worst case, might, on average, have to look through only half of the list for each employee's manager, not through it all. However, this only decreases N^2 to about $N^2/2$, retaining the $O(N^2)$ time bound even in the average case, since the constant of one-half is hidden under the big-O.

In contrast, for some algorithms average-case analysis can reveal significantly better performance. The classical example of this is yet another sorting algorithm, called **quicksort**, which we shall not describe here. Quicksort, also a naturally recursive algorithm, has a worst-case quadratic running time, and hence appears to be inferior to both mergesort and the self-adjusting version of treesort. Nevertheless, its average-case performance can be shown to be $O(N \times \log N)$, matching that of the better sorting algorithms. What makes quicksort particularly interesting is the fact that its average-case performance involves a very small constant. In fact, on only counting comparisons, the time performance of quicksort is a little over $1.4N \times \log N$ on average. Taking into account the fact that it requires only a small fixed amount of additional storage space, and despite its inferior worst-case performance, quicksort is actually one of the best sorting algorithms known, and is definitely the best among the ones mentioned here.

To complete our brief discussion of the sorting methods presented, we should remark that bubblesort is the worst of the lot, having even an average case behavior of $O(N^2)$. (This fact, however, is rather tricky to prove.) Many people are opposed to describing bubblesort in computer science courses, since its elegance is sufficiently misleading, and students might actually be lured into using it in practice. . .

Upper and Lower Bounds

We showed earlier how the naive linear-time algorithm for searching an ordered list can be improved to logarithmic time by using binary search. More precisely, we showed that there was an algorithm that performed such a search using no more than $\log_2 N$ comparisons in the worst case on a list of length N.

Can we do better? Is it possible to search for an element in a million-entry telephone book with fewer than 20 comparisons in the worst case? Is it possible to find an algorithm for the ordered list search problem that requires only $\sqrt{(\log_2 N)}$, or maybe only $\log_2(\log_2 N)$, comparisons in the worst case?

To put these questions into perspective, think of any algorithmic problem as sitting out there, endowed with an inherent **optimal solution**, which is what we are after. Then, along comes someone with an algorithm, say an $O(N^3)$ one (termed **cubic-time**), and thus approaches the desired solution "from above." With this algorithm as evidence, we know that the problem cannot require a higher than cubic running

Figure 6.6

Upper and lower
bounds on an
algorithmic problem.

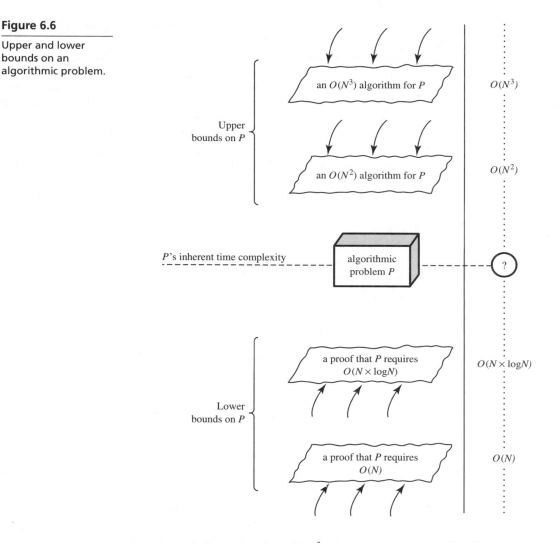

time; it can't be *worse* than $O(N^3)$. Later on, someone else discovers a better algorithm, say one that runs in quadratic time, thus coming closer to the desired optimal solution, also from above. We are now convinced that the problem cannot be inherently worse than $O(N^2)$, and the previous algorithm becomes obsolete. The question is, how far down can these improvements go?

With the "approaching-from-above" metaphor in mind (see Figure 6.6), the discovery of an algorithm is said to place an **upper bound** on the algorithmic problem. Better algorithms bring the problem's best-known time bound downwards, closer to the unknown inherent complexity of the problem itself. The questions we are asking are concerned with the problem's **lower bound**. If we can prove rigorously that algorithmic problem P cannot be solved by any algorithm that requires less than, say, quadratic time in the worst case, then people trying to find efficient algorithms for solving P can give up if and when they find a quadratic-time algorithm, because there is no way they can do better. Such a proof constitutes a lower bound on the algorithmic problem, since it shows that no algorithm can improve on the $O(N^2)$ bound.[3]

In this way, discovering a clever algorithm shows that the problem's inherent time performance is no *worse* than some bound, and discovering a lower bound proof shows that it is no *better* than some bound. In both cases, a property of the *algorithmic problem* has been discovered, not a property of a particular algorithm. This might sound confusing, especially since a lower bound on a problem requires consideration of *all* algorithms for it, while an upper bound is achieved by constructing one particular algorithm and analyzing its time performance (see Figure 6.6).

Achieving a lower bound seems like an impossibility. How do we prove something about all algorithms? How can we be sure that someone will not discover a very subtle but efficient algorithm that we have not anticipated? These are not easy questions to answer, but perhaps contemplation of the following example will give us some partial answers.

A Lower Bound for Telephone Book Search

Before the example, however, we should re-emphasize the fact that any discussion of inherent time complexity, lower bounds included, must be carried out relative to a set of allowed basic instructions. No one can prove that the search problem requires any more than a single time unit if basic instructions like:

search list L for item Y

are allowed. The rules of the game, therefore, must be carefully specified before we make any attempt at proving lower bounds.

We now wish to show that binary search is optimal. In other words, we would like to prove that in general we cannot find a name in a telephone book of length N in fewer than $\log_2 N$ comparisons in the worst case; 20 comparisons are the minimum for a million names, 30 for a billion, 60 for a billion billions, and so on. In more general terms, there is no algorithm for the ordered list searching problem whose worst-case time performance is better than logarithmic.

The rules of the game here are quite straightforward. The only way a proposed algorithm is allowed to extract any kind of information from the inputs is by carrying out two-way comparisons. The algorithm might compare two elements from the input list L among themselves, or an element from L with the input element Y whose position in L is sought for. No other queries can be addressed to the inputs L and Y. However, there are no restrictions on instructions *not* concerning L or Y; any of these can be included, and each will cost only a single time unit.

To show that any algorithm for this problem requires $\log_2 N$ comparisons, we shall argue as follows. Given an algorithm, *any* algorithm, we will show that it cannot possibly better the claimed $\log_2 N$ lower bound on the problem. Accordingly, say we have come up with an algorithm A for the ordered list search problem that is

---

[3] All this, of course, is only insofar as order-of-magnitude improvements are concerned. Decreasing the factor hidden within the big-O might still be possible. Chapters 10 and 11 show that using more liberal notions of an algorithm can change things drastically.

Figure 6.7

A comparison tree for searching in a list.

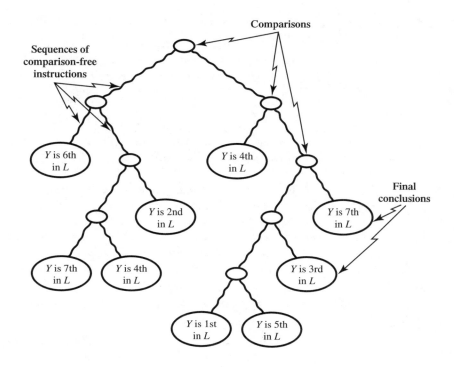

based on two-way comparisons. We shall prove that there are input lists of length N upon which algorithm A will *necessarily* perform $\log_2 N$ comparisons.

■ To that end, let us observe A's behavior on a typical list L of length N. To make life easier, let us stick to the special case in which L consists precisely of the numbers $1, 2, 3, \ldots, N$ in order, and where Y is one of those numbers. We can also safely assume that all comparisons have but two results, "less than" or "more than," since if a comparison yields "equal to," Y has been found (unless some useless comparison of an element with itself was carried out, in which case the algorithm can do without it). The algorithm A, working on our special list L, might perform some number of other actions, but eventually it reaches its first comparison. It then presumably branches off in one of two directions, depending on the (two-way) outcome. In each of these, A might work some more before reaching the next comparison, which again splits A's behavior into two further possibilities. A's behavior can be thus described schematically as a binary tree (see Figure 6.7), in which edges correspond to possible sequences of noncomparison actions, and nodes correspond to comparisons and their branching outcomes. This tree captures A's behavior for all possible lists consisting of the numbers $1, 2, 3, \ldots, N$.

Now, the tree is definitely finite, since A has to terminate on all legal inputs, and its leaves correspond to reaching a final decision concerning Y's position in L, or, in other words, concerning Y's value from among $1, 2, \ldots, N$. Clearly, no two different values of Y can be represented by the same leaf, because that would mean that A produces the same output (that is, position in L) for two different values of Y—obviously an absurdity. Since Y has N possible values, the tree must have at least N possible leaves. (It might have more, since there may be more than one way of reaching the same conclusion about

Y's position.) We now use the following standard fact about binary trees, whose truth you should try establishing:

Any binary tree having at least N leaves has depth at least $\log_2 N$; *that is, the tree contains at least one path from the root whose length is* $\log_2 N$ *or more.*

It follows that our comparison tree contains a path of length at least $\log_2 N$. But a path in the tree corresponds precisely to the execution of the proposed algorithm *A* on some input list of length *N*, with the nodes marking the comparisons made in that very execution (see Figure 6.7). Hence, if there is a path of length at least $\log_2 N$ in the tree, it follows that there is some input list that requires *A* to perform at least $\log_2 N$ comparisons.

This completes the proof that $\log_2 N$ is a lower bound on the number of comparisons, and hence that the algorithmic problem of searching in an ordered list has a logarithmic-time lower bound. Notice how the argument was made general enough to apply to *any* proposed algorithm, as long as it uses comparisons as the sole means for extracting information from the input list.

Closed Problems and Algorithmic Gaps

Lower bounds can be established for many other algorithmic problems. Searching in an *un*ordered list, for example, is the quintessential linear-time problem, and can easily be shown to require *N* comparisons in the worst case. It therefore has a lower bound of $O(N)$ for algorithms based on comparisons. You might want to work out the argument for this.

Several of the problems we have talked about can be construed as variations of unordered search, and are consequently also bounded from below by $O(N)$. These include the **min&max** problem, simple salary summation, maximal polygonal distance, and so on. Notice that for each of these we indeed supplied linear-time algorithms. This means that the upper and lower bounds actually meet (except for the possibly different constant factors). In other words, these algorithmic problems are **closed** as far as big-O time estimates go. We have a linear algorithm, and we know that we can do no better.

Searching in an *ordered* list, as we have shown, is also a closed problem; it has upper and lower bounds of logarithmic-time. Sorting is also closed: on the one hand we have algorithms, like mergesort, heapsort, or the self-adjusting version of treesort, that are $O(N \times \log N)$, and on the other we can prove an $O(N \times \log N)$ lower bound for sorting a list of length *N*. In both these cases the bounds are based on the comparison model, whereby information about inputs is obtained only by two-way comparisons.

Many algorithmic problems, however, do not yet enjoy the property of being closed. Their upper and lower bounds do not meet. In such cases we say that they give rise to **algorithmic gaps**, the best-known upper bound being different from (and therefore higher than) the best-known lower bound. In Chapter 4 we presented a quadratic algorithm for finding minimal railroads (the minimal spanning tree problem), but the best-known lower bound is linear. That is, although we can prove that the problem requires $O(N)$ time (here N is the number of edges in the railroad graph, not the number of nodes), no one knows of a linear-time algorithm, and hence the problem is not closed.

In Chapter 7 we shall see several striking examples of algorithmic gaps that are unacceptably large. For now, it suffices to realize that if a problem gives rise to an algorithmic gap, the deficiency is not in the problem but in our knowledge about it. We have failed either in finding the best algorithm for it or in proving that a better one does not exist, or in both.

Barricading Sleeping Tigers: An Example

The following algorithm uses sorting in a rather unexpected way, and inherits its complexity bounds too.

Assume we are confronted with N sleeping tigers, and to avoid being eaten when one or more of them wake up we are interested in constructing a fence around them. Algorithmically, we are given the precise locations of the tigers, and we want to find the smallest polygon that surrounds them all. Clearly, the problem reduces to finding a minimal sequence of some of the tigers' locations which, when connected by linear pieces of fence (which we shall call **line segments**), will enclose all the others (see Figure 6.8). This enclosure is called the **convex hull** of the set of points.

Note that this problem has been presented in a zoological guise only to make it sound a little more entertaining. The convex hull problem is actually one of the basic problems that arise in computer graphics. Finding fast algorithms for this problem and a number of other problems in computational geometry can make a big difference in the speed and applicability of many graphics applications.

The algorithm now presented is based on the following simple observation. For some line segment connecting two of the points to be part of the convex hull it is necessary and sufficient that all the other points are on the same side of it (or rather, of its extension to a full line).

Figure 6.8

Sleeping tigers and their convex hull.

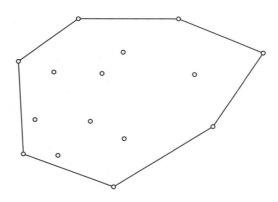

This observation gives rise to a straightforward algorithm: consider each potential line segment in turn, and check whether all the $N - 2$ points that are not on it are on one side of it. The test to decide which side of a line a given point belongs to can easily be carried out in constant time using elementary analytic geometry. Since there are N points, there are N^2 potential segments, one possibly connecting each pair of points, and each of them has to be checked against $N - 2$ points. This yields a cubic (that is, an $O(N^3)$) algorithm, as you can readily see. However, there is a way of doing far better.

Here are the main steps in the proposed algorithm:

(1) find the "lowest" point P_1;

(2) sort the remaining points by the magnitude of the angle they form with the horizontal axis when connected with P_1, and let the resulting list be $P_2, \ldots, P_N$;

(3) start out with P_1 and P_2 in the current hull;

(4) for I from 3 to N do the following:

(4.1) add P_I tentatively to the current hull;

(4.2) work backwards through the current hull, eliminating a point P_J if the two points P_1 and P_I are on different sides of the line between P_{J-1} and P_J, and terminating this backwards scan when a P_J that does not need to be eliminated is encountered.

It may be a little tricky to see what the algorithm is doing, but a glance at Figures 6.9 and 6.10 should help. Figure 6.9 shows the points sorted after step (2) in the order they will be considered in step (4), and Figure 6.10 shows the first few additions and eliminations in step (4). In Figure 6.10 point P_{13} has just been added, and the next step will consider P_{14}. However, since the line between P_{12} and P_{13} goes *between* P_1 and P_{14}, point P_{13} will be eliminated, bringing the hull around the points, above P_{13}. While proving the correctness of this algorithm is an instructive exercise, we are more interested here in its time efficiency. We shall therefore assume that the algorithm is correct and concentrate on its time analysis.

It is easy to see that step (1), which involves a simple search for the point that lies lowest down in the picture, that is, the one with the smallest vertical coordinate, takes

Figure 6.9

The points of Figure 6.8 sorted by angle.

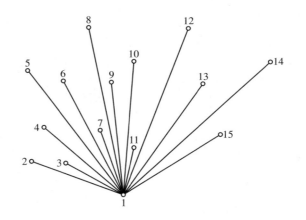

Figure 6.10

First few steps in
barricading the tigers
of Figure 6.8.

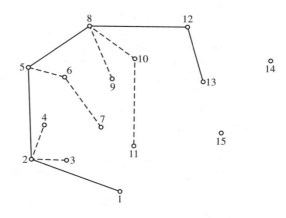

linear time. Now, step (2), the sorting, can be carried out by any efficient sorting
routine. Therefore, since computing an angle or comparing two angles can be carried
out in constant time, step (2) takes total time $O(N \times \log N)$. The interesting part
concerns step (4).

It would appear that the nested loop structure of step (4) yields quadratic time
performance. However, the right way to analyze this part of the algorithm involves
disregarding its structure and accounting for time on a point-by-point basis. Notice
that step (4.2) only eliminates points, and it stops when a point that should not be
eliminated is encountered. Now, since no point gets eliminated more than once,
the total number of times points are considered in the nested loop of step (4.2)
cannot be more than $O(N)$. Since all the remaining parts of step (4) take no more
than linear time too, step (4) in its entirety takes linear time.

The total time of the algorithm, therefore, is:

Step (1)	$O(N)$
Step (2)	$O(N \times \log N)$
Step (3)	$O(1)$
Step (4)	$O(N)$
Total	$O(N \times \log N)$

It is a little surprising that sorting has anything at all to do with finding the
convex hull. It is more surprising that the sorting part of the algorithm is actually
the dominant part as far as computational complexity goes.

■   ■

■ Research on the Efficiency of Algorithms

Finding efficient algorithms for pressing algorithmic problems is one of the most
common research topics in computer science. Indeed, almost all the issues discussed

in this chapter are subjects of considerable research efforts, and most are gathered under the general term **concrete complexity theory**.

In this area, people are interested in developing and exploiting data structures and algorithmic methods in order to improve existing algorithms or to conceive new ones. Many ingenious ideas find their way into sophisticated algorithms, providing at times surprising cuts in running time. Most often, this is done with the practical goal of solving the problem faster by computer. However, at times the driving force is simply the desire to nail down a problem's inherent order-of-magnitude complexity, even if the results, from a practical point of view, are no better than previously known ones.

A good example of this is the railroad layout (spanning tree) problem of Chapter 4. We presented a quadratic-time algorithm for this, which with some effort can be improved to $O(N \times \log N)$. For all practical purposes, this improved algorithm, or any of a number of other algorithms of similar complexity, works just fine. However, complexity theorists are not happy with this, since the best-known lower bound is linear. They want to know whether or not a linear-time algorithm can actually be found for the problem. Recently, using rather clever and complicated techniques, the upper bound has been brought quite close to $O(N)$. Specifically, there is an algorithm that runs in time bounded by $O(f(N) \times N)$, where $f(N)$ is a function that grows incredibly slowly—much, much slower than, say, $\log N$. The following table shows the smallest Ns for the first few values of this function:

Smallest N	such that $f(N)$ is
4	2
16	3
64,000	4
far more than the total number of particles in the known universe	5
absolutely unimaginable	6

Clearly, for all practical purposes an $O(f(N) \times N)$ algorithm is really linear; the value of $f(N)$ is 5 or less for any number we shall ever be interested in. However, we must remember that no matter how slowly growing $f(N)$ is, it would eventually become larger than any constant. Hence, from some point on, that is, for all sufficiently large N, any given linear-time algorithm outperforms the $O(f(N) \times N)$ one, and we say that the former is **asymptotically better** than the latter. Thus, the spanning tree problem is still open, as it still yields an algorithmic gap, and researchers have not given up on it. It is hoped that in the foreseeable future the problem will be closed, one way or another. Either a linear-time algorithm will be discovered, or a nonlinear lower bound proof, matching the known upper bound, will be found.

As mentioned earlier, lower bounds are very hard to come by, and for many problems no one knows of any nonlinear lower bounds. In other words, despite the fact that the best algorithms for some problems are quadratic, cubic, or worse, no one can prove that there does not exist some linear-time algorithm for them out there, awaiting discovery. Methods for proving nonlinear lower bounds are extremely scarce, and researchers expend considerable efforts in trying to find them.

Average-case performance yields another difficult research direction, and there are still many known algorithms for which satisfactory average-case analyses have not been performed.

We have not discussed **space complexity** here at all, but it is worth stating that achieving good upper and lower bounds on the memory space requirements of algorithmic problems is also the subject of considerable research in concrete complexity theory. People are interested not only in separate bounds on time and space, but also in the *joint* time/space complexity of a problem. It might be possible to achieve, say, a linear-space upper bound on a problem with some algorithm and, say, a quadratic-time upper bound with another algorithm, but that does not imply the existence of an algorithm that achieves both simultaneously. It is possible that there is a **time/space tradeoff** inherent in the problem, meaning that we pay for time economy with more space, and for space economy with more time. In such cases researchers try to *prove* that there is such a tradeoff. This usually takes the form of a proof that the performance of any algorithm solving the problem satisfies a certain equation, which holds as either a lower bound or an upper bound (or both). The equation typically captures a three-way relationship between the input length N and the (worst-case) running time and memory space of any solution algorithm.

■ For example, assume that the following equation has been established as both an upper and a lower bound on the time/space complexity of a problem P:

$$S^2 \times T = O(N^3 \times (\log N)^2)$$

This means that if we are willing to spend $O(N^3)$ time we can solve the problem using only $O(\log N)$ space, whereas if we insist on spending no more than $O(N^2)$ time, we would need $O(\sqrt{N} \times \log N)$ space.

The next two chapters will focus on the bad news complexity theory has for us. They will also discuss notions that are even more robust than the big-O notation.

■ Exercises

6.1. Consider the following salary computation problem. The input consists of a number N, a list, $BT(1), \ldots, BT(N)$, of before-tax salaries, and two tax rates, Rh for salaries that are larger than M, and Rl for salaries that are no larger than M. Here Rh and Rl are positive fractions, i.e., $0 < Rh, Rl < 1$. It is required to compute a list, $AT(1), \ldots, AT(N)$, of after-tax salaries, and two sums, Th and Tl, containing the total taxes paid according to the two rates, respectively. Here is a solution to the problem. It calculates the after-tax salaries first and then the tax totals:

for I from 1 to N do the following:
    if $BT(I) > M$ then $AT(I) \leftarrow BT(I) \times (1 - Rh)$;
    otherwise $AT(I) \leftarrow BT(I) \times (1 - Rl)$;
$Th \leftarrow 0$;
$Tl \leftarrow 0$;
for I from 1 to N do the following:
    if $BT(I) > M$ then $Th \leftarrow Th + BT(I) \times Rh$;
    otherwise $Tl \leftarrow Tl + BT(I) \times Rl$.

(a) Suggest a series of transformations that will make the program as efficient as possible, by minimizing both the number of arithmetical operations and the number of comparisons. Estimate the improvement to these complexity measures that is gained by each of your transformations.

(b) How would you further improve the program, if you are guaranteed that no before-tax salary is strictly less than M (i.e., there might be before-tax salaries of exactly M, but not less)? How would you characterize the rate of improvement in this case?

6.2. For the following pairs of time complexities of two algorithms A and B, find the least positive integer N for which algorithm B is better than algorithm A:

A	B
$N/2$	$4 \times \log_2 N$
N^2	$100 \times N \times \log_2 N$
N^6	$6 \times N^5$
3^N	12×2^N
2^N	$4 \times N^{\log_2 N}$
$2^{N \times \log_2 N} N$	100×2^N

6.3. Analyze the worst-case time complexity of each of the four algorithms given in Exercise 5.15 for computing m^n. Count multiplications only.

6.4. Consider the binary search scheme of Figure 6.1, and a telephone book with a million entries given as input to the algorithm.

(a) Describe an input list that exhibits worst-case behavior.

(b) Estimate how many such worst cases there are, and their proportion.

6.5. (a) Write an algorithm for searching an element in a sorted list, based on ternary (three-way) comparisons. A ternary comparison may be written as follows:

compare(L, M, N)
  case $L \leq M \leq N$:   ...   ;
  case $L \leq N \leq M$:   ...   ;
  case $M \leq N \leq L$:   ...   ;
    ...

with as many "case" clauses as necessary. The cost of such a comparison is one time unit.

(b) Given that the cost of each ternary comparison is a single time unit, analyze the worst-case time complexity of your algorithm, and explain why it is no better than binary search in terms of the big-O notation.

6.6. Analyze the time complexity of the following program scheme:

while $N > 0$ do the following:

$$\left[\quad \ldots \quad \right];$$

do the following N times:

$$\left[\quad \ldots \quad \right];$$

$N \leftarrow N/5$;

(Every program segment denoted by ... is executed in some fixed number of time units, and you may assume that the value of N does not change within it. "/" denotes *integer* division, e.g., $4/5 = 0$.)

6.7. Given that the list of employees is of length N, use the checkpoints technique to analyze the time complexity of the algorithm of Figure 2.4.

6.8. Prove that the following algorithms are of linear-time complexity:

(a) The algorithm for counting sentences containing the word "money", presented in Chapter 2.

(b) The algorithm for maximal polygonal distance, presented in Chapter 4.

6.9. (a) Prove that the **treesort** algorithm takes quadratic time in the worst case.

(b) Give an example of a worst-case input to **treesort**.

(c) Prove that the **mergesort** algorithm takes $O(N \times \log_2 N)$ time in the worst case.

(d) What is the average-case time complexity of **mergesort**?

6.10. Analyze the worst-case time complexity of the algorithms for traversing and processing information stored in trees that you were asked to design in Exercises 4.3 and 4.2.

6.11. Analyze the worst-case time and space complexities of the breadth-first algorithm for checking whether a given tree is balanced you were asked to design in Exercise 4.7. Compare them with the complexities of a straightforward depth-first algorithm for the same problem, which uses the algorithm for tree isomorphism that you were asked to design in Exercise 4.6 as a subroutine applied to the offspring of every node containing a binary operation.

6.12. Analyze the worst-case time and space complexities of the dynamic planning algorithm for the integer-knapsack problem you were asked to design in Exercise 4.13.

6.13. Prove a lower bound of $O(N \times \log_2 N)$ on the time complexity of any comparison-based sorting algorithm.

6.14. Explain the relevance, if any, of upper and lower bounds on the worst-case time complexity of the sorting problem to the time complexity of the greedy algorithm for the knapsack problem you were asked to design in Exercise 4.14.

6.15. Recall the problem of detecting palindromes, described in Exercise 5.10. In the following, consider the two correct solutions to this problem: algorithm *Pal1*, presented in Exercise 5.10, and algorithm *Pal4*, which you were asked to construct in Exercise 5.14. Assume that strings are composed of the two symbols "a" and "b" only, and that the only operations we count are comparisons (that is, applications of the **eq** predicate).

(a) Analyze the worst-case time complexity of algorithms *Pal1* and *Pal4*, providing upper bounds for both.

(b) Suggest a good lower bound for the problem of detecting palindromes.

(c) Assume a uniform distribution of the strings input by the algorithms. In other words, for each N, all strings of length N over the alphabet {a, b} can occur as inputs with equal probability. Perform an average-case time analysis of algorithms *Pal1* and *Pal4*.

6.16. A correct solution to Exercise 6.15 shows that the average-case complexity of *Pal4* is *better* than the lower bound on the palindrome detection problem.

(a) Explain why this fact is not self-contradictory.

(b) What does this fact mean with regards to the performance of algorithm *Pal4* on a large set of strings ("most" strings)? What does it mean with regards to the performance on a small set of strings?

(c) How would your answer to (b) change if the worst-case complexity of *Pal4* was significantly *larger* than the lower bound on the problem?

6.17. Assume two algorithms A and B solve the same algorithmic problem, but while the worst-case complexity of A is lower than that of B, the average-case complexity of B is lower than that of A. Would you consider either one of these two algorithms better than the other? If you answer in the affirmative, explain why; otherwise, describe situations and/or applications for which you consider each of the algorithms to be better.

If $m^k = n$ for integers $m, n > 1$, and $k \geq 0$, we say that k is the **logarithm base m of** n. In general, this logarithm need not necessarily be an integer. Let us define the **integer logarithm base** m of n to be the greatest integer $k \geq 0$, such that $m^k \leq n$, and denote it by $k = \lg_m n$. In Exercises 6.18–6.20 you are asked to design a number of algorithms for calculating the integer logarithm function. The only arithmetical operations you may use are addition and multiplication. When analyzing the time complexity of these algorithms, you are to count arithmetical operations only, assuming that every operation takes a single time unit. For memory space analysis, count the number of integers that are stored simultaneously, assuming that an integer can be stored (in a variable or list-element) in a single unit of memory space.

6.18. Design an algorithm $LG1$, with input integers $m, n > 1$, that calculates $\lg_m n$ by repeatedly calculating the powers $m^0, m^1, \ldots, m^k$, until a number k is found satisfying $m^k \leq n < m^{k+1}$. Analyze the time and space complexity of $LG1$.

It is well known that each positive integer k can be written uniquely as a sum of integer powers of 2, i.e., in the form $k = 2^{l_1} + 2^{l_2} + \cdots + 2^{l_j}$, where $l_1 > l_2 > \cdots > l_j \geq 0$. For example, $12 = 2^3 + 2^2$, and $31 = 2^4 + 2^3 + 2^2 + 2^1 + 2^0$. Hence, $m^k = m^{2^{l_1}} \times m^{2^{l_2}} \times \cdots \times m^{2^{l_j}}$, and if we need to calculate $k = \lg_m n$, it is enough to find the appropriate exponents $l_1, l_2, \ldots, l_j$.

6.19. Design an iterative (i.e., nonrecursive) algorithm $LG2$ to calculate $\lg_m n$ by first finding an integer l_1 satisfying $m^{2^{l_1}} \leq n < m^{2^{l_1+1}}$, then finding an integer $l_2 < l_1$, satisfying $m^{2^{l_1}} \times m^{2^{l_2}} \leq n < m^{2^{l_1}} \times m^{2^{l_2+1}}$, and so on. Use a fixed amount of memory space (no lists). Analyze the time and space complexity of algorithm $LG2$.

6.20. The time complexity of the previous algorithm can be improved by calculating each of the values $m^{2^{l_1}}, m^{2^{l_2}}, \ldots, m^{2^{l_j}}$ only once.

(a) Design such an algorithm $LG3$, and analyze its time and space complexity.

(b) Discuss the time/space tradeoff concerning the last two algorithms. Suggest joint time/space complexity measures under which $LG3$ has better/equivalent/worse complexity than $LG2$. What happens when you replace $LG2$ in this analysis with $LG1$?

how long shall it be then?

II Samuel 2: 26

In an acceptable time have I answered thee

Isaiah 49: 8

PART III

Limitations and Robustness

Thou didst set a bound that they might not pass over
PSALM 104: 9

Inefficiency and Intractability

or, You Can't Always Get It Done Cheaply

In the previous chapter we saw that certain algorithmic problems admit solutions that are far more time efficient than their naive counterparts. We saw, for example, that it is possible to search a sorted list in logarithmic time, a result which, when refined, implies that we can search for a name in a million-entry telephone book with only 20 comparisons in the worst case, not a million. In a similar vein, sorting an unsorted million-entry telephone book can be achieved with only several million comparisons, not many billions, as there exist $O(N \times \log N)$ sorting algorithms that outperform the naive quadratic ones.

At this point, you may be unimpressed. You may claim to be sufficiently "rich" to afford a million comparisons for searching a list. Or that a few extra seconds of computer time makes no difference, and hence that linear search is just as good as binary search. This argument gains credence on realizing that it is not a human user, but a computer, that carries out the dull and unimaginative chore of leafing through all the names in the book. A similar argument can be made for sorting too, particularly if the application is such that sorting is to be carried out rarely, and the lists to be sorted never contain more than, say, a million items.

Given this attitude, questions of algorithmic gaps become uninteresting too. Once a reasonably good algorithm has been found for a pressing algorithmic problem, we may not be interested in better algorithms or in proofs that they do not exist.

The purpose of this chapter is to show that the "let's-put-up-with-what-we-have" approach cannot always be adopted. We shall see that in many cases reasonable algorithms, say linear or quadratic ones, do not exist at all. The best algorithms for many important algorithmic problems will be shown to require formidable amounts of time or memory space, rendering them quite useless.

■ The Towers of Hanoi Revisited

Recall the Towers of Hanoi problem of Chapter 2, in which we were asked to produce a sequence of one-ring moves to transfer N rings from one of three pegs to another according to certain rules (see Figure 2.7). You are encouraged to carry out a simple time analysis of the recursive solution **move** described therein, similar to the analysis carried out in Chapter 6 for the **min&max** routine. It will show that the number of single-ring moves produced by the algorithm for the N-ring case, is precisely $2^N - 1$ that is, one less than $2 \times 2 \times 2 \times \ldots \times 2$, with the 2 appearing N times. Since N appears in the exponent, such a function is called **exponential**. It can be shown that $2^N - 1$ is also a lower bound on the required number of moves for solving the problem, so that our solution is really optimal and we cannot do any better.[1]

Is this news good or bad? Well, to answer the question in an indirect way, if the Hindu priests originally confronted with the 64-ring case were to brush up their act and move a million rings every second, it would still take them more than *half a million years* to complete the process! If, somewhat more realistically, they were to move one ring every 10 seconds, it would take them well over *five trillion years* to get the job done. No wonder they believed the world will end before then!

It seems, therefore, that the Towers of Hanoi problem, at least for 64 rings or more, is hopelessly time consuming. While this statement appears hard to contest, it might cause the feeling that the difficulty stems from the desire to output the entire sequence of moves, and since hopelessly many moves are required, it will obviously take hopelessly long to find them and print them all out. We might be tempted, therefore, to expect such devastating time performance to occur only for problems whose outputs are unreasonably lengthy.

To convince ourselves that this is not so, it is instructive to consider **yes/no problems**; that is, algorithmic problems that do not produce any "real" outputs except a "yes" or a "no." These are sometimes called **decision problems**, as their purpose is merely to decide whether a certain property holds for their inputs. Most of this chapter (and the next) will be devoted to decision problems.

■ The Monkey Puzzle Problem: An Example

At some point in life, you may have encountered one or more versions of the very frustrating monkey puzzle (see Figure 7.1). It involves nine square cards whose sides are imprinted with the upper and lower halves of colored monkeys. The objective is to arrange the cards in the form of a 3 by 3 square such that halves match and colors are identical wherever edges meet.

In the general algorithmic problem associated with this puzzle, we are given (descriptions of) N cards, where N is some square number, say, N is M^2, and the problem calls for exhibiting, if possible, an M by M square arrangement of the N cards, so that colors and halves behave as stated. We shall assume that the cards are *oriented*, meaning that the edges have fixed directions, "up," "down," "right," and "left," so that they are not to be rotated. We shall concentrate on the seemingly easier yes/no version, that simply asks whether *any* such M by M arrangement exists, without asking for one to actually be exhibited.

---

[1] Incidentally, the iterative solution presented in Chapter 5 and the recursive one of Chapter 2 produce exactly the same sequence of $2^N - 1$ moves.

Figure 7.1

A 3-by-3 instance of the monkey puzzle.

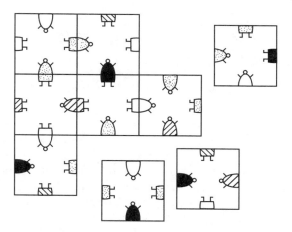

A naive solution to the problem is not too hard to come by. We need only observe that each input involves only finitely many cards, and that there are only finitely many locations to fill with them. Hence, there are only finitely many different ways of arranging the input cards into an *M* by *M* square. Moreover, a given arrangement can easily be tested for legality (that is, that all input cards are indeed used, and that halves and colors match) by simply considering each card and each of the meeting edges in turn. Consequently, an algorithm can be designed to work its way through all possible arrangements, stopping and saying "yes" if the arrangement at hand is legal, and stopping and saying "no" if all arrangements have been considered, and they have all been found to be illegal. Of course, it is possible to make this approach somewhat less brute-force, by avoiding the need to explicitly check extensions of a partial arrangement that has already been shown to be illegal. Some bookkeeping is required to make sure that all possible arrangements are indeed considered and that none is considered twice, but we shall not dwell on the details of the algorithm here—we are more interested in its time performance.

Let us assume that *N* is 25, meaning that the final square is to be of size 5 by 5. Let us also assume that we have a computer capable of constructing and evaluating a billion arrangements every second (that is, one arrangement every nanosecond), including all the bookkeeping involved. This is quite a reasonable assumption, given today's computers. The question is: how long will the algorithm take in the worst case (which is when there is no legal arrangement, so that all possible arrangements are checked)?

If we arbitrarily number the locations in a 5 by 5 grid, there are obviously 25 possibilities for choosing a card to be placed in the first location. Having placed some card in that location, there are 24 cards to choose from for the second location, 23 for the third, and so on. The total number of arrangements can, therefore, reach:

$$25 \times 24 \times 23 \times \ldots \times 3 \times 2 \times 1$$

a number denoted by 25! and called 25 **factorial**. What is astonishing is the *size* of this innocent-looking number; it contains 26 digits, a fact that does not seem alarming until we realize that our billion-arrangements-per-second computer will take well over 490 *million years* to work its way through all 25! arrangements. If

Figure 7.2

Trivial monkey puzzles.

Arrangements always exist

(a)

Arrangements never exist

(b)

we simply increase the size of the square by one, going from a 5 by 5 square to a 6 by 6 one, so that N is 36, things become a *lot* worse. The time it would take to go through all 36! values would be unimaginably long, far, far, FAR longer than the time that has elapsed since the Big Bang.

Obviously, particular monkey card puzzles can be prepared in ways that make life easy. (To give a couple of extreme examples, if all cards are either identical to the one in Figure 7.2(a) or identical to that in Figure 7.2(b), the question has trivial answers.) Moreover, the smarter version of the algorithm, that does not consider extensions of illegal partial arrangements, will perform much better for many input puzzles. However, *worst*-case analysis is the name of our game. The puzzle designer actually strives for sets of cards that admit many *partial* solutions (in which portions of the square are legally covered with cards), but only very few *complete* solutions— maybe only one. This is what prevents the problem from admitting fast and easy solutions. Hence, even the less naive version of the algorithm will exhibit similarly disastrous worst-case behavior.

The brute-force solution, therefore, is quite useless, even for a very small 5 by 5 version (or, say, a 10 by 10 version if the less naive version is used, and we are willing to make do with average-case performance). If you are now expecting a truly clever solution to be presented, which would show how to really solve the problem in a useful way, you are in for a disappointment. The only known solutions that are better than the ones discussed are not sufficiently better as to be reasonable; if N is 25 they would still require, in the worst case, many, many of years of computation for a single instance, and if N is 36, well, . . . forget it . . .

Is there some hidden solution to the monkey puzzle problem, one that would be practical for a reasonable number of cards, say up to 225? By this we mean to ask if there is some easy way of solving the problem, which we have not yet discovered. Perhaps there is an arrangement precisely when the number of distinct cards is a multiple of 17, for some strange reason. The answer to this question is "probably not, but we are not quite sure." We shall discuss this matter further after examining the general behavior of such impractical algorithms as the one just described.

Reasonable vs. Unreasonable Time

The factorial function $N!$ grows at a rate that is orders of magnitude larger than the growth rate of any of the functions mentioned in previous chapters. It grows much, much faster than linear or quadratic functions, for example, and, in fact, easily dwarfs all functions of the form N^K, for any fixed K. It is true that N^{1000}, for example, is larger than $N!$ for many values of N (for all N up to 1165, to be

Function \ N	20	60	100	300	1000
$5N$	100	300	500	1500	5000
$N \times \log_2 N$	86	354	665	2469	9966
N^2	400	3600	10,000	90,000	1 million (7 digits)
N^3	8000	216,000	1 million (7 digits)	27 million (8 digits)	1 billion (10 digits)
2^N	1,048,576	a 19-digit number	a 31-digit number	a 91-digit number	a 302-digit number
$N!$	a 19-digit number	an 82-digit number	a 161-digit number	a 623-digit number	unimaginably large
N^N	a 27-digit number	a 107-digit number	a 201-digit number	a 744-digit number	unimaginably large

Polynomial: $5N$, $N \times \log_2 N$, N^2, N^3

Exponential: 2^N, $N!$, N^N

Figure 7.3

Some values of some functions. For comparison: the number of protons in the known universe has 79 digits; the number of nanoseconds since the Big Bang has 27 digits.

precise). However, for any K, there is some value of N (1165, if K is 1000) beyond which the function $N!$ leaves N^K far behind, very, very quickly.

Other functions exhibit similarly unacceptable growth rates. For example, the function N^N, denoting $N \times N \times N \times \ldots \times N$ with N occurrences of N, grows even faster than $N!$. The function 2^N, that is, $2 \times 2 \times 2 \times \ldots \times 2$, with N occurrences of 2, grows slower than $N!$, but is also considered a "bad" function; it still grows much faster than the N^K functions. If N is 20 the value of 2^N is about a million, and if N is 30 it is about a billion. (This is because 2^N relates to N precisely as N does to $\log_2 N$.) If N is 300 the number 2^N is billions of times larger than the number of protons in the entire known universe. Figures 7.3 and 7.4 illustrate the relative growth rates of some of these functions.

A striking illustration of the differences between these functions is in the running times of algorithms. Figure 7.5 gives the actual running times of several hypothetical algorithms for the monkey puzzle problem for various values of N. It is assumed that the algorithms are run on a computer capable of carrying out a billion instructions per second (that is, one instruction per nanosecond). As can be seen, even the smallest of the "bad" functions appearing therein, 2^N, might require 400 billion centuries for a single instance of the 10 by 10 problem! For functions like $N!$ or N^N, the time is unimaginably worse.

These facts lead to a fundamental classification of functions into "good" and "bad" ones. The distinction to be made is between **polynomial** and **super-polynomial** functions. For our purposes a polynomial function of N is one which is **bounded from above** by N^K for some fixed K (meaning, essentially, that it is no greater in value than N^K for all values of N from some point on). All others are super-polynomial. Thus, logarithmic, linear, and quadratic functions, for example, are polynomial, whereas ones like $1.001^N + N^6$, 5^N, N^N, and $N!$ are exponential or worse. Although there are functions, like $N^{\log_2 N}$ for example, that are super-polynomial but not quite exponential, and others, like N^N, that are super-exponential,

Figure 7.4

Growth rates of some functions.

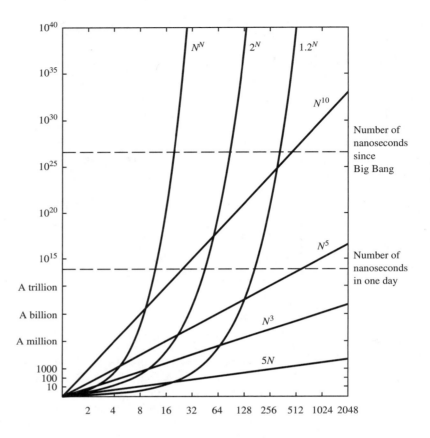

Figure 7.5

Time consumption of hypothetical solutions to the monkey puzzle problem (assuming one instruction per nanosecond). For comparison: the Big Bang was 13–15 billion years ago.

current practice will be followed in abusing the terminology slightly by using "exponential" as a synonym for "super-polynomial" in the sequel.

An algorithm whose order-of-magnitude time performance is bounded from above by a polynomial function of N, where N is the size of its inputs, is called a **polynomial-time algorithm**, and will be referred to here as a **reasonable**

	N Function	20	40	60	100	300
Polynomial	N^2	1/2500 millisecond	1/625 millisecond	1/278 millisecond	1/100 millisecond	1/11 millisecond
	N^5	1/300 second	1/10 second	78/100 second	10 seconds	40.5 minutes
Exponential	2^N	1/1000 second	18.3 minutes	36.5 years	400 billion centuries	a 72-digit number of centuries
	N^N	3.3 billion years	a 46-digit number of centuries	an 89-digit number of centuries	a 182-digit number of centuries	a 725-digit number of centuries

Figure 7.6

The sphere of
algorithmic problems:
Version I.

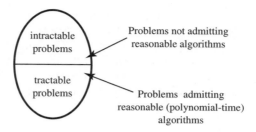

algorithm. Similarly, an algorithm that, in the worst case, requires super-polynomial, or exponential time, will be called **unreasonable**.

As far as the algorithmic problem is concerned, a problem that admits a reasonable or polynomial-time solution is said to be **tractable**, whereas a problem that admits only unreasonable or exponential-time solutions is termed **intractable**.

The discussion and examples surrounding Figures 7.3–7.5 are intended to support this distinction. In general, intractable problems require impractically large amounts of time even on relatively small inputs, whereas tractable problems admit algorithms that are practical for reasonably-sized inputs. We might be justified in questioning the wisdom of drawing the line between good and bad precisely where we did. As already mentioned, an N^{1000} algorithm (which is reasonable by our definition, since N^{1000} is a polynomial function) is worse than a very unreasonable $N!$ algorithm for inputs under size 1165, and the turning point is much larger if N^{1000} is compared, say, with the slower growing exponential function 1.001^N. Nevertheless, the majority of unreasonable algorithms are really useless, and most reasonable ones are sufficiently useful to warrant the distinction made. In fact, the vast majority of polynomial-time algorithms for practical problems feature an exponent of N that is no more than 5 or 6. In Chapter 9 evidence will be presented to the effect that the dichotomy introduced here is actually extremely robust, even more so than the ignoring of constants that comes with the use of the big-O notation.[2]

The sphere of all algorithmic problems can therefore be divided into two major classes as illustrated in Figure 7.6. The dividing line embodies one of the most important classifications in the theory of algorithmic complexity. In Chapter 8 another, even more fundamental, line will be drawn.

■ ■

More on the Monkey Puzzle Problem

The monkey puzzle problem is really worse than anything we have seen so far. It asks only for a simple yes/no answer, yet even when using the best-known algorithms

---

[2] There is a possibility of a dent in this robustness. It concerns the relatively new and exciting area of **quantum computing**, discussed in Chapter 10, which could possibly lead to intractable problems becoming tractable. Why we are being so careful in the wording of this footnote, will be explained there. However, even if this does happen it is still a very long way off, so for now we shall proceed with the knowledge that tractability is a strong and robust notion, insensitive to anything we know about now.

we could spend our entire lifetime on a single, very small instance of the problem and never find out the correct answer. A problem for which there is no known polynomial-time algorithm is thus not much better than a problem for which there is no known algorithm at all. The crucial question here is whether there really is no reasonable solution; in other words, is the monkey puzzle problem *really* intractable?

To sharpen our understanding of the situation, let us focus on several possibly bothersome issues.

1. Computers are becoming faster by the week. Over the past 10 years or so computer speed has increased roughly by a factor of 50. Perhaps obtaining a practical solution to the problem is just a question of awaiting an additional improvement in computer speed.

2. Doesn't the fact that we have not found a better algorithm for this problem indicate our incompetence at devising efficient algorithms? Shouldn't computer scientists be working at trying to improve the situation rather than spending their time writing books about it?

3. Haven't people tried to look for an exponential-time lower bound on the problem, so that we might have a *proof* that no reasonable algorithm exists?

4. Maybe the whole issue is not worth the effort, as the monkey puzzle problem is just one specific problem. It might be a colorful one, but it certainly doesn't look like a very important one.

These points are well taken, but the following unusual situation provides answers to them all. First of all, let us do away with objection number (1). Figure 7.7 shows that even if the fastest computer were to be made 1000 times faster, a 2^N algorithm for the monkey puzzle problem would be able, in a given time frame (say, an hour), to cope with only about 10 more cards than it can today. In contrast, if the algorithm were to take time N it could cope with 1000 times the number of cards it can today. Hence, improving the computer's speed by a mere constant factor, even a large one, will improve things, but if the algorithm is exponential then it will do so only in a very insignificant way.

Let us now relate to point (4)—the two other points are treated implicitly later. It so happens that the monkey puzzle problem is not alone. There are other problems in the same boat. Moreover, the boat is large, impressive, and many-sided. The monkey puzzle problem is just one of close to 1000 diverse algorithmic problems, all of which exhibit precisely the same phenomena. They all admit unreasonable, exponential-time solutions, but none of them is known to admit reasonable ones.

Figure 7.7

Algorithmic improvements resulting from improvements in computer speed.

Function	Maximal number of cards solvable in one hour:		
	with today's computer	with computer 100 times faster	with computer 1000 times faster
N	A	$100 \times A$	$1000 \times A$
N^2	B	$10 \times B$	$31.6 \times B$
2^N	C	$C + 6.64$	$C + 9.97$

Moreover, no one has been able to *prove* that any of them require super-polynomial time. In fact, the best-known lower bounds on most of the problems in this class are $O(N)$, meaning that it is conceivable (though unlikely) that they admit very efficient *linear-time* algorithms.

We shall denote this class of problems **NPC**, standing for the **NP-complete** problems, as explained later. The algorithmic gap associated with the problems in NPC is thus enormous. Their lower bounds are linear, and their upper bounds exponential! The issue is not whether we spend linear or quadratic time in solving them, or whether we need 20 comparisons for a search or a million. It boils down to the ultimate question of whether we can or cannot solve these problems for even reasonably small inputs on even the largest and most powerful computers. It is as simple as that. The location of these algorithmic problems in the sphere of Figure 7.6 is thus unknown, since their upper and lower bounds lie on either side of the dividing line.

There are two additional properties that characterize the special class NPC, and which make it all the more remarkable. However, before discussing them, it should be stressed that the class NPC contains an ever-growing diversity of algorithmic problems, arising in such areas as combinatorics, operations research, economics, graph theory, game theory, and logic. It is worth looking at some of the other problems found there.

Two-Dimensional Arrangement Problems

Some of the most appealing problems in NPC are arrangement problems derived from two-dimensional puzzles like the monkey puzzle. Other good examples are those puzzles, sometimes handed out on airlines, which involve a number of irregular shapes that are to be arranged into a rectangle (see Figure 7.8). The general decision problem calls for deciding whether N given shapes can be arranged into a rectangle, and is in NPC. One reason for the apparent absence of a fast solution is rooted in the existence of many different partial solutions that cannot be extended to complete ones. Sometimes an arrangement puzzle admits only one complete solution.

Figure 7.8

An airline puzzle.

Consider ordinary jigsaw puzzles. They admit virtually no partial solutions except as parts of the unique final solution. Adding a piece to a partially solved jigsaw puzzle is usually just a matter of running through all unused pieces and finding the single piece that will fit. This is a consequence of either the unique shapes of the jigs and jags on individual pieces, or the heterogeneous character of the picture to be formed, or of both. Therefore, as we can verify, an ordinary, "well-behaved" jigsaw puzzle with N pieces can be solved in quadratic time.

However, anyone who has ever labored on a jigsaw puzzle containing lots of sky, sea, or desert knows that not all jigsaw puzzles are that easy. (In such puzzles several parts might appear to fit perfectly in a given place, and some undoing of partial solutions will be necessary in order to obtain a full solution.) A general jigsaw-based algorithmic problem has to cope with all possible input puzzles, including those that involve less heterogeneous pictures and whose pieces contain many identical jigs and jags. The general N-piece jigsaw problem also turns out to be in the class NPC. In essence, it is just the monkey puzzle problem or the irregular shapes problem in disguise.

■ Path-Finding Problems

In Chapter 4 two problems were described, both concerned with finding certain structures of minimal cost in city networks. They involved, respectively, lazy railroad contractors (finding minimal spanning trees) and weary travelers (finding shortest paths). A city network is a graph consisting of N points (the cities), and edges with associated costs (these are the distances between cities). The time behavior of both the algorithms presented in Chapter 4 is quadratic, and therefore both problems are tractable.

Here is another problem, which at first sight looks very similar to the other two. It involves a **traveling salesman** who has to visit each of the cities in a given network before returning to his starting point, whence his trip is complete. The algorithmic problem asks for the cheapest route, namely for a closed **tour** that passes through each of the nodes in the graph and whose total cost (that is, the sum of the distances labeling the edges) is minimal. Figure 7.9 shows a six-city network, in which such an optimal tour is shown.

Figure 7.9

A city network and a minimal round tour.

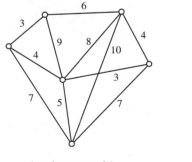

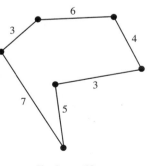

(not drawn to scale)   Total cost: 28

In the yes/no version the inputs include a number K besides the city graph G, and the decision problem asks simply whether there is a tour of G with total cost of no more than K. Thus, for the graph of Figure 7.9, the answer would be "yes" if K is 30, but "no" if K is 27.

Despite its somewhat playful description, the traveling salesman problem, like the minimal spanning tree and shortest path problems, is *not* a toy example. Its variants arise in the design of telephone networks and integrated circuits, in planning construction lines, and in the programming of industrial robots, to mention but a few applications. In all of these, the ability to find inexpensive tours of the graphs in question can be quite crucial.

Again, a naive exponential-time solution is easy to come by. Just consider all possible tours, stopping and saying "yes" if the cost of the tour at hand is no more than K, and "no" if all tours have been considered but have all been found to cost more than K. This is actually an $O(N!)$ algorithm. (Why?) Again, even the case where N is 25 is simply hopeless, and we must realize that while for a traveling salesman with a suitcase full of bits and pieces 25 cities might sound a lot, it is an almost laughable number for the kind of real-world applications mentioned above. The fact is that the traveling salesman problem is also in NPC, rendering the problem insolvable in practice, as far as we know.

It is worth briefly considering some other path-finding problems. Let us see what happens when we leave out edge lengths altogether. Given a graph consisting of points and edges, we can ask simply whether there exists a path, any path, that passes through all points exactly once. Such paths are termed **Hamiltonian**. Figure 7.10(a) shows a graph that has no Hamiltonian path, and Figure 7.10(b) shows how the addition of a single edge can change the situation. Although seemingly much easier, this problem is also in NPC. There is a simple exponential-time algorithm that checks all $N!$ paths, searching for one that reaches each point once, but no one knows of a polynomial-time solution.

Curiously enough, if we are after a path that is to pass through all *edges* exactly once, rather than all points, the story is quite different. Such paths are termed **Eulerian**, and Figure 7.11 is an Eulerian analog of Figure 7.10. At first glance it seems that there is no better way to find an Eulerian path than to similarly go through every possible path. (In the worst case there are about $(N^2)!$ of them. Why?) However,

Figure 7.10

Hamiltonian paths.

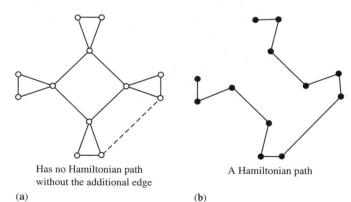

Has no Hamiltonian path
without the additional edge

A Hamiltonian path

(a)

(b)

Figure 7.11

Eulerian paths.

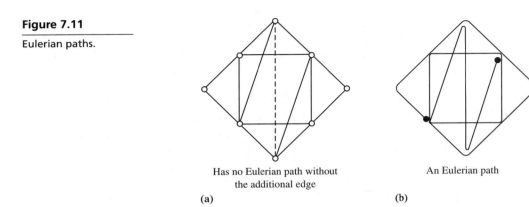

Has no Eulerian path without
the additional edge

(a)

An Eulerian path

(b)

a simple but rather clever polynomial-time solution to the Eulerian path problem was found in 1736 by the great Swiss mathematician Leonhard Euler. The solution is obtained by showing that a graph contains an Eulerian path precisely when it satisfies the following two properties: (1) it is connected (that is, any point is reachable from any other), and (2) the number of edges emanating from any point (with the possible exception of two points) is even. Accordingly, an algorithm need only check whether an input graph satisfies these properties. Checking for the second is trivial, and the first can easily be shown to admit a fast algorithm, one that is actually linear in the number of edges.

Scheduling and Matching Problems

Many NPC problems are concerned, in one way or another, with **scheduling** or **matching**. For example, suppose we are given the particular hours that each of N teachers is available, and the particular hours that each of M classes can be scheduled. In addition, we are given the number of hours each of the teachers has to teach each of the classes. The **timetable problem** asks whether it is possible to match teachers, classes, and hours so that all the given constraints are met, so that no two teachers teach the same class at the same time, and so that no two classes are taught by the same teacher at the same time.

The timetable problem also belongs to the special class NPC. Other matching problems in NPC involve fitting loads of various sizes into trucks with various capacities (sometimes called the **bin-packing problem**), or assigning students to dormitory rooms in a way that satisfies certain constraints.

It must be emphasized that many other scheduling and matching problems are quite tractable, as is the case with arrangements, path finding problems, and so on.

Determining Logical Truth

One of the best-known problems in NPC involves determining the truth or falsity of sentences in a simple logical formalism called the **propositional calculus**. In this language, we are allowed to combine symbols denoting elementary assertions into more complex assertions, using the logical connectives & (denoting "and"), $\vee$ (denoting "or"), $\sim$ ("not"), and $\rightarrow$ ("implies"). Thus, for example, the sentence:

$$\sim(E \rightarrow F) \,\&\, (F \vee (D \rightarrow \sim E))$$

states that (1) it is not the case that the truth of E implies the truth of F, and (2) either F is true or the truth of D implies the falsity of E.

The algorithmic problem calls for determining the **satisfiability** of such sentences. In other words, given a sentence as an input, we want to know whether it is possible to assign "true" or "false" to the basic assertions appearing in it, so that the entire sentence will turn out to be true. An assignment of truth values to the basic assertions is called a **truth assignment**. In the example, we can fix E to be true and D and F to be false. This will cause (1) to be true because E is true but F is not, so that E cannot imply F. Also, (2) is true, despite F's falsity, by virtue of D's falsity.[3] Hence, the sample sentence is satisfiable. You might want to verify that the similar sentence:

$$\sim((D \,\&\, E) \rightarrow F) \,\&\, (F \vee (D \rightarrow \sim E))$$

is unsatisfiable; there is no way to assign truth values to D, E, and F that will make this sentence true.

It is not too difficult to come up with an exponential-time algorithm for the satisfiability problem, where N is the number of distinct elementary assertions in the input sentence. We simply try out all possible truth assignments. There are precisely 2^N of them (why?), and it is easy to test the truth of the formula with respect to each one of these truth assignments in time that is polynomial in N. Consequently, the entire algorithm runs in exponential time. Unfortunately, the satisfiability problem for the propositional calculus is also in NPC, so that the naive exponential-time algorithm is, in essence, the best known. It is impossible, as far as is known at present, to check algorithmically whether even quite short sentences can be made true.

Coloring Maps and Graphs

In Chapter 5 we described the four-color theorem, which proves that any map of countries can be colored using only four colors in such a way that no two adjacent countries are colored the same (see Figure 5.11). It follows that the algorithmic problem of determining whether a given map can be **four-colored**, as this kind of process is termed, is trivial: on any input map the answer is simply "yes." The very same problem, but where only two colors are allowed, is not very hard either. A map can be two-colored exactly when it contains no point that is the junction of an odd number of countries (why?), and this property is easy to check for.

Note that the number of colors is not taken here as part of the input. We are discussing the algorithmic problems obtained by *fixing* the number of colors allowed, and asking whether an input country map can be colored with that fixed number. As we have shown, the cases of two and four colors are trivial. The interesting case

---

[3] A false assertion implies anything. The sentence "if I am an alligator then so are you" is true by virtue of my not being an alligator, regardless of your own standing.

is that of three colors. Determining whether a map can be three-colored is in NPC, meaning that we know of only unreasonable solutions, thus making the problem unsolvable in practice except for extremely small numbers of countries.

A related problem involves coloring graphs. The coloring rule here is similar to that of map coloring, except that nodes (points in the graph) play the role of countries. No two neighboring nodes (that is, nodes connected by an edge) may be monochromatic. In contrast to country maps, whose flatness restricts the possible configurations of bordering countries, any node in a graph can be connected by edges to any other. It is easy to construct graphs that require large numbers of colors. A graph containing K nodes, each connected to all others, clearly requires K colors. Such a graph is called a **clique**. The algorithmic problem asks for the minimal number of colors required to color a given graph. The yes/no version, which asks if the graph can be colored with K colors, where K is part of the input, is also in NPC, and hence is not known to have a reasonable solution. Since the original version is at least as hard as the yes/no version (why?), it too is not known to be solvable in reasonable time.

■ ■

■ Short Certificates and Magic Coins

All these NPC problems seem to require, as part of their inherent nature, that we try out *partial* matchings, *partial* truth assignments, *partial* arrangements, or *partial* colorings, and that we continuously extend them in the hope of reaching a final complete solution. When a partial solution cannot be extended, we apparently have to **backtrack**; that is, to undo things already done, in preparation for trying an alternative. If this process is carried out carefully no possible solution is missed, but an exponential amount of time is required in the worst case.

Thus, given an input to an NPC problem, it appears to be extremely hard to tell whether the answer to the question embodied in the problem is a "yes" or a "no." However, it is interesting that in all these problems *if* the answer happens to be "yes" there is an easy way to convince someone of it. There is a so-called **certificate**, which contains conclusive evidence to the effect that the answer is indeed "yes." Furthermore, this certificate can always be made reasonably short. Its size can always be bounded by a polynomial in N. (In fact, most often it is *linear* in N.)

For example, as discussed earlier, it seems to be notoriously difficult to tell whether a graph contains a Hamiltonian path, or whether it contains one whose length is no greater than some given number K. On the other hand, *if* such a path indeed exists, it can be exhibited (as in Figures 7.9 and 7.10) and easily checked to be of the desired kind, thus serving as an excellent proof that the answer is "yes." Similarly, although it is difficult to *find* a truth assignment that satisfies a sentence in the propositional calculus, it is easy to *certify* its satisfiability, by simply exhibiting an assignment that satisfies it. Moreover, it is easy to verify in polynomial time that this particular truth assignment does the job. In a similar vein, exhibiting a legal arrangement of monkey puzzle cards serves as conclusive evidence that the corresponding algorithmic problem says "yes" when applied to the puzzle as an input. Here, too, the legality of the arrangement (colors and halves match) can be verified easily in polynomial time.

Figuring out whether an NPC problem says "yes" to an input is thus hard, but certifying that it indeed does, *when* it does, is easy.

There is another way of describing this phenomenon. Assume we have a very special magic coin, to be used in the backtracking procedure just described. Whenever it is possible to extend a partial solution in two ways (for example, two monkey cards can be legally placed at a currently empty location, or the next assertion symbol can be assigned "true" or "false"), the coin is flipped and the choice is made according to the outcome. However, the coin does not fall at random; it possesses magical insight, always indicating the best possibility. The coin will always select a possibility that leads to a complete solution, if there is a complete solution. (If both possibilities lead to complete solutions, or if neither does, the coin acts like a normal random coin.)

Technically, we say that algorithms that use such magic coins are **nondeterministic**, in that they always "guess" which of the available options is better, rather than having to employ some deterministic procedure to go through them all. Somehow, they always manage to make the right choice. Clearly, if algorithms were allowed to exploit such magical nondeterminism we might have been able to improve the solutions to certain algorithmic problems, since the work associated with trying out possibilities is avoided. For the NPC problems this improvement is not at all marginal: every NPC problem has a *polynomial-time* nondeterministic algorithm. This fact can be proved by showing that the "short" certificates discussed above correspond directly to the polynomial-time "magical" executions; all we have to do is follow the instructions of the magic coin and when we have a complete candidate solution simply check whether it is legal. Since the coin always indicates the best possibility, we can safely say "no" if the candidate solution is in violation of the rules. A legal solution would have been found by the coin if one existed.

Thus, NPC problems are apparently intractable, but become "tractable" by using magical nondeterminism. This explains part of the acronym NPC: the N and P stand for Nondeterministic Polynomial-time, so that a problem is said to be *in* NP if it admits a short certificate. We now turn to the C, which stands for "Complete."

◼ NP-Completeness: Standing or Falling Together

Besides admitting deterministic solutions that take unreasonable time, and "magical," nondeterministic ones that take reasonable time, NPC problems have an additional, most remarkable, property. Each one's fate is tightly bound to that of all the others. Either *all* NPC problems are tractable, or *none* of them is! The term "complete" is used to signify this additional property, so that, as mentioned, the problems in NP are known as the NP-complete problems.

Let us sharpen this statement. If someone were to find a polynomial-time algorithm for any single NP-complete problem, there would immediately be polynomial-time algorithms for *all* of them. This implies the dual fact: if someone were to prove an exponential-time lower bound for *any* NP-complete problem, establishing that it cannot be solved in polynomial time, it would follow immediately that *no* such

Figure 7.12

Reducing Hamiltonian paths to traveling salesmen.

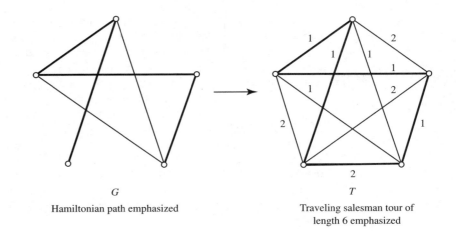

G

Hamiltonian path emphasized

T

Traveling salesman tour of
length 6 emphasized

problem can be solved in polynomial time. In terms of Figure 7.6, it is not known on which side of the line the NP-complete problems belong, but it is known that they all belong on the same side.

This is the ultimate in solidarity, and it is not a conjecture—it has been proved: all the NP-complete problems stand or fall together. We just don't know which one it is. Paraphrasing the brave old Duke of York, we might say:

> *And when they are up they are up*
> *And when they are down they are down*
>
> *And since they can't be halfway up*
> *They are either up or down*

How do we prove such a sweeping claim? Recall that close to 1000 different problems in diverse areas are known to be NP-complete!

The concept that is used to establish this stand-or-fall-together phenomenon is that of a **polynomial-time reduction**. Given two NP-complete problems, a polynomial-time reduction is an algorithm that runs in polynomial time, and reduces one problem to the other, in the following sense. If someone comes along with an input X to the first problem and wants the "yes" or "no" answer, we use the algorithm to transform X into an input Y to the second problem, in such a way that the second problem's answer to Y is precisely the first problem's answer to X.

For example, it is quite easy to reduce the Hamiltonian path problem to the traveling salesman problem.[4] Given a graph G with N nodes, construct a traveling salesman network T as follows. The nodes of T are precisely the nodes of G, but edges are drawn between every two nodes, assigning cost 1 to an edge if it was present in the original graph G, and 2 if it was not. Figure 7.12 illustrates the transformation. It is not too difficult to see that T has a traveling salesman tour of length $N + 1$ or less (passing once through each point) precisely if G contains a Hamiltonian path. Thus, to answer questions about the existence of Hamiltonian paths, take the input graph G and carry out the transformation to T. Then ask whether T has a traveling

---

[4] Here we take the version of the traveling salesman problem that forbids tours to pass through points more than once.

Figure 7.13

Using the reduction of
Figure 7.12.

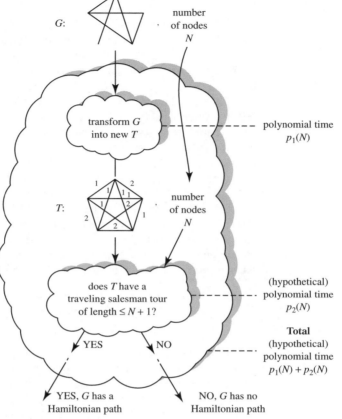

salesman tour that is no longer than $N + 1$, where N is the number of nodes in G. The answer to the first question on G is "yes" precisely when the answer to the second question on T is "yes." Notice, too, that the transformation takes only a polynomial amount of time.

Why is this fact of interest? Because it shows that, in terms of tractability, the Hamiltonian path problem is no worse than the traveling salesman problem; if the latter has a reasonable solution then so does the former. Figure 7.13 illustrates how the reduction is used to obtain a reasonable Hamiltonian path algorithm from a (hypothetical) reasonable traveling salesman algorithm.

Now comes the fact that establishes the common fate phenomenon of the NP-complete problems: every NP-complete problem is polynomially reducible to every other! Consequently, tractability of one implies tractability of all, and intractability of one implies intractability of all.

It is interesting that to establish a newly-considered problem R as NP-complete we need not construct polynomial-time reductions between R and all other NP-complete problems. It suffices, in fact, to polynomially reduce R to a single problem already known to be NP-complete, call it Q, and to reduce another such problem (possibly the same one), call it S, to R. The first of these reductions shows that, in terms of tractability, R cannot be any *worse* than Q, and the second shows that it cannot be any *better* than S. Thus, if Q is tractable so is R, and if R is tractable so is S. But since Q and S are both NP-complete, they stand and fall together, hence R stands and falls with them too, implying its own NP-completeness. It follows that once we know of one NP-complete problem we can show that others are NP-complete too by using the reduction mechanism twice for each new candidate problem. Actually, in practice one carries out only the second of these reductions. To establish the fact that R cannot be any worse than the NP-complete problems, that is, it is *in* NP, it is usually easier to exhibit a short certificate or a polynomial-time magical nondeterministic algorithm than to explicitly reduce R to some known NP-complete problem. Also, to show that a problem R is *complete* in NP, we do not necessarily need a problem previously shown to be NP-complete. Instead, we can use a general argument to show that every problem in NP can be polynomially reduced to R.

Now, clearly all this had to start somewhere; there had to be a *first* problem proved to be NP-complete. Indeed, in 1971 the satisfiability problem for the propositional calculus was shown to be NP-complete, thus providing the anchor for NP-completeness proofs. The result, known as **Cook's theorem**, is considered to be one of the most important results in the theory of algorithmic complexity. Its proof relies on concepts we shall discuss in Chapter 9.

◼ Reducing Oranges to Apples

Polynomial-time reductions between NP-complete problems can be far subtler than the one just given. While it is not at all clear what timetables and monkey puzzles have to do with each other, we know that there *must* be a reduction between them, for they are both NP-complete. Since a new problem requires only one reduction in each direction, often the best-known reduction between two problems consists of a chain of reductions leading through several other NP-complete problems.

It would be fruitless to tire you with one of the really difficult cases, so here is an example of a reduction that is not too difficult but not quite trivial either. We show how to reduce the problem of three-coloring a map to that of satisfiability in the propositional calculus. This establishes that the former cannot be any worse, in terms of tractability, than the latter. Specifically, we have to describe an algorithm that inputs the description of some arbitrary map M, and outputs a propositional sentence F, such that M can be three-colored if, and only if, F is satisfiable. Furthermore, the algorithm must run in polynomial time, which, among other things, implies that the number of symbols in the formula F is allowed to be at most polynomially more than the number of countries in M.

Let M be a given map, assumed to involve the countries $C_1, \ldots, C_N$. We shall describe the sentence F, and argue that its size is polynomial in N. You should be able to see quite easily how this can be turned into a general polynomial-time algorithm that works for every M.

◼ Assuming the three colors are R, B, and Y (red, blue, and yellow), the sentence F involves $3N$ elementary assertions, one for each combination of color and country. The assertion "C_1-is-Y", for example, is intended to mean that country C_1 is colored yellow. We construct F by "and"-ing together two parts.

The first part asserts that each country is colored with exactly one of the three colors, no more and no less. It consists of "and"-ing together the following subsentences for each country C_I:

$$((C_I\text{-}is\text{-}R \ \& \ \sim C_I\text{-}is\text{-}B \ \& \ \sim C_I\text{-}is\text{-}Y)$$

$$\vee \ (C_I\text{-}is\text{-}B \ \& \ \sim C_I\text{-}is\text{-}R \ \& \ \sim C_I\text{-}is\text{-}Y)$$

$$\vee \ (C_I\text{-}is\text{-}Y \ \& \ \sim C_I\text{-}is\text{-}B \ \& \ \sim C_I\text{-}is\text{-}R))$$

meaning that C_I is colored red and not blue or yellow, *or* blue and not red or yellow, *or* yellow and not blue or red. The second part is obtained by identifying all pairs of countries C_I and C_J that are adjacent in the map M, and "and"-ing together the following subsentences for each such pair, asserting that the two countries are not colored with the same color:

$$\sim ((C_I\text{-}is\text{-}R \ \& \ C_J\text{-}is\text{-}R)$$

$$\vee \ (C_I\text{-}is\text{-}B \ \& \ C_J\text{-}is\text{-}B)$$

$$\vee \ (C_I\text{-}is\text{-}Y \ \& \ C_J\text{-}is\text{-}Y))$$

meaning that it is *not* the case that both C_I and C_J are colored red, or both are colored blue, or both are colored yellow.

How long is the sentence F? The first part is linear in N, since it contains one subsentence of fixed length for each country C_I. The second is no worse than quadratic in N, since it contains one fixed-length subsentence for each pair of adjacent countries I and J, and there can be no more than N^2 pairs. Hence, clearly F is polynomial in N.

It remains to show that F is satisfiable if, and only if, M is three-colorable. To prove this, we proceed in both directions. If M is three-colorable by some coloring scheme S (which, it can be assumed, involves the colors red, blue, and yellow), we can satisfy F simply by assigning "true" to the elementary assertion $C_I\text{-}is\text{-}X$ if the scheme S calls for coloring country C_I with color X, and "false" otherwise. It is easy to see that all parts of F are thus satisfied. Conversely, if F is satisfied by some truth assignment S, then M can be colored with three colors by assigning color X to country C_I precisely when the assignment S assigns "true" to the assertion $C_I\text{-}is\text{-}X$. The construction of F guarantees that each country is colored with exactly one color, and that there are no conflicts. This concludes the reduction.

Is P Equal to NP?

Just as NP stands for the class of problems that admit nondeterministic polynomial-time algorithms, P stands for what we have been calling tractable problems; namely, those that admit polynomial-time algorithms. The large class of problems we have been extensively discussing, the NP-complete problems, are the "hardest" problems in NP, in the sense that there are polynomial-time reductions from *every* problem in NP to each of them. If one of them turns out to be easy, that is, in P, then *all* problems in NP are also in P. Now, since obviously P is part of NP (why?), the question really boils down to whether P is equal to NP or not.

The **P** $=$ **NP?** problem, as it is called, has been open since it was posed in 1971, and is one of the most difficult unresolved problems in computer science. It is definitely the most intriguing. Either all of these interesting and important problems can be solved reasonably by computer, or none of them can. Many of the most talented theoretical computer scientists have worked on the problem, but to no avail. Most of them believe that P $\neq$ NP, meaning that the NP-complete problems are inherently *in*tractable, but no one knows for sure. In any case, showing that an algorithmic problem is NP-complete is regarded as weighty evidence of its probable intractability.

Some problems that have been shown to be *in* NP are not known to be either NP-complete or in P. For many years the best-known example of this was the problem of testing a number for **primality**; that is, asking whether it has any factors (numbers that divide it exactly) other than 1 and itself. If the problem is phrased in a form that asks whether the number is *not* a prime, there is an obvious short certificate in case the answer is "yes" (that is, the number is not prime). The certificate is simply a factor that is neither 1 nor the number itself. We check that it is indeed a factor by a simple division. Thus, the *non*primality problem is easily seen to be in NP. On the other hand, if the problem asks whether the number *is* a prime, it is far from obvious that there is a short certificate.[5] Nevertheless, almost 30 years ago the primality problem was also shown to be in NP. Still, just as for all problems that are in NP but are not known to be in P, there was always the nagging possibility that the primality problem would turn out to be intractable.

The big surprise is that primality is in fact in P. Just shortly before this edition of the book was completed, a remarkable polynomial-time algorithm for primality was discovered (nicknamed the AKS algorithm, after the initials of its authors), thus putting to rest one of the most interesting open problems in algorithmics. Chapters 11 and 12 contain more detailed discussions of prime numbers and their detection, and some issues related to their centrality and importance in algorithmics.

Imperfect Solutions to NP-Complete Problems

Many NP-complete decision problems are yes/no versions of what are sometimes called **combinatorial optimization** problems. The traveling salesman problem is a good example. Clearly, the problem of actually *finding* an optimal tour cannot be tractable without the yes/no version being tractable too, since once we have found an optimal tour we can easily check whether its overall length is no greater than a given number K. For this reason, the original problem is also said to be NP-complete, and thus, as far as current knowledge goes, it is intractable.

In some cases, however, we can solve optimization problems in ways that are less than perfect, yet of considerable practical value. The algorithms designed for this purpose are generically called **approximation algorithms**, and are based on the assumption that in many cases a less than optimal tour is better than no tour at all, and a timetable with a few constraint violations is better than no timetable at all.

---

[5] In number-theoretic problems, the size of the input number is not that number itself but, rather, its length in digits, which is on the order of the *logarithm* of the number.

One type of approximation algorithm produces results that are guaranteed to be "close" to the optimal solution. For example, there is a rather clever algorithm for a certain version of the traveling salesman problem (where the graph is assumed to represent a realistic two-dimensional map) that runs in cubic time and produces a tour that is guaranteed to be no longer than 1.5 times the (unknown) optimal tour. The guarantee, of course, is based on a rigorous mathematical proof. Actually, there is a much less sophisticated algorithm that guarantees a tour of no longer than *twice* the optimal tour, and which you might want to try constructing. It is based on finding the minimal spanning tree (see Chapters 4 and 6) and traversing each edge in it twice. (Why is the tour no longer than twice the optimum?)

Another approach to approximation yields solutions that are not guaranteed to be *always* within some fixed range of the optimum, but to be very close to the optimum *almost* always. Here the analysis required is similar to that carried out for the average-case performance of algorithms, and usually involves somewhat sophisticated probability theory. For example, there is a fast algorithm for the traveling salesman problem that for some input graphs might yield tours much longer than the optimum. However, in the vast majority of cases the algorithm yields almost optimal tours. This particular algorithm is based upon a **heuristic**, that is, rule of thumb, whereby the graph is first partitioned into many local clusters containing very few points each. One then finds the optimal tours within each of these, and then combines them into a global tour by a method similar to the greedy algorithm for the spanning tree problem.

Do NP-complete problems always admit fast approximation algorithms? If we are willing to be slightly flexible in our requirements for optimality, can we be sure to succeed? Well, this is a difficult question. People had harbored hopes that powerful approximation algorithms could be found for most NP-complete problems even without knowing the answer to the real P vs. NP question. The hope was that we might be able to come close to the optimal result even though finding the *true* optimum would still be beyond our reach. In recent years, however, this hope has been delivered a crippling blow with the discovery of more bad news: for many NP-complete problems (not all), approximations turn out to be no easier than full solutions! Finding a good approximation algorithm for any one of these problems has been shown to be tantamount to finding a good nonapproximate solution.[6]

This has the following striking consequence. Finding a good approximation algorithm for one of these special NP-complete problems is enough to render all the NP-complete problems tractable; that is, it would establish that P = NP. Put the other way around, if P $\neq$ NP, then not only do the NP-complete problems have no good *full* solutions, but many of them can't even be approximated!

As an example, consider the problem that asks for the minimal number of colors required to color an arbitrary graph. Since this is NP-complete, researchers looked for an approximation algorithm that would come close to the optimal number in a polynomial amount of time. So perhaps there is a method, which, given an input graph, finds a number that is never more than 10% or 20% larger than the minimal number of colors needed to color the network. Well, it turns out that this is as hard as the real thing. It has been shown that if any polynomial-time algorithm can find

---

[6] These results are closely related to the powerful recent characterization of NP in terms of probabilistic interaction, which we discuss in Chapter 12.

a coloring that is within any fixed constant factor of the minimal number of colors needed to color a graph, then there is a polynomial-time algorithm for the original problem of finding the optimal number itself. This has the far-reaching consequence just described: discovering a good approximation algorithm for coloring graphs is just as difficult as showing that P = NP.

■ ■

Provably Intractable Problems

Despite our inability to find reasonable solutions to the numerous NP-complete problems, we are not sure that such solutions do not exist; for all we know, NP-complete problems might have very efficient polynomial-time solutions. It should be realized, however, that many problems (though not the NP-complete ones) have been *proved* to be intractable, and these are not restricted only to ones (like the Towers of Hanoi) whose outputs are unreasonably lengthy. Here are some examples.

Towards the end of Chapter 1 we discussed the problem of deciding whether, given a board configuration of chess, White has a guaranteed winning strategy. As you will have realized, the **game tree** for chess grows exponentially. In other words, if we fix some initial configuration at the root of the tree and each node is extended downwards by descendants corresponding to all possible next configurations, the size of the tree, in general, becomes exponential in its depth. If we want to look N moves ahead we might have to consider K^N configurations, for some fixed number K that is larger than 1.

This fact does not mean that chess, as a game, is intractable. In fact, since there are only finitely many configurations in the entire game (albeit a very large number of them) the winning strategy problem is not really an algorithmic problem, for which we can talk about order-of-magnitude performance. The algorithmic problem commonly associated with chess involves a *generalized* version, where there is a different game for each N, played on an N by N board, the set of pieces and allowed moves being extended appropriately. Generalized chess, as well as generalized checkers, has indeed been shown to have an exponential-time lower bound. It is thus **provably intractable**.

In addition to these somewhat contrived generalizations of fixed-size games, several very simple games whose initial configurations vary in size have also been shown to have exponential-time lower bounds. One of them is called **roadblock**, and is played by two players, Alice and Bob, on a network of intersecting roads, each colored with one of three colors. (Roads may pass under others.) Certain intersections are marked "Alice wins" or "Bob wins," and each player has a fleet of cars that occupy certain intersections. In his (or her) turn, a player moves one of his cars along a stretch of road, all of whose segments must be of the same color, to a new intersection, as long as no cars are met along the way. The winner is the first player to reach one of his "win" intersections.

The algorithmic problem inputs the description of a network, with cars placed at certain intersections, and asks whether Alice (whose turn it is) has a winning

Figure 7.14

A roadblock
configuration that
Alice can win.

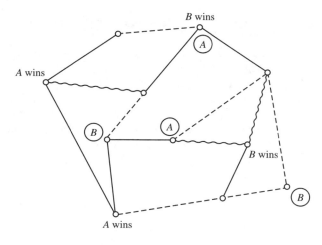

strategy. Figure 7.14 shows a roadblock configuration that Alice can win, no matter what Bob does. (How?)

The roadblock problem has an exponential-time lower bound, meaning that there is a constant number K (greater than 1) such that any algorithm solving the problem takes time that grows at least as fast as K^N, where N is the number of intersections in the network. In other words, while certain configurations might be easy to analyze, there is no practical algorithmic method, and *there never will be*, for determining whether a given player has a guaranteed strategy for winning a roadblock game. For the best algorithm we might design there will always be relatively small configurations that will cause it to run for an unreasonable amount of time.

We should remark that these inherently exponential-time problems do not admit the kind of short certificates that NP-complete problems do. Not only is it provably difficult to tell whether there is a winning strategy for a roadblock player from a given configuration, it is also impossibly time consuming to convince someone that there is one, *if* there is.

A Provably Intractable Satisfiability Problem

Another example of a provably intractable problem involves logical satisfiability. Earlier, we met with the propositional calculus, a formalism that enables us to write sentences consisting of logical combinations of basic assertions. A set of truth values for the basic assertions determines a truth value for the sentence itself. A sentence in the propositional calculus is thus "static" in nature—its truth depends only on the present truth values of its constituents. In Chapter 5 we briefly discussed *dynamic* logics, in which we are allowed to use the construct:

after(A, F)

where A is an algorithm and F is an assertion, or statement. It asserts that F is true after A is executed. Here, of course, the truth of a sentence no longer depends only on the state of affairs at present, but also on the state of affairs after the algorithm is executed.

One version of dynamic logic, called **propositional dynamic logic** (or **PDL** for short), restricts the algorithms, or programs, allowed inside the **after** construct to be combinations of unspecified elementary programs. Just as we can build up complex assertions from basic assertion symbols, using &, ∨, ~, and →, we can now build up complex programs from basic program symbols, using programming constructs such as sequencing, conditional branching, and iteration. Programs and assertions are then combined using the **after** construct. The following is a sentence of PDL, which states that E is false after the two programs inside the **after** are executed in order:

after(**while** E **do** A **end**; **if** E **then do** B **end**, $\sim E$)

This sentence is always true, no matter what assertion E stands for, and no matter what programs A and B stand for, even if B might have the ability to change E's truth value. You are encouraged to convince yourself of this fact.

The satisfiability problem for the propositional calculus is interesting because it concerns the feasibility of reasoning about logical sentences of *static* nature. In the same vein, the satisfiability problem for PDL is interesting because it concerns the feasibility of reasoning about logical sentences of *dynamic* nature, involving programs and some of their most elementary properties. The satisfiability problem for the propositional calculus is NP-complete, and is hence *suspected* to be intractable. The satisfiability problem for PDL, on the other hand, has an exponential-time lower bound, and is hence *known* to be intractable. There is no algorithmic method, and there never will be, which can be used in practice to decide whether PDL sentences can be made true. Any such algorithm will necessarily run for formidable amounts of time on certain sentences of very reasonable size.

We should remark that all of the problems just described (chess, checkers, roadblock, and PDL) happen to admit exponential-time algorithms, so that we have matching upper and lower bounds, and thus we know their tractability status exactly; they are all inherently exponential-time problems.

■ Problems That Are Even Harder!

This chapter has been based on the assumption that algorithmic problems whose best algorithms are exponential in time are intractable. However, there are problems that are even worse. Among these, some of the most interesting ones involve satisfiability and truth determination in various rich logical formalisms.

We have already met with the propositional calculus and PDL, in which basic assertions were simply symbols like E and F that could take on truth values. However, when statements are made about real mathematical objects, such as numbers, we want the basic assertions to be more expressive. We would like to be able to write $X = 15$, or $Y + 8 > Z$; we would like to be able to consider *sets* of numbers or other objects, and talk about all elements in a set; we would like to talk about the *existence* of elements with certain properties, and so on. There are numerous logical formalisms that cater for such desires, and most interesting mathematical theorems, conjectures, and statements can be written in them.

It is, therefore, natural that computer scientists seek efficient methods for determining whether sentences in such formalisms are true; this is one way to establish absolute mathematical truth. Now, we know that satisfiability in the propositional calculus *most probably* cannot be determined in less than exponential time, since the problem is NP-complete, and that truth in PDL *definitely* cannot, since this problem is provably exponential. Several of the more elaborate formalisms are much worse.

Consider the function 2^{2^N} which is $2 \times 2 \times \ldots \times 2$, with 2 appearing 2^N times. If N is 5 the value is well over a billion, while if N is 9 the value is much larger than our friend, the number of protons in the known universe. The function 2^{2^N}, of course, relates to the unreasonable 2^N, just as 2^N relates to the very reasonable function N. It is therefore *doubly* unreasonable, and in fact is referred to as a **double-exponential**. The **triple-exponential** function $2^{2^{2^N}}$ is defined similarly, as are all the K-fold exponential-time functions $2^{2^{\cdots 2^N}}$ with K appearances of 2.

Several formalisms have been shown to have lower bounds of double-exponential time. Among these is a logic known as **Presburger arithmetic**, which allows us to talk about positive integers, and variables whose values are positive integers. It also allows the "+" operation, and the "=" symbol. We combine assertions using the logical operations of propositional calculus, as well as the quantifiers **exists**X and **forall**X. For example, the following formula states that there are infinitely many even numbers, by stating that for every X there is an even Y that is at least as large as X:

forall$X$ **exists**Y **exists**Z $(X + Z = Y$ & **exists**W $(W + W = Y))$

While truth in Presburger arithmetic is provably double-exponential, another formalism, called WS1S, is far worse. In WS1S we can talk not only about (positive) integers, but also about *sets* of integers. We can assert that a set S contains an element X by writing $X \in S$.

■ The following is a true formula of WS1S, stating that every even number is obtained by adding 2 to 0 some number of times.

forall$B$ $((0 \in B$ & **forall**X $(X \in B \rightarrow X + 2 \in B))$
$\rightarrow$ **forall**Y $($**exists**W $(Y = W + W) \rightarrow Y \in B))$

It accomplishes this by asserting that any set B, which contains 0, and contains $X + 2$ whenever it contains X, must contain all even numbers.

WS1S is unimaginably difficult to analyze. It has actually been shown to admit no K-fold exponential algorithm, for any K! (Exclamation mark here, not factorial . . .) This means that for any algorithm A that determines truth of WS1S formulas (and there are such algorithms), and for any fixed number K, there will be formulas of length N, for larger and larger N, that will require A to run for longer than $2^{2^{\cdots 2^N}}$ time units, with K appearances of 2. In such devastating cases we say that the decision problem is provably **nonelementary**. Not only is it intractable, it is not even doubly or triply intractable. Its time performance is worse than any K-fold exponential, and we might justifiably say that it is of *unlimited* intractability.

◼ Unreasonable Amounts of Memory Space

Although we have committed ourselves to concentrate on time performance, we must spend a moment contemplating unreasonable memory-space requirements. There are algorithmic problems that have been proven to have lower bounds of exponential space. This means that any algorithm solving them will require, say, 2^N memory cells on certain inputs of size N. In fact, it can be shown that a consequence of a double-exponential-time lower bound (like that of the truth problem for Presburger arithmetic) is an exponential-space lower bound. Similarly, a nonelementary lower bound on time (like that of truth in WS1S) implies a nonelementary lower bound on space too.

These facts have striking consequences. If a problem has a 2^N lower bound on memory space, then for any algorithm there will be inputs of quite reasonable size (less than 270, to be specific) that would require so much space for intermediate data that even if each bit were to be the size of a *proton*, the whole known universe would not suffice to write it all down! The situation is clearly unimaginably worse for nonelementary space bounds.

◼ ◼

◼ Research on Complexity Classes and Intractability

In the mid-1960s people began to realize the importance of obtaining polynomial-time algorithms for algorithmic problems, and the significance of the dividing line of Figure 7.6 became apparent. Ever since, the issues and concepts discussed in this chapter have been the subject matter of intense and widespread research by many theoretical computer scientists.

Every now and then, a polynomial-time algorithm or an exponential-time lower bound is found for a problem whose tractable/intractable status was unknown. The most striking recent example is primality testing, mentioned earlier. Another is linear planning, better known as **linear programming**. Linear planning is a general framework within which we can phrase many kinds of planning problems arising in organizations where time, resources, and personnel constraints have to be met in a cost-efficient way. The linear planning problem, it must be emphasized, is not NP-complete, but the best algorithm that anyone was able to find for it was an exponential-time procedure known as the **simplex method**. Despite the fact that certain inputs forced the simplex method to run for an exponential amount of time, they were rather contrived, and tended not to arise in practice; when the method was used for real problems, even of nontrivial size, it usually performed very well. Nevertheless, the problem was not known officially to be in P, nor was there a lower bound to show that it wasn't.

In 1979, an ingenious polynomial-time algorithm was found for the problem, but it was something of a disappointment. The exponential-time simplex method outperformed it in many of the cases arising in practice. Nevertheless, it did show that linear programming is in P. Moreover, recent work based on this algorithm has produced more efficient versions, and people currently believe that before long there will be a fast polynomial-time algorithm for linear planning, which will be useful in practice for all inputs of reasonable size.

This kind of work is aimed at improving our knowledge about specific problems, and is analogous to the search for efficient algorithms within P itself, as discussed in Chapter 6.

Work of more general nature involves **complexity classes** such as P and NP themselves. Here we are interested in identifying large and significant classes of problems, all of which share inherent performance characteristics. Using the prefix LOG for logarithmic, P for polynomial, EXP for exponential, and 2EXP for double-exponential, we can write LOGTIME for the class of problems solvable in logarithmic time, PTIME for the class called P above, PSPACE for the problems solvable with a polynomial amount of memory space, and so on. We can then establish the following inclusion relations (where $\subseteq$ means "is a subset of") (see Figure 7.15):

$$\text{LOGTIME} \subseteq \text{LOGSPACE} \subseteq \text{PTIME} \subseteq \text{PSPACE}$$

$$\subseteq \text{EXPTIME} \subseteq \text{EXPSPACE} \subseteq \text{2EXPTIME} \ldots$$

If we add the prefix N for "nondeterministic," writing, for example, NPTIME for NP, we obtain many more classes, and many interesting questions of the interrelationships arise. For example, it is known that NP falls between PTIME and PSPACE, but in many cases no one knows whether the $\subseteq$ symbols represent strict inclusions

Figure 7.15

Some complexity classes with sample problems.

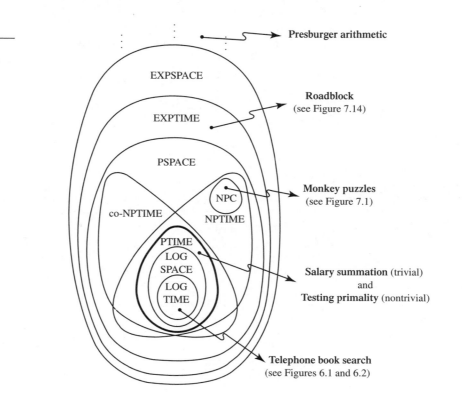

or not. Is there a problem in PSPACE that is not in PTIME? If there is, we would like to know which of the two inclusions in the following sequence is strict:

PTIME ⊆ NPTIME ⊆ PSPACE

The strictness of the first, of course, is just the P vs. NP problem.

We can also consider **dual** complexity classes, such as **co-NP**, for example, which is the class of problems whose **complement**, or dual version (in which the "yes" and "no" answers are interchanged) is in NP. It is not known, for example, whether NP = co-NP. On the other hand, it is known that if NP ≠ co-NP, then also P ≠ NP. The converse, however, is not true; it might be the case that NP and co-NP are equal, while P and NP are not. Many other questions arise, for some of which the answers are known, and for others they are not.

Another important area of research concerns approximate solutions, and solutions guaranteed to be good on average. These are sought for even if a problem is known or suspected to be intractable. Researchers are still trying to understand the connections between a problem's inherent worst-case time complexity, and the availability of fast approximate solutions.

Despite the rather disheartening nature of the facts discussed in this chapter, it appears that most common problems arising in everyday applications of computers can be solved efficiently. This statement is slightly misleading, however, since we tend to equate "common" and "everyday" problems with those that we know how to solve. In actuality, a growing number of problems arising in nontrivial applications of computers turn out to be NP-complete or worse. In such cases, we have to resort to approximation algorithms, or to probabilism and heuristics, as discussed in Chapters 11 and 15.

Before we return to more cheerful material, however, there is worse news to come. Some algorithmic problems admit no solutions at all, not even unreasonable ones.

■ Exercises

7.1. (a) Carry out the recursive analysis described in the text for the procedure **move** (the recursive procedure for solving the Towers of Hanoi problem).
(b) Prove a lower bound of 2^N on the Towers of Hanoi problem.
(c) Calculate the time for Towers of Hanoi with 64 rings according to the following cost: the N rings are of sizes 1 to N; moving a ring of size i takes i time units.

7.2. (a) Redo the calculation of the number of arrangements for the monkey puzzle, for the case where cards *may* be rotated.
(b) How long would an exhaustive search through all the arrangements you calculated in part (a) take, assuming, as in the text, that one billion arrangements can be evaluated every second (regardless of the number of cards such an arrangement contains)?
(c) Why is the suggestion that there might be an arrangement precisely when the number of distinct cards is a multiple of 17 silly? (Hint: try constructing a different set with a different number of cards, but with similar behavior.)

7.3. For each of the following pairs of time complexities of algorithms A and B, find the least positive integer N for which algorithm B is better than algorithm A:

A	B
$2^{(\log_2 N)^3}$	N^{10}
$3^{(\log_2 N)^5}$	$9^{(\log_2 N)^3}$
$N!$	5^N
N^N	$100 \times N!$
$(N^2)!$	$18 \times N^{N^2}$
$2^{2^{2^N}}$	$200 \times (N^2)^{N^2}$

7.4. (a) The following table adds several lines to the table in Figure 7.7. Fill in the missing entries.

	Maximal number of cards solvable in one hour:		
Function	with today's computer	with computer 100 times faster	with computer 1000 times faster
$\log N$	A		
$(\log N)^2$	B		
2^{N^2}	C		
2^{2^N}	D		

   (b) As in the above table, estimate the number of cards solvable in one hour by computers 10, 100 and 1000 times faster, but for the function $N!$, assuming 9 cards are solvable in an hour with present computers.

7.5. (a) Explain why the naive solution to the traveling salesman problem described in the text (considering all possible tours) has time complexity $O(N!)$.

   (b) Explain why the similarly naive solution to the Eulerian path problem given in the text, has time complexity $O((N^2)!)$, rather that $O(N!)$ too.

   (c) Prove the correctness of Euler's algorithm and establish its time complexity.

7.6. (a) For each of the following formulas in the propositional calculus, determine whether it is satisfiable, and if it is, find a satisfying truth assignment:

   $\varphi_1:$ $\sim E$
   $\varphi_2:$ $(\sim E \vee \sim F \vee G)\ \&\ E\ \&\ F$
   $\varphi_3:$ $(E\ \&\ F) \vee (\sim E\ \&\ \sim F)$
   $\varphi_4:$ $(E \vee F) \rightarrow (E \rightarrow \sim F)$
   $\varphi_5:$ $G\ \&\ (E \vee F)\ \&\ \sim(E\ \&\ F)\ \&\ (G \rightarrow E)\ \&\ (G \rightarrow \sim F)$
   $\varphi_6:$ $(E \vee F)\ \&\ \sim(E\ \&\ F)\ \&\ (E \rightarrow G)\ \&\ (G \rightarrow F)$
   $\varphi_7:$ $((E\ \&\ F) \vee (E\ \&\ \sim G))\ \&\ ((\sim E\ \&\ \sim F) \vee (E\ \&\ G))$

   (b) What is the number of truth assignments to a given formula in the propositional calculus with N distinct elementary propositions?

   (c) Show that satisfiability of formulas of length N in the propositional calculus can be checked in time $O(2^N)$. What is the amount of space your algorithm uses?

   (d) Improve the algorithm you proposed in part (c) to answer for a given formula, how many *satisfying* truth assignments it has. Are the time or space complexities of the new algorithm any worse than those of the previous one?

7.7. For each of the following formulas in propositional dynamic logic, determine if it is always true (i.e., true in any initial assignment to the elementary propositions, and under any interpretation of the basic programs):

φ_1 : **after**$(A;B, E) \rightarrow$ **after**$(A,$ **after**$(B, E))$

φ_2 : (**after**(A, E) & **after**$(A, F)) \rightarrow$ **after**$(A, E\&F)$

φ_3 : (**after**(A, E) & **after**$(A, F \rightarrow E)) \rightarrow$ **after**(A, F)

φ_4 : (**after**(A, E) & $(E \rightarrow F)) \rightarrow$ **after**(A, F)

φ_5 : (**after**(A, E) & **after**$(A, E \rightarrow F)) \rightarrow$ **after**(A, F)

φ_6 : (**after**(**if** E **then** A **else if** F **then** $A, E)$ & $(E \vee F)) \rightarrow$ **after**(A, E)

φ_7 : (**after**(**if** E **then** A **else** $(A;B), E)$ & **after**$(A, E \rightarrow$ **after**$(B, E)))$
$\rightarrow$ **after**$(A;B, E)$

φ_8 : (**after**(**while** E **do** $A, G)$ & **after**(**while** F **do** $A, G))$
$\rightarrow$ **after**(**while** $E\&F$ **do** $A, G)$

φ_9 : (**after**(**while** E **do** $A, G)$ & **after**(**while** F **do** $A, G))$
$\rightarrow$ **after**(**while** $E \vee F$ **do** $A, G)$

7.8. In this exercise "number" stands for "positive integer."

(a) State informally the meaning of each of the following formulas in Presburger arithmetic, and determine whether it is always true. Justify your answers.

χ_1 : **forall**X $(X = 1 \vee$ **exists**Y $(X = Y + 1))$

χ_2 : **forall**X **forall**Y **exists**Z $(X = Y + Z)$

χ_3 : $\sim$**forall**X **exists**Y **exists**Z $(X = Y + Z)$

χ_4 : **exists**X $(X + X = X)$

χ_5 : **forall**X **forall**Y
$((\textbf{exists}U$ $(X = U + U)$ & **exists**V $(Y = V + V)) \rightarrow$
exists$W$ $(X + Y = W + W))$

χ_6 : **exists**X **forall**Y (**exists**Z $(Y = Z + Z) \vee$ **exists**Z' $(X = Y + Z'))$

(b) State in Presburger arithmetic the following facts, and determine their truth or falsity:
   i. "The sum of any three odd numbers is even."
   ii. "Every number other than 1 is the sum of two numbers."
   iii. "There are infinitely many numbers divisible by 4."
   iv. "There are finitely many odd numbers divisible by 3."

7.9. Prove that a map can be colored by two colors precisely when every border point touches an even number of countries. (The "rest of the world" is considered to be a country too; a country that touches a border point "twice" is counted twice too.)

7.10. Explain why the optimization version of the graph coloring problem (the problem of finding the minimal number of colors required to color a given graph) is at least as hard as the yes/no version (finding whether a given graph is K-colorable for a given K).

7.11. In the text description reducing the Hamiltonian path problem to the traveling salesman problem, a given graph G with N nodes is transformed into a corresponding network T. Show that T admits a salesman tour of length at most $N + 1$ precisely when G contains a Hamiltonian path.

Let G be a given undirected graph consisting of a set of nodes N and a set of edges E. A subset N' of the nodes N is called a **vertex cover** for G, if for every edge in E, at least one of its endpoints is in N'. A subset N' of the nodes N is called a **dominating set** for G, if every node is either in N' or is connected by some edge from E to a node in N'. A subset N' of the nodes N is called a **clique** of G, if every two nodes in N' are connected by some edge from E.

The **vertex cover** problem is, given a graph G and a positive integer K, to find whether there is a vertex cover for G with at most K nodes. Similarly, the **dominating set** problem is, given a graph G and a positive integer K, to find whether there is a dominating set for G with at most K nodes. The **clique** problem is, given a graph G and a positive integer K, to find whether there is a clique of G with at least K nodes.

You are given the fact (which can be proved by reduction from the propositional satisfiability problem) that the vertex cover problem is as hard as the NP-complete problems.

7.12. (a) Show that the vertex cover problem is, in fact, NP-complete.
   (b) Prove that the clique problem is NP-complete, using the NP-completeness of the vertex cover problem to establish hardness.
   (c) Prove that the dominating set problem is NP-complete, using the NP-completeness of the vertex cover problem for showing hardness.
   (d) Prove that the dominating set problem, when restricted to graphs G that are *trees*, is solvable in polynomial time.

A **tasks instance** consists of a set T of tasks, a positive integer $d(t)$ for every t in T, indicating the *deadline* of task t, and a (noncircular) set of precedence constraints on T of the form "t precedes t'." A **schedule** for the task instance is an arrangement of the tasks of T in a sequence $\sigma : t_1, t_2, \ldots, t_l$ (every task appears in the sequence precisely once), such that all the precedence constraints are satisfied, that is, for any constraint "t_i precedes t_j," the task t_i precedes t_j in σ, namely, $i < j$.

The **task sequencing** problem is, given a tasks instance and a positive integer K, to find whether there exists a schedule σ as above, such that at most K tasks are *overtime* (task t_i is overtime if $d(t_i) \leq i$).

7.13. (a) Establish the NP-completeness of the task sequencing problem, using the NP-completeness of the clique problem you proved in Exercise 7.12(b).
   (b) Show that the task sequencing problem is solvable in polynomial time when restricted to $K = 0$, i.e., when no overtime task is accepted.
   (c) What is the complexity of the sequencing problem (i.e., can you show it to be solvable in polynomial time or is it NP-complete) when restricted to instances with no precedence constraints at all?

7.14. Construct a precise version of the twice-optimal algorithm for the traveling salesman problem hinted at in the text, and establish its correctness (i.e., show that it always produces a correct tour that is no longer than twice the optimal one).

7.15. (a) Prove the following containments and equalities between complexity classes:
   i. PTIME = co-PTIME.
   ii. PTIME $\subseteq$ NPTIME.
   iii. NPSPACE $\subseteq$ PSPACE.
   iv. PSPACE = NPSPACE.
   (b) Explain why your proof of the equality "PTIME = co-PTIME" in part (a) does not work for showing "NPTIME = co-NPTIME."

7.16. (a) Prove the following containments between complexity classes:
   i. LOGTIME $\subseteq$ LOGSPACE.
   ii. LOGSPACE $\subseteq$ PTIME.
   iii. PTIME $\subseteq$ PSPACE.
   iv. NPTIME $\subseteq$ PSPACE.
   v. NPSPACE $\subseteq$ EXPTIME.
   (b) Show that a problem is provably time-nonelementary precisely when it is provably space-nonelementary.

7.17. How would you go about showing that the double-exponential-time lower bound on determining truth in Presburger arithmetic implies an exponential-space lower bound on the problem?

Multitudes, multitudes in the valley of decision

JOEL 4: 14

CHAPTER 8

Noncomputability and Undecidability

or, Sometimes You Can't Get It Done At All!

In April 1984, *Time Magazine* ran a cover story on computer software. In the otherwise excellent article, there was a paragraph that quoted the editor of a software magazine as saying:

> *Put the right kind of software into a computer, and it will do whatever you want it to. There may be limits on what you can do with the machines themselves, but there are no limits on what you can do with software.*

In a way, the results of Chapter 7 already contradict this claim, by showing certain problems to be provably intractable. We might argue, however, that intractability is really a consequence of insufficient resources. Given enough time and memory space (albeit, unreasonably large amounts), perhaps any algorithmic problem can, in principle, be solved by the right software. Indeed, the reasons that people often fail in getting their computers to do what they want seem to fall roughly into three categories: insufficient money, insufficient time, and insufficient brains. With more money one could buy a larger and more sophisticated computer, supported by better software, and perhaps then get the job done. With more time one could wait longer for time-consuming algorithms to terminate, and with more brains one could perhaps invent algorithms for problems that seem to defy solution.

The algorithmic problems we wish to discuss in this chapter are such that no amount of money, time, or brains will suffice to yield solutions. We still require, of course, that algorithms terminate for each legal input within some finite amount of time, but we now allow that time to be unlimited. The algorithm can take as long as it wishes on each input, but it must eventually stop and produce the desired output. Similarly, while working on an input, the algorithm will be given any amount of memory it asks for. Even so, we shall see interesting and important problems, for which there simply are no algorithms, and it doesn't matter how clever we are, or how sophisticated and powerful our computers are.

Such facts have deep philosophical implications, not only on the limits of man-made machines, but also on our own limits as mortals with finite mass. Even if we were given unlimited pencil and paper, and an unlimited life span, there would be precisely-defined problems we could not solve. There are people who are opposed to drawing such extended conclusions from mere algorithmic results for various reasons. In consideration of the fact that the issue in this extended form definitely deserves a much broader treatment, we shall stick to pure algorithmics here, and leave the deeper implications to philosophers and neurobiologists. However, you should keep the existence of such implications in mind.

The Rules of the Game

Just to reclarify things, it should be emphasized that questions regarding the computer's ability to run companies, make good decisions, or love, are not relevant to our present discussions, since they do not involve precisely-defined algorithmic problems.

Another fact worth recalling is the requirement that an algorithmic problem be associated with a set of legal inputs, and that a proposed solution apply to all inputs in the set. As a consequence, if the set of inputs is *finite*, the problem always admits a solution. As a simple example, for a decision problem whose sole legal inputs are the items $I_1, I_2, \ldots, I_K$, there is an algorithm that "contains" a table with the K answers. The algorithm might read:

    (1) if the input is I_1 then output "yes" and stop;

    (2) if the input is I_2 then output "yes" and stop;

    (3) if the input is I_3 then output "no" and stop;

    . . .

    (K) if the input is I_K then output "yes" and stop.

This works, of course, because the finiteness of the set of inputs makes it possible to tabulate all input/output pairs and "hardwire" them into the algorithm. It might be difficult to carry out the tabulation (that is, to *construct* such a table-driven algorithm), but we are not interested in this "meta-difficulty" here. For our present purposes it suffices that finite problems always have solutions. It is the problems with infinitely many inputs that are really interesting. In such cases, a finite algorithm must be able to cope with infinitely many cases, prompting one to question the very existence of such algorithms for all problems.

To be able to state our claims as precisely, yet as generally, as possible, you will have to put up with a certain kind of terminological looseness in this chapter, to be fully justified in the next. Specifically, an arbitrary, but fixed, high-level programming language L is hereby implicitly assumed to be the medium for expressing algorithms, and the word "algorithm" will be used as a synonym for "program in L." In particular, when we say "no algorithm exists," we really mean that no program can be written in the language L. This convention might look a little pretentious here, apparently weakening our claims considerably. Not so. In the next chapter we shall see that, under the unlimited resources assumption, all programming languages are equivalent. Thus, if no program can be written in L, no program can be written in *any* effectively implementable language, running on any computer of any size or shape, now or at any time in the future.

The Tiling Problem: An Example

The following example is reminiscent of the monkey puzzle problem of Chapter 7. The problem involves covering large areas using square tiles, or cards, with colored edges, such that adjacent edges are monochromatic. A tile is a 1 by 1 square, divided into four by the two diagonals, each quarter colored with some color (see Figure 8.1). As with monkey cards, we assume that the tiles have fixed orientation and cannot be rotated. (In this case the assumption is, in fact, necessary. Can you see why?)

The algorithmic problem inputs some finite set T of tile descriptions, and asks whether any finite area, of any size, can be covered using only tiles of the kinds described in T, such that the colors on any two touching edges are the same. It is assumed that an unlimited number of tiles of each type is available, but that the number of types of tiles is finite.

Think of tiling a house. The input T is a description of the various types of tiles available, and the color-matching restriction reflects a rule enforced by an interior designer for aesthetic reasons. The question we would like to ask ahead of time is this: can a room of any size be tiled using only the available tile types, while adhering to the restriction?

This algorithmic problem and its variants are commonly known as **tiling problems**, but are sometimes called **domino problems**, the reason being the domino-like restriction on touching edges.

Figure 8.1

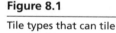

Tile types that can tile any area.

Figure 8.2

Tile types that cannot
tile even small areas.

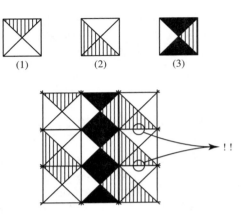

Figure 8.1 shows three tile types and a 5 by 5 tiling, and you should have no
difficulty verifying that the pattern in the lower portion of the figure can be extended
indefinitely in all directions to yield a tiling of any area whatsoever. In contrast, if
we exchange the bottom colors of tiles (2) and (3) it can be shown quite easily that
even very small rooms cannot be tiled at all. Figure 8.2 is meant as an illustration
of this fact. An algorithm for the tiling problem, then, should answer "yes" on the
inputs of Figure 8.1 and "no" on those of Figure 8.2.

The problem is to somehow mechanize or "algorithmicize" the reasoning employed in generating these answers. And here comes the interesting fact: this reasoning is impossible to mechanize. There is no algorithm, and there never will be, for
solving the tiling problem! More specifically, for any algorithm we might design for
the problem, there will always be input sets T (there will actually be infinitely many
such sets) upon which the algorithm will either run forever and never terminate, or
terminate with the wrong answer.

How can we make such a general claim, without restricting the basic operations
allowed in our algorithms? Surely, if *anything* is allowed, then the following two-step
procedure solves the problem:

(1) if the types in T can tile any area, output "yes" and stop;

(2) otherwise, output "no" and stop.

The answer lies in our use of "algorithm" here to stand for a program in a conventional programming language L. No program in any effectively executable language
can correctly implement the test in line (1) of the procedure, and hence, for our purposes, such a "procedure" will not be considered an algorithm at all.

An algorithmic problem that admits no algorithm is termed **noncomputable**; if it
is a decision problem, as is the case here and with most of the examples that follow,
it is termed **undecidable**. The tiling, or domino, problem is therefore undecidable.
There is no way we can construct an algorithm, to be run on a computer, any
computer, regardless of the amount of time and memory space required, that will
have the ability to decide whether arbitrary finite sets of tile types can tile areas of
any size.

Figure 8.3

The sphere of
algorithmic problems:
Version II.

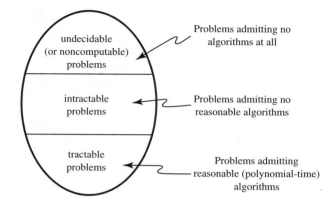

We can now refine the sphere of algorithmic problems appearing in Chapter 7 (see Figure 7.6), taking noncomputable problems into account. Figure 8.3 is the current version.

It is interesting to observe that the following, slightly different-looking problem, is actually equivalent to the one just described. In this version, instead of requiring that T be able to tile finite areas of any size, we require that T be able to tile the entire **integer grid**; that is, the entire infinite plane. One direction of the equivalence (if we can tile the entire plane then we can tile any finite area) is trivial, but the argument that establishes the other direction is quite delicate, and you are encouraged to try to find it for yourself.

Interestingly, the undecidability of this version means that there must be tile sets T that can be used to tile the entire grid, but not periodically. That is, while such a T admits a complete tiling of the grid, the tiling, unlike that of Figure 8.1, does *not* consist of a finite portion that repeats indefinitely in all directions. The reason for this is that otherwise we could decide the problem by an algorithm that would proceed to check all finite areas exhaustively, searching either for a finite area that cannot be tiled at all or for one that admits a repeat in all directions. By "otherwise" we mean that had it been the case that every tile set that admits a complete tiling of the grid would also admit a complete **periodic** tiling, this algorithm would be guaranteed to terminate for every input with the correct result.

■ Unboundedness Can Be Misleading

Some people react to results like this by saying: "Well, obviously the problem is undecidable, because a single input can give rise to a potentially infinite number of cases to check, and there is no way you can get an infinite job done by an algorithm that must terminate after finitely many steps." And indeed, here a single input T apparently requires all areas of all sizes to be checked (or, equivalently, as mentioned above, a single area of infinite size), and there seems to be no way to *bound* the number of cases to be checked.

This unboundedness-implies-undecidability principle is quite wrong, and can be very misleading. It is just like saying that any problem that seems to require

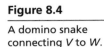

Figure 8.4

A domino snake
connecting *V* to *W*.

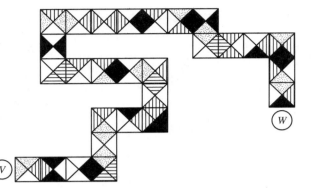

exponentially many checks is necessarily intractable. In Chapter 7 we saw the two problems of Hamiltonian paths and Eulerian paths, both of which seemed to require a search through all of the exponentially many paths in the input graph. The second problem, however, was shown to admit an easy polynomial-time algorithm. With undecidability it is also possible to exhibit two very similar variants of a problem, both of seemingly unbounded nature, which contrast in a rather surprising way to violate the principle.

The inputs in both cases contain a finite set *T* of tile types and two locations *V* and *W* on the infinite integer grid. Both problems ask whether it is possible to connect *V* to *W* by a "domino snake" consisting of tiles from *T*, with every two adjacent tiles having monochromatic touching edges (see Figure 8.4). Notice that a snake originating from *V* might twist and turn erratically, reaching unboundedly distant points before converging on *W*. Hence, on the face of it, the problem requires a potentially infinite search, prompting us to conjecture that it, too, is undecidable.

It is interesting, therefore, that the decidability of the domino snake problem depends on the portion of the plane available for laying down the connecting tiles. Clearly, if this portion is finite the problem is trivially decidable, as there are only finitely many possible snakes that can be positioned in a given finite area. The distinction we wish to make is between two *infinite* portions, and is quite counterintuitive. If snakes are allowed to go anywhere (that is, if the allowed portion is the entire plane), the problem is decidable, but if the allowed area is only a half of the plane (say, the upper half), the problem becomes undecidable! The latter case seems to be "more bounded" than the former, and therefore perhaps "more decidable." The facts, however, are quite different.

In fact, the domino snake problem has been proved to be undecidable for almost any conceivable infinite restriction of the plane, as long as the portion under consideration is unbounded in two orthogonal directions. So, it is undecidable not only in the half-plane, but in the quarter-plane, the one-eighth-plane, etc. The most striking result can be described as establishing that only a single point stands between decidability and undecidability: while the problem, as we have seen, is decidable in the whole plane, it becomes undecidable if even a *single point* is removed from the plane! More specifically, the inputs are the finite set *T* of tile types, the two points *V* and *W* on the infinite integer grid, and a third point *U*. The problem asks whether it is possible to connect *V* to *W* by a legal domino snake constructed from the tiles in *T*, whose tiles are allowed to go anywhere in the plane except through the point *U*.

Word Correspondence and Syntactic Equivalence

Here are two additional undecidable problems. The first, the **word correspondence problem**, involves forming a word in two different ways. Its inputs are two groups of words over some finite alphabet. Call them the Xs and the Ys. The problem asks whether it is possible to concatenate words from the X group, forming a new word, call it Z, so that concatenating the corresponding words from among the Ys forms the very same compound word Z. Figure 8.5(a) shows an example consisting of five words in each group, where the answer is "yes," since choosing the words for concatenation according to the sequence 2, 1, 1, 4, 1, 5 from either the Xs or the Ys yields the same word, "*aabbabbbabaabbaba*." On the other hand, the input described in Figure 8.5(b), which is obtained from Figure 8.5(a) by simply removing the first letter from the first word of each group, does not admit any such choice, as you can verify. Its answer is therefore "no."

The word correspondence problem is undecidable. There is no algorithm that can distinguish, in general, between the likes of Figures 8.5(a) and 8.5(b). The unbounded nature of the problem stems from the fact that the number of words that need to be chosen to yield the common compound word is not bounded. However, here too, we can point to a seemingly "less bounded" variant, in which it seems that there are more cases to check for, but which nevertheless is decidable. In it, the inputs are as before, but there is no restriction on the way choices are made from the Xs and Ys; even the number of words selected need not be the same. We are asking simply if it is possible to form a common compound word by concatenating some words from X and some words from Y. In Figure 8.5(b), which gave rise to a "no" for the standard version of the problem, the word "*babaa*," for example, can be obtained from the Xs by the sequence 3, 2, 2, and from the Ys by 1, 2, and hence is a "yes" in the new version. This more liberal problem actually admits a fast polynomial-time algorithm!

The second problem concerns the syntax of programming languages. Suppose someone provides us with the syntax rules of some language, say in the diagrammatic form of Figure 3.1. If someone else comes along with a different set of rules, we might be interested in knowing whether the two definitions are equivalent, in the sense that they define the same language; that is, the same syntactic class of statements

Figure 8.5

Instances of the word correspondence problem.

	1	2	3	4	5
X	*abb*	*a*	*bab*	*baba*	*aba*
Y	*bbab*	*aa*	*ab*	*aa*	*a*

(a) Admits a correspondence: 2, 1, 1, 4, 1, 5

	1	2	3	4	5
X	*bb*	*a*	*bab*	*baba*	*aba*
Y	*bab*	*aa*	*ab*	*aa*	*a*

(b) Admits no correspondence

(or programs). This problem is of relevance to the construction of compilers, since compilers, among their other chores, are also responsible for recognizing the syntactic validity of their input programs. In order to do so, they have a set of syntactic rules built in. It is quite conceivable that in the interest of making a compiler more efficient, its designer would want to replace the set of rules with a more compact set. Clearly, it is important to know in advance that the two sets are interchangeable.

This problem is also undecidable. No algorithm exists, which, upon reading from the input two sets of syntax rules, will be able to decide in finite time whether they define precisely the same language.

Problems with Outputs Are No Better

We should perhaps re-emphasize the fact that technical convenience is the only reason for limiting ourselves to decision problems here. Each of the undecidable problems we describe has variants that ask for outputs, and which are also noncomputable. Trivial variants are those that are basically decision problems in (a rather transparent) disguise. An example is the problem that asks, for a given set of colored tile types T, to output the size of the smallest area not tileable by T, and 0 if every finite area is tileable. It is clear that this problem cannot be computable, since the distinction in the output between 0 and all the other numbers is precisely the distinction between "yes" and "no" in the original problem.

More sophisticated problems hide the ability to make an undecidable decision far better. The following problem is noncomputable too. In order to define it, let us say that a finite portion of the grid is a **limited area** for a set T of tiles, if it can be tiled legally by T, but cannot be extended in any way by more tiles without violating the tiling rules. Now, the problem involves finding particular sets T that have large limited areas. Specifically, the algorithmic problem is given a number N (which should be at least 2), and is asked to output the size of the largest limited area, for *any* set of tiles, that involves no more than N colors. You should convince yourself that for any $N > 1$ this number is well defined.

It is far from obvious that in order to solve the limited area problem we need the ability to decide the likes of the tiling problem. And so, although the problem gives rise to a well-defined, non-yes/no function of N, this function simply cannot be computed algorithmically.

Algorithmic Program Verification

In Chapter 5 we asked whether computers can verify our programs for us. That is, we were after an **automatic verifier** (see Figure 5.4). Specifically, we are interested in the decision problem whose inputs are the description of an algorithmic problem and the text of an algorithm, or program, that is believed to solve the given problem.

We are interested in determining algorithmically whether the given algorithm solves the given problem or not. In other words, we want a "yes" if for each of the problem's legal inputs the algorithm will terminate and its outputs will be precisely as specified by the problem, and we want a "no" if there is even one input for which the algorithm either fails to terminate or terminates with the wrong results. Note that the problem calls for an algorithm that works for *every* choice of a problem/algorithm pair.

Clearly, the **verification problem** cannot be discussed without being more specific about the allowed inputs. Which programming language is to be used for coding the input algorithms? Which specification language is to be used for describing the input algorithmic problems?

As it happens, even very humble choices of these languages render the verification problem undecidable. Even if the allowed programs can manipulate only integers or strings of symbols, and can employ only the basic operations of addition or attachment of symbols to strings, they cannot be verified algorithmically. Candidate algorithmic verifiers might work nicely for many sample inputs, but the general problem is undecidable, meaning that there will always be algorithms that the verifier will not be able to verify. As discussed in Chapter 5, this implies the futility of hoping for a software system that would be capable of automatic program verification. It also reduces the hope for optimizing compilers capable of transforming programs into optimally efficient ones. Such a compiler might not even be able to tell, in general, whether a new candidate version even solves the same problem as the original program, let alone whether it is more efficient.

Moreover, it is not only verifying that a program meets its full required specification that is undecidable, but even verifying only certain parts thereof. Thus, for example, checking that programs do not have the Year 2000 bug (see Chapters 5 and 13) is also impossible in general. A candidate Y2K detector could do its job well for some kinds of input programs, and it might be able to verify limited kinds of Y2K issues, but as a general solution to the problem it is bound to fail. We can thus forget about a computerized solution to the Y2K problem or other such sweeping attempts at establishing our expectations of software by computer.

Taking this even further, not only is full or partial verification undecidable, we cannot even decide whether a given algorithm merely *terminates* on its legal inputs. Moreover, it is not even decidable whether the algorithm terminates on *one* given input! These problems of termination deserve special attention.

The Halting Problem

Consider the following algorithm A:

    (1) while $X \neq 1$ do the following: $X \leftarrow X - 2$;

    (2) stop.

In other words, A reduces its input X by 2 until X becomes equal to 1. Assuming that its legal inputs consist of the positive integers $\langle 1, 2, 3, \ldots \rangle$, it is quite obvious that A halts precisely for *odd* inputs. An even number will be decreased repeatedly by 2 until it reaches 2, and will then "miss" the 1, running forever through 0, -2, -4, -6, and so on. Hence, for this particular algorithm, deciding whether a legal input will

Figure 8.6

The halting problem.

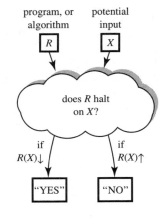

cause it to terminate is trivial: just check whether the input is odd or even and answer accordingly.

Here is another, similar-looking, algorithm B:

(1) while $X \neq 1$ do the following:
    (1.1) if X is even do $X \leftarrow X/2$;
    (1.2) otherwise (X is odd) do $X \leftarrow 3X + 1$;

(2) stop.

The algorithm B repeatedly halves X if it is even, but *increases* it more than threefold if it is odd. For example, if B is run on 7, the sequence of values is: 7, 22, 11, 34, 17, 52, 26, 13, 40, 20, 10, 5, 16, 8, 4, 2, 1, eventually resulting in termination. Actually, if we try running the algorithm on some arbitrary positive integer we will find that it terminates. The sequence of values is often quite unusual, reaching surprisingly high values, and fluctuating unpredictably before it reaches 1. Indeed, over the years B has been tested on numerous inputs and has always terminated. Nevertheless, no one has been able to prove that it terminates for *all* positive integers, although most people believe that it does. The question of whether or not this is the case is actually a difficult open problem in the branch of mathematics known as **number theory**. Now, if indeed B (or any other program) terminates for all its inputs, there *is* a proof of this fact, as discussed in Chapter 5, but for B no one has found such a proof yet. These examples illustrate just how difficult it is to analyze the termination properties of even very simple algorithms.

Let us now define a specific version of the problem of algorithmic termination, called the **halting problem**. We define it here in terms of our agreed-on high-level programming language L.

The problem has two inputs: the text of a legal program R in the language L and a potential input X to R.[1] The halting problem asks whether R would have terminated had we run it on the input X, a fact we denote by $R(X)\downarrow$. The case of R not terminating, or *diverging*, on X is denoted $R(X)\uparrow$ (see Figure 8.6).

[1] We can assume that R expects just one input, since a number of inputs can be encoded into a single string of symbols, with the various parts separated by some special symbol like "#." This point is treated in more detail in Chapter 9.

As already stated, the halting problem is undecidable, meaning that there is no way to tell, in a finite amount of time, whether a given R will terminate on a given X. In the interest of solving this problem, it is tempting to propose an algorithm that will simply run R on X and see what happens. Well, if and when execution terminates, we can justly conclude that the answer is "yes." The difficulty is in deciding when to stop waiting and say "no." We cannot simply give up at some point and conclude that since R has not terminated until now it never will. Perhaps if we had left R just a little longer it *would* have terminated. Running R on X, therefore, does not do the job, and, as stated, nothing can do the job, since the problem is undecidable.

■ Nothing about Computing is Computable!

The fact that verification and halting are undecidable is only one small part of a *far* more general phenomenon, which is actually much deeper and a lot more devastating. There is a remarkable result, called **Rice's theorem**, which shows that not only can we not verify programs or determine their halting status, but we can't really figure out *anything* about them. No algorithm can decide *any* nontrivial property of computations. More precisely, let us say we are interested in deciding some property of programs, which is (1) true of some programs but not of others, and (2) insensitive to the syntax of the program and to its method of operation or algorithm; that is, it is a property of what the program does, of the problem it solves, and not of the particular form that solution takes. For example, we might want to know whether a program ever outputs a "yes," whether it always produces numbers, whether it is equivalent to some other program, etc. etc.

Rice's theorem tells us is that *no* such property of programs can be decided. Not even one. They are *all* undecidable. We can really forget about being able to reason automatically about programs, or to deduce things about what our programs do. This is true whether our programs are small or large, simple or complex, or whether what we want to find out is a general property or something petty and idiosyncratic. Virtually *nothing* about computation is computable!

Now, how about that?

■ ■

■ Proving Undecidability

How do we prove that a problem P is undecidable? How do we establish the fact that no algorithm exists for solving P, no matter how clever the algorithm designer is?

This situation is similar to that described in Chapter 7 for the NP-complete problems. First there has to be one initial problem, whose undecidability is established using some direct method. In the case of undecidability this role is played by the halting problem, which we shall prove undecidable later. Once such a first undecidable problem exists, the undecidability of other problems is established by exhibiting **reductions** from problems already known to be undecidable to the problems in question. The difference is that here a reduction from problem P to problem Q need not necessarily be bounded; it can take any amount of time or memory space. All that is required is that there is an algorithmic way of transforming a P-input into a Q-input, in such a way that P's yes/no answer to an input is precisely Q's answer to the transformed input. In this way, if P is already known to be undecidable Q must be undecidable too. The reason is that otherwise we could have solved P by an algorithm that would take any input, transform it into an input for Q and ask the Q algorithm for the answer. Such a hypothetical algorithm for Q is called an **oracle**, and the reduction can be thought of as showing that P is decidable given an oracle for deciding Q. In terms of decidability, this shows that P cannot be any better than Q.

■ For example, it is relatively easy to reduce the halting problem to the problem of verification. Assume that the halting problem is undecidable (we will actually prove this directly in the next section). To show that the verification problem is undecidable too we have to show that a verification oracle would enable us to decide the halting problem too. Well, given an algorithm R and one of its potential inputs X, we transform the pair $\langle R, X \rangle$, which is an input to the halting problem, into the pair $\langle P, R \rangle$ which is an input to the verification problem. The algorithm R remains the same, and the algorithmic problem P is described by specifying that X is the sole legal input to R, and that the output for this one input is unimportant. Now, to say that R is (totally) correct with respect to this rather simplistic problem P is just to say that R terminates on all legal inputs (i.e., on X) and produces some output, which is really just to say that R terminates on X. In other words, the verification problem says "yes" to $\langle P, R \rangle$ if, and only if, the halting problem says "yes" to $\langle R, X \rangle$. Consequently, the verification problem is undecidable, since otherwise we could have solved the halting problem by constructing an algorithm that would first transform any $\langle R, X \rangle$ into the corresponding $\langle P, R \rangle$, and then use the verification oracle for deciding the correctness of $\langle P, R \rangle$.

Other reductions are far more subtle. What on earth have tiling problems got to do with algorithmic termination? How do we reduce domino snakes to two-way word formations? Despite the apparent differences, these problems are all intimately related, by being interreducible, and in Chapter 9 we shall discuss one of these reductions in some detail.

■ Proving the Undecidability of the Halting Problem

We shall now prove that the halting problem, as described in Figure 8.6, is undecidable. This, as explained earlier, is carried out directly—not by a reduction from some other problem. Now, faithful to our terminological convention, what we really have to show is that there is no program in the agreed-on high-level programming language L that solves the halting problem for programs in L. (As mentioned earlier, this language-dependent fact will be extended into a far more general statement in Chapter 9.)

More precisely, we want to prove the following claim:

There is no program in L which, upon accepting any pair $\langle R, X \rangle$, consisting of the text of a legal program R in L and a string of symbols X, terminates after *some finite amount of time, and outputs "yes" if R halts when run on input X and "no" if R does not halt when run on input X.*

Such a program, if it exists, is itself just some legal program in *L*; it can use as much memory space and as much time as it requests, but it must work, as described, for *every* pair ⟨*R*, *X*⟩.

We shall prove that a program satisfying these requirements is nonexistent, *by contradiction.* In other words, we shall assume that such a program does exist, call it *Q*, and shall derive a downright contradiction from that assumption. Throughout, you should be wary, making sure that anything we do is legal and according to the rules, so that when the contradiction becomes apparent we shall be justified in pointing to the assumption about *Q*'s existence as the culprit.

Let us now construct a new program in *L*, call it *S*, as illustrated schematically in Figure 8.7. This program has a single input, which is a legal program *W* in *L*. Upon reading its input, *S* makes another copy of it. This copying is obviously possible in any high-level programming language, given sufficient memory. Recalling that the (assumed-to-exist) program *Q* expects two inputs, the first of which is a program, the next thing that *S* does is to activate *Q* on the input pair consisting of the two copies of *W*. The first of these is indeed a program, as expected by *Q*, and the other is considered to be an input string, though that string just happens to be the text of the same program, *W*. This activation of *Q* can be carried out by calling *Q* as a subroutine with parameters *W* and *W*, or by inserting the (assumed-to-exist) text

Figure 8.7

Proving undecidability of the halting problem: the program *S*.

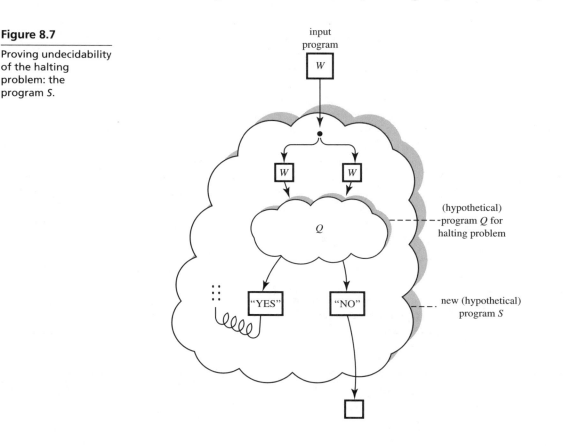

of Q into the right place, and assigning the values W and W to its expected input variables R and X, respectively.

The program S now waits for this activation of Q to terminate, or, in the metaphorical terms used earlier in the book, S's processor Runaround$_S$ waits for Q's processor Runaround$_Q$ to report back to headquarters. The point is that by our assumption Q must terminate, since, as explained, its first input is a legal program in L, and its second, when considered as a string of symbols, is a perfectly acceptable potential input to W. [2] And so, by our hypothesis, Q must eventually terminate, saying "yes" or "no." We now instruct the new program S to react to Q's termination as follows. If Q says "yes," S is to promptly enter a self-imposed infinite loop, and if it says "no," S is to promptly terminate (the output being unimportant). This can also be achieved in any high-level language, by the likes of:

$\cdots$

(17) if $OUT =$ "yes" then goto (17), otherwise stop;

where OUT is the variable containing Q's output. This completes the construction of the (strange-looking) program S, which, it should be emphasized, is a legal program in the language L, assuming, of course, that Q is.

We now want to show that there is something quite wrong with S. There is a logical impossibility in the very assumption that S can be constructed. In exposing this impossibility we shall rely on the obvious fact that, for every choice of a legal input program W, the new program S must either terminate or not. We shall show, however, that there is a certain input program for which S cannot terminate, but it also cannot *not* terminate! This is clearly a logical contradiction, and we shall use it to conclude that our assumption about Q's existence is faulty, thus proving that the halting problem is indeed undecidable.

■ The input program W that causes this impossibility is S itself. To see why S as an input to itself causes a contradiction, assume for the moment that S, when given its own text as an input, terminates. Let us now work through the details of what really happens to S when given its own text as an input. First, two copies are made of the input S (see Figure 8.8), and these are then fed into the (assumed-to-exist) program Q. Now, by our hypothesis, Q must terminate after some finite time, with an answer to the question of whether its first input terminates on its second. Now, since Q is presently working on inputs S and S, and since we assumed that S indeed terminates on S, it must halt eventually and say "yes." However, once it has terminated and said "yes," execution enters the self-imposed infinite loop and never terminates. But this means that on the assumption that S applied to S terminates (an assumption that caused Q to say "yes"), we have discovered that S applied to S does *not* terminate! We thus conclude that it is impossible that S terminates on S. This leaves us with one remaining possibility, namely, that S applied to S does not terminate. However, as can easily be verified with the help of Figure 8.8, this assumption leads in a very similar way to the conclusion that S applied to S *does* terminate, since when Q says "no" (and it *will* say "no" because of our assumption)

---

[2] The fact that the very string W itself is considered an input to the program W should not bother you too much; it is perhaps a little strange, but not impossible. Any compiler written in the language it compiles can compile itself.

Figure 8.8

Proving undecidability
of the halting
problem: *S*
swallowing *S*.

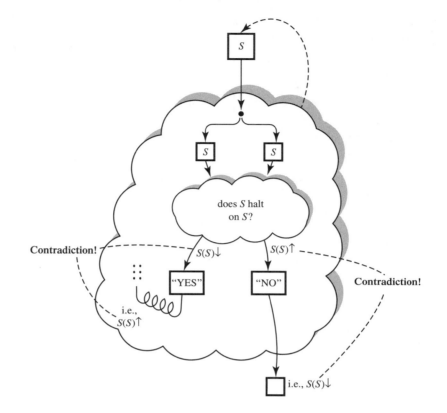

the execution of *S* applied to *S* promptly terminates. Thus, it is also impossible that *S* does not terminate when run on *S*.

In other words, the program *S* cannot terminate when run on itself and it cannot not terminate! Consequently, something is very wrong with *S* itself. However, since all other parts of *S* were constructed quite legally, the only part that can be held responsible is the program *Q*, whose assumed existence enabled us to construct *S* the way we did. The conclusion is that a program *Q*, solving the halting problem as required, simply cannot exist.

The Diagonalization Method

Some people feel a little uneasy with the proof just given, and view it as rather circular-looking. It is a rigorous mathematical proof nonetheless. We might be tempted to propose that strange self-referential programs, such as those whose behavior is exploited in the proof, be somehow outlawed. In this way, perhaps, the halting problem for "well-behaved" programs will be decidable. Well, all that can be said is that the proof holds up very nicely against any such attempts, and, in fact, the self-referential nature of the argument can be completely hidden from an observer. The best evidence of this is in the fact that other undecidable problems are

Figure 8.9

The undecidability proof viewed as diagonalization.

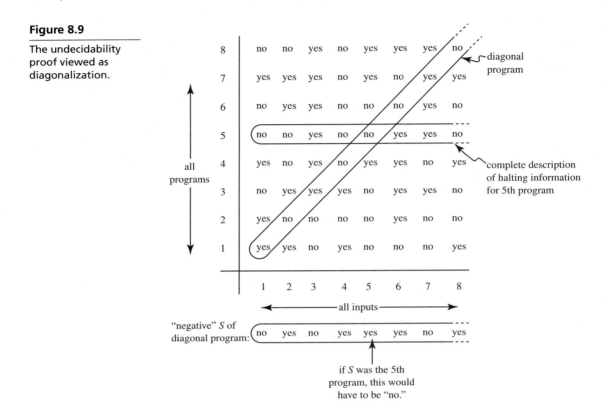

but disguised versions of the halting problem, although they do not seem to have anything at all to do with programs that refer to themselves. The tiling problem, for example, can be shown to encode the halting problem quite directly, as is illustrated in Chapter 9.

In fact, the underlying self-referential nature of this proof is embodied in a fundamental proof technique that goes back to Georg Cantor, a prominent nineteenth-century mathematician, who used it in a nonalgorithmic context. This technique, called **diagonalization**, is used in many other proofs of lower bounds in algorithmics. Let us now try to rephrase the proof that the halting problem is undecidable by using the idea of diagonalization. You should refer to Figure 8.9 in the process.

■ The proof can be visualized by imagining an infinite table, in which we have plotted all the programs in our agreed-upon programming language L against all possible inputs. (It is helpful to imagine inputs to be simply integers.) The programs are listed in the figure vertically on the left, and the inputs horizontally at the bottom. At the junction of the Ith row and Jth column in the figure we have indicated whether the Ith program halts on J or not. In this way, the entire Ith row in Figure 8.9 is a complete, albeit infinite, description of the halting information for the Ith program in L.

We now construct a new imaginary program, which will turn out to be a disguised version of the program S constructed earlier; let us therefore call it S here too. The halting behavior of S is the "negative" of the diagonal line in the table of the figure. In other words, S is constructed so that when run on any input J, it halts just if the Jth program would *not* have halted on J, and does not halt if the Jth program *would* have halted on J.

Given this setup it is easy to argue that the halting problem is undecidable. Assume that it is decidable, meaning that we can decide, with a program Q, whether a given program in L halts on a given input. This means that the imaginary S could actually be written in the language L: given J as an input, it would go through the list of programs in L, find the Jth one, and would then submit that program and the input J to the assumed-to-exist program Q for the halting problem. S itself would then proceed to either halt or enter a self-imposed infinite loop, depending on the outcome of Q's run, as described earlier (see Figure 8.8): the former if Q says "no," and the latter if it says "yes." As you can no doubt see, S indeed behaves as the negative of the diagonal of the table. This, however, leads to a contradiction, since if S is a program in L then it too has to be one of the programs on the list of Figure 8.9, since that list contains *all* programs in L. But it cannot: if S is, say, the 5th program on the list it cannot halt on input 5, since there is a "no" in the table at the junction of the 5th row and 5th column. However, by its construction, S *does* halt on input 5, and this is a contradiction.

A proof like this can be concisely described by saying that we have **diagonalized** over all programs and all inputs, constructing S to be the negative, or opposite, of the diagonal. The contradiction then follows from the impossibility of this S being one of the programs on the list.

Finite Certificates for Undecidable Problems

In Chapter 7 we saw that certain problems that have no known polynomial-time solutions give rise, nevertheless, to polynomially-sized *certificates* for inputs that yield a "yes" answer. Finding such a certificate might take an exponential amount of time, but, once found, it can be checked easily to be a valid proof of the fact that the answer is indeed "yes."

In the context of the present chapter, there is a similar certificate phenomenon, but without the requirement that certificates have to be polynomial in size; they have to be finite, but can be unreasonably long. Just as the problems in NP have reasonably sized certificates, checkable in a reasonable amount of time, despite the fact that they are not known to admit reasonable algorithms, so do some undecidable problems have *finite* certificates, checkable in *finite* time, despite the fact they have no finitely terminating algorithms. In fact, most of the undecidable problems described so far indeed admit finite certificates.

For example, to convince someone that some input yields a "yes" answer to the word correspondence problem, we can simply exhibit the finite sequence of indices that gives rise to the same word when formed from either the Xs or the Ys. Moreover, we can easily check the validity of this (possibly very long, but finite) certificate by concatenating the Xs prescribed by the indices, and then the Ys in the same way, and verifying that both of them result in one and the same word.

As to the halting problem, to convince someone that a program R halts on X, we can simply exhibit the sequence of values of all variables and data structures that constitute a complete **trace** of a legal, finite, terminating execution of R on X. We can then check the validity of the certificate by simulating the action of R on X, comparing the values reached at each step to those in the given sequence, and making sure that the program indeed terminates at the end of the sequence.

Similarly, it is easy to see that a domino snake leading from point V to point W is a perfectly good and checkable finite certificate of the fact that the appropriate inputs to the domino snake problem yield a "yes." As to the ordinary tiling problem, here certificates exist for the "no" inputs, rather than for the "yes" ones. If a set T of tile types *cannot* tile all finite areas of all sizes, there must be some area that cannot be tiled by T in any way. The certificate showing that T yields a "no" will simply be that untileable area itself. To check that this area, call it E, is indeed a certificate, we have to verify that T cannot tile E. Since both T and E are finite, there are only finitely many (albeit an unreasonable number of) possible tilings to try out, and hence the checking can be carried out algorithmically in finite time. In this sense it is the *non*-tiling problem that is comparable to the others; namely, the problem that asks whether it is *not* the case that T can tile all areas.

Problems with Two-Way Certificates Are Decidable

Notice that each of these problems has certificates for only one of the directions, either for "yes"-ness or for "no"-ness. The existence of a certificate for one direction does not contradict the undecidability of the problem at hand, since without knowing ahead of time whether an input is a "yes" or a "no," we cannot exploit the existence of a certificate for one of these to help find an algorithm for the problem. The reason is that any attempt at running through all candidate certificates and checking each for validity will not terminate if the input is of the wrong kind, as it has no certificate at all, and the search for one will never end. This point was implicitly present when it was explained earlier why simulating a given program on a given input cannot serve to decide the halting problem.

The interesting question is whether an undecidable problem can have certificates for both "yes"-ness *and* "no"-ness. Well, it cannot, since if certificates exist for both directions, they *can* be exploited to yield an algorithm for the problem, rendering it decidable. To see how, assume that we have a decision problem, for which each legal input has a finite certificate. The "yes" inputs have certificates of one kind (call them yes certificates), and the "no" inputs have certificates of another kind (no certificates). One kind might consist of finite sequences of numbers, another of certain finite areas of the integer grid, and so on. Assume further that certificates of both kinds are verifiable as such in finite time. To decide whether the problem answers "yes" or "no" to a given input, we can proceed by cycling systematically through all candidate certificates, alternating between those of the two kinds. We thus consider first a yes certificate, then a no certificate, then another yes certificate, and so on, without missing a single one (see Figure 8.10). We are actually trying, simultaneously, to find either a yes certificate or a no certificate, anything that will

Figure 8.10

Deciding a problem *P*
by searching for
certificates of either
kind.

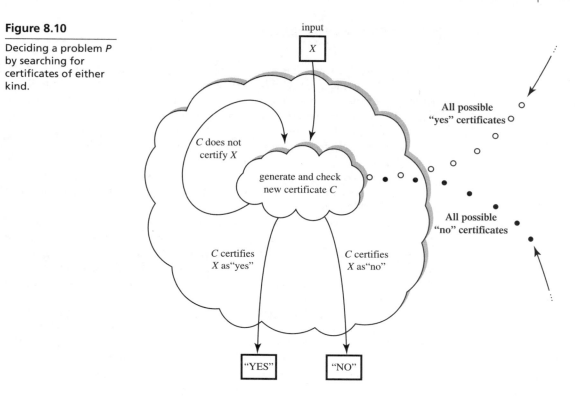

serve to convince us of the status of the problem on the given input. The crucial fact
is that this process is guaranteed to terminate, since every input definitely has either
a yes certificate or a no certificate, and whichever it is, we will find it sooner or later.
Once found, the whole process can be made to terminate, producing "yes" or "no,"
according to the kind of certificate discovered.

Thus, undecidable problems cannot have two-way certificates without contradicting their own undecidability.

Undecidable problems that have one-way certificates, like those we have described, are sometimes termed **partially decidable**, since they admit algorithms
that, in a manner of speaking, come about halfway towards a solution. When applied to an input, such an algorithm is guaranteed to terminate and say "yes," if "yes"
is indeed the answer, but might not terminate at all if the answer is "no." This is the
case for those having yes certificates; the algorithm runs through them all trying to
find a certificate for the "yes"-ness of the input. For problems whose certificates are
of the "no" type, like the tiling problem, the "yes" and "no" switch roles.[3]

---

[3] The technical term used for problems with yes certificates is **recursively enumerable**, or **r.e.** for short.
Thus, the halting and word correspondence problems are r.e., whereas the tiling problem is **co-r.e.**,
meaning that its dual problem (with "yes" and "no" interchanged) is r.e.

■ Problems that Are Even Less Decidable!

As it turns out, all partially decidable problems, including the halting problem, the domino snake problem, the word correspondence problem, and the tiling problem (actually, the non-tiling problem, in which we want a "yes" if the tiles *cannot* tile all areas) are **computationally equivalent**, meaning that each of them is effectively reducible to each of the others. Consequently, although they are all undecidable, each one of them can be decided with the aid of an imaginary subroutine, or oracle, for any one of the others: if we could decide whether a given program halts on a given input, we could also decide whether a given tile set can tile the integer grid, and whether we can form a common word by concatenating corresponding X-words and Y-words, and vice versa.

Again, the situation is similar to that of the NP-complete problems, except that here we *do* know the precise status of the problems in the class, whereas there we do not. All NP-complete problems are **polynomially equivalent**, since there are polynomial-time reductions from each of them to all the others. Partially decidable problems, on the other hand, are merely algorithmically equivalent, with no constraints on the time that reductions can take.

Now, just as there are decidable problems that are even worse than the NP-complete ones, so are there undecidable problems that are even worse than the partially decidable ones. We saw earlier that halting reduces to verification. The converse is not true. It is possible to prove that even if we have a hypothetical oracle for the halting problem, we cannot algorithmically verify programs, nor can we solve the **totality problem**, which asks whether a program halts on *all* its legal inputs. It follows that the verification and totality problems are even worse than the halting problem; they are, so to speak, "less decidable."

Among other things, this means that the totality problem, for example, has no certificates of any kind. This is actually quite intuitive, as there seems to be no finitely checkable way to prove either that a program halts on all of its infinitely many inputs, or that it does not halt (that is, it entails an infinite computation) on at least one of them. The first of these assertions might seem contradictory to the statement made in Chapter 5 to the effect that any correct program indeed has a (finite) proof, proving, in particular, that the program halts on all its inputs. However, while a finite proof of termination for all inputs is guaranteed to *exist*, it cannot qualify as a certificate since it is not necessarily checkable algorithmically. In fact, the logical statements whose truth we need to establish in order to verify the validity of the proof are formulas in a logical formalism which itself is undecidable!

Here is another example. Recall the formalism of Presburger arithmetic, which enables us to talk about the positive integers with "+" and "=". The problem of determining truth of formulas in Presburger arithmetic is decidable, but, as stated in Chapter 7, it has a double-exponential lower bound. Surprisingly, if we add the multiplication operator "×" to the formalism, obtaining a logic called **first-order arithmetic**, the problem becomes undecidable. Moreover, it is not even partially decidable, so that its status is more akin to that of verification and totality than to that of halting, word correspondence, domino snakes, or tiling. Actually, it is even worse than those.

Highly Undecidable Problems

Just as decidable problems can be grouped into various complexity classes, so can *un*decidable problems be grouped into levels, or **degrees**, of undecidability. There are those that are partially decidable, or, we might say, *almost* decidable, and they are all computationally equivalent, and then there are those that are worse. The many worse problems, however, are far from being computationally equivalent among themselves. In fact, there are infinite **hierarchies** of undecidable problems, each level of which contains problems that are worse than all those residing on lower levels.

Besides the low level of undecidability, that of partial decidability, there is another, particularly natural and significant level, that turns out to be much higher. Without getting into too many details, we shall call it simply the level of **high undecidability**, and shall illustrate it here with three examples.[4] It is noteworthy, however, that between these two levels, as well as both below and beyond them, there are many additional levels of undecidability. There is actually an infinite hierarchy of problems, all of which are increasingly "less decidable" than the ones already described but "more decidable" than the highly undecidable problems we now describe. Among these intermediate problems are the problems of totality, verification, and truth in first-order arithmetic. Likewise, there are infinite hierarchies of problems that are all even worse than the following ones.

Two of the three examples we now describe are somewhat surprising, as they seem to be but insignificant variants of problems we have already seen. Consider the satisfiability problem for propositional dynamic logic (PDL). In Chapter 7 the problem was described as (decidable, and) having both upper and lower bounds of exponential time. The programs that can appear in PDL formulas are constructed from unspecified elementary programs using sequencing, conditionals, and iteration. If we leave all other aspects of the formalism as they are, but allow these schematic programs to be constructed using recursion too, the satisfiability problem becomes not only undecidable, but *highly* undecidable! Thus, it is not decidable even if we are given free solutions to all the partially decidable problems described earlier or to the many undecidable problems residing on intermediate levels.

The second example is a subtle variant of the regular tiling, or domino problem, that asks whether the infinite integer grid can be tiled using only tile types appearing in the finite input set T. (This version is preferred here, rather than the equivalent one involving areas of all finite sizes.) In the new variant we add a small requirement: we would like the tiling, whose existence we are asking about, to contain infinitely many copies of one particular tile, say the first tile listed in T. We want a "yes" if there is a tiling of the grid, which contains an infinite **recurrence** of this special tile, and we want a "no" if no such tiling exists, even if other tilings of the entire grid do exist.

It would appear that the extra requirement should make no real difference since, if a finite set of tile types can indeed tile the entire infinite grid, then *some* of the types in the set must occur in the tiling infinitely often. The crucial difference,

---

[4] In technical terms it is called the **inductive/coinductive** level of undecidability.

however, is that here we are pointing to a *specific* tile whose recurrence we are interested in. Despite the apparent similarity, this **recurring dominoes** problem is highly undecidable (in fact, it is computationally equivalent to the aforementioned problem of PDL with recursion). It, too, is not decidable even with free solutions to the many other problems on lower levels.

We will discuss our third example of a highly undecidable problem in a moment.

The Four Fundamental Levels of Algorithmic Behavior

An interesting multi-sided story concerning tiling, or domino, problems emerges. First there are the **bounded** problems, such as whether T can tile an N by N square for a given N. Then there are the **unbounded** problems, such as whether T can tile the infinite integer grid. Finally, there are the **recurring** problems, such as whether T can tile the infinite grid such that a particular given tile recurs indefinitely. The bounded problems can be shown to be NP-complete, and hence are presumably intractable, the unbounded ones are undecidable (but partially decidable), and the recurring ones are highly undecidable.

To complete the picture, there is also a **fixed-width** version of the bounded problem. It asks whether, given the set T and a number N, a rectangle of size C by N can be formed from T, where the width C is fixed and is not part of the input to the problem. (Note that in the special case where C is 1 we are asking about the existence of a *line* of tiles adhering to the coloring restriction.) For each fixed C this problem admits a polynomial-time algorithm, which you might enjoy seeking out.

And so, as summarized in the table below, we have four versions of the tiling problem, which, on the (believable) assumption that P $\neq$ NP (that is, that the NP-complete problems are actually intractable), nicely represent the four fundamental classes of algorithmic behavior illustrated in Figure 8.11.

Type of problem	Algorithmic status
fixed-width bounded	tractable
bounded	intractable
unbounded	undecidable
recurring	highly undecidable

It must be emphasized that it is the property appearing in the left column of the table that is responsible for the fundamental difference in the status of the problems, and not some petty technicalities in the problem's definition. Two arguments can be offered to support this point. First, other problems can similarly be generalized to yield the same four-level behavior. The word correspondence problem, for example, becomes NP-complete if the length of the required sequence of indices according to which the common word is to be constructed is bounded by N; it becomes tractable if to obtain a common word we are to use a fixed-in-advance number of Xs but N of the Ys; and it becomes highly undecidable if we are to detect the existence of an infinite sequence producing a common infinite word, but with one particular index required to occur in the sequence infinitely often.

Figure 8.11

The sphere of
algorithmic problems:
Version III.

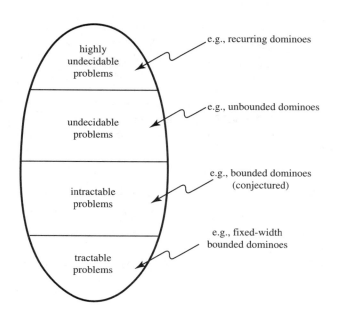

The other justification can be found in the insensitiveness of these four levels to technical variations in the definition of the problems themselves. Numerous variants of these tiling problems can be defined, and as long as the fundamental left-hand characteristic is retained their algorithmic status, as described in Figure 8.11, usually does not change. For example, we can work with hexagonal or triangular tiles instead of squares, and with matching shapes and/or notches instead of colors (so that monkey puzzles or jigsaw puzzles can be the basis for the four-way phenomenon, rather than colored tiles). We can require zigzags or spirals of length N in the fixed-width case, rectangles or triangles of given (input) dimensions in the bounded case, half-grids or a given start tile in the unbounded case, and a recurring color, rather than a tile, or the recurrence restricted to a single row, in the recurring case. In all of these variants, and in many others, the right-hand status in Figure 8.11 remains the same.

It is, therefore, fair to say that this four-level classification is extremely robust, and Chapter 9 will, in fact, provide further weighty evidence to support it.

Before closing, we mention the third example of high (in fact, *extremely* high) undecidability. What we have in mind is the validity of formulas in a powerful logical formalism, called **second-order arithmetic**, which is really a combination of the features found in the three formalisms for reasoning about integers that we discussed earlier: Presburger arithmetic, with its ability to talk about integers involving addition; WS1S, with its ability to talk about *sets* of integers involving addition; and first-order arithmetic, with its ability to talk about integers involving both addition and multiplication. Second-order arithmetic has all of these—it is able to talk about sets of integers with addition and multiplication—and its validity problem is *very* much highly undecidable. How should we explain this "very highly" qualifier? Well, avoiding additional technical details, let us start by saying that first-order arithmetic is a lot worse than "merely" undecidable; in fact, it contains infinitely many levels of increasing undecidability beyond problems like tiling and halting (but it is not quite as highly undecidable as PDL with recursive programs or recurring dominoes). In a similar vein, second-order arithmetic is a lot worse than the "merely" highly undecidable problems (like recursive PDL or recurring dominoes) and actually contains infinitely many levels of increasingly worse complexity than even those!

It is illustrative to summarize the computational complexity of these logics in the following table, which provides another perspective on the levels of difficulty that arise when one takes a problem and repeatedly adds features to it.

Logical formalism	Talks about	Complexity
Presburger arithmetic	integers with +	doubly intractable (double-exponential)
WS1S	sets of integers with +	highly intractable (nonelementary)
First-order arithmetic	integers with + and ×	very undecidable (but not quite highly undecidable)
Second-order arithmetic	sets of integers with + and ×	very highly undecidable

Research on Undecidability

Besides being of obvious relevance to computer science, the undecidability of algorithmic problems is also of interest to mathematicians. It actually forms the basis of a branch of mathematical logic known as **recursive function theory**. (The term is somewhat unfortunately reminiscent of that used to describe self-calling subroutines.) Perhaps surprisingly, many of the basic results, such as the undecidability of the halting problem, were obtained by mathematicians in the mid-1930s, long before working computers were built!

The detailed classification of undecidable problems into the various levels of undecidability is still an active research direction. Much work is devoted to refining and understanding the various hierarchies of undecidability and their interrelationships. Also, scientists are interested in finding simple problems that can serve as the basis for reductions that exhibit the undecidability or high undecidability of other problems. For many problems of interest, such as the satisfiability problem for PDL, or the problem of syntactical equivalence of languages, the line separating the decidable versions from the undecidable ones is not sufficiently clear, and a deeper understanding of the relevant issues is required.

Problems that are not solvable by any kind of effectively executable algorithms actually form the end of the pessimistic part of the story, and it is time to return to happier, brighter issues. It must be remembered, however, that when trying to solve an algorithmic problem there is always the chance that it might not be solvable at all, or might not admit any practically acceptable solution. Figure 8.12 is an attempt at summarizing the situation.

Figure 8.12

Computability: the good and bad news.

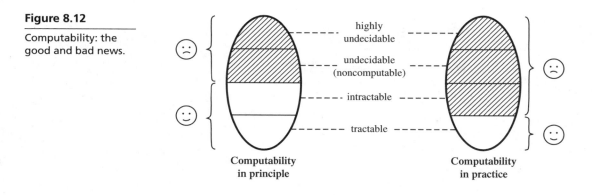

Exercises

8.1. (a) Prove rigorously that the tiles of Figure 8.1 can tile the plane but those of Figure 8.2 cannot.
   (b) Why is the assumption that tiles cannot be rotated necessary (i.e., why does the tiling problem become trivial otherwise)?

8.2. Consider the claim that for any algorithm designed to solve the tiling problem, there is an input set T upon which the algorithm will either run forever or terminate with the wrong answer. Why will there actually be infinitely many such sets?

8.3. (a) Prove the following proposition, known as König's Lemma: A finitely-branching tree (i.e, a tree with finitely many successors to each node) has an infinite path if-and-only-if it has infinitely many nodes. (Note that the branching factor need not be bounded, but merely finite.)
   (b) Prove the equivalence of both versions of the unbounded tiling problem (the problem requiring that the entire integer grid be tileable and the problem requiring that every $N \times N$ grid be tileable) with the aid of König's Lemma. (Hint: consider a tree of expanding tilings.)

8.4. It is shown in the text that "unboundedness implies undecidability" is wrong, but how about:
   (a) "Boundedness implies decidability"?
   (b) "Undecidability implies unboundedness"?
   (c) "Decidability implies boundedness"?

8.5. Determine whether the following versions of the snake problem on the upper half of the plane are decidable. Given a set T of tile types and three *distinct* points V, W, and W' on the upper half of the plane,
   (a) Are both W and W' reachable from V?
   (b) Given specific tiles t and t' of T, are both W and W' reachable from V, by snakes having t and t' placed at the endpoints W and W', respectively?
   (c) Is either W reachable or W' unreachable from V?
   (d) Given specific tiles t and t' of T, is either W or W' reachable from V, by a snake having t or t' placed at the endpoints W or W', respectively?
   (e) Are both W and W' reachable from V by snakes containing at least 5 tiles each?
   (f) Given N, are both W and W' reachable from V by snakes containing at most N tiles each?

(g) Given N, are both W and W' reachable from V by snakes containing at least N tiles each?

8.6. (a) Verify that the word correspondence example in Figure 8.5(b) admits no correspondence.

(b) For each of the following instances of the word correspondence problem, find a correct correspondence whenever it exists, or prove that there is no correspondence otherwise.

Instance	Group	1	2	3	4
i.	X	a	ba	b	abb
	Y	aaa	b	bb	b
ii.	X	a	ba	b	ab
	Y	aaa	b	bb	ba
iii.	X	bb	$bccb$	$bbbb$	$abbb$
	Y	$bbbb$	c	cb	a
iv.	X	ab	a	c	$abca$
	Y	ca	$abac$	bb	ab

8.7. Prove the decidability of the following variants of the word correspondence problem, and devise an appropriate algorithm for each problem.

(a) The bounded version of the word correspondence problem.

(b) The word correspondence problem over a one-letter alphabet.

8.8. Show that the following enriched word correspondence problem is undecidable. Over a two-letter alphabet, we are given *three* groups of words, the Xs, the Ys and the Zs. The problem is to find a sequence of indices such that the relevant words satisfy $X = Y$ but $X \neq Z$.

8.9. For a given set of colored tile types T, let $\max(T)$ be the size of the maximal (finite) square tileable by T, if a maximal such square exists, or 0 otherwise (i.e., when every square is tileable).

(a) Prove rigorously that the variant of the tiling problem, in which we are asked to output $\max(T)$ for a given input T, is undecidable.

(b) Determine the decidability status of the following problem: Given an integer $N > 2$, output a set of tile types T of size N, for which $\max(T)$ is the largest among all tile types of size at most N.

8.10. (a) Write a program which for a given X, terminates with the result "yes" precisely when the $3 \times X + 1$ program halts for X.

(b) For each of the following inputs, calculate the highest number reached during the run of the $3 \times X + 1$ program, and the number of iterations it takes for the program to terminate: 256, 101, 55, 103, 151, 383, 71 209.

8.11. (a) Does the variant of the $3 \times X + 1$ program, in which the assignment "$X \leftarrow 3 \times X + 1$" is replaced by "$X \leftarrow 2 \times X + 1$", halt for every positive integer X?

(b) Prove that the following program terminates for every positive integer X.

> while X is odd do the following:
> $X \leftarrow (3 \times X + 1)/2$.

(Hint: consider the binary representation of an odd X.)

8.12. Formulate the reduction of the halting problem to the verification problem, by writing down the transforming algorithm in detail.

8.13. (a) Assume we never allow a program to be run on precisely its own text. How would you prove the undecidability of the halting problem nevertheless?

   (b) Assume we never allow a program in our programming language L to be run on *any* program text in L. Show that even so the halting problem for programs in L is undecidable.

   (c) Assume that programs in the programming language L must always be run on integer numbers. Show that the halting problem for programs in L is undecidable nevertheless.

8.14. Prove that the following problems are undecidable:

   (a) Given a program P and an input X, determine whether either P does not halt on X, or it halts and produces 8 as its result.

   (b) Given two programs P and Q, and an input X, determine whether either both P and Q halt on X or both do not halt on X.

   (c) Given a program P and two different inputs X and Y, determine whether P halts on both X and Y.

8.15. Let us consider only programs that halt on all inputs.

   (a) Here is a diagonalization "proof" that it is undecidable whether given such a program P and an input X to P, the result is 17. The "proof" is exactly as the proof in the text that the halting problem is undecidable, but with the list of all always-halting programs (instead of all programs) plotted against all inputs, and the yes/no entries asserting whether the result is 17. What is wrong with this proof?

   (b) Show that the problem in part (a) is in fact decidable.

8.16. What would happen to the decidability status of a problem if we were guaranteed that its certificate was not merely finite, but bounded in size (to be specific, let us say that its certificate was no larger than 2^{2^N}, for inputs of size N)?

8.17. Assume that a problem P has the following strange certificates. An input is a yes-input if it has at least 7 yes-certificates, and it is a no-input if it has at least 3 no-certificates. (All certificates are verifiable in finite time.)

   (a) Is P decidable?

   (b) What can you say about the problem if we replace "at least 7" with "at least $7 \times N$," where N is the size of the input?

   (c) What if we replace "at least 7" with "at most 7"?

8.18. Show how to solve the ordinary unbounded domino problem given the recurring domino problem as an oracle.

8.19. Devise polynomial-time algorithms for the fixed-width bounded versions of the following problems.

   (a) The domino problem (i.e., K is fixed, T and N are given, and we are asked whether we can tile an $N \times K$ rectangle).

   (b) The word correspondence problem (i.e., K is fixed, the Xs, Ys, and N are given, and we are asked whether we can concatenate K words from the Xs forming a compound word that can also be formed by concatenating at most N words from the Ys).

8.20. (a) Is the fixed-width unbounded domino problem decidable? (That is, K is fixed, and we are given T, and we are asked whether there is a tiling of an infinite strip of width K.)

   (b) How about the analogous word correspondence problem?

8.21. Show that the regular unbounded version of the tiling problem for equilateral triangles is undecidable.

they shall never see light
PSALM 49: 20

CHAPTER 9

Algorithmic Universality and Its Robustness

he made engines,
invented
by skillful men

II CHRONICLES 26: 15

I know that thou
canst do everything

JOB 42: 2

or, The Simplest Machines That Get It Done

In this chapter we shall examine algorithmic devices of the simplest imaginable kind, strikingly primitive in contrast with today's computers and programming languages. Nevertheless, they are powerful enough to execute even the most complex algorithms.

Given the current trend, whereby computers are becoming more intricate and more sophisticated by the year, this goal might appear to be a mere thought experiment, and probably quite useless. However, our purpose is three-fold. To begin with, it is intellectually satisfying to discover objects that are as simple as possible yet as powerful as anything of their kind. Secondly, we should really justify the sweeping nature of the negative claims made in the last two chapters, concerning problems for which no reasonable solutions exist, and others for which no solutions whatsoever exist. The facts described herein will carry weighty evidence to support these statements. Finally, on purely technical grounds, these primitive devices will be shown to give rise to rigorous proofs of many of the intractability and undecidability results stated earlier.

Let us first see how far we can go in a direct attempt at simplifying things.

An Exercise in Simplifying Data

The first thing to notice is that any data item used by an algorithm, whether as an input, output or intermediate value, can be thought of as a string of symbols. An integer is but a string of digits, and a fractional number can be defined as two strings of digits separated by a slash. A word in English is a string of letters, and an entire text is nothing more than a string of symbols consisting of letters and punctuation marks, spaces included. Some other items we have had occasion to meet earlier in the book are colors, nodes in a graph, lines, monkey halves, rings, pegs, sides of squares, road segments, chess pieces, logical operators, and, of course, the very

Figure 9.1

Linearizing a
two-dimensional
array.

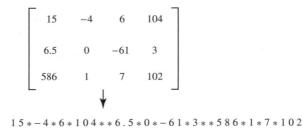

$$15*-4*6*104**6.5*0*-61*3**586*1*7*102$$

texts of programs. In all these cases, we could have easily encoded such objects as numbers, words, or texts, and treated them symbolically throughout.

The number of different symbols used in all such encodings is actually finite, and can always be fixed ahead of time. This is the ingenuity of a standard numbering system, such as the decimal system. We do not need infinitely many symbols, one for each number—10 symbols suffice to encode them all. (The binary system uses just two, 0 and 1.) The same obviously applies to words and texts.

Consequently, we can write any data item of interest along a one-dimensional **tape**, perhaps a long one, which consists of a sequence of **squares**, each containing a single symbol that is a member of some finite **alphabet**.

This idea can be taken much further. It is not too difficult to see that even the most complicated data *structures* can also be "linearized" in this fashion. A vector, for example, is just a list of data items and can be depicted as a sequence of the linearized versions of each of the items, separated by a special symbol, such as "∗". A two-dimensional array can be spread out row by row along the tape, using "∗" to separate items within each row and, say, "∗∗" to separate rows (see Figure 9.1).[1]

Linearizing trees requires more care. If we attempt to naively list the tree's items level by level, the precise structure of the tree may be lost, since the number of items on a given level is not fixed. In the level-by-level encoding in Figure 9.2, for example, there is no way of knowing whether S is an offspring of V or of G. One way of avoiding the problem is to adopt a variant of the nested lists approach of LISP, as illustrated in the examples of SCHEME programs in Chapter 3. (The parentheses are considered as special symbols, like "∗" and "∗∗".) This is especially beneficial when the trees have information only in the leaves. Alternatively, we can refine the method of Figure 9.2 by marking off clusters of immediate offspring, level by level, always starting at the left. Here is the resulting linearization for the tree of Figure 9.2:

$$(T)(V, G)(Q, R, S)(W, L)( )(M, N)( )( )(P)( )$$

You are encouraged to devise algorithms both for representing trees by such lists, and for reconstructing the trees from the lists.

Similar transformations can be carried out for any kind of data structure, however complex. A multitude of variables or data structures can be described in linear fashion using some new symbol to separate their linearized versions from each other. In fact, entire databases, consisting of scores of tables, records, and files, can be encoded as

---

[1] The memory of most kinds of digital computers is really just a one-dimensional array, and two-dimensional arrays are indeed stored in one dimension using some kind of encoding.

Figure 9.2

"Steamrolling" a tree with information loss.

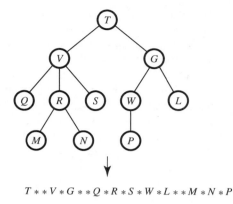

$$T * * V * G * * Q * R * S * W * L * * M * N * P$$

long lists of symbols, with appropriate special-symbol codes signifying breakpoints between the various parts. Of course, it might be very *inefficient* to work with a linear version of a highly structured collection of data. Even the simple clustered-tree representation just given requires quite an unpleasant amount of running around in order to carry out standard tree-oriented chores, such as traversing paths or isolating subtrees rooted at given nodes. However, efficiency is not one of our concerns right now; conceptual simplification is, and once again we find that a linear tape with symbols from a finite alphabet suffices.

Now, algorithms do not deal only with *fixed* amounts of data. They may ask for more as they go along. Data structures may grow in size, and variables may be assigned ever-larger data items; information may be stored, to be used later in the algorithm, and so on. However, given that any such additional data can also be linearized, all we need is to allow our tape, with its marked-off squares, to be of unlimited length. Storing some information will be tediously accomplished by running to some remote, unused part of the tape and storing it there.

The conclusion is this. When it comes to the *data* manipulated by an algorithm, *any* effectively executable algorithm, it suffices to have a one-dimensional tape of potentially unbounded length, divided into squares, each of which contains a symbol taken from a finite alphabet. This alphabet includes the "real" symbols that make up the data items themselves, as well as special symbols for marking breakpoints. It is also assumed to include a special blank symbol for indicating the absence of information, which we shall denote by #, and which is understood to be distinct from the space symbol separating words in a text. Since at any given point in time an algorithm deals with only a finite amount of data, our tapes will always contain a finite **significant portion** of data, surrounded on either side by infinite sequences of blanks. This portion may be very long, and may grow longer as execution proceeds, but it will always be finite.

An Exercise in Simplifying Control

How can we simplify the *control* part of an algorithm? Various languages, we have seen, support various control structures, such as sequencing, conditional branching, subroutines, and recursion. Our question is really about simplifying the work of the processor Runaround, who runs around carrying out basic instructions. For now we shall ignore the basic instructions themselves and concentrate on simplifying the very chore of running around.

One of the things crucial to simplifying control is the finiteness of an algorithm's text. The processor can be in one of only finitely many locations in that text, and hence we can make do with a rather primitive mechanism, containing some kind of **gearbox** that can be in one of finitely many positions, or **states**. If we think of the states of the gearbox as encoding locations in the algorithm, then moving around in the algorithm can be modeled simply by changing states.

At any point during the execution of an algorithm the location to be visited next depends on the current location, so that the next state of our mechanism's gearbox must depend on its current state. However, the new location may also depend on the values of certain data items; many control structures test the values of variables in order to channel control to particular places in the text (for example, to the **then** or **else** clauses of an **if** statement, or to the beginning or end of a **while** loop). This means that a change in the state of our mechanism must be allowed to depend on parts of the data as well as on the current state. But since we have encoded all of our data along a single lengthy tape, we shall have to allow our primitive mechanism to inspect the tape before deciding on a new state.

In the interest of minimalism and simplicity, this inspection will be carried out only one square at a time. At any given moment, only a single symbol will ever be "read." Our mechanism can thus be viewed as having an "eye" of very limited power, contemplating at most one square of the tape at a time, and seeing and recognizing the symbol residing there. Depending upon that symbol and the mechanism's current state, it might "change gear," entering a new state (see Figure 9.3).

As a consequence of the finiteness of the alphabet, we shall see later that the mechanism can actually "remember" the symbol it has seen by entering an appropriately

Figure 9.3

A primitive mechanism: tape, gearbox, and narrow eye.

meaningful new state. This enables it to act according to combined information gathered from several tape squares. However, in order to inspect different parts of the data, we have to allow our mechanism to move along the tape. Again, we shall be very ungenerous, allowing movement to take place only one tape square at a time. The direction of movement (right or left) will also depend both on the current state of the gearbox and on the symbol the eye has just seen.

These observations simplify the control component of an algorithm considerably. What we have is a simple mechanism, capable of being in one of a finite number of gears, or states, chugging along the tape one square at a time. In the process, it changes states and switches directions as a function of the current state and the single symbol it happens to see in front of it.

Simplifying the Basic Operations

Having thus simplified the data and control parts of algorithms, we are left with the basic operations that actually get things done. If processors were just to run around reading parts of the data and changing gears, algorithms could not do very much. We need the ability to *manipulate* the data, to apply transformations to it, to erase, write, or rewrite parts of it, to apply arithmetical or textual operations to it, and so on.

Without offering any kind of justification right now, we shall endow our mechanism with only the most trivial manipulation capabilities. Other than to change states and move one square to the right or left, all it will be allowed to do, when in a particular state and looking at a particular symbol on the tape, is to transform that symbol into one of the other finitely many symbols available. That's all.

The mechanism resulting from this long sequence of simplifications is called a **Turing machine**, after the British mathematician Alan M. Turing, who invented it in 1936.

The Turing Machine

Let us be a little more precise in the definition of Turing machines. A Turing machine M consists of a (finite) set of **states**, a (finite) **alphabet** of symbols, an infinite **tape** with its marked-off squares and a sensing-and-writing **head** that can travel along the tape, one square at a time. In addition, the heart of the machine is a **state transition diagram**, sometimes called simply a **transition diagram**, containing the instructions that cause changes to take place at each step.

A transition diagram can be viewed as a directed graph whose nodes represent the states. We use rounded rectangles (**routangles** in the sequel) for states (see Figure 9.4). An edge leading from state s to state t is called a **transition**, and is labeled with a code of the form $\langle a/b, L \rangle$ or $\langle a/b, R \rangle$, where a and b are symbols. The a part of the label is called the transition's **trigger**, and it denotes the letter read from the tape. The b part is the **action**, and denotes the letter written on the

Figure 9.4

The state transition diagram of a simple Turing machine.

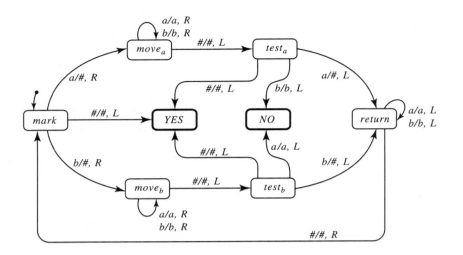

tape. Finally, the L and R part provides the direction to move, with L standing for "left" and R for "right." The precise meaning of a transition from s to t labeled with $\langle a/b, L \rangle$ is as follows (the case for $\langle a/b, R \rangle$ is similar):

> *During its operation, whenever the Turing machine is in state s, and a is the symbol sensed at that moment by the head, the machine will erase the symbol a, writing b in its place, will move one square to the left, and will enter state t.*

To prevent ambiguity as to the machine's next move (that is, in order that its behavior be **deterministic**), we require that no two transitions with the same trigger emanate from a single state. One of the states in the diagram (*mark* in Figure 9.4) is marked with a special small entering arrow and is called the **start state**. Also, states that have no outgoing transitions (*YES* and *NO* in Figure 9.4) are called **halting states**, and are emphasized by thick rountangles. For convenience, several labels may be attached to a single transition (as in the three self-cycling arrows of Figure 9.4).

The machine is assumed to start in its start state on the leftmost nonblank square of the tape, and to proceed step by step as prescribed by the diagram. It halts if and when a halting state is entered.

Detecting Palindromes: An Example

Let us take a closer look at the Turing machine whose transition diagram is shown in Figure 9.4. In particular, let us simulate its actions on a tape consisting of the word "*a b b a*" (surrounded, as explained above, by infinitely many blanks on either side). The machine's head is positioned at the leftmost *a*, and *mark* is the initial state. Figure 9.5 shows the entire simulation, step by step, with the current state indicated by a solid routangle within the miniature version of the transition diagram.

Intuitively, the machine "remembers" the first symbol it has seen (by entering *move*$_a$ or *move*$_b$, according to whether that symbol was *a* or *b*), erases it by replacing

Figure 9.5

A sample run of the Turing machine of Figure 9.4.

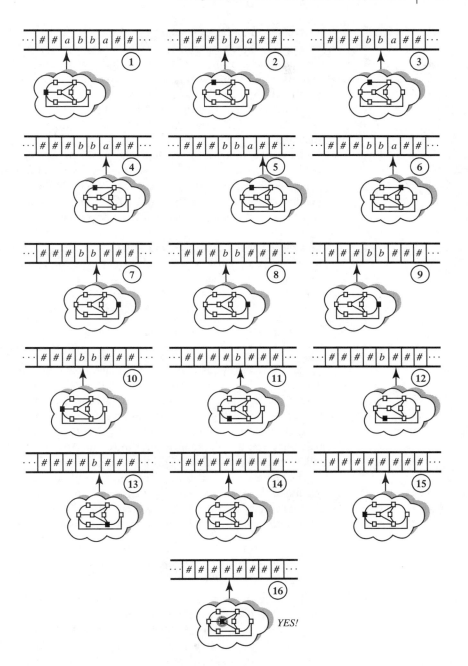

it with a blank, and then runs all the way to the right until it reaches a blank (frame 5). It then moves one symbol to the left, so that it is stationed at the rightmost symbol in state $test_a$ or $test_b$, depending on the symbol it remembered (frame 6). If it were now to sense a symbol different from the one it remembered it would enter the special state *NO*. In our case, however, it remembered an a and now also sees an a, so it erases this rightmost a, and enters *return*, which brings it leftwards all the way to the first blank, in state *mark* (frame 9). As before, the machine now moves one square to the right and remembers the symbol it sees. This symbol, however, is the second one of the original string, since the first was erased earlier. The current rightward run will now compare this second symbol with the string's penultimate symbol (frame 13). This comparison is also successful, and the machine erases the *b* and moves off to the left in search of further symbols. Finding none, and not having reached the *NO* state by virtue of a mismatch, it enters *YES*, indicating that all pairs matched.

In essence, this Turing machine checks for **palindromes**; that is, for words that read the same from either end. (A palindrome would remain the same after being subjected to the reverse algorithm of Chapter 5.) Whenever started at the leftmost symbol of a finite word consisting of *a*'s and *b*'s, it halts in the *YES* state if the word is a palindrome and in *NO* if it isn't. You should simulate the machine also on "*a b a b a*" and "*a b a a b b a a*" to get a better feel for its behavior. Observe that this particular machine uses four fixed states and an additional two for each of the letters in the alphabet. You may also want to extend Figure 9.5 to deal with the case of a three-letter alphabet.

■ Turing Machines as Algorithms

A careful look reveals that a Turing machine can be viewed as a computer with a single fixed program. The software is the transition diagram, and the hardware consists of the tape and head, as well as the (implicit) mechanism that actually moves through the transition diagram changing states and controlling the head's reading, writing, erasing, and moving activities. The computer is thus the same for all Turing machines; it is the programs that are different. As a consequence, people sometimes talk about **programming** a Turing machine, rather than constructing one.

Thus the palindrome example actually shows how a Turing machine can be programmed to solve a decision problem. For a problem P whose legal set of inputs has been encoded as a set of linearized strings, we try to devise a Turing machine M with a start state s and two special states *YES* and *NO*, that does the following:

> For any legal input string X, if M is started in state s at the leftmost symbol of X on an otherwise blank tape containing one copy of X, it eventually enters YES or NO, depending upon whether P's answer to X is "yes" or "no."

Detecting palindromes with a Turing machine may seem easy, but other problems are not. How do we detect strings with the following property. The only appearances of *a*'s in the string are in blocks whose lengths form some initial portion of the sequence of prime numbers 2, 3, 5, 7, 11, ... Within X, the blocks are not required to appear in any particular order. Here we cannot simply run back and forth, erasing symbols; we need the ability to **count** and to compute, and a finite number of states is not sufficient to "remember" arbitrarily large numbers. (The input word, of course, can be arbitrarily long.)

■ The trick is to compute the next prime number on the blank part of the tape, say to the right of the input word X, and then to go searching for a block of *a*'s with precisely the required length. Assuming the current prime has been computed and appears as a string of 1's to the right of X on the tape,[2] the search for the appropriate block of a's can be carried out as follows. The machine repeatedly runs through every block of a's, checking off each a against one of the 1's, by running back and forth and changing both temporarily into some new symbol. If a perfect match is found, the entire block is erased, and the next prime is computed. If not, the block is restored to its original form and the next block is tried. If no matching block is found in the entire string, the machine enters *NO*. If the block matches and the tape contains no more a's, the machine enters *YES*.

Notice how we are using the potentially infinite blank portion of the tape as scrap paper, both to compute and to jot down our current count of the a's.

Turing machines can also be programmed to solve non-yes/no algorithmic problems. The only difference is in the need to produce outputs. By convention, we may agree that when a Turing machine halts (by virtue of its entering any halting state) the output is the string contained between two "!"s on the tape. If there are not precisely two "!"s on the tape at the time of halting we agree that it is as if the machine had entered an infinite loop, and will thus never halt. In other words, if M wants to produce an output, it had better see to it that the output is enclosed between two "!"s, and that it does not use "!"s for any other purpose. (Obviously, it is possible to use this convention for decision problems also, writing "!yes!" or "!no!" on the tape and entering some halting state, rather than entering the special *YES* or *NO* states, as we did with the palindrome machine.)

■   With this definition in mind, it is an instructive exercise to program a Turing machine to add two decimal numbers X and Y. One way of proceeding is as follows. The machine runs to the rightmost digit of X (by reaching the separating symbol "∗" and moving one square to its left) and erases it, while "remembering" it in its state; it will need 10 different states to do so, say *digit-is*-0 through *digit-is*-9. It then runs to the rightmost digit of Y and erases it too, while entering a state that remembers the sum digit of the two numbers and whether or not there is a carry. (These, of course, depend only on the current digit and the memorized one, and can be encoded into, say, states *sum-is*-0-*nocarry* through *sum-is*-9-*nocarry* and *sum-is*-0-*carry* through *sum-is*-9-*carry*.) The machine then moves to the left of what remains of X and writes the sum digit down, having prepared a "!" as a delimiter. The next step is similar, but it involves the currently rightmost digits and takes the carry into account (if there is one). The new sum digit is written down to the left of the previous one, and the process continues. Of course, we have to remember that each of the numbers might run out of digits before the other, in which case after adding the carry (if there is one) to the remaining portion of the larger number, that portion is just copied down on the left. Finally, a second "!" is written down on the extreme left and the machine halts.

Here are the main configurations of the tape for the numbers 736 and 63519:

```
... # # # # # # # # # 7 3 6 ∗ 6 3 5 1 9 # # ...
... # # # # # # # 5 ! 7 3 # ∗ 6 3 5 1 # # # ...
... # # # # # # 5 5 ! 7 # # ∗ 6 3 5 # # # # ...
... # # # # # 2 5 5 ! # # # ∗ 6 3 # # # # # ...
... # # # # 4 2 5 5 ! # # # ∗ 6 # # # # # # ...
... # # # 6 4 2 5 5 ! # # # ∗ # # # # # # # ...
... # # ! 6 4 2 5 5 ! # # # ∗ # # # # # # # ...
```

---

[2] The primality problem itself is discussed, e.g., in Chapters 7 and 11.

Again, the (masochistic) reader might be interested in constructing the entire transition diagram of a Turing machine for decimal addition.

The Church/Turing Thesis

These examples might be a little surprising. A Turing machine has only finitely many states, and can only rewrite symbols on a linear tape one at a time. Nevertheless, we can program it to add numbers. It might be tedious to do the programming (try to construct a Turing machine to *multiply* numbers), and it is no easier to take over the controls and actually carry out a simulation of the machine's actions. Nevertheless, it gets the job done.

With this in mind, let us forget about tedium and efficiency for the time being, and ask ourselves what indeed *can* be done with Turing machines, for whatever cost? Which algorithmic problems can be solved by an appropriately programmed Turing machine?

The answer is not a little surprising, but *very* surprising indeed. Turing machines are capable of solving any effectively solvable algorithmic problem! Put differently, any algorithmic problem for which we can find an algorithm that can be programmed in some programming language, *any* language, running on some computer, *any* computer, even one that has not been built yet but *can* be built, and even one that will require unbounded amounts of time and memory space for ever-larger inputs, is also solvable by a Turing machine. This statement is one version of the so-called **Church/Turing thesis**, after Alonzo Church and Turing, who arrived at it independently in the mid-1930s.

It is important to realize that the CT thesis, as we shall sometimes call it (both for Church/Turing and for Computability Theory), is a thesis, not a theorem, and hence cannot be proved in the mathematical sense of the word. The reason for this is that among the concepts it involves there is one that is informal and imprecise, namely that of "effective computability." The thesis equates the mathematically precise notion of "solvable by a Turing machine" with the informal, intuitive notion of "solvable effectively," which alludes to all real computers and all programming languages, those that we know about at present as well as those that we do not. It thus sounds more like a wild speculation than what it really is: a deep and far-reaching statement, put forward by two of the most respected pioneers of theoretical computer science.

It is instructive to draw an analogy between Turing machines and typewriters. A typewriter is also a very primitive kind of machine, enabling us only to type sequences of symbols on a piece of paper that is potentially infinite in size and initially blank. (A typewriter also has finitely many "states" or modes of operation—upper or lower case, red or black ribbon, etc.) Yet despite this, any typewriter can be used to type *Hamlet* or *War and Peace*, or any other highly sophisticated string of symbols. Of course, it might take a Shakespeare or a Tolstoy to "instruct" the machine to do so, but it can be done. In analogy, it might take very talented people to program Turing machines to solve difficult algorithmic problems, but the basic model, so the CT thesis tells us, suffices for all problems that can be solved at all.

Our exercises in simplification have thus turned out to have profound consequences. Simplifying data down to sequences over a finite alphabet, simplifying control down to a finite number of states that prescribe square-by-square moves along a tape, and adopting symbol rewriting as the only primitive operation, yields a mechanism that is as powerful as any algorithmic device whatsoever.

Evidence for the Church/Turing Thesis

Why should we believe this thesis, especially when it cannot be proved? What evidence is there for it, and how does that evidence fare in an age of day-to-day advances in both hardware and software?

Ever since the early 1930s researchers have suggested models for the all-powerful absolute, or **universal**, computer. The intention was to try to capture that slippery and elusive notion of "effective computability," namely the ability to compute mechanically. Long before the first digital computers were invented, Turing suggested his primitive machines and Church devised a simple mathematical formalism of functions called the **lambda calculus** (mentioned in Chapter 3 as the basis for functional programming languages). At about the same time Emil Post defined a certain kind of symbol-manipulating **production system**, and Stephen Kleene defined a class of objects called **recursive functions**. (As mentioned in the research section of Chapter 8, this "recursive" has a meaning that is somewhat different from the one used throughout this book.) All these people tried, and succeeded, in using their models to solve many algorithmic problems for which there were known "effectively executable" algorithms. Other people have since proposed numerous different models for the absolute, universal algorithmic device. Some of these models are more akin to real computers, having the abstract equivalent of storage and arithmetical units, and the ability to manipulate data using control structures such as loops and subroutines, and some are purely mathematical in nature, defining classes of functions that are realizable in a step-by-step fashion.

The crucial fact about these models is that they have *all* been proven equivalent in terms of the class of algorithmic problems they can solve. And this fact is still true today, even for the most powerful models conceived.

That so many people, working with such a diversity of tools and concepts, have essentially captured the very same notion is evidence for the profundity of that notion. That they were all after the same intuitive concept and ended up with different-looking, but equivalent, definitions is justification for equating that intuitive notion with the results of those precise definitions. Hence the CT thesis.

Computability is Robust

The CT thesis implies that the most powerful super-computer, with the most sophisticated array of programming languages, interpreters, compilers, assemblers, and what have you, is no more powerful than a home computer with its simplistic programming language! Given an unlimited amount of time and memory space, both can solve precisely the same algorithmic problems. The noncomputable (or undecidable) problems of Chapter 8 are solvable on neither, and the computable (or decidable) problems mentioned throughout are solvable on both.

As a result of the CT thesis the class of computable, effectively solvable, or decidable algorithmic problems becomes extremely *robust*. It is invariant under changes in the computer model or programming language, a fact alluded to in Chapter 8. Proponents of a particular computer architecture or programming discipline must find reasons other than raw computational power to justify their recommendations, since problems solvable with one are also solvable with the other, and all are equivalent to the primitive machines of Turing or the various formalisms of Church, Post, Kleene, and others.

The line drawn between the decidable and the undecidable in Chapter 8 (see Figures 8.3, 8.11 and 8.12) is thus fully justified, as is our reliance on an unspecified language L for discussing undecidability therein. Moreover, it is intellectually satisfying to be able to point to a most simple model that is as powerful as anything of its kind.

Variants of the Turing Machine Model

The robustness afforded by the CT thesis starts with variants of the Turing machines themselves. As it turns out, it is possible to limit the machines in a number of ways without reducing the class of problems they can solve. For example, we can require that (unlike the erasing effect of the palindrome machine) inputs are to be kept intact, and that the "work areas" of the tape are to be cleared up, so that upon halting, the tape is to contain only the input and output, surrounded by blanks. We can define Turing machines with a tape that is infinite to the right only, the input appearing justified to the left, and the machine being constrained never to attempt to move "off" the leftmost square. Both variants can solve precisely the same problems as the basic model, and therefore they are really no weaker.

In a similar vein, adding any powerful (but "effectively executable") feature to the machines also yields precisely the same class of solvable problems, so that in the context of raw computability this extra power is merely an illusion. For example, we can allow many tapes, each with its own read/write head, in such a way that the transitions are based on the entire set of symbols seen simultaneously by the heads; the actions specify a new symbol to be written on each tape and a direction for each head to move in. Similarly, we can define machines involving **two-dimensional** tapes, giving rise to four, not two, possible moving directions, and so on. None of these extensions can solve problems that the basic model cannot.

One of the most interesting extensions involves **nondeterministic** Turing machines. The idea is to allow many transitions with the same trigger to emanate from a state. The machine then has a choice of which transition to take. The way a nondeterministic machine is said to solve a decision problem is very similar to the way "magical nondeterminism" was defined in Chapter 7: whenever there *is* a choice to be made, the machine can be thought of as making the best one—that is, the one that will eventually lead to a "yes" answer, if that is at all possible. In this way, the nondeterministic Turing machine says "yes" to input X precisely if there exists some sequence of choices that leads to the *YES* state, even if there are others that don't (for example, they lead to *NO* states or into infinite loops). Thus, what is really happening is that the machine considers all possible computation paths, saying "yes" if at least one of them results in a "yes," and "no" otherwise. Here too, perhaps somewhat surprisingly, no solving power is gained. Even this "magical" notion of computation does not enable us to solve any algorithmic problems that could not have been solved without it.

Folding Over an Infinite Tape: An Example

As explained earlier, scores of distinct models of computation, often of radically different nature, have been suggested over the years and have all been proven equivalent, thus providing weighty evidence of the truth of the CT thesis.

How do we establish such equivalences? How do we show that even two similar variants of the Turing machine model (let alone two completely different models) give rise to the very same class of solvable problems? The answer lies in the notion of **simulation**, whereby we show that for each machine of one type there is an *equivalent* machine of the other. In other words, we show how to *simulate* one type of machine on another.

For example, suppose we wish to show that machines with a two-way infinite tape are no more powerful than those with a tape that is infinite only to the right. Assume we are given a machine that employs a two-way infinite tape. We can construct an equivalent new machine, whose one-way tape is "viewed" as a two-way tape folded over into two merged halves. Figure 9.6 shows the correspondence between the tapes. The simulating machine will first spread out its input so that its contents are in the odd-numbered squares and the rest contain blanks. This blank portion will correspond to the left, totally blank, part of the simulated tape, folded over. The new machine will then simulate the old, but moving two squares at a time, as if it were on the right-hand part of the original tape, until it reaches the leftmost square. It then "shifts gear," also moving two squares at a time, but on the even-numbered squares, as if it were on the left-hand part of the original tape. The precise details are somewhat tedious, and are omitted here, but conceptually the simulation is quite simple. Other simulations can be quite intricate, even conceptually. In all cases, however, simulation techniques exist; hence there are Turing machines for solving any problem that can be solved on even the most sophisticated modern computers.

Counter Programs: Another Very Primitive Model

On the face of it, there is little reason to choose the Turing machine model above all others to be the one the CT thesis mentions explicitly. The thesis might have talked about the model underlying a large IBM or Cray computer. In fact, one of the most striking formulations of the thesis does not mention any particular model at

Figure 9.6

"Folding over" a
two-way infinite tape.

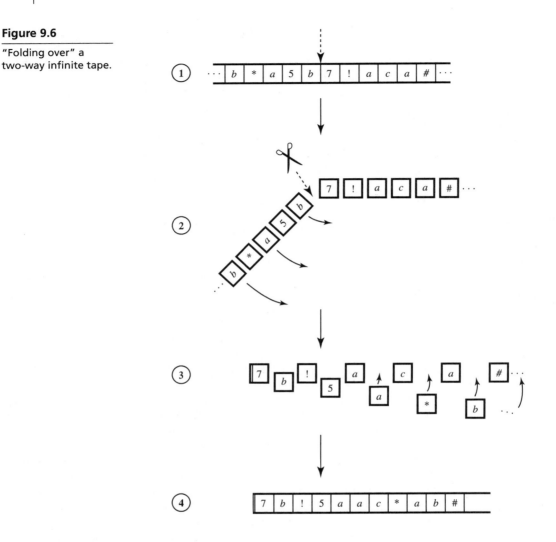

all, but rather states simply that all computers and all programming languages are equivalent in computational power, given unlimited time and memory space.

However, as we shall see later, there are technical reasons for investigating extremely primitive models. Accordingly, we now describe the **counter program** model, which is another one of the truly simple, yet universal, models of computation.

Instead of arriving at them by starting out with general algorithms and simplifying things, we shall first define the counter programs themselves and then try to see how they relate to Turing machines. A counter program can manipulate non-negative integers stored in variables. The model, or language, allows just three types of elementary operations on variables, interpreted in the standard way (where, by convention, $Y - 1$ is defined to be 0 if Y is already 0):

$$X \leftarrow 0, \qquad X \leftarrow Y + 1, \qquad \text{and} \qquad X \leftarrow Y - 1$$

The variables are called counters because the limited operations enable them, in essence, only to count. The control structures of a counter program include simple sequencing and the conditional **goto** statement:

if $X = 0$ **goto** G

where X is a variable and G is a label that is possibly attached to a statement. A counter program is just a finite sequence of optionally labeled statements. Execution proceeds in order, one statement at a time, branching off to the specified statement when a **goto** is encountered and the appropriate variable is indeed zero. A counter program halts if and when it attempts to execute a nonexistent statement, by reaching the end of the sequence or by trying to go to a nonexistent label.

Here is a counter program that computes $X \times Y$, the product residing in Z upon termination:

$$U \leftarrow 0$$
$$Z \leftarrow 0$$
$$A : \textbf{if } X = 0 \textbf{ goto } G$$
$$X \leftarrow X - 1$$
$$V \leftarrow Y + 1$$
$$V \leftarrow V - 1$$
$$B : \textbf{if } V = 0 \textbf{ goto } A$$
$$V \leftarrow V - 1$$
$$Z \leftarrow Z + 1$$
$$\textbf{if } U = 0 \textbf{ goto } B$$

You might want to ponder this program for a while. First, there is a **goto** G but no statement labeled G. This is in accordance with our convention, and the program halts in a normal fashion when it attempts to carry out that **goto**. We have also used two small tricks, achieving, respectively, the effect of the statement $V \leftarrow Y$ and the unconditional instruction **goto** b, both of which are not really allowed by the formal syntax. The product $X \times Y$ is computed by two nested loops. The outer loop repeatedly adds Y to an initially zeroed Z, X times, and the inner one carries out the addition by repeatedly adding 1 to Z, V times, where V is initialized to Y each time around. Tricky, maybe, but it works.

How powerful are counter programs? Can they solve really complicated problems? The answer is: they are precisely as powerful as Turing machines, and hence as powerful as any computer whatsoever.

Turing Machines vs. Counter Programs

Since counter programs manipulate numbers only, this last statement requires clarification. It might make sense to claim that counter programs can solve the *numerical* problems that are solvable by Turing machines (especially having seen how tediously Turing machines add numbers). But how, for example, does a counter program find shortest paths in a graph, or occurrences of "money" in a text? Turing machines are capable of these feats because, as shown earlier, every kind of data structure, graphs and texts included, can be encoded as a sequence of symbols on a tape. But

Figure 9.7

Encoding a Turing
machine's tape and
position as two
numbers.

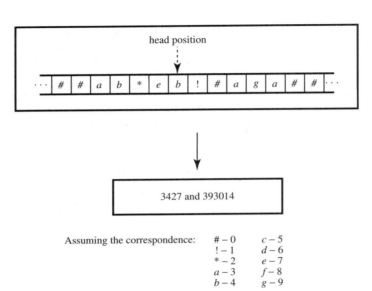

Assuming the correspondence:

# – 0	c – 5
! – 1	d – 6
* – 2	e – 7
a – 3	f – 8
b – 4	g – 9

can such objects be encoded also as numbers, to be manipulated by mere one-step increments and decrements?

The answer is yes. If the alphabet used in these sequences were to contain precisely 10 symbols we could easily associate them with the 10 decimal digits, and we would then have no problem viewing any (finite) sequence as a number. Using standard methods, the same can be done for an alphabet of *any* (finite) size, since non-negative integers can be represented in a uniform and unambiguous way using any fixed number of digits. Binary numbers involve only two digits, and those involving 16 are called **hexadecimal** numbers.[3] Thus, using an easily programmable encoding mechanism, any finite sequence of symbols over a finite alphabet can be viewed as a number.

To see how a Turing machine tape can be viewed as consisting of numbers, recall that at any point during a Turing machine's execution (assuming it starts on a finite input) only a finite portion of the tape contains nonblank information; the rest is all blank. Consequently, this significant part of the tape, together with the head's position, can be represented simply by two numbers, encoding the two portions of the tape lying on either side of the machine's head. To make things easier, it is useful to represent the right-hand portion in reverse, so that the least significant digits of both numbers are close to the head. Figure 9.7 shows the numerical representation of a tape assuming, for simplicity, an alphabet of 10 symbols. On this basis, it is possible to carry out a simulation of any Turing machine with a counter program.

■ How? Well, two variables are used to carry the two crucial values encoding the nonblank portions of the tape on either side of the head and (implicitly) the head position itself; another variable is used for the state. The subtlety of the simulation is in the fact that

---

[3] The binary representation is particularly useful when real digital computers are involved, because of the 0/1 nature of bits, and the hexadecimal notation likewise, since one hexadecimal digit is represented precisely by four binary digits, or bits.

the effect of one step of the Turing machine is quite "local." One side of the tape gets "longer" because the head moves away from it, adding a new symbol to its "end," and the other gets shorter, losing its last symbol (unless the machine moves off the nonblank portion into the all-blank area, in which case the side which was to become empty gets a new blank symbol for nothing, in effect making the entire relevant part of the tape one symbol longer). All these changes can be simulated in the counter program by relatively straightforward arithmetical manipulation of the two main variables.

As a consequence, the entire transition diagram of the Turing machine can be "worked" into the counter program by "chunks," each of which simulates one transition of the diagram. To actually simulate the workings of the machine, the program repeatedly inspects the state-carrying variable and the symbol seen by the head (that is, the least significant digit of the right-hand number), executes the relevant chunk, and changes the value of the state variable.

And so, programs that can merely increment and decrement integers by 1 and test their value against 0 can be used to do anything any computer can do. Not only can they calculate numerically, but, in principle, they can also represent, traverse, and manipulate any kind of data structure, including lists, graphs, trees, and even entire databases.

As to the other direction, namely that Turing machines can do anything counter programs can, we can simulate counter programs with Turing machines as follows. The values of the various counters are spread out on the tape, separated by "∗"s. The simulating machine uses special states to represent the different statements in the program. Entering each such state triggers a sequence of transitions that carries out the statement itself. Again, the details are omitted.

It is perhaps of interest to the minimalists among us that we can always do with only *two* counters. It is possible to simulate any counter program with one that uses only two variables, though this simulation is more complicated.

Turing machines and counter programs both achieve universality by making use of a potentially infinite amount of memory, but in different ways. With Turing machines, the *number* of objects containing information (the tape's squares) is potentially unbounded, but the *amount* of information in each is finite and bounded. With counter programs it is the other way around. There are only finitely many variables in any given program, but each can contain an arbitrarily large value, thus, in effect, encoding a potentially unbounded amount of information.

Simulations as Reductions

When we say that one computational model can simulate another we are really saying that we have a *reduction* (in the sense of Chapter 8) between the two models. This point of view provides a firm mathematical basis for certain discussions in earlier chapters. Whenever we talked about programs that accept other programs as inputs we were not being restrictive at all. Since effective simulations exist between any two sufficiently powerful models of computation, we can always start with a program or algorithm in any language or model and translate it into the language we happen to be working with.

Consider, for example, the undecidability of the halting problem, as proved in Chapter 8. Proper use of the reductions associated with the CT thesis enables us to show that this result is extremely general. It can first be proved rigorously for Turing machines by (1) assuming that the input program W in Figure 8.7 is the description of some Turing machine, and (2) constructing the hypothetical program S also as a Turing machine (quite an easy adaptation of the construction given therein). The contradictory nature of this construction is then established, resulting in the seemingly humble conclusion that no Turing machine exists that solves the halting problem for Turing machines. This result, however, is not humble at all. In fact, it proves that the halting problem is undecidable in a very strong sense: no effective language or model L_1 can possibly solve the halting problem for programs in the universal language or model L_2. (A special case is when L_1 and L_2 are one and the same language.) This is because if, for some universal L_1 and L_2, this version of the halting problem were decidable, so would the Turing machine version be. (Can you see why?)

It is these language- and model-independent facts, coupled with the confidence we have in the Church/Turing thesis, that justify our use in previous chapters of phrases concerning the nonexistence, for certain problems, of *any* algorithms, written in *any* languages and run on *any* computers, now or in the future.

Universal Algorithms

The CT thesis talks about universal models, or languages. One of its most interesting consequences is the existence of **universal algorithms**. A universal algorithm has the ability to act like any algorithm whatsoever. It accepts as inputs the description of *any* algorithm A and *any* legal input X, and simply runs, or **simulates**, A on X, halting if and when A halts, and producing the outputs that would have been produced if A had indeed been run on X. Thus, fixing the input algorithm A and letting X vary has the effect of making the universal algorithm behave precisely like A.

In a sense, a computer, or an interpreter (see Chapter 3), is very much like a universal algorithm: we present it with a program and an input and it runs the former on the latter. However, the term "universal" suggests independence, meaning that a universal algorithm should be *insensitive* to the choice of a language or machine, whereas computers and interpreters are not. It would thus appear that *no* universal algorithm could ever be implemented, since both the universal algorithm itself and its input algorithms must be written in some language, intended for some machine.

To our help comes again the CT thesis, with its simulations between models, and its claim that all programming languages and computation models are equivalent. To obtain a universal algorithm we have only to use some language L_1 to write an effectively executable program U, which accepts as inputs any program written in some fixed universal language or model L_2, and any input, and simulates the running of that program on that input. Once written, U can be thought of as being language- and machine-independent because, by the thesis, (1) it could have been written in *any* universal language, running on *any* machine, and (2) it can simulate *any* effectively

Figure 9.8

A universal program
written in language L_1
for programs in L_2.

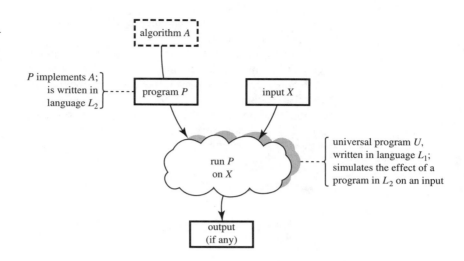

executable algorithm, written in *any* language. That is, given an algorithm A and
input X, rewrite A in the language L_2 (this is possible by the thesis), and submit the
new program with X to U (see Figure 9.8).

Turing machines are a perfect candidate for both L_1 and L_2, and indeed it is not
too difficult to construct a so-called **universal Turing machine**—namely, one that
can simulate the effect of arbitrary Turing machines on arbitrary inputs. But to do
so we must first find a way to describe any Turing machine as a linear sequence of
symbols, suitable for input on a tape. In fact, we have only to describe the machine's
transition diagram, which must be linearized into a sequence of symbols, suitable
for writing down on a Turing machine tape. This is done easily, since each transition
can be given by its source and target states, followed by the $\langle a/b, L \rangle$ or $\langle a/b, R \rangle$
label. By convention, the list of transitions will be preceded by the name of the start
state. Here, for example, is the initial part of an encoding of the Turing machine of
Figure 9.4:

mark $**$ *mark YES* $\langle \#/\#, L \rangle * mark\ move_a\ \langle a/\#, R \rangle * move_a\ move_a\ \langle a/a, R \rangle * \ldots$

The universal Turing machine U accepts as inputs such a description of any Turing
machine M, followed by a finite sequence X that is viewed as a potential input to M
(the description of M and the input X are separated, say, by "$\$$"). It then proceeds
to simulate M's action on a tape that contains the input X surrounded by blanks,
with the very same consequences: if M would not have halted on such a tape, then
neither does U, and if it would, then so does U. Furthermore, if and when U halts,
the tape looks precisely as it would have looked upon M's termination, including
the output enclosed between "!"s.

To really construct a universal Turing machine is an interesting exercise, not
unlike the task of writing an interpreter for a simple programming language L
in the language L itself. There exist, in fact, extremely concise universal Turing
machines with only very few states. In a similar vein, of course, it is also possible
to construct a **universal counter program**, which accepts as inputs two numbers,
the first encoding an input counter program, and the other its potential input, and
simulates the one on the other. In fact, being just another counter program itself, the

universal counter program can therefore be constructed with only two counters, as already mentioned.

More important than the number of states or counters, however, is the profound nature of a universal algorithm or machine U. Once constructed, U is a *single* object of *maximal* algorithmic power, and its significance cannot be overestimated. If a universal algorithm were written for use on a personal desk computer it would literally be able to simulate even the largest and most sophisticated mainframe computer, provided that it was given enough time, that a description of the simulated machine were given as its first input, and that sufficiently many memory units were available.

A Slight Modification of Counter Programs

We will now make a slight change in the primitive instructions of counter programs; the reason will become apparent in the next section. As defined earlier, counter programs can only add or subtract 1 to a counter. Thus, if they are to work on the numbers that represent Turing machine tapes, they would have to do so one *unit* at a time, whereas the Turing machines work on their tapes one *symbol* at a time. And since the Turing machine tape is thought of as representing numbers in, say, decimal notation, Turing machine numbers are manipulated one digit at a time, which is exponentially more efficient than working on them one unit at a time (unless the Turing machine operates on a one-letter alphabet, which is a very uninteresting case). And so, while counter programs based on $+1$ and -1 instructions alone are indeed as powerful as Turing machines, they are exponentially slower. This is not because of some inherent limitation of the counter program model itself, but because the primitive instructions are exponentially weaker. To remove this discrepancy, counter programs must be allowed to manipulate whole digits, be they binary, decimal, or otherwise. (Why is the particular choice of the number base unimportant here?) In essence, the programs are to be allowed to work on **nonunary** numbers, and they must be given the ability to attach and detach digits to numbers in constant time. Accordingly, let us add two instructions to the repertoire of basic operations of counter programs:

$$X \leftarrow X \times 10 \qquad \text{and} \qquad X \leftarrow X/10$$

(By convention, the division operator ignores fractions.) The new operations clearly add no computational power to the model, as they could have been simulated by the $+1$ and -1 operations. However, they do enable us to compare Turing machines and counter programs in a more realistic way, as will now be shown.

Tractability Is also Robust

By providing reductions between all sufficiently powerful models of computation, we convince ourselves that the class of problems solvable by these models is insensitive to the differences between them. By labeling the problems in the class

computable (or **decidable**, if we are interested in the yes/no case), we express our opinion that the notion we have captured is important and profound. This is the crux of the Church/Turing thesis.

With a small effort, however, we can do even better. Careful inspection shows that if both models involved in such a reduction deal with numbers (or whatever representation of them the model supports) in a nonunary fashion, then all these reductions take polynomial time; that is, they are *reasonable* in the sense of Chapter 7. For example, the transformation described earlier from a Turing machine and its input into an equivalent counter program and its corresponding input takes time that is only polynomial in the length of the descriptions of the former. Moreover—and this fact is not true without allowing the $X \times 10$ and $X/10$ operations—the time taken by the resulting counter program to run on the transformed input (assuming that it halts) is at most only polynomially longer than the time the Turing machine would have taken to run on the original input.[4]

It follows, of course, that if the Turing machine solves some algorithmic problem in polynomial time, then, not only does the corresponding counter program also solve the problem, it does so in polynomial time too. The converse reduction, from counter programs to Turing machines, is also polynomial-time, so that the dual fact holds too: if a counter program solves some problem in polynomial time then so does the resulting equivalent Turing machine.

The conclusion is that Turing machines and counter programs (with the $X \times 10$ and $X/10$ instructions) are **polynomially equivalent**. The class of problems having reasonable solutions (that is, polynomial-time ones) is the same for both models. The really surprising fact is that this polynomial-time equivalence holds not only for the reductions among these very primitive models, but also for the reductions between them and even the most sophisticated models. Turing machines and counter programs are obviously very inefficient even for quite trivial tasks, having to either shuttle back and forth on a tape, or repeatedly increase and decrease counters. However, they are only *polynomially* less efficient than even the fastest and most intricate computers, which support the most advanced programming languages with the most sophisticated compilers. In solving some algorithmic problem, the Turing machine or counter program resulting from the appropriate reduction might take *twice* as much time as it takes a fast computer, or a *thousand* times as much, or even that amount of time *squared*, *cubed*, or raised to the power 1000, but not *exponentially* as much.

■ More concisely, if a fast computer solves a certain problem in time $O(f(N))$, for some function f of the input length N, then there is an equivalent Turing machine that will take no more than time $O(p(f(N)))$, for some fixed polynomial function p. In particular, if f itself is a polynomial, meaning that the fast computer solves the problem *reasonably*, then some very primitive-looking Turing machine also solves it reasonably—in polynomial time $p(f(N))$, to be precise. Thus, the time might grow from, say, $O(N^2)$ to $O(N^5)$ or $O(N^{85})$, but not to $O(2^N)$. In fact, most known reductions involve *lower-order* polynomials of no more than about N^4 or N^5, so that "good" polynomial-time algorithms on one model will not become unacceptably worse on another.

---

[4] For counter programs time is measured by the number of instructions executed, and for Turing machines by the number of steps taken.

The conclusion is this: not only is the class of *computable* problems robust (that is, insensitive to model or language), but so is the class of *tractable* problems. This is really a refinement of the CT thesis that takes running time into consideration too. We should take note that the refined thesis does not hold for certain models that incorporate unlimited amounts of **concurrency**, as explained in Chapter 10, and for this reason it is sometimes called the **sequential computation thesis**. The term "sequential" is meant to capture algorithmic executions that proceed in a sequential, stepwise manner, rather than by carrying out lots of things simultaneously.

The refined CT thesis thus claims that all sequential universal models of computation, including those that have not yet been invented, have polynomially-related time behaviors, so that the class of problems solvable in reasonable time is the same for all models. Thus, the refined thesis justifies another of the lines appearing in our sphere of algorithmic problems, the one separating the tractable from the intractable (see Figures 7.6, 8.3, 8.11, and 8.12).

Many other complexity classes, such as NP, PSPACE, and EXPTIME (see Figure 7.15) are also robust in the same sense, justifying much of the language- and model-independent research in complexity theory. However, some classes, like the problems solvable in *linear* time, are not, and can be highly sensitive to changes in the model. A Turing machine with an additional counter, for example, can compare the number of a's and b's appearing in a sequence in linear time, but bare Turing machines require $O(N \times \log N)$ if a rather clever method is used, and take quadratic time if they naively run back and forth. (Can you find the $O(N \times \log N)$ method?)

Incidentally, the polynomial-time version of the CT thesis could not have been formulated as early as the 1930s because complexity theory did not exist then. The significance of the class P was only recognized in the late 1960s, and gained credence a few years later with the realization of the importance of the P vs. NP problem.

(Although we have not defined it precisely, it happens that the line separating the undecidable from the *highly* undecidable in Figures 8.11 and 8.12 is also robust in the sense of the present discussion. Thus, all universal models of computation give rise to the same division, and the recurring domino problem, for example, is highly undecidable in them all.)

■ Turing Machines and the P vs. NP Problem

The NP-complete problems of Chapter 7 deserve special mention here. In most textbooks P and NP are introduced in terms of the rigorous notion of Turing machine computations; NP is defined to contain precisely those decision problems solvable by *nondeterministic* Turing machines running in polynomial time, while P is defined to contain those solvable by *ordinary* Turing machines in polynomial time. Once such formal definitions are given, the refined CT thesis is stated as claiming that all reasonable sequential computation models are polynomially equivalent to ordinary Turing machines, and the ramifications of this fact can then be discussed. In contrast, we have introduced the notions of P and NP in Chapter 7 without a precise model, stating the CT thesis first, and only later introducing formal models such as Turing machines. The reasons for this are pedagogic in nature; the consequences remain the same.

Now, had nondeterministic Turing machines satisfied the criterion of sequentiality, the refined thesis would have implied a positive solution to the P vs. NP problem, since it would have equated the classes of problems solvable in polynomial time on both versions of Turing machines. As it happens, nondeterministic machines are not considered sequential, since they employ "magic" to make the best choices, and without magic they would have had to try out many possibilities *simultaneously* to find the best one. (Trying them out sequentially would take exponential time.) Therefore, the thesis does not apply to such machines, and it thus cannot help much with regards to P vs. NP.

Formulating the P vs. NP problem in this formal fashion is interesting because it implies that to solve the problem in the negative (that is, to show that P $\neq$ NP) we need only show that the simple and primitive model of Turing machines cannot solve some NP-complete problem in less than exponential time. For example, if someone were to show that the monkey puzzle problem cannot be solved on any Turing machine in polynomial time, it would follow from the refined thesis that it cannot be solved in polynomial time on *any* sequential model, and hence that it is truly intractable. And, as we know, if the monkey puzzle problem is intractable, then so are *all* the NP-complete problems, yielding P $\neq$ NP.

Using Turing Machines for Lower Bound Proofs

To prove an *upper* bound on an algorithmic problem—that is, to find a good algorithm—the richest and most powerful formalism available should be used. In fact, researchers typically employ very high-level programming constructs and intricate data structures to devise nontrivial algorithms. They then rely on the robustness afforded by the variants of the Church/Turing thesis to make claims about the implications of those algorithms to *all* models. Thus, if someone ever manages to prove that P $=$ NP, the chances are that it will be done using a very high-level model, with perhaps complicated data structures, to describe a sophisticated polynomial-time algorithm for some NP-complete problem. However, when proving *lower* bounds, primitive models are much better suited, since they employ only a few extremely simple constructs and there is less to worry about, so to speak. Thus, if someone ever proves that P $\neq$ NP, the chances are that it will be done using a very primitive model, like Turing machines or counter programs.

Turing machines are, in fact, used widely in lower bound proofs of all kinds. As an example, it is instructive to get a feeling for how Turing machines can be used to show the undecidability of the tiling problem. (Undecidability, of course, is a kind of lower bound—it brings bad news about the status of the problem.) It is easier to discuss a version of the tiling problem that is slightly less general than the simple unbounded domino problem of Chapter 8. This particular version of the problem asks whether the set T of tile types can be used to tile the upper half of the infinite integer grid, but with the additional requirement that the first tile in T, call it t, is to be placed somewhere along the bottom row. To show that this tiling problem is undecidable we describe a reduction of the halting problem for Turing machines to it (actually, the *non*halting problem, as explained below). In other words, we want to show that if we could decide the tiling problem we could also decide whether a given Turing machine M can halt on a given input X.

Figure 9.9

Reducing halting
Turing machines to
tiling half-grids.
(Notice how "yes" and
"no" switch roles.)

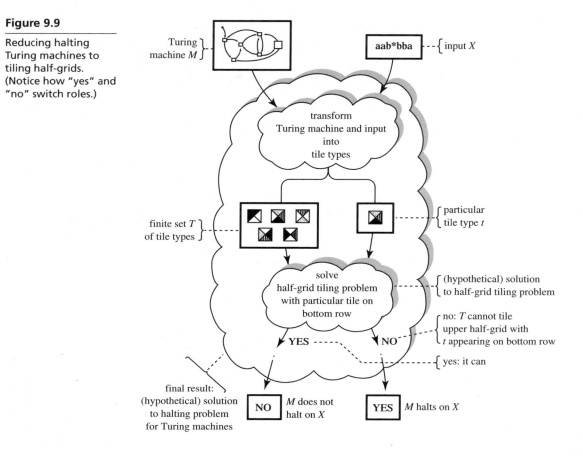

Assume, then, that we have a hypothetical solution to the tiling problem just
described. We are now given a Turing machine M and an input word X. We would
like to show how to construct a set of tile types T, containing a particular tile t, such
that M does not halt on X precisely if T can tile the upper half-grid with t appearing
somewhere along the bottom row. See Figure 9.9. We shall not describe the details
of the transformation itself, only its uderlying idea. You are invited to try to work
out these details.

The idea is very simple. The tile set T is constructed in such a way that tiling the
half-grid in the upward direction corresponds to making progress in the computation
of the Turing machine M on X. The effect is achieved by making each row of tiles
encode, using appropriate colors, the current contents of M's infinite tape, together
with the current state and the location of the head within the tape. (Since there
are only finitely many states and symbols, combinations of them can be encoded
with finitely many colors.) In this way, each legal tiling of a row represents a legal
configuration (that is, complete status) of the Turing machine. Moreover, the tiles
are constructed to guarantee that progressing upward from tiled row to tiled row
is possible only in precise accordance with the instructions given in M's transition
diagram. This is done by allowing in T only tiles whose bottom colors (which
merely "copy" M's previous configuration from the previous row of tiles by the

color-matching constraint) are related to the top colors (which encode M's new configuration) by the legal transitions in M's transition diagram. In this way, the ability to extend part of a tiling upwards by one more row is precisely the same as the ability to carry out one more step of M's computation, reaching a new configuration. The special tile t, the one that has to appear in the bottom row, is constructed to encode the start state of the Turing machine and the beginning of the input word X. Other bottom row tiles encode the rest of X, guaranteeing that the first row in any possible tiling faithfully represents the starting configuration of the machine.

We are thus mapping Turing machine computations onto tiled portions of the upper half of the grid, where the horizontal dimension corresponds to memory space (the tape) and the vertical dimension to time. It is then fair to say that tiling with colored tiles and computing with algorithms are almost the same thing.

Figure 9.10 shows the tiling that results from the tile set constructed for the palindrome machine of Figure 9.4 and the input sequence "$a\,b\,b\,a$". The figure is thus a faithful tile version of the computation depicted in Figure 9.5. (For conciseness, we have abbreviated the names of states as follows: *mark* becomes mk, *move$_a$* becomes mv_a, *test$_a$* becomes ts_a and *return* becomes rt. Also, to make the connection with Figure 9.4 clearer, we write the explicit combinations of symbols instead of the colors that encode them.) Notice how the rows correspond perfectly to the frames of Figure 9.5. In this example the tiling cannot be continued upwards because the machine halts and cannot continue its computation.

From all this it follows that any possible tiling of the entire upper half-grid with the tile types of T, in which t appears in the bottom row, corresponds directly to an infinite computation of M on X. Consequently, if the half-grid tiling problem were decidable, i.e., if we could decide whether T can tile the half-grid with t appearing in the first row, the non-halting problem for Turing machines would be decidable too, as illustrated in Figure 9.9. But since the halting problem is not decidable, neither is the nonhalting problem (why?), so that as a result the tiling problem cannot be decidable either.

One-Way Turing Machines, or Finite-State Automata

We have seen that certain restrictions on Turing machines (such as using a tape that is infinite only to the right) do not detract from the universality of the model; the class of solvable problems remains the same even when the model is so restricted. Clearly, not all restrictions have this property. Machines that are required to halt immediately upon starting cannot do very much, and the same goes for those that are not allowed to halt at all. These examples, however, are not very interesting. In the interim many kinds of limitations can be imposed on universal models of computation, and on Turing machines in particular, which result in weaker classes of problems that are nevertheless of great interest.

One obvious approach is to restrict the machine's use of resources. We already know that the class P is obtained by allowing only Turing machines that halt within a polynomial amount of time. PSPACE is the class obtained by allowing Turing

Figure 9.10

The tiling
corresponding to the
computation of
Figure 9.5.

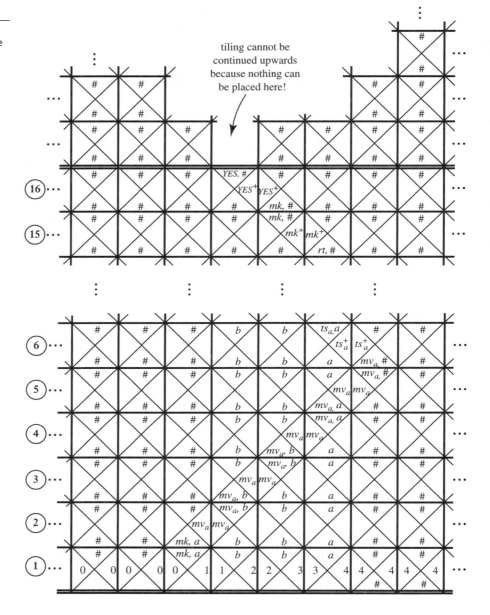

machines access to only a polynomial amount of tape (any attempt to go beyond the
limit is punished, say, by halting in state *NO*). Other complexity classes can similarly
be defined as consisting of the problems solvable by appropriately resource-bounded
Turing machines.

There is, however, another approach to restricting the Turing machine model.
It involves limiting the machine's very mechanism. One of the most interesting of
these downgrades is obtained by allowing Turing machines to travel along the tape in
only one fixed direction—say to the right. The result is a device called a **finite-state
automaton**, or simply a **finite automaton** for short.

Let us think about this for a moment. If the machine is not allowed to move left it cannot inspect any square more than once. In particular, it cannot make use of anything it writes down itself, save to produce output, since it cannot go back to read its own notes, so to speak. Therefore, if the discussion is restricted to *decision* problems, which do not produce outputs anyway, we can assume that finite automata do not write at all; saying "yes" or "no" can be achieved via two special halting states, and the new symbols it writes down as it moves along are worthless, having no effect whatsoever on the automaton's final verdict. Moreover, to the right of the input sequence the tape contains only blanks; thus, the automaton might as well stop when it reaches the end of the input sequence, since it is not going to see anything new that will make a difference.

In conclusion, a finite automaton solving a decision problem acts as follows. It simply runs through the input sequence of symbols, one by one, changing states as a result of the current state and the new symbol it sees. When it reaches the end of the input sequence it stops, and the answer depends upon whether it stopped in state *YES* or *NO*. (By convention, we shall consider stopping in any other state to be like saying "no," so that a finite automaton need not have a *NO* state; if it is in the *YES* state when it reaches the end of the input the answer is "yes," and otherwise it is "no.") We can describe a finite automaton as a state transition diagram, just as we did for Turing machines, but now we have no need for the $\langle b, L \rangle$ or $\langle b, R \rangle$ part of the labels; a transition is labeled only with the symbol that triggers it.

The Power of Finite Automata

What are finite automata capable of? Figure 9.11 shows a finite automaton that decides whether or not its input sequence of a's and b's contains an even number of a's. (What does the automaton of Figure 9.12 do?) Answering questions of **parity**

Figure 9.11

A finite automaton that detects words with an even number of a's.

Figure 9.12

What does this automaton detect?

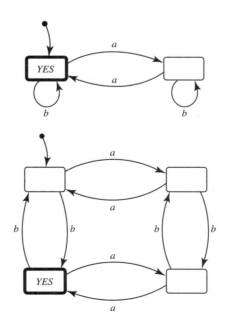

(that is, evenness and oddness) might appear at first to require the ability to count. It does not. The automaton of Figure 9.11 does the job not by counting how many a's it has seen, but by alternating between two states that indicate the current parity status of that number.

In fact, it is quite easy to show that finite automata *cannot* count. As an illustration, let us convince ourselves that no finite automaton can decide whether its input sequence contains precisely the same number of a's and b's.

■ The proof will be by way of contradiction. Assume that some automaton F *can* indeed solve this decision problem, meaning that for any sequence of a's and b's, F says "yes" precisely if the number of occurrences of both is equal. Denote by N the number of states in F. Consider the sequence X that consists of precisely $N + 1$ a's followed by $N + 1$ b's. Obviously, our automaton must say "yes" when handed X as an input, since X has the same number of a's and b's.

The argument now uses the so-called **pigeonhole principle**: if all the pigeons have to enter pigeonholes, but there are more pigeons than holes, then at least one hole will have to accommodate more than one pigeon. In our case the pigeons are the $N + 1$ a's constituting the first half of the input sequence X, and the holes are the N states of the automaton F. As F moves along X there must be at least two different tape squares, or positions, within the initial sequence of a's where F will be in the same state. For definiteness, assume that N is 9, that the two positions are the third and the seventh, and that the common state entered in the two cases is s (see Figure 9.13). Now, F cannot move backwards, cannot jot any information down, and acts solely on the basis of the one symbol it sees and its current state. It is therefore obvious that when it reaches the seventh square its behavior on the rest of the input will not depend on anything it has seen earlier except by way of the fact that it is now in state s. Consequently, if we were to *remove* squares 3 through 6, resulting in a sequence of 6 a's, not 10, followed by the 10 b's, the automaton F would still reach the third a in state s and would proceed just as if it had reached the seventh a in the original sequence. In particular, since it said "yes" on the original sequence, it will say "yes" on the new one. But the new sequence has

Figure 9.13

Applying the pigeonhole principle to a finite automaton.

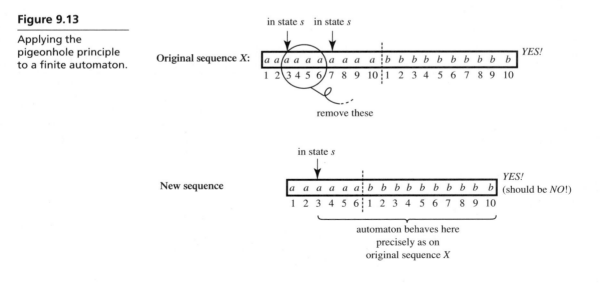

Figure 9.14

An automaton describing a simple digital watch.

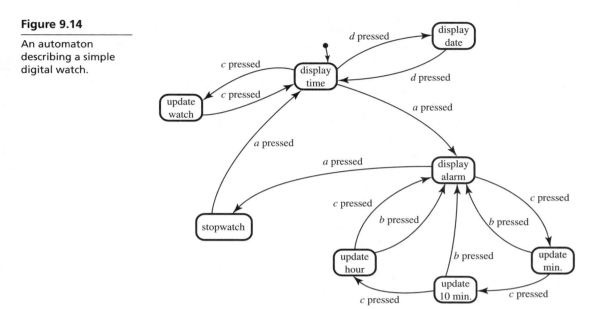

6 a's and 10 b's, and our assumption to the effect that F says "yes" only on sequences with the same number of a's and b's is thus contradicted. The conclusion is that no finite automaton can solve this decision problem.

You might enjoy constructing a similar proof, also using the pigeonhole principle, to show that finite automata cannot detect palindromes.

Finite automata are indeed very limited, but they do capture the way many everyday systems work. For example, Figure 9.14 shows a finite-state automaton describing part of the behavior of a simple digital watch, with four control buttons, $a, b, c,$ and d. The names of the states are self-explanatory, and we can associate with each state detailed descriptions of the actions that are carried out therein. Notice that the input symbols are really the **signals**, or **events**, that enter the system from its outside environment—in this case, the user pressing buttons. An input word is thus just a sequence of incoming signals. In Chapter 14 we shall further discuss this correspondence.

■ ■

Research on Abstract Models of Computation

In a sense, the material of this chapter forms the underpinnings of nearly all the topics mentioned in the book so far. Primitive models of computation, whether they are universal, like Turing machines and counter programs, or less powerful, like finite automata or resource-bounded models, are extremely important objects for research in computer science. They focus attention on the essential properties of real algorithmic devices, such as computers and programming languages, and give rise to fundamental and robust notions that are insensitive to the particular device used.

In Chapters 7 and 8 we touched upon the research areas of computational complexity and undecidability, both of which use the likes of Turing machines and counter programs in an essential way. Finite automata are the basis of a very large body of research, of both theoretical and practical nature, which has fundamental implications to such diverse areas as the design of power stations and the understanding of the brain.

Other restrictions of Turing machines have been, and are still being, heavily studied, in the research areas of **automata** and **formal language theory**. Notable among these are **pushdown automata**, which can be viewed as finite automata endowed with a stack, upon which symbols can be pushed, read off the top, and popped. Pushdown automata are of importance in a variety of endeavors, including compiler design and structural linguistics, as they can be used to represent recursively-defined syntactical structures, such as computer programs or legal sentences in English. It turns out, for example, that in terms of the classes of problems they can solve, nondeterministic pushdown automata are more powerful than deterministic ones, a fact that is not true either for the weaker finite automata or for the stronger Turing machines. For example, a nondeterministic pushdown automaton can be constructed to detect palindromes (how?), but it is possible to prove that no deterministic pushdown automaton can do so.

Researchers are interested in decision problems involving the models themselves. For example, we know that algorithmic equivalence is undecidable, so that, in particular, it is undecidable whether two given Turing machines solve the same algorithmic problem. However, if we go all the way down to finite automata, equivalence becomes decidable. As to pushdown automata, the story is as follows. For the nondeterministic case, equivalence is undecidable, which is an old and well-known result. In contrast, for *deterministic* pushdown automata the question was considered to be one of the hardest unresolved problems in the theory of automata and formal languages. A few years ago it was finally resolved, in the affirmative. Hence, we now know that equivalence is decidable for deterministic pushdown automata too, resulting in an interesting decidability difference between the deterministic and nondeterministic versions of the same model of computation.

By the way, whenever such decision problems are found to be decidable, research turns to the task of determining their computational complexity, and, here too, many interesting and applicable results have emerged.

Scientists are also interested in finding the right "CT thesis" for certain variants of the standard notions of computability and tractability. One case that has been addressed is that of databases, where the following questions are of interest. What is the basic universal notion of a "computable" query on a database or knowledge base? What are the "Turing machines" of databases? There is no real value in trying to answer the question naively by encoding databases on Turing machine tapes and appealing to the standard theory of Turing machines. While this can be done, of course, the resulting linearization of the databases may, by its very nature, enforce an order on sets of data items that are not intended to be ordered in any particular way (say a list of equally important employees). Queries should not be allowed to make use of an ordering on such data items, and any proposed universal model or language for database queries should reflect that fact.

The research areas of computability theory, automata and formal language theory, recursive function theory, and complexity theory, are thus closely interrelated. Ever since the pioneering work of the 1930s, abstract models of computation have played a crucial role in obtaining fundamental results in these areas, thus forming the basis for many of the most important developments in algorithmics.

■ Exercises

9.1. (a) Write an algorithm for "linearizing" a two-dimensional array A. The input includes two positive integers M and N, and an array A of size $M \times N$. The expression $A[I, J]$ returns the value of A at the Ith row and Jth column. The result of the linearization should be produced in a vector B, such that each $B[K]$ can be a value in the linearized form, an *intra-rows* separator, or an *end-of-vector* marker.

   (b) Write an algorithm which, given a linearized list, reconstructs the original two-dimensional array A. The number of rows and columns is not given as part of the input; rather, it too should be calculated by the algorithm.

   (c) Write subroutines that perform the following operations on a two-dimensional array given in the linearized form. Do not reconstruct the array.
   - Return $A[I, J]$.
   - Replace $A[I, J]$ by the new value E.
   - Zero all elements of row number I.
   - Delete all elements of column number J. (In other words, the array A is "collapsed" by eliminating the entire column.)
   - Add a new column after column J, such that the value of A at row I and the new column is the maximum value of row $I - 1$ in the original array. (At the first row take the maximum of the last row.)

9.2. (a) Write an algorithm for "linearizing" a tree using the method described in the text. The tree is given by a pointer to its root R, and can be accessed by the operations **value**(N), **#offspring**(N) and **offspring**(I, N), returning for a (pointer to) node N the value stored in it, the number of its offspring, and a pointer to its Ith offspring, respectively. The result of the linearization should be produced in a vector B, such that each $B[K]$ can be a value, a left or right parenthesis symbol, or the *end-of-vector* marker.

   (b) Write an algorithm which, given a linearized tree, reconstructs the original tree. You may use the operations **value**$(N) \leftarrow E$, **#offspring**$(N) \leftarrow I$, and **offspring** $(I, N) \leftarrow M$, with the obvious semantics.

   (c) Write subroutines that perform the following operations on a linearized tree. Do not reconstruct the tree.
   - Return the index (in B) of the Ith offspring of the node stored at index K.
   - Return the value of the Ith offspring of the node stored at index K.
   - Delete the leaf stored at index K.
   - Return the number of offspring of the node stored at index K.
   - Add an Ith offspring with value E to the node stored at index K. That is, the previous Ith offspring becomes the $I + 1$st, etc. If the node stored at index K has less than $I - 1$ offspring, add enough offspring, all with the value E.

9.3. (a) Construct a Turing machine that performs unary addition.

   (b) Construct the complete transition table (or diagram) of a Turing machine that performs binary addition.

(c) Construct the complete transition table (or diagram) of a Turing machine that performs decimal addition.

(d) Describe informally an algorithm that, given an integer $N > 1$, produces a Turing machine description for performing N-ary addition.

9.4. Describe informally Turing machines that, given a linearized two-dimensional array in the form shown in Figure 9.1, and the appropriate parameters, perform the operations described in Exercise 9.1(c).

9.5. Describe informally the operation of a Turing machine that solves the general monkey puzzle problem.

9.6. Does the CT thesis hold for a computer with an input device of unlimited size, say, a PC with an unlimited stock of *read-only* diskettes, but with only a limited amount of additional memory, say, nothing additional except a 40 MB disk? Justify your answer rigorously. (Hint: either sketch a simulation of a Turing machine on such a computer, or exhibit a decidable problem that is not solvable on it.)

9.7. Show that none of the following limitations on Turing machines actually weakens the formalism. That is, for each Turing machine in the standard formalism, show that there exists one that obeys the limitation but computes precisely the same function.

(a) The machine is not permitted to simultaneously write on the tape and move its head on a single transition.

(b) There exists an upper bound of five on the number of times the machine is allowed to write on any tape square.

9.8. Show that none of the following additions to Turing machines actually adds computational power to the formalism. That is, for each Turing machine with the additional feature, show that there exists a standard one that computes precisely the same function.

(a) The machine may, in a single transition, exchange two tape symbols throughout the entire tape.

(b) The machine may have several tapes, with one head operating on each tape (simultaneous transitions).

(c) The machine has two tapes, and can switch tapes at will. That is, the tape presently considered "first" becomes "second" and vice versa. The head's position on each actual tape is preserved.

(d) The machine operates on a two-dimensional tape (a grid), with **left**, **right**, **up**, and **down** movements.

9.9. Describe in detail a (possibly nondeterministic) Turing machine that solves the word correspondence problem whenever a correspondence exists, and may not halt otherwise. For simplicity, consider only instances with three Xs and three Ys. You may employ any convenient representation of the input.

9.10. Write counter programs that compute the following:

(a) The integer power function N^M.

(b) The least prime number greater than a given integer N.

(c) The integer square root (i.e., the integer part of the square root) of a given integer N. (For example, the integer square roots of 12, 16, and 26, are 3, 4, and 5, respectively.)

9.11. Write a modified counter program which, for a given integer N, checks whether the decimal string representing X forms a palindrome. (For example, 121 and 3663 are palindromes, but 12 is not.)

9.12. Write a universal Turing machine simulator in some high-level programming language.

9.13. Write a universal counter program simulator in some high-level programming language.

9.14. Explain why the choice of the number base is unimportant when referring to the modification of counter programs that enables them to manipulate whole digits.

9.15. (a) Why does the polynomial-time equivalence of models of computation prove that EXPTIME is robust too?

(b) Does the same hold for NP and PSPACE? If not, what additional fact do we need to make it hold?

9.16. Assume we could establish linear-time equivalence of models of computation. What other complexity classes would become robust in the sense described in the text?

9.17. Find the $O(N \times \log N)$ method hinted at in the text for comparing the number of a's and b's in a sequence by an ordinary Turing machine.

9.18. (a) Show in detail how to construct the tile set T suggested in the text, with the property that the given Turing machine halts on the given input precisely if T can tile the upper half-grid with a specific tile t appearing somewhere along the bottom row.

(b) Enhance the method used in the text to prove that the problem of whether T can tile the *entire* grid with t appearing somewhere is undecidable.

(c) Explain why the fact that the halting problem in undecidable implies that the nonhalting problem is undecidable too?

9.19. Construct in detail finite automata that perform the following tasks.

(a) Recognize a sequence of symbols representing a PASCAL real number.

(b) Recognize a sequence of symbols representing a comment in C, C++, or JAVA.

(c) Add 1 to a binary number. That is, convert a sequence of the form $a_1, a_2, \ldots, a_k$, $k \geq 1$, where all the a_i's are either 0 or 1, representing the binary number $A = a_k a_{k-1} \ldots a_1$, into a sequence $b_1, b_2, \ldots, b_n$, $n \geq k$, representing the binary number $B = b_n b_{n-1} \ldots b_1$, such that $B = A + 1$.

(d) Add 3 to a decimal number.

9.20. Prove that deterministic finite automata (acceptors) are closed under union, intersection, concatenation, iteration, and complementation. That is, given two deterministic automata A and B, show that:

(a) There exists a deterministic automaton C which accepts a sequence precisely if at least one of A or B accepts it.

(b) There exists a deterministic automaton C which accepts a sequence precisely if both A and B accept it.

(c) There exists a deterministic automaton C which accepts a sequence precisely if it is the concatenation $w = w_1 w_2$ of two sequences w_1 and w_2, such that A accepts w_1 and B accepts w_2.

(d) There exists a deterministic automaton C which accepts a sequence precisely if it is the concatenation $w = w_1 w_2 \ldots w_k$ of k sequences, for some $k \geq 1$, such that A accepts each of the sequences w_i.

(e) There exists a deterministic automaton C which accepts a sequence precisely if A does not accept it.

9.21. Prove that deterministic and nondeterministic finite automata have equivalent computational power. (Hint: given a nondeterministic automaton A, construct a deterministic one whose states are labeled by subsets of the set of states of A.)

9.22. Construct a nondeterministic finite automaton and an equivalent deterministic one, that accept those sequences over the set of symbols $\{a, b, c, d\}$, such that at least one symbol appears precisely twice along the sequence.

9.23. Prove the decidability of the following problems for finite automata:

(a) The nonemptiness problem (i.e., given an automaton A, does it accept any sequence at all?).

(b) The equivalence problem (i.e., given two automata A and B, do they accept precisely the same sequences?).

9.24. Show that for decision problems, Turing machines that are not allowed to write at all are really equivalent to finite automata.

9.25. Use the results you have proved in Exercises 9.20 and 9.23, in order to prove that the unrestricted word correspondence problem, described in Chapter 8, is decidable. (Hint: given the Xs and Ys, construct a nondeterministic automaton that recognizes sequences that are formed from one or more segments, each segment being one of the Xs, and a similar automaton for the Ys.)

9.26. Prove that the following sets of symbol sequences cannot be recognized by finite automata:

(a) Well-formed arithmetic expressions, constructed from integers, arithmetic operators ("+", "−", "×", and "/"), and left and right parentheses.

(b) Legal LISP lists.

The model of pushdown automata is an extension of that of finite automata. We will consider pushdown acceptors only. A pushdown automaton has, in addition to an internal state and a read-only, right-moving-only head, an unbounded stack, i.e., a LIFO store of which symbols from a special finite *stack alphabet* can be pushed, popped (whenever there is any element to be popped), and compared against the top element. (Stacks as data types are described in the text in Chapter 2.)

In addition to using its internal state and input symbol to determine its next transition, a pushdown automaton also uses the value of the **top** element of the stack to make the transition. Upon performing a transition, the automaton may **pop** the top element from the stack, and may in addition **push** another symbol into it.

9.27. Construct (nondeterministic) pushdown automata that recognize the following sets.

(a) Palindromes.

(b) Arithmetic expressions, as defined in Exercise 9.26(a).

(c) Well-formed formulas in the propositional calculus.

9.28. Consider the "programming language" of modified counter programs. A **syntactically legal program** is a sequence of symbols as defined in the text, including separating blanks and **end-of-line** symbols separating sentences. An identifier or label name is any nonempty string of letters and digits beginning with a letter. The syntactical part of a compiler is concerned with recognizing syntactically legal programs.

(a) Construct a pushdown automaton that recognizes syntactically legal counter programs.

(b) Another method for recognizing programs is to separate the task into two subtasks: **lexical analysis** and **parsing**.

■ Construct a **lexical analyzer** for counter programs, i.e., a deterministic finite automaton, which inputs a counter program and produces a sequence of **token symbols**. These are *single* symbols that stand for a whole token, such as "an identifier," "an assignment arrow," "a + symbol," "an end-of-sentence symbol," "the **goto** token," etc.

■ Construct a **parser**, i.e., a pushdown automaton that accepts a sequence of token symbols precisely if it is produced by the lexical analyzer upon reading a syntactically legal counter program.

(c) Discuss the methodological and computational differences between the above two methods for recognizing syntactically legal programs. Can you provide a quantitative measure that can be used to exhibit some of these differences?

9.29. Show that pushdown automata with *two* stacks are computationally equivalent to Turing machines.

All things come alike to all

ECCLESIASTES 9: 2

PART IV

Relaxing the Rules

so shall it be easier for thyself

EXODUS 18: 22

CHAPTER 10

Parallelism, Concurrency, and Alternative Models

*many shall run to
and fro, and
knowledge shall
be increased*

DANIEL 12: 4

or, Getting Lots of Stuff Done at Once

The fact that computing doesn't bring only good news has pushed researchers in a number of directions, intended to try and alleviate the problem. In this chapter we shall discuss some of the most interesting of these: **parallelism** and **concurrency**, **quantum computing**, and **molecular computing**. Each of these represents a new algorithmic paradigm, and they all do so by relaxing a fundamental assumption underlying conventional computing, namely that an algorithm is carried out by the little processor Runaround, working all on its own. Parallelism and concurrency concern setting things up directly so that several processors (or several little Runarounds) do the work together, in cooperation. Quantum computing transfers computation into the mysterious realm of quantum mechanics, whereby parallelism stems from the ability of particles to be in more than one place simultaneously. And molecular, or biological, computing represents an attempt to have molecules do the work for us by massive, seemingly redundant, parallelism.

To get a feeling for parallelism, consider the following. Several years ago there was a contest in the Los Angeles area for the world title in fast house building. Certain rigid rules had to be adhered to, involving things like the number of rooms, the utilities required, and allowed building materials. No prefabrication was permitted, but the foundations could be prepared ahead of time. A house was deemed finished when people could literally start living in it; all plumbing and electricity had to be in place and functioning perfectly, trees and grass had to adorn the yard, and so on. No limit was placed on the size of the building team.

The winning company used a team of about 200 builders, and had the house ready in a little over *four hours*!

This is a striking illustration of the benefits of parallelism: a single person working alone would need a lot more time to complete the house. It was only by working together, amid incredible feats of cooperation, coordination, and mutual effort, that the task could be accomplished in so short a time. Parallel computation allows many computers, or many processors within a single computer, to work on a problem together, in parallel.

Quantum computing is a brand new approach to computation, based on quantum mechanics, that tantalizing and paradoxical piece of twentieth-century physics. So far, a few surprisingly efficient quantum algorithms have been discovered for problems not known to be tractable in the "classical" sense. However, to work they require the construction of a special **quantum computer**, something that as of now is still very much nonexistent. Molecular computing, another very recent paradigm, has enabled researchers to coax a molecular solvent to solve instances of certain NP-complete problems, which raises interesting and exciting possibilities.

The rest of the chapter discusses these ideas, with parallelism and distributed concurrency—the more classical of them—being treated in quite a bit more detail.

Parallelism, or Joining Forces

Our main aim in this chapter is to examine the consequences of having many processors achieve algorithmic goals jointly, by working together. This relaxation is motivated in part by the desire to exploit **parallelism** in hardware, namely, the availability of so-called **parallel computers**, which consist of many separate processing elements, cooperating and working in parallel. Later we shall also generalize the rigid input/output notion of an algorithmic problem to cases involving **perpetuity**, or **ongoing behavior**, that need not lead to termination at all. Such problems stem from **distributed** environments of inherently parallel nature, such as flight reservation systems or telephone networks, and are also related to the system development issues discussed in Chapters 13 and 14.

Parallelism Helps

The house building story makes it obvious that doing things in parallel can work wonders. Let us see what these wonders boil down to in terms of algorithmic efficiency.

If an algorithm calls for the sequence of instructions:

$$X \leftarrow 3; \ Y \leftarrow 4,$$

then we could obviously save time by carrying them out simultaneously, in parallel. We must be very careful, however, not to "parallelize" just anything; if the instructions were:

$$X \leftarrow 3; \ Y \leftarrow X$$

the story would be quite different, since following a parallel execution Y's new value might be X's *old* value, rather than its new one, 3. Here the effect of the second instruction depends on the results of the first, and hence the two cannot be parallelized. Of course, they can be modified in ways that will circumvent the problem, but in their original form they must be carried out in order.

To further illustrate the point, consider the problem of digging a ditch, one foot deep, one foot wide, and 10 feet long. If a single person can dig a one-by-one-by-one

Figure 10.1

Summing salaries in
logarithmic time.

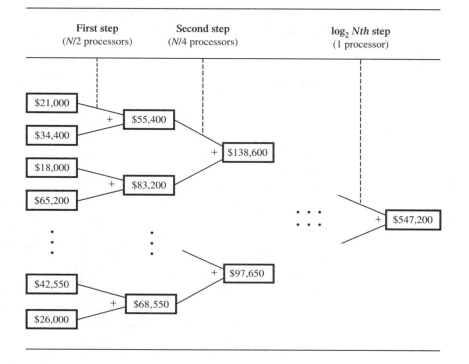

foot ditch in, say, an hour, 10 people could dig the desired ditch in one hour in the obvious way. Parallelism is at its best here. However, if the desired ditch is to be one foot wide, one foot long, and 10 feet *deep*, parallelism will achieve nothing, and even 100 people would need 10 hours to get the job done.[1]

Some algorithmic problems can easily be parallelized, despite the fact that the first solutions that come to mind are heavily sequential; they are not really **inherently sequential**. Many of them can be solved far more efficiently by parallel processing. Consider the salary summation problem of Chapter 1. It would perhaps appear necessary to run through the list of employees in order, yielding the linear algorithm described therein. Not so. A parallel algorithm can be devised that will run in logarithmic time—a momentous improvement indeed, as shown in Chapter 6. The method is to first consider the entire list of N employees in pairs, $\langle first, second \rangle$, $\langle third, fourth \rangle$, and so on, and to sum the two salaries in all pairs *simultaneously*, thus yielding a list of $N/2$ new numbers (recall that N is the total number of employees). This takes the time of only one addition, which we count here as a single time unit. The new list is then also considered in pairs, and the two numbers in each are again added simultaneously, yielding a new list of $N/4$ numbers. This continues until there is only one number left; it is the sum of the salaries in the entire list. Figure 10.1 illustrates this simple idea. As explained in Chapter 6, the number of times N can be divided by 2 until it reaches 1 is about $\log_2 N$, and hence the logarithmic time bound. With the numbers of Chapter 6 in mind, it follows that 1000 salaries can be

---

[1] A similar example involves nine couples trying to have a child in one month, rather than one couple having it in nine months...

summed in the time it takes to carry out just 10 additions, and a million salaries can be summed in the time of only 20 additions.

Fixed vs. Expanding Parallelism

Notice that to simultaneously carry out the 500 additions required in the first step of summing 1000 salaries, we need 500 processors. The *same* ones can then be used to carry out the 250 additions of the second stage in parallel (half of them, of course, would be idle), then the 125 additions of the third stage, and so on. Of course, a large number of processors alone is not enough; we also have to arrange the data in such a way that the right numbers are quickly accessible to the right processors when they need them. This is why good data structures and communication methods are crucial to fast parallel algorithms. However, concentrating on the number of processors at the moment, we see that in order to achieve the reduction from linear to logarithmic time we need $N/2$ processors, a number that depends on N, the length of the input. Indeed, this is necessarily the case, for if we had only a fixed number of processors we could not improve things beyond the constant hidden under the big-O: we might be able to do things twice as fast, or 100 times as fast, but it would still be linear, that is, $O(N)$, and there would not be an order-of-magnitude improvement.

You might claim that a growing number of processors is just not feasible. But then neither is a growing amount of time or memory. The purpose of complexity measures is to provide means for estimating the inherent difficulty of solving algorithmic problems as inputs become larger, the estimate being given as a function of the size of the input. If we are going to be summing lists of no more than a million salaries, and if we have half a million processors at hand, we will need very little time (roughly that of 20 additions). If we have fewer processors we can parallelize up to a point; that is, up to a certain depth in the tree of Figure 10.1. From that point on, a mixture of parallelism and sequentiality will have to be used. Clearly, the result will not be as good.

To achieve an order-of-magnitude improvement, therefore, requires **expanding parallelism**—that is, a number of processors that grows as N grows. However, that number need not necessarily be $N/2$. For example, it is possible to add the salaries in a list of length N in time $O(\sqrt{N})$ if $\sqrt{N}$ processors are available—for example, a million salaries in the time of about 1000 additions with 1000 processors. (Can you see how?) Of course, the time of 1000 additions is not as good as that of 20, but then 1000 processors are fewer than half a million, so that we get what we pay for, so to speak.

Sorting in Parallel

Sorting a list of length N (for example, putting a jumbled telephone book into order) is an excellent problem for discussing the benefits of parallel processing. Consider the mergesort algorithm of Chapter 4 (see Figure 4.3). It called for splitting the input list into halves, sorting them both recursively, and then merging the sorted halves. The merge is achieved by repeatedly comparing the currently smallest (first) elements in the halves, resulting in one of them being sent off to the output. The algorithm can be described schematically as follows:

subroutine **sort-**L:

(1) if L consists of one element then it is sorted;

(2) otherwise do the following:
    (2.1) split L into two halves, L_1 and L_2;
    (2.2) call **sort-**L_1;
    (2.3) call **sort-**L_2;
    (2.4) merge resulting lists into a single sorted list.

In Chapter 6 it was claimed that the time complexity of this algorithm is $O(N \times \log N)$. Now, obviously, the two activities of sorting the halves (lines (2.2) and (2.3) in the algorithm) do not interfere with each other, since they involve disjoint sets of elements. Therefore, they can be carried out in parallel. Even parallelizing the sorting of the halves only once, on the *top* level of the algorithm, resulting in the need for just two processors, would improve things, but only within the big-O constant, as already explained. However, we can carry out the two sorts in parallel on *all* levels of the recursion, yielding the following:

subroutine **parallel-sort-**L:

(1) if L consists of one element then it is sorted;

(2) otherwise do the following:
    (2.1) split L into two halves, L_1 and L_2;
    (2.2) call **parallel-sort-**L_1 and **parallel-sort-**L_2, simultaneously;
    (2.3) merge resulting lists into a single sorted list.

If followed meticulously, this algorithm can be seen to work very much like the tree-based parallel summation algorithm of Figure 10.1. First, after diving down to the bottom level of the recursion, it simultaneously compares the two elements in each of the $N/2$ pairs, arranging each pair in the right order. It then, again simultaneously, merges each pair of pairs into a sorted four-tuple, then each pair of four-tuples into an eight-tuple, and so on. The first step takes the time of only one comparison, the second takes three (why?), the third seven, the fourth fifteen, and so on. Assuming for simplicity's sake that N is a power of 2, the total number of comparisons is:

$$1 + 3 + 7 + 15 + \cdots (N - 1)$$

which is less than $2N$. Hence the total time is linear. The price paid for improving $O(N \times \log N)$ to $O(N)$ is the need for $N/2$ processors. Here, too, there is a tradeoff; we can sort N elements in time $O(N \times \log N)$ with one processor, or in linear time with a linear number of processors. Actually, as we shall see later, we can do even better.

The Product Complexity: Time × Size

The number of processors required by a parallel algorithm as a function of the length of its input is one way of measuring the complexity of the hardware required to run the algorithm. By abusing terminology slightly, we can call this measure simply the **size complexity** of the algorithm, with the understanding that we do not mean either the length of the algorithm or the amount of memory it requires, but, rather, the size of the required army of processors.

Since both time measure and size play a role in the analysis of parallel algorithms it is not clear how we should determine the relative superiority of such algorithms. Is a slightly faster algorithm better, even if it uses many more processors? Or should we make a small sacrifice in size in order to yield a significant saving in time? One approach to estimating the quality of a parallel algorithm is to combine both measures—multiplying time by size (see Figure 10.2). The algorithm with a better **product complexity** is considered better. It is noteworthy that the best product measure cannot be any less than the lower bound on the problem's sequential-time complexity, because it is possible to sequentialize any parallel algorithm. This is done by simulating the actions of the various processors on a single processor, in an order that is consistent with the order prescribed by the parallel algorithm. (For example, if we were sequentializing the parallel mergesort algorithm, we would be allowed to sort the two halves in any order, but both sorts would have to be completed before the merging could be carried out.) The overall time this simulation takes is roughly the total of all the time taken by all the processors; that is, the product time × size of the original parallel algorithm. Thus, if, hypothetically, we could find a parallel sorting algorithm that took logarithmic time and used only $O(N/\log N)$

Figure 10.2

The performance of some sorting algorithms.

Name	Size (no. of processors)	Time (worst case)	Product (time × size)
SEQUENTIAL			
Bubblesort	1	$O(N^2)$	$O(N^2)$
Mergesort	1	$O(N \times \log N)$	$O(N \times \log N)$ (optimal)
PARALLEL			
Parallelized mergesort	$O(N)$	$O(N)$	$O(N^2)$
Odd-even sorting network	$O(N \times (\log N)^2)$	$O((\log N)^2)$	$O(N \times (\log N)^4)$
"Optimal" sorting network	$O(N)$	$O(\log N)$	$O(N \times \log N)$ (optimal)

processors, a sequentialized version could be derived that would run in time that was on the order of the product, which is linear (why?). But this would contradict the $O(N \times \log N)$ lower bound on sequential sorting.

The best we can hope for, then, is a parallel sorting algorithm that exhibits the optimal product performance of $O(N \times \log N)$. In this sense, the sequential merge-sort algorithm, for example, is optimal. But then again, it is not a parallel algorithm. Particularly intriguing is the question of whether or not there exists a parallel, comparison-based, sorting algorithm that runs in logarithmic time but requires only a linear number of processors. This, in a way, would represent the ideal parallel sorting routine—extremely fast, but of reasonable size. As we shall see, this problem has been solved in the affirmative.

Networks: Fixed-Connection Parallelism

So far, we have said nothing about the way different processors cooperate. Obviously, they do not work in total seclusion, since they have to pass on intermediate results to each other. Even the simple parallel summation algorithm of Figure 10.1 requires some kind of cooperation, between the processors that produce intermediate sums and those that use them next. The performance of a parallel algorithm can vary greatly under different cooperation methods.

One approach advocates **shared memory**, which means, roughly, that certain variables or data structures are shared by many processors. Within this approach, it is important to specify whether the sharing is only in **reading** the values from the relevant memory, or also in **writing** them. If the latter approach is chosen, we have to decide how to resolve writing conflicts (for example, two processors attempting to write simultaneously into the very same variable or memory location), and the particular method chosen can make quite a difference in the resulting algorithmic power.

Unrestricted shared memory is considered unrealistic, mainly because when it comes to building real parallel computers the pattern of interconnection becomes impossibly complicated. Either each processor has to be connected to essentially every memory location, or (if the memory is physically distributed between the processors) every processor has to be connected to every other one. In both cases this is usually a hopeless situation: if the required number of processors grows with N, as is the case with all nontrivial parallel algorithms, the interconnections quickly become unreasonably intricate.

A more realistic approach is to use **fixed-connection networks**, or just **networks** for short, and to design parallel algorithms specifically for them. The word "fixed" implies that each processor is connected to at most some *fixed* number of **neighboring processors**. In many cases it also means that the entire network is constructed as a special-purpose machine, solving one particular algorithmic problem very efficiently. The processors in a special-purpose network typically have very limited computational capabilities.

One well-known class of networks is the **boolean networks**, or **boolean circuits**, named after the nineteenth-century logician George Boole, who invented the rules for manipulating the logical values true and false (and hence also the rules for manipulating the corresponding bit values, 1 and 0). In a boolean network the processors are called **gates**, and they compute simple logical functions of one or two bit values. An AND gate produces a 1 precisely when both of its inputs are 1s, an OR gate produces a 1 precisely when at least one of its two inputs is 1, and a NOT gate inverts the value of its single input.

■ In a certain sense, every effectively solvable algorithmic problem P can be solved by an effectively computable **uniform collection** of boolean networks. To be able to state this fact more precisely, think of the inputs of P as being encoded using just 0s and 1s. The claim is that, for every such problem P, there is an algorithm (say a Turing machine) that accepts a number input N and outputs the description of a boolean network that solves the problem P for inputs consisting of N bits. However, this somewhat strange kind of universality is not our reason for introducing networks. We are more interested in networks that are especially designed to yield efficient solutions to specific problems.

■ The Odd-Even Sorting Network

Special-purpose networks have been found for many problems, but most notably for sorting and merging. A **sorting network** can be viewed as a special-purpose computer architecture, providing a fixed interconnection pattern of extremely simple processors, which cooperate to sort N elements in parallel. Most sorting networks employ only one very simple kind of processor, called a **comparator**, which inputs two elements and outputs them in order, as shown in Figure 10.3.

Let us illustrate the approach with the so-called **odd-even sorting network**. This network is constructed recursively, using a rule for constructing the network for N elements from networks for $N/2$ elements. We shall not provide a description of this general rule here, but will illustrate with an example. Figure 10.4 shows the network for the case when N is 8, with an example input list written in along the lines. The portions of the network enclosed in dashed lines represent two odd-even networks for 4 elements each. In a similar vein, a network for 16 elements would have at its left-hand side two networks for 8 elements, identical to that of Figure 10.4. The remaining portions of the odd-even network consist of various subnetworks for merging sorted lists. What is clever about all of this is the way the subnetworks are put together, as you will discover if you try to define the general recursive construction rule.

The time taken by the odd-even sorting network can be shown to be $O((\log N)^2)$, and its size (number of processors) is $O(N \times (\log N)^2)$, hence it is not optimal, as the product of these is more than the optimum (see the table in Figure 10.2). A breakthrough of sorts was achieved in 1983 with the advent of an ingenious sorting network that uses $O(N \times \log N)$ processors and takes only logarithmic time. Later,

Figure 10.3

A comparator used in sorting networks.

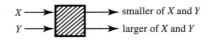

Figure 10.4

The odd-even sorting network for eight elements.

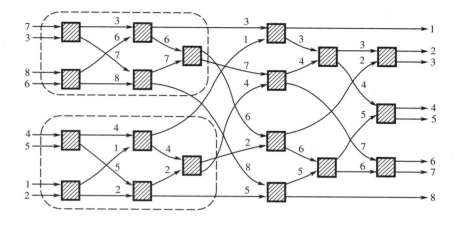

this solution was combined with a variation of the odd-even network, to finally yield an optimal logarithmic-time network of linear size. This, then, is the optimal parallel sorting algorithm mentioned earlier. Unfortunately, besides being extremely complicated, the big-O constants in both of these logarithmic-time networks are huge, rendering them quite useless in practice for reasonably-sized N. In contrast, the constants for many of the theoretically worse networks are very small; those of the odd-even network, for example, are less than 1 (about $\frac{1}{2}$ for the time measure and $\frac{1}{4}$ for size). Specifically, we can construct an odd-even sorting network with a little over 1000 comparators, which will sort 100 elements in the time it takes to carry out just 25 comparisons. For 1000 elements it would take just the time of about 55 comparisons, but we would need about 23,000 comparators. If time is a crucial factor, and the lists to be sorted will all be of roughly the same length, a sorting network such as this one becomes quite practical.

More About Networks: Computing Weighted Averages

In the odd-even network each comparator is used only once in sorting a given list. The input list arrives all together, and the entire life cycle of each comparator consists of waiting for its own two inputs, comparing them, sending the maximum and minimum along the appropriate output lines, and shutting itself off.

Other kinds of networks are characterized by processors that are activated repeatedly within a single run, in a regular kind of pattern. Such networks are sometimes termed **systolic**, the word deriving from the physiological term "systole," which refers to the repeated contractions responsible for pumping blood through our bodies.

As an example, consider a teacher who is interested in computing the final grades of N students in a course in which there are M examinations. Each examination has a different **weight** associated with it, and the final grade is to be the weighted average of those M examinations. The input grades are arranged in an N by M array, and the weights are given by a list of M fractions, totaling 1. For each student, it is required to multiply each grade by the appropriate weight and then to sum the M results.

Figure 10.5

A systolic network for computing weighted averages.

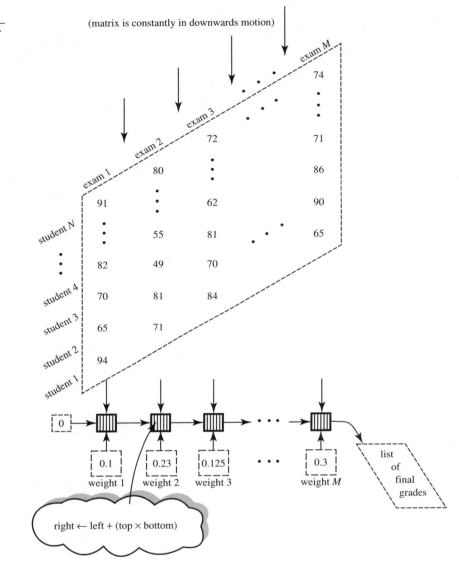

The final output is to be a list of the N final grades. A sequential algorithm would obviously take time $O(N \times M)$, since one multiplication has to be performed for each grade and each of the N students has a grade in each of the M exams.

Figure 10.5 shows a systolic network for solving this problem (which, in mathematical terminology is called the **matrix-by-vector multiplication problem**). The network consists of a linear arrangement of M interconnected processors. The array of grades, the **matrix**, in technical terms, is fed into the network from the top in the fashion shown, a diagonal row at a time. Thus, the network first accepts the grade of student 1 in exam 1, then, simultaneously, student 2's grade in exam 1 and student

1's grade in exam 2, then, simultaneously, student 3's grade in exam 1, 2's grade in exam 2 and 1's grade in exam 3, and so on. The final step is to accept student N's grade in exam M. The vector of weights, on the other hand, is constantly available along the bottom lines. Zeros are fed in from the left, and the output vector is produced at the right, an element at a time. (This linear configuration is sometimes called a **pipeline arrangement**, referring to the way in which each processor pipes its output to the one to its right.) Each processor on its own is extremely simple: whenever it receives a set of new inputs it just multiplies its top and bottom ones, adds the product to the left-hand input and sends the result off to the right. The algorithm induced by this network is clearly linear in $N + M$. Figure 10.6 shows a simple step-by-step simulation of the network for the case of four students and three exams.

Systolic networks have been constructed to solve many problems. The arrangement of processors is typically linear, rectangular, or diamond shaped, and the processors are either square, resulting in a so-called **mesh-connected array**, or hexagonal, resulting in a **beehive**, as in Figure 10.7.

■ ■

Can Parallelism Be Used to Solve the Unsolvable?

The facts we have discussed so far leave no doubt that parallelism can be used to improve the time behavior of sequential algorithms. Problems that require a certain amount of time for sequential solution can be solved faster, even in order-of-magnitude terms, if (expanding) parallelism is allowed. It is natural to ask whether parallelism can be used to solve problems that could not have been solved at all without it. Can we devise a parallel algorithm for an undecidable problem? The answer is no, since, as explained earlier, every parallel algorithm can be simulated sequentially by a single processor, running around and doing everyone's work in an appropriate order. In this sense, the Church/Turing thesis applies to parallel models of computation too: the class of solvable problems is insensitive even to the addition of expanding parallelism.

The next question to ask is whether parallelism can turn *in*tractable problems into tractable ones. Is there a problem requiring an unreasonable (say, an exponential) amount of time for sequential solution that can be solved in parallel in a reasonable (that is, polynomial) amount of time?

To be able to better appreciate the subtlety of this question, let us first consider the NP problems of Chapter 7. As you may recall, all problems in NP have reasonable solutions that are nondeterministic; they employ a magic coin, which, if tossed when confronted with a choice, will use its wizardry to point to the direction that leads to a positive answer, if there is such a direction. Now, if we have an unlimited number of processors, we do not need the magic coin: whenever a "crossroad" is reached we can simply send new processors off to follow both possibilities simultaneously. If one of the processors sent off ever comes back and says "yes," the entire process halts and says "yes" too; if the predetermined polynomial amount of time has elapsed

Figure 10.6

Simulating the
behavior of the
network of Figure
10.5.

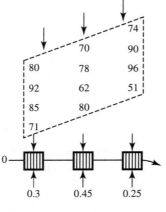

(a)

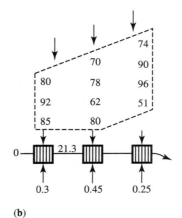

(b)

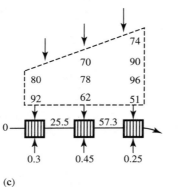

(c)

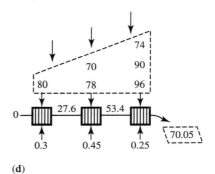

(d)

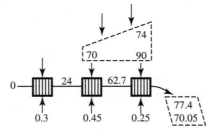

(e)

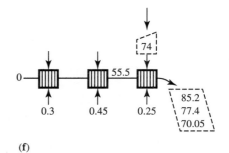

(f)

(g)

Figure 10.7

Two typical
arrangements of
processors for systolic
networks.

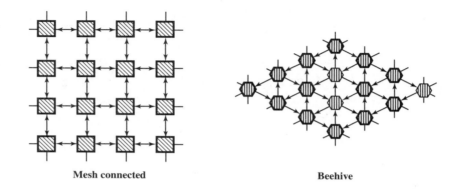

Mesh connected   **Beehive**

and none has said "yes," the process halts and says "no." Since the NP-ness of the
problem guarantees that if the answer is "yes" it will indeed be found by the magic
coin in a polynomial amount of time, our exhaustive, multiple-processor traversal
of all possibilities will find the "yes" in the same amount of time too. If it does not,
then the answer must be "no."

The consequence is clear. The problems in NP, including the NP-complete ones,
such as monkey puzzles, traveling salesmen, and timetables, all have polynomial-
time parallel solutions. However, three comments should be made, before you rush
off to tell everyone that intractability is but a slightly bothersome consequence of
conventional one-processor models of computation, and that it can be eliminated
by using parallel computation. The first is that the number of processors required
to solve an NP-complete problem in a reasonable amount of time is itself exponential. If we want to find out, in fewer than billions of years of computer time,
whether our local high school can come up with a class schedule to satisfy all
of its constraints, we would need a wholly unreasonable computer containing trillions of intricately connected processors. This is something we shall return to in a
moment.

The second comment is rooted in the fact that the NP-complete problems are not
known to be intractable—they are merely conjectured to be so. Thus, the fact that
we can solve NP-complete problems in parallel in polynomial time does not imply
that parallelism can rid a problem of its inherent intractability, since we do not know
whether or not the NP-complete problems are actually intractable.

Finally, even if we have a parallel algorithm that uses only a polynomial number
of instructions but requires an exponential number of processors, it is far from clear
that we can really run the algorithm in polynomial time on a real parallel computer.
In fact, there are results that show that under quite liberal assumptions about the
width of communication lines and the speed of communication, a super-polynomial
number of processors would require a super-polynomial amount of real time to carry
out even a polynomial number of steps, no matter how the processors are packed
together. These results are based on the inherent limitations of three-dimensional
space. Thus, the complexity analysis of parallel computation with unreasonable size
seems to require more than merely estimating the number of processing steps; the
amount of communication, for example, is also crucial.

The question thus remains: can we use parallelism, even with unreasonably many
processors, to solve in a reasonable amount of time a problem that we can *prove*

to be unsolvable sequentially in reasonable time? And this question is still open, as will now be shown.

The Parallel Computation Thesis

In Chapter 9 we saw that the Church/Turing thesis holds also in a refined sense, whereby, under very natural assumptions, all sequential models of computation are equivalent to within a polynomial amount of time. As a consequence, tractability, and not only decidability, is insensitive to the choice of such a model. The thesis claims that this situation will not change as new models are proposed.

A similar claim holds for *parallel* models of computation. Under natural assumptions, all universal models of expanding parallelism that have been suggested so far, including numerous variants of shared-memory models, communication-based models, uniform classes of networks, etc., can be shown to be polynomial-time equivalent. Each model can be simulated by the other with at most a polynomial loss of time. This means that, as in the sequential case, the class of problems solvable in parallel in polynomial time is also robust, in its own way; it does not depend on the particular kind of parallel computer model chosen, nor on the programming language used to program it.

As in the sequential case, we have to be careful here. Models that allow *concurrent* reading and writing of the same variable may be exponentially more efficient than ones which allow only reading and writing by one processor at a time. Without getting into the details, it should be said that in order for this claim to be true the basic instructions related to the simultaneous manipulation of low-level elements must be of similar nature (just as the basic instructions for manipulating numbers have to be comparable in order for the polynomial-time equivalence of sequential models to hold).

This fact leads to one part of the so-called **parallel computation thesis**. It claims that this situation too will not change as new models are suggested. In other words, up to polynomial differences, the important complexity classes for parallel computation are also robust, and will remain so even as science and technology make progress. This half-thesis, however, is not quite enough, as it talks about parallelism only. We also want to know whether there is any inherent relationship *between* sequentiality and parallelism, as far as efficiency is concerned. All we know is that parallelism does not help in solving totally *un*solvable problems; but just how much better can it make things for problems that *are* solvable?

To our help comes the second part of the parallel computation thesis. It claims that (again, up to polynomial differences) parallel time is the same as sequential memory space. If we can solve a problem sequentially using a certain amount of space for inputs of length N, then we can solve it in parallel in time that is no worse than a polynomial in that amount of space. It might be that amount squared, cubed, or maybe even raised to the 100th power, but it will not be exponential in it. The converse holds too: if we can solve a problem in parallel in a certain amount of time for inputs of length N, we can also solve it sequentially using memory space that is bounded by a polynomial in that amount of time. Of particular interest is the special case of this general fact, in which the original amount of space is itself a polynomial: any problem solvable sequentially using only a polynomial amount of memory space is solvable in parallel in a polynomial amount of time, and vice versa. Symbolically:

Sequential-PSPACE = *Parallel*-PTIME

Thus, the question of whether there are intractable problems that become tractable with the introduction of parallelism boils down to whether the sequential complexity class PSPACE contains intractable problems; that is, ones that can be proved to admit no polynomial-time sequential solutions. This question, phrased purely in sequential terms, is still open, and, like the P vs. NP problem, is probably very difficult too.

Nick's Class: Towards Reasonable Parallelism

In general, polynomial-time parallel algorithms cannot be claimed to be reasonable, since they may require a totally unreasonable (that is, exponential) number of processors. Moreover, one of the purposes of introducing parallelism is to drastically *reduce* running time. In fact, one of the objectives here is to find **sublinear** algorithms; that is, algorithms that are parallel to such an extent that they do not even read the entire input sequentially (otherwise they would require at least linear time). Hence, it would appear that *Parallel*-PTIME is not the best choice for the class of problems that are tractable in the presence of parallelism. What then is the "right" definition of parallel tractability?

One of the most interesting proposals regarding this question is a class of problems called NC (**Nick's class**, after one of its first investigators). A problem is in NC if it admits a very fast parallel solution, which requires only polynomially many processors. "Very fast" is taken to mean that it runs in **polylogarithmic** time; that is, in time that is some fixed power of the logarithm of N, like $O(\log N)$ or $O((\log N)^2)$. Salary summation, sorting, weighted average computation, and a host of other problems are all in NC (the first two by the algorithms described earlier, and the third by an algorithm not described here). The NP-complete problems, for example, may or may not be in NC—we do not know. All we were able to show was that they admit polynomial-time parallel solutions; being in NC is a stronger requirement.

The class NC is robust in the same sense that classes like P, NP, and PSPACE are. It remains insensitive to differences between the various models of parallel computation, and hence can be used in the investigation of the inherent power of parallelism. It can be shown, for example, that all problems in NC are also in P (that is, in *Sequential*-PTIME), but the converse is not known to be true: is there a problem that is tractable in the sequential sense (that is, in P) but not in this parallel sense? Here too, as in the P vs. NP question, most researchers believe that the two classes are distinct, so that P is different from NC. In particular, the problem of finding the greatest common divisor of two integers (its gcd) is in P—Euclid found a polynomial-time algorithm for it as early as 2300 years ago, as mentioned in Chapter 1. However, the gcd problem is suspected not to be in NC. No one knows how to exploit parallelism to significantly speed up the computation of this most important quantity, the way we can speed up sorting and salary summation. That is, each step of the classical gcd algorithm depends on previous steps, and no one has been able to find a way to remove some of this dependence so that parallelism can be exploited beneficially.

Thus, we have

$$\text{NC} \subseteq \text{P} \subseteq \text{NP} \subseteq \text{PSPACE}$$

and many computer scientists believe that all three inclusions are actually strict. Recalling the aforementioned connection between PSPACE and *Parallel*-PTIME, this set of conjectured inequalities can be described (from right to left) by saying:

1. There are problems that can be solved in reasonable sequential space—that is, in reasonable parallel time (but unreasonable hardware size)—that cannot be solved in reasonable sequential time even with magical nondeterminism.

2. There are problems solvable in reasonable sequential time with magical nondeterminism that cannot be solved in such time without it.

3. There are problems solvable in reasonable sequential time that are not solvable in very little parallel time with reasonable hardware size.

However, none of these inequalities is actually known to be strict, and hence it is just possible (though very unlikely) that these classes of problems are actually all equal. It should be mentioned that, as with NP vs. P, the P vs. NC question also gives rise to a natural notion of completeness. Thus, although we do not know whether P = NC, it is very helpful to show that a problem is P-*complete*, implying that if it is in NC then all the problems in P are in NC too.

Distributed and Ongoing Concurrency

It would be nice to be able to end the discussion of explicit simultaneity here. And why not? We have discussed parallel algorithms and their complexity, and have seen how they can improve things, and to what extent. We have even admitted that we do not know nearly as much about parallelism as we should. What, then, is missing?

Well, introducing parallelism in order to solve conventional algorithmic problems more efficiently is only one of its facets. The other has to do with situations in which parallelism is not something we introduce in order to improve things, but something we have to live with because it's just there.[2] Also, it has to do with a different kind of algorithmic problem, which does not always involve transforming inputs that are given at the start into desired outputs that are produced at the end. Rather, it is what one finds in many (indeed, most!) of the reactive and embedded systems we shall discuss in Chapter 14. The problem involves specifying protocols of desired behavior over time, so that the various properties required of that behavior are guaranteed to hold. What makes these problems particularly difficult is that in many cases the protocol that has to be described as their solution is not required to terminate at all. It merely has to sit there forever, doing things that are always in accordance with those requirements.

---

[2] To keep the distinction clear we shall use the term **concurrency**, rather than parallelism, for this case.

In contrast with Chapters 13 and 14, here we are not interested in the general problem of methods and languages for engineering the development of large and complex systems, but in the small-scale, but ever so subtle, algorithmic problems that arise therein.

Let us consider an example. Suppose a certain hotel has only one bathroom on each floor. (Many inexpensive hotels are of this kind.) Also, suppose there is heating only in the rooms—the corridor is unpleasantly chilly. (Many inexpensive hotels satisfy this assumption too.) Every now and then guests have to take showers. (Most guests in such hotels indeed do.) How should they go about satisfying these needs? They cannot line up in front of the bathroom door, because of the shivering factor involved.

If a guest simply tries the bathroom door once in a while he or she might stay unclean forever, since quite possibly it will be occupied whenever the attempt is made. This is true despite the fact that showers take only a finite amount of time; someone else might always manage to get in first. We assume that the guests come from a variety of countries and all speak different languages, so that direct communication is out of the question.

One apparent solution calls for attaching a small blackboard to the exterior of the bathroom door. Any guest leaving the bathroom erases the room number written on the blackboard (it will be his or her own) and writes down the number of the next room in some fixed order. (Think of the rooms on the floor as being arranged in a cyclic order, so that each room has a unique predecessor and successor.) Unclean guests simply walk up to the bathroom door every now and then, entering if their own room number is written on the blackboard, and returning to their room if it is not. Apparently, every guest will eventually get a turn to shower.

However, this solution still has severe problems. First, it is possible that room number 16 is never occupied, that its occupant never wants to take a shower, or he has just been kidnapped, never to be seen again. The blackboard will then have a 16 written on it forever, and none of the other guests will ever become clean. Secondly, even if all rooms are inhabited by live, available people, this solution imposes an impossible one-shower-per-cycle discipline on all guests, forcing the more fastidious ones to shower as rarely as those who could not care less.

This problem illustrates some of the main issues arising in the design of systems that are inherently **distributed**. Distributivity is a special kind of concurrency, where the concurrent components are physically remote. Accordingly, people concern themselves not only with figuring out what each component should do, and doing the software engineering and project management the way it should, but also with minimizing the amount of communication that takes place between the components. Communication, whether explicit or implicit (say in the form of shared memory), can become extremely expensive in a distributed system. As before, we shall use the term "processors" for the separate entities, or components, in a distributed system.

The processors in an inherently concurrent or distributed system are not required to achieve a mere input/output relationship, but rather to exhibit a certain desired behavior over time. In fact, the system might not be required to terminate at all, just as in the shower problem. Parts of the desired behavior can be stated as **global constraints**. The shower, for example, carries with it a constraint stating that it can accommodate at most one person at a time, and another relevant constraint states that everyone needs the shower from time to time. Thus, the shower is really a **crucial resource**, of the kind everyone needs for some finite amount of time, after which it can be given up for the benefit of someone else. Another important constraint in the shower problem is that we must prevent **deadlock** situations, in which no progress can be made by any processor (for example, in the blackboard solution when guest 16 never shows up), and **starvation** situations—sometimes called **lockouts**—in which one or more of the processors, but not every one of them, is prevented from making progress (for example, when guests are instructed to simply try the bathroom door once in a while and the unlucky ones might be kept out forever).

These notions are typical of many real-world systems, of the kind discussed in Chapters 13 and 14. Most standard computers, for example, have several crucial resources, such as tape and disk drives, printers and plotters, and communication channels. In a way, a computer's memory can also be viewed as a crucial resource, since we would not like two jobs that run together to simultaneously write on to the same location. A flight reservation system, to give another example, is highly distributed. It might consist of a worldwide network containing one large computer in New York, another in Los Angeles, and 2000 terminals. It would be embarrassing if two of the terminals assigned seat 25D on the same flight to two different passengers. A flight reservation system is also not permitted to terminate. It has to keep working, continuously making its resources available to any processors who request them, while preventing deadlock and starvation.

These are really not algorithmic problems in the usual sense of the word. They involve different kinds of requirements, and are not solved by ordinary algorithms. A solution has to dictate **algorithmic protocols** for the behavior of each of the processors, which guarantee fulfillment of all the requirements and constraints specified in the problem, and for the entire (potentially infinite) lifetime of the system.

Solving Hotel Shower Problems

The blackboard suggested for the problem of showering in inexpensive hotels can be thought of as shared memory, and the shower as a crucial resource. Notice that we have skirted the problem of writing conflicts by allowing no more than one guest to write on the blackboard at any one time.

Let us now describe a satisfactory solution to this problem. Actually, we shall solve a more difficult problem, in which there *are* bathrooms in every room, yet no more than one guest is allowed to take a shower at any given time. (The reason might have to do with the pressure or temperature of the water, another reasonable assumption for inexpensive hotels.) This situation is clearly more delicate, since there is no direct way of knowing if anyone is indeed taking a shower. Nevertheless, the solution must ensure that everyone showers, but that two guests never shower simultaneously.

A more general description of the problem is as follows. There are N processors, each of which has to repeatedly carry out certain "private" activities, followed by a **critical section**:

life cycle of the Ith processor:

(1) do the following again and again forever:
    (1.1) carry out *private activities* (for example, eat, read, sleep);
    (1.2) carry out *critical section* (for example, take a shower).

The private activities are processor I's own business—they have nothing to do with anyone else. The critical section, on the other hand, is everyone's business, since no two processors may be in their critical section simultaneously. The problem is to find a way to enable the N processors to live their life forever, without deadlock or starvation, while respecting the critical nature of the critical sections. We must instruct the processors to carry out certain actions, like inspecting blackboards and writing on them, before and/or after they enter their critical sections, so that these requirements are met. When presented in this form, the problem is sometimes called the **mutual exclusion problem**, as processors have to be guaranteed exclusivity in entering the critical sections.

We shall discuss a solution for the case of two guests, or processors, P_1 and P_2. The more general case for N processors is presented later. We shall be using three variables, X_1, X_2, and Z, which, in the shower example, are represented by three small areas on a blackboard that hangs in the corridor. Z can be either 1 or 2, and both processors can change its value. In such cases we say that Z is a **shared variable**. The Xs can be either *yes* or *no*, and they can be read by both processors but changed only by the processor with the corresponding index; that is, P_1 can change X_1 and P_2 can change X_2. In such cases we say that the Xs are **distributed variables**. The initial value of both the Xs is *no*, and that of Z is either 1 or 2, it does not matter. Here are the protocols for the two processors:

protocol for P_1:

(1) do the following again and again forever:
  (1.1) carry out *private activities* until entrance to critical section is desired;
  (1.2) $X_1 \leftarrow yes$;
  (1.3) $Z \leftarrow 1$;
  (1.4) wait until either X_2 becomes *no* or Z becomes 2 (or both);
  (1.5) carry out *critical section*;
  (1.6) $X_1 \leftarrow no$.

protocol for P_2:

(1) do the following again and again forever:
  (1.1) carry out *private activities* until entrance to critical section is desired;
  (1.2) $X_2 \leftarrow yes$;
  (1.3) $Z \leftarrow 2$;
  (1.4) wait until either X_1 becomes *no* or Z becomes 1 (or both);
  (1.5) carry out *critical section*;
  (1.6) $X_2 \leftarrow no$.

What is happening here? Well, think of X_1 as being an indication of P_1's desire to enter its critical section: X_1 being *yes* means that it would like to enter, and X_1 being *no* means that it has finished and would like to go back to its private activities. X_2 plays the same role for P_2. The third variable, Z, is a **courtesy indicator** of sorts: after P_1 has made it clear that it wants to enter its critical section it immediately sets Z to 1, indicating, in a very generous fashion, that, as far as it is concerned, P_2 can enter if it wants to. It then waits until either P_2 has indicated that it has left its own critical section and is back to its private activities (that is, X_2 is *no*), or P_2 has set the courtesy variable Z to 2, generously giving P_1 the right of way. P_2 acts in a similar way. (We can think of Z as representing the processors' signatures in a logbook. The last to sign in is the one who, most recently, has given the other the right of way.) The waiting in clause (1.4) is sometimes called **busy waiting**, as the processor cannot simply idle until it is prodded by someone else. Rather, it has to keep checking the values of Z and the other processor's X variable itself, while doing nothing else in the meantime.

■ Let us now see why this solution is correct. Well, first of all, we claim that P_1 and P_2 cannot possibly be in their critical sections simultaneously. Assume that they can. Obviously, during the time they are in their critical sections together, both X_1 and X_2 have the value *yes*, so that the last processor to enter must have entered by virtue of the Z part of its waiting test in clause (1.4), since the other's X value was *yes*. Obviously, the two processors couldn't have passed their tests at the very same time. (Why?) Let us say that P_1 passed the test first. Then Z must have been 1 when P_2, later, passed *its* test. This means that between the moment P_2 set Z to 2 in its clause (1.3) and the moment it passed its test in clause (1.4), P_1 must have set Z to 1, and from that point on P_2 did nothing else until it entered its critical section by virtue of the fact that Z is 1. But then how did P_1 manage to enter its critical section earlier? It could not have entered by virtue of the fact that Z is 2 because, as we have just said, it set Z to 1 after P_2 set it to 2. Also, it could not have entered by virtue of X_2 being *no* because X_2 was set to *yes* by P_2 before it set Z to 2. And so there is no way for P_2 to enter its critical section as long as P_1 is in its own critical section. A similar argument holds for the dual possibility, where P_1 enters while P_2 is already in. The conclusion is that mutual exclusion indeed holds.

Let us see why starvation and deadlock are impossible. (Here starvation occurs when one of the processors wants to enter its critical section but is forever prevented from doing so, and deadlock occurs when neither processor can make progress.) The first thing to note is that it is impossible for both processors to be stuck in their (1.4) clauses together, because Z is always either 1 or 2, and one of them can therefore always free itself from the wait. Now, assume that P_1 is forced to stay in its (1.4) clause, while P_2 does not. If P_2 never wants to enter its critical section, that is, it stays in clause (1.1), the value of X_2 will be *no* and P_1 will be free to enter whenever it wants to. The only other possibility is that P_2 continues to cycle around its protocol forever. In such a case it will sooner or later set Z to 2, and since it can never change it back to 1 (only P_1 can), P_1 will eventually be able to pass its test and enter (1.5). Thus, starvation and deadlock are prevented, and the solution satisfies all the requirements.

■ Things Are Trickier Than They Seem

This two-processor solution appears at first sight to be quite elementary, and the correctness argument, while slightly involved, does not look overly complicated either. However, this kind of simplicity can be quite deceptive. As an illustration of just how delicate things really are, let us study a minor variation of the foregoing solution.

What would happen if we switched the order of clauses (1.2) and (1.3) in the protocols? In other words, when P_1, for example, wants to enter its critical section, it first does P_2 the courtesy of setting Z to 1, letting it through if it wants, and only then sets X_1 to *yes* to indicate its own desire to enter. On the face of it, there seems to be no difference: P_1 can still enter its critical section only if P_2 is either disinterested (that is, if X_2 is *no*) or is explicitly giving P_1 the right of way (that is, if Z is 2). What can go wrong?

At this point you should try to work through the informal proof of correctness given, but for the amended version, to see where it fails. It does fail, and here is a scenario that leads to both processors being in their critical sections simultaneously. Initially, as agreed on, X_1 is *no* and X_2 is *no*, and both processors are busy with their private activities. Now comes the following sequence of actions:

1. P_2 sets Z to 2;
2. P_1 sets Z to 1;
3. P_1 sets X_1 to *yes*;
4. P_1 enters its critical section, by virtue of X_2 being *no*;
5. P_2 sets X_2 to *yes*;
6. P_2 enters its critical section, by virtue of Z being 1.

The problem, of course, is that now P_2 can take a shower (that is, enter its critical section) even though P_1 is taking one itself, because P_1 was the last to be courteous, and hence Z's value is 1 when P_2 indicates its desire to enter. In the original protocol this was impossible, since the last thing P_2 was required to do before entering was to set Z to the unfavorable value 2.

Thus, even this apparently simple solution for two processors hides a certain amount of subtlety. Let us now look at the general solution for N processors, which is even more delicate.

◼ A Solution to the *N*-Processor Mutual Exclusion Problem

When there are more than two guests it is not enough just to say "I would like to take a shower" and then to be courteous to one of the others. Neither will it do any good to be courteous to *all* the others together and hope that everything will work out nicely. We have to make our processors more sophisticated.

◼ Processors will be instructed to increase their insistence on entering the critical section as they keep waiting. Each processor will thus run through a loop, each execution of which will correspond to being at a higher level of insistence. The number of levels is precisely N, the total number of processors, and the first level (actually the zeroth) indicates disinterest in entering the critical section. Each of the insistence levels has its own courtesy variable, and at each level a processor is courteous to everyone else by writing its own number in that variable. Once a processor has indicated its desire to increase its level of insistence, and has been courteous to all the others, it waits to increase the level until either all the others are less insistent than itself or it has been given the courtesy of proceeding to the next level by someone else. The critical section is finally entered when the green light for proceeding beyond the highest level appears. Upon leaving the critical section, a processor starts the whole procedure anew at the zeroth level.

Here is the protocol for the Ith processor. In it, the vector Z is indexed by the insistence levels, not by the processors. Thus, processor I sets $Z[J]$ to I (not $Z[I]$ to J as with the X vector) to indicate that on level J it gives the right of way to everyone else. It is worth noting that if $N = 2$ these protocols are precisely the ones just presented, so that this is indeed a direct extension of the two-processor solution.

protocol for Ith processor, P_I:

  (1) do the following again and again forever:
      (1.1) carry out *private activities* until entrance to critical section is desired;
      (1.2) for each J from 1 to $N - 1$ do the following:
          (1.2.1) $X[I] \leftarrow J$;
          (1.2.2) $Z[J] \leftarrow I$;
          (1.2.3) wait until either $X[K] < J$ for all $K \neq I$, or $Z[J] \neq I$;
      (1.3) carry out *critical section*:
      (1.4) $X[I] \leftarrow 0$.

It is possible to provide an informal proof of correctness for this general case, along the lines of the proof for the two-processor case. Here we show that at each level the processors proceed only one at a time, so that, as a special case, there is at most one processor in the critical section at any given time. Freedom from deadlock and starvation is established similarly.

Safety and Liveness Properties

Distributed concurrent systems are in many senses more demanding than normal sequential systems. The difficulties start with the very task of specifying the problem and the properties desired of a solution. The "algorithmic problems" associated with such systems can no longer be defined naively by specifying a set of legal inputs together with a function describing the desired outputs. Correctness no longer consists simply of termination plus the generation of correct outputs, and efficiency can no longer be measured naively as the number of steps taken before termination or the size of memory used. Consequently, techniques developed for proving the correctness or estimating the efficiency of conventional algorithms are insufficient when it comes to protocols that solve problems of concurrent and distributed nature. Some aspects of these problems are discussed later on, in Chapters 13 and 14.

It turns out that most correctness requirements of protocols for ongoing concurrent systems fall into two main categories, **safety** and **liveness** properties. Safety properties state that certain "bad" things must never happen, or, equivalently, that the corresponding "good" things will *always* be the case, and liveness properties state that certain "good" things will *eventually* happen. Mutual exclusion—preventing two processors from being in their critical sections simultaneously—is a safety property, since it asks for a guarantee that there will *always* be at most one processor in a critical section, whereas preventing starvation is a liveness property, since it asks for a guarantee that any processor wanting to enter its critical section will *eventually* be able to do so.

Interestingly, the partial correctness and termination properties of conventional algorithms are special cases of safety and liveness. Partial correctness means that the program must never terminate with the wrong outputs—clearly a safety property—and termination means that the algorithm must eventually reach its logical end and terminate—clearly a liveness property.

To show that a given protocol violates a safety property, it is enough to exhibit a finite, legal sequence of actions that leads to the forbidden situation. This was done for the erroneous version of the two-processor solution to the shower problem, and is just like showing that an algorithm violates partial correctness by exhibiting a terminating execution sequence with the wrong results. Showing that a *liveness* property is violated is quite a different matter. We must somehow prove the existence of an *infinite* sequence of actions that *never* leads to the promised situation. This difference is actually one way of characterizing the two classes of properties.

When it comes to ongoing concurrency, testing techniques are usually of little help. We can become reasonably convinced of the correctness of an ordinary sorting algorithm by trying it out on a number of standard lists of elements, and on some "borderline" cases, such as lists with one element or none, or lists with all elements equal. On the other hand, many of the errors that turn up in the realm of concurrent systems have nothing to do with unexpected inputs. They stem from unexpected interactions between processors, and the unpredictable order in which actions are carried out. Proving the correctness of such systems, therefore, is more slippery and error prone than that of conventional, sequential algorithms. A number of published "solutions" to concurrent programming problems were later found to contain subtle errors that eluded reviewers and readers alike, despite the presence of seemingly valid arguments of correctness.

The need for formal verification is thus more acute here than in the sequential case, and several approaches have indeed been proposed. Typically, those that deal with safety properties are extensions of the intermediate-assertion method for verifying partial correctness, and those tailored for liveness properties expand upon the method of convergents for proving termination (see Chapter 5).

Showing that the parallel mergesort algorithm, for example, is partially correct requires, among other things, a formal proof that the two processors assigned to sorting the two halves of a list in parallel, on any level of the recursion, do not interfere with each other. In this particular case, the processors working in parallel do not interact at all, and such a proof is relatively easy to come by. When processors *do* interact, as in the solution to the shower problem, things become much trickier. We have to somehow verify the behavior of each individual processor in isolation, taking into account all possible interactions with others, and then combine the proofs into one whole.

Intermediate assertions cannot be used here in the usual way. A claim that an assertion is true whenever a certain point in the protocol of processor P is reached no longer depends on P's actions alone. Moreover, even if the assertion is indeed true at that point, it might become false before P's next action, because another processor was quick enough to change the value of some variable in the interim. Certain formal proof methods overcome this problem by requiring the separate proofs to satisfy some kind of **interference freedom** property, which has to be proved separately.

All this sounds quite complicated. In fact, it is. One of the reasons for presenting only an informal proof of correctness for the simple solution to the two-processor mutual exclusion problem was the rather technical nature of the formal proofs. In principle, however, there *are* adequate proof methods, and, as in the sequential case, formal proofs *do* always exist if the solutions are indeed correct, though discovering them is, in principle, non-computable.

Temporal Logic

In previous chapters dynamic logics were mentioned. These are formal frameworks that can be used to specify and prove various properties of algorithms. It would be nice if we were able to use such logics for specifying and proving the safety and liveness properties of concurrent systems. As mentioned in Chapter 5, the central logical construct used in dynamic logics is **after**(A, F), which means that F is true after A terminates. Such logics are thus based on the input/output paradigm—that of relating the situation before executing part of an algorithm to the situation after the execution. When dealing with concurrency it seems essential to be able to talk directly also about what is happening *during* execution.

A formalism that has proved to be far more fitting here is **temporal logic**, or **TL**. It is a variant of a classical logic known to mathematicians as **tense logic**, especially tailored for algorithmic purposes. Its formulas make statements about the truth of assertions as time goes by, and can also refer explicitly to the current location of control in the protocols. Two of the central constructs here are **henceforth**(F) and **eventually**(F). The first states that F is true from now on—until termination if the protocol terminates, and forever if it does not—and the second states that F will eventually become true, that is, at some point in the future. Recalling our use of the symbol $\sim$ to denote "not," the first of these constructs can be used to state safety properties, by writing **henceforth**$(\sim F)$ (that is, F will never become true), and the second to state liveness properties.

As an example, consider the solution of the two-processor shower problem, and the following formulas of TL:[3]

$$P_1\text{-}\textbf{is-at-}(1.4) \rightarrow \textbf{eventually}(P_1\text{-}\textbf{is-at-}(1.5))$$

$$P_2\text{-}\textbf{is-at-}(1.4) \rightarrow \textbf{eventually}(P_2\text{-}\textbf{is-at-}(1.5))$$

$$\sim (P_1\text{-}\textbf{is-at-}(1.5) \mathrel{\&} P_2\text{-}\textbf{is-at-}(1.5))$$

The first two formulas state that if a processor is waiting to enter the critical section then it will eventually enter, and the third states that both processors will never be in their critical section simultaneously. Taken together, and stated to be true at all points of the computation (using **henceforth**), these formulas assert that the solution is correct. A formal proof of this involves logical manipulation that adheres to the strict axiomatic rules of temporal logic, which we shall not dwell upon here.

---

[3] The fact that processor P is at location G in the protocol is described by the construct $P\text{-}\textbf{is-at-}G$.

However, to make a comparison with the proof methods of Chapter 5, it turns out that pure safety properties (like that in the third formula above) can be proved in a manner similar to that of the invariant assertion method for partial correctness. Eventualities (like those in the first two formulas) can be proved by first analyzing each possible single step of the protocols, and then using mathematical induction to deduce eventualities that become true within some number of steps from those that become true in less.

As mentioned, if the protocols are indeed correct, a proof of correctness exists, and if found, parts of it can be checked algorithmically. Actually, in many applications of temporal logic each variable has only a finite number of possible values (the mutual exclusion protocol discussed earlier employs three variables, each with only two possible values). These **finite-state protocols**, as they are sometimes called, *can* be verified algorithmically. That is, there are algorithms that accept as inputs certain kinds of protocols and the temporal logic formula asserting correctness, and verify the former against the latter. Thus, while finding proofs of correctness for the **transformational**, or **computational**, parts of concurrent systems is not possible in general, it is possible to effectively find proofs of the **control parts**, such as the mechanisms for scheduling processors and preventing starvation and deadlock, as these usually involve variables with a finite range only. However, these automatic verifiers are not always as efficient as we would hope, since, among other things, the number of combinations of values grows exponentially with the number of processors. Thus, even short and innocent-looking protocols may be quite difficult to verify automatically, and in hand-produced proofs, of course, subtle errors are the rule, not the exception.

Over the past several years, powerful methods have been developed for verifying concurrent systems against formulas of temporal logic. Using **model checking**, for example, it is possible to construct computer-aided proofs that a system satisfies temporal logic formulas, including safety and liveness properties. This might come as something of a surprise, given the undecidability of verification, as discussed in Chapter 8. Moreover, even if we restrict ourselves to **finite-state systems**, by, e.g., forbidding variables to take on values above a certain finite bound, and by *a priori* limiting the number of components in the system, the corresponding verification problems are intractable. Still, there are ways to deal with these issues, that work extremely well in many of the cases that arise in practice. There is indeed high hope for verification, even in the slippery realm of concurrency.

Fairness and Real-Time Systems

There are two additional issues that deserve mention here, although neither of them will be treated in any detail. The first concerns a global assumption that is usually made when dealing with ongoing concurrency. We typically make no assumptions about the relative speed of the processors involved in solving problems of concurrency, but we do assume that they all respond and make progress within some finite, though possibly lengthy, amount of time. In our solutions to the mutual exclusion problem we used this assumption, of course, since otherwise P_1 could reach clause (1.3) and never get round to setting Z to 1 and proceeding.

This assumption is sometimes called **fairness**, since if you think of concurrency as being implemented by a central processor, sometimes called a **scheduler**, who gives each of the concurrent processors a turn in carrying out a few instructions, then to say that each processor eventually makes progress is just like saying that the simulating processor is being fair to all, eventually giving each one its turn.

Consider the following protocols for two processors P and Q.

protocol for P:

(1) $X \leftarrow 0$;

(2) do the following again and again forever:
    (2.1) if $Z = 0$ then stop;
    (2.2) $X \leftarrow X + 1$.

protocol for Q:

(1) $Z \leftarrow 0$;

(2) stop.

Let Z's initial value be 1. If we do not assume fairness, P may be continuously given the right to proceed, with poor Q being forever left out of the game. This, of course, leads to an infinite loop. The only way to ensure that the protocols terminate is to let Q make progress. On the other hand, under the fairness assumption, this concurrent algorithm terminates, setting X to some unknown, possibly very large, non-negative integer. The way it does so is as follows. The scheduler is free to schedule P and Q to take turns any way it wants, and, in particular, it can let P execute many times before it lets Q in for the first time. However, it must let Q take a turn at some point in time, by the fairness assumption. Thus, P will increment X from 0 some unknown number of times, but once Q gets the green light execution will terminate. Obviously, the final value of X can be any number from 0 up, but the process will eventually terminate, as a result of the fairness.

Of course, that these protocols might produce very large numbers is based on the assumption that some processors can be arbitrarily slower than others. Stronger notions of fairness are sometimes useful, especially those that bound the **delay** that can occur between actions. We might want to say that Q has a slower response than P, but that it is no worse than twice as slow. Such fairness assertions are quantitative in nature, and introduce **timing** issues into the game.

An additional complication arises in systems for which timing constraints are crucial, particularly in **real-time** systems. These are required to respond to certain events immediately, or at least within unnoticeable and negligible amounts of time. Examples include flight control, missile guidance, and fast communication systems. Here, too, temporal logic can help, using the special **nextstep** operator, which talks about what will be true one time unit from the present instant. It is possible, for example, to write a TL formula that states that whenever one given fact is true some other one will become true at most, say, 10 steps later. This still does not solve the problems of programming such systems, which are usually not only time critical but also large and complex. More will be said about methods for describing their behavior in Chapter 14.

The Dining Philosophers Problem

One of the most popular examples of ongoing concurrency, which illustrates many issues of synchronization and cooperation, is the following. We have a table, around which are seated N philosophers. In the center there is a large plate containing an unlimited amount of spaghetti. Half-way between each pair of adjacent philosophers there is a single fork (see Figure 10.8). Now, since no one, not even a philosopher, can eat spaghetti with one fork, there is a problem. The desired life cycle of a philosopher consists of carrying out his private activities (for example, thinking, and then writing up the results for publication), becoming hungry and trying to eat, eating, and then back to the private activities, *ad infinitum*. (A related, but somewhat less manageable, problem involves Chinese philosophers, with rice and chopsticks replacing spaghetti and forks.)

How should the philosophers go about their rituals without starving? We can instruct them to simply lift up the forks on either side when hungry, and eat, laying the forks down again when finished. This solution will not work, since one or both of the forks may be taken by neighboring philosophers at the time. Also, two adjacent philosophers may try to pick up the same fork at the same time. Using forks that are beyond a philosopher's reach is forbidden. Here, eating can be considered a critical section of sorts, as two adjacent philosophers cannot eat simultaneously, and the forks are crucial resources of sorts, as they cannot be used by two philosophers simultaneously.

Figure 10.8

The dining philosophers.

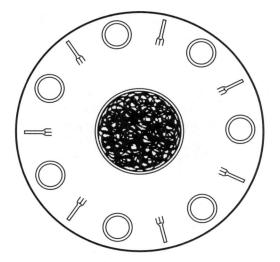

This problem also typifies many real-world situations, such as computer operating systems, for example, in which many processors compete for certain shared resources. The interconnection pattern of such systems is usually quite sparse (not all resources are accessible to each processor) and the number of resources is too small for everyone to be happy together.

One solution to the problem involves introducing a new player into the game, the dining room doorman. Philosophers are instructed to leave the room when they are not interested in eating, and to try to re-enter when they are. The doorman is required to keep count of the philosophers currently in the room, limiting their number to $N - 1$. That is, if the room contains all but one philosopher, the last one will be kept waiting at the door until someone leaves. Now, if at most $N - 1$ philosophers are at the table at any one time, then there are at least two philosophers who have at least one neighbor absent, and thus at least one philosopher can eat. (Why?) When properly formalized, this solution can be shown to be satisfactory. However, it uses an additional person (whose monthly salary will probably be more than the sum needed for buying an additional set of forks, at least for reasonably small N).

Can the dining philosophers problem be solved without a doorman, and without resorting to shared memory or its equivalents? In other words, is there a fully distributed, fully symmetric solution to the problem, one that does not employ any additional processors? Here "fully distributed" means that there is no central shared memory and the protocols may use only distributed variables (shared, say, only by two neighboring philosophers). "Fully symmetric" means that the protocols for all the philosophers are essentially identical—we do not allow different philosophers to act differently, and we do not allow them to start off with different values in their variables. These conditions might sound a little too restrictive. However, if the philosophers have different programs or different initial values, it is like saying that they use their own personal knowledge and talents in the mundane quest for food. We would like to save all that for thinking and publishing; eating should be a procedure that is standard and common to all.

The answer to these questions is no. To solve the problem we need something more, such as shared memory, direct communication between processors, special centralized controlling processors, or the use of different information for different philosophers.

■ Why? The argument is really quite simple. Think of a correct solution as one that guarantees all the desired properties, even against the most malicious scheduler (that is, even against a scheduler that tries as hard as it can to cause deadlock or starvation). In other words, to show that there is no fully distributed, fully symmetric solution, it suffices to exhibit one particular order in which the philosophers are scheduled to carry out the actions in a candidate solution, and then to show that something must go wrong. Assume, therefore, that we have some such candidate solution. Also, assume we have numbered the philosophers $1, 2, \ldots, N$. (The philosophers themselves are not aware even of their own numbers; they are not allowed to have any private information that might turn out to be useful.)

The schedule we adopt is the following. At each stage, every philosopher in the order $1, 2, \ldots, N$ is allowed to carry out one basic action. An action might be a **busy wait** test, in which case testing and deciding whether to wait or to proceed are taken together as one indivisible basic action. It is possible to show that at each stage precisely the same action is carried out by each processor. This follows from the facts that both the initial situation and the protocols are fully symmetric, there are no processors other than the philosophers themselves, and the table and its contents are symmetrically cyclic. Consequently, the situation at the end of each stage will still be fully symmetric; that is, the values of the variables will be the same for all philosophers, as will their locations within the protocols. Now, could any philosopher have eaten within one or more of the stages? No, because stages involve basic actions only, and at the end of a stage the fact that a philosopher is eating or has eaten will be detectable. But it is impossible for all the philosophers to be eating at once, and the process of two philosophers eating, one after the other, cannot be carried out within one stage. It thus follows from the necessary symmetry that at the end of every stage no philosopher will have eaten. Hence, none ever will.

In Chapter 11 we shall see that the dining philosophers problem *can* be solved in a fully distributed and fully symmetric fashion, but with a more liberal notion of correctness.

■ Semaphores

There are many programming languages that support concurrency one way or another, and these include object-oriented languages and visual formalisms for system development, of the kinds discussed later on, in Chapter 14. We shall not describe any of these languages here, but shall briefly consider one of the main constructs invented especially for dealing with concurrency. It underlies parts of the way concurrency is implemented in some of these languages, and can be used explicitly in others.

We already know that shared memory and direct communication represent the two main approaches for describing the cooperation that is to take place between concurrently executing processes. If the former is used, there must be a mechanism for solving the writing conflicts that shared memory raises. One of the most popular of these is the **semaphore**.

A semaphore is a special kind of programming element that employs two operations to control the use of critical sections (such as those that entail writing into a portion of shared memory). An attempt to enter such a section is represented by the **request** operation, and **release** indicates an exit. A semaphore S can actually be viewed as an integer-valued variable. Executing **request**(S) is an atomic action that tries to decrease S by 1, doing so without interruption if its value is positive and waiting for it to become positive otherwise. The effect of **release**(S) is simply to increment S by 1. The important point is that, by its very definition, a semaphore S yields to only one request or release operation at a time. In a typical use of semaphores to achieve mutual exclusion, S is given an initial value of 1, and each processor's critical section is enclosed as follows:

```
    . . .
request(S);
    carry out critical section;
release(S);
    . . .
```

This results in allowing only one processor at a time into its critical section. The first one that tries to enter succeeds in decreasing S to 0 and enters. The others must wait until the first one exits, incrementing S to 1 in the process. A semaphore that starts with 1, and hence takes on only the values 1 and 0, is termed a **binary semaphore**. A simple way of using semaphores for critical sections that can handle up to K processors at a time is to use a non-binary semaphore with initial value K. (Why does this have the desired effect?) In the dining philosophers problem, for example, the doorman can be modeled by a semaphore with an initial value of $N - 1$, controlling a critical section that includes the activities involved in trying to eat, eating, and leaving the room. The use of each fork can be modeled by a binary semaphore.

It is noteworthy that this simple definition of semaphores does not assume that all processors waiting at blocked **request** operations are eventually given the right to enter when S becomes nonzero. It is quite possible that a malicious implementation of semaphores always gives the right of way to the most recently arrived processor, locking others out forever. This is one of the cases in which some kind of **fairness** assumption appears to be necessary, whereby, say, each processor that is waiting is guaranteed eventual progress.

Semaphores can thus be described as a very simple data type, whose operations (increment, test-and-decrement) are *guarded* against writing conflicts by a built-in mechanism of mutual exclusion. Mutual exclusion for more complicated data types that employ many operations can be achieved by surrounding each occurrence of a writing operation with the appropriate semaphore operations. However, in a sense, semaphores are like **goto** statements; too many **request** and **release** operations sprinkled all over a lengthy program may become unclear and susceptible to errors. Semaphores can be used to solve the standard kinds of problems in programming concurrency, but they do constitute an *un*structured programming construct.

◼ ◼

Research on Parallelism and Concurrency

If we have claimed in previous chapters that intensive research is being carried out on many of the topics discussed, then this is truer than ever in the realm of parallelism and concurrency. Researchers are trying to come to terms with virtually all aspects of algorithmic cooperation, and it would not be too much of an exaggeration to say that the research of most computer scientists has some connection to the topics discussed in this chapter.

Intensive research is being carried out in finding fast parallel algorithms for a variety of algorithmic problems, and the solutions employ a wide spectrum of sophisticated data structures and mechanisms for concurrency. Many problems (such as gcd computation) have resisted attempts to usefully exploit any kind of parallelism. Boolean circuits and systolic networks are also the subject of much current research, and interesting connections have been discovered between these approaches and conventional sequential algorithmics.

The abstract complexity theory of parallelism poses a number of important, and apparently very difficult, unresolved questions, concerning classes like NC and PSPACE, some of which were described earlier. While, as we have seen, sequentiality already poses many unresolved problems, parallelism undoubtedly raises many more. In fact, it seems clear that we understand the fundamentals of sequential algorithms far better than those of parallel algorithms, and there is a long and difficult way ahead.

Other subjects of current research include parallel computer design, proof and analysis techniques for reasoning about concurrent processes, and the creation of useful and powerful concurrent programming languages.

As illustrated by the house building story early in the chapter, concurrency is a fact of life, and the better we understand it the more we can use it to our advantage. In a way, recent scientific and technological advances in concurrency are ahead of each other. Many of the best parallel algorithms known cannot be implemented because existing parallel computers are inadequate in some way. On the other hand, we still do not know enough about designing concurrent programs and systems to take full advantage of the features those same computers do offer. The work continues, however, and significant results are continuously being achieved, though the deep issues around the true complexity of parallelism remain elusive.

We now turn to two more recent approaches to parallelism, which attack it from completely different angles.

Quantum Computing

So what's all this fashionable new quantum computing stuff? Well, it is a deep and complicated topic, relying on complex mathematical and physical material, and thus very hard to describe in the expository fashion of this book. Quantum computing is based upon quantum mechanics, a remarkable topic in modern physics, which is unfortunately slippery and difficult to grasp, and is often counterintuitive. A naive attempt to employ worldly common sense to understand it can easily become a hindrance to comprehension rather than an aid. The following sections will thus treat the topic extremely superficially, even applying the standards of this technicality-avoiding book. We apologize for this. The bibliographic notes, however, contain several pointers to surveys in the literature for the more curious, mathematically adept reader.

On the brighter side, there is a chance—a very small one as of the time of writing—that quantum computing could bring with it good news of the kind alluded to in this book. How, why, and when, are the questions we shall try to address, very briefly, as we go along.

One of the main advantages of quantum physics is its ability to make sense out of certain experimental phenomena on the particle level that classical physics seemed unable to. Two of the main curiosities of the quantum world, stated very informally, are that a particle can no longer be considered to be at a single location in space at a particular time, and that its situation (including locations) can change as a result of merely observing it. The first of these seems like good news for computing: might we not be able to exploit the property of being at many places together to carry out massive parallelization of a computation? The second, however, seems like bad news: trying to "see" or "touch" a value during a computation, say, to carry out a comparison or an update, could change that value unpredictably!

Quantum computation is a very recent idea. The early work was motivated by the assertion that if a computer could be built that operates according to the laws of quantum physics, rather than those of classical physics, one might be able to obtain an exponential speedup for certain computations.

A quantum computer, like a classical one, is to be based on some kind of finite-state element, analogous to the classical two-state bit. The quantum analog of a bit, called a **qubit** and pronounced "queue-bit," can be envisioned physically in a number of ways: by the direction of photon polarization (horizontal or vertical), by nuclear spin (a special two-valued quantum observable), or by the energy level of an atom (ground or excited). The two so-called **basis states** of a qubit, analogous to the 0 and 1 of an ordinary bit, are denoted by $|0\rangle$ and $|1\rangle$, respectively. What we *don't* have in a quantum system is the simple deterministic notion of the qubit being in one basis state or another. Rather, its notion of being or not being is indeterminate: all we can say about the status of a qubit is that it is in both of the states simultaneously, each with a certain "probability."[4] But, as if to deliberately make things even less comprehensible to mortals, these are not ordinary, positive-valued probabilities, like being in state $|0\rangle$ with probability $\frac{1}{4}$ and in $|1\rangle$ with probability $\frac{3}{4}$. These "probabil-ities" can be negative, even imaginary (i.e., complex numbers that involve square roots of negatives), and the resulting combination state is called a **superposition**. Once we "take a look" at a qubit, i.e., make a measurement, it suddenly decides where to be, we see it in one basis state or the other, the probabilities disappear, and the superposition is forgotten.[5] This kind of "forced discreteness" is what leads to the adjective "quantum."

So much for a single qubit. What happens with many qubits taken together, side by side, which we need as the basis for true quantum computation? How are the states of several qubits combined to obtain a compound state of the entire computing device? In the classical case, any collection of N bits, each of which can be in two states 0 or 1, gives rise to 2^N compound states. In the quantum world of qubits we also start with the 2^N compound states built from the basis states of N qubits (in the case of two qubits, for example, the four compound states are denoted $|00\rangle$, $|01\rangle$, $|10\rangle$ and $|11\rangle$). To these we then apply complex combinations, just as we did for a single qubit. However, here, the way the combinations are defined gives rise to an additional crucial twist called, appropriately, **entanglement**: some of the compound states are clean composites that can be obtained—using an operation called a "tensor product"—from the states of the original qubits, but some cannot; they are entangled. Entangled qubits, a term that comes with a precise mathematical rendition, represent an intrinsically nonseparable "mish-mash" of the

---

[4] Perhaps we should call this "To qubee or not to qubee"...

[5] Specifically, a superposition is what is sometimes called a complex unit-length linear combination of the basis states. That is, the coefficients are two complex numbers c_0 and c_1 satisfying $|c_0|^2 + |c_1|^2 = 1$. After measuring, we will "see" a 0 with probability $|c_0|^2$ and a 1 with probability $|c_1|^2$.

original qubits. They have the weird property of instant communication: observing one and thus fixing its state causes the other to lock in the dual state simultaneously, no matter how far away they are from each other. Entanglement turns out to be a fundamental and indispensable notion in quantum computation, but unfortunately further discussion of its technicalities and the way it is exploited in the computations themselves is beyond the scope of this book.

Quantum Algorithms

What have people been able to do with quantum computation?

A few facts have to be stated up front. First, full, general-purpose quantum computing subsumes classical computation. That is, if and when built, a quantum computer will be able to emulate classical computations without any significant loss of time. Second, although seemingly weaker, a classical computer can simulate any quantum computation, but this could entail an exponential loss of time. The fact that this simulation is possible means that quantum computation cannot destroy the Church/Turing thesis: computability remains intact in the world of quantum computation too. If and when actual quantum computers are built, they will not be able to solve problems not solvable without them.

This having been said, the big question is whether the exponential loss of time in the second statement is indeed insurmountable. Just like we did with parallelism, we ask whether there are provably intractable problems that become tractable in the quantum world. That is, is there a problem with an exponential-time lower bound in the classical models of computation that has a polynomial-time quantum algorithm? And here too, if we use QP to stand for *quantum*-PTIME, we have:

$$\text{PTIME} \subseteq \text{QP} \subseteq \text{PSPACE} \ (= \text{parallel-PTIME})$$

Thus, reasonable, i.e., polynomial, quantum time lies around the same place as NP, i.e., between reasonable deterministic time and reasonable memory space. Unfortunately, as before, we do not know whether either of these inclusions is strict.

Computation complexity aside, and the technological issue of actually building a quantum computer notwithstanding, there have already been some extremely exciting developments in quantum algorithmics. Here are some of the highlights.

Quantum parallelism has indeed been achieved, whereby a superposition of the inputs is used to produce a superposition of outputs. Interestingly, although this seems like one is indeed computing lots of stuff in parallel, the outputs cannot be naively separated out and read from their superposition; any attempt at reading, or measuring, will produce only one output and the rest will simply be lost. What is needed is for the algorithm to cleverly compute **joint properties** common to all outputs, and make do with them. Examples might include certain arithmetical aggregate values of numerical outputs, or the "and"s and "or"s of logical yes/no outputs.[6]

---

[6] However, there are results that show that this ability is inherently limited. While the use of quantum parallelism can often yield significant gains in efficiency, it is unable to deliver each and every desired joint property.

Later, a rather surprising quantum algorithm was discovered for searching in an unordered list, say a large database. Instead of around N operations, an item can be found with $\sqrt{N}$ operations only (the square root of N). This is counterintuitive, almost paradoxical, since it would appear necessary to at least look at all N inputs in order to figure out whether what you are looking for is indeed there.

However, the big surprise, and indeed the pinnacle of quantum algorithms so far, is **Shor's factoring algorithm**. We have mentioned factoring several times in the book, and its importance as a central algorithmic problem is indisputable. As we have seen, factoring has not yet been shown to be tractable in the usual sense—it is not known to be in PTIME (which, as we now know, is not the case for primality testing) and the very fact that it appears to be computationally difficult plays a critical role in cryptography, as we shall see in Chapter 12. So much so, in fact, that a significant part of the walls that hold up modern cryptography would come tumbling down if an efficient factoring algorithm would be available. It is against this background that one should view the significance of this work, which provides a polynomial-time quantum algorithm for the problem.

To appreciate the subtlety of quantum factoring, consider a naive algorithm that attempts to find the factors of a number N by trial and error, going through all pairs of potential factors and multiplying them to see if their product is exactly N. Why shouldn't we be able to do this using grand-scale quantum parallelism? We could use quantum variables to hold a superposition of all candidate factors (say, all numbers between 0 and $N - 1$), then compute, in parallel, and in the best quantum spirit, all products of all possible pairs of these numbers. We could then try to check whether there was a pair that did the job. Unfortunately, this wouldn't work, since taking a look at—that is, carrying out a measurement of—this enormous superposed output would not say much. We might just happen to hit upon a factorization, but we might also land on any other of the many products that are different from N. And as we have already mentioned, once you measure, that's what you get to see, and the rest is lost. So, just the mish-mashing of lots of information, that alone, is not enough.

It turns out that things have to be arranged so that there is **interference**. This is a quantum notion, whereby the possible solutions "fight" each other for supremacy in subtle ways. The ones that turn out not to be good solutions (in our case, pairs of numbers whose product is not N) will interfere *de*structively in the superposition, and the ones that are good solutions (their product is N) will interfere *con*structively. The results of this fight will then show up as varying amplitudes in the output, so that measuring the output superposition will give the good solutions a much better shot at showing up. We should remark that it is the negative numbers in the definition of superposition that make this kind of interference possible in a quantum algorithm.

This is easier said than done, and it is here that the mathematics of quantum computing get complicated and are beyond the scope and level of our exposition. But what we can say is that the right kind of entanglement has been achieved for factoring. The algorithm itself is quite remarkable, both in its technique, and as we shall see later, in its ramifications. Its time performance is roughly cubic, that is, not much more than M^3, where M is the number of digits in the input number N. For the more technically interested reader, the algorithm involves an efficient quantum method to compute the order of a number Y modulo N, that is, to find the least integer a such that $Y^a = 1 \pmod{N}$. This is known to be enough to enable fast factoring, and the rest of the work is done using conventional algorithms.

This algorithm hasn't yet turned a provably intractable problem into a tractable one, for two reasons, one of which we have repeatedly mentioned and one of which we have hinted at but will shortly address in more detail. First, factoring isn't *known* to be intractable; we simply haven't been able to find a polynomial-time algorithm for it. It is conjectured to be hard, but we are not sure. Second, the practical difficulties of building a quantum computer are truly formidable.

Can There Be a Quantum Computer?

When discussing parallelism earlier, we noted that there is a certain mismatch between existing parallel algorithms and the parallel computers that have been built to run them. To be efficiently implemented, many known algorithms require hardware features not yet available, and, dually, the theory of parallel algorithms has yet to catch up with what the available hardware *is* able to do.

In the realm of quantum computation the situation is less symmetric. We have at our disposal some really nice quantum algorithms, but no machines whatsoever to run them on.

Why? Again, this issue revolves around deep technicalities, but this time the barrier preventing a detailed exposition here is not the mathematics but the physics. So, again, we shall only provide a very brief account, and the interested reader will have to seek more information elsewhere. The bibliographic notes provide some pointers.

At the time of writing (mid 2003), the largest quantum "computer" that has actually been built consists of a mere seven qubits (and it has been able to successfully factor the number $15 = 3 \times 5 \ldots$). What is the problem? Why can't we scale up?

Despite the fact that the quantum algorithms themselves, and the factoring one in particular, are designed to work according to rigorous and widely accepted principles of quantum physics, there are severe technical problems around the actual building of a quantum computer. First, experimental physicists have not managed to be able to put even a small number of qubits (say, 10) together and control them in some reasonable way. The difficulties seem beyond present-day laboratory techniques. A particularly troubling issue is **decoherence**: even if you could gather a good number of qubits and cause them to behave nicely themselves, things that reside close to a quantum system have the pushy habit of affecting it. The quantum behavior of anything surrounding a quantum computer—the casing, the walls, the people, the keyboard, *anything!*—can mess up the delicate setup of constructive and destructive interference within the quantum computation. Even a single naughty electron can affect the interference pattern that is so crucial for the correct execution of the algorithm, by becoming entangled with the qubits participating in that execution, and as a result the desired superposition could fail.

The computer thus has to be relentlessly isolated from its environment. But it also has to read inputs and produce an output, and its computational process might have to be controlled by some external elements. Somehow, these contradictory requirements have to be reconciled.

What kind of sizes do we really need? Some small-scale quantum coding protocols require only something like 10 qubits, and even the quantum factoring algorithm needs only a few thousand qubits to be applicable in real-world situations. But since experimental physics can deal with only seven qubits right now, and even that is extremely difficult, many people are pessimistic. A true breakthrough is not expected any time soon. On the brighter side, the excitement surrounding the topic is already bringing about a flurry of ideas and proposals, accompanied by complex laboratory experimentation, so that we are bound to see interesting advances as time goes by.

In summary, Shor's polynomial-time quantum factoring algorithm constitutes a major advance in computing research by any measure. However, at the moment it must be relegated to the status of shelfware, and it is probably destined to remain that way for quite some time.

Intractability hasn't been beaten yet.

Molecular Computing

To wrap up our discussion of models of computation aimed at trying to alleviate some of the bad news, we mention one more: **molecular computing**, sometimes called DNA computing.

The main approach here is based on letting the computation happen essentially on its own, in a carefully concocted "soup" of molecules, that play with each other, splitting, joining, and merging. Thus, you get billions or trillions of molecules to tackle a hard problem by brute force, setting things up cleverly so that the winning cases can later be isolated and identified.

In a 1994 experiment molecules were made to solve a small instance of the Hamiltonian path problem, which, as explained in Chapter 7, is really a sort of unit-length version of the traveling salesman problem. Later, other problems—essentially all problems in NP—were shown to be amenable to similar techniques.

That nature can be tuned to solve real-world algorithmic problems, essentially all by itself, and on a molecular scale, is rather astonishing. While the original experiment for a seven-city instance took several days in the laboratory, the problem was solved later by others in less of a brute-force fashion, and for much larger instances (50–60 cities). Dedicating molecular biology labs to this kind of work can result in a significant speeding up of the process, and indeed lots of work is underway to try to get the techniques to scale up.

From a puristic point of view, things are reminiscent of conventional parallel algorithms: although in principle the time complexity of such molecular algorithms is polynomial because of the high degree of parallelism that goes on within the molecular soup, the number of molecules involved in the process grows exponentially.

But on the positive side, one of the main advantages of using DNA is its incredible information density. Some results show that DNA computations may use a billion times less energy than an electronic computer doing the same things, and could store data in a trillion times less space.

In any case, molecular computing is definitely another exciting area of research, catching the imagination and energy of many talented computer scientists and biologists. We are bound to see a lot of exciting work in this area in the future, and some specific difficult problems might very well become doable for reasonably-sized inputs. Still, we must remember that it can definitely not eliminate noncomputability, nor is it expected to do away with the woeful effects of intractability.

■ Exercises

10.1. Devise a parallel algorithm that sums N salaries in time $O(\sqrt{N})$ with $\sqrt{N}$ processors.

10.2. Can you use parallelism to improve upon the quadratic algorithm given in Chapter 1 (see also Chapter 6) for the salary summation problem, in which we sum only salaries of employees earning more than their managers? What is the time complexity of your solution, and how many processors does it require?

10.3. Justify rigorously the time analysis of the parallel version of mergesort given in the text.

10.4. (a) How many processors do you need in order to solve the satisfiability problem for the propositional calculus in parallel polynomial time? Explain your algorithm.
   (b) What additional assumption do you need in order to show that the number of processors you employed in the previous question is actually necessary?
   (c) Is it possible to solve the satisfiability problem for PDL presented in Chapter 7 in parallel time $O(N)$ and size $O(N)$?

10.5. (a) Construct an algorithm which, given N a power of 2, outputs the odd-even sorting network for N elements.
   (b) Carry out a rigorous time and size analysis of the odd-even sorting network.

An *L by M matrix* A is an array of L rows and M columns, with a typical element $A[I, J]$ located at the intersection of row I and column J. Let A be an L by M matrix and B be an M by N matrix; that is, the number of columns in A equals the number of rows in B. The *product* of A and B is defined to be the L by N matrix C whose elements are given by

$$C[I, J] = \sum_{K=1}^{M}(A[I, K] \times B[K, J]).$$

That is, the element located at row I and column J of the product matrix C is obtained by summing the products of all M corresponding pairs of elements of As Ith row and Bs Jth column. Thus, the matrix-by-vector multiplication defined in the text is the special case of the matrix-by-matrix multiplication defined above, in which the matrix B has just one column (i.e., $N = 1$, namely, B is a vector).

Consider for example a set of M commercial products, each of which is produced by every one of a group of N manufacturers. Consider L stores, each of which sells every one of the M products, but assume that each store buys all the products it sells from precisely one of the L manufacturers. Let A be the L by M matrix containing at $A[I, K]$ the quantity of the Kth product bought by the Ith store each year. Let B be the M by L matrix containing at $B[K, J]$ the price of a unit of the Kth product sold by the Jth manufacturer. Then, if the L by N matrix C is the product of A and B, it contains at $C[I, J]$ the total price per year of all M products to be paid by the Ith store if bought from the Jth manufacturer.

10.6. Devise a systolic array that computes matrix multiplication.

10.7. Show that any problem solvable in NEXPTIME has a parallel algorithm that runs in exponential time. How many processors may such an algorithm require?

10.8. Consider the search problem, in which a given ordered list of length N (with possible multiplicities) is to be searched for the index of an item equal to a given value X, if any such index exists. The binary search algorithm presented in Chapter 6 solves the problem in sequential time $O(\log N)$.

    (a) How would you drastically improve the time complexity of the problem by employing as many processors as you need? Analyze the parallel time and size complexity of your algorithm.

    (b) Consider a stronger model of parallel computation in which many processors can simultaneously read the contents of any single memory location. How would you significantly improve upon the time complexity of the binary search algorithm by employing the more reasonable number of only $\log N$ processors? Explain where exactly in your algorithm do you exploit the "multiple reading" feature of the model, and why it is necessary there.

10.9. Show that weighted average computation (matrix-by-vector multiplication) is in NC.

10.10. Prove the following relations between complexity classes:

    (a) Sequential-PSPACE = Parallel-PTIME.
    (b) NC $\subseteq$ Sequential-PTIME.

10.11. Prove the correctness of the protocol for the N-processor mutual exclusion problem given in the text.

10.12. (a) Construct a protocol for a three-processor mutual exclusion problem, in which the critical section can accommodate one or two processors simultaneously, but not all three.

    (b) Prove the correctness of your protocol.

    (c) Can you generalize your protocol to N processors with at most two in the critical section simultaneously?

    (d) How about N processors with at most L, $1 \leq L < N$, in the critical section simultaneously?

10.13. For each of the following formulas in propositional temporal logic, determine if it is always true.

    φ_1: **henceforth**$(E \,\&\, F) \rightarrow$ **eventually**(E)

    φ_2: **eventually**$(E \,\&\, F) \rightarrow$ **henceforth**(E)

    φ_3: **henceforth**$(E \,\&\, F) \rightarrow ($**henceforth**$(E) \,\&\,$ **henceforth**$(F))$

    φ_4: $($**henceforth**$(E) \,\&\,$ **henceforth**$(F)) \rightarrow$ **henceforth**$(E \,\&\, F)$

    φ_5: **henceforth**$(E \rightarrow F) \rightarrow ($**henceforth**$(E) \rightarrow$ **henceforth**$(F))$

    φ_6: $($**henceforth**$(E) \rightarrow$ **henceforth**$(F)) \rightarrow$ **henceforth**$(E \rightarrow F)$

    φ_7: **henceforth**$($**eventually**$(E)) \rightarrow$ **eventually**$($**henceforth**$(E))$

    φ_8: **eventually**$($**henceforth**$(E)) \rightarrow$ **henceforth**$($**eventually**$(E))$

    φ_9: **henceforth**$(\sim\!E) \rightarrow \sim$**eventually**$(E)$

    φ_{10}: **eventually**$(\sim\!E) \rightarrow \sim$**henceforth**$(E)$

10.14. Consider the doorman solution to the dining philosophers problem.

(a) Formalize the problem to be solved—lack of starvation—by a temporal logic formula using the following set of atomic assertions:

Private$_I$: Philosopher I is carrying out his or her private activity.
Hungry$_I$: Philosopher I is hungry.
Eating$_I$: Philosopher I is eating.

(b) Explain why if there are at most $N - 1$ philosophers at the table at any particular time, then at least one of them can eat.

(c) Write a rigorous version of the solution and prove its correctness.

Two are better than one; because they have a good reward for their labour

ECCLESIASTES 4: 9

Probabilistic Algorithms

or, Getting It Done by Tossing Coins

In the previous chapter we took steps that landed us outside the standard framework of algorithmic problems and their solutions. We allowed parallel algorithms, ones that employ a number of little Runarounds rather than a single one. This departure required little justification, as it can easily be seen to improve performance. We also discussed harnessing the tantalizing power of quantum mechanics or the forces that govern molecular interactions in our quest for massive parallelism. All in all, we concentrated on doing many things at once—not just one.

In this chapter we shall take a more radical step, renouncing one of the most sacred requisites in all of algorithmics, namely, that a solution to an algorithmic problem must solve that problem correctly, for all possible inputs. We cannot completely abandon the need for correctness, since, if we do, any algorithm would "solve" any problem. Nor can we afford to recommend that people solve algorithmic problems with algorithms that they *hope* will work, but whose performance they can only observe, not analyze. What we are interested in are algorithms that might not always be correct, but whose possible incorrectness is something that can be safely ignored. Moreover, we insist that this fact be justifiable on rigorous mathematical grounds.

If we assume that spinning a revolver's barrel is a truly random way of selecting one of its six bullet positions, then some people might consider the chances of getting killed in a single attempt at Russian roulette unlikely. Most people would not. Let us now suppose that the revolver has 2^{200} bullet positions, or (equivalently) that the trigger in an ordinary six-bullet revolver is actually pulled only if the single bullet always ended up in the shooting position in 77 consecutive spins. In such a case, the chances of getting killed in a single (77-spin) play are many orders of magnitude smaller than the chances of achieving the same effect by drinking a glass of water, driving to work, or taking a deep breath of air. Clearly, in such a case the chances *can* be safely ignored; the probability of a catastrophe is unimaginably minute.

This chapter is concerned with one of the ways that **probability theory** can be exploited in algorithmic design. We shall consider algorithms that in the course of their action can toss fair coins, yielding truly random outcomes. The consequences of adding this new facility turn out to be quite surprising. Rather than constituting a step backwards, leading to algorithms that produce unpredictable results, the new ability will be shown to be extremely useful and capable of yielding fast probabilistic solutions to problems that have only very inefficient conventional ones. The price paid for this is the possibility of error, but, as in the 77-round version of Russian roulette, this possibility can be safely ignored. Curiously, in Chapter 12 we shall see that probabilism, or randomization, in algorithmics is most advantageous when used together with negative results, concerning problems for which no good solutions are known, not even probabilistic ones.

More on the Dining Philosophers

In Chapter 10 we became acquainted with the dining philosophers, and saw that the problem admits no deadlock-free solutions if we insist on total symmetry and use no centralized variables. The rules prescribed that a candidate solution must work correctly even against the most malicious scheduler; for example, even for the case in which everyone becomes hungry and tries to lift up the forks at precisely the same time.

We now show that the problem *is* solvable if we let the philosophers toss coins. The basic idea is to use coin tossing to break the symmetry in the long run. Specifically, consider the following candidate solution:

protocol for each philosopher:

(1) do the following again and again forever:
    (1.1) carry out *private activities* until hungry;
    (1.2) toss coin to choose a direction, *left* or *right*, at random;
    (1.3) wait until fork lying in chosen direction is available, and then lift it;
    (1.4) if other fork is not available do the following:
        (1.4.1) put down fork that was lifted;
        (1.4.2) go to (1.2);
    (1.5) otherwise (i.e., other fork is available) lift other fork;
    (1.6) *critical section*: eat to your heart's content;
    (1.7) put down both forks (and go back to (1.1)).

This solution can be shown to be deadlock free **with probability 1.** What does this mean? Well, it means that in the course of an infinite time period, the chances of a deadlock occurring are zero. Not just small, or negligible, but zero!

This statement requires further clarification. It is possible that the system of philosophers will deadlock, but the chances that deadlock will occur, relative to the chances that it will not, are nil. Let us consider a scheduler that causes all philosophers to become hungry simultaneously. Say the philosophers are all positioned at clause (1.2) together. One way for the system to deadlock is that all philosophers, simultaneously, choose the same direction in (1.2), say *right*, lift up their right-hand fork, discover that the other fork is not available (in (1.4)), put down the right-hand fork (in (1.4.1)), go back to (1.2) and again, all choose the same direction, perhaps *left* this time, again lift up the appropriate fork, then put it down, then choose the same direction again, and so on, *ad infinitum*. This is clearly a deadlock situation, since no philosopher can eat.

That the philosophers are all perfectly synchronized, reaching the same instruction at one and the same time, is the devious work of this special scheduler, and scheduling is not something that is chosen at random; our solutions must work even against the worst of schedulers. Coin tossing may only be used within the protocols to influence the behavior of individual processors, but not to influence the order or timing in which they are told to carry out their instructions. It follows that malicious scheduling cannot be the reason that a particular scenario such as this one has zero chance of happening; the scheduler might just behave in precisely this way. The real reason has to do with the probability that certain outcomes will occur as a result of the coin-tossing activities. To achieve deadlock under this scheduler, all *N* coins have to indicate the same direction, each and every time they are tossed. This can be shown to be a **zero-probability** event, to use the terminology of probability theory. There is no real chance that this will indeed happen in the process of tossing *N* coins, simultaneously, and infinitely often. (Is this true for all *N*? What happens when *N* is 1?) In other words, in an infinite execution of these protocols for *N* philosophers the apparent symmetry will be broken with probability 1, that is, for sure, by some unequal set of outcomes in one of the coin-tossing stages. It is easy to see that such a break in symmetry results in at least one eating philosopher, so that deadlock is avoided.

It is important to realize that the preceding argument does not constitute a *proof* that the protocol is deadlock free with probability 1. We have only discussed one particular scheduler, and one particular set of coin tosses that results in deadlock, showing it to be of zero probability. What if the coin indicates *left* for even-numbered philosophers and *right* for odd-numbered ones, and the scheduler repeatedly gives the former philosophers one turn and then the latter ones one turn? What if there are seven philosophers and they are given turns in a cyclic fashion, skipping two each time? Generalizing the argument to hold for all schedulers is not straightforward, but it can be done, so that the protocol just presented is indeed deadlock free under *any* scheduling. However, this solution is still not satisfactory, since it admits lockouts, or starvation.

■ Here is a scheduler that, with certainty, will cause all but one philosopher to be locked out; in other words, they will all be deprived of food with probability 1.

The scheduler first arranges a situation in which all philosophers are at (1.2). It will now work things in such a way as to guarantee that, with probability 1, one of the philosophers, say Plato, will eat infinitely often, while each of the others will eventually eat a last supper and thereafter starve forever. The idea is based on the fact that if a philosopher is given the opportunity of eating repeatedly until his coin toss in (1.2) happens to yield some particular desired direction, then with probability 1 the desired direction will indeed eventually appear. Utilizing this fact, the scheduler will now ignore everyone but Plato, letting him find his forks and eat repeatedly as long as he draws *right* in the coin toss of (1.2). Plato will be stopped when he draws *left* for the first time, and, as mentioned, with probability 1 this will indeed happen. Plato is now left in limbo after this last execution of (1.2) but before the check-and-lift instruction of (1.3), and his right-hand neighbor is given the green light. She, too, is allowed to eat repeatedly until she draws *left*, at which time he is also left lingering after the completion of (1.2) and the execution of (1.3). This goes on around the table in cyclic counterclockwise order, giving each philosopher the floor (and the spaghetti) until he or she draws *left*. When this is over, all philosophers are ready to carry out clause (1.3), with *left* being their chosen direction. Since the probability is 1 that each philosopher's eating spree will eventually terminate with the coin showing *left*, the probability of reaching this common situation is also 1. Now, all the philosophers are allowed by the scheduler to materialize their most recent choice of *left*, and to pick up their left-hand fork. None yet has started (1.4).

From this point on, our scheduler will only allow Plato to eat; all others will starve forever. The way to achieve this is as follows. Plato's right-hand neighbor is allowed to proceed. She looks to her right, sees that the fork is unavailable (*her* right-hand neighbor has it), puts down her left-hand fork and tosses the coin again. This goes on without her eating until she draws *right*. She is then left in limbo by the scheduler, before (1.3), so that she has not even determined that her right-hand fork is unavailable, and control goes to *her* right-hand neighbor (the second from Plato). This philosopher is similarly given the opportunity to proceed (similarly without succeeding to eat) until he also draws *right*, and is stopped at the same point, just before (1.3). This procedure is carried out for all philosophers, in counterclockwise order around the table, up to, but excluding, Plato himself. The situation now is that all forks are on the table, except Plato's left-hand one, which he is holding, and all the other philosophers are ready to look to their right in (1.3). Now Plato is allowed to proceed, which he does by lifting his right-hand fork and eating. In fact, he is allowed to go through his entire protocol repeatedly as long as he chooses *left* in (1.2), eating well each time, and is stopped by the scheduler when he draws *right* for the first time. Now the situation is exactly as it was after Plato's initial eating spree, but with *right* being his latest choice, not *left*. The scheduler now continues precisely as before, but with the directions reversed throughout, going around from neighbor to left-hand neighbor in clockwise order, waiting for them all to draw *left*, until Plato is reached. Again, he eats repeatedly until he draws *left*, and the whole procedure repeats itself.

Except for Plato, all philosophers clearly starve after the initial round of eating is over. Plato, on the other hand, eats infinitely often. Furthermore, all the eventualities that were invoked in describing this most malicious scheduler actually occur with probability 1. Consequently, all philosophers except for Plato will be starved with probability 1. Thus, as we said, the protocol presented earlier avoids deadlock but, unfortunately, it admits starvation.

There is an extension of the protocol that yields zero probability of starvation too. This version will not be presented here, except to remark that it uses the same coin-tossing mechanism for choosing directions, as well as variables that are somewhat similar to those used in the solution to the shower problem. Among these are two variables for each philosopher—one notifies the two neighbors that he or she desires to eat, and the other (shared by the philosopher and his or her neighbors) indicates which of them ate last. None of the variables is centralized, as each is shared by at most two locally adjacent philosophers.

And so, in fact, there *is* a fully symmetric, fully distributed solution to the dining philosophers problem, and it is quite satisfactory, in spite of the proof in Chapter 10 that such a solution does not exist.[1] It exists only in the presence of the more liberal notion of correctness used here: not absolute correctness, but, rather, correctness with probability 1.

Probabilistic Algorithms for Conventional Algorithmic Problems

We have seen that the dining philosophers problem, with the requirements of symmetry and distributivity, cannot be solved without the help of randomization. However, there is something a little disconcerting about the probabilistic solutions just discussed. They seem to rely for their success on the infinite, perpetual nature of the protocols, since in such solutions what causes certain events to occur with probability 1 is the fact that we are reasoning about an infinite time span, and things can happen arbitrarily far into the future. Indeed, we get the feeling that, if presented with some version of the problem that involves finite time spans only, the entire probabilistic building constructed above would collapse, and there would not be much that we could say. Somehow, it appears that the really interesting problem is this: can probabilism, or randomization, improve things when it comes to ordinary, conventional algorithmic problems, those that accept inputs and have to halt with the desired outputs? And the answer to this is also a resounding yes.

Before giving concrete examples, let us imagine the following situation, which is not unlike the Russian roulette story, except that we prefer to talk about people's money, not their lives. Let us assume that, for some unexplained reason, all our money was tied up to the monkey puzzle problem of Chapter 7 in the following way. We are given a single large instance of the problem (say 225 monkey cards), and are told that our money will be doubled if we give the right yes/no answer to the question of whether the cards can be arranged in a legal 15 by 15 square. We are also told that we lose the lot if we give the wrong answer. Moreover, our money is unavailable until we give *some* answer. Since the monkey puzzle problem is NP-complete, we have a problem of our own. What shall we do?

We could run our favorite exponential-time algorithm on the input cards, hoping that this particular set is an easy one, so that the algorithm will be able to deal with it reasonably fast, or we could position ourselves on the floor and start trying things out on our own. Given the discussions in Chapter 7, these possibilities have certain obvious drawbacks. Alternatively, realizing the hopelessness of the situation, we might simply toss a coin, say yes or no at random, and hope for the best. Is there any better way?

Remaining in an imaginary mode of thought, suppose we were offered an algorithm that solved the monkey puzzle problem, but with a slight chance of error.

---

[1] The reason the proof there no longer holds in the present context, is that it was crucially based on the fact that an algorithm always does the very same thing each time it is run on the same inputs. Probabilistic algorithms can act differently in different runs under the exact same circumstances.

Say we were guaranteed that, randomly, once in every 2^{200} executions, it gave the wrong answer. This would be an excellent way of resolving the dilemma. We would undoubtedly just run the algorithm on the input cards and present our tormentor with the answer. The chances of losing our money would be, as in the 77-round Russian roulette game, far less than the chances of getting run over in crossing the road to the computer center, and far, far less than the chances that, during execution, a hardware error will occur in the computer on which the algorithm is implemented.

The fact is that for many algorithmic problems, including some that appear to be intractable, such algorithms do exist (not, as far as we know, for the monkey puzzle problem, but for many similar ones). These algorithms are probabilistic in nature, as they employ random coin tossing, and are thus sometimes called **probabilistic**, or **randomized** algorithms. For all practical purposes that come to mind such algorithms are perfectly satisfactory, whether it is an individual's money or life, a company's financial future, or an entire country's security or welfare that is at stake.

Let us now look at an example of a remarkable probabilistic solution to a problem, which for a very long time was thought to be intractable.

■ Generating Large Primes

Chapter 7 mentioned **prime numbers**, or just **primes** for short. A prime is a positive integer whose only **factors** (that is, numbers that divide it exactly, with no remainder) are 1 and the number itself. Other numbers are termed **composite**; they are just the multiples of the primes. The first few primes are 2, 3, 5, 7, 11, 13, 17, 19, 23, 29, 31, . . . There are infinitely many prime numbers, and they are spread out over the entire spectrum of positive integers in the following way. The number of primes less than a given number N is on the order of $N / \log N$. As specific examples, there are 168 primes less than 1000, about 78,500 primes less than a million, and about 51 million primes less than a billion. Among all 100-digit numbers, roughly one in every 300 is prime, and for 200-digit numbers it is about one in every 600.

The primes undoubtedly constitute the most interesting class of numbers ever to have caught mathematicians' attention. They play a central role in the branch of mathematics known as **number theory**, and have many remarkable properties. Their investigation has led to some of the most beautiful results in all of mathematics. Moreover, as we shall see in Chapter 12, prime numbers are fast becoming indispensable in several exciting applications of algorithmics, where it is important to be able to generate large primes reasonably fast.

Suppose now that we are interested in generating a new large prime number, say 150 digits long. If only we had a good way of *testing* the primality of large numbers, we would be able to take advantage of the way the primes are distributed among all positive integers to find a 150-digit prime in a moderate amount of time. To do so, we would simply generate, at random, odd 150-digit numbers repeatedly (by tossing coins to choose the digits), and test each one for primality until we hit one that is prime. There is a very high likelihood (more than 90%) that we will find one within the first 1000 attempts, and a good chance that we will find one after far less. In any event, if we are careful not to choose the same number twice we are sure to find one before long. The problem of *generating* large primes efficiently is therefore reduced to that of *testing* the primality of large numbers.

But how do we test a number for primality? Here is one straightforward way. Given a number N, divide it by all numbers from 2 all the way to $N - 1$. If any of these are found to divide N evenly, stop and say no, since you have just found a factor of N other than 1 and N itself. If all the $N - 2$ divisions are found to leave remainders, stop and say yes, N is a prime. This algorithm is fine, except that it is unreasonably inefficient. In fact, as explained in Chapter 7, it runs in exponential time, where the size of the input is taken to be the number of digits in N.[2] Testing numbers of 10 or 15 digits in this way is feasible, but testing 150-digit numbers is not, as it would take billions of years on the fastest computers (see Chapter 7). Of course, this algorithm can be improved by dividing the candidate number N only by 2 and by the odd numbers from 3 to the square root of N, or, more significantly, by carefully leaving out all multiples of divisors already considered. However, no such naive improvements eliminate the super-polynomial time that the solution takes, and hence this brute-force approach is quite useless.

Until very recently, primality was not known to be in P. As mentioned in Chapter 7, it has been known for almost 30 years to be in NP, and thus to have short certificates, but no one knew of any polynomial-time algorithm for testing primality, and there was always the possibility that the problem would turn out to be intractable. In the absence of a truly polynomial-time solution to the problem, several ingenious circumventing approaches had been developed over the years. They included a polynomial-time algorithm for primality testing that relied for its correctness on a deep, but unproven, conjecture in mathematics, called the **extended Riemann hypothesis**. Had this conjecture ever been proved to be true, the primality problem would have automatically become a member of P. Moreover, even without relying on the Riemann hypothesis, people had been able to come up with algorithms for primality testing that run in "almost" polynomial time. The one that for a long time was best in terms of order-of-magnitude performance ran in time $O(N^{O(\log\log N)})$, which can be considered very close to polynomial time, since $\log\log N$ grows ever so slowly: if the base of the logarithm is 2, the first N for which $\log\log N$ reaches 5 is more than four billion.

Very recently, primality was shown to be in P. We shall not describe the algorithm here, except to make two remarks. First, this is an extremely important result, both because of the classical nature of the primes and their importance in algorithmics (see Chapter 12), and because it puts to rest one of the most well-known open problems in algorithmics. Second, the exponent of the polynomial in this so-called AKS algorithm is still rather high (12 in the original algorithm, which was later brought down to 8) and its performance is still painfully slow. In that respect it is not unlike the polynomial-time algorithm for linear programming, mentioned towards the end of Chapter 7. Still, given that the polynomial-time primality algorithm is so new, many people expect it to be refined and improved considerably, so that it will eventually become practical.

---

[2] We repeat a crucial fact, which appeared in a footnote in Chapter 7: in number-theoretic problems the size N of the numerical input is not the number itself, but its length in digits, which is essentially its *logarithm*.

Nevertheless, there *are* extremely fast and fully practical polynomial-time algorithms for testing primality, which were in fact available long before the AKS algorithm was discovered. They are probabilistic.

▧ Probabilistic Algorithms for Testing Primality

In the mid-1970s two very elegant probabilistic algorithms for testing primality were discovered. These were among the first probabilistic solutions to be found for hard algorithmic problems, and they have triggered extensive research that has led to randomized algorithms for many other problems. Both algorithms run in time that is a (low-order) polynomial in the number of digits in the input number N, and both can test the primality of a 150-digit number with a negligible probability of error in a few seconds on a medium-sized computer!

The algorithms are based on searching at random for certain kinds of certificates, or **witnesses**, to N's compositeness. If such a witness is found, the algorithm can safely stop and say "no, N is not prime," since it has acquired indisputable evidence that N is composite. However, the search must be constructed in such a way that at some reasonably early point in time the algorithm will be able to stop searching and declare that N is prime, with a very small chance of being wrong. Notice, of course, that we cannot simply define a witness to be a number between 2 and $N - 1$ that divides N exactly, although obviously such a finding constitutes undisputed evidence that N is composite. The reason is that there are exponentially many numbers between 2 and $N - 1$ (that is, exponentially many relative to the number of digits in N), and if we want to give up and declare N to be prime with a small chance of being wrong, we would have had to check almost all of them, which is unreasonable. The idea, therefore, is to find a different definition of a witness, one that is also rapidly testable, but with the property that, if N is indeed composite, more than half of the numbers between 1 and $N - 1$ are witnesses to N's compositeness. In this way, if we choose at random a single number K between 1 and $N - 1$, and N is indeed composite, the probability that K will serve to convince us of that fact is greater than $\frac{1}{2}$. Now we can understand better why the naive idea of making K a witness if it divides N will not do: in general, far fewer than half of the numbers between 1 and $N - 1$ divide a composite number N exactly. The definition of a witness has to be more subtle.

Before seeing a satisfactory approach to witness definition, it is worth understanding why this "more-than-half-are-witnesses" property is so significant. The secret lies in the idea of repeatedly testing many different potential witnesses. If we choose just one K at random, and say "yes, N is prime" if K is found not to be a witness to N's compositeness, we have a chance of less than $\frac{1}{2}$ of being wrong, since at least half of the numbers from which we have chosen would have caused us to say no if the answer is indeed no. Now, if we choose *two* such Ks at random, independently, and say yes if *neither* of them is found to be a witness, the probability that we are wrong is reduced to $\frac{1}{4}$, the reason being that there is one chance in four that although N is really composite we have landed twice on a nonwitness, while again, at least half of the possibilities for each choice would have led us to the right answer. If we choose *three* Ks the probability of error becomes $\frac{1}{8}$, and so on. This fact translates

Figure 11.1

The scheme of a
probabilistic
primality-testing
algorithm.

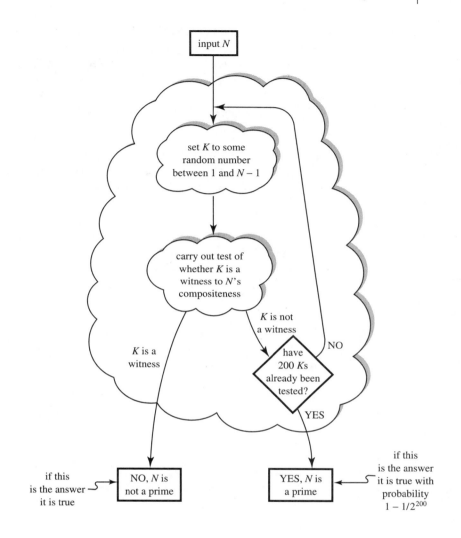

immediately into an algorithm. Choose, say, 200 random numbers between 1 and
$N - 1$ and test each for being a witness to N's compositeness. Stop and say no if
(and when) any one of them is found to be a witness, and stop and say yes if they
all pass the witness-testing procedure in the negative. Since the choices of the Ks
are mutually independent, the following statement holds (see Figure 11.1):

> *Whenever this algorithm is run on a prime number, the answer is sure to be
> yes. When it is run on a composite number, the answer will almost certainly
> be no, and the probability that it will be yes (when it should not) is less than 1
> in 2^{200}.*

It seems unnecessary to repeat the Russian roulette story here, or the breathing,
drinking, or crossing-the-road facts, but you will undoubtedly agree that this performance is perfectly satisfactory for any practical purpose, including cases where
a person's money or life depend on giving a correct answer. If a user is not satisfied

with this incredible success probability, he can instruct the algorithm to try 201 Ks instead of 200, and thus halve the chance of error, or, say, 500 Ks, making it an incredibly small $\frac{1}{2^{500}}$. In practice, we might add, running such algorithms on as little as 50 Ks has proved to be quite adequate.

We are left with having to exhibit a workable definition of a witness to N's compositeness, and it is here that the two algorithms differ. Here is a brief description of one of them.

■ We shall need a few notions from elementary number theory. For two positive integers K and N, we say that K is a **quadratic residue modulo** N if there is some X such that X^2 and K yield the same remainder when divided by N. This is denoted by:

$$X^2 \equiv K(\mathrm{mod}\ N)$$

If K and N have no common factors and N is odd, we associate a special number (that is always either 1 or -1) with the pair $\langle K, N \rangle$. This number is known as the **Jacobi symbol** of K and N, and we shall denote it here by $Js(K, N)$. If N is a prime, then define $Js(K, N)$ to be 1 if K is a quadratic residue modulo N, and -1 otherwise. If N is not a prime, then $Js(K, N)$ is defined to be the grand product of the Jacobi symbols of K and each of the prime factors of N, where each factor appears in the product as many times as it appears in N's unique decomposition into prime factors. For example, since $261 = 3 \times 3 \times 29$, we have:

$$Js(35, 261) = Js(35, 3) \times Js(35, 3) \times Js(35, 29)$$

Now, $Js(35, 3)$ and $Js(35, 29)$ can be shown, respectively, to be -1 and 1 (the latter because $8^2 = 64$, and 64 and 35 yield the same remainder modulo 29). Hence, the final value for $Js(35, 261)$ is:

$$-1 \times -1 \times 1 = 1$$

If K is the number chosen at random from among $1, 2, \ldots, N - 1$, first determine if K and N, the number whose primality we are trying to test, have any factors in common other than 1. If they do, then obviously N is not a prime and the test is over. Assume, therefore, that they do not. Now compute:

$$X \leftarrow K^{(N-1)/2}(\mathrm{mod}\ N)$$

that is, set X to the remainder obtained when $K^{(N-1)/2}$ is divided by N. Also, compute:

$$Y \leftarrow Js(K, N)$$

If $X \neq Y$ we say that K is a witness to N's compositeness, and the entire procedure stops and says "no, N is not a prime." If, on the other hand, $X = Y$, K is not a witness.

It is possible to show, using number-theoretic arguments, that for every *prime* N the resulting X and Y are equal, so that if indeed the K chosen gives rise to $X \neq Y$ we are fully justified in concluding that N is not prime. On the other hand, $X = Y$ does not guarantee that N *is* a prime. However, it so happens (though this is by no means easy to prove) that if N is really not prime, then the equality $X = Y$ holds for at most *half* of the $N - 2$ numbers between 1 and $N - 1$. Thus, as required, the probability of erring in giving the indicated yes/no answers for a randomly chosen N is no more than $\frac{1}{2}$, so that reiterating the procedure for, say, 200 such Ks yields the desired algorithm.

To complete the story, we must be able to tell efficiently whether K and N have any common factors, and to compute X and Y rapidly. The former can be achieved by applying Euclid's fast gcd algorithm, and for the latter there are also fast algorithms that we shall not dwell upon here.

This completes the brief discussion of a fast probabilistic algorithm for testing primality. It is noteworthy that the other solution yields even smaller error probabilities, in the sense that the fraction of witnesses to N's compositeness among the numbers from 1 to $N - 1$ is at least $\frac{3}{4}$, not $\frac{1}{2}$. Thus, as more Ks are chosen at random, the probability of error diminishes twice as fast. A 1-in-2^{200} effect can thus be achieved with 100 random Ks, not 200.

And so, we have extremely fast probabilistic algorithms for testing primality, which are far better in practice—at least for the time being—than any others, including the recent nonprobabilistic polynomial-time AKS algorithm. In contrast, the problem of finding the *factors* of a number, even a number known ahead of time to be composite, does not seem to admit even a probabilistic solution that runs in polynomial time. Thus, while primality testing has become tractable both in principle (AKS) and in practice (the probabilistic algorithms), factoring has become so in neither. As promised, we shall see some surprising applications of fast primality testing in the next chapter, and interestingly, they hinge on precisely this difference between primality testing and factoring.

Fast Probabilistic Pattern Matching

Testing for primality is a striking example of a difficult problem that becomes solvable when coin tossing is allowed. In a more humble vein, there are many examples of problems that do have reasonable solutions, but for which randomization can nevertheless improve things significantly. Let us consider an example.

Suppose we wish to determine whether a given pattern of symbols occurs in a lengthy text.[3] Assume that the pattern is of length M and the text of length N; see Figure 11.2. Clearly, any algorithm that solves the problem must, in the worst case, consider every position in the entire text, so that $O(N)$ is clearly a lower bound on the time complexity of the problem. (Can you formulate a precise argument to that end?) A naive algorithm calls for running through the text, and at each position checking whether the next M symbols of the text match the M symbols of the pattern perfectly. This may give rise to a worst-case time behavior of $O(N \times M)$, which is inadequate unless the pattern is very short. If we are looking for a short word in the *Encyclopedia Britannica*, for example, this procedure may be feasible, even though N is approximately a billion. However, if the *Britannica* is to be searched for a symbol string of length 1000, or a million, the naive algorithm is hopelessly slow. While there are a number of rather clever linear-time algorithms for this problem,

---

[3] **Bioinformatics**, the scientific field that deals with the use of computing for analyzing biological data, requires pattern matching of many different kinds. In fact, it is fair to say that the heart of the algorithmic difficulties in analyzing DNA sequences, and other results of the various genome-related projects, lies in pattern matching and data mining (the latter mentioned in Chapter 2).

Figure 11.2

The pattern-matching problem.

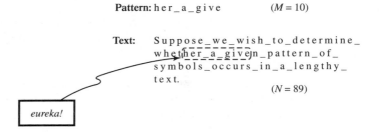

Pattern: h e r _ a _ g i v e   (*M* = 10)

Text: S u p p o s e _ w e _ w i s h _ t o _ d e t e r m i n e _
w h e t h e r _ a _ g i v e n _ p a t t e r n _ o f _
s y m b o l s _ o c c u r s _ i n _ a _ l e n g t h y _
t e x t.

(*N* = 89)

eureka!

they are somewhat intricate, and their constants are too high to be of much help when *M* is also large. Most of them also require a considerable amount of memory space. Enter coin tossing.

The following algorithm uses an idea called **fingerprinting**. Instead of comparing the pattern, symbol by symbol, with every possible block of *M* contiguous symbols of text, we use a fingerprinting function that associates a number with each symbol string of length *M*. Then, as the algorithm runs through the text considering each *M*-symbol block in turn, it is these representative numbers, rather than the strings themselves, that are compared. This sounds quite straightforward, but does not seem to constitute an improvement over the $O(M \times N)$ upper bound, since we still have to consider each of the *M* letters in each of the possible *N* or so potential locations of the pattern. However, we can improve things if the following two requirements can be met: (1) the fingerprint number is itself much shorter than *M*, ideally of length log *N* or log *M*, and (2) the fingerprint of an *M*-symbol block is computable in time less than $O(M)$, ideally in constant time. Requirement (1) is not satisfied by a simple translation of an *M*-block of symbols into digits (as was done in Chapter 9 in the reductions between Turing machines and counter programs). The fingerprint function must be more subtle.

Here is what we shall do. A prime number *K* of about log *N* binary digits is chosen at random, and the fingerprint of an *M*-symbol block *B* is taken to be the remainder obtained when the digitized version of *B* is divided by *K*. Thus, for the *Britannica* we would need a prime number of length about 30 binary digits, or about 10 decimal ones.

■ Requirement (1) is satisfied by this definition, because remainders of divisions by *K* are between 0 and $K - 1$, and are hence no longer than log *N*, which is on the order of the length of *K* itself. Requirement (2) is also satisfied. To see how, suppose (as in Chapter 9) that the text is constructed from an alphabet of 10 symbols, so that it can be considered simply as a lengthy decimal number. In this way, *M*-symbol blocks become simply *M*-digit numbers, which, to make things a little easier, are considered in reverse, the least significant digit being the leftmost one. In general, computing the fingerprint of an *M*-digit number (i.e., its remainder modulo *K*) takes a *non*constant amount of time, depending on *M*. However, here we are traveling along a lengthy string of digits, and we can use the fingerprint of one *M*-digit number to rapidly compute that of the next. For example, consider the text

9 8 3 3 4 1 1 5 8 6 4 4 9 3 2 2 9 1 6 1 5 . . .

Let *M* = 6, and assume, as illustrated, that we have reached the ninth position (i.e., the second 8 from the left), having already computed the fingerprint *J* to be the remainder of the number 394,468 modulo the chosen prime K. The new fingerprint, call it J', is the remainder of 239,446 modulo K. Using the fact that the second of these six-digit numbers is obtained from the first by subtracting 8, dividing by 10 (leaving 39,446) and then adding 200,000, J' can be obtained from J with three simple arithmetical operations, carried out modulo K, i.e., with remainders modulo K in mind. Each of these operations takes only constant time, since, for example, there are only 10 possibilities for the number that has to be added, 200,000 in this example, and the remainders of these modulo K can be computed in advance and kept in a table. Consequently, the entire algorithm (which runs through the entire text, comparing every M symbols with the pattern until it finds matching fingerprints) can easily be seen to run in low-order linear time. More precisely, it takes time $O(N + M)$, with a very small constant and negligible memory space.

This is the good news. The bad news is that the algorithm, as it stands, may err. Obviously, if the fingerprints turn out to be unequal, the real strings (the pattern and the M-symbol block against which it is being checked) must be unequal too. However, the converse is not necessarily true. Two different M-symbol blocks might have the very same fingerprint, since they are only required to yield the same remainder when divided by K, a property shared by many different numbers. The algorithm might thus find incorrect "matches." However, like any good story, this one has a happy ending too.

It can be shown that in our case the probability that one of the M-symbol blocks in the text will have the same remainder when divided by the random prime number K as does the M-symbol pattern, although they are *un*equal as symbol strings, is about 1 in N. In other words, even if a malicious adversary tries to set up a text and pattern that will generate many different blocks with the same fingerprint, the fact that K is chosen at random *after* the text and pattern are given guarantees that, probabilistically speaking, a mismatch will erroneously be declared to be a match only roughly once during an entire run of the algorithm. To make sure that even this remote event will not lead to the wrong answer, we can modify the algorithm so that when a fingerprint match is found the algorithm will actually check the supposedly matching blocks, symbol for symbol, before stopping and declaring a match. If it so happens that this is the one case in which the fingerprint comparison errs, the algorithm will continue to search for other matches. As mentioned, there is only a very small chance that many of these expensive double-checks will be necessary. Usually there will be roughly one in each run of the algorithm, and this will not change its $O(M + N)$ performance.

What emerges here is a choice of two versions of this algorithm. The first, in which no double-check is made when fingerprints are found to match, is guaranteed to run in linear time but (with low probability) it might err, and the second, in which double-checks are made, is guaranteed not to err but (with low probability) it might run for longer than linear time. There are names for these different kinds of probabilistic algorithms. Those that are always fast and probably correct are dubbed **Monte Carlo**, and those that are always correct and probably fast are termed **Las Vegas**. The probabilistic primality-testing algorithms are thus of the Monte Carlo variety, and for pattern matching we have one of each.

Probabilistic Complexity Classes

Probabilistic algorithms can be formalized using **probabilistic Turing machines**. These are nondeterministic Turing machines, in which the choices are made by tossing normal, unbiased coins, not magical ones. The class RP (standing for **Random Polynomial-time**) is defined as the class of decision problems for which there is a polynomial-time probabilistic Turing machine with the following property. If the correct answer for an input X is *no*, the machine says *no* with probability 1, and if the correct answer is *yes*, the machine says *yes* with probability greater than $\frac{1}{2}$. Of course, the interest in RP problems stems from the fact that for any given X these possibly erroneous algorithms can be reiterated many times, achieving a diminishing probability of error, as explained in detail earlier. The complement class, co-RP, contains those problems whose complements are in RP. A co-RP problem thus admits a probabilistic polynomial-time Turing machine that with probability 1 says *yes* for yes inputs, and with probability greater than $\frac{1}{2}$ says *no* for no inputs.

The class RP lies between P and NP. Every tractable problem, that is, one that is solvable in conventional polynomial time, is in RP (why?), and every RP problem is in NP, and is thus solvable by magical nondeterminism in polynomial time. (Why?) The co-RP problems are similarly between P and co-NP (see Figure 11.3, and compare with Figure 7.15). Here too, some researchers believe that the inclusions in the sequence:

$$P \subseteq RP \subseteq NP$$

are strict, but no one knows for sure. For example, just as primality has turned out to be in P, so might all the NP problems, causing this three-way hierarchy to collapse. It is thus interesting that in the realm of reasonable time we do not know whether coin tossing provides any real additional power, or whether magical coin tossing provides even more.

Figure 11.3

Random polynomial-time complexity classes.

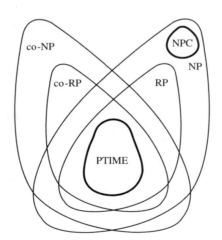

As far as universal algorithmic power goes, the Church/Turing thesis extends to probabilistic algorithms too. Randomization, like concurrency, cannot be used to solve the noncomputable, or the undecidable, at least not under these definitions: it is possible to simulate every probabilistic Turing machine by a conventional Turing machine, and, moreover, this can be done with at most an exponential loss of time. Thus, coin tossing does not extend our absolute algorithmic capabilities, but it does allow us to make better use of them. Perhaps it will eventually be possible to exploit coin tossing to solve in practice *provably* intractable problems. As of now, however, we know of no fast probabilistic algorithm for any provably intractable problem. And some problems that are conjectured to be intractable are also conjectured to remain so even in the face of probabilism. Factoring numbers is one example, and we shall have occasion to return to it later.

Research on Probabilistic Algorithms

Although by now it must sound repetitious, the topics discussed in this chapter are also the subject of intensive research. Randomization in algorithmics is an extremely exciting idea. Numerous new applications have been found, and many results have been established since this area of research started in earnest about 25 years ago.

As with parallelism and concurrency, researchers are working in essentially two different directions. The first is the search for efficient randomized algorithms for conventional input/output-oriented algorithmic problems (this is analogous to the quest for efficient parallelized algorithms for such problems), and the second is finding ways to utilize coin tossing in the solution of problems of an inherently perpetual, ongoing nature, which typically involve distributed processing. Probabilistic primality testing is an example of the former and the coin-tossing protocol for the dining philosophers is an example of the latter. Researchers are interested in both kinds of probabilistic algorithms, Monte Carlo and Las Vegas, and in others too, and also in the relationships between them.

Some of the most difficult problems arise when concurrency and randomization are combined. If in Chapter 10 we claimed that concurrency renders specification and verification subtle and slippery, adding coin tossing makes them doubly so. Verifying formally that the probabilistic dining philosophers protocol is deadlock free with probability 1, is a very delicate and tedious chore. Researchers are interested in finding satisfactory proof methods for probabilistic protocols and algorithms, and also in constructing probabilistic dynamic logics, which enable many different properties of such algorithms to be stated and proved in rigorous mathematical fashion.

The classification of algorithmic problems into probabilistic complexity classes is another interesting research topic. Classes such as RP, co-RP, and their intersection (sometimes called ZPP), as well as a number of additional classes, are being investigated, both from a concrete point of view and from a more abstract one. In the concrete approach, the aim is to try to find interesting problems that reside in these classes and to prove that others do not. In the abstract approach, the aim is to seek the inherent properties of these classes, and their relationship to other complexity classes, both probabilistic and nonprobabilistic ones.

■ As an example, recall the boolean networks of Chapter 10. There we claimed that every effectively computable algorithmic problem can be solved by a *uniform* set of boolean circuits. That is, for every such problem there is an effective way of generating the circuit that solves the problem for inputs of a given size N. It is easy to see that if the original problem is in P, that is, it is solvable in polynomial time, then these circuits can be made to be of size polynomial in N. It has been shown that problems in RP, that is, those solvable in *random* polynomial time, also have polynomial-sized circuits, and this is true even if the problem at hand is not known to be in P. However, we do not know whether these circuits can be uniformly constructed in polynomial time. If we did, we would have a proof that any problem in RP is actually in P. (How?)

As we shall see in Chapter 12, a new, extremely interesting aspect of randomization and probabilistic computing arises from its use in interactive protocols. The combination has far-reaching consequences to many issues in complexity theory and the hardness of algorithmic problems, and was mentioned in Chapter 7 in connection with the hardness of approximating NP-complete problems. These ideas are the subject of some of the most intensive research in the theory of computing in the past decade.

A particularly interesting direction of research is the connection between probabilistic algorithms and the probabilistic analysis of conventional algorithms. In Chapter 6 we briefly discussed the average-case behavior of sequential algorithms and in Chapter 7 we mentioned certain approximation approaches to NP-complete and other problems. In both cases probabilistic reasoning is involved, since certain assumptions have to be made about the probability with which certain inputs occur. The analysis addresses questions regarding the algorithm's behavior on average, or on "almost all" inputs. In this way, probability dictates the form that the inputs will take, while the algorithm itself is totally deterministic. Here things are the other way around. Instead of worrying about the probabilistic distribution of the inputs, the algorithm itself, by tossing coins, generates the probabilities that we later reason about. It turns out that for some purposes, these two approaches are actually equivalent. In a certain technical sense, the results of the coin tossing can be regarded as additional inputs, given at the start, and conversely, generating a probabilistic distribution on the real inputs can be shifted into the algorithm itself. Thus, the probabilistic complexity of conventional algorithms and the conventional complexity of probabilistic algorithms can be viewed as two sides of the same coin, so to speak.

One issue that has not been addressed at all here is the way in which computers can be made to toss fair, unbiased coins. Allusion has repeatedly been made to this ability in the algorithms presented, but the implicit assumption that it can be done is unjustified, since a real digital computer is a totally deterministic entity, and hence, in principle, all of its actions can be predicted in advance. Therefore, a computer cannot generate truly random numbers, and hence cannot simulate the truly random tossing of fair coins. There are a number of ways of overcoming this problem. One is to appeal to a physical source. For example, our computer could be attached to a small robot hand, which in order to choose 0 or 1 at random scoops up a handful of sand from a large container, counts the sand grains contained therein, decides 0 if the number is even and 1 otherwise, and then tosses the sand back into the container. This approach has several obvious drawbacks. However, there are more practical physical methods of obtaining truly random numbers, employed by smartcards and similar devices.

Another approach involves so-called pseudo-random numbers. In a word, a **pseudo-random** sequence is one that cannot be distinguished from a truly random sequence in polynomial time. In the next chapter we discuss **one-way functions**, which are computable in polynomial time, but whose inverses are intractable to compute. It can be shown that if provably one-way functions exist (that is, if we could *prove* that the hard direction of these functions is really intractable), then pseudo-random number **generators** also exist. A generator is given a single number, the **seed**, as an input, and it thereafter keeps producing pseudo-random numbers forever. Thus, rather curiously, the very ability to generate the random numbers that are needed in probabilistic algorithms also hinges on conjectures regarding the intractability of other problems. If problem P is truly hard, then problem Q can be made easy by appealing to a probabilistic algorithm that uses P's hardness to generate coin tosses that are impossible to distinguish from truly random tosses.

Thus, the last word has not been said even about the most fundamental issue underlying the application of randomization to algorithmics: the possibility of algorithmically simulating a true, or almost true, random choice.

Theorems that Are Almost True?

At the end of Chapter 5 we discussed the four-color theorem, whose proof was carried out in part using a computer program. In a sense, this theorem cannot be claimed to have been proved in full, since no one has proved the correctness of the program, the compiler, or the operating system involved. On the other hand, if we really want to be certain that the theorem is true, we can always try to prove the correctness of these pieces of software. Thus, the proof of the theorem is amenable to formal verification, at least in principle.

It is interesting to imagine a different situation, which, as far as we know, has not occurred yet. What would happen if some important problem in mathematics were to be resolved with the help of a *probabilistic* algorithm, say of the Monte Carlo variety, with a diminishing probability of error? Could we then put a "Q.E.D." at the end of the proof? The difficulty here is that even after formally verifying program, compiler, and operating system, we will only have established rigorously that the process admits an error with, say, probability $1/2^{200}$. What shall we do? Shall we claim an *almost theorem*, or a *very high probability theorem*? Will mathematicians have sufficient confidence in such a result to base further developments on it? We shall probably just have to wait and see.

Some people dismiss the whole issue by pointing out that all mathematical proofs have some chance of being wrong, as they are carried out by error-prone humans. And indeed, many proofs, even published ones, have been found to be flawed. This actually happened to the four-color theorem itself on a number of previous occasions.

Here the situation is different, since we *do* have a rigorously verified proof of the theorem. However, one of its components, the probabilistic algorithm, is provably correct with very high probability only, a probability that can be made as high as desired by running the algorithm a little longer. As long as we use probabilistic algorithms only for petty, down-to-earth matters such as wealth, health, and survival, we can easily make do with very-likely-to-be-correct answers to our questions. The same, it seems, cannot be said for our quest for absolute mathematical truth.

Exercises

11.1. Why is playing Russian roulette with a 2^{200}-bullet revolver the same as playing the 77-round version described in the text with a normal 6-bullet revolver?

11.2. Here is a recursive version of the **quicksort** algorithm. It performs in-place sorting of an array A of size N, and is very efficient on the average, as mentioned in Chapter 6.

> call **quicksort-of** 1 **and** N.

The subroutine **quicksort** is defined by:

> subroutine **quicksort-of** F **and** T:
> if $F < T$ then do the following:
>   call **partition-of** F **and** T;
>   call **quicksort-of** F **and** $M - 1$;
>   call **quicksort-of** $M + 1$ **and** T;
> return.

The subroutine **partition** produces an output value in the variable M and is defined by:

> subroutine **partition-of** F **and** T:
> $X \leftarrow A[F]$;
> $L \leftarrow F$;
> $H \leftarrow T + 1$;
>   while $L < H$ do the following:
>   repeat $L \leftarrow L + 1$ until either $A[L] \geq X$ or $L = T$;
>   repeat $H \leftarrow H - 1$ until $A[H] \leq X$;
>   if $L < H$ then do the following:
> $Y \leftarrow A[L]$;
> $A[L] \leftarrow A[H]$;
> $A[H] \leftarrow Y$;
> $A[F] \leftarrow A[H]$;
> $A[H] \leftarrow X$;
> $M \leftarrow H$;
>   return.

(a) Study the algorithm, and prove its correctness.

(b) Analyze the worst-case time and space complexity of the algorithm.

(c) Show that the average-case time complexity of **quicksort** is $O(N \log N)$, assuming a uniform probability distribution for the input list. That is, the probability of any element being the Ith smallest one is uniform, for each location I.

11.3. Design an efficient probabilistic algorithm that, given two positive integers $A < B$, generates a random integer N in the range $A \leq N \leq B$. You may toss a given fair coin, an action that takes one time unit. For each of the following cases, calculate how many times your algorithm tosses the coin and how many bits of working space the algorithm uses (the space required for storing input and output is not counted).

(a) Assuming that $A = 0$ and $B = 2^K - 1$ for some positive integer K.

(b) Assuming that $0 = A < B$.

(c) Assuming that $0 \leq A < B$.

11.4. Design an efficient probabilistic algorithm which, given an integer N, generates a random permutation of the integers $1, 2, \ldots, N$. Again, you have access to a fair coin. What is the time and space complexity of your algorithm?

11.5. Prove a lower bound of $O(N)$ on the pattern matching problem.

11.6. Consider the fingerprinting idea for pattern matching described in the text.

(a) Prove that the probability that one of the M-symbol blocks will have the same remainder when divided by the random number K as does the M-symbol pattern, although they are *not* equal, is $O(1/N)$.

(b) Design a detailed Monte Carlo version of the fingerprinting algorithm.

(c) Design a detailed Las Vegas version of the fingerprinting algorithm.

11.7. Design Monte Carlo algorithms that perform the following numerical tasks. You may use the random number generator you have designed in Exercise 11.3.

(a) Given three positive numbers A, D, and E, approximate the area of the closed figure formed by the parabola

$$y = \frac{x^2}{A}$$

and the horizontal line

$$y = D$$

in the standard Cartesian grid, up to an error of at most $\pm E$. (Hint: the figure is bounded by the rectangle whose sides lie on the horizontal lines $y = 0$ and $y = D$ and the vertical lines $x = A + D$ and $x = -A - D$. Therefore, the ratio between the areas of the figure and the entire rectangle equals the limit of the proportion of random points within this rectangle that fall into the figure.)

(b) Given a positive integer N, approximate the value of the constant π, the ratio between the length of a circle and its diameter, up to the Nth decimal digit. (Hint: consider a circle with radius 1 bounded by some square, and draw random points inside the square.)

11.8. Consider the problem of testing the primality of a given positive integer.

(a) Design a deterministic algorithm for testing primality, following the hints provided in the text for improving the naive solution, and analyze its time and space complexity.

(b) Division is a relatively complex arithmetic operation. Analyze the complexity of your algorithm when counting division operations only, and compare it to the naive version.

11.9. (a) Euclid's fast algorithm for computing the greatest common divisor of two given positive integers X and Y, is based upon the following arithmetical equality for $X \geq Y$:

$$\gcd(X, Y) = \begin{cases} Y & \text{if } X \bmod Y = 0 \\ \gcd(Y, X \bmod Y) & \text{if } X \bmod Y > 0 \end{cases}$$

Design a procedure implementing Euclid's algorithm and analyze its time complexity.

(b) Design in detail the probabilistic algorithm for testing primality described in the text. You may use as subroutines Euclid's fast gcd algorithm and other algorithms you have supplied as answers to previous exercises.

11.10. Show how to simulate a probabilistic Turing machine by a conventional Turing machine.

11.11. Prove the following containments between complexity classes:
(a) P ⊆ RP.
(b) RP ⊆ NP.
(c) P ⊆ co-RP.
(d) co-RP ⊆ co-NP.

And we have cast lots

NEHEMIAH 10: 35

for they have chosen their own ways

ISAIAH 66: 3

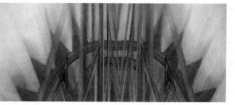

CHAPTER 12

Cryptography and Reliable Interaction

or, Getting It Done in Secret

Let us now turn to a new and exciting application area of algorithmics. Its novel feature is the fact that the methods used to solve problems in this area exploit the difficulty of solving other problems. This in itself is quite surprising, as we would expect negative results that establish lower bounds on the solvability of algorithmic problems to be of no practical value, except in preventing people from trying to improve on these bounds. Not so. Problems for which no good algorithms are known are crucial here.

The area in general is that of **cryptography**, and it concerns the need to communicate in secure, private, and reliable ways. Cryptography has numerous diverse applications in military, diplomatic, financial, and industrial circles. The need for good cryptographic protocols is greatly enhanced by the fast proliferation of computer-based communication systems, most notably the Internet, of course. Increasingly, computers are becoming responsible for storing, manipulating, and transmitting anything from contracts, strategic commands, and business transactions, to ordinary confidential information such as military, medical, and personal data. This situation, in turn, makes problems of eavesdropping and tampering all the more acute.

One of the basic problems in cryptography is that of encrypting and decrypting data. How should we encode an important message in such a way that the receiver should be able to decipher it, but not an eavesdropper? Moreover, can the message be "signed" by the sender, so that (1) the receiver can be sure that the sender alone could have sent it, (2) the sender cannot later deny having sent it, and (3) the receiver, having received the signed message, cannot sign any message in the sender's name, not even additional versions of the very message that has just been received? The signature issue is relevant to numerous applications, such as money transfer orders and electronic contracts. We could continue at length with such questions and their motivating examples, as there are many, and each raises new challenges. For some of these, elegant and useful solutions have been found, whereas for others there are none. We shall start by concentrating on the encryption and signature problems.

Conventional cryptosystems are based on **keys**. These are used to translate a message M into its encrypted form, the **ciphertext** H, and then to decrypt it back into its original form. If we denote the general encryption procedure associated with the key by *Encr*, and the corresponding decryption procedure by *Decr*, we may write:

$$H = Encr(M) \quad \text{and} \quad M = Decr(H)$$

In other words, the encrypted version H is obtained by applying the *Encr* procedure to the message M, and the original M can be retrieved from H by applying the *Decr* procedure to H. A simple example that we have all used in our childhood calls for the key K to be some number between 1 and 25, for *Encr* to be the procedure that replaces every letter with the one residing K positions further along in the alphabet, and for *Decr* to replace every letter with the one residing K positions earlier. In this way, *Encr* and *Decr* are mutually dual; *Decr* is *Encr*'s inverse. (For purposes of counting letters the alphabet is considered to be cyclic; *a* follows *z*.)

This standard approach can be illustrated using the metaphor of a locked box. To exchange secret messages with a friend we should first prepare a box with a securable latch. Then we should buy a padlock with two keys, one for us and one for our friend. Thereafter, sending a message involves putting it in the box, locking the box using the key, and sending the box to its destination. No one can read the message *en route* unless they have the key, and since there are only two keys, kept by the sender and the intended receiver, the system is quite secure.

This approach has several drawbacks. First, it does not address the signature issue. Receivers can make up fake messages of their own and claim that they were sent by the sender, and the sender in turn can deny having sent authentic messages. Another major drawback concerns the need to cooperate in the selection and safe distribution of keys. In general, there are more than two parties involved in a communication network, and to enable privacy between any two there must be some secure way of distributing pairs of keys, one for each pair of parties. Given that the main applications of modern cryptography are in computerized environments, the digital keys cannot be distributed along the same (unsafe) communication channels as the encrypted messages. It would thus be necessary to resort to other far more expensive methods, such as personal delivery by a trusted courier. This is clearly not feasible in applications involving many parties.

■ Public-Key Cryptography

In 1976 a novel approach to the encryption, decryption, and signature problems was proposed, the **public-key cryptosystem**. It is perhaps best explained by a variant of the locked box metaphor. The idea is to use a different kind of padlock, one that can be locked without a key, by simply clicking it shut. Opening such a lock, however, requires a key. To set up the mechanism for exchanging secret information, each potential user of the system goes out on his own and purchases such a padlock and key. He then writes his name on the padlock, and places it on the table, in public view. The key, however, is kept by the purchaser. Now, assume party B (say, Bob) wants to send a message to party A (say, Alice). Bob puts the message into a box, goes to the table, picks up Alice's padlock and locks the box with it. For this, no key is needed. The box is then sent to Alice, who uses her key to open the lock and read the message. No one other than Alice has the key, and thus the message is safe. Notice that no prior communication or cooperation between Alice and Bob is needed. Once any party has decided to join the game, has bought a padlock and has made it public, that party can start receiving messages.

To understand how public-key systems can be used in digital, computerized environments, let us assume that messages are (perhaps lengthy) sequences of digits. Thus, some direct and straightforward method of translating symbols into digits has already been applied. Alice's padlock is just the encryption function $Encr_A$ that transforms numbers into other numbers, and Alice's key is a secret way of computing the decryption function $Decr_A$. Thus, each party makes their encryption procedure public but keeps their decryption procedure private. To send a message to Alice, Bob uses Alice's public encryption procedure $Encr_A$ and sends Alice the number $Encr_A(M)$. Now Alice can decipher it using her private procedure $Decr_A$. For the method to work, both functions must be easy to compute, and the duality equation:

$$Decr_A(Encr_A(M)) = M$$

must hold for every message M. Most importantly, however, it should be impossible to deduce a method for computing the decryption function $Decr_A$ from the publicly known encryption function $Encr_A$. Here "impossible" really means "computationally infeasible," so that what we really need is an appropriate kind of **one-way trapdoor function**; that is, a function $Encr$ for each user, which is easy to compute, say in low-order polynomial time, but whose inverse function $Decr$ cannot be computed in polynomial time unless that user's secret key is known. The analogy to trapdoors is obvious: a trapdoor cannot be activated unless the existence or location of the secret lever or button is known. Later we shall discuss such functions.

As far as signatures go, it is obvious that, unlike a handwritten one, a digital signature that is to be used in a computerized cryptosystem must not only be a function of the signing party, but also of the message that is being signed. Otherwise, the receiver could make changes to the signed message before showing it to a neutral judge, or even attach the signature to a totally different message. If the message is a money transfer order, the receiver can simply add a couple of crucial zeros to the sum and claim the new signed message to be authentic. Thus, signatures must be different for different messages.

To use one-way trapdoor functions for signing messages we require that the $Encr$ and $Decr$ functions are **commutative** that is, not only should the decryption of any encrypted message yield that message in its original form, but also the *en*cryption of a *de*crypted message has to yield the original message. Thus we require, for each party A, both:

$$Decr_A(Encr_A(M)) = M \qquad \text{and} \qquad Encr_A(Decr_A(M)) = M$$

Since a message is but a number and both $Encr_A$ and $Decr_A$ are functions on numbers, it makes sense, at least mathematically, to apply $Decr_A$ to a message M. But what *practical* sense does it make? Why would anyone be interested in applying a decryption function to an unencrypted message? The answer is simple. In order to sign it! Here is the way it works (see Figure 12.1).

Figure 12.1

Sending signed and
encrypted messages
using public-key
cryptography.

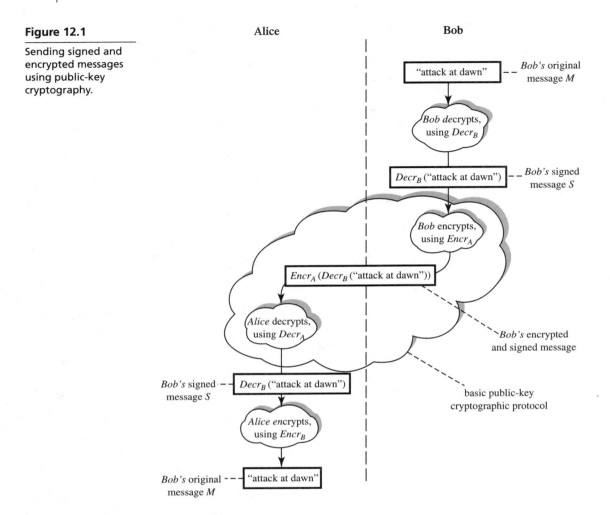

If Bob wants to send Alice a *signed* message M, Bob first computes his special message-dependent signature S, by applying his own private decryption function $Decr_B$ to M. Thus:

$$S = Decr_B(M)$$

He then encrypts the signature S in the usual public-key fashion, using Alice's public encryption function $Encr_A$, and sends the result, namely, $Encr_A(Decr_B(M))$, to Alice. Upon receiving this strange-looking number, Alice first decrypts it using her private decryption function $Decr_A$. The result is $Decr_A(Encr_A(S))$, which is really $Decr_A(Encr_A(Decr_B(M)))$. However, since $Decr_A$ undoes anything that $Encr_A$ has tied up, the result of this will be just S, or $Decr_B(M)$. (Notice that Alice cannot yet read the message M, nor is she in any way convinced that Bob was really the sender.) Finally, Alice applies Bob's public encryption function $Encr_B$ to S, yielding

$$Encr_B(S) = Encr_B(Decr_B(M)) = M$$

Thus, all at once, Alice sees the message M and can also be quite sure that only Bob could have sent it. This follows from the fact that the functions are such that no number will result in M when subjected to $Encr_B$ unless that number was precisely $Decr_B(M)$, and no one besides Bob could have produced $Decr_B(M)$, since the decryption function $Decr_B$ is Bob's closely guarded secret. Moreover, Alice cannot sign any other message in Bob's name, since signing entails applying Bob's secret function $Decr_B$ to the new message.

However, there is still the possibility that Alice will be able to send the very same message M to some other party, say Carol, but with Bob's signature. The reason is that during the process Alice has possession of $Decr_B(M)$, which she can then encrypt using $Encr_C$, sending the result to Carol, who will think it came from Bob. This might be critical in case the message M is "I, General Bob, hereby order you to set out on the following dangerous mission: ..." To prevent this situation, the name of the receiver of the message (and possibly also the date) should always be included, as in "I, General Bob, hereby order you, Major Alice, to set out on the following dangerous mission: ..." Such mischief on Alice's behalf (and at Carol's expense) would then become impossible. Of course, this means that it should be impossible for Alice to compute the function $Decr_B$ without the right key, even for some slightly modified message M' which is very close to the message M for which she has access to $Decr_B(M)$.

The concept of public-key cryptography thus sounds very promising. To make it work, however, requires that we find appropriate definitions of the keys and the corresponding $Encr$ and $Decr$ procedures, which enjoy all the nice properties we have discussed. In other words, we are interested in one-way trapdoor functions, and if we want to use the signature feature they must also satisfy the mutual inverse property.

It is by no means clear that such functions exist. In fact, it could be argued that the requirements are paradoxical, almost self-contradictory. Where do we find a one-way function with a really hard-to-compute inverse? Taking square roots, for example, is not that much harder than its converse, squaring, and moving backwards in the alphabet is as easy as moving forwards. In addition, the difficult direction must become easy to compute if the secret key is known. Are there such functions? We shall now see that there are, but the difficulty of computing the inverse without the key will rest on conjectured, not proven, intractability. The question of whether there are such functions with *provably* intractable inverses is still open.

◼ The RSA Cryptosystem

About a year after the concept of public-key cryptosystems emerged, the first method to implement it was found. The resulting system, called the **RSA cryptosystem**, after the initials of its inventors, is described here. Since then, several other definitions have been suggested, some of which have consequently been shown not to be secure. The RSA approach, however, remains one of the most interesting of them all, and, as explained later, there is reason to believe that it is really unbreakable.

It is important to understand what it means for a public-key cryptosystem to be broken, or cracked. Since the integrity of a public-key system hinges on the difficulty of computing the $Decr$ functions without the right keys, breaking such a system involves finding a fast algorithm for computing the *Decr* function given knowledge of the corresponding *Encr* function. If signatures are used, one might also have knowledge of several examples of messages M and their ciphertexts $Decr(M)$. Thus, while cracking certain kinds of conventional cryptographic methods might require lucky guesses, or sophisticated ways of finding some secret code or number, cracking public-key cryptosystems is really tantamount to finding clever polynomial-time algorithms for certain problems that are believed to be of inherent super-polynomial time behavior. And this is algorithmic work *par excellence*.

The RSA system is based on the contrast between testing primality and factoring. The former, as we have seen, can be carried out very fast, using a probabilistic algorithm, and perhaps in the future also using a fast version of the new non-probabilistic polynomial-time algorithm. However, for the latter there are no known fast methods, not even probabilistic ones, and factoring is actually conjectured not to be even in the probabilistic/randomized class RP.

Each party, say Alice, secretly and at random, chooses two large prime numbers P and Q, of length, say, around 300 digits, and multiplies them, resulting in the product $N = P \times Q$. Alice keeps the primes secret, but makes their product (as well as another quantity, as explained later) public.[1] The crucial fact is that, given the product, no one except Alice herself can find the two prime factors in a reasonable amount of time. Here are the details.

■ Before choosing the two primes, Alice needs to select another number, G, called the **public exponent**. This should be an odd number, preferably prime, and need not be too large. This number can be the same for all participants; a favorite choice is the prime $2^{16} + 1 = 65,537$. When choosing her prime numbers P and Q, Alice needs to make sure that neither $P - 1$ nor $Q - 1$ have any common factors with G, except, of course, the trivial factor 1. Finally, Alice computes her **private exponent**, K, to be the **multiplicative inverse** of G modulo $(P - 1) \times (Q - 1)$, meaning that $K \times G$ yields a remainder of 1 when divided by $(P - 1) \times (Q - 1)$. Symbolically:

$$K \times G \equiv 1 \ (\mathrm{mod} \ (P - 1) \times (Q - 1))$$

This completes Alice's process of going out and buying a padlock and key. The padlock is the pair $\langle G, N \rangle$, which is made public, and the secret key is K. The prime factors of N, namely, P and Q, are also kept secret. To be quite precise, we should indicate that these are all Alice's numbers, by writing them as P_A, Q_A, N_A, K_A, and G_A. Other parties choose their own numbers P_B, P_C, Q_B, Q_C, etc.

What do the encryption and decryption procedures look like? Well, assume Bob wants to send a message M to Alice. To encrypt it, he uses Alice's public pair $\langle G_A, N_A \rangle$. Bob first breaks M up into blocks of numbers, each between 0 and $N_A - 1$. Hereafter, we can assume that there is only one such number M, since the entire process is carried out for each of them. To obtain the ciphertext H, Bob raises M to the power G_A, modulo N_A:

$$H = Encr_A(M) = M^{G_A} \ (\mathrm{mod} \ N_A)$$

---

[1] We have chosen to describe this process in a somewhat personalized fashion. In actuality, when the RSA procedure is used in practice—and it is employed extensively by one's computer when sensitive information is sent over the Internet—the steps we describe here are done in a way that is transparent to the user. Hence, for example, the two prime numbers are "chosen" for Alice by the software implementing the method, and she doesn't really have to do anything like that on her own.

That is, H is the remainder obtained when M^{G_A} is divided by N_A. This completes the definition of the encryption procedure. Notice that since all arithmetic is done modulo N_A, all numbers involved are between 0 and $N_A - 1$ so that both the message and its ciphertext are within the same range of numbers. Decryption is very similar: Alice, upon receiving the ciphertext H, raises it to the power of her secret key K_A, also modulo N_A. Thus:

$$Decr_A(H) = H^{K_A} \ (\text{mod } N_A)$$

The origin of the terms *public exponent* and *private exponent* should now be clear. It is now easy to see that:

$$Decr_A(Encr_A(M)) = Encr_A(Decr_A(M)) \equiv M^{G_A \times K_A} \ (\text{mod } N_A)$$

It is not so easy to see, but it is true nevertheless, that by the special way K_A was derived from G_A, P, and Q, this last quantity is just M (mod N_A), so that decrypting the encrypted message yields the message in its original form. The fact that not only $Decr_A(Encr_A(M))$ yields M but also $Encr_A(Decr_A(M))$ and that this is true for *any* M, is what makes the RSA method fitting for signatures too.

Of course, we have to show how all the computations involved can indeed be carried out efficiently, and that $Decr_A(M)$ cannot be computed without knowledge of Alice's key K_A. The entire setting-up process starts with each party choosing two large primes, a feat that can be achieved quite painlessly using a fast primality-testing algorithm repeatedly for random 300-digit numbers, as explained earlier. Of course, the chance that two parties will come up with precisely the same primes is negligible.

The last step of preparation is to compute K from G, P, and Q (we omit the A subscript here for clarity). This, as well as the actual computations of M^G and H^K modulo N, can be carried out quite rapidly using relatively simple procedures for exponentiation modulo N and for a certain version of the greatest common divisor (gcd) algorithm. The details are omitted as they are somewhat technical in nature.

As far as the security of the RSA system goes, it can be shown that if we can factor large numbers in reasonable time the system is immediately broken, since then an adversary could take the public product N, find its factors (that is, the two secret primes P and Q), and use them, together with the public exponent G, to compute the private exponent K. Dually, all the approaches suggested so far for attempting to break the RSA system have been shown that to work they must yield fast solutions to the factoring problem too. In other words, as of now, for every approach suggested as an attack on the security of the RSA system, it has been shown that either it will not work, or that if in principle it does work, it results in a fast algorithm for factoring. However, since factoring is strongly conjectured to have no fast algorithm, not even a probabilistic one, and none of the proposed attacks on the RSA system have yielded such an algorithm, people strongly believe RSA to be safe.

There is a slightly different version of the RSA system whose security is *provably* equivalent to fast factoring. In other words, it has been shown that any method for cracking that particular cryptosystem will yield a fast factoring algorithm. Obviously, since we don't know the precise status of the factoring problem, whether this cryptosystem is better or worse than the original RSA is unclear.

It is worth re-emphasizing the fundamental facets of algorithmics that are involved in such ideas as the RSA cryptosystem. They include conventional sequential algorithms, apparently intractable algorithmic problems, probabilistic algorithms, and, if the method is to work reasonably fast on large numbers, then either very efficient programming or the design of special-purpose hardware.

Playing Poker Over the Phone

Public-key cryptographic functions can be used in many seemingly unrelated applications. Consider two people, Alice and Bob, who want to play poker over the phone. We can assume that each player has access to a computer, in case there are computations to be carried out during the game, and that digital information can be transmitted over the telephone line. There is no neutral referee who will deal the cards or who has global knowledge of the players' hands and/or of the cards remaining in the deck; everything must be carried out by the two players themselves. It is not too difficult to imagine less playful situations of similar nature, such as digital contract negotiations.

Obviously, each player must have some information that can be kept secret during the game, such as his hand of cards. Now, in an ordinary face-to-face game, a player cannot claim to have an ace unless he can demonstrate it by actually exposing the ace as one of the cards being held. The electronic analog of this is to wait until the game is over, and then allow each player to inspect the other's entire sequence of moves, including his private activities. This will prevent ordinary kinds of cheating.

Cheating, however, is not the only problem. A little thought reveals that dealing the cards constitutes the real challenge. We have to design a protocol that starts out with 52 (digitally represented) cards, and results in each of the two players holding a random hand of five cards, with the remaining 42 left in a pile for future use. What makes the problem far from trivial is that we must ensure that neither of the players knows the other player's hand. At first sight this sounds impossible. We can start out by somehow encrypting and shuffling the cards. However, since at least one of the players must be able to decrypt the encryption that is used, it would appear that one of them will know which of the cards has been dealt to the other, or that one of them will be able to arrange for himself to have a particularly good hand. Can we prescribe a fair and random deal? The answer is yes.

The idea is to use one-way trapdoor functions, as in public-key cryptography, but in this case we require them to be commutative; that is, for any message M we must have:

$$Encr_B(Encr_A(M)) = Encr_A(Encr_B(M))$$

This ensures that if a message is encrypted by Alice and then by Bob it can be decrypted first by Alice and then by Bob, since the double encryption will yield $Encr_B(Encr_A(M))$, which is the same as $Encr_A(Encr_B(M))$, whereby Alice's decryption will yield $Decr_A(Encr_A(Encr_B(M)))$, which is just $Encr_B(M)$, and finally, Bob's decryption will yield $Decr_B(Encr_B(M))$, which is simply the original M. The RSA functions can be shown to satisfy this additional commutativity requirement, and hence they would appear to be adequate for the present application too.

Figure 12.2

Dealing cards over the phone (we use *E* and *D* as abbreviations for *Encr* and *Decr*).

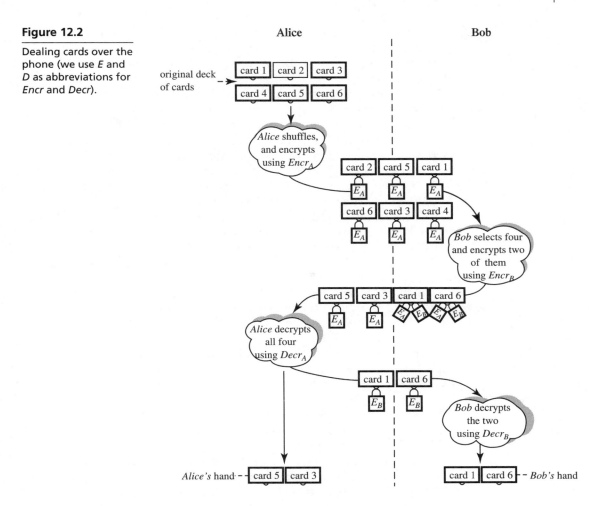

In terms of locked boxes, commutativity means that the latch has enough room for two padlocks that can be clicked shut, side by side in any order, rather than one over the other. In this way, the first padlock to be attached need not be the last one to be removed.

As before, each player starts by selecting his own personal *Encr* and *Decr* functions. However, in contrast to public-key cryptography, none of the information is made public until the game is over, not even the encryption functions. Here is how our players Alice and Bob go about dealing themselves five cards out of a pack of 52. (Figure 12.2 illustrates the procedure, and for simplicity it shows the dealing of two cards each, out of a total of six.) First, Alice uses her own encryption function $Encr_A$ to encrypt descriptions of the 52 cards. Recall that the entire game sequence is later checked, with both players' functions being exposed, so that Alice cannot encrypt an illegal set of cards, having, say, 20 aces. Using coin tossing, or any other means, Alice then shuffles the encrypted deck and sends the resulting list to Bob. Even though he knows precisely what the 52 encrypted messages look like when decrypted, Bob has no way of knowing which card is which, since they arrive in an order unknown to him, and $Encr_A$ and $Decr_A$ are Alice's closely kept secrets.

Now for the dealing itself. Bob selects 10 encrypted cards, five of which he encrypts a second time using his own function $Encr_B$. He then sends Alice all 10. Thus, Bob now has 42 boxes locked with Alice's padlock, and Alice has 10—five locked with her own padlock and five locked with both padlocks. Alice now unlocks her own 10 locks; that is, Alice decrypts the 10 messages received from Bob using her decryption function $Decr$. The first five of these now become unencrypted card descriptions, and henceforth Alice regards them as her hand. The other five are still locked with $Encr_B$ (here is where commutativity is needed—the reader should check this), and Alice sends them back to Bob. Upon receipt, Bob unlocks them using $Decr_B$, thus exposing his own five-card hand.

The hands are obviously disjoint, and are all different from the remaining 42 cards. Moreover, neither player knows what the other player's hand is. Bob does not know anything about Alice's hand, although Bob was the one who actually dealt the cards, because he selected the 10 cards from a shuffled deck that was encrypted using a function he has no way of decrypting. Similarly, Alice does not know anything about Bob's hand, although Alice does know how to decrypt the original encryptions, because Bob's five cards were encrypted a second time (by Bob) using a function that Alice has no way of decrypting. Thus the deal appears to be valid, fair, and as secure as any dealing method.

You should now have no difficulty figuring out how the game continues. The only nontrivial part is when a player has to take a new card from the remaining pile, a procedure that can be carried out using precisely the same idea as in dealing the initial hands.

Despite these facts, it turns out that there are rather serious problems when it comes to implementing this dealing protocol. It has been shown, for example, that the RSA encryption functions are inadequate here. While messages encrypted using them cannot, as far as we know, actually be *deciphered* in reasonable time, certain *partial* information *can* be extracted from them. Thus, it is possible to manipulate the encrypted version of a card and figure out certain mathematical properties of its original (digital) version, which follow from the particular way the RSA functions are defined. For example, it may be possible to find out whether the number encoding a card has the same remainder when divided by some special prime as some other square number. This is a little like saying that one player can figure out the color (red or black) of the other's cards—clearly an unacceptable compromise in most card games.

One *ad hoc* way to overcome such problems is for Alice to describe the cards prior to encryption in her own informal language, the precise form the description takes being unknown to Bob ahead of time, or to insert random letters and digits therein; a similar idea would be used by Bob too. In this way there would appear to be no way for one player to gain anything from knowing such arithmetical properties of the original unpredictable descriptions of the other's cards. We should realize, however, that this approach might not be really secure, as we cannot *prove* that no relevant information about the cards leaks out. Other, more provably secure, protocols for dealing cards have indeed been discovered. They are themselves probabilistic, but are considerably more complicated than the simple and elegant one described here.

Interactive Proofs

Let us return for a moment to the class NP. We have seen that problems in NP are characterized as being solvable in polynomial time with the help of a magic coin. Equivalently, the problems in NP are those that admit a "yes"-certificate of polynomial size. This second characterization can be rephrased in terms of a kind of game between a **prover** and a **verifier**. Alice, the prover, is all-powerful, and she is trying to convince Bob, the verifier, who has only deterministic polynomial-time power, that an input X to the problem is a "yes" input. For specificity, let us take a particular problem in NP, say three-colorability of a graph. Alice wants to convince Bob that the graph G can be colored with three colors. (Recall that the rule is that no two adjacent nodes may be monochromatic.) Since Bob has only polynomial-time power, he cannot verify that fact on his own. Accordingly, Alice, who has unlimited power, simply sends Bob a three-coloring of G. Clearly, Bob, even with his limited power, can verify that the coloring is legal and will thus become convinced that G is indeed three-colorable. Obviously, there is no way Alice can convince Bob that a graph is three-colorable if it is not. Thus, we may say that a decision problem P is in NP if, for each input X, whenever X is a "yes" input then Alice can convince Bob of that fact in polynomial time, but if X is a "no" input then neither Alice nor any other prover can convince Bob otherwise.

This little game is quite simple, and it requires a single round only: Alice sends the polynomially-sized certificate to Bob, who promptly verifies that it is indeed a certificate. This setup has been generalized in several ways, leading to stronger notions of proving and verifying. The basic idea is to turn the process into an interactive one, with many rounds, and to allow the verifier to flip coins and ask the prover questions, all in polynomial time. Thus, Alice remains all-powerful, but Bob now has the power of a *probabilistic* polynomial-time machine. Moreover, in the good spirit of the previous chapter, we also make the basic notion of proving probabilistic. Specifically, we require only that Alice can convince Bob of the "yes"-ness of an input to P with overwhelmingly high probability, whereas a prover can (wrongly) convince Bob that a "no" input is really a "yes" input only with negligibly low probability. This extension leads to a class of problems known as IP, standing for **interactive polynomial time**.

It is worth pausing to assess the significance of this notion. The conventional game associated with NP is very much like the standard way of proving a statement to someone in writing, say, as part of a mathematical publication: You supply what you claim is a complete proof, using all the ingenuity you can muster, and I then check to see whether I believe it or not. (We shall be returning to this version of proof a little later on.) The new notion is a powerful, yet very natural, extension, more akin to the way people prove statements to each other orally: You supply some information; I ask questions, perhaps involving random elements that you did not know I would choose; you then supply answers and more information; I continue to pester you with questions; etc. This continues until I become convinced (in the probabilistic sense of the word, that is, with very high probability) that you are right. And, of course, we require that the entire procedure take only a reasonable, viz. polynomial, amount of time.

What is the precise power of this combination of interaction and coin tossing? What decision problems can be solved using the new procedure? In other words, we would like to know exactly which problems are in IP. From the previous discussion it is clear that IP contains all of NP, including, of course, the NP-complete problems. However, it is not at all clear that the addition of interaction and coin tossing gets us anything new. Indeed, it is not an easy task to come up with an interactive protocol for a problem that is not known to be in NP. Nevertheless, recently the question was settled in its full generality, with the establishment of the surprising result that IP is, in fact, exactly PSPACE. The power of probabilistic polynomial-time interaction is thus exactly the same as the power of polynomial space! For each problem in PSPACE, "yes"-ness can be proved in polynomial time using interaction and randomness. Put another way, extending the stringent, one-pass proof procedure to admit a more relaxed probabilistic and interactive proof protocol (required to use only a reasonable amount of time), is exactly the same as dumping proof protocols altogether, in favor of a conventional computation that uses a reasonable amount of memory space (but might require an unreasonable amount of time).

A further liberty has also been taken, with the definition of the class MIP, standing for **multiple-prover interactive proofs**. Here, the interactive proofs are allowed to be carried out by more than one prover (but still only one verifier), though the provers are not allowed to communicate. This class has been shown to be identical to NEXPTIME, i.e., the class of problems computable with an exponential amount of time using a magic coin. This fact is especially interesting, since NEXPTIME is known to be *strictly* larger than P or even NP (which is not the case for PSPACE), so that multi-prover proofs with normal coins are more powerful than direct proofs with magic coins.

Zero-Knowledge Protocols

To illustrate interactive proofs it is beneficial to give an example of an exciting variant thereof. Suppose Alice wants to convince Bob that she knows a certain secret, but she does not want Bob to end up knowing the secret himself. This sounds impossible: how do you convince someone that you know, say, what color tie the President of the United States is wearing right now, without somehow divulging that priceless piece of information to the other person or to some third party?

As another down-to-earth example, consider the *Where's Waldo?* book. Each of its pages contains a very intricate illustration with many different characters, and the issue is to find Waldo, a predefined, rather colorful, character. Suppose Alice and Bob are looking at one of the pages, and Alice claims that she knows where Waldo is. Bob doesn't believe her, and Alice wants to convince him that she isn't lying. However, she wants to do this without revealing to him Waldo's actual location, so that he can go on trying, eating his heart out that she has found Waldo but he hasn't . . . How can she do this?

There are many solutions, and here is one. Alice and Bob first photocopy the relevant page. Bob then prints some regular, but nonforgeable pattern on the back of the copy (e.g., he repeats some nonsense word densely, and with random directionality, all over it). With her back to Bob, Alice now cuts out Waldo's image from that copy, destroying the leftovers, and triumphantly shows it to Bob, who sees that it is indeed Waldo, and sees that it has his pattern on the back. Alice could not have guessed the pattern, so she cannot have been cheating, and Bob cannot discern from seeing the small cutout where in the large page was this image of Waldo actually taken from. So she has proved to him that she indeed knows where Waldo is, but Bob learns nothing (or almost nothing) from what he sees.

Presidents' ties and Waldo images aside, the issue in question is to devise an interactive probabilistic protocol, built around a fixed algorithmic problem P, whereby Alice can convince Bob in polynomial time that a given X is a "yes" input of P, but in such a way that when the interactive exchanges are over Bob knows nothing about the *proof* of the "yes"-ness of X. He knows, with overwhelming probability, that X is indeed a "yes," and hence that Alice was right, but that is the only new information he has gained from the process. In particular, he cannot (in polynomial time) even prove that very fact to someone else! Such seemingly paradoxical protocols are dubbed **zero-knowledge**.

Before giving an example of one, it is worth noting that zero-knowledge protocols have many applications in cryptography and secure communications. For example, we might want to devise smartcards that will enable workers to enter a sensitive establishment, but while we want the gates to open only for bearers of a legal card, we do not want the establishment's personnel to know exactly who they have admitted. Or suppose a group of people want to set up a joint bank account. They would like to be able to withdraw and transfer money electronically, and would like the bank to enforce certain rules (e.g., a limit on the daily amounts withdrawn). However, suppose they also want to prevent the bank personnel from being able to simulate a withdrawal on their own, or even from knowing exactly which of them withdraws, only that the money was withdrawn legally and according to the rules. Such cases call for the ability to convince a verifier that you know some secret, some key or code, but without divulging anything more than that fact itself.

■ Zero-Knowledge Three-Coloring

Here, then is a zero-knowledge protocol. It will be described as if it takes place between two real people, but it is not too difficult to turn it into a full-fledged algorithmic protocol, suitable for electronic applications. It is based on three-colorability.[2]

Alice shows Bob a graph G (see Figure 12.3), and claims that it can be colored with three colors. Bob, in the polynomial time available to him, cannot verify that fact on his own, so Alice now attempts to prove it to him. She takes the graph away, and secretly colors it with three colors, say, red, blue, and yellow. She then carefully covers the colored nodes with small coins, and places the graph in Bob's view (see Figure 12.4(a)). She also tells Bob what colors she has used.[3] Bob is, of course, skeptical, but despite the fact that she is interested in eliminating his skepticism,

---

[2] Actually, zero-knowledge protocols can be shown to exist whenever ordinary interactive protocols exist, i.e., for all problems in PSPACE. However, when one goes beyond NP, the protocols become far more complicated, and cannot be described in an appealing intuitive manner. Hence the choice of three-colorability, which is NP-complete, as an example.

[3] When this protocol is carried out electronically, the secret coloring and covering, and the stages that come thereafter, must be carried out using appropriate cryptographic means.

Figure 12.3

A graph.

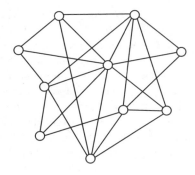

Alice is not willing to expose the coloring. In fact, she is not interested in exposing the coloring of any three nodes, since this would compromise something of the coloring strategy itself. Instead, she says that she is willing to expose any pair of neighboring nodes. So Bob chooses an edge in the graph, at random, and Alice removes the coins from the nodes at its ends (see Figure 12.4(b)). Bob observes that there are two different colors on these two nodes, and that the two colors are from among the three Alice listed. Now, clearly, if he discovers that the exposed nodes violate one of these properties, then he has shown that the coloring is not legal, thus shattering Alice's claim. If the two colors are different and from among the three

Figure 12.4

Covering a three-coloring and exposing a pair of adjacent nodes.

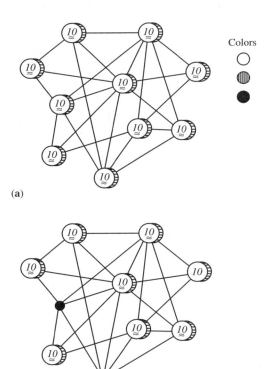

(a)

(b)

Figure 12.5

The three-coloring of the graph of Figure 12.3.

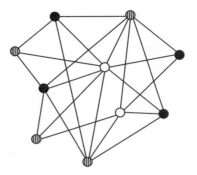

Alice listed, Bob cannot complain, but neither is he sure that the entire graph is colored legally. Now comes the trick. Rather than agreeing to expose more nodes, Alice takes back the graph, and recolors it, this time using, say, brown, black, and white, and she again tells him which colors she used, covers the nodes and shows Bob the graph. He, again, chooses an edge, and Alice promptly uncovers the two nodes at its ends. Again, Bob sees two different colors from the three she said she has used. This procedure continues several more times, until Bob is happy.

Should Bob ever be really happy? Well, let us look at things from his point of view. Let us say that G contains N edges (N can be at most the square of the number of nodes). After Alice passed the first test, i.e., Bob was happy with the colors he saw in the first round, he is obviously not sure Alice can three-color the entire graph, but he knows that he had a chance of 1 in N of catching her if she does not, since he gets to choose any edge, and Alice had no idea which he would choose when she colored and covered the nodes. Hence, the probability that she could pass this first test without really knowing how to color G is $1 - 1/N$, which is actually $(N - 1)/N$. Now, the second test was completely independent of the first one, from Alice's point of view, so that the probability that she could pass the first *two* tests without knowing how to color the graph is $((N - 1)/N)^2$. And, as the process continues, the probability decreases through increasingly larger powers of $(N - 1)/N$, thus rapidly approaching 0 as the number of succesful tests increases. Bob can therefore stop the process whenever he is satisfied that this probability is negligably low. He will then be overwhelmingly convinced that Alice can three-color the graph. (In fact, she can. See Figure 12.5.) In practice, a relatively small number of rounds suffices, even for large graphs.

What about Bob's knowledge? Well, since he keeps seeing different colors, and since Alice does not indicate the correspondence between the color sets in the various tests, Bob has no knowledge of the color relationships between any three nodes, and his isolated knowledge about many pairs of nodes is of no help, since the colors are always different.[4] This argument can be formalized to show that Bob has zero-knowledge of the coloring scheme, and that in polynomial time he cannot find out anything that he could not have found out without the information he gets from Alice (unless, of course, P = NP). In particular, as mentioned above, he cannot

---

[4] Actually, Alice can use the same three colors each time, but permuted, so that given any two tests Bob never knows the actual correspondence between the colors.

even prove to someone else that G can be three-colored, although he himself is fully convinced. Thus, this is a zero-knowledge protocol *par excellence*, and once again we have a remarkable application that utilizes in a crucial way both the good news and the bad that algorithmics has to offer.

Probabilistically Checkable Proofs

So we know about interactive proofs, in which the verifier becomes convinced of the correctness of what the prover is trying to prove in the probabilistic sense. And we also know about doing so without giving the verifier any new information. We now return to the noninteractive notion of proof, where the proof is given in writing: we still have a verifier, Bob, but instead of a prover Alice interacting with him, there is a static, unchanging document of proof that she has prepared in advance and has given him. This is the kind of certificate we have alluded to when discussing NP in terms of certificates of "yes"-ness. So the input we are trying to establish as a "yes" input is of size N, and the length of the proof document is polynomial in N.

The subtlety of the difference is in the fact that a fixed certificate of proof cannot lie. In the interactive prover/verifier model, Alice can change the proof in midflight, so to speak, giving different answers to Bob's probes, in order to make his job more difficult. A fixed, written proof, on the other hand, does not change. As discussed earlier, the difference between the two setups is the difference between a person trying to convey to you a proof of some mathematical statement in an interactive session, say in front of a blackboard, vs. you trying to become convinced of a written proof of that statement, say in a published paper. So, the game now is not Alice trying to turn Bob into a believer, but Bob *checking* her proof and deciding on his own whether to believe it or not.

What does Bob do? He reads some parts of the proof, *any* parts he wants, and carries out his own thinking, *any* kind he wants, then reads some more and thinks some more, and at the end of the day he must be convinced that the proof is correct. As usual, the day must end within a polynomial amount of time, and the conviction is in the probabilistic sense, i.e., Bob has to be sure the proof is correct with a negligible chance of error. In the true spirit of this chapter and the previous one, we also allow Bob's thinking itself to be probabilistic; that is, he can carry out a polynomial-time probabilistic computation with coin tossing to help him decide what he wants to do next.

To finish formalizing this notion of proof, we must say what we mean by allowing Bob to read any parts of the proof he wants. The most natural way to model this kind of activity is to view the proof as a sequence of bits of polynomial length, and to allow Bob to probe it for information whenever he feels like it. This last phrase means that from the point of view of anyone other than Bob himself, the probes are random, because we have no way of knowing in advance which parts of the proof he will ask to see.

This model of proof is called **PCP**, standing for **probabilistically checkable proofs**. In order to assess the difficulty of checking proofs in this fashion, we measure two quantities, both as functions of N (the input size): the number of coin tosses Bob needs in his thinking, and the number of bits from the proof that he needs to probe. The second of these is particularly important, as it captures how much of a possibly lengthy proof Bob needs to even look at in order to be convinced of its correctness. It is not too difficult to show that NEXPTIME, which we know to be equivalent to the set MIP of problems provable in polynomial time using multi-party interaction, is actually also the set of problems that admit probabilistically checkable proofs, in which Bob can toss any number of coins and ask to see any number of bits from the proof.[5]

The remarkable result about PCP is this: all NP problems can be checked using a constant number of probes of the proof! Let us say this more carefully. For any problem in NP, including the most difficult ones therein—the NP-complete problems—"yes"-ness can be proved by using proof certificates for which the verifier need only check a portion of *fixed* size, whose length is unrelated to the particular instance case he is trying to be convinced of. This has the rather amazing consequence that if you are willing to make do with conviction with overwhelming probability, most mathematical statements can be proved using reasonably-sized proofs that can be checked by reading only a very small, fixed-sized, random part of the proof.[6]

■ ■

▦ Research on Cryptography

The subject matter of this chapter constitutes one of the "hottest" research areas in computer science, and, just as it has always been, it is also an attractive area of work in more covert establishments, such as intelligence agencies and other, less legal or acceptable realms too. Cryptography, digital signatures, electronic commerce and "electronic cash," computerized contract signing, and the security and fault tolerance of large systems, are but some of the buzzwords driving such research. As explained earlier, besides the highly applicative nature of such work, its appeal stems from the fact that it exploits not only ideas leading to efficient solutions to certain algorithmic problems, but also *negative* results regarding the (apparent) difficulty of solving others. It is of interest that in virtually all of these applications the negative results are based on deep conjectures concerning non-polynomial-time lower bounds on certain problems.

Interaction and zero-knowledge proofs are also being researched intensively, and one of the most active areas of work is in probabilistically checkable proofs. The reason is that such proofs have a close relationship to issues regarding the difficulty of approximating NP-complete problems, which were discussed in Chapter 7; actually, certain PCP results lead to nonapproximability results. However, the connection is beyond the scope of this book.

---

[5] The phrase "any number" here means a polynomial number, since Bob only has a polynomial amount of time at his disposal.

[6] This fixed fraction can actually be made incredibly small; under certain technical assumptions about the setup you only need to look at three (!) bits of the proof.

■ Exercises

12.1. Extend the method described in the text for dealing cards in playing poker over the phone to three players. The players conduct "conference conversations," that is, every message sent by one player goes simultaneously to the other two. Assume a central pile and fixed turns of the players. The first to move starts the dealing process.

12.2. Assume N employees, $N > 2$, want to collectively calculate their average salary, but without any of them discovering the actual salary of any other. Consider the following probabilistic solution:

The employees are given labels 1 through N, with the Ith employee earning salary S_I. They all execute the same procedure. In the first stage, the Ith employee privately performs the following:

- Generate $N - 1$ random numbers:

$$X_I^1, \ldots, X_I^{I-1}, X_I^{I+1}, \ldots, X_I^N$$

- Calculate

$$X_I^I = S_I - \left(X_I^1 + \ldots + X_I^{I-1} + X_I^{I+1} + \ldots + X_I^N\right)$$

- Send X_I^J to the Jth employee. (Thus, the Ith employee receives the values $X_1^I, \ldots, X_{I-1}^I, X_{I+1}^I, \ldots, X_N^I$.)
- Calculate the sum

$$Y^I = X_1^I + X_2^I + \ldots + X_N^I$$

- Publish the value Y^I.

In the second stage, all employees calculate together

$$Y = \frac{Y^1 + Y^2 + \ldots + Y^N}{N}$$

Prove the following facts, establishing the correctness of the algorithm:

(a) The final value Y is indeed the average salary.

(b) No employee has a way of deducing the salary of any other (that is, there is no algorithm that, based on the information available to the Ith employee, can calculate the salary of any other employee).

(c) Assume there are L gossips among the employees, who are willing to cooperate by sharing their information. Then they can compute at most the average of the other $N - L$ employees. That is, if $L < N - 1$, they cannot deduce the salary of any of the other $N - L$ employees, but only their average salary.

12.3. Devise a rigorous version of the zero-knowledge protocol for three-colorability described in the text. Recall that you have to carry out all the actions electronically, and hence have to use appropriate cryptographic methods.

A talebearer reveals
secrets: but he that is
of a faithful spirit
conceals the matter

PROVERBS 11: 13

PART V

The Bigger Picture

greater and mightier than thyself
DEUTERONOMY 9: 1

but hear the small as well as the great
DEUTERONOMY 1: 17

CHAPTER 13

Software Engineering

a soft tongue breaks the bone

PROVERBS 25: 15

Let us rise up and build

NEHEMIAH 2: 18

or, Getting It Done When It's Large

A famous anecdote tells of an attempt to give an idea of what computer programming is to a group of executives in a firm that employed programmers. In one week they were taught how to program, and were given a small problem to solve. Each executive was given a professional programmer as an assistant. Having successfully solved the problems assigned to them with just "a little" help, the executives came out of this experience with the feeling that programming is after all quite easy, and that there is no reason why their programmers couldn't complete their assignments on time, just as they did themselves.

Of course, there is a big difference between large programming projects, involving millions of lines of code or even more, and small programming exercises of a few dozen lines. Such a large quantitative difference makes for a qualitative difference in the complexity of the task, and requires a completely different kind of management. One person can easily keep track of all the details of a small problem in his or her head. As the problem becomes larger, this becomes more difficult, and the need arises for written records of the purposes of the various components that make up the project and the relationships between them. Without such documentation, it is easy to make assumptions about how a certain component is to be used when programming it, but to violate these assumptions when programming other components that use it. This can already happen when the program consists of some hundreds of lines.

As projects get larger, they grow beyond the ability of one programmer to handle. Large projects require a team of programmers working together, or even several teams, each dealing with a different part of the overall project. Very large projects, such as modern operating systems, are composed of tens of millions of lines of code and employ hundreds of programmers or even more. Parts of the overall project may be developed by different companies. This makes hidden assumptions and other kinds of errors inevitable. Unfortunately, even employing the best tools and methods available today does not guarantee bug-free programs, as anyone who has used a computer for any length of time knows.

This chapter discusses the general problems that arise in engineering large software systems, and the main processes and methodologies employed in addressing them.

◼ Hidden Assumptions in Spaceflight

There are, unfortunately, many examples of hidden assumptions in software development leading to sometimes catastrophic failures. The following examples are famous incidents in the history of spaceflight.

NASA launched the Mars Climate Orbiter in 1998. Its mission was to orbit Mars and report on its weather conditions, in preparation for the Mars Polar Lander, which was supposed to land on Mars in 1999. The orbiter reached Mars on September 23, 1999, but was then lost. It has been determined by the investigation board that the orbiter's trajectory was about 170 kilometers too low, due to the fact that one part of the orbiter's ground-control program used English units while other parts expected the data in metric units. This happened in spite of the existence of a clear specification that indicated the correct units to use, as well as state-of-the-art development methodologies used by NASA. Among the contributing factors mentioned in the investigation board's report was insufficient communication between the development and operations teams.

The Mars Polar Lander, which was supposed to land on Mars about six weeks later, was lost as well. The review board has identified a software failure as the most probable cause for this loss. The lander's engines must be shut down as soon as it lands, otherwise it will tip over. Sensors on the landing legs of the Polar Lander generate a signal upon surface contact. The sensors may occasionally generate spurious signals, and the software is programmed to ignore such signals by comparing two consecutive signals and acting on them only if both show the same value. However, when the lander legs are deployed from their stowed position to the landing position, the sensors may generate longer "contact" signals. This in itself is not a problem, since the legs are deployed at an altitude of about 1500 meters, while the software will not shut down the engines until radar reports that the lander is less than 40 meters above the surface. Unfortunately, the spurious signal detected at deployment is not erased, and causes engine shutdown as soon as the lander reaches an altitude of 40 meters. This is enough to cause it to crash to the surface. The report states:

> *This behavior was understood and the flight software was required to ignore these events; however, the requirement did not specifically describe these events, and consequently, the software designers did not properly account for them.*

Another spectacular example of hidden assumptions is the explosion that took place in the maiden flight of the European Space Agency's Ariane 5 rocket on June 4, 1996. About 40 seconds after the launch, the rocket made an abrupt change of path, and as a result broke up and exploded. The inquiry board traced the failure to a software error of a certain type. The programming language used allowed the program to recover from such errors, and four possible cases out of seven were indeed adequately protected. The reason that the other three cases were not protected was not documented in the code, but was later traced to an analysis that showed that this kind of error cannot occur in these cases. As it turned out, this analysis was indeed correct for earlier models of Ariane, for which the software was written. When this software was reused for the Ariane 5, which has different flightpath characteristics, it failed. Without getting into more details here, it should be noted that while this was the primary fault, it combined with a series of other aspects of the system to create the catastrophic failure.

The Problem With Software

These examples clearly demonstrate the need for a disciplined method of writing programs, to ensure their reliability. The study of such methods is called **software engineering**. It involves technical aspects, such as programming languages and tools for tasks like testing, debugging, and verification, as well as management practices. Software engineering is different from other engineering disciplines because of the different nature of its subject matter: algorithms and programs. These are of a discrete nature; that is, they deal with individual and separate entities, namely, bits. In contrast, other engineering disciplines deal with physical phenomena, which are usually of a continuous nature.

An important measure of the complexity of a system is the number of qualitatively different states it can have. For example, while a car may be driven at an infinite number of speeds between zero and, say, 150 kilometers per hour, for the purpose of controlling the car using a manual transmission there are up to just seven different states: between three and five forward gear ratios, a neutral position, and reverse. In each of these states, the car's speed is a simple function of the engine speed.

While the variables of a continuous system can take on infinitely many values, they usually have a relatively small number of qualitatively different states. Discrete systems, and particularly computers, have a huge number of states. If you add a single bit to the computer's memory, you multiply the number of states by two, since each old state splits into two new ones: one in which the value of the additional bit is zero, and another in which it is one. The number of possible states for a computer with a memory of just 280 bits exceeds the total estimated number of atoms in the universe! Modern computers have memories containing billions of bits, with an unimaginable (but nevertheless finite) number of possible states. The complexity of computer-based systems is therefore much higher than that of continuous systems, making them less predictable.

As a result of this difference, continuous systems are more amenable to mathematical analysis, and they enable engineers to rely on **safety factors**. For example, when designing a bridge for a certain load, the design always assumes a bigger load. With a safety factor of three, the bridge should theoretically support three times the required load. This will require sturdier construction, which can even make up for some design defects. However, a single bit error in a computer program can cause it to go completely off-track, causing catastrophic failure. This magnification effect of discrete systems makes the notion of safety factors for software meaningless, and thus removes one of the most powerful engineering tools from the realm of software engineering.

Analysis methods for discrete systems also lag behind those for continuous systems. For example, there is a large body of knowledge related to the verification of computer programs, as described in Chapter 5. This research has even led to some commercially successful verification projects. However, these require large investments of effort by highly-skilled researchers, and it is at present impossible to formally verify much of the software being written. Such efforts are therefore mostly focused on the cores of safety-critical systems. For the rest, we must make do with less effective but more practical methods.[1]

Software is a much more flexible medium than the physical materials used in other engineering disciplines. Once a bridge is built, it will take a very substantial reason to replace it. Similarly, when you buy a computer, you expect to use it for some years before replacing it with a new one. However, since computer programs are apparently so easy to change—it only involves changing the contents of the computer's hard disk—customers often expect (and many times get) frequent replacements for their software (usually called "upgrades"). The flip side of this coin is that software producers do not worry about the quality of their initial product in the same way that hardware manufacturers do. Instead, they rely on upgrades to provide solutions to problems discovered after the product is already on the market. This does little to create a feeling of trust in the software industry.

Worse yet, the assumption that software is easy to modify is fallacious. The great complexity of software systems on the one hand, and the size of the problems that such systems are expected to solve on the other, mean that programs are very complex, way beyond our analysis capability. Typically, therefore, an attempt to fix one bug may create several others. Software engineering methodologies, such as those discussed in this chapter, can be used to alleviate this problem. However, they come with a cost of their own, which should be factored into the total cost of modification.

A recent famous example is the Y2K bug, which was mentioned in Chapter 5. At the close of the twentieth century there was a lot of software in operation that was built on the assumption that years can be represented using two digits. For example, the number "80" would represent the year 1980; logically, the number "01" would represent the year 1901. Even though there weren't any electronic computers in 1901, it would still be necessary to refer to that date; for example, it could be the birth date of someone who in 1980 was entitled to social security benefits. However, as the year 2000 approached, it became obvious that it would also be necessary to represent years such as 2001, but the number "01" was already taken! (The first actual cases of this problem occurred in 1998, with some credit cards whose expiration date was 2000 being rejected by computers thinking it was 1900.) This problem is similar to that underlying the story about the old Danish lady from the beginning of Chapter 5.

At the time the programs were written, this choice of representation was reasonable. Some of these programs were written in the 1960s, and nobody expected them still to be in operation more than 30 years later. At the time, memory and disk sizes were much smaller and more expensive than those of today, and storing the redundant "19" digits in every date field would have been excessively costly. (Amazingly, some programs written in the early 1990s still continued to use the two-digit representation, although there was really no excuse for that so close to 2000.) There

---

[1] One of the things we know about this problem is that it not solvable by a computer *in principle* (see Chapter 9). This still does not preclude a partial solution that works for many if not most practical cases, but even that much is not easily available today.

were a great many such programs, since dates crop up almost everywhere. To give just one example, dates occur in the control programs for some elevators since they must keep track of their maintenance schedule.

Unfortunately, the inexorable march of time turned these programs, which were correct when written, into erroneous ones. This caused a scramble to rectify the problem in the mid to late 1990s, which proved to be an immense undertaking. The assumption that years are represented using two digits was spread throughout the programs. It was necessary to examine each line of code to determine whether it manipulated dates in any way. If so, it had to be corrected in a way consistent with the new strategy for dates. This project, which was very successful on the whole, took up a large investment of time and money, and delayed other plans for software development.

As we saw in Chapter 8, the software verification problem is undecidable, and therefore there is no real hope that somebody will someday write a program that is able to discover all occurrences of some similar bug. Automatically correcting bugs is likewise noncomputable. While it is possible to develop tools that help people discover and correct bugs (and this was indeed done by so-called **Y2K factories** in the late 1990s), the process can never be fully automated.

Modularity and Interfaces

When you buy a new car, you get an owner's manual, which explains the instruments and controls, where the fuses are located, how to change tires, and other technical details. In the section about light controls, you will find explanations about how to operate the headlights, the turn signals, the parking lights, and so on, but not instructions that tell you to use the right-turn signal before you wish to turn right, which fuse to check if the lights don't turn on, or which countries require you to drive with your headlights on during the day. These are important issues you need to know in order to operate your car; however, like many other issues related in one way or another to the car's lights, they appear elsewhere in the owner's manual or in completely different documents. It may be nice to have all the relevant details in one place, but there are just too many of them. In order to be able to access this information quickly and accurately, it must be divided into separate topics, each of which appears in a different section of some document. And the division must be logical enough to allow us to figure out where to find anything we need.

The same principle holds for computer programs. An often overlooked aspect of programs is that they are written for people more than for computers. At first, this seems absurd: computer programs are obviously written for computers to execute, and the compiler doesn't really care how clearly written the program is. However, programmers need to read and understand these programs while they are writing them, and while modifying them. Since software modification is so common, any successful program will have to be modified during its lifetime, and the programmers responsible for the modifications will not necessarily be those who wrote the program in the first place. Even the original programmer will typically not remember the details of the program after a few months. Therefore, organization of the program by chapter and verse is as important for computer programs as it is for the car's owner manual, and for the same reasons: so that people are able to find the information they need.

Computer programs need to be broken up into small and coherent parts, called **modules**, each of which can be understood separately. This is particularly important when each module has to be developed by a separate programming team. However, if there are many connections between the modules, they cannot be understood in isolation, and the teams developing them cannot work separately, because every decision one team makes may affect many other teams, and the whole process bogs down. Therefore, modules must be relatively independent; this goal is called **modularity**.

Of course, modules cannot be completely independent, since some (the **clients**) need to use services provided by other modules (the **suppliers**). However, modularity implies that there should be a minimal amount of information that needs to be shared between the client and supplier modules. This information is called the **interface** of the supplier module, and it should include all the details that the clients need to know about *what* services the supplier offers, but nothing about *how* it performs those services. For example, the interface of a module that implements queues consists of the methods used to perform the various queue operations (adding and removing elements, getting the front element, etc.), but not the implementation of those methods.

Interfaces should be clearly documented, ideally in a formal way that allows the compiler to check that programmers do not create undesirable dependencies. This goal is called **information hiding**, which means that the client is not allowed to depend on the implementation of the supplier module, only on its interface.[2] This enables a Lego-style approach to building large systems, in which modules may be replaced by other implementations of the same interface.

Different types of programming languages have different ways of breaking a program into modules. The notion of a module may be as simple as a collection of functions written in a single file. It may be more sophisticated, and some languages distinguish explicitly between the interface and the implementation of a module. However, a language that does not support modularity in one way or another is simply unusable for large projects.

For example, in object-oriented languages classes are the natural modular unit. Abstract classes with no implementation are pure interfaces (and, indeed, this is their name in JAVA). The Queue class of Chapter 3 is an example. As mentioned there, this interface can be implemented by such classes as LinkedQueue, and the programmer of the client module need not be aware of which particular implementation is used. It is easy for the compiler to check that an appropriate implementation is indeed in use.

JAVA interfaces contain the names and parameter types of all methods that clients can invoke on Queue objects. Unfortunately, this is not all the information that the

---

[2] The term "information hiding" is misleading in that it seems to imply that the programmer of the client module is not allowed to *know* anything about the implementation. This is not quite true; the programmer may know everything about the implementation (and he may even be the one writing it), provided no use is made of this knowledge in the client program.

programmer of a client module needs to know; missing is the *meaning* of these methods, which distinguishes stacks from queues, for example. This is provided by the assertions of the design-by-contract methodology, as described in Chapter 5. An interface with a contract contains the full information needed by clients.

There are many methodologies that attempt to guide the process of breaking up a large problem into relatively independent modules. We will not get into the details of these methodologies here. Suffice to say that this task is still more of an art than a science, and requires a lot of experience.

Life-Cycle Models

In order to develop management methods for software engineering, it is first necessary to understand the process of creating software. This process turns out to be quite complex and difficult to formalize. There are various models of it, called **life-cycle models**; each model takes a different view of the process and as a result supports different methodologies. All life-cycle models are based on the following types of activities, which we will illustrate with the example of a word-processing program.

> **Requirements acquisition.** (Also called **requirements analysis**.) This is the process of discovering what the customer really needs. Customers may be knowledgeable about their own business domain, but they often do not understand the algorithmic and system implications of introducing a computer-based system into their business. This may lead to misunderstandings, which must be carefully elucidated in order to lead to a successful result. The result of this activity is usually a **requirements document**.
>
> Sometimes there is no customer to work with, as when a company makes software products to be sold off-the-shelf. In this case, the producer needs to anticipate customer needs, which makes requirements acquisition harder, not easier! (And, indeed, quite a few products end up with low sales because this process failed to anticipate what the customers really needed.)
>
> In our word-processing example, the requirements document will contain a list of the customer's specific needs, such as the use of complex mathematical notation, a spelling checker, and automatic generation of address labels.
>
> **Design.** In this process, the problem is broken up into modules, and appropriate algorithms and data structures are chosen to represent the problem domain and perform the required operations. This activity demands a thorough understanding of algorithmics in order to make choices that will ensure correctness and efficiency of the resulting product.
>
> The design of the example word processor may specify modules for such tasks as the graphical user interface, text handling, mathematical typesetting, and letter composition (including the generation of address labels). The design for the text-handling module would specify the data structure for holding the contents of the text; this could be, for example, a list of characters, with special symbols denoting linebreaks, or a list of lines, each of which is a vector

containing the characters that appear in the line. This module will also specify the algorithms used to perform such actions as justifying lines and checking the spelling.

Implementation. This is the process of translating the design into a specific programming language. First, each module is implemented separately. Then, the modules are put together to form the complete system; this process is called **integration**, and is often the stage where hidden assumptions manifest themselves.

Our word processor is now cast into a specific programming language, and it is possible to experiment with it (or with parts of it) and see what it really does.

Validation. This is the process of making sure that each module, as well as the complete system, fulfill their specifications. Validation can take many forms. It usually includes extensive testing of the separate modules (called **unit testing**) and of the complete system (called **integration testing**). Unfortunately, as mentioned in Chapter 5, testing is insufficient for finding all bugs. Formal verification can ensure that the system fulfills its specification, but, as mentioned earlier, is not yet practical for general use. Also, the fact that the system fulfills the specification still does not necessarily mean that it does what the customer wanted! Verification requires a formal specification to check the program against, but translating the requirements into a formal specification is a hard problem, and as error-prone as programming. There is no foolproof way to check the specification against the customer's requirements, since these are in the customer's brain and are inaccessible to our formal tools.

In a well-designed process, each module of the word-processing application can be tested separately. This requires special test programs to be written, since modules are not designed to work on their own. However, this "extra" work is well worth the effort, since it is much easier to find and correct problems in a single module than in a complete system.

Maintenance. This word is used here in a special technical sense. Unlike mechanical systems, computer programs are not subject to environmental processes that can cause them to overheat, run down, or otherwise lose their operational characteristics. It isn't necessary to "overhaul" a program after 200,000 miles or 10 years (whichever comes first)—it will continue to function indefinitely in exactly the same way as on the first day. This is exactly the problem! In order to remain useful, programs must change. Changes can be required because of changes in the program's operating environment; for example, when the customer changes from a mainframe to a personal computer, or when upgrading the operating system. The operating environment includes much more than the computer itself: for example, the program may need to be modified when state laws that govern the behavior of the application domain change, as could happen to cashier's software when a new type of tax is legislated. Changes may also be the result of new customer requests; as customers start using a new system, they discover more things they would like the program to do for them. Finally, and sadly, modifications may be required to fix bugs that the supplier didn't discover before the program was released to customers.

New customer requests appearing after the system's deployment are almost always inevitable, since introducing a computerized system into an environment that previously didn't have one changes that environment. What initially may have been a labor-saving program performing a task that could otherwise have been carried out manually now becomes an essential part of the business. For example, an accountant may start using the computer as a convenience. Discovering that this expedites his or her work might result in a decision to take on new clients. Now, however, the accountant is dependent on the computer, and can't do without it. For example, if unusual tasks that the software couldn't handle were previously done manually, with a larger clientele these too must be automated.

Statistics show that the greatest investment in software is in the maintenance stage; this could reach 80% of the total! It is therefore a good idea to make a great effort in the other activities mentioned above to facilitate future maintenance. Most software engineering methodologies are based on this premise.

If the postal service changes from five-digit zip codes to nine-digit codes, we will hasten to the supplier of our word-processing application to modify the address label generator to support nine-digit codes. If the original design treated five as a "magic number" without giving thought to the possibility that it might change, it is quite likely that this assumption is embedded in many parts of the program. It will then be very difficult to modify, and the supplier will charge a large fee for doing so. In this case, we might spend our money better by switching to a different supplier.

In fact, the change to nine-digit zip codes is a real example, which caused a lot of expense for those suppliers that weren't prepared for it. It is, however, dwarfed by the example of the Y2K problem already discussed.

The Waterfall Model

The most basic life-cycle model is called the **waterfall model**. It assumes that the activities mentioned above follow each other in strict order. The name of this model comes from the view of the activities following each other like water falling off a cliff in a series of steps (see Figure 13.1). In this view, a requirements document must be fully prepared before it is possible to start the design. Furthermore, once the design has started, the requirements document is frozen, and cannot be modified. The reason for this is that any changes in the requirements made after design or, worse yet, after implementation, necessitate going back to the beginning, and modifying the design (and implementation) accordingly. This could be extremely costly. Indeed, modifications to early stages of the process require changes in subsequent stages. Later stages add lots of detail, and changing them is therefore more complicated. As a result, the further back in the process a change is made, the more costly it is. It has been estimated that the cost of fixing an error in the requirements phase grows by a factor of 10 if its discovery is delayed until the implementation phase, and by a factor of 100 if it is discovered when the system is already in operation.

Figure 13.1

The waterfall model.

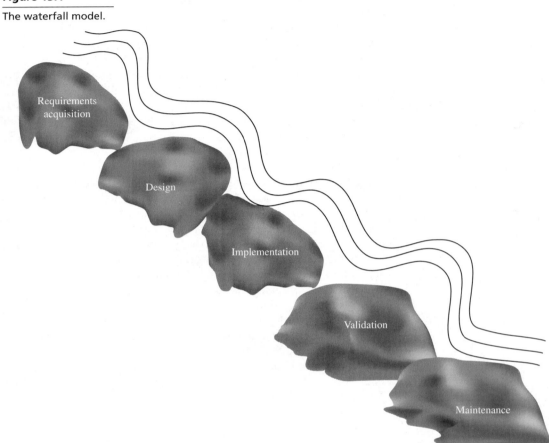

Unfortunately, at the earlier stages, in which we make the most important and influential choices, we understand the problem only in rather vague terms. As we move along in the design and implementation, our understanding of the problem grows until, when we get to the point where we really understand it, we have no meaningful choices to make! In practice, wrong decisions will inevitably be made in early stages, and these will have to be corrected later. This means that a lot of effort must be applied to the validation of the requirements and the design, before starting the implementation. This is quite difficult, and there are not that many satisfactory formal tools to help in these tasks. Often we have to make do with less precise but still useful methods, such as **design reviews**, where the requirements and design are presented to the most experienced people available, who try to uncover any flaws.

Since the cost of making changes in the requirements and design is so high, it is necessary to anticipate them in advance. With some experience, it is possible to do this reasonably well, but clearly changes will have to be made. Consequently, the waterfall model is usually shown with "backward flow" that admits this reality, but methodologies based on the waterfall model offer little support when this happens.

The advantage of the waterfall model is that it makes the process visible and thus easier to manage. The process is document-oriented, and each stage of the model has a clear definition of what products (often called **deliverables**) are to be available when it is done. These products, which may be documents or programs, are the obvious points of control for the entire process. Management (and also the customer) can use the deliverables to keep track of the project's progress.

This strength of the model is also a weakness, since the effort spent on documenting the process is sometimes better spent on ensuring that it will result in a satisfactory product. Furthermore, when requirements change, it is practically impossible to start the process from scratch. As a result, developers "fake it," by attempting to modify existing documents to make them look as if the new requirements had been in there from the beginning. While this is useful (and has even been legitimized by some influential methodologists), it is necessarily error-prone. As more changes are made, the structure becomes riddled with gaps that the patches don't quite fill. Eventually, each addition creates more problems than it fixes, at which point the entire process gets out of control.

Evolutionary Development

The waterfall model certainly has the order of the activities right; a program written without a good design will be flawed, and a design done without a good understanding of the requirements will not lead to a solution of the customer's problem. However, it is only possible to evaluate the final product at the end of this lengthy process, and as we have said, early errors are very costly to fix. The **evolutionary development** model tries to reduce this risk by advocating the production of an initial working version as quickly as possible. The customer can provide useful feedback on the suitability of the product by actually using it. This is much more likely to uncover hidden assumptions and other problems than any amount of document reading. The feedback from this is then used to create the second version, which even lead to a third one.

Each version is produced according to the activities specified by the waterfall model, but more quickly and with much less documentation. Consequently, the resulting systems may be less well structured and therefore more costly to maintain. The model is best applied when the risk of early errors is particularly high, as when creating a new type of application with which the developer (and possibly even the customer) has no experience.

In order to get to a working version as quickly as possible, it is usually produced as a barebones system, concentrating on the most crucial features and omitting the rest. Such a version is called a **prototype**. Further versions elaborate on the initial prototype by adding more features, until a full-featured final system is obtained. This process is called **exploratory programming**. A more radical approach is to throw away the initial prototype and start from scratch the second time. This approach, called **rapid prototyping**, has the advantage that the initial prototype can be created very quickly, since its internal quality is not important. Having learned from their initial experience, the developers can now build a second prototype of higher quality, without having to worry about retrofitting new insights into the old design. Furthermore, the rapid prototype can be written in a different programming language than the second one. Some languages, such as LISP, are eminently suitable for rapid prototyping because they relieve the programmer of some of the more tedious aspects of other languages, such as the need to declare the types of all variables. The resulting speed of development makes up for the risks inherent in ignoring these. The second prototype can then be written more carefully in a more restrictive language.

If the developers have a thorough understanding of the problem domain, evolutionary development may not be necessary, since they could probably produce a detailed specification without experimentation. This would be the case, for example, if an experienced software team were to work on a new product that was similar to ones they had developed previously. Rapid prototyping is particularly useful when the problem to be solved requires particularly innovative ideas, or is simply not sufficiently well understood, as, for example, in artificial intelligence.

The Spiral Model

The spiral life-cycle model is a generalization of the previous ones (see Figure 13.2). It is based on an iterative process, and thus allows evolutionary development as well as rapid prototyping, where each cycle can be based on the waterfall model. The main contribution of the spiral model is its focus on risk management. Each iteration

Figure 13.2

The spiral model. (After Boehm, 1988[3].)

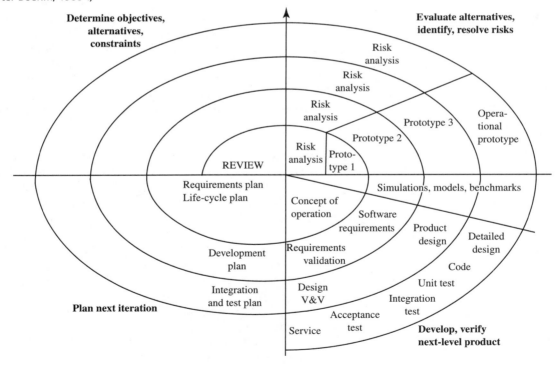

---

[3] B. W. Boehm, "A spiral model of software development and enhancement," IEEE Computer, 21(5), pp. 61–72, 1988.

in the spiral starts with a phase where the objectives of the iteration are determined, together with alternative ways of achieving them (top left of Figure 13.2). This is followed by a risk assessment phase, in which the risks associated with each alternative are investigated (top right of the figure). For example, the choice of hardware platforms, programming language, and software tools could be evaluated at this stage. For new technology, where the risk is particularly high, it may be necessary to perform a small-scale technology evaluation in order to correctly assess and reduce the associated risk. After an alternative has been chosen, it is pursued and evaluated in the third phase (bottom right of the figure). This evaluation is then used to plan the next iteration (bottom left). The spiral model itself does not specify the details of each iteration, which could follow the waterfall model, or allocate the activities some other way.

Like the waterfall model, the spiral model is primarily aimed at process control, and is therefore also document-based. In fact, it has additional deliverables, resulting from the additional three phases added for risk management. This is considered a small price to pay in high-risk projects.

Object-Oriented Development

As we saw in Chapter 3, object-oriented programming languages grew out of the need to model real-world events. It is therefore natural that the concepts of classes and objects are particularly suitable for requirements acquisition and design. The stages of object-oriented software engineering are similar to those of the other methodologies shown above. However, object-oriented methodologies have the important advantage of employing a common vocabulary across activities, based on the notions of classes and objects. For example, a program to manage a store in a supermarket chain is naturally specified in terms of objects denoting customers, cashiers, point-of-sale terminals, grocery items, warehouses, suppliers, etc. The design phase may add other types of objects for internal algorithmic purposes, but this is an elaboration of the specification rather than a completely different type of document.

In earlier methodologies, the transition between activities involves shifts between different formalisms. This need to switch representations is one of the weak points of non-object-oriented methodologies, since it is likely to sever the link between related activities. For example, it is not uncommon for programmers to ignore the designs laid out for them because they are couched in a formalism that is not directly related to the programming language they use. The common vocabulary in object-oriented methodologies makes this much less likely to happen. It also allows some mixing between activities; for example, design might be interleaved with programming. In this way, the experience gained in implementing one part of the system may clarify issues useful in the design of other parts. As long as the process is well managed, this can speed the development by providing more timely feedback without a negative impact on quality.

One of the important goals of software engineering has always been **reuse**: the ability to use artifacts (programs, designs, and even requirements) generated for one project in a subsequent project. The advantage of reuse is obvious: it allows the developer to create new projects quickly after an initial investment in the first project of its kind.[4] Object technology offers a technical means for achieving reuse. Since classes encapsulate data types with their associated operations, they are the natural unit to be reused. This is one of the major benefits of object-oriented development.

Extreme Programming

The basic tenet of the waterfall model is that the cost of change increases dramatically over time, so that errors early in the development process become more and more costly to repair as we go from stage to stage. As a result, it is necessary to anticipate future changes as much as possible, and to account for them in the design. This could make the design more complex and unwieldy than necessary.

Recently, a technique called **refactoring** has been developed in order to help solve this problem. Instead of freezing the design when starting the implementation, this view takes the opposite approach: the design should be flexible and should change together with the implementation. This is not easy to do. What usually happens is that the implementation is modified in response to pressure from customers, changing environments, and bug discoveries, but it is done by "patches" that attempt to modify some aspect of the program without an overall view. As a result, the program drifts away from the original design and becomes harder and harder to modify. The refactoring methodology attempts to preserve the quality of the design in spite of changes to the code. Programming alternates between modifications that add new functionality or fix bugs, and refactoring activity, which improves the structure of the program without affecting its functionality.

This is similar to what happens when you need to make modifications to your home. For example, when you add a new electric outlet you first break open the wall in order to access the wiring. After installing the new wires and outlet, you then cover up the hole and repaint the wall. These last actions have nothing to do with the way the new outlet functions; it will supply electricity even if you don't cover up the hole. They are done in order to restore the wall to its original condition.

One expert in object technology has compared cleaning up the design to paying off debts, whereas modifying the program while messing up the design is like taking a loan. An unpaid loan accrues interest and, if unpaid for a long time, may grow beyond the borrower's ability to pay. Similarly, if the program is allowed to drift away from the design too much, it becomes unmanageable. Eventually it will become impossible to make further modifications, since every such attempt will introduce more problems than it solves. Occasionally it is useful to borrow money, but the debt should be paid as soon as possible. Similarly, it is sometimes useful to make quick changes to the program in order to take advantage of some opportunity. However, the program should be refactored as soon as possible in order to realign it with a good design.

Refactoring offers a suite of detailed methods for improving the design of a program without affecting its functionality. In this way, new insights about the structure of the program are leveraged to improve its design. Such insights may be

---

[4] There are also risks in reuse, as demonstrated by the story of the Ariane 5 explosion mentioned at the beginning of this chapter. Unfortunately, these are much less obvious.

gained during the process of adding new functionality, finding and correcting bugs, or during code reviews.

With refactoring it is possible to correct design errors (or otherwise modify the initial design) without incurring a great penalty even much later in the process. This may not be effective in very large projects, but it works quite well in small to medium-sized projects. Because design errors are not as prohibitive, the initial design can be kept simple, and this simplifies later stages as well. All this leads to a completely different style of development, called **extreme programming**.

The extreme programming methodology highly prizes simplicity. It is called "extreme" because it takes every good practice to the utmost. For example, it advocates frequent and automated testing (which is a basic premise for refactoring as well). Evolutionary development is also taken to its logical conclusion, at a number of levels. First, system integration is performed often (at least once a day). This means that a full working system is continuously available. Although such an interim version of the system may not fulfill all the requirements, it can be used to evaluate the current status of the development in the most direct way—by actually using it. Second, development is based on short cycles (of about three weeks), each of which compresses requirements acquisition, design, implementation, and validation into a single continuous activity. Finally, customer releases are made every few months, which means that the customer must be involved in the project all the time, rather than just at the initial stage. Indeed, an on-site customer representative is a basic requirement for extreme programming.

In extreme programming, code reviews are performed continuously through the practice of **pair programming**, in which every programming activity is carried out by two people. At any point one of the pair will be using the computer to write or modify the program, while the other "looks over his (or her) shoulder" to try and identify problems, from typing mistakes to logical errors. Periodically, the "driver" and "navigator" switch roles. It might seem that two people doing the work of one will be half as productive. However, studies have shown that pair programming is almost as productive as two people working separately in terms of the amount of work performed, but it results in significantly higher-quality programs.

There is still not enough experience with this methodology for a full evaluation, but when it works it appears to be very effective. We expect it to gain a significant place beside the other, more heavyweight, methodologies.

The Psychology of Software Engineering

Methodology designers often tend to forget the most important factor in software engineering: the analysts, designers, programmers, and managers. These are all human, with human strengths and weaknesses. One of the weaknesses is a tendency to break the rules, which makes it hard to enforce a methodology's requirements. It is possible to make programmers produce voluminous documentation; it is almost impossible to force them to produce *useful* documentation. People's tendency to break rules is also a strength, if used properly. For example, there are many stories about projects saved by people going beyond their job descriptions to report and even fix a problem they noticed.

It is well known, though often forgotten, that there are many factors that have a large impact on people's performance and productivity apart from methodological ones. A famous anecdote tells of a large common room for students in a university's computing center that had a number of vending machines at one end. When a couple of students complained about the noise emanating from that corner of the room, the administration moved the machines to a different location. Immediately afterwards, a more serious problem manifested itself: the two consultants provided by the computing center to help students with their problems found themselves swamped, with long lines forming in front of their room. It turned out that the noise around the vending machines was often made by students talking to each other about their computing problems, and since the problems were often similar, most of them were solved on the spot. Only unusual problems were referred to the consultants. With the removal of this informal but highly effective service, the whole situation changed for the worse.

In recent years, several methodologies that try to address the human issue have appeared. Instead of calling themselves "lightweight methodologies," which is a negative term that distinguishes them from other, "heavyweight" methodologies, they have taken to calling themselves **agile**. This term underlies the change of focus from document-based management to people-based management. Agile methodologies, of which extreme programming is one example, attempt to give people the motivation and support they need to do their job, and trust them to do it well. As a result, they place strong emphasis on communication between customers, designers, and programmers, and advocate that they all work in close proximity; if possible, in the same room. When team members communicate effectively, much less paper documentation is required. Instead of tracking progress by secondary documentation, agile methodologies use working software. It is much easier to evaluate a working product than a design document. Of course, this implies that the process must support the production of stable versions frequently. As a result of this philosophy, teams using agile methodologies can respond to changes more readily than those using fixed plans.

Traditional methodologies following the "production line" strategy and view developers (such as analysts, designers, coders, and testers) as interchangeable within their particular categories. Agile methodologies focus instead on individual craftsmanship, without rigid boundaries, and where developers gain knowledge and experience by working with others. They start as apprentices, doing the simpler and more tedious parts of the work, but are not kept away from tasks that require more expertise. As they make progress, they take on some of the more complex tasks, until they reach the position where they become craftsmen themselves. It is important to understand that this does not correspond to the usual progression from programmer to manager. A craftsman takes on more responsibilities than an apprentice, including management responsibilities, but that does not preclude him or her from doing what he does best—actual software development. Needless to say, this approach emphasizes the individual rather than the process, and is much favored by the developers themselves.

It is clear that larger teams, or those developing life-critical applications, must use more formal processes with more documentation than smaller teams developing less critical software. Indeed, there are many varieties of agile methodologies, geared towards different types of projects. As the approach becomes better known and more prevalent, it will probably be put to the test in larger organizations, including those that develop critical applications. Aficionados of agile software development methodologies claim that there is nothing that cannot be done using these methodologies. Time will tell if they are right.

Professional Ethics

Because of the ever-growing use of software in many critical systems on the one hand, and our insufficient ability to verify its correctness on the other, great emphasis must be put on the integrity and professionalism of the people who specify, design, and develop computer-based systems. They must do their best to ensure that the software they develop is of the highest quality according to the best available practices of the art.

The two major professional computing organizations, the ACM and the IEEE Computer Society, have prepared ethics codes for computer professionals. These detail specific responsibilities of system developers with respect to society in general, and the organizations they work for in particular. For example, they are instructed to contribute to society and human well-being in their work, to avoid harming others, to be honest and fair, and to respect privacy, confidentiality, and the intellectual property of others. They should strive for the highest quality and effectiveness of their professional work, should educate the public as to the implications of computerized systems, and should further their own technical education. Managers should create working environments that make it easy for employees to follow the code, and they must make sure that the needs of all people who are affected by their products are taken into account.

A related issue concerns certification. Should computer professionals be certified by one of the professional societies, and should such certification be a requirement for working on critical projects? The IEEE Computer Society has a voluntary certification program for its members, which, in addition to the technical requirements for certification, also requires adherence to the code of ethics. Such programs, together with the inclusion of ethics courses in the computer science curriculum, are expected to lead to higher ethical standards in the profession and thus to higher-quality products.

Research on Software Engineering

In the late 1970s a job candidate arrived at one of IBM's research centers for a job lecture and interview. The topic he lectured on had something to do with comparing programming languages. About 15 minutes into his talk it became clear that he was planning to exhibit a method for comparing the syntax of programming languages.

One of the people in the audience, an expert on formal languages, put up her finger and said kind of meekly, "But that problem is undecidable."[5] The job-seeker turned around to her and said, "Oh, but that's just a theoretical result; I'm going to show you a real practical algorithm." Of course he never got the job...

In engineering disciplines there tends to be continuous tension between theory and practice, and it takes time for theoretical ideas to percolate to the practitioners. Certain ideas catch on quickly, others take more time, and some remain as pure theory (which often doesn't detract from their importance).

In algorithmics, efficiency considerations (Chapter 6) have had a more immediate appeal to practitioners than correctness (Chapter 5). This is probably due to two reasons. First, a grossly inefficient program is unusable, whereas a program with some rarely-manifested bugs in it can still be used (albeit with some frustration). Second, the discovery of a new, more efficient algorithm, something most often done by the theoreticians, is usually simple to translate into code, and once that is done, the code can be used in many programs. Proving program correctness, on the other hand, is notoriously difficult, and has to be carried out separately for each new program.

Research on the correctness of algorithms has influenced software engineering in a number of ways. The most intensive use of formal methods in industry is in verification, that is, formally proving that a product satisfies its specification. We shall see more of this in Chapter 14. There are also quite sophisticated tools that can help verify a proof outlined by an expert. These tools have two benefits. First, they construct completely formal proofs, at a level of detail unachievable by a human (not because this is too intellectually challenging for humans, but for the opposite reason: it is too long and tedious). Second, they allow their users to concentrate on high-level concepts and strategies, letting the tool fill in the details. Still, verification requires a lot of time and effort, and has been applied mostly by hardware manufacturers, since hardware errors are much more costly to fix than software errors. For example, all of the elementary floating point operations on the AMD Athlon microprocessor were mechanically verified to be compliant with the standard specification. The work was done at AMD before the Athlon was first fabricated, and discovered several bugs. Motorola and Intel have also had impressive successes in using verification tools.

An important contribution of formal research methods to programming practice is design by contract, which was mentioned in Chapter 5. The assertions that can be written in languages such as EIFFEL are not strong enough to express all the mathematical properties of the program needed for verification. However, they are executable, in the sense that a computer can check that they are true during the execution of the program. Thus, design by contract is a good example of useful formal reasoning about programs. It increases the quality of programs as well as development speed (when taking into account that it allows early discovery of bugs), and this makes up for the extra effort required in writing the assertions. Furthermore, it encourages programmers to think about the formal properties of their code, and even to prove to themselves (without automated assistance, for the time being) that

---

[5] This specific problem is called the equivalence problem for context-free languages, and has been proved to be undecidable.

they are correct. As theorem-proving tools become more sophisticated, they will be able to offer more help in this process.

Research has also led to advances in requirements and specification languages, mainly ones that are both visual and mathematically formal, and which are used to specify complex behavior. The next chapter discusses these.

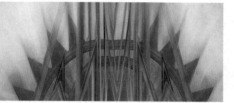

Wisdom has built her house

PROVERBS 9: 1

So he built the house, and finished it

I KINGS 6: 9

Reactive Systems

or, Getting It to Behave Properly Over Time

The previous chapter dealt with the general problems that arise when we have to devise not just algorithms and programs but large and complex systems. In this chapter, we concentrate on one especially problematic type of system, and on its most difficult and slippery facet. The kinds of systems we have in mind are predominantly reactive in nature, and the difficult aspect is to specify, analyze, and implement their behavior over time.

Some systems are indeed complex, but are **transformational** in nature; they are of an input/process/output type, with their prescribed work being carried out repeatedly for each new set of inputs. This means that they owe their complexity to computations and to the flow of data. In these cases, we might say that our friend, little Runaround, has lots of thinking to do or lots of lifting and carrying. A typical component of such a system waits for all of its input data to arrive, processes it, sends off its output data to some other components, and goes back to sleep until prompted by new input data. Systems of this kind can be described and analyzed in a satisfactory manner by **data-flow** techniques, which identify the processing taking place inside the various components and the data that flows between them.[1] Thus, the dynamic behavior of a transformational system is, by and large, determined by the flow connections between the components or objects.

Far more problematic are those systems (especially the large and complex ones) that are heavily **control driven**, or **event driven**. Such systems have been termed **reactive**. Their role in life is to react to many different kinds of events, signals, and conditions in intricate ways. Reactive systems need not necessarily be concurrent or distributed, although many of them are. Many are also time-critical, often having to respond to events in real time. Here, little Runaround, or many of them if the

---

[1] Most of the cloud-like figures in this book are data-flow diagrams of sorts. Typically, they describe processing activities in clouds and data in rectangles, with arrows prescribing the data flow itself. The meaning of these diagrams is usually quite obvious, although no rigorous conventions were imposed regarding when and why the data indeed flows.

system is also concurrent, has to be extremely alert, responsive, and fast. In fact, it is no exaggeration to say that a vast portion of computerized systems are reactive, or have dominant reactive parts. Examples include relatively small systems, such as video cassette recorders (VCRs), mobile phones, and ATMs, and far larger and complex ones, such as automotive and avionics systems, chemical plants, control systems, telephone and communication controllers, industrial robots, and interactive software packages such as word processors and program editors. These systems have to maintain intricate dynamic relationships with their environment, reacting properly, and on time, to buttons being pressed, temperatures rising above critical levels, receivers being hung up, cursors being moved on a screen, and so on. Often they also contain extensive reactive interaction internally; that is, between the various components constituting the system. And in the age of the Internet, more and more web-intensive systems are also reactive, with manipulation in one place causing reactions in another, and with lots of this reactivity happening simultaneously.

Thus, the dominant part of the complexity of a reactive system does not stem from complex computations or the flow of data, but from intricate cause/effect, trigger/response patterns, usually coupled with a high degree of concurrency and timing aspects too.

The main problem with reactivity is to specify the system's behavior over time, clearly and correctly, and in ways that can be easily and reliably implemented, analyzed, and verified. What will happen and when? Why will these things happen, and what else will they cause to happen in their wake? Can other things happen in the interim? Are certain things mandatory but others merely allowed to happen? What are the time constraints on something happening? What is the result of expected things not happening when they should? What things may *not* happen, under any circumstances? And on and on.

Interestingly, reactivity is not an exclusive characteristic of man-made computerized systems. It occurs also in biological systems, which, despite being a lot smaller than we humans and our home-made artifacts, can also be a lot *more* complicated. And it occurs also in economical and social systems, which are a lot larger than a single human. These, too, have an intricate reactive nature, and being able to fully understand and analyze them, and possibly to predict their future behavior, involves the same kind of thinking required for computerized systems. This leads to the belief that some of the solutions offered by computer science and systems engineering can also be used to deal with such noncomputerized reactivity. Dually, we might also be able to learn much about how to deal with computerized reactivity by observing Mother Nature dealing with her own reactive systems.

Visual Formalisms for Reactive Behavior

The main artifact needed for developing a reliable reactive system is an overall system model, which consists of a carefully linked comprehensive representation of the system's structural and behavioral aspects. It serves as a vehicle for the specifiers and designers to capture their thoughts and incorporates elements from the requirements and the design, and can then lead all the way down to successful implementation. In some ways, a model is like the set of plans drawn by an architect to describe a house or a bridge. The difference, however, is in the dynamics: reactive systems change over time; they do things; they behave. And this is not true of houses or bridges. Thus, while the structural description of a reactive system can be considered to be its backbone, its behavior is, in a crucial sense, its heart and soul. Behavior in a reactive system is like the engine in an automobile; neither can "move" without it. Also, behavior over time is much less tangible than the overall functionality of a reactive system or its physical structure, and more than anything else it is this aspect that renders the development of reactive systems so difficult and error-prone.

One approach to the problem of specifying such systems are **visual formalisms**, languages that are diagrammatic and intuitive, yet mathematically rigorous. All other things being equal, pictures are usually better understood than text or symbols, and if used properly they can serve to enable thinking on a higher level of abstraction than text. But these languages are not merely graphics. Just as high-level programming languages require not only editors and display utilities but also—and far more importantly!—compilers, interpreters, and debugging tools, so do languages for modeling the behavior of reactive systems require a lot more than pretty diagrams with nice graphical editors. We need means for running, or executing, the models, and means for compiling them down into conventional code, an activity called **code generation** or **code synthesis**.

Thus, visual formalisms for reactive behavior, just like conventional languages for programming computation, must come complete with a syntax that determines what is allowed and a semantics that determines what the allowed things mean. Visuality is often based on the use of boxes and arrows, with topological relationships between them, such as encapsulation, connectedness, and adjacency. Such languages are often hierarchical and modular.

There are many languages for specifying reactive behavior, several of which can be classified as full-fledged visual formalisms. Some of the most interesting are Petri nets and SDL diagrams—visual formalisms both—and Esterel, Signal and Lustre, which in appearance are more like programming languages, though they have graphical front-ends too. We now describe one example of a visual formalism for reactive behavior, called **statecharts**.

Statecharts for Reactive Behavior

Finite state machines and their associated state transition diagrams appear to be a satisfactory starting point for specifying reactive behavior. We identify the system's states, or modes of operation, and proceed to specify the events and conditions that cause transitions between states, and the actions (for example, the sending and receiving of data, the starting or stopping of activities, and so on) that are carried out within them. Chapter 9 contained a simple example of a diagram describing part of the behavior of a digital watch (see Figure 9.14).

However, there are several problems with the naive use of state diagrams for complex cases. First, the diagrams are "flat," whereas reactive behavior of even relatively small systems falls naturally into levels of detail. (Cutting electrical power is a very high-level event, whereas moving a screen cursor over some icon is a low-level one.) These levels are beneficial not only for clarity and comprehension but also during the development process itself. Consider the watch of Figure 9.14. We might like to continue specifying it further by describing the behavior of the stopwatch feature itself (for example, how and when it is started and stopped), and the various possibilities of updating. All we have for updating is a state named *update-watch*, which presumably denotes, or contains, a number of **substates** that deal with updating the seconds, minutes, hours, and months, much as there are three states for updating the alarm.

Second, state diagrams are sequential and do not cater naturally for concurrency. As an example, suppose our watch has a light for illumination, which can be turned on or off independently of other things that are happening elsewhere. If the light is a totally separate entity controlled, say, by a separate button, then all we need is a new two-state diagram describing it as a separate system. In truth, however, the light feature in a digital watch is less straightforward. It may not always be applicable—perhaps it does not work in the stopwatch state.

Of course, it is possible to combine the light information with the rest of the description, yielding two states for each of the old ones; one for the case where the light is on, and one for when it is off.[2] However, if this approach is adopted in general for dealing with concurrency, it results in an **exponential blow-up** in the number of states that must be explicitly described. (Why?) Obviously, these problems, which arise even in such small systems as digital watches, are far more acute in large and complex reactive systems, which typically have huge numbers of states.

In an attempt to address these shortcomings, state diagrams have been extended, yielding a language called **statecharts**. Figure 14.1 shows a statechart for a more detailed version of the watch of Figure 9.14, which now includes a light component, refinements of the stopwatch and update states, and the beeping status. (For brevity, we have omitted the word "pressed" from the button-pressing events.)

Statecharts allow for multi-level states, decomposed in an and/or fashion, and thus support compact specification. To capture the hierarchy of states, the rountangles of regular state diagrams can be arranged in a clustered, encapsulated fashion. The state *update-watch* of Figure 14.1, for example, consists of the six enclosed substates, related among themselves by an exclusive "or": being in *update-watch* actually means being in precisely one of its six substates. We might have grouped these six states together for clarity, or for purposes of gradual development. We might have first decided that there will be a state for updating (as indeed we have; see Figure 9.14) and only later on went ahead and carried out the refinement itself. Moreover, the six updating states have at least one real property in common: they all respond to the pressing of *b* by stopping the updating process and returning to *display-time*. If "flat" diagrams were used this would require six separate arrows, one coming out of each state. If we are in *update-watch* and button *b* is pressed, we leave and enter *display-time*. However, since being in *update-watch* is being in any one of the substates, the desired effect follows. Similarly, if the battery is removed

---

2 It is also possible to specify the light as a separate object, and to then program the interaction between the objects. We shall return to this possibility later.

Figure 14.1

Statechart for a more detailed version of the digital watch of Figure 9.14.

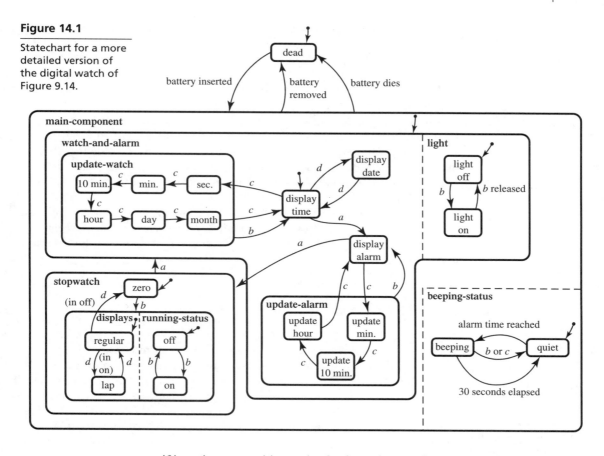

or if it expires, a transition to the *dead* state is caused, no matter what state we were in. These are sometimes called **interrupts**.[3]

To specify **concurrent** state components, statecharts use dashed-line partitioning. These add the dimension of simultaneity, and are called **orthogonal** components of the statechart. The relationship between orthogonal components is not "or" but "and." For example, if we are in the *stopwatch* state of Figure 14.1, but not in *zero*, then we must be simultaneously both in *displays* and in *running-status*. Within each of these there are two possibilities, related by "or," and resulting in a total of four possible state configurations. To contrast with these four, consider the *light* component, where we have added two states instead of the 12 we would have needed without orthogonal components, and *beeping-status*, where two are added instead of 29. (Where did the 12 and 29 come from?) This reduction in size helps overcome the exponential blow-up problem discussed earlier.

The small arrows denoting start states in ordinary state diagrams can appear on any level in a statechart. Here they are called **defaults**. Within the high-level state *main-component*, for example, the combined state consisting of the orthogonal

---

[3] Notice that we have not given the six updating states any inner description, and the particular method by which the updating is carried out is left unspecified. Later, a designer can fill in this lower level information, or delegate the job to someone else.

components *watch-and-alarm* and *light* is the default, so that if a battery is inserted when in the dead state, we enter this combination, and not *stopwatch*. (Of course, we also enter *quiet* in state *beeping-status*.) Now, within each of these orthogonal components there is also a default arrow—there must be one, otherwise we would not know which of their substates to enter—so that we really end up in the configuration ⟨*display-time*, *light-off*, *quiet*⟩.

Statecharts have a number of additional features, such as the ability to specify timing constraints, and the possibility of basing transitions on past behavior. We should remember, however, that formalisms like statecharts are capable of describing only the control part of a reactive system, and not its data flow or structural aspects. The behavioral specification must be combined with a specification of the system's structure, just as the nonengine parts of an automobile must be combined with the engine, and these connections are not that straightforward. One of the most widely-used approaches to this is to combine a language for reactive behavior, like statecharts, with the ideas of object-orientation. We shall discuss this approach later.

Model Execution

One of the most interesting notions to have come out of research in systems and software engineering is that of **executable specifications**, or, to fit in better with the terminology used here, **executable models**. Executing a model can be done either directly, in a manner analogous to running an interpreter on a conventional computer program, or indirectly, by compiling down into code and running the code. A number of powerful tools that support such capabilities are available.

The core of model execution is the ability to carry out a single **step** of the system's dynamic operation, with all the consequences taken into account. During a step, the environment can generate external events, modify the values of conditions and variables, etc. Such changes then affect the status of the system: they trigger new events, they activate and deactivate activities, they modify conditions and variables, and so on. And, of course, each of these changes, in turn, may cause many others, often yielding intricate chain reactions. In many kinds of systems, time and timing constraints play an important role in determining how a step is executed.

The semantics of the formalism used to specify behavior must contain all the information needed to capture these changes precisely. Calculating the effect of a step from the current status and the changes made by the environment, usually involves complicated algorithmic procedures, which are derived from, and reflect, that semantics. In the case of statecharts, the execution mechanism has to be able to follow the dynamics of all the orthogonal components in all active statecharts,[4] taking into account chain reactions of events and state changes, and carrying out all the changes they prescribe, including any actions that are associated with states or transitions.

---

[4] As we shall see later, a typical system will have many statecharts active simultaneously, one for each live system component or object.

The simplest way to execute, or "run," the model using a computerized tool is in a step-by-step interactive fashion. At each step, the user emulates the system's environment, by generating events and changing values. The tool, in turn, responds by transforming the system into the new resulting status. If the model is represented visually, the change in status will be reflected visually too, say, by changes in color or emphasis in the diagrams.

In way of illustration, let us return for a moment to the watch example of Figure 14.1. One can conclude easily by observing the topological properties of the chart that the light's behavior is not applicable to the stopwatch states, since it is orthogonal to the *watch-and-alarm* state, and exclusive to *stopwatch*. However, this relationship between the light and *watch-and-alarm* has more subtle implications that cannot easily be seen without actually executing the model. In particular, suppose we are in the configuration ⟨*hour, light-off, beeping*⟩, meaning that we are updating the hour, the light is off, and the beeper is beeping because the alarm time has arrived. (This is like saying that we have the watch in our hands and we are actually "running" it, starting in the described situation.) Now we press button *b*. What happens? Well, whether we like it or not, three seemingly unrelated things will happen simultaneously. The beeping will stop (by virtue of the "*b* or *c*" transition to *quiet*), the light will turn on until *b* is released, and the updating will end, with the watch returning to *display-time*! When this sequence is run using a tool that executes statecharts these changes will show up in the statechart in an animated fashion, usually in a special coloring of the states the system is currently in and the recently traversed transitions.

By interactively executing scenarios that reflect the way we expect our system to behave we are able to verify that it will indeed do so, prior to final implementation. If we find that the system's response is not as expected, we can go back to the model, change it, and run the same scenario again. This is analogous to single-step, or batch debugging of conventional programs. During an execution, the user plays the role of all parts of the model that are external to the portion being executed, even if those parts will eventually be specified and thus become internal.

Once we have the basic ability to execute a step, our appetite grows. We might now want to see the model executing noninteractively. To check, for example, that a telephone call connects when it should, we may prepare the relevant sequence of events and signals in a batch file, set up the model to start in the initial status, and ask our tool to execute steps iteratively, reading in the changes from the file. The graphic feedback from such a batch execution becomes an (often quite appealing) animation of the diagrams. In fact, we need not restrict ourselves to running self-devised scenarios: we might want to see the model executing under circumstances that we do not care to specify in detail ourselves. We might like to see its performance under *random* conditions, and in both typical and less typical situations. We might want to incorporate **breakpoints** into the execution mechanism, causing it to suspend and the tool to take certain actions when particular situations come up. These actions can range from temporarily entering interactive mode for the purpose of monitoring careful step-by-step progress, to executing a piece of ready-made code that describes a low-level activity.

These abilities get to the heart of the need for executable models—to minimize the unpredictable in the development of complex reactive systems.

All of this can be taken a lot further, with model executions themselves being programmed, or *meta*-programmed, using external means. Thus, the executing tool can be set up to look out for predefined breakpoints and accumulate information regarding the system's progress as it takes place. As an example, we might want to know how many times, in a typical flight of the aircraft we are specifying, the radar loses a locked-on target. Since it might be difficult for the engineer to put together a typical flight scenario, we can tap the power of our tool by instructing it to run many typical scenarios, using the accumulated results to calculate average-case information. The tool would then follow typical scenarios by generating random numbers to select new events according to predefined probability distributions. The statistics are then gathered using appropriate breakpoints and simple calculations. The basic ideas behind these techniques are, of course, well known in program testing and debugging. However, the point here is to extend them to apply to high-level visual formalisms used to model complex reactive behavior, long before the costly stages of implementation and deployment of the final system.

Executing the model may uncover a bug, i.e., behavior that is different from what we intended. Obviously, if this happens, we would like to find out what caused the anomalous behavior. Why did something unexpected happen? Why didn't something else happen, even though we thought it should? What would have happened if some external event had occurred, or had occurred earlier or later? And so on. Many such questions refer to the behavior of the model before the point at which the bug was discovered. In order to be able to answer such questions, the tool needs to keep a history of its past actions, together with the reasons for them. In the absence of such information, we are reduced to rerunning the model from the start many times, pausing at various points in order to observe intermediate states and see where its behavior diverges from what we expect.[5]

The next step in this growing appetite for analysis capabilities of reactive behavior is, of course, verification, in the sense of Chapter 5. A typical property that we very often want to verify is **reachability**, which determines whether, when started in some given initial situation, the system can ever reach a situation in which some specified condition becomes true. This condition can be made to reflect undesired or desired situations. Moreover, we could imagine the test being set up to report on the first scenario it finds that leads to the specified condition, or to report on all possible ones, producing the details of the scenarios themselves. Are such tests realistic? Could we subject the model to a reachability test, for example, after which we will know for sure whether there is *any* possibility of it occurring, under any possible circumstances?

The answer is just like the one we gave when discussing verification in Chapter 5 and the limitations of computing in Chapters 7 and 8: in principle no, but in many practical situations yes. Indeed, recent years have seen a considerable amount of work dedicated toward taking program verification a major step further, leading to the possibility of verifying visual models for complex reactive behavior. We believe that automatic verification of critical properties in reactive systems will become

---

[5] The ability to answer "why," "why not," and "what if" questions is useful for any type of program, but particularly so for reactive systems, whose behavior over time is usually a lot more complicated than that of transformational systems or sequential programs.

commonplace, and that the methods and tools for behavioral modeling will become more and more powerful, offering means to routinely verify properties as the model gets developed.

Code Synthesis

As explained earlier, direct model execution is analogous to running programs using an interpreter. Many tools, however, generate automatically from the model code in some conventional language, like C++ or JAVA, and then execute that code. This is the analog of compilation. When you view the model in execution you can't really tell the difference.[6] One of the main uses of code generator output is in observing the system performing under circumstances that are close to those of the real world. For example, the code can be ported to, and executed in, the actual target environment, or, as is often the case in earlier stages, in a simulated version of the target environment. The code can thus be linked to a **graphical user interface (GUI)** of the system—an on-screen mock-up of the system's control boards, complete with images of displays, switches, levers, dials, and gauges—that represents the actual user interface of the final system. The GUI can then be manipulated with mouse and keyboard in a realistic way. An important point is that the simulated system's behavior is not driven by hastily-written code prepared especially for prototype purposes, but by code that was generated automatically from a model that will typically have been thoroughly tested and analyzed before being subjected to code generation. Moreover, when parts of the real target environment are available, they too can be linked to the code, and the runs become even more realistic.

Code generation from models of reactive behavior built with visual formalisms can thus be used for goals that go beyond the development team. Code-driven system GUIs can be used as part of the standard communication between customer and contractor or contractor and subcontractor. It is not unreasonable for such a running version of the system model to be a required deliverable in certain development stages.

A good code-generation facility will also have a debugging mechanism, with which the user can trace the executing parts of the code back up to the graphical model. Breakpoints can be inserted to stop the run when specified events occur, at which point the model's status can be examined, and elements can be modified on the fly prior to resuming the run. If substantial problems arise, changes can be made in the original model, which is then recompiled down into code and rerun. Trace files can be requested, recording crucial information for future inspection, and so on.

---

[6] The code generated from such models need not necessarily result in software; it could be code in a hardware description language, leading to hardware designs. Moreover, the code can be tailored for specific implementations, as is the case, for example, in real-time systems, where some tools are able to generate code optimized to run on particular real-time operating systems.

■ Two Styles of Behavior

How is the structure of a reactive system specified, and how is this specification combined with its behavior? There have been several methods proposed for this, and one of the more widespread is to base the entire modeling and development process on the object-oriented paradigm. This leads to so-called **object-oriented specification and analysis**. The main idea is to lift concepts up from the level of object-oriented programming, as described in Chapter 3, to the modeling level, and to use visual formalisms. For the system's structure, a diagrammatic language called **object model diagrams** is used to specify classes and their interrelationships. As to specifying behavior, most object-oriented modeling approaches base an object's behavior on a state machine, and many recommend that a statechart be constructed for each class, capturing the desired behavior of any instance thereof. When an instance of a class is created, a copy of the class statechart starts its operation, controlling the behavior of that instance.

The details of this connection between structure and behavior are a lot more complicated than can be conveyed here. Classes represent dynamically changing collections of concrete objects, and behavioral modeling must address issues related to object creation and destruction, message delegation, relationship modification and maintenance, event queuing, class aggregation, inheritance, multi-thread processing, and so on. The links between behavior and structure must be defined in sufficient detail and with enough rigor to support the construction of tools that enable the kinds of model execution and code generation discussed above.[7] Figure 14.2 illustrates these basic parts of system modeling.

Put in different words, behavior is specified in this setup in an object-by-object state-based fashion, by providing the reactivity of each object using, say, a statechart.

Figure 14.2

Modeling a reactive system.

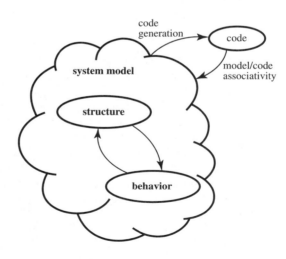

---

[7] When a tool generates code for such a model, each statechart is translated into code for the object in some object-oriented programming language, such as C++ or JAVA, and these pieces of code are appropriately inserted into a piece of skeleton code for the system's structure, most of which is generated from the object model diagram.

If it were a football game we were devising, this approach would require us to program each of the players in detail—and, for that matter, also the referees, the ball, the wooden frames of the goals, and so on—specifying the way they respond and react to each event or happening that comes their way. Once this is done we can "execute" the system, or simulate the game, since we have full information about each possible trigger/response pair available for each object.

So far, so good. However, when people think about reactive systems, they most often think naturally in terms of **scenarios** of behavior. You do not find too many people saying things like "Well, the recording mechanism of my VCR can be in idle mode, or in recording mode, or in mid-selection mode; in the first case, here are the possible inputs and the VCR's reactions, . . . ; in the second case, here is what happens, etc." Rather, you find them saying things like "If I press this button, and then turn this dial to point here, then the following shows up on the display," or less detailed things like, "Selecting the date and time, and then pressing Record, causes the VCR to do the following . . . " They also talk about **forbidden scenarios**, such as "As long as it is connected to the power outlet, the VCR will never switch off while the cassette spool is rotating." Many people find it a lot more natural to describe and discuss a reactive system's behavior by its scenarios rather than by the state-based reactivity of each of its components. This is particularly true of some of the early and later stages of the system development process—e.g., during requirements capture and analysis, and during testing and maintenance.

Thus, we have an interesting and subtle dichotomy here. One side has state-based behavioral descriptions, which remain within the object, and are based on providing a complete description of the reactivity of each one. A sort of **intra-object** approach: "all pieces of stories for each object." The other side has scenario-based behavioral descriptions, which cut across the boundaries of the objects of the system in order to provide understandable descriptions of scenarios of behavior (and forbidden behavior). A sort of **inter-object** approach: "each story given via all of its relevant objects." The latter is more intuitive and natural for humans to grasp and is therefore fitting in the requirement and testing stages, but the former approach seems to be the one needed for implementation. Indeed, it appears that implementing a system would require each of the objects to be supplied with the full description of the behavioral reactions it supports, so that it can be executed directly or subjected to a process that would generate code that implements that description.

Figure 14.3 is an attempt to illustrate these two approaches graphically. On the left we have each object filled with all of its little pieces of behavior—the global behavior of the entire system being derived from the grand combination of all these—and on the right we have each sequence of behavior moving through all of its relevant objects.

If we wanted to describe the "behavior" of a typical office, for example, it would be a lot more natural to describe the inter-object scenarios, such as how an employee mails off 50 copies of a document (this could involve the employee, the secretary, the copy machine, the mail room, etc.), the office activities that are not allowed to occur unless initiated by the top-level boss, or how information about vacation days and sick leave is organized and forwarded to the payroll office. Contrast this with the intra-object style, whereby we would have to provide complete information on the modes of operation and reactivity of the boss, the secretary, the employees, the copy machine, the mail room, etc.

Figure 14.3

Intra-object vs.
inter-object modeling
of reactivity.

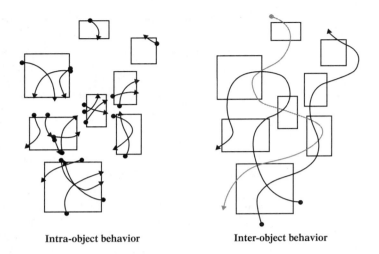

Intra-object behavior   Inter-object behavior

Thus, in contrast to scenarios, used typically to specify requirements in the early stages of the system's development, modeling with statecharts or directly with code is typically carried out at a later stage (usually design), and it results in a behavioral specification for each object instance (or task, or process), providing details of its behavior under all possible conditions and in all of the "stories." This object-by-object specification will later be tested against the scenarios and will evolve into the system's implementation, since at the end of the day the final system will consist of code (or hardware) driving the dynamic behavior of each object.

Underlying this process is the assumption—which we will soon challenge—that inter-object scenario-based behavior is not executable or implementable. Indeed, how would a system described by scenarios operate? What would it do in general dynamic circumstances? How do we know at each point which scenarios should kick in and start operation? How should we proactively make sure that things that have to happen indeed happen, things that may happen will sometimes happen, and things that may not happen will indeed not happen? How do we enforce all of this, and what do we do when we encounter underspecification (missing information), overspecification (nondeterminism), and contradictions (clashes between "must"s and "must-not"s)?

LSCs for Inter-Object Behavior

A visual formalism that has been used for many years to specify scenarios, originating in the telecommunications industry, is the language of **message sequence charts (MSCs)**. Scenarios are specified in MSCs as sequences of message interactions between object instances. MSCs are popular in the object-oriented world in the requirements phase, where engineers identify the **use-cases**—general patterns of high-level behavior—and then specify the scenarios that instantiate them. This captures the desired interrelationships amongst the object instances and between them and the external environment (e.g., the user).

Figure 14.4

A message sequence
chart.

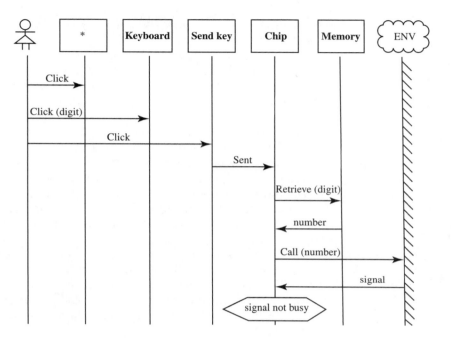

Object instances are represented in MSCs by vertical lines, and messages between these instances are represented by horizontal (or sometimes down-slanted) arrows. Conditional guards, depicted as elongated hexagons, specify statements that are to be true when reached. The overall effect of such a chart is to specify a scenario of behavior, consisting of messages flowing between objects and thing having to be true along the way. Figure 14.4 shows a simple example of an MSC for the quick-dial feature of a cellular telephone. The sequence of messages it depicts consists of the following: the user clicks the ∗ key, and then clicks a *digit* on the keyboard, followed by the *Send key*, which sends a *Sent* indication to the internal *Chip*, which, in turn, sends the digit to the *Memory* to retrieve the telephone number associated with the clicked digit. The chip then sends out that number to the environment (e.g., the cellular company's antenna) to carry out a *Call*, following which a signal is received from the environment. Finally, the chart contains a guarding condition that states that the signal is indeed not busy.

The semantics of MSCs is existential: a chart asserts that the scenario it describes represents a possible sequence of occurrences in the life of the system. The time-dependent meaning of the scenario itself is determined by two simple rules. First, along a vertical object line time progresses from top to bottom. Second, the event of a message being sent precedes the event of it being received.[8] Thus, MSCs do not really say much about what the system will actually do when run. They can be used to say what might possibly occur, but not what must occur. In the chart of Figure 14.4, for example, we may ask whether the *Memory* can "decide" not to send back a number in response to the request from the *Chip*? Does the condition

---

[8] There can also be **synchronous** messages, for which the two events are simultaneous.

that asserts that the signal is not busy really *have* to be true? What happens if it is not?

Such charts can indeed be used to capture sample scenarios of expected behavior, to be checked later against the final executable system. However, they are not enough if we want to use them to actually state and assert what the system does. We would like to be able to say what may happen and what must happen, and—as mentioned above—also what may *not* happen. Such forbidden behaviors are sometimes called **anti-scenarios**. If they occur during system execution there is something very wrong: either something in the behavioral specification was not properly asserted, or else the implementation does not correctly satisfy the specification. We would also like to be able to specify multiple scenarios that combine with each other, or even with themselves, in subtle ways. We want to be able to specify generic scenarios, i.e., ones that stand for many specific scenarios, in that they can be instantiated by different objects of the same class. We want variables and means for specifying timing constraints, and so on.

MSCs have been extended in several ways to help remedy some of these issues. One recent extension, called **live sequence charts**, or **LSCs**, takes its name from the ability to specify liveness, i.e., things that must occur. LSCs allow the distinction between possible and necessary behavior, both globally, on the level of an entire chart, and locally, when specifying events, guarding conditions, and progress over time within a chart.

Thus, there are two types of charts in the LSCs language: **universal** (annotated with a solid borderline) and **existential** (annotated with a dashed borderline). Universal charts are the more interesting ones, and are used to specify scenario-based behavior that applies to all possible system runs. A universal chart has two parts, turning it into a kind of if-then construct: a **prechart**, which specifies the scenario which, if satisfied, forces the system to also satisfy the second part, the **main chart**. A collection of universal LSCs thus provides a set of action/reaction pairs of scenarios, which must be satisfied at all times during any system run.[9]

Within an LSC, the live elements, termed **hot**, signify things that must occur, and the others, termed **cold**, signify things that may occur. Hot elements make it possible to enforce behavior (and anti-behavior too), and cold elements can be used to specify control structures like branching and iteration. Figure 14.5 shows a universal LSC that is actually an enriched version of the MSC in Figure 14.4. The first three events are in the prechart, and the rest are in the main chart. Hence, the LSC states that whenever the user clicks *, followed by a *digit*, followed by the *Send key*, the rest of the scenario must be satisfied. (In particular, if the three prechart events are not completed, e.g., the user fails to click the *Send key*, no harm is done and nothing is expected from the system.) The messages in the main chart are hot (depicted by solid arrows, in contrast to the dashed ones in the prechart), as are the vertical lines. Thus, progress along all lines in the main chart must occur, and the messages must be sent and received, in order for the chart to be satisfied. In addition, a loop has been added, within which the chip can make up to three attempts to receive a non-busy signal from the environment. The loop is controlled by the cold (dashed line) condition: as long as the signal is busy the three-round loop

---

[9] We will not discuss existential LSCs here, except to note that their main role is to be monitored during testing, making them similar to conventional MSCs.

Figure 14.5

An LSC.

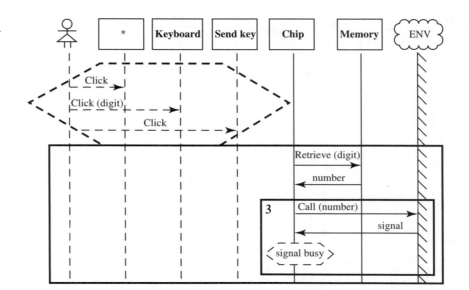

continues, but if it is not the loop is exited (which means that the entire chart has been satisfied).

In this example we exploited the semantics of a cold condition: if it is true when reached during a system run then fine, but even if it is false nothing bad happens and execution simply moves up one level, out of the innermost chart or subchart. In contrast, a hot condition *must* be true when reached. If it is false that is very bad indeed; in fact, it is an unforgivable error, or violation, and the system must abort. For example, one nice way to specify an anti-scenario using hot conditions (e.g., an elevator door opening when it shouldn't, or a missile firing when the radar is not locked on the target) is to include the entire unwanted scenario in the prechart, followed by a main chart that contains a single hot condition that is always false. (Why does this work?)

LSCs support many additional features, which will not be described in detail here. The language is actually powerful enough to specify most aspects of reactive behavior. Figure 14.6 is part of a full specification of a multi-telephone exchange, which we shall not explain any further. Among other things, it contains symbolic instances that refer to any phone or channel, binding conditions, if-then-else constructs, a hot condition, and more.

Figure 14.7 shows a simple use of time in an LSC, coupled with assignment statements and a cold condition. The prechart shows the Queen of Hearts instructing the White Rabbit to come to her place in five seconds, and then proceeding to look at her watch, noting the time. As a result, the White Rabbit meets Alice and tells her he is late (the message is cold, so he doesn't *have* to do this, but *can*). Alice hurries the White Rabbit up, and upon arriving at the Queen's place he dutifully reports his arrival. The Queen then checks to see whether more than five seconds have elapsed. If indeed this is the case, she issues an order to remove the White Rabbit's head; otherwise (i.e., if the cold condition is false) the scenario terminates peacefully, and the White Rabbit remains with his anatomy intact . . .

Figure 14.6

A more complex LSC.

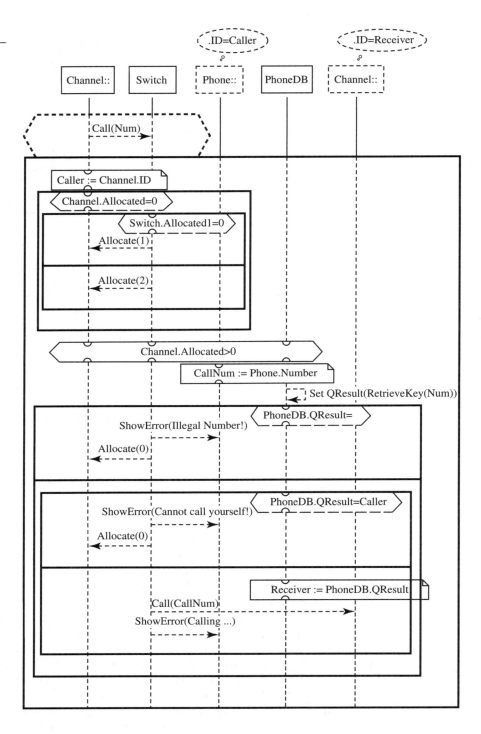

Figure 14.7

Alice in LSC-land.

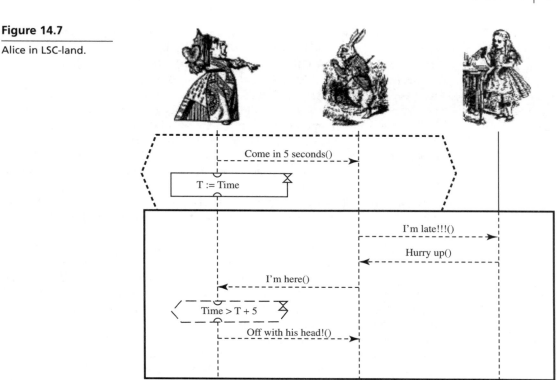

The Play-In/Play-Out Approach

A two-faceted methodology has been developed recently around LSCs, called **play-in/play-out**. It allows the user to specify scenario-based inter-object behavior conveniently, and to then execute it directly. Thus, it is really just a means for programming a system using LSCs and then running the program. The first technique involves a user-friendly means to "play in" behavior directly from the system's GUI (or some abstract version thereof, such as an object model diagram), during which LSCs are generated automatically. The second technique makes it possible to "play out" the behavior, that is, to execute the system as constrained by the grand sum of the scenario-based information, thus simulating the system's behavior exactly as if it were specified in the conventional state-based intra-object fashion. These techniques are supported by a tool called the *Play-Engine*.

The main idea of the play-in process is to raise the level of abstraction in behavioral specification, and to work with a lookalike version of the system under development not only in running the model but in preparing it too. This enables people who are unfamiliar with LSCs, or who do not want to work with such formal languages directly, to specify the behavioral requirements of systems using a high-level and intuitive mechanism. These could include domain experts, application engineers, requirements engineers, and even potential users.

What "play-in" means is that the system's developer first builds the GUI of the system, with no behavior built into it, but with a division into objects and their basic isolated capabilities. For example, a switch is given with its ability to be on or off, and a calculator display is specified as being able to show any sequence of up to, say, 10 characters. For GUI-less systems, or for sets of internal objects, we can simply use a structural representation, such as an object model diagram as a GUI. In any case, the user "plays" the GUI by clicking buttons, rotating knobs, and sending messages to objects, in an intuitive drag-and-drop manner. By similarly playing the GUI, often using the mouse to select among possibilities, the user describes the desired reactions of the system and the conditions that may or must hold. As this is being done, the corresponding LSCs are constructed automatically. The desired modalities of the chart being constructed and its elements (universal/existential, hot/cold) can be selected in the process.

In play-out, the user simply plays the GUI application as he or she would have done when executing a conventional intra-object state-based model, but limited to end-user and external environment actions.

The play-out process calls for the play-engine to monitor the applicable precharts of all universal charts, and if successfully completed to then execute their main charts, looking out for violations. The underlying mechanism can be likened to an over-obedient citizen who walks around holding the Grand Book of Rules at all times. Such people do nothing unless asked to, and never do anything if it violates some other rule. To achieve this, they constantly scan and monitor all rules at all times and upon executing any action (e.g., lifting a finger), they repeatedly carry out any required consequences thereof. Clearly, in so acting, there might be choices to be made, and inconsistencies in the rules could be discovered.

A stronger means for executing the LSCs, is to use a technique called **smart play-out**, in which powerful model-checking techniques from program verification are utilized to compute the best way for the system to respond to a user action, thus avoiding many of the pitfalls of naive execution. The details, however, will not be described here.

There are two ways to exploit the ability to execute LSCs. The first is to view LSCs as enriching a conventional system development cycle, and the second is to use them as the implementable behavioral specification itself, which could lead to a new kind of development cycle. In the first approach, executable scenario-based behavior offers improvements to some of the standard stages of system development: more convenient requirement capture, the ability to specify more powerful behavioral requirements, a means for executing rich use cases, tools for the dynamic testing of requirements prior to building the actual system model or the implementation, and a means for testing systems by dynamic and run-time comparison of two dual-view executables.

The second approach, however, is more radical. It calls for considering the possibility of an alternative way of designing the actual behavior of a system, which is scenario-based and inter-object in nature. This view proposes the idea that LSCs (or some other comparable inter-object language, such as **timing diagrams** or **temporal logic**) can actually constitute the implementation of a system. The play-out mechanism would then constitute a sort of "universal reactive system" that executes a collection of LSCs in an interpretive fashion, as if it were a conventional implementation. In this view, behavioral specification of a reactive system would not have to involve much intra-object modeling (e.g., by state machines or statecharts or code). This idea is still quite preliminary, but it appears to be promising, since scenario-based behavior is the way most people think about reactivity. Once it becomes possible to capture that thinking in a natural way and to execute it directly, we will have a means for specifying the implementable behavior of our systems that is well matched to the way we think of it. And this could make a difference in the quality, reliability, and expedition of complex system development.

Developing Real-Time Systems

Some reactive systems, called **real-time systems**, are characterized by the fact that time plays a crucial role in their behavior. It is not good enough that such a system react correctly to its stimuli, it must do so within stringent prespecified time limits. For example, an aircraft collision-avoidance system must issue a warning early enough to give the pilot time to carry out actions to avoid the collision, and an anti-braking system in an automobile must operate fast enough to prevent an accident. Similarly, an anti-missile system must identify the trajectory of the incoming missile in time to launch its own intercepting weapon.

Developing real-time systems is particularly difficult, since the actual time taken by each element of the system must be factored into the calculation of its reaction times. In particular, conventional operating systems are usually inappropriate for the deployment of real-time systems, since they don't provide the necessary time guarantees. Special **real-time operating systems** exist for this purpose; these typically offer more limited services than their general-purpose counterparts, but they guarantee strict response times.

Specifying the behavior of real-time systems is also particularly difficult, since besides the issues of reactivity and conventional computation, they have to adhere to the critical timing constraints. While many approaches to reactive system specification can deal with real-time aspects too, a recent proposal is tailored specifically for time-dependent reactivity. It is called MASS, an acronym for *marionettes activation scheme specification* language. The marionette metaphor suggests separating the activation mechanism from the actions of the puppets. In MASS, the nonreactive aspects of the system can be specified using any of a wealth of proposed formalisms for sequential programs or transformational systems. The reactive aspects, particularly the time-dependent ones, are captured by a set of **reactions**, each of which specifies the response of the system to some event, with a possible time limit. For example, the reaction

$$[\text{Switch} > \text{On} \rightarrow \text{Activate-furnace}] < 2\text{sec}$$

means that within two seconds from the time the switch was turned on, the task Activate-furnace must be finished. The details of what exactly is involved in this task are specified separately, since it does not interact with any other activities in the system.

Reactions can also have aborting events; for example, the reaction

[Train-out → Gate(Open)] : Train-in < 15sec

specifies that the gate must finish opening no more than 15 seconds from when the train moved out of the railroad crossing; however, if another train enters the crossing before that task finishes, it is aborted. Another reaction, such as

[Train-in → Gate(Close)] < 10sec

specifies that the gate should finish closing within 10 seconds of the Train-in event. Here, the first reaction must be aborted, otherwise there will be conflicting requirements.

In this example too, the details of how the gate opens and closes can be specified by other means and can be implemented in any programming language for which timing constraints can be derived; in practice, this limits the selection to assembly languages, or low-level languages like C. Thus, MASS allows the designer of a real-time system to concentrate on the real-time activation aspects of the system without having to worry about the specifics of the activated tasks at the same time.

Research on Reactive Systems

Most of the topics mentioned in the research section of the previous chapter apply to large computerized systems of all kinds, the special case of reactive systems being no exception. The same applies to the research topics of correctness and verification from Chapter 5. If anything, many issues become more acute when systems are reactive, and especially when they also have stringent real-time constraints.

In addition, there is a lot of research being carried out on visual formalisms, their convenience and power of expression, and their implementation and analysis. One notable effort is the **unified modeling language**, the **UML**, which purports to collect under a single roof many interrelated diagrammatic notations for system development (not necessarily reactive systems). The behavioral heart of the UML is an object-oriented version of statecharts. MSCs are also part of the UML, and are used for specifying requirements and test sequences, under the name of **sequence diagrams**. The UML is an official standard for system development, coordinated and issued by the Object Management Group. It represents an ongoing effort, with periodic calls going out for proposals and extensions, and with new versions of the standard being issued from time to time.

The UML team has made extensive attempts to define and write down the meanings of the various languages that constitute it, and their interconnections, but these efforts are informal and often incomplete. Another concern some people have with the UML is its vast scope, involving many different languages used for many different purposes. In particular, the UML provides several different languages for specifying reactive behavior, and these can easily be used to inadvertently specify things more than once in different ways. This raises subtle issues of consistency that have not yet been adequately dealt with. Since the UML is an accepted standard, and will probably only grow in usage, semanticists are busy at work trying to define some of the more central parts of the UML in a rigorous fashion, rendering it amenable to computerized analysis, and to figure out ways of ensuring consistency of UML models.

Verification of reactive systems is a topic of extensive work, and some verification techniques have been adapted to work for visual reactive models, and are being incorporated into industry-scale development tools. In all probability, this trend will continue, and the foreseeable future should bring with it the ability to automatically verify certain critical properties of complex systems.

The relationship between inter-object and intra-object behavior, and the emergence of languages such as LSCs, raise many issues related to the difference between requirements on behavior and conventional implementable behavior. While verification concerns checking that the former is true of the latter, a different topic of research concerns synthesizing the latter *from* the former. See Figure 14.8, which shows the system model from Figure 14.2 on the right, as it relates to the requirements on the left. The relationships are (1) making sure that the latter holds for the former (by testing and verification) and (2) constructing the former from the latter (by methodologies and synthesis). For example, it would be nice if we could provide an efficient algorithm for synthesizing compact statecharts from LSCs. Unfortunately, the worst-case complexity of most versions of the synthesis problem for finite-state systems is very bad—at least exponential time. The good news, however, is that although the same is true for the verification problem for such systems, it has not prevented the development of extremely useful verification tools. In any case, synthesis is a topic of much research too.

Figure 14.9 is a modification of Figure 14.2, intended to illustrate the possibility of using played inter-object behavior as the actual implementation of a reactive system. This idea requires much further research too, such as: developing methodologies for doing so and heuristics for figuring out what kinds of systems would be most amenable to the approach; developing criteria and guidelines for establishing the completeness of such a specification; and developing algorithms for determining the internal consistency of a scenario-based specification and the equivalence of such a specification to a conventional one. In addition, smart play-out seems to be

Figure 14.8

The system model
vis-à-vis the
requirements.

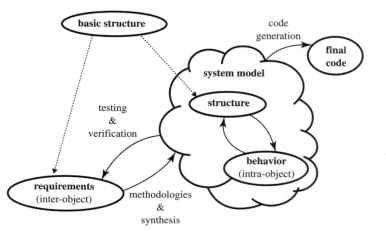

Figure 14.9

Basing system development on played inter-object behavior.

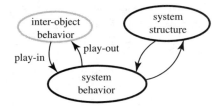

an interesting line of future work, whereby verification techniques are used not to prove something about a model or a program, but to actually help *run* it, in ways that avoid violations and pitfalls, thus contributing to a "correct" execution thereof. It seems that these and other related topics will occupy researchers in this area for quite a while.

Finally, a tantalizing new area of research involves using techniques, languages, and tools for reactive system development in order to model nature. It appears that many kinds of biological systems exhibit reactivity to a great degree and on many levels of detail, including the molecular and cellular level, as well as the level of an entire organism. The past few years have seen a surge of work in this area, and it is possible that we will start seeing intricate models of complex biological systems built using techniques that come out of computer science. Such models will be used not only to aid biologists in visualizing and comprehending biological systems in animated behavior, but also to uncover gaps or errors in biological knowledge, and even to contribute to actual discoveries by making predictions that will drive lab experiments.

■ Exercises

14.1. Why does the naive approach for combining states to deal with concurrency in reactive systems yield an exponential blow-up in the number of states?

14.2. Consider Figure 14.1 and the accompanying text. Explain where the numbers 12 and 29 that are mentioned in the text come from.

14.3. Construct statecharts for a simple VCR and a simple ATM.

14.4. Construct LSCs for a simple VCR and a simple ATM.

I will give thee thanks, for thou hast answered me

PSALMS 118: 21

Algorithmics and Intelligence

or, Are They Better at It Than Us?

The question of whether computers can think, someone once said, is just like the question of whether submarines can swim. The analogy is quite apt. Although we all know more or less what submarines are capable of—and indeed they *can* do things that are akin to swimming—"real" swimming is something we associate with entities of organic nature, such as humans and fishes, not with submarines. Similarly, although by now the reader must have a pretty good idea of what algorithmics is all about, and hence of the capabilities of computers, real thinking is associated in our minds with human beings, and perhaps also with apes and dolphins, but not with silicon-based collections of bits and bytes.

This somewhat less technical chapter is concerned with the relationship between machine-based computation and human intelligence. The issue is an emotionally loaded one, and almost anything anyone says about it causes heated controversy. For our own part, we shall try to avoid these controversies as best as we can. Instead, we shall discuss the relevance or irrelevance of the field of algorithmics as described in this book to the computer-based simulation of human intelligence. Mostly problems and difficulties rather than solutions will be pointed out.

The area of research most relevant to this chapter is **artificial intelligence**, or **AI** for short. In most places, AI is carried out in computer science departments, while in others there is either a separate department for AI or an interdepartmental group connected, perhaps, to computer science, cognitive psychology, and neurobiology. In many universities nowadays, all these disciplines have been amalgamated into **brain science** or **cognitive science** centers. The fact that this is the closing chapter should not lead the reader to conclude that the sole reason for studying algorithmics is rooted in the possibility that one day we shall be able to computerize intelligence. However intriguing this idea may sound, the task of writing this book has not been undertaken in order to report on the scientific basis for artificial intelligence. Algorithmics stands on its own merit, and a strong case for its importance, depth, and applicability can easily be made, whether the subject matter of this chapter is considered or not. Here we deal with a new, "softer" dimension. It is a fascinating and exciting one, but it is also controversial and speculative. Mainly, as we shall see, it is quite different.

In purely technical terms, it might be said that the present chapter focuses on another liberty that can be taken when designing algorithms, to be added to those of parallelism and coin tossing that were treated in Chapters 10 and 11. This liberty involves the introduction of rules of thumb, educated guesses of sorts, or, to use the accepted term, **heuristics**. The nature of this new facility and its motivating examples set it apart from virtually all of the issues discussed heretofore, and this is the reason for its being treated last. While heuristics represent the special nature of the *control* part of intelligent programs, there are also difficulties involved in representing and manipulating the *data* relevant to them, namely, **knowledge** in its various guises.

Some Robot Stories

Talking of swimming, here is what happened in the 1970s, when in some circles there was a lot of naive excitement around the possibility of building truly intelligent robots, in one of the most respectable centers of American computer science. A delegation from the U.S. Navy visited the center to find out whether they could use the knowledge accumulated there to build a robot that, all on its own, would be able to dive underneath ships and carry out submerged maintenance chores. The scientists proudly showed these people the results of their latest efforts in robotics—a computerized robot arm connected to a video camera, which could read in, comprehend, and execute commands such as "build a tower of three blocks," or "place the red pyramid on the blue block." Out of courtesy, the members of the delegation listened, observed, and then politely took their leave, deeply disappointed. These people had no idea of the incredible difficulty involved in achieving even such mundane behavior in an automatic computerized system. At one stage in the development of its controlling software, the robot arm would try to build three-block towers starting at the top! It was no small matter to "teach" the robot about gravity, even within its very limited world of a few blocks and pyramids.

Another story involving the same group of researchers tells of a commercial company that claimed to have manufactured a robot that would carry out routine housekeeping tasks in response to commands given in plain English, such as "wash the dishes," or "make lunch for four." The company was to demonstrate the robot's abilities in public at one of the local department stores. The scientists of the group, knowing fully well what could be achieved with the current state of the art, were certain that this was a fraud. Thus, while the many spectators who had gathered to behold the miracle were busy up front taking in the scene, they were busy behind the scene trying to discover the trick. Surely enough, after a while they found the person who was using a radio transmitter to physically control the robot's movements, giving the impression that it was responding to the instructor's commands.

These stories seem to contradict the statement made in Chapter 1, to the effect that computers can control extremely sophisticated industrial robots that construct complex items consisting of numerous components. There is no contradiction. Those robots are programmed to carry out long and intricate sequences of operations by a carefully prepared recipe. In general, they can be reprogrammed to carry out different tasks, and sometimes they are able to adapt their behavior somewhat to accommodate changing situations. However, they are not able to take a look at their surroundings, decide what has to be done, and then make a plan and execute it to completion. For this reason no one knows how to program a robot to build a bird's nest from a pile of twigs. There have been some successes in dealing with very limited worlds of blocks and pyramids, but not with twigs of all shapes and sizes, or with a large and diverse array of machine components. Dealing with these requires levels of intelligence that are far beyond present-day capabilities. Even the ability to take in a simple scene such as a normal living room (using some visual sensory equipment) and "understand" it, something every child can do, is far beyond current possibilities.

Another example given in Chapter 1 concerned the contrast between computerized tomography (synthesizing a cross-section of the brain from a large number of X-ray images taken from increasing angles) and the ability to deduce a person's age from an ordinary photograph. Here, too, there is no contradiction. While the former task is carried out with the aid of complex, but well-defined, algorithmic procedures, the second requires real intelligence. Computerizing intelligence, making it algorithmic, is something about which we know far too little.

Algorithmic Intelligence?

What *is* intelligence? There is nothing to be gained by competing with philosophers, cognitive psychologists, and AI researchers regarding this question. However, from a layman's point of view it would appear that the very notion of artificial intelligence, or, to rename it to fit in with the rest of the book, **algorithmic intelligence**, is a contradiction in terms. We tend to view intelligence as our quintessential *non*programmable, and hence nonalgorithmic, feature. To many people the very idea of an intelligent machine does not sound right.

Various arguments have been put forward to render unthinkable the concept of an intelligent thinking machine. To think, some say, necessarily involves emotions and feelings, and no computer can hate, love, or become angry. Others claim that thinking intelligently necessarily entails originality, and no computer can originate anything unless programmed ahead of time to do so, in which case it is no longer original. In this view, a computer can never be called "intelligent." On the other hand, many people believe that the human brain is itself just a machine, albeit a complex one. Thus, according to the Church/Turing thesis (see Chapter 9), an electronic computer can in principle simulate the human mind, and can act as though it were intelligent. This is called the **weak AI** claim. Going a step further, proponents of the **strong AI** claim hold that such a computer would truly be conscious.

We shall have more to say about this debate below. It does appear, however, that a machine claimed to be intelligent must, at the very least, be able to exhibit human-like intellectual behavior. For this we do not require it to walk, see, or talk like a human, only to reason and respond like one. Furthermore, whatever the agreed-on criteria for intelligence turn out to be, *someone* ought to be able to check whether a candidate machine fulfills them. And who, if not a real, intelligent human being, is qualified to carry out such a test? This brings us to the idea that a machine ought to be labeled intelligent if it can convince an average human being that in terms of its intellect it is no different from another average human being.

The Turing Test

How can we set up things to make such a test possible? In 1950 Alan Turing[1] proposed the following method, now commonly called the **Turing test**. The test takes place in three rooms. In the first there is a human interrogator, call her Alice, in the next there is another human, and in the third the candidate computer. The interrogator Alice knows the other two only by the names Bob and Carol, but does not know which is the human and which is the computer. The three rooms are equipped with computer terminals, and Alice's terminal is connected to those of Bob and Carol (see Figure 15.1). Now, Alice is given, say, an hour in which to determine the correct identities of Bob and Carol. Alice is free to address any questions or statements whatsoever to either of them, and the computer has to make its best effort to deceive Alice, giving the impression of being human. The computer is said to pass the test if Alice does not know which of Bob or Carol is really the computer after the allotted time has elapsed. (Actually, we require the computer to pass a *number* of one-session tests, with different interrogators, in order to minimize the possibility that Alice simply guesses which is which.)

Figure 15.1

The Turing test (*A*, *B*, and *C* are Alice, Bob, and Carol).

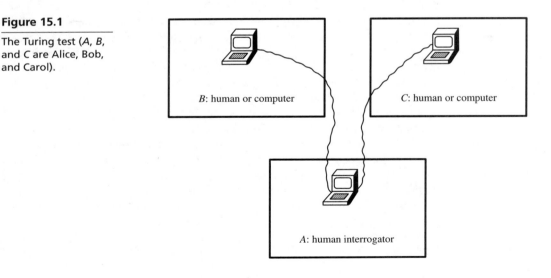

B: human or computer

C: human or computer

A: human interrogator

---

[1] This is the same Turing from the thesis and the machines.

Let us try to get a feel for the immense difficulty involved. Consider how an intelligent program would have to react to the following questions by Alice:

1. Are you a computer?
2. What is the time?
3. When was President Kennedy assassinated?
4. What is $2\,276\,448 \times 7\,896$?
5. Can White win in one move from the following chess position: . . .?
6. Describe your parents.
7. How does the following poem strike you: . . .?
8. What do you think of Charles Dickens?
9. What is your opinion on space exploration programs, in view of the fact that millions of people around the globe suffer from starvation?

Notice that the programmed computer must be able to converse freely in a natural language such as English. We waive the need for it to hear and talk, and hence the electronic links. However, understanding and synthesizing language are considered to be two of the cornerstones of human intelligence, and thus they are required prerequisites here.

The first two questions are rather easy. The answer to the first should be "no," and for the second the program can utilize a built-in clock that is present in most computers. Question (3) requires the program to be able to access a very large pool of knowledge, comparable to the knowledge of a human being. Question (4) looks easy—computers seem to do best on such questions—but it is nevertheless subtle, since the computer must wait for a while before answering; an immediate answer would give away its identity. Question (5), of course, requires it to have some knowledge of chess, including the ability to reason about a new position. Although answers to the likes of question (6) could be prepared in advance, Alice might respond to an answer by pursuing a certain unexpected detail to which the computer might not have a ready-made answer. Questions (7), (8), and (9) are far more difficult, as they illustrate the need for exhibiting preferences, opinions, positions, and emotions, explaining them and relating them to others. In short, the competing computer must be endowed with a real personality.

One of the difficulties in programming a computer to pass the Turing test is the great diversity of areas that the conversation can lead to. There have been some apparent successes in imitating human conversation in very limited areas of discourse. A program called ELIZA, written in 1966, was able to give an impressive performance as a psychoanalyst. So impressive, in fact, that people were known to actually "confide" in the program in ways they would never confide in a human being! Here are a couple of typical exchanges:

Person: My wife says I am often depressed.
ELIZA: I'm sorry to hear you are depressed.
Person: The truth is I am quite unhappy.
ELIZA: Do you think coming here will help you not to be unhappy?
Person: Well, perhaps by talking to you I will find out why I hate my brother.
ELIZA: Tell me more about your family.

The interesting thing about ELIZA is the fact that it cannot be said to be intelligent by any reasonable measure. In fact, despite its apparent sophistication, ELIZA is really quite dumb, so that insofar as it gives the impression of being a thoughtful therapist, it is really a shrewd cheat. At times, it simply zeros in on a particular word or phrase that it has been taught to look out for, and responds by choosing, virtually at random, one of a small number of fixed responses. An excellent example of this is the response "Tell me more about your family," triggered by the word "brother." Other times, ELIZA merely turns an incoming sentence into a question or a somewhat content-free statement, as in the exchange concerning the person's unhappiness. To do this, it utilizes a simple mechanism for figuring out the coarse structure of the input sentences.

Strange things happen on really trying to test ELIZA's intelligence, instead of just pouring out one's problems. In fact, if we said "I was a sister in a monastery in Burma," or even "I admire Sister Teresa," the program might very well respond with the same irrelevant response: "Tell me more about your family." Its response to the question about space exploration programs is bound to be equally amusing. ELIZA, of course, has no chance of passing the Turing test. In fact, it was not intended to. The motivation behind ELIZA was to show that it is easy to *appear* intelligent, at least for a short while, to a sympathetic observer, and within a narrow domain of discourse. To be *really* intelligent, however, is quite a different matter.

To further appreciate the difference between the genuine intelligence required to pass Turing's test, and the shallow, yet deviously deceptive nature of ELIZA's conversational abilities, here is a hypothetical exchange between the Turing test interrogator Alice and a really intelligent candidate, say Bob:

Alice: What is a zupchok?

Bob: I have no idea.

Alice: A zupchok is a flying, novel-writing whale. It has been carefully cultivated in a laboratory over several generations to ensure that its fins evolve into wing-like things that enable it to fly. It has also been gradually taught to read and write. It has a thorough knowledge of modern literature, and has the ability to write publishable mystery stories.

Bob: How weird!

Alice: Do you think zupchoks exist?

Bob: No way. They cannot.

Alice: Why?

Bob: For many reasons. First of all, our genetic engineering capabilities are far from adequate when it comes to turning fins into wings, not to mention our inability to cause 10-ton engineless creatures to defy gravity just by flapping those things. Secondly, the novel-writing part does not even deserve responding to, since writing a good story requires much more than the technical ability to read and write. The whole idea seems ridiculous enough. Don't you have anything more interesting to talk about?

To carry out this conversation, Bob, be it the human or the computer, must display very sophisticated abilities. It must possess a large amount of *knowledge* on specific topics, such as whales, flying, novel writing, and gravity. It must be able to *learn* about a totally new concept, taking in the definitions and relating them to what it already knows. Finally, it must be able to *deduce* things from all of this, such as the fact that genetic engineering is more relevant to zupchoks than, say, mathematics, or Chinese philosophy. (In this particular case it must also have a sense of humor.)

Strong AI and the Chinese Room

Suppose a computer program is created, which can pass the Turing test. According to the strong AI claim, this program would be considered to be intelligent and conscious. A famous thought experiment, called the **Chinese room argument**, tries to refute this kind of claim. Here is how it goes. Consider a modified version of the program, which converses in Chinese rather than in English. It is essentially a set of precise instructions to the computer, and can be translated into a series of similar instructions rendered in English, for a human to follow. (This would be long and tedious, but still possible in principle, and the Chinese input/output parts of it might contain "dumb" things like "if you are looking at this Chinese character and square number 159 in your notebook contains 1, write 0 in square 243 and move to the next character to the right.") Suppose now that a book containing the complete set of English instructions is given to a person, who understands and speaks English but not Chinese, and who is then locked in a room with a slot for communication with the outside world. Questions, written in Chinese, are inserted through the slot, and the person locked in the room follows the instructions in the book in order to produce an answer, again in Chinese. Since the person is following the original computer program, his or her responses must be considered to be intelligent according to the Turing test. However, clearly the occupant of the so-called Chinese room has no understanding of the content of the communications but is merely following the instructions in his book. Thus, the Chinese room and its occupant cannot be described as conscious, or even intelligent, and therefore neither can the original program!

Many articles and books have been written to support one or the other side of this debate, but we shall not discuss them any further here. While the philosophers debate and argue, AI researchers are still trying to develop truly intelligent programs. Still, it should be noted that a program that is able to pass the Turing test will not put an end to the issue; rather, it will probably only serve to intensify it. If such a program insisted that it was conscious, would you believe it? For that matter, you could ask the same question of human beings too: are we truly intelligent, or are we just simulating intelligence by virtue of the programming of our brains?

Playing Games

Turing's test seems to provide a nice sufficient condition for a computer to possess full human-like intelligence. However, most AI researchers have not set themselves the goal of writing programs that can pass the Turing test, since it involves much that is not directly related to pure intelligence. For example, in order to pass the Turing test, the computer would have to be programmed to hide its own super-human proficiencies, as seen in question (4) above. This is similar to what has happened in other fields. For example, for many years people have tried to achieve "artificial flight" by trying to imitate birds. Success has been achieved by turning to completely different methods, and we attribute to modern airplanes the ability to fly, even though they will not fool anyone for a minute into thinking they are birds.

Modern AI research can be roughly divided into analysis and synthesis. The goal of the first is to understand the nature of intelligence; often, this involves the study of how humans learn, reason, deduce, and make plans, and duplicating these abilities in computer programs. This line of research therefore has a lot in common with fields such as psychology and neurobiology, in addition to mathematics and algorithmics. The second approach aims to build "smart" computer programs that can perform useful tasks. How similar these are to human intelligence is less important.

Initial work in the 1950s and 1960s was aimed at building general methods for solving a variety of particular problems. This has been found to be much more difficult than originally thought, and later work turned to more narrow fields in order to leverage specialized knowledge associated with specific topics. Game playing is one of the specialized areas in which AI research has achieved significant results. It seems proper to start the discussion with a short news bulletin.

- In 1979, a computer program beat the world champion in backgammon. (This did not make the program the new champion, as the game was not played in an official tournament, but the win was a win nevertheless.) We must realize that a backgammon match involves many single games, so that the luck factor, introduced by the tossing of dice, is minimized and the quality of play dominates.
- In 1994, the world champion checkers player, Marion Tinsley, resigned the title to the computer program Chinook. This program won the Man–Machine Checkers Championship, which takes place between the best human player and the best program player. (This special title was created so that it would be possible to have both a human world champion and a computer world champion.)
- In 1997, the world champion chess player, Gary Kasparov, lost to the computer Deep Blue by 3.5 to 2.5 in six games. This match followed a 4–2 win by Kasparov in 1996. In early 2003, Kasparov rallied round and tied 3–3 with Deep Junior, the program that took the World Computer Chess Championship title in 2002.

While programs can now play superb games of backgammon, checkers, and chess, they are still not perfect. There are other games, such as Go, at which computers don't perform that well at all. Why can't programs always play a *perfect* game? Why can't a computer run through all possible moves and always make the best one? The answer lies in **game trees**, which were mentioned in Chapter 2 (see Figure 15.2). In tic-tac-toe (noughts and crosses), for example, there is no difficulty. The first player has nine possible moves, to which his opponent can respond in one of eight ways, to which the first can respond in one of seven, etc. The game tree thus consists of a root with nine offspring, each of which has eight offspring, and so on. Some nodes in this tree are **terminal**, meaning that they represent either a win for one of the players or a full board with no win. In any event, any sequence of nine moves leads to a terminal node. The tree is thus of maximum depth 9, with maximum outdegree

Figure 15.2

A game tree.

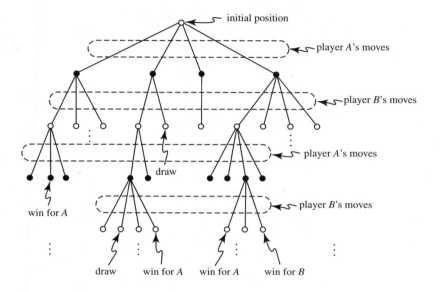

of 9 at the root. Altogether, there are no more than 9!, or 362,880, possibilities to check; hence a program can easily be written to efficiently play perfect tic-tac-toe.

With chess, on the other hand, the story is quite different. White has 20 possible first moves, and the average number of possible next moves from an arbitrary chess position is around 35. Thus the tree's outdegree is about 35 on average. The depth of the tree is the number of moves (twice the number of rounds of the game), which can easily reach 80 or 100. This means that the number of possibilities to check in a typical game might be 35^{100}. In Chapter 7 we saw some such numbers, and we recall that 35^{100} is many, many orders of magnitude larger than the number of protons in the universe, or the number of nanoseconds since the Big Bang. Consequently, even if we ignore the bookkeeping and memory involved in a brute-force trip through all possible moves, and assume that each of them can be tested in one nanosecond, no program will ever play perfect chess. The numbers for checkers are not quite as large, but perfect checkers is also out of the question. The numbers for Go are even higher than for chess; for example, the number of possible moves in each position is typically around 200 rather than 35, and the game goes on for about 300 moves!

How, then, do good chess programs operate? Well, they indeed carry out massive searches through large parts of the game tree, but they also use heuristics, or rules of thumb. In the context of games, heuristics are used to help decide which parts of the game tree will be considered in an attempt to choose a good move. A typical heuristic search uses intuitive rules, incorporated into the program by the programmer, to ignore certain parts of the game tree. For example, it might be decided that, if in the last five moves nothing has changed within the four-square vicinity of a certain pawn, that pawn will not be moved, and hence the search can ignore all parts of the tree that are located beneath the corresponding node. Such a rule might turn out to be very insightful—it definitely results in smaller trees to be considered—but, of course, it could cost the game; Gary Kasparov might have advanced that very pawn to win in three moves. This is a very simple-minded example, and the heuristics embodied in real chess-playing programs are usually far more sophisticated. However, they are heuristics nevertheless, and using them raises the possibility that we might miss the best move.

More About Heuristics

A nice way to explain the nature of heuristic search is to consider a person who has lost a contact lens. One possibility is to carry out a **blind search**, by bending over and feeling around for the lens at random. Another possibility is a **systematic search**, which involves continuously extending the area searched, in a methodical and organized manner (say, in ever-larger circles around a central point). This search is bound to succeed eventually, but might be very time consuming. A third possibility is an **analytic search**, whereby the precise mathematical equations governing the fall of the lens are calculated, taking into account wind, gravity, air friction, and the precise topography, tension, and texture of the surface. This too, if done correctly, is guaranteed to succeed, but for obvious reasons it is impractical.

In contrast to these methods, most of us would approach the problem using a **heuristic search**. First, we would identify the approximate direction of the fall and make an educated guess as to the distance the lens could have made by falling, and then we would limit the search to the resulting area. Here, of course, the search might not be successful, but there seems to be a reasonably good chance that it will. (There is, of course, a fifth approach, the **lazy search**, which calls for searching for the closest optician and having a new lens made . . .)

The main disadvantage of heuristics is in the fact that they do not guarantee success. It is always possible that a rule of thumb will fail for a particular case. As far as advantages go, besides having the potential to drastically reduce running time, heuristics are usually amenable to improvements or replacement as we become more acquainted with the problem at hand and the ways human beings tackle it. In the context of algorithmics, however, the most important characteristic of a heuristic is the fact that its performance is not subject to analysis. We can decide upon a chess heuristic, incorporate it into our chess-playing program, and from then on we will be able to assess its performance only by observation. It might play 100 excellent games before we discover that it has a serious weakness which, once known to an opponent, worsens its game dramatically.

In a sense, employing heuristics is a little like tossing coins, in that we do not necessarily cover all possibilities and might miss out on a good solution as a consequence. In Chapter 11 we saw how things can be improved by following the whims of random coin tosses. In other words, the search space of all possibilities was reduced, and some directions were left unexplored. Thus, we were willing to label a number "prime" although we had not checked all possible witnesses to its nonprimality. There too, success is not guaranteed; hence it is tempting to view coin tossing as a *blind* heuristic, a sort of intuitionless rule of thumb. There is a major difference, however. In the realm of probabilistic algorithms, analysis replaces intuition. By employing carefully defined sets of ignorable possibilities, and using randomization to decide which to actually ignore, we are able to analyze the probability of success rigorously, making precise statements about the algorithm's performance. With heuristics we typically cannot.

Although the probabilistic primality-testing algorithm (and for that matter almost any algorithm, even a simple sorting routine) definitely *looks* intelligent—indeed, it does its thing much better than the average human being—we do not think of it as being truly intelligent. While its construction might have required intuitive ingenuity on the part of the designer, its performance is not based on intuition, and can be analytically accounted for. A chess-playing program, on the other hand, might be considered intelligent, as it uses nonprobabilistic rules of thumb, the results of which we cannot predict or analyze. This, then, is one possibility for interpreting our feeling that real intelligence is nonprogrammable; just replace nonprogrammable by nonanalyzable. AI is typified by programs that are based on rules that *appear* to be helpful, but whose helpfulness has not been rigorously analyzed.

This crude attempt to define AI by some property of the resulting programs is not quite fair. Most people would prefer to define it by subject matter. Moreover, certain directions in AI research have lately become quite precise and analytic. In many cases the heuristics employed are more than just educated guesses; they are actually based on well-defined mathematical models and formulas. In computerized vision, for example, the heuristics used in detecting motion and in comprehending stereoscopic pairs of pictures are based on complicated mathematics, and strongly supported conjectures are made about the way the resulting programs behave on random inputs. The same can be said about motion planning in robotics. In such cases, the heuristic algorithms are closer to the approximation algorithms of Chapter 7 than to probabilistic ones, since the heuristics used are usually conjectured either to guarantee a good solution on average or to produce a bad one extremely rarely. We can thus call the resulting algorithms **conjectured** approximation algorithms—the only thing missing is a proof of the conjectured property. Obviously, once a proof is found we would not expect the discipline of AI to give up the algorithm just because its behavior has been precisely analyzed.

■ ■

Evaluating and Searching

The account given of heuristics in computerized chess was also overly simplistic. In actuality there is much more going on than a few simple rules that cause the program to ignore parts of the game tree. For example, there has to be a way to evaluate the quality of positions in the tree. As a simple example, consider a node for which it has been decided to ignore all but two of White's possible next moves. Assume that the first of these can lead eventually to 10 terminal nodes, three of which represent a win for White, one a win for Black, and six draws, and in the other the numbers are not 10, 3, 1, and 6, but, say, 8, 4, 3, and 1. How should the program (that plays White) compare these situations in order to choose the next move? The problem becomes much more acute when even in the directions that are considered we want to stop searching at a certain depth. In such a case, the most distant positions reached in the search do not give rise to definite win/lose/draw information; we only have the information that is implicit in the board configuration itself. In such a case, the evaluation function is far less obvious.

The problem of evaluating situations and assigning them numerical values to help in reaching a decision is one of the main challenges of heuristic programming, and it is not restricted only to game playing. Consider a program for carrying out medical diagnosis. Here too, there is a tree, the nodes of which represent combinations of symptomatic problems and queries to the patient, with the terminal nodes representing final diagnoses. Here too, the tree is enormous; furthermore, some nodes correspond to various kinds of medical tests, which carry their own risks. Thus, a heuristic search must take place, with the patient's observable symptoms and his answers to queries prescribing the directions that will be pursued and the tests that will be performed. The evaluation problem here, which determines how relevant a particular set of possibilities is to the sought-after final diagnosis, is just as difficult.

Whether in chess, in medicine, or elsewhere, once an evaluation function for the search tree has been defined, there still remains the problem of exploiting the values of nodes in the tree to efficiently search through its relevant parts. Here, work in AI has resulted in a number of powerful search methods that have many applications in nonheuristic algorithmics too. Many of these are based on a fundamental search strategy called the **minimax** method, which is best explained in the framework of game trees.

Figure 15.3(a) shows part of a game tree for a two-person game, like tic-tac-toe or chess, together with previously established values for each terminal node. (The terminal nodes in the figure are either real end positions of the game or intermediate positions, beyond which we have decided not to search.) The root represents a board position with player Alice to go, and the values represent the strength of the positions from Alice's point of view. Thus, 999 represents a win for Alice and 0 a win for Bob. Intermediate values reflect the relative chances of Alice winning from the corresponding positions, as prescribed by some heuristic evaluation function. One possible move must be chosen for Alice that will maximize her ability to win.

The basic idea is to repeatedly propagate values upwards in the tree, starting at the bottom. If the current parent node represents an Alice-move then the *maximum* of the values of the offspring nodes is attached to the parent, and if it represents a Bob-move then the *minimum* value is taken. The rationale for this is clear: Bob is assumed to play in a reasonable manner, and hence will make every effort to *maximize* his own chances of winning, which is to say that he will try to *minimize* Alice's chances of doing so. In other words, Alice should make the best move (that is, the one with maximal value) under the assumption that, following it, Bob will make *his* best move (i.e., the one with minimum value of Alice's function), following which Alice will make her best next move, and so on. Figure 15.3(b) shows the tree with these min and max values inserted.

This process can be shortened by observing that in some cases even partial information regarding the values of a node's second-generation offspring (that is, its grandchildren) is sufficient for determining its final value. In Figure 15.4, for example, there is no point in evaluating the rightmost of the five second-generation subtrees, since the minimum of the three leftmost ones is 42, which is greater than 27, the known value on the right. The minimum of 27 and any possible value of the root of the rightmost tree will be no more than 27 itself, and hence the maximizing that will be carried out to determine the value at the root necessarily leads to a value of 42. A similar case occurs when the node in question represents a Bob-move rather

Figure 15.3

Propagating values by
the minimax method.

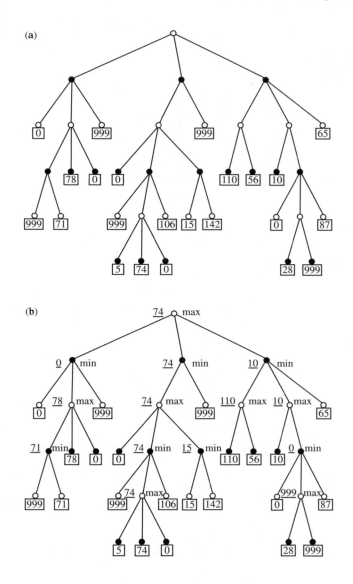

than an Alice-move, but with maximum and minimum changing places. Methods have been found to traverse the tree during the propagation process in such a way as to take advantage of these savings. One of the better known of these, which will not be described here, is called **alpha-beta pruning**.

In summary, a heuristic search consists of:

1. heuristics embodied in a valuation function;

2. rules as to how deep the lookahead from any given position will be (this is usually a function of the position in question); and

3. an efficient propagation procedure for determining the values and actually making the choices.

Figure 15.4

A subtree that need not be evaluated in the minimax method.

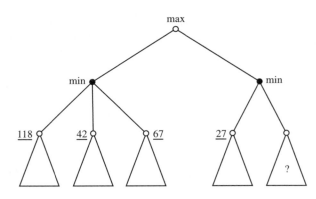

Knowledge Representation

We need more than just heuristics to achieve algorithmic intelligence. We have to find ways to represent the **knowledge** that intelligent algorithms manipulate. If the *control* parts of an AI program are special, being based upon the "soft" notion of heuristics, then the *data* parts are also special, being based upon the "soft" notion of knowledge.

That twice four is eight and that France is in Europe is knowledge, but so is the fact that all giraffes have long necks, that Alan Turing was brilliant, and that academics who do not publish perish. But what is "long," and what is "brilliant," and is "perish" meant literally? Furthermore, how do we represent such facts in our minds or in our algorithmic knowledge bases, and how do we use them? No program can be labeled intelligent, be it one that operates in a narrow domain, such as chess or blocks and pyramids, or a general-purpose candidate for passing the Turing test, unless it has an appropriate mechanism for storing, retrieving, and manipulating knowledge. The problem of **knowledge representation** is indeed one of the central issues in artificial intelligence.

The difficulty is rooted in the fact that knowledge does not consist only of a large collection of facts, but also of the many intricate relationships between them. These relationships have numerous facets and attributes which in turn, spawn other, higher-level relationships with other items of knowledge. We know very little about the way we ourselves store and manipulate the immense quantities of knowledge accumulated over our lifetimes. In fact, there is evidence that a human's knowledge base is dynamic and associative, and does not necessarily work in ways that are suggestive of the workings of current-day digital computers.

Many models of knowledge have been suggested for use by intelligent programs. Some are based on pure computer science concepts, such as relational or hierarchical databases, and others on logical formalisms, such as the predicate calculus or modal logic. Certain programming languages, such as LISP and PROLOG, which are discussed in Chapter 3, are more suitable for manipulating knowledge than others. PROLOG, for example, is quite apt when it comes to knowledge items involving simple relationships like "John is Mary's father," or even "a parent of any ancestor of Mary is also an ancestor of Mary." However, once outside a small well-defined domain of discourse the relationships required become far more intricate, and such models become vastly inadequate. Retrieving those knowledge items that are relevant to some decision that the program has to make becomes a formidable task. The "right" model for the algorithmic representation of knowledge is thus yet to be found.

Knowledge-Based Systems

One approach to the problem is that of **production rules**. A simple production rule might state that if X is a company and Y manages that company then Y works for X. A more complex one, relevant perhaps to a scene comprehension program, would state that whenever three lines are found to meet at a single point then it is possible that they represent the corner of a three-dimensional cube, unless one of the angles is less than $45°$ and another more than $90°$. Some special-purpose programs have been dubbed **knowledge-based systems**, or **expert systems**,[2] as they are based on rules that a human expert employs in solving a particular problem. A typical knowledge-based system is constructed by questioning the expert about the ways he utilizes expertise in tackling the problem at hand. The (human) questioner, sometimes called a **knowledge engineer**, attempts to discover and formulate the rules used by the expert, and the knowledge-based system then uses these rules to guide the search for a solution to a given instance of the problem. The heart of a knowledge-based system is the set of **rules**, given in some format, and a corresponding search mechanism for finding the rules that are applicable. The resulting systems are also called **production systems** or **rule-based systems**.

Knowledge-based systems with acceptable levels of performance have been constructed for carrying out limited forms of medical diagnosis, allocating resources such as airport gates to arriving flights, planning and scheduling operations for spacecraft, and logistics planning. Such systems save many millions of dollars for the corporations that use them. In fact, the U.S. Defense Research Projects Agency (DARPA), for many years the major funding agency for AI research in the United States, has stated that the transportation planning and scheduling system used in the 1991 Gulf War more than paid back for DARPA's total investment in AI over a period of 30 years!

We must realize, however, that besides the reliance on heuristic search, the rules that control the search are formed by questioning experts who might not always operate according to rigid rules. The chances of unexpected, perhaps catastrophic, behavior in a knowledge-based system are therefore non-negligible. Some people put it this way: "Would you be willing to be taken care of by a computerized intensive care unit that was programmed according to the knowledge-based system paradigm?" Under a rare set of circumstances, the unit could administer the wrong medicine or shut a crucial valve at the wrong moment. Its behavior is governed by rules that were formulated by interviewing expert doctors who might not necessarily

---

[2] The term "expert systems" is inaccurate, though catchy, since it focuses on performance rather than on mechanisms. Computer programs can perform much better than any human expert on many tasks, such as sorting a large amount of data. However, these are not considered to be expert systems, because they are not knowledge-based. On the other hand, some knowledge-based systems are very useful in practice, even though they may not achieve the performance level of a human expert.

act in an unusual case according to any well-formed rules. (Of course, similar things have happened with *non*heuristic programs because of inadequate software engineering practices, as we saw in the case of the Therac-25 in Chapter 5.)

Attempts could possibly be made to subject critical knowledge-based systems to precise analytic techniques, enabling us to verify formally that certain safety properties hold for any application of the underlying rules. Since, as explained in Chapter 10, safety properties usually assert that bad things will not happen, it would appear that rule-based systems would be amenable to such an approach.

Knowledge in Learning, Planning, and Deduction

The problem of knowledge representation is indeed fundamental to the mechanization of any kind of intelligence, and it resurfaces in **learning**, **planning**, and **deduction**. Here are some typical examples that further illustrate the need for sophisticated representation of knowledge.

No program can be said to be truly intelligent if it never learns, being forever doomed to repeating its previous mistakes, and never getting any better. Consider a checkers program that learns. It might be assumed to know the rules and then simply to learn how to avoid the mistakes it makes as it plays more games. However, even here an algorithmic point of view presents serious representational problems. Do we simply make a list of the positions and moves that turned out to be bad, and henceforth repeatedly run through them to avoid making the same mistakes again? Or do we try to remember and update more general rules of good play, which will be used to modify the program's heuristics? These questions become all the more difficult when the subject area is wider. How do children learn? How do they represent the knowledge that enables them to recognize familiar faces or synthesize new sentences they have never really heard before? How does an adult remember and retrieve the knowledge that enables him to learn how to write an essay, to organize personal finances, or to adapt to a new environment?

Earlier we mentioned deduction as one of the kinds of intelligence required for passing the Turing test. Programs have been written that do a reasonably good job of proving theorems in high school geometry. They are able to accumulate relevant facts and deduce new ones from them. How is it done? Do these programs simply keep a list of known theorems and a few logical inference rules (such as "if P is true and P always implies Q, then Q is true too")? Or are they familiar with more complex chains of reasoning that are geared towards producing interesting theorems? Again, these questions become all the more difficult when the knowledge relevant to the desired deductions is not restricted to a narrow domain. How does a person's knowledge enable him to conclude that it will probably rain tomorrow, to decide upon the proper school for a child, or to prove a really deep theorem in algebraic topology?

Most of our discussion so far has been related to the *internal* activities of intelligent programs. The need for them to talk, walk, or see has been repeatedly waived, concentrating instead on comprehension, learning, and deduction. However, a more general view of intelligent machines requires that they also have the ability to physically imitate humans. In their most general form, they must be able to understand and synthesize human speech, as well as to perform physical tasks in the classical robot-like spirit. Here too, the problem of knowledge representation is a fundamental one. Some AI systems can understand simple views of blocks and pyramids using appropriate visual sensory equipment, and others can understand clearly spoken elementary English using audio equipment. How do they do so? Do the vision-based programs simply know about every possible combination of locations for the appropriate objects, or do they recognize various configurations of line junctions and utilize rules for deducing the overall arrangement from them? What happens if a new kind of object, say a cylinder, is introduced? Do the speech-recognition programs have a database consisting of the wave profiles for all possible pronunciations of each word? Or do they have built-in rules that enable them to combine spoken word segments into a whole? Again, if the domain is much broader, like those encountered by a human viewing new surroundings or listening to a rich and diverse conversation, things become far more complicated. How do human beings comprehend the variety of colors, lines, and shapes that make up the interior of a living room? How do they identify movement and distance from observing things with two eyes over some short period, and how do they understand foreign accents?

The ability to plan is another intelligent skill. Some robots that operate within carefully limited surroundings are capable of planning a sequence of movements that will take them to their destination. How do they do so? Do they simply carry out a search through possibilities, heuristic or otherwise? Or do they utilize more subtle knowledge that enables them to make plans with the aim of achieving more general goals? Again, wider domains make things much harder. How does a person plan a trip, outline a scheme for ending the year with a positive balance, or devise a strategy to win a war?

If intelligence is a wellspring of life, as the book of Proverbs would have it, then the problem of knowledge representation is definitely its cornerstone, and to find out whether we can breathe life—so to speak—into a computer requires finding a suitable solution to that problem.

Intelligence Without Knowledge Representation?

The "classical" approach to AI, based on the so-called **knowledge-representation hypothesis**, assumes that cognition based on internally-represented knowledge is the key to intelligence. This hypothesis allowed researchers to concentrate on algorithms for learning, planning, deduction, etc., while largely ignoring the environment in which the intelligent agent is supposed to be situated. Even research on computer vision and robotics was conceived of as aiming to develop the mechanisms that allow the intelligent agent to perceive its environment and act within it, but to be still no more than input and output for some other central cognitive component.

This basic model was challenged in the mid-1980s. The claim was that the interaction between perception and action can create complex behavior, and that there is no need for a "cognitive" component based on an internal representation of knowledge, which has symbolic reasoning capabilities. Cognition emerges out of this interaction, but is not programmed in. In this view, the "classical" decomposition of intelligence followed by most AI researchers is premature. Human-level intelligence is too complex, and we know far too little about it to be able to identify its components successfully. Instead, researchers following this view attempt to build complete systems that interact with their environment, starting with small ones, which are as intelligent as, say, insects, and building upwards.

This approach decomposes intelligent behavior according to its actions rather than its functions. Thus an intelligent system should not be viewed as consisting of different functions leading from perception to action through intermediate cognitive tasks like modeling and planning. Rather, it is made up from various *skills*, each of which goes all the way from perception to action. In a robot, for example, such skills might include avoiding collisions, exploring and parsing the visible space, searching for specific objects (such as electrical outlets for recharging itself . . .), and so on.

Indeed, a number of robots (including a commercial autonomous household vacuum cleaner) have been produced in this fashion. Their intelligence level can be compared to that of some insects (which is nothing to sneeze at!), but this is still a far cry from human-level intelligence. It remains to be seen whether this behavior-based approach to AI will indeed scale up successfully in future.

Prospects for Artificial Intelligence

The term "artificial intelligence" was first coined in connection with the 1956 Dartmouth Conference. This was a meeting of leading researchers in a variety of scientific domains, who tried to set the research agenda for the fledgling field. Their mood was very optimistic, and they expected major breakthroughs within 10 years. The most significant outcome of subsequent research was the realization of how difficult the problems really were. As a consequence, the reputation of the field inevitably suffered.

How have we been doing in the half-century or so that has elapsed? While nothing approaching real artificial intelligence has yet been developed, turning to more specialized problems has produced some impressive successes, both scientifically and commercially. For example, computers today can understand spoken commands, recognize faces and objects in pictures, and produce passable translations of technical documents. As mentioned earlier, knowledge-based systems are used in many commercial and engineering endeavors, often behind the scenes.

In fact, many things that we have been used to reading about in science fiction stories[3] now appear in newspapers describing ongoing research or sometimes even existing systems. They include wearable computers that are constantly connected to a worldwide information network; virtual and augmented reality; "smart dust," that is, numerous tiny sensors that function together as a distributed computer; "intelligent

---

[3] *Hard science fiction*, as distinct from fantasy, refers to explorations of alternative possible futures based on a self-consistent and scientifically plausible extrapolation of the present.

rooms" that respond via wall-sized displays to spoken commands, hand gestures, and facial expressions; and, on a more sombre note, government monitoring of all internet communications.

In spite of these achievements, AI is as controversial nowadays as it was at the start. It has become clear that systems built using AI techniques can be very useful in practice even without achieving human-level intelligence. Some people (including many AI researchers) believe that the ultimate goal of true machine intelligence is unachievable. Others foresee a future in which machine intelligence will eventually surpass human intelligence, possibly even leading to an amalgamation of people and computers. One famous inventor and author predicted in 1999 that by 2029 there will be direct neural connections between human brains and computers, and machines' claims to being conscious will largely be accepted. By 2099, the prediction continues, there will no longer be any clear distinction between humans and computers. We leave it to the reader to decide whether this is possible, likely, or even desirable . . .

Understanding Natural Language

To end this chapter on a lighter note, it seems worthwhile to further illustrate the difficulty of mechanizing the comprehension of ordinary natural language. The problem is really much harder than it appears.

We shall concentrate here on understanding the language—not merely recognizing the words—but it is instructive to first see what can happen when a speech-recognition program makes mistakes. The sentence "His presence made all the difference" can be easily misunderstood and interpreted as "His presents made all the difference." Similarly, "Any Japanese car responds well" can be heard as "Any Japanese corresponds well," and the well-known American statement "I pledge allegiance to the flag," when said fast, can be understood as "I led the pigeons to the flag." Speech-recognition programs are a pun lover's paradise.

When it comes to semantics the subtleties are much greater. A sentence cannot always be understood without the context in which it appears, and without knowing about the special nuances, phrases, and slang of the language at hand. Sometimes it is also necessary to be familiar with the idiosyncrasies of the person who is speaking. A famous example involves the aphorism "The spirit is willing but the flesh is weak." As the story goes, this sentence was subjected first to a program that carried out a simple dictionary-based translation into Russian and then to one that translated it back into English. The result was "The vodka is strong but the meat is rotten." How inspiring!

Problems can arise when parts of a sentence are ambiguous. Consider the following:

> *Jim sat down at the table and found a large fruit salad on a plate next to the basket of bread. It took him a while, but he finally managed to eat and digest it all.*

What did Jim eat? Was it the salad, the bread, or both? In some context it might be the plate, the basket, or even the table! Here grammar alone is of little help; it is the meaning of things that an intelligent program must be able to grasp. The following sentences are grammatically identical but they differ in the relationship between their various parts.

> *The lost children were found by the searchers.*
> *The lost children were found by the mountain.*
> *The lost children were found by the afternoon.*

Obviously, the correct interpretation depends on the meaning of the words "searchers," "mountain," and "afternoon." The same phenomenon occurs in the following.

> *The thieves stole the jewels, and some of them were subsequently sold.*
> *The thieves stole the jewels, and some of them were subsequently caught.*
> *The thieves stole the jewels, and some of them were subsequently found.*

In this case, the word "sold" refers to the jewels, "caught" refers to the thieves, and "found" can refer to either. Actually, even that much is not obvious. It is possible that the story takes place in a country where thieves are sold as slaves, rendering the first sentence ambiguous too. If the second sentence had "threw the jewels out of the window" instead of "stole the jewels," it would also be ambiguous.

Again, the knowledge issue appears in all its severity. We utilize an enormous amount of knowledge in disambiguating and understanding ordinary English, besides just the words and the grammar. Identifying that knowledge, and representing it in ways that capture its intricate interrelationships, enabling useful retrieval, re-emerges as the central and fundamental problem.

To emphasize this problem, think of the task of translating a murder mystery from English to Spanish. Certain nouns in English, such as actor/actress or waiter/waitress, are gender specific, while others, such as teacher or secretary, are gender neutral. In Spanish, however, "secretary" has two gender-specific forms: "secretario" and "secretaria." Now suppose that our famous but eccentric detective finds the murderer in the last chapter of the book, based on the information that the secretary is male, whereas we have been subtly led to believe otherwise up to that point. A clever translation program might discover this information, and proceed to translate all references to "the secretary" into the male form, "secretario." This would require quite a bit of intelligence on the part of the program, since it would need to correlate information appearing in the entire book. Unfortunately, this is a very nonintelligent thing to do, as it spoils the whole point of the book! Translating the book without totally ruining it for the reader requires a far deeper understanding of the story. Once that is achieved, perhaps some creative way of hiding the murderer's gender can be found. Such deep levels of understanding require, among other things, reasoning about the readers' knowledge while reading the book, which is far beyond the capabilities of current story-understanding systems.

Let us end our discussion with some hypothetical exchanges between a human being and a futuristic intelligent phone-answering machine.[4]

Machine: Hello, this is Jim's phone.
Voice: Hello. I would like to talk to Jim.
Machine: Jim isn't here. Can I help you?
Voice: This isn't stuff I can share with a machine. When will he be here?
Machine: Who is this calling?
Voice: This is Bill Bixlot.
Machine: I'm sorry, Mr. Big-Slut, but Jim will not be here in the foreseeable future. Thank you for calling, Bill. *(Click.)*
Voice: Damn!

Machine: Hello, this is Jim's phone.
Voice: Oh, hello, you darling machine. I just wanted to check that we're still on for dinner and whatever.
Machine: Of course, Sue. I have you for Thursday at the usual spot.
Voice: This is Jim's fiancee, Barbara. Who is Sue?
Machine: Oh, Barbara, I didn't recognize your voice. I have never heard of anyone named Sue.
Voice: But you just said he was meeting with Sue on Thursday.
Machine: Oh *that* Sue. Are you sure you have the right number? This is Bill Finch's phone.
Voice: You can't pull that trick on me. Tell Jim it's all over!
Machine: You have reached a nonworking number. Please check your listing and redial. *(Click.)*

Machine: Hello, this is Jim's phone.
Voice: Oh, it's you. Listen, this is his boss. I really need to get Jim right away. Can you locate him and have him call me?
Machine: I'm sorry, Mr. Hizboss, Jim is playing golf this afternoon and left orders not to be disturbed.
Voice: He is, is he? Well, look, I'm thin on patience this afternoon. This is *his boss* calling, you idiot, not Mr. Hizboss. Get Jim. Now!
Machine: I'm pleased to hear that you are spending time with your patients this afternoon, Dr. Thin. Business must be good. If you want to reach Jim's boss just dial 553–8861. Certainly you would never find him here in Jim's office; we have him listed in our directory under the alias of The Monster.
Voice: Take this message, you son of a chip, and get it straight. Tell him he is not worth the keys on your keyboard. He is fired! *(Click.)*

---

[4] These conversations are based on those appearing in a 1986 essay by Robert W. Lucky. They have been modified, and are included with permission.

> *Machine:* Hello, this is Jim's phone.
> *Voice:* Are you satisfied with your present investments? Have you considered the advantages of tax-free municipal bonds? To hear more, please give your name and address after the beep. *(Beep.)*
> *Machine:* Er, . . . this is Jim's phone.
> *Voice:* Thank you Mr. Jimzfone. Let me tell you more about our unusual investment opportunities . . .

One of the main advantages of pure algorithmics over heuristic-based AI is the ability to analyze the behavior of its algorithms; namely, to prove that they always produce the correct result, and to provide analytic lower and upper bounds on their complexity. Heuristic algorithms don't usually enjoy these properties. Often, they run in a reasonable amount of time on only some of their inputs but not on others, and characterizing in advance which are which is impossible. The usefulness of such algorithms can only be evaluated empirically, over time, after they have been run in numerous real-world situations. Safe use of heuristic algorithms is in a setting where they are allowed to fail. They can be used in an advisory capacity, but should not be allowed to make final critical decisions on their own; human judgment must always be applied. If a heuristic algorithm is deemed necessary for the operation of a critical system like a nuclear reactor, this indicates the need to simplify the system to the point where a purely analytic algorithm (or a human operator) will do.

Having said that, we must keep in mind that some problems cannot be solved by a fully analyzable algorithm. A great many interesting and practical problems are intractable or even undecidable (see Chapters 7 and 8), and we know very little about whether approximation, parallelism, or randomization can make a significant difference (see Chapters 7, 10, and 11). Instead of giving up on these problems altogether, we can try looking for heuristic solutions. A solution that works in only, say, 80% of the cases may still be useful and can save a lot of manual effort, provided that it is subject to human supervision. And this is true even if we have no idea how to identify those 80%.

Perhaps, instead of AI, "artificial intelligence," the emphasis should be on IA, **intelligence augmentation**, which is the development of computerized tools that enhance human intelligence and improve its functioning. Combining the best aspects of human and machine intelligence may bring about what neither can do on its own.

Such knowledge is too wonderful for me;
it is high, I cannot attain unto it

PSALM 139: 6

for I am more brutish than a man,
and have not the understanding of a man

PROVERBS 30: 2

Postscript

Better is the end of a thing than the beginning of it

ECCLESIASTES 7: 8

Well, we have come a long way. Starting from the basic notion of an algorithmic problem and its solution, we have discussed the basic ways in which algorithms are constructed and written, as well as their correctness and efficiency. We have seen intractable problems and noncomputable ones, and have shown that these notions are insensitive to the choice of the model of computation and the language in which solutions are written. We have also discussed concurrency, probabilism, quantum computing, heuristics, software engineering, and complex systems.

In retrospect, we have identified three distinct kinds of complexity with which algorithmics tries to cope. In each, there remain serious obstacles that seem to require significant new ideas in order to be overcome.

The first is **computational complexity**, where we search for efficient solutions to well-defined algorithmic problems. Efficiency is based on resources such as computation time, memory space, and hardware size. New algorithmic problems pose new challenges—to find the most efficient algorithms and to prove matching lower bounds. This is particularly acute when the problem at hand is conjectured, but not known, to be intractable. From the fundamentalist's point of view, the main obstacles here are reflected in the many open questions involving complexity classes and their interrelationships. In particular, the P vs. NP and P vs. RP problems stand out as being not only very difficult but also of great interest, both theoretical and practical.

The second kind of complexity can be termed **behavioral complexity**, or **system complexity**. Here we are interested in designing extremely complex computerized systems, typically ones that are concurrent, distributed, and reactive in nature. Efficiency here is secondary; the main problem is in dealing with the intricacy of the system's desired behavior. Again, each new system presents a new challenge—to provide designs, algorithms, and protocols that are clear and well structured, and that yield the desired behavior under all circumstances. For the fundamentalist, the problem is to develop rigorous methods, languages, and analysis tools for the sound and painless development of reliable systems.

The third kind of complexity might be called **cognitive complexity**. It has to do with pseudo-algorithmic problems, which, by their very nature, are not amenable to precise definition, though we need only look around to see them continuously being solved by noncomputerized beings. They involve knowledge and intelligence, and are usually aimed at achieving human-like effects. Here too, new problems present brand new challenges—to design systems that will exhibit intelligent behavior in the appropriate realms. From a fundamentalist's point of view, the main problem is to understand how intelligent beings operate, and to represent the complex knowledge relevant to that operation in ways that are amenable to algorithmic manipulation and analysis.

There have been major advances on all of these issues since the first version of this book was prepared around 20 years ago. However, these three areas of complexity still stand out as being fundamental in nature, and are still far from being satisfactorily handled. We can only hope that similar expositions of algorithmics in the future will be able to report on breakthroughs in coping with the three types of complexity.

Even the most attentive readers will not have become competent computer professionals by reading this book. It is hoped, however, that they have acquired a reasonably detailed understanding of some of the most fundamental issues in the young and exciting field of computer science. In the coming years, algorithmics is expected to emerge as an even more influential area of interest, improving and expanding the ways computers are applied to real-world problems, and applied even more extensively to understanding and analyzing nature.

And it shall be,
when thou hast made an end of reading this book,
that thou shalt bind a stone to it, and cast it
into the midst of [the river] Perat

JEREMIAH 51: 63

Selected Solutions

■ Chapter 2

2.5. (a) The loop

> for I going from M to N do S

is simulated by the sequence of statements

> $I \leftarrow M$;
> while $I \leq N$ do the following:
>> S;
>> $I \leftarrow I + 1$

where I is a new integer variable, not appearing in S.

(b) The conditional statement

> if E is true then do S

is simulated by the sequence of statements

> $B \leftarrow$ true;
> while both E and B are true do the following:
>> S;
>> $B \leftarrow$ false

where B is a new Boolean variable, not appearing in E and S.
The statement

> if E is true then do S else do T

is simulated by the sequence of statements

> $B \leftarrow$ true;
> while both E and B are true do the following:
>> S;
>> $B \leftarrow$ false;

        while B is true do the following:
            T;
            $B \leftarrow$ false

    where B is a new Boolean variable, not appearing in E, S, and T.

(c) We introduce two new labels L and M not appearing in S. Now, the loop

        while E is true do S

    is simulated by the sequence of statements

        L: if E is not true then goto M;
              S;
              goto L;
        M:

(d) The loop

        while E is true do S

    is simulated by the statement

        if E is true then do the following:
            repeat S until E is false

2.8.   We can simulate the loop

        while E is true do S

    by a single call to a recursive procedure

        call **simulate-while**

    which is defined by

        subroutine **simulate-while**:
            if E is true then do the following:
                S;
                call **simulate-while**;
            return.

2.10.   The following algorithm checks whether the vector P of length N represents any permutation of A_N. It uses a vector A of length N that contains Boolean values (true or false) to keep track of the integers already encountered in P. The result is set into the variable E, which is true upon termination of the algorithm precisely if P indeed represents a permutation.

        for I going from 1 to N do the following:
            $A[I] \leftarrow$ false;
        $I \leftarrow 1$;
        $E \leftarrow$ true;
        while E is true and $I \leq N$ do the following:
            $J \leftarrow P[I]$;
            if $1 \leq J \leq N$ and $A[J]$ is false then do the following:
                $A[J] \leftarrow$ true;
                $I \leftarrow I + 1$;
            otherwise
                $E \leftarrow$ false.

2.11.   Here is an algorithm which, given N, prints all the permutations of A_N. It uses two vectors A and P of length N each. The vector A contains Boolean values and represents those integers already considered in the current permutation being generated in the vector P.

for I going from 1 to N do the following:
$\quad A[I] \leftarrow$ true;
call **perms-from** 1.

where the subroutine **perms**, with local variable J, is defined by

subroutine **perms-from** K:
$\quad$ if $K > N$ then do the following:
$\quad\quad$ **print**("New permutation: (");
$\quad\quad$ for J going from 1 to N do **print**($P[J]$);
$\quad\quad$ **print**(")");
$\quad$ otherwise (i.e., $K \le N$) do the following:
$\quad\quad$ for J going from 1 to N do the following:
$\quad\quad\quad$ if $A[J]$ is true then do the following:
$\quad\quad\quad\quad P[K] \leftarrow J$;
$\quad\quad\quad\quad A[J] \leftarrow$ false;
$\quad\quad\quad\quad$ call **perms-from** $K + 1$;
$\quad\quad\quad\quad A[J] \leftarrow$ true;
$\quad$ return.

2.12. (b) We prove that the following permutations cannot be obtained by a stack:

i. The permutation $(3, 1, 2)$. In order to print 3 first, the input integers 1 and 2 have to be previously pushed on to the stack. But this can only happen in the order 1, 2, so that 2 will necessarily be on the top. Now, 2 has to be popped and immediately printed, otherwise it is lost.

ii. The permutation $(4, 5, 3, 7, 2, 1, 6)$. In order to print 4 first, the integers 1, 2, and 3 must be pushed (in this order) on to the stack. After printing 5, the integer 3 has to be popped and printed. Now, in order to print 7, the input 6 has to be first pushed on to the stack. Therefore, the integer at the top of the stack is now 6, and 2 cannot be printed before it.

(c) It is easy to check all $4! = 24$ permutations of A_4 and find that precisely 10 of them cannot be obtained by a stack. Alternatively, the number of permutations of A_N that can be obtained by a stack is given by the formula

$$\frac{(2 \times N)!}{N! \times (N + 1)!}$$

which we will not prove here. Therefore, A_4 has

$$\frac{(2 \times 4)!}{4! \times (4 + 1)!} = \frac{8!}{4! \times 5!} = 14$$

permutations obtained by a stack, so that $24 - 14 = 10$ permutations are not.

2.15. The following algorithm prints the series of operations on one or two stacks for obtaining a given input permutation. The variable R is true at the end precisely if the permutation can be obtained by one stack. The algorithm uses two stacks, S and S', with the **push**, **pop**, and **is-empty** operations. The result is produced in the variable E, which is true upon termination precisely when the input permutation can be obtained by a single stack.

$E \leftarrow$ true;
$I \leftarrow 1$;
while input is not empty do the following:
$\quad$ **read**(Y);
$\quad$ while $Y > I$ do the following:
$\quad\quad$ **push**(I, S);
$\quad\quad$ **print**("**read**(X)");

$$\text{print(``\textbf{push}(X, S)'');}$$
$$I \leftarrow I + 1;$$
if $Y = I$ then do the following:
    print("**read**(X)");
    print("**print**(X)");
    $I \leftarrow I + 1;$
otherwise (i.e., $Y < I$) do the following:
    pop(Z, S);
    print("**pop**(X, S)");
    while $Z \neq Y$ do the following:
        $E \leftarrow$ false;
        push(Z, S');
        print("**push**(X, S')");
        pop(Z, S);
        print("**pop**(X, S)");
    print("**print**(X)");
    while **is-empty**(S') is false do the following:
        pop(Z, S');
        print("**pop**(X, S')");
        push(Z, S);
        print("**push**(X, S)").

▨ Chapter 4

4.2. (b) The following algorithm calculates the number of nodes the tree T has at depth $K > 0$. The result is returned in the variable S.

    $S \leftarrow 0$;
    call **count-nodes-of** T **and** 0.

The recursive subroutine **count-nodes** is defined by

    subroutine **count-nodes-of** N **and** D:
        if $D = K$ then do the following:
            $S \leftarrow S + 1$;
        otherwise (i.e., $D < K$) do the following:
            $DX \leftarrow D + 1$;
            $I \leftarrow 1$;
            while N has an Ith offspring do the following:
                $NI \leftarrow I$th offspring of N;
                call **count-nodes-of** NI **and** DX;
                $I \leftarrow I + 1$;
    return.

4.3. (a) Here is an algorithm that prints the sum of the contents of the nodes at each depth of the tree T. We use a special item denoted by \$ to separate between nodes from different depths inside the queue Q. Initially Q is empty.

    $L \leftarrow 0$;
    add(T, Q);
    repeat the following:
        $L \leftarrow L + 1$;
        $S \leftarrow 0$;
        add$(\$, Q)$;

> **remove**(V, Q);
> while V ≠ $ do the following:
>> S ← S + contents of V;
>> I ← 1;
>> while V has an Ith offspring do the following:
>>> VI ← Ith offspring of V;
>>> **add**(VI, Q);
>>> I ← I + 1;
>> **remove**(V, Q);
>> **print**("Sum of contents at level ", L, " is ", S);
> until **is-empty**(Q).

4.6. Here is an algorithm that checks whether the expressions represented by the trees E_1 and E_2 are isomorphic, and returns the result in R. Actually, the algorithm is not limited to binary trees nor to any specific set of arithmetic operations.

> R ← true;
> call **check-isomorphic-of** E_1 **and** E_2.

The recursive subroutine **check-isomorphic** is defined by

> subroutine **check-isomorphic-of** E_1 **and** E_2:
>> if either of E_1 or E_2 (or both) has first offspring then do the following:
>>> if contents of E_1 ≠ contents of E_2 then R ← false;
>>> otherwise (i.e., E_1 and E_2 have equal contents) do the following:
>>>> I ← 1;
>>>> repeat the following:
>>>>> if E_1 has an Ith offspring then do the following:
>>>>>> EI_1 ← Ith offspring of E_1;
>>>>>> R_1 ← true;
>>>>> otherwise R_1 ← false;
>>>>> if E_2 has an Ith offspring then do the following:
>>>>>> EI_2 ← Ith offspring of E_2;
>>>>>> R_2 ← true;
>>>>> otherwise R_2 ← false;
>>>>> if both R_1 and R_2 are true then do the following:
>>>>>> call **check-isomorphic-of** EI_1 **and** EI_2;
>>>>>> I ← I + 1;
>>>>> otherwise, if either of R_1 or R_2 is true then R ← false;
>>>> until at least one of R, R_1, or R_2 is false;
> return.

4.7. Here is an algorithm that checks whether the expression represented by the tree T is balanced. It is based on the observation that the expression is balanced precisely if at every depth of T, either all nodes contain integers or they all contain the same arithmetical operation (binary and unary "−" being considered different). We use a queue Q to perform a breadth-first traversal of the tree and the special item $ to separate between nodes from different depths inside the queue Q. Initially Q is empty. The result is set in the variable R, which is true upon termination precisely if the expression is balanced.

> R ← true;
> **add**(T, Q);
> while R is true and **is-empty**(Q) is false do the following:
>> **add**($, Q);
>> **remove**(V, Q);
>> I ← 1;

> while V has an Ith offspring do the following;
>> $VI \leftarrow I$th offspring of V;
>> **add**(VI, Q);
>> $I \leftarrow I + 1$;
> **remove**(W, Q);
> while R is true and $W \neq \$$ do the following:
>> if $I > 1$ and contents of $V \neq$ contents of W then $R \leftarrow$ false;
>> $J \leftarrow 1$;
>> while R is true and $J < I$ do the following:
>>> if W has a Jth offspring then do the following:
>>>> $WJ \leftarrow J$th offspring of W;
>>>> **add**(WJ, Q);
>>>> $J \leftarrow J + 1$;
>>> otherwise $R \leftarrow$ false;
>> **remove**(W, Q).

4.13. (a) Here is a dynamic planning algorithm for the integer-knapsack problem. It operates in N stages. Let M_T be the maximal number of available items of type T that can be put into the knapsack, i.e., M_T is the minimum of $Q[T]$ and C div $W[T]$, where the "div" operation denotes integer division that returns the integer part of the quotient. The Tth stage of the algorithm consists of M_T substages. After executing the Jth substage of the T'th stage, the algorithm has computed the most profitable fillings for the knapsacks of capacities $K = 1, 2, \ldots, C$, using only the items of types 1 through $T - 1$, and at most J items of type T.

These fillings are represented by a vector A of length $C + 1$ and a two-dimensional array B of size $(C + 1)$ by N, as follows. The profit of the best filling for a knapsack of weight capacity K, where $0 \leq K \leq C$, is stored at $A[K]$. The number of items of type T' that are put into the knapsack is $B[K, T']$.

The following dynamic rule is used to generate this filling:

At any substage of stage T, $A[K]$ is the maximum of the following two values at the previous substage:

$$A[K] \quad \text{and} \quad A[K - W[T]] + P[T]$$

Therefore, after completion of the N'th stage, the algorithm has computed the most profitable fillings for all capacities smaller than or equal to C using available items of all N types.

Here is the algorithm:

> for K going from 0 to C do the following:
>> $A[K] \leftarrow 0$;
>> for T going from 1 to N do $B[K, T] \leftarrow 0$;
> for T going from 1 to N do the following (N stages):
>> $M \leftarrow$ minimum of $Q[T]$ and C div $W[T]$;
>> for J going from 1 to M do the following (M substages):
>>> for K' going from 0 to $C - J \times W[T]$ do the following:
>>>> $K \leftarrow C - K'$;
>>>> $KX \leftarrow K - W[T]$;
>>>> $AX \leftarrow A[KX] + P[T]$; (alternative profit)
>>>> if $A[K] < AX$ then do the following:
>>>>> $A[K] \leftarrow AX$;
>>>>> $B[K, T] \leftarrow B[KX, T] + 1$;
>>>>> for T' going from 1 to $T - 1$ do $B[K, T'] \leftarrow B[KX, T']$;
>> for T going from 1 to N do $F[T] \leftarrow B[K, T]$.

Note that a "for-do" loop does nothing if the initial value of the running variable exceeds its upper bound.

(b) The output of the dynamic planning algorithm for the given input is $F = [0, 1, 3, 2, 1]$, with the total profit of the snapsack 194.

4.14. (a) Here is a greedy algorithm for the knapsack problem. It is based on the observation that a most profitable filling of the knapsack consists of filling the knapsack by as large a quantity as possible of the "best" type, then as large a quantity as possible of the second "best" type, etc., where the "quality" of type I is measured by its *specific profit* (per weight unit) defined by $P[I]/W[I]$. This specific profit of type I is calculated and stored until its use in the vector item $S[I]$.

for I going from 1 to N do the following:
    $S[I] \leftarrow P[I]/W[I]$;
    $F[I] \leftarrow 0$;
$I \leftarrow 0$;
$T \leftarrow 0$;
repeat the following:
    $I \leftarrow I + 1$;
    call **find-max-of** S **into** K;
    $S[K] \leftarrow 0$;
    $FK \leftarrow W[K] \times Q[K]$;
    if $T + FK \leq C$ then do the following:
        $F[K] \leftarrow Q[K]$;
        $T \leftarrow T + FK$;
    otherwise (i.e., $T + FK > C$) do the following:
        $F[K] \leftarrow (C - T)/W[K]$;
        $T \leftarrow C$;
until either $T = C$ or $I = N$.

The subroutine **find-max** sets K to the index of the maximal element in vector S. Its implementation is straightforward and we omit it.

(b) The output of the greedy algorithm is $F = [0, 1, 1.8, 5, 1]$, with the total profit of the knapsack 200.

Chapter 5

5.2. If the algorithm to be verified does not halt on some input, the proposed verifier will not halt either. Hence, in order to be able to follow the strategy described we must assume that algorithms that are input to the verifier halt on all their legal inputs. This assumption cannot, in general, be tested.

5.9. Here is a possible construction of **equal**(X, Y). We have inserted invariants in the appropriate places, which can be used as the basis of a proof of partial correctness, and a convergent for proving termination.

subroutine **equal**(X, Y):
    { Invariant: "$X = S1$ and $Y = S2$, for some symbol strings $S1, S2$" }
    $E \leftarrow$ true;
    while $X \neq \Lambda$ and E is true do the following:
        { Invariant: "$S1 = S2$ if-and-only-if both $X = Y$ and E is true" }
        { Convergent: Number of symbols in X }
        if $Y = \Lambda$ then $E \leftarrow$ false;

otherwise (i.e., if Y is not empty)
  if **eq**(**head**(X),**head**(Y)) then
      $X \leftarrow$ **tail**(X);
      $Y \leftarrow$ **tail**(Y);
  otherwise $E \leftarrow$ false;
if $Y \neq \Lambda$ then $E \leftarrow$ false;
{ Invariant: "$S1 = S2$ if-and-only-if E is true" }
return.

5.12.   (a) *Pal2* is partially correct. Following is an invariant which, when attached to the point prior to the execution of the loop, can be used to prove partial correctness: "S is a palindrome if-and-only-if both X is a palindrome and E is true."

      (b) *Pal2* does not terminate on nonpalindrome input strings. Take S to be any nonpalindrome, say "ab". Algorithm *Pal2*, when given S as input, will eventually reach a state in which E is false but X is not empty, and will remain in it forever.

5.13.   (a) *Pal3* is not partially correct. Take S to be any palindrome composed of an odd number of symbols, say the one symbol string "a". Algorithm *Pal3*, when given this input S, will terminate with the wrong answer, namely, E is false.

      (b) *Pal3* terminates on every input string, since the length of X decreases on every iteration of the loop except the last one.

5.15.   For the first three algorithms, we briefly present the invariants and convergents to be used in the proofs. For the fourth, we show these in place in the text of the algorithm.

- Algorithm *Pwr1*: Assume we have added a counter C to the algorithm, counting the number of times the loop has been executed. Then, the invariant to be used is "$PW = m^C$." Also, the difference between n, the total number of iterations to be executed, and the current value of C, is an appropriate convergent.
- Algorithm *Pwr2*: The assertion "$PW = B^E$" is invariant upon every return from the subroutine **compute-power**. The depth of nested recursive calls is bounded by the parameter E, which decreases on every nested call to the subroutine, hence the algorithm terminates.
- Algorithm *Pwr3*: The assertion "$PW \times B^E = m^n$" is invariant upon entering the loop. The variable E at this location is an appropriate convergent.
- Algorithm *Pwr4*: Here is the annotated version.

     subroutine **times-power-of** Q, B, **and** E:
        { Invariant: "$Q \times B^E = m^n$" }
        { Convergent: E }
        if $E = 0$ then $PW \leftarrow Q$;
        otherwise, if E is an even number then
           call **times-power-of** Q, $B \times B$, **and** $E/2$;
        otherwise (i.e., if E is an odd number)
           call **times-power-of** $Q \times B$, B, **and** $E - 1$;
        { Invariant: "$PW = m^n$" }
        return.

     call **times-power-of** 1, m, **and** n.
     { Invariant: "$PW = m^n$" }

To prove termination of *Pwr4*, observe that the value of the parameter E decreases on every recursive call to **times-power**, so the depth of recursive calls is bounded by n, the value of E in the initial call to **times-power**.

5.19.   (a) Define two programs to be equivalent with respect to some agreed-upon output variables, if the following holds: "for every legal input, either both programs diverge, or they both terminate and produce the same result in the output variables."

(b) A partial correctness proof of two algorithms (with respect to some common specification) does not necessarily establish equivalence under this definition. For example, algorithms *Pal1* and *Pal3* given above are both partially correct, yet they are not equivalent according to this strong definition, since *Pal1* terminates on every legal input while *Pal3* does not. Here is a weaker notion of equivalence, with the property that a proof of partial correctness of two algorithms with respect to the common specification establishes that they are indeed equivalent: "for every legal input on which both programs terminate, they produce the same result in the output variables."

(c) This is a topic for discussion. In one sense, the answer should be "no." If you are given two arbitrary algorithms, and you know nothing about their intended role, there is no criterion against which you can measure their equivalence, especially if they have different sets of internal variables. You do not even have a way of figuring out which variables in each program hold the intended results. On the other hand, there is a sense in which you might want the answer to be "yes." Assume that one algorithm is incorporated as a subprogram in a larger system (which may have access to all of its variables), and the other algorithm (perhaps a more efficient one) is to replace the first one. In order to guarantee that the behavior of the larger system will not be affected by this change, we want to prove that both algorithms are equivalent, without having to specify their intended role, and indeed, without having even to specify output variables. This can be done by first insisting that both algorithms use exactly the same variables, and then defining them to be equivalent if for every set of initial values of these variables, either both algorithms diverge, or they both terminate with the same values in all variables. Due to the absence of a specification of correctness, this kind of equivalence is much harder to prove.

◼ Chapter 6

6.2. The least integers are 44, 997, 7, 7, 22, and 6, respectively.

6.6. For simplicity, assume that the input N to the program scheme is a power of 5, i.e. N equals 5^L for some integer $L \geq 0$ (which means that L is essentially $\log_5 N$). Let K_1 and K_2 be the constant number of time units required to execute the first and second "...", respectively. We may also assume that K_1 includes the time required for the division of N by 5. When $N > 0$, the scheme takes K_1 time units to execute the first "...", and then runs for $K_2 \times N$ units executing the inner loop. It then repeats this process with N being reduced to $N/5$, and so on. This gives rise to the following pair of recurrence equations, where $C(N)$ denotes the number of time units required to execute the scheme with input N:

$$C(1) = K_1 + K_2$$
$$C(N) = K_1 + (K_2 \times N) + C(N/5) \qquad \text{for } N > 1$$

The solution of this pair of equations for N a power of 5, is

$$C(N) = C(5^L) = K_1 \times (L + 1) + K_2 \times (5 \times N - 1)/4,$$

i.e.,

$$C(N) = O(\log_5 N + N) = O(N)$$

It is thus of interest that, although the scheme contains two nested loops, each governed by N, the time complexity is linear, not quadratic. The reason, of course, is the reduction of N by a multiplicative constant before re-execution of the outer loop.

6.9. (a) As explained in the text, **treesort** first transforms its input list into a binary search tree, and then traverses the tree in a left-first manner, sending the contents of each node to the output on the second visit. The complexity of the algorithm will be seen to be dominated by the first stage, since the traversal takes only a constant amount of time for each node, and is thus linear in total.

As to the construction of the search tree, we observe that in the process of placing an input value in its final location node in the tree, it is compared with each of the node's ancestors (i.e., those residing along the path leading from the root of the tree to the new location). These are all the comparisons associated with that particular input value. It follows that the total number of comparisons carried out for the nodes residing along a given path of the tree can be calculated as follows: 0 comparisons for the root, plus 1 comparison for the immediate successor of the root, plus 2 comparisons for the next node down, and so on. In general, this sum is $O(M^2)$, where M is the length of the path. The total number of comparisons carried out for *all* nodes in the tree is the sum of these totals, taken over all paths of the tree.

Rather than trying to calculate this sum for various kinds of trees, we show that among all search trees with N nodes (call them N-trees), the most expensive one in terms of the number of comparisons required for its construction is a "thin" tree, i.e., one containing a single branch of length N. This we now prove by induction on N. Clearly the only 1-tree is that containing a single node—the root—which is also a thin tree. Now assuming that the most expensive N-tree is a thin tree of length N, we show that the most expensive $(N + 1)$-tree is a thin tree of length $N + 1$. Suppose we are about to place the last integer of a list of length $N + 1$ in a tree constructed in the first stage of **treesort**. The total number of comparisons made when placing the previous N integers in their positions in the tree cannot be more than the cost of a thin tree of length N, by the induction hypothesis. Hence, the cost of the $(N + 1)$-tree cannot be more than the cost of a thin N-tree plus the cost of placing the last integer in its right place. Obviously, this cost is maximal when the last integer has to be compared with *all* the previous N ones; and this, by the workings of the second stage of **treesort**, can happen only when the temporary search tree constructed for the first N integers *is* a thin tree, and the last node is to be placed at the end of its single branch, forming a thin $(N + 1)$-tree.

Thus, as claimed, thin trees are the most expensive. By our remark above concerning the cost of constructing a single branch in a search tree, it follows that the total complexity of constructing the tree in the second stage of **treesort**, and hence also the worst-case time complexity of the entire algorithm, is bounded by $O(N^2)$.

(b) As is shown in (a), a worst-case input to **treesort** is a list that yields a thin tree, i.e., one containing a single branch, when subjected to the first stage of the algorithm. It is easy to see that if the input is already sorted (in ascending or descending order) this will indeed happen.

(c) We have to count only comparisons, and these are all performed in the merging stage of **mergesort**. An input list of length N can be repeatedly split into halves at most $1 + \log_2 N$ times. Thus, there are at most $O(\log N)$ stages to the algorithm. We claim that the total number of comparisons carried out during such a stage is at most N. The reason is that each comparison causes one of the numbers to be placed on the merged list, and, moreover, after being placed on the merged list such a number does not participate in any further comparisons during that stage. Hence, the overall time complexity of the algorithm is $O(N \times \log N)$.

(d) Given an input list to **mergesort** of length N, it will always be split at most $\log N$ times. Now, the number of comparisons carried out during such a split/merge stage is easily seen to be at least $N/2$ (this occurs when the input is already sorted). Hence, the algorithm takes time $O(N \times \log N)$ for *every* input of length N, which is thus a bound on the average-case time complexity too.

6.15. (a) Worst-case time analysis of both algorithms yields upper bounds of $O(n)$, where n is the length of the string. This bound occurs, for example, on an input string that *is* a palindrome.

(b) Palindromes of length n cannot be detected with fewer than $n/2$ symbol comparisons in the worst case, otherwise we would be able to exhibit nonpalindrome strings that are tagged as palindromes by the algorithm in question. Hence, we have a lower bound of $n/2$ on the problem.

(c) Algorithm *Pal1* requires $O(n)$ comparisons on *every* string, hence this is also its average-case complexity.

The average-case analysis of *Pal4* is harder. Fix an integer n, and for simplicity assume that n is even, i.e., $n = 2k$ for some integer $k > 0$. Let $s = a_1 a_2 \ldots a_k b_k \ldots b_2 b_1$ be a typical string of length n. Call s an i-*nonpalindrome*, for some $i \in \{1, 2, \ldots, k\}$, if $a_j = b_j$ for all $j < i$, but $a_i \neq b_i$. Obviously, every string of length n, is either a palindrome or an i-nonpalindrome for precisely one i. Now, recalling that we are talking about a two-symbol alphabet, we note that for every $i \in \{1, 2, \ldots, k\}$, there are precisely 2^{n-i} i-nonpalindromes, while *Pal4* executes i operations when given such a string. Also, there are 2^k palindromes of length n, and *Pal4* executes k operations on each. Hence, since we assume a uniform distribution of strings, the number of operations that algorithm *Pal4* executes on the average for strings of length n, is

$$\frac{(k \times 2^k) + \Sigma_{i=1}^k(i \times 2^{n-i})}{2^n} = \frac{(k \times 2^k) + \Sigma_{i=1}^k \Sigma_{j=k}^{n-i} 2^j}{2^n}$$

$$= \frac{(k \times 2^k) + \Sigma_{i=1}^k(2^{n-i+1} - 2^k)}{2^n} = \frac{2^{n+1} - 2^{k+1}}{2^n} < 2$$

In a similar fashion, one can show that if n is odd, the average number of operations is less than 4. Thus, quite surprisingly, the average-case complexity of *Pal4* is $O(1)$, that is, a constant.

6.18. Here is a construction of $LG1$:

{ Invariant: "$m, n > 1$" }
$M \leftarrow m$;
$K \leftarrow 0$;
while $M \leq n$ do the following:
    { Invariant: "$M = m^{K+1} \leq n$" }
    { Convergent: $\lg_m n - K$ }
    $M \leftarrow M \times m$;
    $K \leftarrow K + 1$;
{ Invariant: "$m^K \leq n < m^{K+1}$" }

It can easily be seen that this algorithm takes $O(\log_m n)$ time and $O(1)$ space.

6.19. Algorithm $LG2$ can be constructed as follows:

{ Invariant: "$m, n > 1$" }
$M \leftarrow 1$;
$M_1 \leftarrow m$;
$K \leftarrow 0$;
while $M_1 \leq n$ do the following:
    { Invariant: "$K = 2^{l_1} + \ldots + 2^{l_i}$ for some $l_1 > \ldots > l_i \geq 0$, such that
        $M = m^K \leq n < m^{K+2^{l_i}}$ and $M_1 = M \times m$" }
    { Convergent: $\lg_m n - K$ }
    $M \leftarrow M_1$;
    $M_1 \leftarrow M_1 \times m$;
    $M_2 \leftarrow m \times m$;
    $K_2 \leftarrow 1$;

while $M_1 \leq n$ do the following:
$\quad$ { Invariant: "$K = 2^{l_1} + \ldots + 2^{l_i}$ for some $l_1 > \ldots > l_i \geq 0$, and
$\quad\quad\quad K_2 = 2^l$ for some $l < l_i - 1$, such that
$\quad\quad\quad m^{K+2 \times K_2} \leq n < m^{K+2^{l_i}}$ and
$\quad\quad\quad M = m^{K+K_2}$ and $M_1 = m^{K+2 \times K_2}$ and $M_2 = m^{2 \times K_2}$" }
$\quad$ { Convergent: $\lg_m n - K - K_2$ }
$\quad M \leftarrow M_1$;
$\quad M_1 \leftarrow M_1 \times M_2$;
$\quad M_2 \leftarrow M_2 \times M_2$;
$\quad K_2 \leftarrow K_2 + K_2$;
$M_1 \leftarrow M \times m$;
$K \leftarrow K + K_2$;
{ Invariant: "$m^K \leq n < m^{K+1}$" }

For the time complexity analysis, denote the value of $\lg_m n - K$ at any stage of the computation by L. Let $C_1(L)$ be the time complexity of performing the outer loop with a particular initial value L, and $C_2(L, K_2)$ be the time complexity of performing the inner loop with initial values of L and K_2. With the aid of the invariants and convergents listed in the algorithm, we get the following recurrence equations:

$$C_1(L) = \begin{cases} O(1) & \text{if } L = 0 \\ O(1) + C_2(L, 1) + C_1(L/2) & \text{if } L > 0 \end{cases}$$

$$C_2(L, K_2) = \begin{cases} O(1) & \text{if } L < 2 \times K_2 \\ O(1) + C_2(L, 2 \times K_2) & \text{otherwise} \end{cases}$$

It can easily be shown that $C_2(L, 1) = O(\log_2 L)$, and thus $C_1(L) = O((\log_2 L)^2)$. Hence, if we remove the bases of the logarithms, we conclude that the total time complexity is bounded by $O((\log(\log n))^2)$.

Since the algorithm uses only a fixed number of variables, by our convention that storing an integer takes one memory space unit the space complexity is constant, i.e., $O(1)$.

Chapter 7

7.2. (a) Assume the cards of the monkey puzzle can be rotated, and let us recalculate the number of arrangements in a 5 by 5 grid. Since there are 25 cards, each of which can be rotated into one of 4 orientations, we have 25 possibilities for choosing a card to be placed in the first location, and for every card we have 4 possibilities for choosing an orientation. Thus, we have 25×4 possibilities for the placement of a card in the first position. Similarly, there are 24×4 possibilities for the second position, 23×4 for the third position, and so on. All together, there are

$$(25 \times 4) \times (24 \times 4) \times \ldots \times (1 \times 4) = 25! \times 4^{25}$$

arrangements in the worst case. (This number, written in decimal, has 41 digits!)

(b) An exhaustive search would take over 1.7464×10^{34} seconds, i.e., over 5.5×10^{26} years!

(c) We will prove the following stronger claim, which implies that the number of distinct cards cannot be the factor that determines the existence of an arrangement:

For every positive integer N,

■ there is a choice of N^2 distinct cards that can be arranged to form a legal N by N square; and

■ there is a choice of $(N + 1)^2$ distinct cards that cannot be arranged into an $N + 1$ by $N + 1$ square.

The proof is by induction on the number of cards N. Clearly, a single card is arrangeable into a 1 by 1 square, and it is easy to come up with four distinct cards that are not arrangeable into a 2 by 2 square. Assume the claim holds for some N, and we will prove it for $N + 1$. The second part of the claim is trivial, since we can take any $(N + 2)^2$ distinct cards, one of which has colors that do not match any other card at all. For the first part of the claim, consider an N by N arrangeable instance, existing by the inductive hypothesis. We can design $N + N + 1$ new cards that will match the right-hand side and top edges of the N by N arrangement. All we have to consider is that, for example, a card designed for the right column will match the right edge of the existing card to its left, and its bottom and top edges will match its designed neighboring cards. Notice that for any new card there are no matching constraints whatsoever on either its right-hand side or top edge. We can use these "free" edges in order to guarantee that all the new cards in the next step of the induction are distinct, by assigning them some unique new color.

7.3. The least integers are 9, 3, 12, 7, 3, and 2, respectively.

7.5. (a) The naive solution to the traveling salesman problem that considers all possible tours has time complexity of the order of the number of possible tours in a given graph, since every tour can be checked in linear time as to whether it satisfies the given constraint. The number of tours starting at node n_0 of the graph equals, in the worst case, the number of possible arrangements of the other $N - 1$ nodes of the graph in a sequence, which is $(N - 1)!$. Since all tours are actually cyclic, there is no loss of generality in starting at n_0, so that $(N - 1)!$ is the number of tours in general too. The time complexity of the solution is thus a linear function of N multiplied by $(N - 1)!$, which is $O(N!)$.

(b) For an Eulerian path, arrangements of the *edges* of the graph should be considered, rather than nodes. Since the number of edges is at most N^2 (an edge between every two nodes), the time complexity of a naive solution to the Eulerian path problem is $O((N^2)!)$.

(c) Euler's algorithm checks that the given graph satisfies two properties:

- Connectivity—every two nodes that are *endpoints* of some edges are reachable from each other.

- The number of edges emanating from any point (except, possibly, two points) is even. It is easy to see that the existence of an Eulerian path implies the above two properties. Any point that is internal to the path (i.e., any point in the path that is not an endpoint) must have an even number of edges emanating from it, since every such edge appears precisely once along the path, and has the point common with precisely one adjacent edge on the path. If the endpoints are distinct (i.e., the Eulerian path is not a cycle), then by the same argument each endpoint has an even number of *internal* edges, plus a single end-edge.

  The claim that a graph that satisfies the above two properties has an Eulerian path is proved by induction on the number of edges in the graph, as follows. A graph with one edge obviously satisfies both properties, and has an Eulerian path—the single edge itself. Assume now that the claim holds for all graphs with at most K edges, for some positive K, and prove it for graphs with $K + 1$ edges. Let G be a given graph with $K + 1$ edges that satisfies both properties. If there are two points in G with an odd number of edges emanating from each one, pick an edge e emanating from any one of these two points, otherwise pick any edge e of G. Denote by G' the graph resulting from the deletion of e from G. It is easy to see that G' satisfies the second property, and it is either connected or consists of two connected subgraphs. If G' is connected, then by the inductive hypothesis, G' has an Eulerian path with an endpoint belonging to e. Hence the path can be extended by attaching e to its endpoint to form an Eulerian path in G. If G' is not connected, it consists of two connected subgraphs, each of which has an Eulerian path by the inductive hypothesis. Since both endpoints of e are endpoints of these two paths in G', they can be merged via e into a single Eulerian path of G.

7.8. As in the exercise, "number" stands for "positive integer" here.

(a) Meaning and truth of formulas.

χ_1 : "Every number other than 1 is the successor of some number."
The formula is always true.

χ_2 : "The sum of every two numbers is a number too."
The formula is always true.

χ_3 : "Not every number is the sum of two numbers."
The formula is always true—1 is not the sum of any two numbers.

χ_4 : "Some number equals twice itself."
The formula is false—no such number exists. (Recall that here zero is not considered a number.)

χ_5 : "The sum of two even numbers is even."
The formula is always true.

χ_6 : "There exists a number X that is greater than every odd number."
The formula is false—every given X is smaller than the odd number $X + X + 1$.

(b) Formalization in Presburger arithmetic.

i. "**forall**X **forall**Y **forall**Z
$(\sim$**exists**U $(X = U + U \vee Y = U + U \vee Z = U + U) \rightarrow$
exists$V$ $(X + Y + Z = V + V))$"

This formula is false. Actually, the sum of any three odd numbers is odd too.

ii. "**forall**X $(X = 1 \vee$ **exists**Y **exists**Z $(X = Y + Z))$"

This formula is always true.

iii. "**forall**X **exists**Y **exists**Z $(X + Y = Z + Z + Z + Z)$"

This formula is always true—the numbers 4, 8, 12, 16, ..., are all divisible by 4.

iv. "$\sim$**forall**X **exists**Y
(**exists**Z $(X + Y = Z + Z + Z)$ & $\sim$**exists**Z' $(X + Y = Z' + Z'))$"

This formula is false—the odd numbers 3, 9, 15, 21, ..., are all divisible by 3.

7.9. Let us define the *order* of a border point in a map to be the number of countries it touches. The *order* of an entire map is the maximal order of any border point on the map. It is easy to see that in any map that can be colored by two colors, the order of every border point is even. For the other direction, we prove by induction on the order of maps, that if the order of all border points is even then the map can be colored by two colors.

Let M be a map of order two. We can certainly color the "rest of the world" by, say, white. Then, every country that has a common border with this white "rest of the world" is colored by, say, black. Two such countries can have no common border, since otherwise there should be a border point that touches both and the rest of the world as well, thus having order at least three, which is impossible by our assumption of maximal order two. We now continue and color white all countries that touch a black colored country, and again, no borders may exist between two such countries. The process of alternately coloring by white and black continues until all the map M is colored.

Assume now that the claim holds for all maps of order at most K, and we prove it for maps of order $K + 1$. If K is even then the claim holds vacuously for the odd number $K + 1$. Therefore, assume that K is odd, hence $K + 1$ is even. Let M be a map of order $K + 1$ all of whose border points are of even order. Choose a point P on M of order $K + 1$. Let C_1, C_2, C_3 be three countries that P touches, such that C_1 is adjacent to C_2 with a borderline that ends at P and similarly C_2 is adjacent to C_3. Let us join C_1 and C_3 into a single country via a narrow strip taken out of the part of C_2 that touches P. Now P has order $K - 1$. Since we consider maps with a finite number of countries only, there are finitely many points with order $K + 1$ in M. Perform similar changes to these points, and call the resulting map $\hat{M}$. The order of $\hat{M}$ is $K - 1$ and all its border points have even order, thus, by the inductive hypothesis $\hat{M}$ can be colored by two colors. Note that, by the construction, C_2 must be colored by a different color than the joint country consisting of C_1, C_3, and the strip. Hence, if we now restore the situation to the original map M, removing all strips but leaving the coloring (except for the strips, which are recolored by the color of their original country), the map will be legally colored by two colors.

7.12. (a) Since we are given the NP-hardness of the vertex cover problem, we have to show only that it is in NP. We provide a nondeterministic polynomial-time algorithm for the problem. Given a graph G and a positive integer N, the algorithm guesses a subset N' of N of size at most K, and then verifies in polynomial time that N' is a vertex cover by simply examining all edges of G.

(b) The clique problem is in NP, since any subset N' of the nodes of a graph can be tested for being a clique in polynomial time. For the NP-hardness direction, we employ a polynomial reduction from the NP-hard vertex cover problem. That is, we provide a polynomial transformation from instances $\langle G, K \rangle$ of the vertex cover problem to instances $\langle \hat{G}, \hat{K} \rangle$ of the clique problem, such that G has a vertex cover of size at most K precisely when $\hat{G}$ has a clique of size at least $\hat{K}$, thus showing that the clique problem is at least as hard as the vertex cover problem (up to a polynomial). In fact, the proof shows that, in a certain technical sense, the two problems are mutually dual.

Given the graph G with nodes N and edges E, we construct $\hat{G}$ whose set of nodes $\hat{N}$ is exactly N, and whose set of edges $\hat{E}$ is the complement of E, i.e., $\hat{E}$ contains an edge between n and n' precisely when E does not. Without loss of generality, we may assume that K is smaller than J, the size of N. We thus set $\hat{K} = J - K$. Assume N' is a vertex cover for G of size at most K and let $N'' = N - N'$ be the set of all nodes of N not in N'. Every two nodes in N'' have an edge connecting them in $\hat{E}$, since otherwise, by the construction of $\hat{E}$, these nodes would have an edge connecting them in E, in contradiction to the fact that N' is a vertex cover for G. Therefore, N'' is a clique in $\hat{G}$ of size at least $\hat{K}$. Similarly, if N'' is a clique in $\hat{G}$ of size at least $\hat{K}$, the set $N' = N - N''$ of all nodes of N not in N'' is a vertex cover for G of size at most K.

7.16. (a) i. A deterministic algorithm that takes at most logarithmic time cannot use more than a logarithmic amount of space, since it can ask for at most one space unit at each step of its computation.

ii. An algorithm that uses logarithmic space has a number of possible configurations (i.e., "snapshots" of the entire current situation) that is at most exponential in this amount, i.e., polynomial. Here is why. Say we are talking about a fixed Turing machine that uses K squares of its tape. The number of possible symbols (including a blank) that each square can contain is fixed, say C_1. The number of internal states of the machine is fixed, say C_2, and the head can be in any of the K positions. The total number of configurations is therefore $C_2 \times C_1^K$. Since K is a logarithmic function of N, the size of the input, this expression is polynomial in N.

Now, since the algorithm is deterministic, it does not repeat any configuration twice (otherwise it enters an infinite loop). Hence, it runs in polynomial time.

iii. A deterministic algorithm that takes at most polynomial time cannot use more than a polynomial amount of space; see the solution to the first part above.

iv. A nondeterministic polynomial-time algorithm uses a polynomial amount of space, since space is counted as the maximal amount used in any of the possible computations. We can deterministically trace all possible computations of such an algorithm by traversing its tree of configurations without any additional amount of space other than a small amount for the bookkeeping involved.

v. According to Exercise 7.15(a), PSPACE = NPSPACE, thus it is enough to consider deterministic polynomial-space bounded algorithms. Such an algorithm has at most an exponential number of configurations. Thus, similarly to the solution to the second part above, the algorithm runs in exponential time. Alternatively, we may want to directly consider nondeterministic polynomial-space bounded algorithms. The number of possible configurations of such an algorithm is exponential as well. Since no configuration has to be repeated along a halting computation, we can deterministically traverse its tree of configurations in exponential time.

(b) In the spirit of the solutions in part (a), if a problem is solvable by an algorithm that runs in time bounded by a K-fold exponential, then its space is bounded by a K-fold exponential. Similarly, if an algorithm uses an amount of space that is bounded by a K-fold exponential, then it can be simulated by an algorithm that runs in time bounded by a $(K + 1)$-fold exponential. Therefore, a problem is provably time-nonelementary, i.e., it has no algorithm whose time complexity is any K-fold exponential, precisely when the problem has no algorithm whose space complexity is any J-fold exponential, namely, it is provably space-nonelementary.

7.17. Suppose the problem of determining truth in Presburger arithmetic has an algorithm that requires $O(f(N))$ space, where $f(N)$ is less than an exponential. This algorithm has time complexity $2^{O(f(N))}$, since no configuration has to be repeated. Thus the problem is solvable in time less than double-exponential, which is a contradiction. Therefore, the problem has an exponential-space lower bound.

Chapter 8

8.3. (a) One direction of the lemma is trivial, since an infinite path contains infinitely many nodes. For the other direction, assume that a finitely-branching tree T has infinitely many nodes. We will exhibit an infinite path $n_0, n_1, \ldots$ in T. Every node n in this path will have the following *infinity property*: The subtree of T rooted at n has infinitely many nodes. To construct the path, we start by letting n_0 be the root of T. Since T has infinitely many nodes, n_0 has the infinity property, and since n_0 has finitely many siblings, it has at least one sibling that has the infinity property. Take one such sibling to be n_1. Similarly, for every integer i, once we have shown the existence of the finite path $n_0, n_1, \ldots, n_i$, such that each node in it has the infinity property, it follows from the finite branching of T that n_i has a sibling n_{i+1} with the infinity property too. Thus, this finite path can be extended indefinitely, providing the desired infinite path.

(b) The existence of a tiling for the entire integer grid certainly implies the existence of a tiling for every finite square ($N \times N$ grid). For the other direction, assume the existence of tilings for every finite square. Consider the tree whose nodes represent legal tilings, constructed as follows: The root of the tree is the trivial tiling of the 0×0 (empty) grid. If a node of the tree represents an $N \times N$ tiling, then its siblings are precisely all the $(N + 2) \times (N + 2)$ tilings that can be formed by taking the parent's tiling and surrounding it legally by another "layer" of tiles. (That is, the sibling contains the tiling of its parent as the tiling of its internal $N \times N$ subgrid.) Now, since every node represents a tiling of a finite portion of the integer grid and there are only finitely many given tile types, the constructed tree is finitely (although not necessarily boundedly!) branching. Moreover, each legal finite tiling must occur somewhere in this tree. Now, since there are infinitely many finite tileable squares, the tree has infinitely many nodes. Thus, by König's Lemma, there is an infinite path in the tree. But such a path can easily be seen to represent a tiling of the entire infinite integer grid.

8.5. (a) We show the undecidability of the problem presented in the exercise (call it problem (a)) by reduction from the undecidable ordinary snake problem on the upper half of the plane (call it simply the snake problem). Here is an algorithm that solves the snake problem using an oracle Q for problem (a). Given an input $\langle T, V, W \rangle$ for the snake problem, the algorithm asks the oracle Q for its answers to inputs of the form $\langle T, V, W, W' \rangle$, where W' is a point adjacent to W on the upper half of the plane. The algorithm answers "yes" precisely when Q answers "yes" for *some* of these inputs. (There are three or four possibilities for W', depending on whether W is adjacent to the borderline of the half-grid). It is easy to show that this algorithm is correct, since any acceptable snake from V to W must pass through one such W'.

(d) We show problem (d) undecidable by reduction from the ordinary snake problem. Assuming an oracle Q for problem (d), the following algorithm solves the snake problem given the input $\langle T, V, W \rangle$. Choose arbitrarily a new distinct point W' on the upper half of the plane, and let T' be T augmented with an additional tile type t', defined to have new distinct colors on each of its sides. Thus, no tiled snake can reach a point tiled with t'. For each tile type t of T, the algorithm asks the oracle Q whether either of W or W' is reachable from V by a snake constructed using the tile types T', and having a tile of type t placed at W or a tile of type t' placed at W'. Since no legal snake of length greater than 1 can contain type t', it follows that W is reachable from V using tile types from T precisely when there exists a tile t of T such that the corresponding question posed to the oracle has a "yes" answer. Thus, the algorithm answers "yes" precisely when Q answers "yes" at least once.

(e) We show the undecidability of problem (e) by reduction from the ordinary snake problem. Assume an oracle Q for problem (e), and construct an algorithm for the snake problem as follows. Given an input $\langle T, V, W \rangle$, the algorithm uses Q to check whether there exists an acceptable snake of length at least 5 from V to W passing through some of the points W' adjacent to W. If there exists such a snake, the algorithm answers "yes." Otherwise it checks whether there exists a snake shorter than 5 from V to W by performing an exhaustive search through all possible "short" snakes, and answering "yes" if such a snake is found and "no" otherwise.

(f) Since for every given N there are finitely many snakes of length at most N departing from any point on the grid, the problem can be shown decidable by employing an exhaustive search algorithm. The algorithm simply iterates through all the bounded length snakes departing from V, and answers "yes" precisely when there exist two such snakes on the upper half of the grid reaching W and W'.

8.8. We show undecidability by reduction from the ordinary word correspondence problem. Assume an oracle Q for the enriched problem, and construct an algorithm for the ordinary problem as follows: Given input words groups Xs and Ys, construct the Zs so that each Z word is longer than the corresponding X word, say by adding one letter to the X word. Now the algorithm runs the oracle Q with these given Xs and Ys and constructed Zs, and answers the same answer as Q. Obviously, there is a sequence of indices such that $X = Y$ precisely if there is a sequence of indices such that $X = Y$ and $X \neq Z$, since no sequence of indices will ever satisfy $X = Z$.

8.10. (b) The following table contains the results of the required calculations.

Input	Highest number	Number of iterations
256	256	8
101	304	25
55	9232	112
103	9232	87
151	1024	15
383	13,120	45
71,209	3,079,780	174

8.11. (a) No. It is easy to see that among the positive integers the "$2 \times X + 1$" program halts precisely on the powers of 2 (i.e., on the inputs 1, 2, 4, 8, ...). Thus, it does not halt on integers that have odd divisors, such as 3, 5, 6, ...

(b) For a positive integer N, denote by oddity(N), the length of the rightmost string of consecutive 1 digits in the binary representation of N, if N is odd, and 0 otherwise. (For example, oddity(183) = 3, since the binary representation of 183 is 10110111, oddity(36) = 0, and oddity(15) = 4.) It is easy to see that for every odd integer X, oddity(X) = $1 +$ oddity(($3 \times X + 1)/2$), and thus "oddity(X)" is an appropriate convergent for the given program.

8.13. (a) If programs are not allowed to be run on precisely their own text, a proof of the undecidability of the halting problem can proceed similarly to the proof presented in the text, except that whenever the original proof assumes some program P to be run on its own text P, we run it on the text of another program P', which is just P prefixed by some vacuous statement, say "$X \leftarrow X$."

(b) If programs are not allowed to be run on any program text in L, we change the proof of the undecidability of the halting problem as follows: Whenever a program P is assumed to run on its own text in the original proof, we instead run a program P' on the text P''. P'' is the text of P prefixed by some agreed upon symbol, say ¶, such that the new text $P'' = \P P$ is not a legal program text in L. P', on the other hand, is the legal program in L that ignores any ¶ symbol which prefixes its input, and afterwards proceeds exactly as P.

(c) The diagonalization proof of the undecidability of the halting problem described in the text (see Figure 8.9) can be applied to L programs (programs that accept only integer inputs) as well. It only remains to show that integer numbers can effectively represent all programs of L. Specifically, we have to show that there exists a *computable, one-to-one* correspondence between the set of all L programs and the set of all positive integers. This means that we have to order the programs in L in some fashion, and then exhibit two effective procedures. The first inputs any integer i, and halts, producing the ith program in the ordering of L, and the second (which cannot itself be in L!) inputs any program L, and if it is the ith program in our ordering, it outputs the integer i.

To order L, consider the *lexicographical* ordering between programs. That is, assume all programs of L are listed in an infinite dictionary in which every program is but a long (but finite) word, composed of symbols from a fixed finite alphabet. The alphabet contains letters, digits, special symbols, blanks, etc. (See the discussion on simplifying data in Chapter 9 of the text.) The programs are sorted in the standard lexicographical manner, extended to handle the special symbols of L. Since the alphabet is finite, it is possible to compute, for any given integer i, which is the ith program in the dictionary, and vice versa. Thus, the correspondence between L programs and their index in the dictionary is effectively computable, as desired.

8.17. (a) P is decidable. The proof is the same as for the problems with two-way certificates described in the text, except that instead of searching for some yes- or no-certificate for the given input, the search is for either 7 yes-certificates or 3 no-certificates.

(b) Given the input, its size N is determined, and thus the search for either $7 \times N$ yes-certificates or 3 no-certificates is also guaranteed to terminate, hence the problem is decidable too.

(c) The problem is not necessarily decidable, since there is not enough information for deciding that an input is a no-input, just from searching through the list of certificates. At any stage in such a process, additional no-certificates might still be found if the search is continued, so that we can never be sure that we can stop and say "no."

8.18. Given an oracle Q for the recurring domino problem, the ordinary domino problem can be solved by repeatedly asking the oracle for the existence of a tiling with the recurring tile type

t, for each of the tile types t in the input set T. Since any tiling must have some tile type t recurring in it, there exists a tiling precisely when the oracle answers "yes" to *some* t. And since there are only finitely many such questions to be addressed to Q, the process, given Q, terminates.

8.20. (a) The problem is decidable. Given T, we can construct all legal tilings of $1 \times K$ rectangles. Say there are n such tilings. Then, an exhaustive search through all strips of width K and height at most $n + 1$ can determine whether there is a way of stacking these rectangles atop each other, so that one of them occurs twice. Such a repeat appearance is a necessary and sufficient condition for the existence of a tiling of the infinite strip of width K.

◾ Chapter 9

9.3. (a) The unary addition of M and N means simply the concatenation of two strings formed of M and N consecutive "1" symbols, respectively. Assume that input to the Turing machine is given by these two unary numbers listed on the tape with some delimiter in between. To form their sum, the machine only needs to replace the delimiter by a "1" symbol and then delete the last "1" symbol to the right.

   (d) Given an integer $N > 1$, the algorithm constructs a Turing machine whose inputs are X and Y, two N-ary integers, and its output is their sum $X + Y$, all numbers written using the appropriate N digits. The input is listed on its tape from left to right as follows: the number X, the special delimiter \$, the number Y, the special delimiter #. Assume that both X and Y have the same number of digits, by padding the smaller number with enough "0" symbols on its left.

   The Turing machine is constructed so that it cycles in a loop, performing the following sequence of operations at each cycle, as long as it is applicable. Upon entering the cycle, the machine records one carry digit C, initially set to 0, in its internal state.

   - Move to the square adjacent on the left to the leftmost \$ symbol. It contains the current digit D_1 of X to be added. Record the sum $T_1 = C + D_1$ in the internal state (there are only finitely many possible values for this sum) and write \$ on this square.
   - Move to the square adjacent on the left to the leftmost # symbol. It contains the current digit D_2 of Y to be added. Record the sum $T_2 = T_1 + D_2$ in the internal state and write # on this square. Note that T_2 might be a two-digit number.
   - Move to the rightmost # symbol. Write the rightmost (less significant) digit of T_2 on this square, and record the left digit of T_2 (or 0 if there is no digit) as the carry C for the next cycle.

   When the machine exits the above loop, its tape contains a block of several \$ and # symbols, followed by the N-ary representation of $X + Y$. The delimiters may now be replaced by "0" symbols or blanks.

9.6. The CT thesis does not hold for a computer with a limited amount of memory. This can be proved from the existence of problems that are hard in complexity *space* classes. Take for example a problem that is EXPSPACE-hard, such as determining the truth of formulas in Presburger arithmetic. Since the problem is doubly-exponential-time complete, it is also exponential-space hard. Thus, there exist infinitely many formulas in Presburger arithmetic that require more work space than is available in the main memory of the computer plus the 40 MB disk. Yet, each of these formulas is presentable to the computer via its unlimited input device. Therefore, the decidable problem of determining the truth of formulas in Presburger arithmetic is unsolvable on the limited computer.

9.7. (b) Given a standard Turing machine M, construct an equivalent machine $\hat{M}$ that writes on any tape square at most five times. The tape symbols of $\hat{M}$ are those of M except that they contain an additional coded "counter" that counts the number of times the square has been written. (For example, for any symbol a of M, the machine $\hat{M}$ has the symbols $a.1, a.2, a.3, a.4$, and $a.5$.) $\hat{M}$ operates similarly to M but keeps updating these counters each time it writes on its tape. Once any such counter reaches four, $\hat{M}$ puts a special delimiter # on the right of the written part of its tape, then copies the whole written tape to the right of the delimiter, turning all symbols into their ".1" versions in the process. It then resumes its simulation of M without ever passing to the left of the # symbol again.

9.8. (c) By part (b), a Turing machine with several tapes is equivalent to a standard one. Given a machine M with two tapes that can switch heads, we construct an equivalent machine $\hat{M}$ that has two tapes but cannot switch heads. The transition table of $\hat{M}$ contains two copies of the transition table of M, where in the second copy the operations on the first and second tape are interchanged. $\hat{M}$ operates similarly to M, except that when M switches tapes, the internal control of $\hat{M}$ switches from a state in one copy of the transition table to the corresponding state in the other copy.

(d) We simulate a Turing machine M that operates on a two-dimensional tape by a machine $\hat{M}$ that operates on an ordinary one-dimensional tape as follows. Each square of M is represented by a square of $\hat{M}$ containing the same symbol and preceded by an unbounded (but finite) number of squares with symbols that encode the coordinates of M's square relative to the grid, using, say, two decimal numbers and appropriate delimiters. Of course, the set of symbols used to encode the coordinates has to be disjoint from the original set of tape symbols of M. In carrying out a move of M, $\hat{M}$ calculates the coordinates of the neighboring square that the machine has to move to on a separate tape, and then searches for it on its one-dimensional tape. If such a square does not appear then it is added on the right.

9.9. We describe a nondeterministic Turing machine that solves the word correspondence problem but may not halt. That is, if there exists a correspondence for a given instance of the problem, then the machine *has* a computation that determines that fact, but other legal computations of the machine on this instance may diverge (i.e., the machine does not halt). For instances with no correspondence, the machine always diverges.

The machine has the X_i and Y_i words written appropriately on its input tape. In addition, it has a working tape on which it tries to write a word that exhibits a correspondence of the given input instance. (By Exercise 9.8, this does not add any computational power.) The working tape may contain symbols from the words alphabet and blanks, possibly marked by either of the special symbols $\$_X$ and $\$_Y$, denoting the ends of the words formed by Xs and Ys, respectively. The machine performs the following sequence of operations repeatedly:

- Guess (a nondeterministic choice) an integer i between 1 and 3.
- Move to the square marked by $\$_X$ (initially the beginning of the tape) and erase the $\$_X$ marker.
- Write X_i beginning from the previously marked square, but in doing so, if a square is already written and contains a word symbol, verify that the written symbol and the current X_i symbol are identical. If they are not identical—diverge.
- Mark by $\$_X$ the square following the last symbol of X_i.
- Carry out the above operations with Y_i and the marker $\$_Y$.
- Halt and output "yes" if both markers $\$_X$ and $\$_Y$ are now placed on the same square.

9.11. Here is a modified counter program that checks whether the decimal representation of X is a palindrome. The result is produced in the variable U, where the value 0 is interpreted as "no" and 1 is interpreted as "yes." The comments on the right provide a higher-level description of the program.

$$U \leftarrow 0 \qquad \} \quad U \leftarrow 0$$
$$Y \leftarrow 0 \qquad \} \quad Y \leftarrow 0$$
$$Z \leftarrow X + 1$$
$$Z \leftarrow Z - 1 \qquad \Big\} \quad Z \leftarrow X$$

repeat

$A :$
$$V \leftarrow Z + 1$$
$$V \leftarrow V - 1$$
$$V \leftarrow V / 10$$
$$V \leftarrow V \times 10$$
$$W \leftarrow Z + 1$$
$$W \leftarrow W - 1$$
$B :$ **if** $V = 0$ **goto** C
$$W \leftarrow W - 1$$
$$V \leftarrow V - 1$$
if $U = 0$ **goto** B

$W \leftarrow Z \bmod 10$

$C :$ $\quad Y \leftarrow Y \times 10$
$D :$ **if** $W = 0$ **goto** E
$$W \leftarrow W - 1$$
$$Y \leftarrow Y + 1$$
if $U = 0$ **goto** D

$Y \leftarrow Y \times 10 + W$

$E :$ $\quad Z \leftarrow Z / 10 \qquad \} \quad Z \leftarrow Z / 10$
if $Z = 0$ **goto** F
if $U = 0$ **goto** A $\qquad$ **until** $Z = 0$

$F :$ **if** $Y = 0$ **goto** G
if $X = 0$ **goto** J
$$Y \leftarrow Y - 1$$
$$X \leftarrow X - 1$$
if $U = 0$ **goto** F $\qquad$ **if** $\quad X = Y$
$G :$ **if** $X = 0$ **goto** H
if $U = 0$ **goto** J
$H :$ $\quad U \leftarrow U + 1 \qquad \}$ **then** $U \leftarrow 1$

The reader is urged to turn this program into a more efficient one, similarly to the modification asked for in Exercise 5.14.

9.15. (a) It follows from the rules of arithmetic that a polynomial function applied to an exponential function is an exponential function too. (For example, the fourth power of 2^N is $(2^N)^4 = 2^{4 \times N}$.) This applies to big-O notations too. Thus, an exponential-time algorithm in one model of computation has an exponential-time version in any other polynomial-time equivalent model of computation.

(b) The polynomial-time equivalence of models on its own does not suffice for proving the robustness of NP and PSPACE. For showing the robustness of NP, we need a *non-deterministic* polynomial-time equivalence of models of computation, requiring that a nondeterministic algorithm in one model has an equivalent algorithm in any other model, whose nondeterministic time is at most polynomial in that of the first algorithm. Similarly, for showing the robustness of PSPACE, we need a polynomial-*space* equivalence of models of computation.

We should add that both kinds of reductions do indeed exist, and hence both classes NP and PSPACE *are* robust.

9.21. A deterministic automaton is just a special case of a nondeterministic one. For the other direction, let A be a nondeterministic automaton (an acceptor). We will show how to construct a deterministic automaton $\hat{A}$ that accepts an input sequence precisely when A does. The proof can easily be extended to finite automata that are not acceptors.

Let S be the set of states of A. The set of states T of $\hat{A}$ consists of (representations of) all the *subsets* of S. For a subset t_1 in T and an input symbol a, let t_2 be the subset in T consisting of all states s_2 in S for which there exists a state s_1 in t_1 and a transition of the automaton A from s_1 to s_2 labeled by a. We then construct a transition of $\hat{A}$ from t_1 to t_2 labeled by a. The single initial state of $\hat{A}$ consists of the set containing precisely the initial state of A. A state t in T is terminal if it contains at least one terminal state s of A. Note that this construction yields a deterministic automaton $\hat{A}$.

It is now possible to prove that an input sequence x is accepted by $\hat{A}$ precisely when there exists an accepting run of A on x.

9.24. For one direction, the model of finite automata acceptors is just a special case of that of Turing machines that are not allowed to write at all. For the other direction, let M be a (deterministic) Turing machine that does not write at all. We sketch the construction of a (nondeterministic) finite automaton $\hat{M}$ that accepts precisely the same input sequences as M. By Exercise 9.21, the automaton $\hat{M}$, and thus the machine M too, is equivalent to a deterministic finite automaton. Slight modifications to the proof show that the above claim holds for *nondeterministic* Turing machines that are not allowed to write as well.

Let Q be the set of states of M and q_0 its initial state. The set of states $\hat{Q}$ of $\hat{M}$ consists of (representations of) all the sequences of the form $p_1, q_1, p_2, q_2, \ldots, p_k, q_k, p_{k+1}$, consisting of $2 \times k + 1$ elements of Q, for some $k \geq 0$, such that no two p's and no two q's are identical. Since Q is finite, it follows that $\hat{Q}$ is finite too. The sequence $p_1, q_1, p_2, q_2, \ldots, p_k, q_k, p_{k+1}$ is intended to represent, for a given boundary between two consecutive tape squares, any computation of M that "crosses" this boundary, as follows:

- In the first crossing, M crosses from left to right (a *right crossing*) while entering internal state p_1.
- In the second crossing, M crosses from right to left (a *left crossing*) while changing its internal state to q_1.

.

.

.

- In the last crossing, M right-crosses the specified boundary while changing the internal state to p_{k+1}. Note that this is the $(2 \times k + 1)$th crossing, but only the $(k + 1)$th right crossing.

Thus, the p's depict the right crossings of the specified boundary while the q's depict the left crossings. The odd length of the sequence guarantees that the computation eventually right-crosses without left-crossing any more, that is, the head "remains" on the portion of the tape to the right of the specified boundary.

We can now construct a transition of $\hat{M}$ from one sequence in $\hat{Q}$ to another sequence in $\hat{Q}$ labeled by a, if these two sequence can be *merged* in a way that consecutive states in the merged sequence are consistent with the transitions of M labeled by a, and all right moves are from some p to some q while all left moves are from some q to some p. We leave further details of the construction of the transitions to the reader.

Finally, we set the singleton sequence q_0 to be the initial state of $\hat{M}$, and all singleton sequences q, where q is a terminal state of M, to be the final states of $\hat{M}$. It can now be shown that any accepting computation of M can be simulated by an accepting computation of $\hat{M}$ and vice versa.

9.25. Let the Xs and Ys be given. For any i, it is easy to construct a deterministic automaton A_i that recognizes one word only—X_i. By Exercise 9.20(a), we can construct a deterministic automaton A that accepts a sequence precisely if it is one of the Xs. By Exercise 9.20(d), we can construct a deterministic automaton A^+ that accepts a sequence precisely if it consists of the concatenation of one or more of the Xs. We can similarly construct a deterministic automaton B^+ that accepts repetitions of the Ys.

Finally, the existence of an unrestricted correspondence between the Xs and Ys is represented by a word accepted by both A^+ and B^+. For this, we construct an automaton $A^+ \cap B^+$ accepting their intersection (Exercise 9.20(b)), and check its emptiness (Exercise 9.23(a)).

9.27. (c) We describe a pushdown automaton M that recognizes fully-parenthesized propositional formulas. That is, a well-formed formula is either:

   i. a propositional variable, formed by a letter followed by zero or more letters and digits;

   ii. the negation "$(\sim\varphi)$" of a well-formed formula φ;

   iii. an application "$(\varphi \vee \psi)$", "$(\varphi \mathbin{\&} \psi)$", "$(\varphi \to \psi)$", or "$(\varphi \equiv \psi)$" of a binary operator to two well-formed formulas φ and ψ.

The automaton has nine states: $q_0, q_1, q_2, q_3, q_4, q_5, q_6, q_7$, and q_8. The initial state is q_0 while q_7 and q_8 are the terminal ones. The stack alphabet consists of three symbols: "{", "[", and "(". The following table contains the transitions of M:

	Conditions			Operations
Current state	Input	Top of stack	Next state	Operation on stack
q_0	letter		q_7	
q_0	"("		q_1	push "{"
q_1	letter		q_2	
q_1	"("		q_1	push "["
q_1	"$\sim$"		q_3	
q_2	letter or digit		q_2	
q_2	binary operator		q_3	
q_3	letter		q_4	
q_3	"("		q_1	push "("
q_4	letter or digit		q_4	
q_4	")"	"("	q_5	pop "("
q_4	")"	"["	q_6	pop "["
q_4	")"	"{"	q_8	pop "{"
q_5	")"	"("	q_5	pop "("
q_5	")"	"["	q_6	pop "("
q_5	")"	"{"	q_8	pop "{"
q_6	binary operator		q_3	
q_7	letter or digit		q_7	

The intended purpose of the states is as follows:

- At q_0, M records the *first* left parenthesis by pushing "{" into the stack.
- At q_1, M checks the first symbol of a *left* subformula. A left parenthesis in this stage is recorded by pushing "[" into the stack.
- At q_2, M looks for a binary operator following a propositional variable.
- At q_3, M checks the first symbol of a *right* subformula. A left parenthesis in this stage is recorded by pushing "(" into the stack.
- At q_4 and q_5, M checks that right parentheses properly match left parentheses as recorded in the stack.
- At q_6, M looks for a binary operator following a right parenthesis.
- At q_7 and q_8, M is ready to accept its input.

It can now be shown that M has an accepting run on an input sequence precisely when the sequence is a well-formed formula.

9.29. Pushdown automata with *two* stacks can easily be simulated by Turing machines with two working tapes used to store the stacks. For the other direction, we sketch the idea of simulating a given Turing machine M by a pushdown automaton A with two stacks: a "left" stack and a "right" stack.

A configuration of M is represented as follows:

- The state of A records the state of M and the current symbol on the tape square pointed to by M's head.
- The left stack contains the portion of the tape to the left of M's head, with the rightmost symbol on the top of the stack.
- The right stack contains the portion of the tape to the right of the head, with the leftmost symbol on the top.

A move of M to the left is simulated by popping one symbol from the left stack, pushing the symbol written by M on the current square onto the right stack, and appropriately updating A's internal state. A move to the right is similarly simulated by a pop from the right stack and a push onto the left one.

The automaton A begins by reading its input tape from left to right and pushing all the symbols it encounters into the left stack. It then transfers all these symbols (in reverse order) into its right stack, ending in a situation representing the initial configuration of M. Now A simply proceeds to simulate the operations of M, as described above.

■ Chapter 10

10.1. The algorithm employs $\sqrt{N}$ processors, and its N input salaries are equally distributed between the processors, namely, $\sqrt{N}$ input salaries each. At the first stage, in parallel, each processor sums its $\sqrt{N}$ input salaries. Each processor needs sequential-time $O(\sqrt{N})$ for this, so that the first stage takes parallel-time $O(\sqrt{N})$. At the second stage, one of the processors sums the $\sqrt{N}$ results obtained in the first stage. The entire execution requires parallel-time $O(\sqrt{N})$.

10.4. (a) The number of processors needed is exponential in the number of distinct propositional variables in the input formula, that is, exponential in the size of the input in general. Every processor considers a different truth assignment to the variables and then evaluates the truth value of the entire formula in this particular assignment. This takes parallel polynomial time. The algorithm answers "yes," namely the formula is satisfiable, precisely when at least one processor evaluates it to true. Additional polynomial time is required for the processors to come to an agreement on the answer, since they can be arranged in the leaves of a tree of polynomial depth, and pipeline their results towards the root of the tree.

(b) What is needed is an exponential-time lower bound on sequential solutions to the problem, since this will imply that it cannot be solved in parallel polynomial time using less than an exponential number of processors. The reason is that a solution employing less than an exponential number of processors can be simulated on a single processor requiring less than exponential time (the product complexity), thus contradicting the lower bound.

(c) The satisfiability problem for PDL is exponential-time complete, thus, as explained in part (b), its exponential-time lower bound implies that it cannot be solved in parallel polynomial time with a polynomial number of processors. In particular, it cannot be solved in parallel time $O(N)$ and size $O(N)$.

10.7. A problem solvable in nondeterministic exponential time has an algorithm that runs in exponential time but may make at most an exponential number of nondeterministic decisions.

Every decision is among at most a polynomial number of alternative choices. Such an algorithm can be simulated deterministically by employing a polynomial number of processors at each decision point, each of which simulates the computation resulting from deciding on one particular choice.

The number of processors required for this simulation is at most as the number of nodes in a tree of exponential depth and polynomial branching, which is double-exponential.

10.8.   (a)   The search problem can be solved in parallel constant time $O(1)$. This is done by assigning one processor to each of the N items in the input list. Now, any processor whose item has value X, checks whether it has the highest index in the list whose item is X, by examining the next item in the list. The processor with the highest index whose item is X (and there can be at most one such processor), outputs its index. Now, if the item of a processor is *not* X, then the processor attempts to detect whether X does not appear in the list at all, by checking if its own item is smaller than X and the next one is larger than X. If it determines that this is indeed the case (and there can be at most one such processor), it outputs "no." This is a parallel constant-time algorithm that employs N processors.

      (b)   The following algorithm uses the idea of binary search, but instead of halving the list it divides it into $\log N$ parts. The algorithm works as follows: At the first stage it divides the input sorted list containing N items into $\log N$ equal-sized regions, and allocates each of the $\log N$ processors to one such region. These processors determine (in parallel) whether the value X should appear within their regions by examining the items at the boundaries of the region. Then the processor J in whose region X should appear (or the first-numbered one that has actually *found* X) writes its index and status on a special memory location M.

At the second stage, all $\log N$ processors *simultaneously* read the contents of the location M. If X has been found, they all terminate. Otherwise, the algorithm further divides the Jth region into $\log N$ subregions, with each processor working on its own subregion in parallel as before. This stage would require parallel time $O(\log(\log N))$ had the processors not been able to read location M simultaneously. In the stronger model considered here both stages take parallel constant time.

These stages are repeated until X is found or until each subregion has length 1 and X is not found therein. The number of repeated divisions of a list of size N by $\log N$ is at most

$$\log_{\log N} N = \frac{\log N}{\log(\log N)}$$

Therefore, the parallel-time complexity of the algorithm is $O(\log N / \log(\log N))$.

10.12.   (a)   We extend the solution to the two-processor mutual exclusion problem presented in the text to a solution to the three-processor mutual exclusion problem in which the critical section can accommodate at most two processors simultaneously.

The processors are P_1, P_2, and P_3. Each processor P_I can write in its own distributed variable $X[I]$, whose value can be either *yes* or *no*. We use a shared variable Z that can be 1, 2, or 3. Initially, all the $X[I]$s are set to *no*. The protocols for the three processors are symmetric.

        protocol for the Ith processor, P_I:

           do the following again and again forever:

               carry out *private activities* until entrance to critical section is desired;

               $X[I] \leftarrow yes$;

               $Z \leftarrow I$;

               wait until either $X[K] = no$ or $Z = K$ (or both) for some $K \neq I$;

               carry out *critical section*;

               $X[I] \leftarrow no$.

(b) We first prove mutual exclusion. Assume the requirement of mutual exclusion is not satisfied, that is, all three processors are in their critical sections simultaneously. When entering the critical section, processor P_I has already set the variable $X[I]$ to *yes*. Assume $Z = K$ for some K from among 1, 2, or 3. The setting of Z to K was obviously performed by P_K before continuing to its waiting phase, and no processor could have changed Z since then. Therefore, P_K should have entered its critical section by virtue of another processor, P_L, having not set $X[L]$ to *yes* yet. But in order for P_L to enter its critical section, it has to first change Z to L, which is a contradiction.

To show the impossibility of both starvation and deadlock, it is enough to show that no processor can be stuck in its waiting phase, provided no processor is stuck in its critical section. In case all three processors are waiting, since $Z = K$ for some K, both processors with an index different from K can enter the critical section. This means that there is no deadlock. Moreover, since once in its critical section, a processor P_K is guaranteed to exit it, any other processor P_L waiting to enter the critical section will eventually enter it by virtue of either $X[K]$ being set to *no* or Z being set a value other than L. Therefore, no starvation can occur either.

(c) We generalize the protocol of part (a) to N processors with at most two in the critical section simultaneously. The idea is, as in the analogous generalization in the text, to have several levels of insistence, with the processor passing from one level to a higher one until entering its critical section. However, since two processors can be in their critical sections simultaneously, we need one level less, namely, $N - 1$ levels (including the zeroth level of private activities).

Again, each processor P_I has a distributed variable $X[I]$ that can be any integer between 0 and $N - 2$, the initial value of which is 0. The vector Z consists of the shared variables $Z(1)$ through $Z(N - 2)$, each of which can be an integer between 1 and N.

protocol for the Ith processor, P_I:
  do the following again and again forever:
    carry out *private activities* until entrance to critical section is desired;
    for each J from 1 to $N - 2$ do the following:
      $X[I] \leftarrow J$;
      $Z[J] \leftarrow I$;
      wait until either $X[K] < J$ for $N - 2$ processor indices K,
        or $Z[J] \neq I$;
    carry out *critical section*;
    $X[I] \leftarrow 0$.

(d) The solution given in part (c) can be extended to N processors with at most L in the critical section simultaneously, by simply having $N - L + 1$ levels of insistence in the protocols.

10.14. (a) For every philosopher I, we define two formulas. The first, φ_I, states that once the philosopher is granted the possibility of eating, he or she eventually finishes eating (i.e., gets back to his or her private activities). It is formalized by

$$\varphi_I : \quad \text{Eating}_I \rightarrow \textbf{eventually}(\text{Private}_I)$$

The second formula, ψ_I, states that once the philosopher is hungry, he or she eventually gets to eat. It is formalized by

$$\psi_I : \quad \text{Hungry}_I \rightarrow \textbf{eventually}(\text{Eating}_I)$$

Now, lack of starvation for a system of N philosophers is formalized by

$$\textbf{henceforth}(\varphi_1 \& \dots \& \varphi_N) \rightarrow \textbf{henceforth}(\psi_1 \& \dots \& \psi_N)$$

(b) Any philosopher who cannot eat must have at least one neighbor holding a common fork. Suppose, without loss of generality, that the right neighbor holds her left fork. If this philosopher cannot eat either, then her right neighbor must hold his left fork, and so on. Finally, the first philosopher is shown to hold his left fork too. Therefore, a situation where no philosopher can eat is one in which either all N philosophers hold their left forks or all hold their right forks. But if there are at most $N - 1$ philosophers at the table and N forks at any particular time, such a situation is impossible, and at that time at least one philosopher can eat.

■ Chapter 11

11.3. The following is an algorithm for generating a random integer N in the range $A \leq N \leq B$. It uses the arithmetic function $\lg_2 X$, which denotes the integer part of the logarithm base 2 of X. (See Exercises 6.18–6.20 for the calculation of this function.)

$$H \leftarrow B - A;$$
$$N \leftarrow 0;$$
while $H > 0$ do the following:
$$\quad L \leftarrow \lg_2(H + 1);$$
$$\quad H \leftarrow H + 1 - 2^L;$$
$$\quad M \leftarrow 0;$$
$$\quad \text{do the following } L \text{ times:}$$
$$\qquad R \leftarrow \text{choose 0 or 1 at random;}$$
$$\qquad M \leftarrow 2 \times M + R;$$
$$\quad N \leftarrow N + M;$$
$$N \leftarrow N + A.$$

The number of coin tosses the algorithm requires is

$$\lg_2 H + 1 + \lg_2(H + 1 - 2^{\lg_2(H+1)}) + \ldots + 1 \leq \frac{\log_2 H \times (1 + \log_2 H)}{2}$$

namely, $O((\log(B - A))^2)$. A careful construction of a Turing machine that performs this algorithm requires only $\log_2(B - A)$ bits for the generation of a random number between 0 and $B - A$. Since this number should be added to A, the total number of working bits is $\log_2 B$. Now to the special cases (a) and (b):

(a) When $A = 0$ and $B = 2^K - 1$, the algorithm tosses precisely K coins and uses K bits.
(b) When $0 = A < B$, the algorithm tosses at most $\frac{\log_2 B \times (1 + \log_2 B)}{2}$ coins and uses at most $\log_2 B$ bits.

11.7. We employ the algorithm from Exercise 11.3 as a subroutine, and call it **random-int-between** A **and** B. It generates a random integer N in the range $A \leq N \leq B$. We define a subroutine **random** which, given three numbers L, H, and E, with $L < H$ and $E > 0$, generates in X a random number from among the set

$$\{L, \ L + E, \ L + 2 \times E, \ \ldots, \ L + K \times E\}$$

where K is the largest integer for which $L + K \times E \leq H$.

subroutine **random-of** L, H, **and** E:
$$\quad C \leftarrow \text{integer part of } (H - L)/E;$$
$$\quad \text{call } \textbf{random-int-between } 0 \textbf{ and } C;$$
$$\quad X \leftarrow L + X/E;$$
$$\quad \text{return.}$$

(a) The following program produces in S an approximation of the required area. It repeatedly generates random points (X, Y) in the rectangle represented by $0 \leq X \leq A + D$ and $0 \leq Y \leq D$. The variable T counts the current number of such points generated, while

F counts the number of those points that fall inside the figure, namely, those that satisfy $Y \geq X^2/A$. The variable R records the previous ratio between F and T. The algorithm initially sets this ratio to be $1/2$, and terminates when the last point generated has changed the ratio by an amount that would not affect the calculation of the area by more than the given error E. Finally, the area is calculated in S as the computed ratio R of the area the figure and that of the bounding rectangle. Note that the required figure is symmetric with respect to the y-axis, thus the correct ratio needs to be calculated for its right half only.

$E \leftarrow E/(2 \times (A + D) \times D)$;
$T \leftarrow 2$;
$F \leftarrow 1$;
repeat the following:
    $R \leftarrow F/T$;
    call **random-of** 0, D, **and** E;
    $Y \leftarrow X$;
    call **random-of** 0, $A + D$, **and** E;
    $T \leftarrow T + 1$;
    if $Y \geq X^2/A$ then $F \leftarrow F + 1$;
until $R - F/T \leq E$;
$S \leftarrow 2 \times (A + D) \times D \times R$.

(b) The following program produces in P an approximation of π. The idea is that a quarter of the circle with radius 1 can be bounded inside a square of size 1 by 1 whose sides lie on the axes and the lines $x = 1$ and $y = 1$. The area of this circle is precisely π.

$E \leftarrow (0.1)^{N+1}$;
$T \leftarrow 2$;
$F \leftarrow 1$;
do the following:
    $R \leftarrow F/T$;
    call **random-of** 0, 1, **and** E;
    $Y \leftarrow X$;
    call **random-of** 0, 1, **and** E;
    $T \leftarrow T + 1$;
    if $X^2 + Y^2 \leq 1$ then $F \leftarrow F + 1$;
until $R - F/T \leq E$;
$P \leftarrow 4 \times R$.

11.10. We show how to simulate a given probabilistic Turing machine M, defined to accept an input precisely if it halts in a "yes" state with probability greater than $1/2$, on a conventional Turing machine as follows. We construct a Turing machine $\hat{M}$ that operates on two-dimensional tapes and accepts an input precisely if M accepts it. We can then deduce, using the result of Exercise 9.8(d), that M is equivalent to a conventional Turing machine.

The machine $\hat{M}$ simulates a possible execution of M using a pair of consecutive rows, one for simulating the single-dimensional tape of M and one for recording the probability of the particular execution. Initially, only one pair of rows exists: the input row, and the probability row containing 1. $\hat{M}$ uses a "time-sharing" method for simulating repeatedly one move of each of the executions of M. Whenever a coin toss is to be performed, the simulation duplicates the row representing the tape, one copy for each outcome of the coin toss, and attaches the correct probability (i.e., half of the probability of the duplicated execution) to each copy. Whenever a "yes" state is reached, $\hat{M}$ sums the probabilities of all executions reaching a "yes" state so far. If this sum is larger than $1/2$, $\hat{M}$ halts in an accepting state; otherwise it proceeds. Clearly, $\hat{M}$ halts in an accepting state on a given input precisely if M accepts it.

■ Chapter 12

12.2. (a) To show that Y is indeed the average salary, consider the following equalities based on the performance of the algorithm:

$$
\begin{aligned}
N \times Y &= \sum_{I=1}^{N} Y^{I} \\
&= \sum_{I=1}^{N} \sum_{J=1}^{N} X_{J}^{I} \\
&= \sum_{I=1}^{N} \left(X_{I}^{I} + \sum_{\substack{J=1 \\ J \neq I}}^{N} X_{J}^{I} \right) \\
&= \sum_{I=1}^{N} \left(S_{I} - \sum_{\substack{J=1 \\ J \neq I}}^{N} X_{I}^{J} + \sum_{\substack{J=1 \\ J \neq I}}^{N} X_{J}^{I} \right) \\
&= \sum_{I=1}^{N} S_{I} - \sum_{I=1}^{N} \sum_{\substack{J=1 \\ J \neq I}}^{N} X_{I}^{J} + \sum_{I=1}^{N} \sum_{\substack{J=1 \\ J \neq I}}^{N} X_{J}^{I} \\
&= \sum_{I=1}^{N} S_{I}
\end{aligned}
$$

That is,

$$
Y = \frac{\sum\limits_{I=1}^{N} S_{I}}{N}
$$

as required.

(b) We prove the claim by contradiction. Assume the Ith employee has an algorithm A that, given the information available to her, calculates the salary of another employee—the Jth one (i.e., $I \neq J$).

The information available to the Ith employee includes:

- her salary S_{I}
- $N - 1$ random numbers she generates:

$$
X_{I}^{1}, \ldots, X_{I}^{I-1}, X_{I}^{I+1}, \ldots, X_{I}^{N}
$$

- $N - 1$ values she receives:

$$
X_{1}^{I}, \ldots, X_{I-1}^{I}, X_{I+1}^{I}, \ldots, X_{N}^{I}
$$

- N published values:

$$
Y^{1}, \ldots, Y^{I-1}, Y^{I+1}, \ldots, Y^{N}
$$

We first observe that the result of the algorithm cannot depend on the value X_{I}^{J} sent to the Jth employee. The reason is that since the number of employees N is larger than 2, there is at least one more employee, say the Kth one, who sends a value X_{K}^{J} to the Jth employee, to which the Ith employee has no direct access. Consider the situation in which the sum $X_{K}^{J} + X_{I}^{J}$ is constant, and all other values do not change. In particular, the value of S_{J}, which is unknown to the Ith employee, and Y^{J}, which is known to her, do not change, and therefore algorithm A should return the same value, S_{J}, regardless of any change to X_{I}^{J}.

Consider now a different salary $\hat{S}_J$ of the Jth employee, and a run of our probabilistic distributed algorithm that generates precisely the same random numbers except for X_I^J. Since this is a random number, we are free to consider any value for it, and require algorithm A to calculate $\hat{S}_J$ correctly. We thus choose the value generated by the Ith employee and sent to the Jth one to be $\hat{X}_I^J = X_I^J + S_J - \hat{S}_J$. It is easy to see that the value published by the Jth employee, Y^J does not change either, and therefore, according to our first observation, algorithm A must return the old salary, S_J, which contradicts the assumption.

(c) The proof that when $L < N - 1$ there is no algorithm for computing the salary of any employee outside the group of L gossips is the same as in part (b). It is based on the fact there are at least two nongossips and the values sent among them are not known to the gossips.

Without loss of generality, assume the gossips are the employees labeled 1 through L. Then they can compute the the average salary of the other $N - L$ employees as follows. Since they know each other's salary, they can compute the average salary Y_g of the gossips by

$$Y_g = \frac{\sum_{I=1}^{L} S_I}{L}$$

Let Y_n be the average salary of the nongossips. It is easy to see that the average salary of all N employees satisfies the following equation:

$$N \times Y = L \times Y_g + (N - L) \times Y_n$$

Therefore, the L gossips can calculate the average salary of the other employees by

$$Y_n = \frac{N \times Y - L \times Y_g}{N - L}$$

Chapter 14

14.2. The *light* component is attached as an orthogonal component to *watch-and-alarm*, which has 12 internal states. In order to represent the fact that the two internal states of the *light* component are independent of these 12 without orthogonal states, we would need to duplicate them, and have a copy of each of them for each of the two states of *light*. We thus have 12 *additional* states.

We have just shown that without orthogonal states the *main-component* would have 24 states. Similarly, the *stopwatch* would have $2 \times 2 + 1 = 5$ states. Thus, the two-state *beeping-status* component, which is orthogonal to all of these, would require the duplication of these 29 states, namely, the *addition* of 29 new ones.

Like a kiss on the lips, it is when one gives a right answer

PROVERBS 24: 26

Bibliographic Notes

◼ General

The purpose of these bibliographic notes is twofold. The first is to provide the reader with additional sources in which to find more detailed accounts of the topics discussed. The second is to credit the people responsible for the research reported and to point to the original publications outlining their ideas and results.

This introductory section provides information about books relevant to the entire field of algorithmics, as well as the names and publishers of periodicals and newsletters that publish papers spanning the field. The sections following provide detailed bibliographic notes for each chapter. These notes are structured so that general information about books and periodicals relevant to the subject matter of the chapter appears first. The notes are then developed, in parallel with the chapter itself, providing credits for the results mentioned, with pointers to their original published versions. Whenever appropriate, additional pointers to particularly informative, important, or influential publications have been included. We use the novel method of having the bibliographic notes point back to the page numbers of the relevant parts of the text, which we feel significantly increases the convenience of use.

Obviously, it is impossible to even come close to covering all that is relevant to algorithmics. Moreover, many profound and fundamental results do not get referred to here at all, since considerations of space and structure have prevented their inclusion in the text itself. Many of these can be found by following the references that appear in the papers and books that are included.

One final background comment. Since the first edition of this book appeared in 1987, there has been a major change in the way people search for information, including scientific information. We mean, of course, the internet. The change is profound, sweeping, and revolutionary. People visit technical libraries much less, browsing the internet extensively for what they are looking for. There are essentially two kinds of browsing: (1) looking for the information itself on the internet, and (2) searching the the internet for pointers to where in the conventional published literature the information appears. The second of these might be termed "meta-browsing." In fact, when revising and extending these bibliographic notes, working from the version that appeared in the second edition of this book, extensive use was made of meta-browsing; in seeking new books and papers, in double-checking details of the references themselves, etc. However, very little of the first kind of browsing was done, so that with very few exceptions information that appears on the internet but has not been published in the usual scholarly fashion (as books, or as articles in archival journals and conference proceedings) will not be reflected in these bibliographic notes. There are many reasons for this, one of which has to do with reliability of the contents.

■ ■

The Biblical quotations in this book are all taken from a translation prepared by the main author's late father, Harold Fisch:

- *The Holy Scriptures*, English text revised and edited by H. Fisch, Koren Publishers, Jerusalem, 1969.

As will be seen, there are excellent textbooks on almost all of the specific subareas of algorithmics. However, there are precious few that attempt to provide a more general treatment. Three exceptions are:

- J. G. Brookshear, *Computer Science: An Overview*, 6th edn, Addison-Wesley, 1999.
- L. Goldshlager and A. Lister, *Computer Science: A Modern Introduction*, 2nd edn, Prentice-Hall International, 1988.
- I. Pohl and A. Shaw, *The Nature of Computation: An Introduction to Computer Science*, W. H. Freeman & Co., 1981.

These are textbooks for introductory computer science courses and contain brief but informative accounts of many of the subjects treated in this book. In addition, they discuss a number of other topics, such as operating systems and computer architecture.

The following book is a hands-on introduction to computer science, which touches on many of the topics discussed in this book, such as programming paradigms, abstraction, compilation and interpretation, and more.

- H. Abelson and G. J. Sussman, *Structure and Interpretation of Computer Programs*, 2nd edn, MIT Press, 1996.

There is an excellent handbook of theoretical topics in computer science, though by now some of its chapters might be a little dated. Its two volumes contain detailed technical articles on many of the topics discussed in this book. We shall refer to several of these in the appropriate chapters. The general reference is:

- *Handbook of Theoretical Computer Science*, vols A and B, J. van Leeuwen, ed., Elsevier and MIT Press, 1990.

Turning for a moment from the spirit of computing to its flesh and bones and the link between the three, one of the best places to read about computers and the difficulty people have in getting acquainted with them is:

- J. Shore, *The Sachertorte Algorithm and Other Antidotes to Computer Anxiety*, Viking Penguin, 1985.

There are several periodicals that publish papers in virtually all areas of algorithmics:

- *Journal of the Association for Computing Machinery*, often abbreviated *J. Assoc. Comput. Mach.*, or just *J. ACM*; published by the ACM.
- *SIAM Journal on Computing*, abbreviated *SIAM J. Comput.*, or sometimes just *SICOMP*; published by SIAM, the Society for Industrial and Applied Mathematics.
- *Information and Computation* (formerly *Information and Control*), abbreviated *Inf. and Comput.*, or *Inf. and Cont.*; published by Elsevier.
- *Journal of Computer and System Sciences*, abbreviated *J. Comput. Syst. Sci.*, or sometimes just *JCSS*; published by Elsevier.
- *Theoretical Computer Science*, abbreviated *Theor. Comput. Sci.*, or sometimes just *TCS*; published by Elsevier.
- *The Computer Journal*, abbreviated *Comput. J.*; published by Oxford University Press.
- *Fundamenta Informaticae*, abbreviated *Fund. Inf.*; published by IOS Press, under the auspices of the European Association for Theoretical Computer Science (EATCS).
- *Information Processing Letters*, abbreviated *Inf. Proc. Lett.*, or sometimes just *IPL*; contains short papers or communications and is published by Elsevier.
- *Computing Surveys*, abbreviated *Comput. Surv.*; contains lengthy survey papers and is published by the ACM.
- *International Journal of Foundations of Computer Science*, abbreviated *Int. J. Found. Comput. Sci.*, or sometimes just *IJFCS*; published by World Scientific.

The following journals are of a somewhat more elementary and widespread nature, and occasionally contain relevant articles:

- *Communications of the Association for Computing Machinery*, abbreviated *Comm. Assoc. Comput. Mach.*, or sometimes just *CACM*; published by the ACM.
- *Computer*, sometimes called *IEEE Computer*; published by the IEEE.

The following non-refereed newsletters contain short papers, communications, and announcements relevant to many aspects of algorithmics:

- *ACM SIGACT News*; published by ACM's Special Interest Group on Automata and Computability Theory.
- *Bulletin of the EATCS*; published by the European Association for Theoretical Computer Science.

In addition to these, the following journal publishes short reviews of books and papers in computer science, algorithmics included:

- *Computing Reviews*, abbreviated *Comput. Rev.*, or sometimes just *CR*; published by the ACM.

There are several annual or biannual conferences, symposia, and colloquia that are devoted to algorithmics at large, and numerous others that concentrate on specific subjects. They will not be listed here, but will be referenced as the occasion arises. Nevertheless, the reader should keep in mind that many are sponsored by the various subgroups of the ACM and the IEEE, and the proceedings of many others appear in the Springer-Verlag series of Lecture Notes in Computer Science.

■ Chapter 1

The following books shed light on the history of computing:

- *A History of Computing in the Twentieth Century*, N. C. Metropolis et al., eds, Academic Press, 1980.
- F. G. Ashherst, *Pioneers of Computing*, Frederick Muller, 1983.
- W. Aspray, *John von Neumann and the Origins of Modern Computing (History of Computing)*, MIT Press, 1990.
- M. R. Williams, *A History of Computing Technology*, 2nd edn, Wiley-IEEE Press, 1997.
- M. Campbell-Kelly and W. Aspray, *Computer: A History of the Information Machine*, Basic Books, 1997.
- G. Ifrah, *The Universal History of Computing: From the Abacus to the Quantum Computer*, John Wiley & Sons, 2002.
- C. Wurster, *Computers: An Illustrated History*, TASCHEN America Llc, 2002.

It is also worth reading the following biographies of two of the most influential pioneers of computer science:

- A. Hyman, *Charles Babbage, Pioneer of the Computer*, Princeton University Press, 1985.
- A. Hodges, *Alan Turing: The Enigma*, Simon & Schuster, 1983.

The following journals are devoted entirely to the history of computation, and often contain illuminating papers on the origins and insights of the early researchers:

- *IEEE Annals of the History of Computing*, abbreviated *Ann. Hist. Comput.*; a quarterly published by IEEE.
- *Journal of the Association for History and Computing*, abbreviated *J. Assoc. Hist. Comput.*; published by AAHC, the American Association for History and Computing.
- *History and Computing*; published by Edinburgh University Press and AHC, the Association for History and Computing.

The analogy between computer science and surgery [p. 6] appears in:

- E. W. Dijkstra, "On a Cultural Gap," *The Mathematical Intelligencer* 8 (1986), pp. 48–52.

A detailed, illustrated account of Babbage's analytical engine [p. 7] appears in:

- A. G. Bromley, "Charles Babbage's Analytical Engine, 1838," *Ann. Hist. Comput.* 4 (1982), pp. 196–217.

The latest ACM curriculum of the core part of computer science, and reports of a joint IEEE/ACM task force on curricula for computing [p. 8] can be found in:

- P. J. Denning et al., "Computing as a Discipline," *Comm. Assoc. Comput. Mach.* 32 (1989), pp. 9–23.

- http://www.acm.org/education/curr91/homepage.html
- http://www.computer.org/education/cc2001

The mousse recipe [p. 10] is from page 73 of:

- P. C. Sinclair and R. K. Malinowski, *French Cooking*, Weathervane Books, 1978.

Chapter 2

There are numerous excellent textbooks devoted to algorithms and data structures. In the notes for Chapters 4, 5, and 6 a number of those that emphasize design methods, design through correctness proofs, and design for efficiency, respectively, are listed. Here are some that are fitting for this less specific chapter:

- A. V. Aho, J. E. Hopcroft, and J. D. Ullman, *Data Structures and Algorithms*, Addison-Wesley, 1983.
- E. Horowitz and S. Sahni, *Fundamentals of Data Structures in Pascal*, 4th edn, W. H. Freeman & Co., 1999.
- D. E. Knuth, *The Art of Computer Programming, vol. 1: Fundamental Algorithms*, 3rd edn, Addison-Wesley, 1997.
- T. A. Standish, *Data Structures, Algorithms and Software Principles*, Addison-Wesley, 1994.
- N. Wirth, *Algorithms and Data Structures*, Prentice-Hall, 1986.
- T. H. Cormen, C. E. Leiserson, R. L. Rivest, and C. Stein, *Introduction to Algorithms*, 2nd edn, MIT Press, 2001.

The following early monographs have been extremely influential:

- E. W. Dijkstra, "Notes on Structured Programming," in *Structured Programming*, Academic Press, 1972.
- C. A. R. Hoare, "Notes on Data Structuring," in *Structured Programming*, Academic Press, 1972.

The following are expositions of several of the issues treated in this chapter:

- D. E. Knuth, "Algorithms," *Scientific American* 236:4 (1977), pp. 63–80.
- N. Wirth, "Data Structures and Algorithms," *Scientific American* 251:3 (1984), pp. 60–9.

Apart from the general periodicals listed earlier, here are some additional journals that publish papers on algorithms and data structures:

- *Journal of Algorithms*, abbreviated *J. Algs.*; published by Elsevier.
- *Journal of Complexity*, abbreviated *J. Complex.*; published by Elsevier.
- *Discrete & Computational Geometry*, abbreviated *Disc. Comput. Geom.*; published by Springer-Verlag.

- *Combinatorica*; published by Springer-Verlag.
- *Journal of Symbolic Computation*, abbreviated *J. Symb. Comput.*; published by Elsevier.
- *Computing*; published by Springer-Verlag.
- *BIT*; published by Kluwer Academic Publishers.

The bubblesort algorithm [pp. 21–3], as well as a host of other sorting methods, is described in detail in Knuth's encyclopedic volume:

- D. E. Knuth, *The Art of Computer Programming, vol. 3: Sorting and Searching*, 2nd edn, Addison-Wesley, 1998.

The controversy surrounding the "goto" statement [pp. 23–4] is generally considered to have originated in the following letter to the editor:

- E. W. Dijkstra, "Go To Statement Considered Harmful," *Comm. Assoc. Comput. Mach.* 11 (1968), pp. 147–8.

More about this controversy, as well as the possibility of eliminating certain control structures in favor of a set of minimal ones [pp. 32–3], can be found in the following papers:

- D. E. Knuth, "Structured Programming with go to Statements," *Comput. Surv.* 6 (1974), pp. 261–301.
- D. Harel, "On Folk Theorems," *Comm. Assoc. Comput. Mach.* 23 (1980), pp. 379–89.

The following book is devoted to the idea (put forward by many researchers) of writing only well-structured programs that use only a few selected control constructs:

- R. C. Linger, H. D. Mills, and B. I. Witt, *Structured Programming: Theory and Practice*, Addison-Wesley, 1979.

A good place to read about various flowchart techniques and notations [pp. 24–6] is:

- T. R. G. Green, "Pictures of Programs and Other Processes, or How To Do Things with Lines," *Behaviour and Information Technology* 1 (1982), pp. 3–36.

There are many places to read about gradual, top-down design of large algorithms and programs, using subroutines or other similar means [pp. 26–30]. Apart from Dijkstra's notes on structured programming, the following have been particularly influential:

- N. Wirth, "Program Development by Stepwise Refinement," *Comm. Assoc. Comput. Mach.* 14 (1971), pp. 221–7.
- D. L. Parnas, "A Technique for Software Module Specification with Examples," *Comm. Assoc. Comput. Mach.* 15 (1972), pp. 330–6.
- E. Yourdon and L. L. Constantine, *Structured Design: Fundamentals of a Discipline of Computer Program and Systems Design*, Prentice-Hall, 1979.

Recursion [pp. 30–1] is a fascinating subject and a wealth of interesting material about it can be found in:

- E. Roberts, *Thinking Recursively*, John Wiley & Sons, 1986.
- D. R. Hofstadter, *Gödel, Escher, Bach: An Eternal Golden Braid*, Basic Books, 1979.

The recursive solution to the Towers of Hanoi problem [pp. 31–2] appears in almost any elementary book on algorithms, including several of those already mentioned.

Treesort [pp. 40–3] is described in detail and is traced back to its many independent inventors in Knuth's volume on sorting and searching previously mentioned, where it is called tree insertion sort.

Self-adjusting data structures [p. 43] appear routinely in many of the algorithms described in the general books listed for this chapter. Perhaps the most well known are balanced binary trees, which are discussed in detail in Knuth's volume on sorting and searching. The following chapter contains material on this subject too.

- K. Mehlhorn and A. Tsakalidis, "Data Structures," in *Handbook of Theoretical Computer Science*, vol. A, J. van Leeuwen, ed., Elsevier and MIT Press, 1990, pp. 301–41.

There are numerous books devoted to databases [pp. 44–5]. They contain a wealth of information on various database models, languages, and design methods. Here are some:

- C. J. Date, *An Introduction to Database Systems*, 8th edn, Addison-Wesley, 2004.
- J. D. Ullman, *Principles of Database and Knowledge-Base Systems: The New Technologies*, W. H. Freeman & Co., 1989.
- R. Elmasri and S. B. Navathe, *Fundamentals of Database Systems*, 3rd edn, Addison-Wesley, 2002.
- D. Maier, *The Theory of Relational Databases*, Computer Science Press, 1983.
- A. Silberschatz, H. F. Korth, and S. Sudarshan, *Database System Concepts*, 3rd edn, McGraw-Hill, 1999.

The following paper is considered to have been one of the most influential in shaping the prevalent approaches to databases:

- E. F. Codd, "A Relational Model for Large Shared Data Banks," *Comm. Assoc. Comput. Mach.* 13 (1970), pp. 377–87.

The following periodicals and newsletter publish papers about database systems:

- *ACM Transactions on Database Systems*, abbreviated *ACM Trans. Database Syst.*, or sometimes just *TODS*; published by the ACM.
- *Data and Knowledge Engineering*, abbreviated *Data & Knowl. Eng.*; published by Elsevier.
- *Information Systems*, abbreviated *Inf. Syst.*; published by Elsevier.
- *ACM SIGMOD Record*; published by ACM's Special Interest Group on Management of Data.

Data mining and data warehousing [p. 45] are discussed in:

- T. Hastie, T. Tibshirani, and J. Friedman, *The Elements of Statistical Learning: Data Mining, Inference, and Prediction*, Springer-Verlag, 2001.

- J. Han and M. Kamber, *Data Mining: Concepts and Techniques*, Morgan Kaufmann, 2000.
- *Advances in Knowledge Discovery and Data Mining*, U. M. Fayyad, G. Piatetsky-Shapiro, P. Smyth, and R. Uthurusamy, eds., AAAI Press, 1996.
- B. Devlin, *Data Warehouse: From Architecture to Implementation*, Addison-Wesley, 1996.

The following periodical publishes articles on data mining and knowledge discovery:

- *ACM SIGKDD Explorations*; published by the ACM's Special Interest Group on Knowledge Discovery and Data Mining.

Chapter 3

There are a number of books on the general principles of designing programming languages. Here are some:

- T. W. Pratt and M. V. Zelkowitz, *Programming Languages: Design and Implementation*, 4th edn, Prentice-Hall, 2001.
- H. F. Ledgard and M. Marcotty, *The Programming Language Landscape*, 2nd edn, Science Research Associates, 1986.
- J. E. Nicholls, *The Structure and Design of Programming Languages*, Addison-Wesley, 1975.
- M. L. Scott, *Programming Language Pragmatics*, Morgan Kaufmann, 2000.
- R. D. Tennent, *Principles of Programming Languages*, Prentice-Hall International, 1981.

The following one emphasizes abstract data types:

- D. M. Harland, *Polymorphic Programming Languages*, Halstead Press, 1984.

In addition, the following volume contains an extensive collection of some of the central papers in the programming language area, discussing both principles and specific languages:

- *Programming Languages: A Grand Tour*, 3rd edn, E. Horowitz, ed., W. H. Freeman & Co., 1995.

The history of programming languages is described in a paper by P. Wegner in this "grand tour," and also in:

- *History of Programming Languages*, R. L. Wexelblat, ed., Academic Press, 1981.
- *History of Programming Languages*, vol. 2, T. J. Bergin and R. G. Gibson, eds., Addison-Wesley, 1996.
- J. E. Sammet, *Programming Languages: History and Fundamentals*, Prentice-Hall, 1969.

An exposition of several issues related to programming languages and their structure is:

- L. G. Tesler, "Programming Languages," *Scientific American* 251:3 (1984), pp. 70–8.

The following periodicals contain papers about the principles of programming languages:

- *ACM Transactions on Programming Languages and Systems*, abbreviated *ACM Trans. Prog. Lang. Syst.*, or simply *TOPLAS*; published by the ACM.
- *Computer Languages, Systems and Structures*, abbreviated *Comput. Lang., Syst. Struc.*; published by Elsevier.
- *Science of Computer Programming*, abbreviated *Sci. Comput. Prog.*; published by Elsevier.
- *ACM SIGPLAN Notices*; published by ACM's Special Interest Group on Programming Languages.
- *Formal Aspects of Computing*, abbreviated *Form. Aspects Comput.*; published by Springer-Verlag.

The BNF notation for syntax definitions [p. 51] appears in:

- J. Backus, "The Syntax and Semantics of the Proposed International Algebraic Language of the Zurich ACM-GAMM Conference," *Proc. Int. Conf. on Information Processing*, UNESCO, pp. 125–32, 1959.

It was used extensively in the celebrated and extremely influential definition of the language ALGOL 60:

- P. Naur, ed., "Revised Report on the Algorithmic Language Algol 60," *Comm. Assoc. Comput. Mach.* 6 (1963), pp. 1–17.

Syntax diagrams for defining the syntax of programming languages [Figure 3.1, p. 51] appear in:

- K. Jensen and N. Wirth, *PASCAL User Manual and Report*, 3rd edn, Springer-Verlag, 1984.

Turning to semantics [pp. 52–3], the following early papers have been particularly influential in research on the semantics of programming languages:

- D. S. Scott and C. Strachey, "Towards a Mathematical Semantics for Computer Languages," *Proc. Symp. on Computers and Automata*, Polytechnic Inst. of Brooklyn Press, pp. 19–46, 1971.
- D. S. Scott, "Mathematical Concepts in Programming Language Semantics," *Proc. 1972 Spring Joint Computer Conference*, AFIPS Press, Montvale, NJ, pp. 225–34, 1972.

Several books treat the semantics of programming languages in depth, among which are:

- J. E. Stoy, *Denotational Semantics: The Scott–Strachey Approach to Programming Language Theory*, MIT Press, 1977.
- J. W. de Bakker, *Mathematical Theory of Program Correctness*, Prentice-Hall International, 1980.

- D. A. Schmidt, *Denotational Semantics: A Methodology for Language Development*, McGraw-Hill, 1988.
- L. Allison, *A Practical Introduction to Denotational Semantics*, Cambridge University Press, 2002.

Good early survey papers on semantics are:

- R. D. Tennent, "The Denotational Semantics of Programming Languages," *Comm. Assoc. Comput. Mach.* 19 (1976), pp. 437–53.
- D. S. Scott, "Logic and Programming Languages," *Comm. Assoc. Comput. Mach.* 20 (1977), pp. 634–41.

The following books discuss the compilation process in detail [pp. 55–7]:

- A. Aho, R. Sethi, and J. D. Ullman, *Compilers: Principles, Techniques, and Tools*, Addison-Wesley, 1986.
- S. S. Muchnick, *Advanced Compiler Design and Implementation*, Morgan Kaufmann, 1997.
- A. W. Appel and J. Palsberg, *Modern Compiler Implementation in Java*, 2nd edn, Cambridge University Press, 2002.

The following influential early paper discusses the possibility of defining special, self-tailored abstract data types [pp. 58–9]:

- J. V. Guttag and J. J. Horning, "The Algebraic Specification of Abstract Data Types," *Acta Inf.* 10 (1978), pp. 27–52.

Books on specific programming paradigms are mentioned later. However, the following one introduces and contrasts a number of paradigms, including imperative, functional, and logic programming:

- H. Abelson and G. J. Sussman, *Structure and Interpretation of Computer Programs*, 2nd edn, MIT Press, 1996.

FORTRAN [pp. 60–1] was designed by J. Backus and a team of scientists from IBM in 1954. One of the many books describing it is:

- D. D. McCracken, *A Guide to FORTRAN Programming*, John Wiley & Sons, 1961.

Later versions are described in:

- W. Brainerd, "FORTRAN 77," *Comm. Assoc. Comput. Mach.* 21 (1978), pp. 806–20.
- J. C. Adams, W. S. Brainerd, J. T. Martin, B. T. Smith, and J. L. Wagener, *Fortran 95 Handbook*, MIT Press, 1997.

COBOL [pp. 60–1] was designed in 1959 by a technical committee sponsored by the US Department of Defense. Two of the many books describing it are:

- D. D. McCracken and U. Garbassi, *A Guide to COBOL Programming*, 2nd edn, John Wiley & Sons, 1970.
- D. M. Collopy, *Introduction to COBOL: A Guide to Modular Structured Programming*, Prentice-Hall, 1999.

There are many books on PL/I, [pp. 61–4] most of which are out of print. One classic is:

- G. M. Weinberg, *PL/I Programming: A Manual of Style*, McGraw-Hill, 1970.

A more recent book is:

- R. A. Vowels, *Introduction to PL/I, Algorithms, and Structured Programming*, 3rd edn, Vowels, 1997.

PASCAL [p. 63] was designed by N. Wirth and was first described in:

- N. Wirth, "The Programming Language PASCAL," *Acta Informatica* 1 (1971), pp. 35–63.

An important paper assessing the language, and written by its inventor, is:

- N. Wirth, "An Assessment of the Programming Language PASCAL," *IEEE Trans. Soft. Eng.* SE-1 (1975), pp. 192–8.

The C language [pp. 63–4] was designed by B. W. Kernighan and D. M. Ritchie. Their book is the classic reference for the language:

- B. W. Kernighan and D. M. Ritchie, *The C Programming Language*, 2nd edn, Prentice-Hall, 1988.

In the following influential paper, J. Backus (mentioned above as the developer of FORTRAN and the BNF notation) called for the development of functional programming languages [pp. 65–8] based on a small set of strong primitives, in order to facilitate reasoning about such programs and proving them correct:

- J. Backus, "Can Programming Be Liberated from the von Neumann Style? A Functional Style and Its Algebra of Programs," *Comm. Assoc. Comput. Mach.* 21 (1978), pp. 613–41.

LISP [pp. 65–7] was designed by J. McCarthy in 1960, based on the lambda calculus [p. 67] of A. Church and S. C. Kleene. An excellent reference to the lambda calculus is:

- H. P. Barendregt, *The Lambda Calculus: Its Syntax and Semantics*, 2nd edn, North Holland, 1984.

The LISP language is described in many places, among which are:

- J. Allen, *The Anatomy of LISP*, McGraw-Hill, 1978.
- P. H. Winston and B. K. P. Horn, *LISP*, 3rd edn, Addison-Wesley, 1989.
- G. L. Steele, *Common Lisp, the Language*, 2nd edn, Digital Press, 1990.

In addition to Abelson and Sussman's book mentioned above, the following books describe the SCHEME dialect of LISP:

- B. Harvey and M. Wright, *Simply Scheme*, 2nd edn, MIT Press, 1999.
- R. K. Dybvig, *The Scheme Programming Language*, 3rd edn, MIT Press, 2003.

Here are introductions to functional programming using HASKELL and MIRANDA:

- P. Hudak, *The Haskell School of Expression*, Cambridge University Press, 2000.
- S. Thompson, *Haskell: The Craft of Functional Programming*, 2nd edn, Addison-Wesley, 1999.
- S. Thompson, *Miranda: The Craft of Functional Programming*, Addison-Wesley, 1995.

PROLOG [pp. 68–70] was designed by A. Colmerauer in 1970, based upon ideas of R. Kowalski. The underlying approach is described in:

- R. Kowalski, "Algorithm = Logic + Control," *Comm. Assoc. Comput. Mach.* 22 (1979), pp. 424–36.
- J. W. Lloyd, *Foundations of Logic Programming*, 2nd edn, Springer-Verlag, 1987.

Good books for reading about the language are:

- W. F. Clocksin and C. S. Mellish, *Programming in PROLOG*, 5th edn, Springer-Verlag, 2003.
- L. Sterling and E. Shapiro, *The Art of Prolog*, 2nd edn, MIT Press, 1994.

The following two books are good places to read about object-oriented programming [pp. 70–5]. The first is based on EIFFEL (although the word "EIFFEL" appears in it only once), and the second on JAVA:

- B. Meyer, *Object-Oriented Software Construction*, 2nd edn, Prentice-Hall, 1997.
- B. Liskov with J. Guttag, *Program Development in Java: Abstraction, Specification, and Object-Oriented Design*, Addison-Wesley, 2000.

A critical look at the principles of object-oriented programming through a comparison of the strengths and weaknesses of three influential languages is:

- I. Joyner, *Objects Unencapsulated: Java, Eiffel, and C++??*, Prentice-Hall, 1999.

SIMULA [p. 70] was developed by O.-J. Dahl and K. Nygaard. It is described in:

- O.-J. Dahl and K. Nygaard, "SIMULA—an ALGOL-Based Simulation Language," *Comm. Assoc. Comput. Mach.* 9 (1966), pp. 671–8.
- G. M. Birtwistle, O.-J. Dahl, B. Myhrhaug, and K. Nygaard, *Simula Begin*, Van Nostrand Reinhold, 1973.

SMALLTALK [p. 72] was developed by the Learning Research Group at XEROX PARC (Palo Alto Research Center), as part of the pioneering development of a personal computer that included a bit-mapped display, a mouse, and overlapping windows. This was done years before the ideas were commercialized by other companies. The following books describe the language and its innovative programming environment:

- A. Goldberg and D. Robson, *Smalltalk-80: The Language*, Addison-Wesley, 1989.
- A. Goldberg, *Smalltalk-80: The Interactive Programming Environment*, Addison-Wesley, 1984.

C++ [p. 72] was developed by B. Stroustrup at AT&T Bell Labs. His definitive book on the language is:

- B. Stroustrup, *The C++ Programming Language*, 3rd edn, Addison-Wesley, 2000.

JAVA [pp. 72–4] was developed at Sun Microsystems by J. Gosling, and was originally intended for programming "smart" consumer electronic devices. The official description of the language is:

- K. Arnold and J. Gosling, *The Java Programming Language*, 3rd edn, Addison-Wesley, 2000.

EIFFEL [pp. 74–5] was developed by B. Meyer, according to his theoretical approach to object-oriented programming. The general approach is described in his textbook cited above, and the language itself is described in the following book:

- B. Meyer, *Eiffel: The Language*, Prentice-Hall, 1992.

The design of the EIFFEL libraries is interesting in its own right; it is described in:

- B. Meyer, *Reusable Software: The Base Object-Oriented Component Libraries*, Prentice-Hall, 1994.

Chapter 4

There are several excellent books on algorithms, which, among other things, emphasize design paradigms and methods. They include:

- A. V. Aho, J. E. Hopcroft, and J. D. Ullman, *The Design and Analysis of Computer Algorithms*, Addison-Wesley, 1974.
- E. Horowitz, S. Sahni and S. Rajasekaran, *Computer Algorithms*, Computer Science Press, 1997.
- T. H. Cormen, C. E. Leiserson, R. L. Rivest, and C. Stein, *Introduction to Algorithms*, 2nd edn, MIT Press, 2001.
- S. Baase and A. Van Gelder, *Computer Algorithms: Introduction to Design and Analysis*, 3rd edn, Addison-Wesley, 1999.
- D. Kozen, *The Design and Analysis of Algorithms*, Springer-Verlag, 1992.
- U. Manber, *Introduction to Algorithms: A Creative Approach*, Addison-Wesley, 1989.
- A. V. Aho and J. D. Ullman, *Foundations of Computer Science*, W. H. Freeman & Co., 1995.
- M. Sipser, *Introduction to the Theory of Computation*, Brooks Cole, 1996.
- G. Brassard and P. Bratley, *Fundamentals of Algorithmics*, Prentice-Hall, 1995.

A more elementary book is:

- R. G. Dromey, *How to Solve it by Computer*, Prentice-Hall, 1982.

Apart from these, there are many books that are organized around specific kinds of algorithms, but implicitly contain also a wealth of information about algorithmic methods. Here are some:

- S. Even, *Graph Algorithms*, Computer Science Press, 1979.
- G. H. Gonnet, *Handbook of Algorithms and Data Structures*, Addison-Wesley, 1984.
- T. C. Hu and M. T. Shing, *Combinatorial Algorithms*, Dover Publications, 2002.
- K. Mehlhorn, *Data Structures and Algorithms 1: Sorting and Searching*, Springer-Verlag, 1984.
- K. Mehlhorn, *Data Structures and Algorithms 2: Graph Algorithms and NP-Completeness*, Springer-Verlag, 1987.
- K. Mehlhorn, *Data Structures and Algorithms 3: Multi-Dimensional Searching and Computational Geometry*, Springer-Verlag, 1990.
- D. E. Knuth, *The Art of Computer Programming, vol. 1: Fundamental Algorithms*, 3rd edn, Addison-Wesley, 1997.
- D. E. Knuth, *The Art of Computer Programming, vol. 2: Seminumerical Algorithms*, 3rd edn, Addison-Wesley, 1997.
- D. E. Knuth, *The Art of Computer Programming, vol. 3: Sorting and Searching*, 2nd edn, Addison-Wesley, 1998.
- E. L. Lawler, *Combinatorial Optimization: Networks and Matroids*, Dover Publications, 2001.
- C. H. Papadimitriou and K. Steiglitz, *Combinatorial Optimization: Algorithms and Complexity*, Prentice-Hall, 1982.
- E. M. Reingold *Combinatorial Algorithms: Theory and Practice*, Prentice-Hall, 1977.
- R. Sedgewick and P. Flajolet, *An Introduction to the Analysis of Algorithms*, Addison-Wesley, 1995.
- R. E. Tarjan, *Data Structures and Network Algorithms*, CBMS-NSF Regional Conf. Series in Appl. Math., SIAM Press, 1983.

Two books on computational geometry [pp. 83–5] are Mehlhorn's third volume above and:

- F. P. Preparata and M. I. Shamos, *Computational Geometry: An Introduction*, Springer-Verlag, 1991.

An excellent survey is:

- F. F. Yao, "Computational Geometry," in *Handbook of Theoretical Computer Science*, vol. A, J. van Leeuwen, ed., Elsevier and MIT Press, 1990, pp. 343–89.

The mergesort algorithm [pp. 86–7] is described in many of the books listed, but (as mentioned earlier in connection with bubblesort and treesort) Knuth's volume on sorting and searching is by far the most comprehensive reference.

The greedy spanning tree algorithm [pp. 88–9] is from:

■ R. C. Prim, "Shortest Connection Networks and Some Generalizations," *Bell Syst. Tech. J.* 36 (1957), pp. 1389–401.

Another important paper on minimal spanning trees is:

■ J. B. Kruskal, Jr. , "On the Shortest Spanning Subtree of a Graph and the Traveling Salesman Problem," *Proc. Amer. Math. Soc.* 7 (1956), pp. 48–50.

An early paper relevant to both spanning trees and shortest path algorithms is:

■ E. W. Dijkstra, "A Note on Two Problems in Connexion with Graphs," *Numerische Mathematik* 1 (1959), pp. 269–71.

The history of spanning tree algorithms, which apparently starts well before Prim and Kruskal, is traced in:

■ R. L. Graham and P. Hell, "On the History of The Minimal Spanning Tree Problem," *Ann. Hist. Comput.* 7 (1985), pp. 43–57.

Here are books in which dynamic programming (called dynamic planning in the text) [pp. 89–91] is outlined in more detail:

■ R. E. Bellman, *Dynamic Programming*, Princeton University Press, 1957 (paperback edition, Dover Publications, 2003).
■ S. E. Dreyfus and A. M. Law, *The Art and Theory of Dynamic Programming*, Academic Press, 1977.
■ D. Bertsekas, *Dynamic Programming and Optimal Control*, 2nd edn, Athena Scientific, 2001.

Two very influential papers concerning algorithmic problems on graphs are:

■ R. E. Tarjan, "Depth First Search and Linear Graph Algorithms," *SIAM J. Comput.* 1 (1972), pp. 146–60.
■ J. E. Hopcroft and R. E. Tarjan, "Efficient Algorithms for Graph Manipulation," *Comm. Assoc. Comput. Mach.* 16 (1973), pp. 372–8.

Good surveys of graph algorithms appear in:

■ T. H. Cormen, C. E. Leiserson, R. L. Rivest, and C. Stein, *Introduction to Algorithms*, 2nd edn, MIT Press, 2001.
■ J. van Leeuwen, "Graph Algorithms," in *Handbook of Theoretical Computer Science*, vol. A, J. van Leeuwen, ed., Elsevier and MIT Press, 1990, pp. 525–631.

Heaps [pp. 91–2] are discussed in great detail in most books on algorithms and data structures. See, e.g., the books listed at the beginning of the notes for Chapter 2.

The following book describes nondestructive algorithms [pp. 92–4] and appropriate analysis methods:

■ C. Okasaki, *Purely Functional Data Structures*, Cambridge University Press, 1998.

On-line algorithms [pp. 94–5] are described in:

- A. Borodin and R. El-Yaniv, *Online Computation and Competitive Analysis*, Cambridge University Press, 1998.

Chapter 5

There are several books devoted to methods and tools for the verification of algorithms and programs. Here are some:

- Z. Manna, *Mathematical Theory of Computation*, McGraw-Hill, 1974.
- S. Alagić and M. A. Arbib, *The Design of Well-Structured and Correct Programs*, Springer-Verlag, 1978.
- J. W. de Bakker, *Mathematical Theory of Program Correctness*, Prentice-Hall International, 1980.
- J. Loeckx and K. Sieber, *The Foundations of Program Verification*, 2nd edn, John Wiley & Sons, 1987.
- N. Francez, *Program Verification*, Addison-Wesley, 1991.
- K. R. Apt and E.-R. Olderog, *Verification of Sequential and Concurrent Programs*, Springer-Verlag, 1991.
- Z. Manna and A. Pnueli, *Temporal Verification of Reactive Systems: Safety*, Springer-Verlag, 1995.
- E. M. Clarke, O. Grumberg, and D. A. Peled, *Model Checking*, MIT Press, 2000.

In addition, the following early books contain informative chapters on correctness and verification:

- R. Bird, *Programs and Machines: An Introduction to the Theory of Computation*, John Wiley & Sons, 1976.
- J. M. Brady, *The Theory of Computer Science: A Programming Approach*, Chapman & Hall, 1977.
- S. A. Greibach, *Theory of Program Structures: Schemes, Semantics, Verification*, Springer-Verlag, 1975.
- E. V. Krishnamurthy, *Introductory Theory of Computer Science*, Springer-Verlag, 1983.

Apart from the general periodicals listed earlier, the following more specific journals publish many papers pertaining to algorithmic correctness:

- *ACM Transactions on Programming Languages and Systems*, sometimes abbreviated *ACM Trans. Prog. Lang. Syst.*, or simply *TOPLAS*; published by the ACM.
- *Acta Informatica*, abbreviated *Acta Inf.*; published by Springer-Verlag.
- *Science of Computer Programming*, abbreviated *Sci. Comput. Prog.*; published by Elsevier.
- *Journal of Automated Reasoning*, abbreviated *J. Autom. Reas.*; published by Kluwer Academic Publishers.

- *IEEE Transactions on Software Engineering*, abbreviated *IEEE Trans. Soft. Eng.*; published by the IEEE.

- *Formal Aspects of Computing*, abbreviated *Form. Aspects Comput.*; published by Springer-Verlag.

- *Software and System Modeling*, abbreviated *Soft. Syst. Modeling*, or simply *SoSyM*; published by Springer-Verlag.

Some of the stories of computer errors [p. 99] are among numerous ones that are reported regularly in:

- *ACM Software Engineering Notes*; published by ACM's Special Interest Group on Software Engineering.

Good places to read about syntactic analysis and error handling in compilation [pp. 101–3] include:

- A. V. Aho, R. Sethi, and J. D. Ullman, *Compilers: Principles, Techniques, and Tools*, Addison-Wesley, 1986.

- R. Allen, K. Kennedy, and J. R. Allen, *Optimizing Compilers for Modern Architectures: A Dependence-Based Approach*, Morgan Kaufmann, 2001.

- S. S. Muchnick, *Advanced Compiler Design and Implementation*, Morgan Kaufmann, 1997.

Good places to read about testing [pp. 103–4] are:

- C. Kaner, J. Falk, and H. Q. Nguyen, *Testing Computer Software*, 2nd edn, John Wiley & Sons, 1999.

- B. Hetzel, *The Complete Guide to Software Testing*, 2nd edn, John Wiley & Sons, 1993.

- R. V. Binder, *Testing Object-Oriented Systems: Models, Patterns, and Tools*, Addison-Wesley, 1999.

- B. Marick, *The Craft of Software Testing: Subsystem Testing, Including Object-Based and Object-Oriented Testing*, Prentice-Hall, 1994.

- G. J. Myers, *The Art of Software Testing*, John Wiley & Sons, 1979.

The mermaid aphorism [p. 104] appears on page 17 of:

- G. D. Bergland, "A Guided Tour of Program Design Methodologies," *Computer* 14 (1981), pp. 13–37.

The aphorism about the absence/presence of errors [p. 104] appears on page 6 of:

- E. W. Dijkstra, "Notes on Structured Programming," in *Structured Programming*, Academic Press, 1972.

The notion of partial correctness [p. 106] appears in:

- Z. Manna, "The Correctness of Programs," *J. Comput. Syst. Sci.* 3 (1969), pp. 119–27.

The statement about the time software is released for use [p. 107] appears on page 1330 of:

- D. L. Parnas, "Software Aspects of Strategic Defense Systems," *Comm. Assoc. Comput. Mach.* 28 (1985), pp. 1326–35.

Provocative but important papers on the (im)possibility of proving correctness of programs are:

- R. A. De Millo, R. J. Lipton, and A. J. Perlis, "Social Processes and Proofs of Theorems and Programs," *Comm. Assoc. Comput. Mach.* 22 (1979), pp. 271–80.
- J. H. Fetzer, "Program Verification: The Very Idea," *Comm. Assoc. Comput. Mach.* 31 (1988), pp. 1048–63.

Both the intermediate assertion (invariant) method for proving partial correctness [pp. 108–9], and the convergence method (sometimes called the well-founded sets method) for proving termination [pp. 109–14] are due to R. W. Floyd. They were first described as proof methods in the following paper, although they have their roots in much earlier work of Turing, von Neumann, and others:

- R. W. Floyd, "Assigning Meanings to Programs," *Proc. Symp. on Applied Math.* (vol. 19: "Mathematical Aspects of Computer Science"), American Math. Soc., Providence, RI, pp. 19–32, 1967.

Three important and influential papers expounding upon Floyd's methods are:

- C. A. R. Hoare, "An Axiomatic Basis for Computer Programming," *Comm. Assoc. Comput. Mach.* 12 (1969), pp. 576–83.
- S. Cook, "Soundness and Completeness of an Axiom System for Program Verification," *SIAM J. Comput.* 7 (1978), pp. 70–90.
- E. M. Clarke, "Programming Language Constructs for which it is Impossible to Obtain Good Hoare-Like Axioms," *J. Assoc. Comput. Mach.* 26 (1979), pp. 129–47.

Besides the books on verification recommended earlier, excellent surveys of the methods and ideas that originated in the work of Floyd, Hoare, and Cook are:

- K. R. Apt, "Ten Years of Hoare's Logic: A Survey," *ACM Trans. Prog. Lang. Syst.* 3 (1981), pp. 431–83.
- P. Cousot, "Methods and Logics for Proving Programs," in *Handbook of Theoretical Computer Science*, vol. B, J. van Leeuwen, ed., Elsevier and MIT Press, 1990, pp. 841–993.

An efficient algorithm for finding a minimal set of checkpoints to which assertions can be attached for proving correctness [p. 114] appears in:

- A. Shamir, "Finding Minimum Cutsets in Reducible Graphs," *SIAM J. Comput.* 8 (1979), p. 645–55.

That a partially correct program can, in principle, always be proved correct [p. 114]—a kind of completeness result—is established in Cook's paper above. That a totally correct program can also be so proved is established in:

- D. Harel, "Arithmetical Completeness in Logics of Programs," *Proc. Int. Colloq. on Automata, Lang. and Prog.*, Lecture Notes in Computer Science, vol. 62, Springer-Verlag, pp. 268–88, 1978.

A large amount of information on a variety of such completeness results can be found in:

- D. Harel, D. Kozen, and J. Tiuryn, *Dynamic Logic*, MIT Press, 2000.

A good place to read about mathematical induction [p. 116] and the ways it is used in program verification is:

- M. Wand, *Induction, Recursion, and Programming*, Elsevier Science, 1980.

The simple iterative solution to the Towers of Hanoi problem [p. 118] appears in:

- R. E. Allardice and A. Y. Fraser, "La tour d'Hanoï" *Proc. Edinburgh Math. Soc.*, 2 (1884), pp. 50–3.

The following books contain detailed approaches to as-you-go verification [pp. 118–19], by providing methodologies for constructing well-structured and correct programs:

- E. W. Dijkstra, *A Discipline of Programming*, Prentice-Hall, 1976.
- D. Gries, *The Science of Programming*, Springer-Verlag, 1981.
- J. C. Reynolds, *The Craft of Programming*, Prentice-Hall International, 1981.
- Z. Manna and R. Waldinger, *The Deductive Foundations of Computer Programming*, Addison-Wesley, 1993.

The design by contract methodology [pp. 119–20] is elucidated in:

- B. Meyer, *Object-Oriented Software Construction*, 2nd edn, Prentice-Hall, 1997.
- R. Mitchell and J. McKim, *Design by Contract, by Example*, Addison-Wesley, 2002.

Here are some pointers to early work on computer-aided program verification [pp. 120–1]:

- R. S. Boyer and J S. Moore, *The Computational Logic Handbook*, Academic Press, 1997.
- R. L. Constable et al., *Implementing Mathematics with the Nuprl Proof Development System*, Prentice-Hall, 1986.
- M. J. Gordon, A. J. R. G. Milner, and C. P. Wadsworth, *Edinburgh LCF: A Mechanised Logic of Computation*, Lecture Notes in Computer Science, vol. 78, Springer-Verlag, 1979.

Model checking [p. 121] is discussed in detail in:

- K. L. McMillan, *Symbolic Model Checking: An Approach to the State Explosion Problem*, Kluwer Academic Publishers, 1993.
- E. M. Clarke, O. Grumberg, and D. A. Peled, *Model Checking*, MIT Press, 2000.

Three basic papers on dynamic logics [pp. 22–3] are:

- A. Salwicki, "Formalized Algorithmic Languages," *Bull. Acad. Polon. Sci., Ser. Sci. Math. Astron. Phys.* 18 (1970), pp. 227–32.
- V. R. Pratt, "Semantic Considerations on Floyd-Hoare Logic," *Proc. 17th IEEE Symp. on Foundations of Computer Science*, IEEE Press, pp. 109–21, 1976.
- M. J. Fischer and R. E. Ladner, "Propositional Dynamic Logic of Regular Programs," *J. Comput. Syst. Sci.* 18 (1979), pp. 194–211.

The entire area has been surveyed in:

- D. Harel, D. Kozen, and J. Tiuryn, *Dynamic Logic*, MIT Press, 2000.

Good places to read about program synthesis [p. 123] are:

- N. Dershowitz, *The Evolution of Programs*, Birkhäuser, 1983.
- Z. Manna and R. Waldinger, *The Deductive Foundations of Computer Programming*, Addison-Wesley, 1993.

Two early papers on program transformations [p. 123] are:

- J. Darlington and R. M. Burstall, "A System which Automatically Improves Programs," *Proc. 3rd Int. Conf. on Artificial Intelligence*, pp. 479–85, 1973.
- S. L. Gerhart, "Proof Theory of Partial Correctness Verification Systems," *SIAM J. Comput.* 5 (1976), pp. 355–77.

An early survey of implemented systems that aid in program testing is:

- H. Partsch and R. Steinbrüggen, "Program Transformation Systems," *Comput. Surv.* 15 (1983), pp. 199–236.

Building upon the work of many predecessors, the four-color problem [pp. 123–5] was finally solved by K. I. Appel and W. Haken, and was first announced in:

- K. I. Appel and W. Haken, "Every Planar Map is Four Colorable," *Bull. Amer. Math. Soc.* 82 (1976), pp. 711–12.

A detailed account of the problem and its solution can be found in:

- T. L. Saaty and P. C. Kainen, *The Four Color Problem: Assaults and Conquest*, Dover, 1986.

Chapter 6

Most of the books recommended in the notes for Chapter 4 are also relevant here, since they typically spend considerable time analyzing the efficiency of the algorithms they present. Four of them are mentioned here again, followed by several additional books. These all contain a good overview of the subject of algorithmic efficiency, with examples of a variety of algorithms:

- T. H. Cormen, C. E. Leiserson, R. L. Rivest, and C. Stein, *Introduction to Algorithms*, 2nd edn, MIT Press, 2001.
- D. Kozen, *The Design and Analysis of Algorithms*, Springer-Verlag, 1992.
- A. V. Aho, J. E. Hopcroft, and J. D. Ullman, *The Design and Analysis of Computer Algorithms*, Addison-Wesley, 1974.
- E. Horowitz, S. Sahni, and S. Rajasekaran, *Computer Algorithms*, Computer Science Press, 1997.
- M. Hofri, *Analysis of Algorithms: Computational Methods & Mathematical Tools*, Oxford University Press, 1995.
- P. W. Purdom, Jr., and C. A. Brown, *The Analysis of Algorithms*, Holt, Rinehart & Winston, 1997.
- G. J. E. Rawlings, *Compared to What?: An Introduction to the Analysis of Algorithms*, W. H. Freeman & Co., 1991.
- R. Sedgewick and P. Flajolet, *An Introduction to the Analysis of Algorithms*, Addison-Wesley, 1995.
- C. H. Papadimitriou, *Computational Complexity*, Addison-Wesley, 1994.

A useful book whose title speaks for itself is:

- J. L. Bentley, *Writing Efficient Programs*, Prentice-Hall, 1982.

Its author, J. L. Bentley, has written a column on efficient algorithms in the *Comm. Assoc. Comput. Mach.* Some of these appear in:

- J. L. Bentley, *Programming Pearls*, 2nd edn, Addison-Wesley, 1999.
- J. L. Bentley, *More Programming Pearls: Confessions of a Coder*, Addison-Wesley, 1988.

Two handbooks containing much of the mathematics used in typical analysis of algorithmic efficiency are:

- D. H. Greene and D. E. Knuth, *Mathematics for the Analysis of Algorithms*, 3rd edn, Birkhäuser, 1990.
- R. L. Graham, D. E. Knuth, and O. Patashnik, *Concrete Mathematics: Foundation for Computer Science*, 2nd edn, Addison-Wesley, 1994.

As far as periodicals are concerned, besides the ones listed in the general section of the notes, those listed in the notes for Chapter 2 are relevant here too.

The history of the big-O notation (which, strictly speaking, should be called the *big-Omicron* notation) [pp. 132–3] and its adoption in computer science is traced in:

- D. E. Knuth, "Big Omicron and Big Omega and Big Theta," *SIGACT News* 8:2 (1976), pp. 18–24.

Several variants of binary search [pp. 133–6, 146–8], as well as their analysis and origins, appear in Knuth's volume on searching and sorting:

- D. E. Knuth, *The Art of Computer Programming, vol. 3: Sorting and Searching*, 2nd edn, Addison-Wesley, 1998.

Treesort, mergesort, and heapsort [pp. 142–3] are also analyzed in detail in Knuth's volume, as is quicksort [p. 136]. Quicksort was invented by C. A. R. Hoare and first appeared in:

- C. A. R. Hoare, "Quicksort," *Comput. J.* 5 (1962), pp. 10–15.

An extensive survey of methods for average-case analysis [pp. 143–4] is:

- J. S. Vitter and P. Flajolet, "Average-Case Analysis of Algorithms and Data Structures," in *Handbook of Theoretical Computer Science*, vol. A, J. van Leeuwen, ed., Elsevier and MIT Press, 1990, pp. 431–524.

The convex hull algorithm [pp. 149–51], sometimes called the *Graham scan*, appears in:

- R. L. Graham, "An Efficient Algorithm for Determining the Convex Hull of a Finite Planar Set," *Inf. Proc. Lett.* 1 (1972), pp. 132–3.

Two books devoted to computational geometry, which among many other topics include more efficient convex hull algorithms, are:

- F. P. Preparata and M. I. Shamos, *Computational Geometry: An Introduction*, Springer-Verlag, 1991.
- K. Mehlhorn, *Data Structures and Algorithms 3: Multi-Dimensional Searching and Computational Geometry*, Springer-Verlag, 1990.

A survey of the subject is:

- F. F. Yao, "Computational Geometry," in *Handbook of Theoretical Computer Science* vol. A, J. van Leeuwen, ed., Elsevier and MIT Press, 1990, pp. 343–89.

Almost linear algorithms for the spanning tree problem [p. 152] appear in:

- M. L. Fredman and R. E. Tarjan, "Fibonacci Heaps and their Uses in Improved Network Optimization Algorithms," *J. Assoc. Comput. Mach.* 34 (1987), pp. 596–615.
- H. N. Gabow, Z. Galis, T. H. Spencer, and R. E. Tarjan, "Efficient Algorithms for Finding Minimal Spanning Trees in Undirected and Directed Graphs," *Combinatorica* 6 (1986) pp. 106–22.

Chapter 7

The following book is devoted in its entirety to intractability. It concentrates on the class of NP-complete problems and related issues and, in addition, contains a detailed annotated list of the numerous problems known in 1979 to have been NP-complete:

- M. R. Garey and D. S. Johnson, *Computers and Intractability: A Guide to NP-Completeness*, W. H. Freeman & Co., 1979.

Between 1981 and 1992, one of the authors of this book, D. S. Johnson, wrote a periodical column in the *Journal of Algorithms*, called "The NP-Completeness Column: An Ongoing Guide." Together, the book and the many columns provide a list of hundreds of known NP-complete problems, which, as of the early 1990s came as close to being really complete as anything of its kind.

Many books contain chapters that discuss intractable problems and NP-completeness. They include:

- M. D. Davis, R. Sigal, and E. J. Weyuker, *Computability, Complexity, and Languages: Fundamentals of Theoretical Computer Science*, 2nd edn, Academic Press, 1994.
- J. E. Hopcroft, R. Motwani, and J. D. Ullman, *Introduction to Automata Theory, Languages and Computation*, 2nd edn, Addison-Wesley, 2001.
- E. Horowitz, S. Sahni, and S. Rajasekaran, *Computer Algorithms*, Computer Science Press, 1997.
- E. V. Krishnamurthy, *Introductory Theory of Computer Science*, Springer-Verlag, 1983.
- H. R. Lewis and C. H. Papadimitriou, *Elements of the Theory of Computation*, 2nd edn, Prentice-Hall, 1997.
- M. Machtey and P. Young, *An Introduction to the General Theory of Algorithms*, North Holland, Amsterdam, 1978.
- K. Mehlhorn, *Data Structures and Algorithms 2: Graph Algorithms and NP-Completeness*, Springer-Verlag, 1984.
- C. H. Papadimitriou and K. Steiglitz, *Combinatorial Optimization: Algorithms and Complexity*, Prentice-Hall, 1982.
- C. H. Papadimitriou, *Computational Complexity*, Addison-Wesley, 1994.

Two excellent expository articles on the subject of intractability, which were an inspiring source in the preparation of parts of Chapter 7, are:

- H. R. Lewis and C. H. Papadimitriou, "The Efficiency of Algorithms," *Scientific American* 238:1 (1978), pp. 96–109.
- L. J. Stockmeyer and A. K. Chandra, "Intrinsically Difficult Problems," *Scientific American* 240:5 (1979), pp. 140–59.

The following survey papers, written by three researchers who have made fundamental contributions to the subject matter of this chapter, are very informative:

- M. O. Rabin, "Complexity of Computations," *Comm. Assoc. Comput. Mach.* 20 (1977), pp. 625–33.
- S. A. Cook, "An Overview of Computational Complexity," *Comm. Assoc. Comput. Mach.* 26 (1983), pp. 401–8.
- R. M. Karp, "Combinatorics, Complexity, and Randomness," *Comm. Assoc. Comput. Mach.* 29 (1986), pp. 98–109.

Here is an additional extensive survey:

- D. S. Johnson, "A Catalog of Complexity Classes," in *Handbook of Theoretical Computer Science* vol. A, J. van Leeuwen, ed., Elsevier and MIT Press, 1990, pp. 67–161.

The tables and graph appearing in Figures 7.3, 7.4, 7.5, and 7.7, [pp. 163–6] are based in part on those appearing in Garey and Johnson's book and the two *Scientific American* articles previously mentioned.

The following early papers have been most influential in laying the foundations for complexity theory and in recognizing the importance of the dichotomy between polynomial and super-polynomial time [pp. 163–5]:

- M. O. Rabin, "Degree of Difficulty of Computing a Function and a Partial Ordering of Recursive Sets," Technical Report No. 2, Hebrew University, Branch of Applied Logic, Jerusalem, 1960.
- A. Cobham, "The Intrinsic Computational Difficulty of Functions," *Proc. 1964 Int. Congress for Logic, Methodology, and Phil. of Sci.*, Y. Bar-Hillel, ed., North Holland, pp. 24–30, 1965.
- J. Edmonds, "Paths, Trees, and Flowers," *Canad. J. Math.* 17 (1965), pp. 449–67.
- J. Hartmanis and R. E. Stearns, "On the Computational Complexity of Algorithms," *Trans. Amer. Math. Soc.* 117 (1965), pp. 285–306.
- M. Blum, "A Machine Independent Theory of the Complexity of Recursive Functions," *J. Assoc. Comput. Mach.* 14 (1967), pp. 322–36.

The identification of the class of NP-complete problems [p. 167], together with the landmark result (Cook's Theorem) that established the NP-completeness of the satisfiability problem [pp. 170–1, 176], appears in:

- S. A. Cook, "The Complexity of Theorem Proving Procedures," *Proc. 3rd ACM Symp. on Theory of Computing*, ACM Press, pp. 151–8, 1971.

Similar results were obtained independently, but a little later, by L. A. Levin in:

- L. A. Levin, "Universal Search Problems," *Problemy Peredaci Informacii* 9 (1973), pp. 115–16 (in Russian). English translation in *Problems of Information Transmission* 9 (1973), pp. 265–6.

The significance of these discoveries was recognized in the following extremely important paper, in which several other problems (including the traveling salesman problem, three-colorability, and Hamiltonian paths [pp. 168–70]) were shown to be NP-complete using polynomial-time reductions:

- R. M. Karp, "Reducibility Among Combinatorial Problems," in *Complexity of Computer Computations*, R. E. Miller and J. W. Thatcher, eds., Plenum Press, pp. 85–104, 1972.

That the traveling salesman problem remains NP-complete not only for general graphs but even for city networks with Euclidean distances is shown in:

- C. H. Papadimitriou, "The Euclidean Traveling Salesman Problem is NP-Complete," *Theor. Comput. Sci.* 4 (1977), pp. 237–44.

That the timetable problem is NP-complete [p. 170] is shown in:

- S. Even, A. Itai, and A. Shamir, "On the Complexity of Timetable and Multicommodity Flow Problems," *SIAM J. Comput.* 5 (1976), pp. 691–703.

The nursery rhyme on the brave old Duke of York (often misquoted, called the *grand* old Duke of York) [p. 174] can be found on p. 138 of:

- W. S. Baring-Gould and C. Baring-Gould, *Annotated Mother Goose*, Clarkson N. Potter, 1962.

That the primality problem is in NP [p. 178] is shown in:

- V. R. Pratt, "Every Prime has a Succint Certificate," *SIAM J. Comput.* 4 (1975), pp. 214–20.

The polynomial-time algorithm for primality (the AKS algorithm), was proved in:

- M. Agrawal, N. Kayal, and N. Saxena, "PRIMES is in P," manuscript, August 2002.

This paper has not been officially published yet, but you can find it easily—as well as many descriptions thereof and even some simplifications—on the internet. (Try searching for the phrase "Primes is in P".)

Approximation algorithms [pp. 178–80] appear in many of the books and papers mentioned above. The following books are devoted to the subject:

- V. V. Vazirani, *Approximation Algorithms*, Springer-Verlag, 2001.
- G. Ausiello, P. Crescenzi, G. Gambosi, V. Kann, A. Marchetti-Spaccamela, and M. Protasi, *Complexity and Approximation: Combinatorial Optimization Problems and Their Approximability Properties*, Springer-Verlag, 1999.
- *Approximation Algorithms for NP-Hard Problems*, D. S. Hochbaum, ed., Brooks Cole, 1996.

The 1.5-times-the-optimum algorithm for the traveling salesman problem [p. 179] is due to N. Christofides. The heuristic algorithm for the same problem, which is almost always good [p. 179], appears in:

- R. M. Karp, "The Probabilistic Analysis of Partitioning Algorithms for the Traveling-Salesman Problem in the Plane," *Math. Oper. Res.* 2 (1977), pp. 209–24.

An excellent collection of papers on the traveling salesman problem is:

- *The Traveling Salesman Problem: A Guided Tour of Combinatorial Optimization*, E. L. Lawler et al., eds., John Wiley & Sons, 1985.

That certain NP-complete problems cannot be approximated unless P = NP [pp. 179–80] was proved in the following series of papers:

- U. Feige, S. Goldwasser, L. Lovász, S. Safra, and M. Szegedy, "Approximating Clique is Almost NP-Complete," *J. Assoc. Comput. Mach.*, 43 (1996), pp. 268–92.
- S. Arora and S. Safra, "Probabilistic Checking of Proofs: A New Characterization of NP," *J. Assoc. Comput. Mach.*, 45 (1998), pp. 70–122.
- S. Arora, C. Lund, R. Motwani, M. Sudan, and M. Szegedy, "Proof Verification and Intractability of Approximation Problems" *J. Assoc. Comput. Mach.* 45 (1998), pp. 501–55.

The proof that establishes this fact for graph coloring [pp. 179–80] appears in:

- C. Lund and M. Yannakakis, "On the Hardness of Approximating Minimization Problems," *J. Assoc. Comput. Mach.* 41 (1994), pp. 960–81.

An early influential inapproximability result for graph coloring appears in:

- M. R. Garey and D. S. Johnson, "The Complexity of Near-Optimal Graph Coloring," *J. Assoc. Comput. Mach.* 23 (1976), pp. 43–9.

The first proof that a problem of interest has an exponential-time lower bound [p. 180] appears in:

- A. R. Meyer and L. J. Stockmeyer, "The Equivalence Problem for Regular Expressions with Squaring Requires Exponential Time," *Proc. 13th Ann. Symp. on Switching and Automata Theory*, IEEE Press, pp. 125–9, 1972.

That generalized chess and checkers are provably intractable [p. 180] is shown, respectively, in:

- A. S. Fraenkel and D. Lichtenstein, "Computing a Perfect Strategy for $n \times n$ Chess Requires Time Exponential in n," *J. Combinatorial Theory*, Series A31 (1981), pp. 199–214.
- J. M. Robson, "*N* by *N* Checkers is Exptime Complete," *SIAM J. Comput.* 13 (1984), pp. 252–67.

Roadblock [pp. 180–1] is described in the *Scientific American* paper by Stockmeyer and Chandra previously mentioned and was proved to be intractable in:

- L. J. Stockmeyer and A. K. Chandra, "Provably Difficult Combinatorial Games," *SIAM J. Comput.* 8 (1979), pp. 151–74.

Propositional dynamic logic [p. 182] was defined and shown to be intractable in:

- M. J. Fischer and R. E. Ladner, "Propositional Dynamic Logic of Regular Programs," *J. Comput. Syst. Sci.* 18 (1979), pp. 194–211.

That Presburger arithmetic requires double-exponential time [p. 183] is shown in:

- M. J. Fischer and M. O. Rabin, "Super-Exponential Complexity of Presburger Arithmetic," in *Complexity of Computation*, R. M. Karp, ed., *Amer. Math. Soc.*, Providence, RI, pp. 27–41, 1974.

That WS1S requires nonelementary time [p. 183] is shown in:

- A. R. Meyer, "Weak Monadic Second Order Theory of Successor is not Elementary Recursive," in *Logic Colloquium*, R. Parikh, ed., Lecture Notes in Mathematics, vol. 453, Springer-Verlag, pp. 132–54, 1975.

A good survey of many upper and lower bounds on the complexity of certain satisfiability problems is:

- J. Ferrante and C. W. Rackoff, *The Computational Complexity of Logical Theories*, Lecture Notes in Mathematics, vol. 718, Springer-Verlag, 1979.

The simplex method for linear programming [p. 184] was discovered in the early 1950s by G. B. Dantzig and a detailed account appears in:

- G. B. Dantzig, *Linear Programming and Extensions*, Princeton University Press, 1963.

The first polynomial-time algorithm for the problem appeared in the influential paper:

- L. G. Khachiyan, "A Polynomial Algorithm in Linear Programming," *Doklady Akademiia Nauk* SSSR 244 (1979), pp. 1093–6 (in Russian). English translation in *Soviet Mathematics Doklad* 20 (1979), pp. 191–4.

Another polynomial-time algorithm for linear programming, which performs better than Khachiyan's in practice, appears in:

- N. Karmarkar, "A New Polynomial-Time Algorithm for Linear Programming," *Combinatorica* 4 (1984), pp. 373–95.

Chapter 8

Historically, the interest in noncomputability and undecidability dates back to a plan devised by the great mathematician David Hilbert. At the turn of the last century, Hilbert proposed that all mathematical problems should be encoded in some suitable logical formalism, and an algorithm be found for determining truth therein. That this is essentially impossible was proved in 1931 by K. Gödel in the following landmark paper, which showed that truth in the first-order predicate calculus is not even partially decidable (a result sometimes referred to as Gödel's Incompleteness Theorem):

- K. Gödel, "Über formal unentscheidbare Sätze der Principia Mathematica und verwandter Systeme, I," *Monatshefte für Mathematik und Physik* 38 (1931), pp. 173–98.

An English translation of this paper, entitled "On Formally Undecidable Propositions of Principia Mathematica and Related Systems," appears in the following book, which constitutes a collection of many of the early pioneering papers on the subject matter of this chapter:

- *The Undecidable: Basic Papers on Undecidable Propositions, Unsolvable Problems and Computable Functions*, M. Davis, ed., Raven Press, 1965.

An early and clear exposition of the subject matter of this and the next chapter is:

■ B. A. Trakhtenbrot, *Algorithms and Automatic Computing Machines*, D. C. Heath & Co., 1963.

Many books contain material about undecidable and noncomputable problems. Here are some:

■ R. Bird, *Programs and Machines: An Introduction to the Theory of Computation*, John Wiley & Sons, 1976.

■ G. S. Boolos, J. P. Burgess, and R. C. Jeffrey, *Computability and Logic*, 4th edn, Cambridge University Press, 2002.

■ W. S. Brainerd and L. H. Landweber, *Theory of Computation*, John Wiley & Sons, 1974.

■ J. M. Brady, *The Theory of Computer Science: A Programming Approach*, Chapman & Hall, 1977.

■ N. J. Cutland, *Computability: An Introduction to Recursive Function Theory*, Cambridge University Press, 1980.

■ G. Rozenberg and A. Salomaa, *Cornerstones of Undecidability*, Prentice-Hall, 1994.

■ M. D. Davis, R. Sigal, and E. J. Weyuker, *Computability, Complexity, and Languages: Fundamentals of Theoretical Computer Science*, 2nd edn, Academic Press, 1994.

■ F. C. Hennie, *Introduction to Computability*, Addison-Wesley, 1977.

■ J. E. Hopcroft, R. Motwani, and J. D. Ullman, *Introduction to Automata Theory, Languages and Computation*, 2nd edn, Addison-Wesley, 2001.

■ A. J. Kfoury, R. N. Moll, and M. A. Arbib, *A Programming Approach to Computability*, Springer-Verlag, 1982.

■ E. V. Krishnamurthy, *Introductory Theory of Computer Science*, Springer-Verlag, 1983.

■ H. R. Lewis and C. H. Papadimitriou, *Elements of the Theory of Computation*, 2nd edn, Prentice-Hall, 1997.

■ M. Machtey and P. Young, *An Introduction to the General Theory of Algorithms*, North Holland, 1978.

■ R. Sommerhalder and S. C. van Westrhenen, *The Theory of Computability: Programs, Machines, Effectiveness and Feasibility*, Addison-Wesley, 1988.

■ R. W. Floyd and R. Beigel, *The Language of Machines: An Introduction to Computability and Formal Languages*, W. H. Freeman & Co., 1994.

The most mathematically detailed and comprehensive treatment of recursive function theory, which includes noncomputability as a subarea, is:

■ H. Rogers, *Theory of Recursive Functions and Effective Computability*, McGraw-Hill, 1967 (reprinted by MIT Press, 1987).

Three influential early books are:

■ S. C. Kleene, *Introduction to Metamathematics*, North Holland, 1952 (eighth reprint, 1980).

■ M. Davis, *Computability and Unsolvability*, McGraw-Hill, 1958. (Second edition published by Dover Publications in 1982).

- M. L. Minsky, *Computation: Finite and Infinite Machines*, Prentice-Hall, 1967.

The following book contains a somewhat unusual and entertaining account of the subject:

- D. R. Hofstadter, *Gödel, Escher, Bach: An Eternal Golden Braid*, Basic Books, 1979.

In addition to the periodicals mentioned in the general section of these notes, the following journals contain papers on recursive function theory, and hence also on undecidability and noncomputability:

- *Journal of Symbolic Logic*, abbreviated *J. Symb. Logic*, or sometimes just *JSL*; published by the Association for Symbolic Logic.
- *Zeitschrift für Mathematische Logik und Grundlagen der Mathematik*, abbreviated *Zeitschr. Math. Logik und Grundlagen Math.*, or sometimes simply *ZML*; published in Berlin by VEB Deutscher Verlag der Wissenschaften.

The quotation from *Time Magazine* [p. 191] is by E. Baxter, managing editor of Personal Software magazine, and appeared on pages 44–5 of the April 16, 1984 issue.

Tiling, or domino problems [pp. 193–5] were introduced by H. Wang in the following paper, which also contains a proof of the undecidability of a slightly restricted version:

- H. Wang, "Proving Theorems by Pattern Recognition," *Bell Syst. Tech. J.* 40 (1961), pp. 1–42.

The unrestricted version was proved undecidable in:

- R. Berger, "The Undecidability of the Domino Problem," *Memoirs Amer. Math. Soc.* 66 (1966).

A fascinating book about tilings of the plane is:

- B. Grünbaum and G. C. Shephard, *Tilings and Patterns*, W. H. Freeman & Co., 1987.

The two results stating that the domino snake problem is undecidable in the half-plane but is actually decidable in the whole plane [p. 196] appear, respectively, in:

- H.-D. Ebbinghaus, "Undecidability of Some Domino Connectability Problems," *Zeitschr. Math. Logik und Grundlagen Math.* 28 (1982), pp. 331–6.
- Y. Etzion-Petrushka, D. Harel, and D. Myers, "On the Solvability of Domino Snake Problems," *Theoret. Comput. Sci.* 131 (1994), pp. 243–69.

The second-listed paper also contains the stronger undecidability results about domino snakes [p. 196], including the one that talks about removing a single point only.

The word correspondence problem [pp. 197–8], sometimes called *Post's correspondence problem*, or simply PCP, was introduced and proven undecidable by E. L. Post in:

- E. L. Post, "A Variant of a Recursively Unsolvable Problem," *Bull. Amer. Math. Soc.* 52 (1946), pp. 264–8.

The problem of deciding the equivalence of syntactic definitions of programming languages [pp. 197–8] is known better as the equivalence problem for context-free grammars and was proven undecidable in:

- Y. Bar-Hillel, M. Perles, and E. Shamir, "On Formal Properties of Simple Phrase Structure Grammars," *Zeit. Phonetik, Sprachwiss. Kommunikationsforsch.* 14 (1961), pp. 143–72.

That program verification is noncomputable [pp. 198–9] follows from the fact that truth in the first-order predicate calculus is undecidable, and is thus due, in essence, to K. Gödel, as discussed at the beginning of this section.

The following paper discusses the $3x + 1$ algorithm [p. 194] and its variants in great detail:

- J. C. Lagarias, "The $3x + 1$ Problem and its Generalizations," *Amer. Math. Monthly* 92 (1985), pp. 3–23.

Its author, Lagarias, has also written an unpublished manuscript titled "$3x + 1$ Problem Annotated Bibliography."

That the halting problem is undecidable [pp. 199–201, 202–205] is due, in essence, to A. Turing, in his extremely important paper:

- A. Turing, "On Computable Numbers with an Application to the Entscheidungsproblem," *Proc. London Math. Soc.* 42 (1936), pp. 230–65. Corrections appeared in: ibid., 43 (1937), pp. 544–6.

Rice's theorem [p. 201] is from:

- H. G. Rice, "Classes of Recursively Enumerable Sets and Their Decision Problems," *Trans. Amer. Math. Soc.* 74 (1953), pp. 358–66.

Rogers' book referenced earlier contains detailed accounts of the results on recursive enumerability [pp. 208–9] and hierarchies of undecidable problems, as well as the fact that the totality problem is not r.e. [p. 210]. Many of these results are based on important early work of S. C. Kleene in:

- S. C. Kleene, "Recursive Predicates and Quantifiers," *Trans. Amer. Math. Soc.* 53 (1943), pp. 41–73.

That PDL with recursion is highly undecidable [p. 211] is proved in:

- D. Harel, A. Pnueli, and J. Stavi, "Propositional Dynamic Logic of Non Regular Programs," *J. Comput. Syst. Sci.* 26 (1983), pp. 222–43.

Recurring domino problems are defined and shown to be highly undecidable [pp. 211–12] in:

- D. Harel, "Effective Transformations on Infinite Trees, with Applications to High Undecidability, Dominoes, and Fairness," *J. Assoc. Comput. Mach.* 33 (1986), pp. 224–48.

The high undecidability of second-order arithmetic [pp. 213–14], and many related facts, are established in Kleene's paper cited above.

▆ Chapter 9

The material of this chapter is traditionally treated together with that of the previous one. Consequently, the list of books and periodicals mentioned at the beginning of the notes for Chapter 8 serves this chapter too.

▆   ▆

Turing machines [pp. 223–8] were invented by Alan Turing and were first described in his fundamental paper:

- A. Turing, "On Computable Numbers with an Application to the Entscheidungsproblem," *Proc. London Math. Soc.* 42 (1936), pp. 230–65. Corrections appeared in: ibid., 43 (1937), pp. 544–6.

The Church/Turing thesis [pp. 228–9] is named after Alonzo Church and Alan Turing. Ideas leading to it appear in Turing's paper and in the following extremely important paper:

- A. Church, "An Unsolvable Problem of Elementary Number Theory," *Amer. J. Math.* 58 (1936), pp. 345–63.

Fascinating historical accounts of the evolution of the lambda calculus, recursive function theory, and the Church/Turing thesis are:

- S. C. Kleene, "Origins of Recursive Function Theory," *Ann. Hist. Comput.* 3 (1981), pp. 52–67.
- M. Davis, "Why Gödel Didn't Have Church's Thesis," *Inf. and Cont.* 54 (1982), pp. 3–24.
- J. B. Rosser, "Highlights of the History of the Lambda-Calculus," *Ann. Hist. Comput.* 6 (1984), pp. 337–49.

An interesting approach to modifying the thesis so as to capture terminating computations in real programming languages appears in:

- Y. Gurevich, "Logic and the Challenge of Computer Science," in *Current Trends in Theoretical Computer Science*, E. Börger, ed., Computer Science Press, 1988.

The following paper proposes a definition of computable queries for databases [pp. 248–9]. It actually applies to most kinds of structures, including sets, trees, graphs, and hierarchical directory structures. Thus it implicitly establishes an appropriate CT thesis for computing on structures:

- A. K. Chandra and D. Harel, "Computable Queries for Relational Data Bases," *J. Comput. Syst. Sci.* 21 (1980), pp. 156–78.

The lambda calculus [p. 229] was the result of work by Church and Kleene, appearing explicitly in:

- S. C. Kleene, "A Theory of Positive Integers in Formal Logic," *Amer. J. Math.* 57 (1935), pp. 153–73, 219–44.

It is described in great detail in:

- H. P. Barendregt, *The Lambda Calculus: Its Syntax and Semantics*, 2nd edn, North Holland, 1984.

Post's production systems [p. 229] appear in the following important paper:

- E. L. Post, "Formal Reductions of the General Combinatorial Decision Problem," *Amer. J. Math.* 65 (1943), pp. 197–215.

Kleene's definition of recursive functions [p. 229] is based on that of Gödel, and appears in:

- S. C. Kleene, "General Recursive Functions of Natural Numbers," *Math. Ann.* 112 (1936), pp. 727–42.

Three of the first papers to prove the equivalence of these formalisms are:

- S. C. Kleene, "λ-Definability and Recursiveness," *Duke Math. J.* 2 (1936), pp. 340–53.
- E. L. Post, "Finite Combinatory Processes—Formulation 1," *J. Symb. Logic* 1 (1936), pp. 103–5.
- A. M. Turing, "Computability and λ-Definability," *J. Symb. Logic* 2 (1937), pp. 153–63.

As mentioned earlier, the definitive reference on recursive functions and their properties is:

- H. Rogers, *Theory of Recursive Functions and Effective Computability*, McGraw-Hill, 1967 (reprinted by MIT Press, 1987).

Many variants of Turing machines, in particular, nondeterministic and multi-tape machines [pp. 230–1], as well as the reduction from two-way to one-way infinite tapes [pp. 231–2], are described in many books, the most influential of which is the following (which, as listed earlier, was published more than 20 years later in a second edition):

- J. E. Hopcroft and J. D. Ullman, *Introduction to Automata Theory, Languages and Computation*, Addison-Wesley, 1979.

Counter programs, sometimes called counter machines [pp. 231–3], are described in many of the aforementioned books, but constitute a particularly important part of:

- M. L. Minsky, *Computation: Finite and Infinite Machines*, Prentice-Hall, 1967.

That two counters suffice [p. 235] is proved in Minsky's book, and originally in:

- M. L. Minsky, "Recursive Unsolvability of Post's Problem of 'Tag' and Other Topics in the Theory of Turing Machines," *Annals Math.* 74 (1961), pp. 437–55.

A more elegant proof (which forms the basis of the treatment herein) is given in:

- P. C. Fischer, "Turing Machines with Restricted Memory Access," *Inf. and Cont.* 9 (1966), pp. 364–79.

An important paper related to particularly interesting sublanguages of the language of counter programs (a hierarchy of *primitive recursive* variants) is:

- A. R. Meyer and R. Ritchie, "The Complexity of Loop Programs," *Proc. ACM National Conf.*, ACM Press, pp. 465–9, 1967.

The concept of a universal program [pp. 236–8] is, again, due to Alan Turing. In his 1936 paper, he actually constructed a universal Turing machine and argued its importance.

The following is an exposition of Turing machines and related topics:

- J. E. Hopcroft, "Turing Machines," *Scientific American* 250:5 (1984), pp. 70–80.

A good survey of machines and simulations between them is:

- P. van Emde Boas, "Machine Models and Simulations," in *Handbook of Theoretical Computer Science*, vol. A, J. van Leeuwen, ed., Elsevier and MIT Press, 1990, pp. 1–66.

The connection between Turing machines and complexity classes such as PTIME was made in the early work on complexity theory; for example, in:

- J. Hartmanis and R. E. Stearns, "On the Computational Complexity of Algorithms," *Trans. Amer. Math. Soc.* 117 (1965), pp. 285–306.

The class NP has been defined using nondeterministic Turing machines [pp. 240–1] ever since Cook's original paper:

- S. A. Cook, "The Complexity of Theorem Proving Procedures," *Proc. 3rd ACM Symp. on Theory of Computing*, ACM Press, pp. 151–8, 1971.

The reduction of the halting problem to a half-plane tiling problem [pp. 241–4] is based on the original proof in:

- H. Wang, "Proving Theorems by Pattern Recognition," *Bell Syst. Tech. J.* 40 (1961), pp. 1–42.

Finite automata [pp. 244–7] seem to have originated in the following pioneering work on modeling nervous activity:

- W. S. McCulloch and W. Pitts, "A Logical Calculus of the Ideas Immanent in Nervous Activity," *Bull. Math. Biophysics* 5 (1943), pp. 115–33.

Two important early papers are:

- S. C. Kleene, "Representation of Events in Nerve Nets and Finite Automata," in *Automata Studies*, C. E. Shannon and J. McCarthy, eds., *Ann. Math. Studies* 34 (1956), pp. 3–41. (Earlier version: RAND Research Memorandum RM-704, 1951.)
- M. O. Rabin and D. Scott, "Finite Automata and their Decision Problems," *IBM J. Res.* 3 (1959), pp. 115–25.

Proving limitations of finite automata by the pigeonhole principle [p. 246] (leading to the so-called pumping lemma) is based upon proofs in:

- Y. Bar-Hillel, M. Perles, and E. Shamir, "On Formal Properties of Simple Phrase Structure Grammars," *Zeit. Phonetik, Sprachwiss. Kommunikationsforsch.* 14 (1961), pp. 143–72.

Pushdown automata [p. 248] first appeared in explicit form in:

- A. G. Oettinger, "Automatic Syntactic Analysis and the Pushdown Store," *Proc. Symp. in Applied Math.* 12, Amer. Math. Soc., pp. 104–29, 1961.

Several important papers on the subject were written in the late 1950s by N. Chomsky, among which are:

- N. Chomsky, "Three Models for the Description of Language," *IRE Trans. Inf. Theory* 2 (1956), pp. 113–24.
- N. Chomsky, "On Certain Formal Properties of Grammars," *Inf. and Cont.* 2 (1959), pp. 137–67.

That equivalence for DPDAs is decidable [p. 248] was proved in:

- G. Sénizergues, "The Equivalence Problem for Deterministic Pushdown Automata is Decidable," *Proc. Int. Colloq. on Automata, Lang. and Prog.*, Lecture Notes in Computer Science, vol. 1256, Springer-Verlag, pp. 671–81, 1997.

A strengthening of this result appears in:

- C. Sterling, "An Introduction to Decidability of DPDA Equivalence," *Proc. 21st Conf. on Foundations of Software Technology and Theoretical Computer Science*, Lecture Notes in Computer Science, vol. 2245, Springer-Verlag, pp. 42–56, 2001.
- C. Sterling, "Deciding DPDA Equivalence is Primitive Recursive," *Proc. Int. Colloq. on Automata, Lang. and Prog.*, Lecture Notes in Computer Science, vol. 2380, Springer-Verlag, pp. 821–32, 2002.

A detailed and insightful historical survey of the development of formal languages and automata theory is:

- S. A. Greibach, "Formal Languages: Origins and Directions," *Ann. Hist. Comput.* 3 (1981), pp. 14–41.

Many of the books mentioned in the notes for Chapter 8 contain thorough treatments of finite automata, pushdown automata, and related formalisms. There are also many books devoted exclusively to automata and formal language theory. They include:

- S. Ginsburg, *Algebraic and Automata-Theoretic Properties of Formal Languages*, North Holland, 1975.
- M. A. Harrison, *Introduction to Formal Language Theory*, Addison-Wesley, 1978.
- A. Salomaa, *Jewels of Formal Language Theory*, Computer Science Press, 1981.

Chapter 10

This chapter is really divided into several parts: parallelism (that is, solving algorithmic problems efficiently using parallel processes), concurrency (that is, dealing with the design and behavior of concurrent protocols and systems), and then quantum and molecular computing.

Here are some books devoted to parallel algorithms:

- J. JaJa, *An Introduction to Parallel Algorithms*, Addison-Wesley, 1992.
- F. T. Leighton, *Introduction to Parallel Algorithms and Architectures: Arrays, Trees, Hypercubes*, Morgan Kaufmann, 1992.

- S. G. Akl, *Parallel Computation: Models and Methods*, Prentice-Hall, 1996.
- M. J. Quinn, *Designing Efficient Algorithms for Parallel Computers*, McGraw-Hill, 1987.
- I. Parberry, *Parallel Complexity Theory*, John Wiley & Sons, 1987.
- A. Gibbons and W. Rytter, *Efficient Parallel Algorithms*, Cambridge University Press, 1988.

Here are some books that treat the specification and design of concurrent protocols:

- M. Ben-Ari, *Principles of Concurrent Programming*, Prentice-Hall, 1982.
- R. E. Filman and D. P. Friedman, *Coordinated Computing: Tools and Techniques for Distributed Software*, McGraw-Hill, 1984.
- G. R. Andrews, *Concurrent Programming: Principles and Practice*, Pearson Education, 1991.
- N. Lynch, *Distributed Algorithms*, Morgan Kaufmann, 1997.
- R. Milner, *Communication and Concurrency*, Prentice-Hall, 1989.
- C. A. R. Hoare, *Communicating Sequential Processes*, Prentice-Hall, 1985.
- R. Milner, *Communicating and Mobile Systems: The Pi-Calculus*, Cambridge University Press, 1999.
- K. M. Chandy and J. Misra, *Parallel Program Design: A Foundation*, Addison-Wesley, 1988.
- F. Andre, D. Herman, and J.-P. Verjus, *Synchronization of Parallel Programs*, MIT Press, 1985.
- E. V. Krishnamurthy, *Parallel Processing: Principles and Practice*, Addison-Wesley, 1989.

The following books contain articles relevant to parallelism and concurrency:

- *Concurrency Verification: Introduction to Compositional and Noncompositional Methods*, W.-P. de Roever et al., eds., Cambridge University Press, 2001.
- *Algorithms, Software and Hardware of Parallel Computers*, V. E. Kotov and J. Miklosko, eds., Springer-Verlag, 1984.
- *Logics and Models of Concurrent Systems*, K. R. Apt, ed., NATO ASI Series, vol. 13, Springer-Verlag, 1985.
- *The Origins of Concurrent Programming: From Semaphores to Remote Procedure Calls*, P. Brinch Hansen, ed., Springer-Verlag, 2002.

A good book that discusses parallel computers is:

- R. W. Hockney and C. R. Jesshope, *Parallel Computers 2: Architecture, Programming and Algorithms*, 2nd edn, Adam Hilger Ltd, 1988.

Here are some books on quantum and molecular computation:

- C. P. Williams and S. H. Clearwater, *Explorations in Quantum Computing*, Springer-Verlag, 1998.

- M. A. Nielsen and I. L. Chuang, *Quantum Computation and Quantum Information*, Cambridge University Press, 2000.

- M. Hirvensalo, *Quantum Computing*, Springer-Verlag, 2000.

- C. S. Calude and G. Păun, *Computing with Cells and Atoms: An Introduction to Quantum, DNA and Membrane Computing*, Taylor & Francis, 2001.

- G. Păun, G. Rozenberg, and A. Salomaa, *DNA Computing: New Computing Paradigms*, Springer-Verlag, 1998.

- M. Sipper, *Machine Nature: The Coming Age of Bio-Inspired Computing*, McGraw-Hill, 2002.

- A. Ehrenfeucht, T. Harju, I. Petre, D. M. Prescott and G. Rozenberg, *Computation in Living Cells: Gene Assembly in Ciliates*, Springer-Verlag, 2004.

Some surveys are:

- D. Aharonov, "Quantum Computation," *Annual Reviews of Computational Physics VI*, D. Stauffer, ed., World Scientific, 1998.

- A. Berthiaume, "Quantum Computation," in *Complexity Theory Retrospective II*, L. A. Hemaspaandra and A. L. Selman, eds., Springer-Verlag, 1997, pp. 23–51.

- D. P. DiVincenzo, "Quantum Computation," *Science* 270 (1995), pp. 255–61.

- S. A. Kurtz, S. R. Mahaney, J. S. Royer, and J. Simon, "Biological Computing," in *Complexity Theory Retrospective II*, L. A. Hemaspaandra and A. L. Selman, eds., Springer-Verlag, 1997, pp. 179–95.

- L. Kari, "DNA Computing: The Arrival of Biological Mathematics," *The Mathematical Intelligencer* 19:2 (1997), pp. 9–22.

Apart from the periodicals mentioned in the general section, the following journals publish papers relevant to the subjects of this chapter:

- *Journal of Parallel and Distributed Computing*, abbreviated *J. Par. Dist. Comput.*; published by Elsevier.

- *International Journal of Parallel Programming*, abbreviated *Int. J. Parallel Prog.*; published by Kluwer/Plenum.

- *Distributed Computing*, abbreviated *Dist. Comput.*; published by Springer.

- *ACM Transactions on Programming Languages and Systems*, abbreviated *ACM Trans. Prog. Lang. Syst.*, or sometimes simply *TOPLAS*; published by the ACM.

- *Science of Computer Programming*, abbreviated *Sci. Comput. Prog.*; published by Elsevier.

- *Software: Practice and Experience*, abbreviated *Softw. Pract. Exp.*; published by John Wiley & Sons.

- *Journal of Systems and Software*, abbreviated *J. Syst. Softw.*; published by Elsevier.

- *IEEE Transactions on Software Engineering*, abbreviated *IEEE Trans. Soft. Eng.*; published by the IEEE.

- *IEEE Transactions on Computers*, abbreviated *IEEE Trans. Comput.*; published by the IEEE.

- *IEEE Transactions on Parallel & Distributed Systems*, abbreviated *IEEE Trans. Par. Dist. Syst.*; published by the IEEE.

- *Concurrency and Computation: Practice & Experience*; published by John Wiley & Sons.

- *Quantum Information & Computation*, abbreviated *Quant. Inf. Comput.*; published by Rinton Press.

- *International Journal of Quantum Information*, abbreviated *Int. J. Quant. Inf.*; published by World Scientific.

- *Quantum Computers and Computing*; published by the Russian Academy of Science.

- *Journal of Computational Biology*, abbreviated *J. Comput. Biol.*; published by Mary Ann Liebert, Inc.

The ditch-digging example [pp. 258–9] is due to A. Pnueli, and the child-having one [p. 259: footnote] is based on a sentence appearing on page 17 of the following insightful book (this is the original version; a new edition was published in 1995):

- F. P. Brooks, Jr., *The Mythical Man-Month*, Addison-Wesley, 1979.

There are three places in which to read in detail about parallel sorting algorithms [pp. 260–7]. The first, of course, is:

- D. E. Knuth, *The Art of Computer Programming, vol. 3: Sorting and Searching*, 2nd edn, Addison-Wesley, 1998.

The second is the following survey:

- D. Bitton, D. J. DeWitt, D. K. Hsaio, and J. Menon, "A Taxonomy of Parallel Sorting," *Comput. Surv.* 16 (1984), pp. 287–318.

The third source for parallel sorting algorithms is the entire April 1985 issue (vol. C-34, no. 4) of *IEEE Transactions on Computers*, which contains several articles on parallel sorting.

An influential paper on boolean networks [pp. 263–4] is:

- A. Borodin, "On Relating Time and Space to Size and Depth," *SIAM J. Comput.* 6 (1977), pp. 733–44.

The odd-even sorting network [pp. 264–5] was invented by K. E. Batcher and is described in:

- K. E. Batcher, "Sorting Networks and their Applications," *Proc. 1968 Spring Joint Comput. Conf.*, AFIPS Press, pp. 307–14, 1968.

The logarithmic-time sorting network with $O(N \times \log N)$ processors [pp. 264–5], sometimes called the *AKS network*, after its inventors (not to be confused with the inventors of the AKS primality algorithm), appears in:

- M. Ajtai, J. Komlós, and E. Szemerédi, "Sorting in $c \log n$ Parallel Steps," *Combinatorica* 3 (1983), pp. 1–19.

The optimal sorting network [pp. 264–5] is based on the AKS network and appears in:

- T. Leighton, "Tight Bounds on the Complexity of Parallel Sorting," *IEEE Trans. Comput.* C-34 (1985), pp. 344–54.

An excellent survey of the AKS network and related issues is:

- N. Pippenger, "Communication Networks," in *Handbook of Theoretical Computer Science*, vol. A, J. van Leeuwen, ed., Elsevier and MIT Press, 1990, pp. 805–33.

A relatively early survey of parallel algorithms on graphs, including ones for finding minimal spanning trees and traveling salesman paths, is:

- M. J. Quinn and N. Deo, "Parallel Graph Algorithms," *Comput. Surv.* 16 (1984), pp. 319–48.

Systolic networks [pp. 265–8] were first studied in:

- H. T. Kung, "Let's Design Algorithms for VLSI Systems," *Proc. Conf. Very Large Scale Integration: Architecture, Design, Fabrication*, California Inst. Tech., pp. 65–90, 1979.
- H. T. Kung and C. E. Leiserson, "Algorithms for VLSI Processor Arrays," in *Introduction to VLSI Systems*, C. Mead and L. Conway, eds., Addison-Wesley, 1980, pp. 271–92.

A good exposition is:

- H. T. Kung, "Why Systolic Architectures?" *Computer* 15-1 (1982), pp. 37–46.

The results about the limitations of parallelism when it comes to actually configuring processors in three-dimensional space [p. 269] appear in:

- P. M. B. Vitányi, "Locality, Communication and Interconnect Length in Multicomputers," *SIAM J. Comput.* 17 (1988), pp. 659–72.

The parallel computation thesis [pp. 270–1] was first proposed in:

- A. K. Chandra and L. J. Stockmyer, "Alternation," *Proc. 17th IEEE Symp. on Foundations of Computer Science*, IEEE Press, pp. 98–108, 1976.

Additional evidence for it appears in:

- L. M. Goldschlager, "A Universal Interconnection Pattern for Parallel Computers," *J. Assoc. Comput. Mach.* 29 (1982), pp. 1073–86.

An important paper leading to this thesis is:

- V. R. Pratt and L. J. Stockmeyer, "A Characterization of the Power of Vector Machines," *J. Comput. Syst. Sci.* 12 (1976), pp. 198–221.

The class NC [pp. 271–2], *Nick's Class*, is named after N. Pippenger, who first defined and investigated it. The two relevant papers are:

- N. Pippenger, "On Simultaneous Resource Bounds (preliminary version)," *Proc. 20th IEEE Symp. on Foundations of Computer Science*, IEEE Press, pp. 307–11, 1979.

- S. A. Cook, "Towards a Complexity Theory of Synchronous Parallel Computation," *L'Enseignement Mathématique* 27 (1981), pp. 99–124.

The following are detailed and informative surveys of results and open questions concerning NC and several of its interesting subclasses:

- S. A. Cook, "A Taxonomy of Problems with Fast Parallel Algorithms," *Inf. and Cont.* 64 (1985), pp. 2–22.
- D. S. Johnson, "A Catalog of Complexity Classes," in *Handbook of Theoretical Computer Science*, vol. A, J. van Leeuwen, ed., Elsevier and MIT Press, 1990, pp. 67–161.
- R. M. Karp and V. Ramachandran, "Parallel Algorithms for Shared-Memory Machines," in *Handbook of Theoretical Computer Science*, vol. A, J. van Leeuwen, ed., Elsevier and MIT Press, 1990, pp. 869–941.

Several solutions to mutual exclusion problems [pp. 274–6] are surveyed in many of the books mentioned earlier. The solution presented here, both the two-processor version and the general version [pp. 277–8], appears in:

- G. L. Peterson, "Myths about the Mutual Exclusion Problem," *Inf. Proc. Lett.* 12 (1981), pp. 115–16.

Safety and liveness [p. 278] are discussed in many of the books on concurrent protocols listed above. The early papers on these include:

- L. Lamport, "Proving the Correctness of Multiprocess Programs," *IEEE Trans. Soft. Eng.* SE-3 (1977), pp. 125–43.
- S. Owicki and L. Lamport, "Proving Liveness Properties of Concurrent Programs," *ACM Trans. Prog. Lang. Syst.* 4 (1982), pp. 455–95.

Here are some more of the basic papers that discuss correctness proofs for concurrent protocols [pp. 279–80]:

- S. Owicki and D. Gries, "Verifying Properties of Parallel Programs: An Axiomatic Approach," *Comm. Assoc. Comput. Mach.* 19 (1976), pp. 279–85.
- K. R. Apt, N. Francez, and W. P. de Roever, "A Proof System for Communicating Sequential Processes," *ACM Trans. Prog. Lang. Syst.* 2 (1980), pp. 359–85.
- J. Misra and K. M. Chandy, "Proofs of Networks of Processes," *IEEE Trans. Soft. Eng.* SE-7 (1981), pp. 417–26.

A good survey is:

- L. Lamport and N. Lynch, "Distributed Computing: Models and Methods," in *Handbook of Theoretical Computer Science*, vol. A, J. van Leeuwen, ed., Elsevier and MIT Press, 1990, pp. 1157–99.

Temporal logic [pp. 280–1] was suggested for use in the context of algorithmic specification and verification in:

- A. Pnueli, "The Temporal Semantics of Concurrent Programs," *Theor. Comput. Sci.* 13 (1981), pp. 45–60.

The following books discuss temporal logic in detail:

- Z. Manna and A. Pnueli, *The Temporal Logic of Reactive and Concurrent Systems: Specification*, Springer-Verlag, 1992.
- D. M. Gabbay, I. Hodkinson, and M. Reynolds, *Temporal Logic: Mathematical Foundations and Computational Aspects*, vol. 1, Oxford University Press, 1994.
- D. M. Gabbay, M. A. Reynolds, and M. Finger, *Temporal Logic: Mathematical Foundations and Computational Aspects*, vol. 2, Oxford University Press, 2000.

Here are some detailed surveys of temporal logic and its uses:

- A. Pnueli, "Applications of Temporal Logic to the Specification and Verification of Reactive Systems: A Survey of Current Trends," in *Current Trends in Concurrency*, J. de Bakker et al., eds., Lecture Notes in Computer Science, vol. 224, Springer-Verlag, pp. 510–84, 1986.
- E. A. Emerson, "Temporal and Modal Logic," in *Handbook of Theoretical Computer Science*, vol. B, J. van Leeuwen, ed., Elsevier and MIT Press, 1990, pp. 995–1072.

An interesting recent approach to dealing with concurrency, which is different from temporal logic, can be found in:

- V. R. Pratt, "Modelling Concurrency with Partial Orders," *Int. J. Parallel Prog.* 15 (1986), pp. 33–71.

There are many good places to read about the automatic verification of finite-state protocols [p. 281]. Here are some:

- E. M. Clarke, E. A. Emerson, and A. P. Sistla, "Automatic Verification of Finite-State Concurrent Systems Using Temporal Logic Specifications," *ACM Trans. Prog. Lang. Syst.* 8 (1986), pp. 244–63.
- E. M. Clarke, O. Grumberg, and D. A. Peled, *Model Checking*, MIT Press, 2000.
- R. P. Kurshan, *Computer-Aided Verification of Coordinating Processes: The Automata-Theoretic Approach*, Princeton University Press, 1995

The definitive reference on fairness in its various guises [pp. 281–3] is:

- N. Francez, *Fairness*, Springer-Verlag, 1986.

The dining philosophers problem [pp. 283–5] was introduced by E. W. Dijkstra and is described, for example, in:

- E. W. Dijkstra, "Hierarchical Ordering of Sequential Processes," *Acta Inf.* 1 (1971), pp. 115–38.

Solutions to it appear in many of the books on concurrency mentioned earlier. That there is no fully distributed, fully symmetric solution with no new processors [pp. 284–5] was observed in:

- N. A. Lynch, "Fast Allocation of Nearby Resources in a Distributed System," *Proc. 12th ACM Symp. on Theory of Computing*, ACM Press, pp. 70–81, 1980.

A good survey of the features present in many concurrent programming languages [pp. 285–6] is:

- G. R. Andrews and F. B. Schneider, "Concepts and Notations for Concurrent Programming," *Comput. Surv.* 15 (1983), pp. 3–43.

Two extremely influential books on language constructs for concurrency are:

- R. Milner, *A Calculus of Communicating Systems*, Springer-Verlag, 1980.
- C. A. R. Hoare, *Communicating Sequential Processes*, Prentice-Hall, 1985.

Semaphores [pp. 285–6] were described in:

- E. W. Dijkstra, "Cooperating Sequential Processes," in *Programming Languages*, F. Genuys, ed., Academic Press, 1968.

Some of the earliest proposals pertaining to quantum computation [pp. 287–92] are:

- C. Bennett, "Logical Reversibility of Computation," *IBM J. Research and Development* 17 (1973), pp. 525–32.
- P. Benioff, "The Computer as a Physical System: A Microscopic Quantum Mechanical Hamiltonian Model of Computers as Represented by Turing Machines," *J. Stat. Phys.* 22 (1980), pp. 563–91.
- R. Feynman, "Quantum Mechanical Computers," *Optics News* 11 (1985), pp. 11–20.
- D. Deutsch, "Quantum Theory, the Church-Turing Principle, and the Universal Quantum Computer," *Proc. R. Soc. London* A400 (1985), pp. 97–117.

Some early results on the limitations of quantum parallelism [p. 289; footnote] appear in:

- R. Josza, "Characterizing Classes of Functions Computable by Quantum Parallelism," *Proc. R. Soc. London* A435 (1991), pp. 563–74.

The $\sqrt{N}$ quantum search algorithm [p. 290] was described in:

- L. Grover, "A Fast Quantum Mechanical Algorithm for Database Search," *Proc. 28th Ann. ACM Symp. on Theory of Computing*, ACM Press, pp. 212–19, 1996.

Shor's polynomial-time quantum factoring algorithm [pp. 290–1] is from:

- P. Shor, "Algorithms for Quantum Computation: Discrete Logarithms and Factoring," *Proc. 35th IEEE Ann. Symp. on Foundations of Computer Science*, IEEE Press, pp. 124–34, 1994.
- P. Shor, "Polynomial-time Algorithms for Prime Factorization and Discrete Logarithms on a Quantum Computer," *SIAM J. Comp.* 26 (1997), pp. 1484–509.

Shor's work is based on:

- D. Simon, "On the Power of Quantum Computation," *Proc. 35th Ann. IEEE Symp. on Foundations of Computer Science*, IEEE Press, pp. 116–23, 1994.

There is quite a lot of information on the difficulties of building a quantum computer [pp. 291–2] in the books and surveys listed at the beginning of the notes for this chapter. The 7-qubit machine [p. 291] is described in:

- E. Knill, R. Laflamme, R. Martinez, and C.-H. Tseng, "An Algorithmic Benchmark for Quantum Information Processing," *Nature* 404 (2000), pp. 368–70.

The first molecular computation, solving a seven-city instance of the traveling salesman problem [p. 292], was carried out by L. M. Adelman, and reported upon in:

- L. M. Adelman, "Molecular Computation of Solutions to Combinatorial Problems," *Science* 266 (1994), pp. 1021–4.

See also:

- L. M. Adelman, "Computing with DNA," *Scientific American* 279 :2 (1998), pp. 54–61.

The stronger results regarding NP-complete problems in general [p. 292] appear in:

- R. J. Lipton, "DNA Solution of Hard Computational Problems," *Science* 268 (1994), pp. 542–5.

Some results on the energy-saving potential of molecular computers appear in:

- E. Baum, "Building an Associative Memory Vastly Larger Than the Brain," *Science* 268 (1995), pp. 583–5.

▓ Chapter 11

Many of the books on algorithms listed in the notes for earlier chapters contain material on probabilistic algorithms and the probabilistic analysis of conventional algorithms. The following concentrate on these topics:

- R. Motwani and P. Raghavan, *Randomized Algorithms*, Cambridge University Press, 1995.
- N. Alon and J. H. Spencer, *The Probabilistic Method*, 2nd edn, John Wiley & Sons, 2000.
- M. Hofri, *Probabilistic Analysis of Algorithms*, Springer-Verlag, 1987.

As far as periodicals go, the ones listed in the general section and in the notes for Chapter 2 are relevant here too.

The probabilistic solutions to the dining philosophers problem [pp. 298–301], including the argument that the first one admits lockouts [pp. 299–300], appear in:

- D. Lehmann and M. O. Rabin, "The Advantages of Free Choice: A Symmetric and Fully Distributed Solution to the Dining Philosophers Problem," *Proc. 8th ACM Symp. on Principles of Programming Languages*, ACM Press, pp. 133–8, 1981.

That the primality problem is in NP [p. 303] is shown in:

- V. R. Pratt, "Every Prime has a Succint Certificate," *SIAM J. Comput.* 4 (1975), pp. 214–20.

The primality-testing algorithm that runs in polynomial time but depends on the extended Riemann hypothesis [p. 303] appears in:

- G. L. Miller, "Riemann's Hypothesis and Tests for Primality," *J. Comput. Syst. Sci.* 13 (1976), pp. 300–17.

The $O(N^{O(\log \log N)})$ algorithm for the problem [p. 303] appears in:

- L. Adelman, C. Pomerance, and R. S. Rumely, "On Distinguishing Prime Numbers from Composite Numbers," *Ann. Math.* 117 (1983), pp. 173–206.

The polynomial-time algorithm for primality (the AKS algorithm) [p. 303], was presented in:

- M. Agrawal, N. Kayal, and N. Saxena, "PRIMES is in P," manuscript, August 2002.

The first papers containing nontrivial randomized, probabilistic algorithms appear to be the following, containing the two independent algorithms for testing primality [pp. 304–7].

- M. O. Rabin, "Probabilistic Algorithm for Testing Primality," *J. Number Theory* 12 (1980), pp. 128–38.
- R. Solovay and V. Strassen, "A Fast Monte-Carlo Test for Primality," *SIAM J. Comput.* 6 (1977), pp. 84–5.

A preliminary version of Rabin's algorithm appeared in the following influential paper:

- M. O. Rabin, "Probabilistic Algorithms," in *Algorithms and Complexity: Recent Results and New Directions*, J. F. Traub, ed., Academic Press, pp. 21–40, 1976.

Two important papers on nonprobabilistic pattern matching [p. 313] are:

- D. E. Knuth, J. H. Morris, and V. R. Pratt, "Fast Pattern Matching in Strings," *SIAM J. Comput.* 6 (1977), pp. 323–50.
- R. S. Boyer and J. S. Moore, "A Fast String Searching Algorithm," *Comm. Assoc. Comput. Mach.* 20 (1977), pp. 762–72.

The probabilistic fingerprinting algorithm for the problem [pp. 308–9] appears in:

- R. M. Karp and M. O. Rabin, "Efficient Randomized Pattern-Matching Algorithms," *IBM J. Res. Dev.* 31 (1987), pp. 249–60.

The following paper surveys pattern-matching algorithms, including the two mentioned above:

- A. V. Aho, "Algorithms for Finding Patterns in Strings," in *Handbook of Theoretical Computer Science*, vol. A, J. van Leeuwen, ed., Elsevier and MIT Press, 1990, pp. 255–300.

The following paper contains a short, but informative, survey of the various approaches to probabilistic algorithms:

- R. M. Karp, "Combinatorics, Complexity, and Randomness," *Comm. Assoc. Comput. Mach.* 29 (1986), pp. 98–109.

An influential paper on probabilistic Turing machines and probabilistic complexity classes [p. 310] is:

- J. Gill, "Computational Complexity of Probabilistic Turing Machines," *SIAM J. Comput.* 6 (1977), pp. 675–95.

Here are three good places to read about these complexity classes and their interrelationships:

- D. S. Johnson, "A Catalog of Complexity Classes," in *Handbook of Theoretical Computer Science*, vol. A, J. van Leeuwen, ed., Elsevier and MIT Press, 1990, pp. 67–161.
- S. Zachos, "Robustness of Probabilistic Computational Complexity Classes under Definitional Perturbations," *Inf. and Cont.* 54 (1982), pp. 143–54.
- U. Schöning, *Complexity and Structure*, Lecture Notes in Computer Science, vol. 211, Springer-Verlag, 1986.

Important work towards providing proof methods for verifying probabilistic algorithms [p. 311] appears in:

- D. Kozen, "Semantics of Probabilistic Programs," *J. Comput. Syst. Sci.* 22 (1981), pp. 328–50.
- D. Lehmann and S. Shelah, "Reasoning with Time and Chance," *Inf. and Cont.* 53 (1982), pp. 165–98.
- S. Hart, M. Sharir, and A. Pnueli, "Termination of Probabilistic Concurrent Programs," *ACM Trans. Prog. Lang. Syst.* 5 (1983), pp. 352–80.
- Y. A. Feldman and D. Harel, "A Probabilistic Dynamic Logic," *J. Comput. Syst. Sci.* 28 (1984), pp. 193–215.
- Y. A. Feldman, "A Decidable Propositional Probabilistic Dynamic Logic with Explicit Probabilities," *Inf. and Cont.* 63 (1984), pp. 11–38.

That problems in RP have polynomial-sized boolean circuits [p. 312] is proved in:

- L. Adleman, "Two Theorems on Random Polynomial Time," *Proc. 19th IEEE Symp. on Foundations of Computer Science*, IEEE Press, pp. 75–83, 1978.

An interesting paper that discusses the two approaches to probabilism in algorithmics and their relationship [p. 312] is:

- A. C. Yao, "Probabilistic Computations: Towards a Unified Measure of Complexity," *Proc. 18th IEEE Symp. on Foundations of Computer Science*, IEEE Press, pp. 222–7, 1977.

An early and extremely influential paper related to random and pseudo-random numbers [pp. 312–13] is:

- A. Kolmogorov, "Three Approaches to the Concept of the Amount of Information," *Probl. Inf. Transm.* 1 (1965), pp. 1–7.

Information about pseudo-random numbers in the polynomial-time sense discussed in the text [p. 313] can be found in:

- A. Shamir, "On the Generation of Cryptographically Secure Pseudo-Random Sequences," *ACM Transactions on Computer Systems* 1 (1983), pp. 38–44.
- A. C. Yao, "Theory and Applications of Trapdoor Functions," *Proc. 23rd IEEE Symp. on Foundations of Computer Science*, IEEE Press, pp. 80–91, 1982.
- M. Blum and S. Micali, "How to Generate Cryptographically Strong Sequences of Pseudo-Random Bits," *SIAM J. Comput.* 13 (1984), pp. 850–64.

Detailed accounts of random and pseudo-random numbers appear in:

- D. E. Knuth, *The Art of Computer Programming, vol. 2: Seminumerical Algorithms*, 3rd edn, Addison-Wesley, 1997.
- O. Goldreich and L. Lovasz, *Modern Cryptography, Probabilistic Proofs and Pseudo-randomness*, Springer-Verlag, 1999.

An interesting exposition of some related issues is:

- G. J. Chaitin, "Randomness and Mathematical Proof," *Scientific American* 232:5 (1975), pp. 47–52.

Chapter 12

There are many books that deal extensively with cryptography. Here are some of the ones that provide good treatment of the scientific aspects of the topic:

- A. G. Konheim, *Cryptography: A Primer*, John Wiley & Sons, 1981.
- D. E. R. Denning, *Cryptography and Data Security*, Addison-Wesley, 1982.
- O. Goldreich and L. Lovasz, *Modern Cryptography, Probabilistic Proofs and Pseudo-randomness* , Springer-Verlag, 1999.
- O. Goldreich, *Foundations of Cryptography: Basic Tools*, Cambridge University Press, 2001.

A very useful survey article is:

- R. L. Rivest, "Cryptography," in *Handbook of Theoretical Computer Science*, vol. A, J. van Leeuwen, ed., Elsevier and MIT Press, 1990, pp. 717–55.

There are several periodicals that publish papers on cryptography. Two that are devoted to the subject are:

- *Journal of Cryptology*, abbreviated *J. Crypt.*; published by Springer-Verlag.
- *Cryptologia*; published by the United States Military Academy.

Public-key cryptography [pp. 318–21], together with the idea of using the scheme for signatures [pp. 321–2], was proposed in the following important paper:

- W. Diffie and M. Hellman, "New Directions in Cryptography," *IEEE Trans. Inform. Theory* IT-22 (1976), pp. 644–54.

The RSA cryptosystem [pp. 321–4] is named after its inventors, and appears in:

- R. L. Rivest, A. Shamir, and L. M. Adleman, "A Method for Obtaining Digital Signatures and Public-Key Cryptosystems," *Comm. Assoc. Comput. Mach.* 21 (1978), pp. 120–6.

The version that is provably as difficult to crack as it is to factor large numbers [p. 323] appears in:

- M. O. Rabin, "Digitalized Signatures and Public-Key Functions as Intractable as Factorization," Technical Report MIT/LCS/TR-212, Mass. Inst. of Tech., Cambridge, MA, 1979.

An early expository survey of public-key cryptography is:

- M. E. Hellman, "The Mathematics of Public-Key Cryptography," *Scientific American* 241:2 (1979), pp. 146–57.

The card-dealing protocol [pp. 324–6] appears in:

- A. Shamir, R. L. Rivest, and L. M. Adleman, "Mental Poker," in *The Mathematical Gardner*, D. A. Klarner, ed., Wadsworth International, Belmont, CA, 1981.

That information might leak when cryptographic functions, such as the RSA ones, are used naively in the card dealing protocol [p. 326] was shown in:

- R. J. Lipton, "How to Cheat at Mental Poker," *Proc. AMS Short Course on Cryptology*, American Mathematical Society, 1981.

A more complex probabilistic protocol for dealing cards, which does not suffer from these drawbacks, appears in the following paper:

- S. Goldwasser and S. Micali, "Probabilistic Encryption," *J. Comput. Syst. Sci.* 28 (1984), pp. 270–99.

Three of the many interesting "how to" papers on cryptographic protocols, secret-keeping protocols and similar issues are:

- A. Shamir, "How to Share a Secret," *Comm. Assoc. Comput. Mach.* 22 (1979), pp. 612–13.
- M. Blum, "How to Exchange (Secret) Keys," *ACM Trans. Comput. Syst.* 1 (1983), pp. 175–93.
- A. C. Yao, "How to Generate and Exchange Secrets," *Proc. 27th IEEE Symp. on Foundations of Computer Science*, IEEE Press, pp. 162–7, 1986.

Interactive proofs and zero-knowledge protocols [pp. 327–29] were first considered in:

- S. Goldwasser, S. Micali, and C. Rackoff, "The Knowledge Complexity of Interactive Proof Systems," *SIAM J. Comput.* 18 (1989), pp. 186–208.

For the proof that IP = PSPACE [p. 328], one has to read the following two papers:

- C. Lund, L. Fortnow, H. Karloff, and N. Nisan, "Algebraic Methods for Interactive Proof Systems," *J. Assoc. Comput. Mach.* 39 (1992), pp. 859–68.
- A. Shamir, "IP = PSPACE," *J. Assoc. Comput. Mach.* 39 (1992), pp. 869–77.

The zero-knowledge approach to playing *Where's Waldo* is from:

- M. Naor, Y. Naor, and O. Reingold, "Applied Kid Cryptography, or How to Convince Your Children That You Are Not Cheating," unpublished manuscript, 1999.

The zero-knowledge protocol for three-coloring a graph [pp. 329–32] appears in:

- O. Goldreich, S. Micali, and A. Wigderson, "Proofs that Yield Nothing But Their Validity, or All Languages in NP Have Zero-Knowledge Proof Systems," *J. Assoc. Comput. Mach.* 38 (1991), pp. 691–729.

One of the most important papers on probabilistically checkable proofs [pp. 332–3] is:

- U. Feige, S. Goldwasser, L. Lovász, S. Safra, and M. Szegedy, "Approximating Clique is Almost NP-complete," *J. Assoc. Comput. Mach.*, 43 (1996), pp. 268–92.

The ultimate result on these, that problems in NP can be checked using only a constant number of probed bits, is from:

- S. Arora and S. Safra, "Probabilistic Checking of Proofs: A New Characterization of NP," *J. Assoc. Comput. Mach.*, 45 (1998), pp. 70–122.

Chapter 13

There are many books devoted to the various aspects of software engineering. The two most popular ones are:

- R. S. Pressman, *Software Engineering: A Practitioner's Approach*, 5th edn, McGraw-Hill, 2001.
- I. Sommerville, *Software Engineering*, 6th edn, Addison-Wesley, 2000.

The following books focus on object-oriented software engineering:

- B. Liskov with J. Guttag, *Program Development in Java: Abstraction, Specification, and Object-Oriented Design*, Addison-Wesley, 2000.
- B. Meyer, *Object-Oriented Software Construction*, 2nd edn, Prentice-Hall, 1997.

- I. Jacobson, M. Christerson, P. Jonsson, and G. Övergaard, *Object-Oriented Software Engineering: A Use Case Driven Approach*, Addison-Wesley, 1992.
- B. Bruegge and A. H. Dutoit, *Object-Oriented Software Engineering: Conquering Complex and Changing Systems*, Prentice-Hall, 2000.

The following book concentrates on the economic aspects of software development:

- B. W. Boehm, *Software Engineering Economics*, Prentice-Hall, 1981.

For many years, F. P. Brooks managed some of IBM's largest software projects, including the OS/360 mainframe operating system. His insights from this experience (both good and bad, including the infamous "multi-million dollar mistake") are discussed in his influential book:

- F. P. Brooks, Jr., *The Mythical Man-Month: Essays on Software Engineering*, special anniversary edn, Addison-Wesley, 1995.

The following journals publish articles on software engineering:

- *IEEE Transactions on Software Engineering*, abbreviated *IEEE Trans. Soft. Eng.*; published by the IEEE.
- *ACM Transactions on Software Engineering and Methodology*, abbreviated *ACM Trans. Soft. Eng. Meth.*, or simply *TOSEM*; published by the ACM.
- *IEEE Software*; published by the IEEE.
- *Advances in Engineering Software*, abbreviated *Adv. in Eng. Soft.*; published by Elsevier.
- *Information and Software Technology*, abbreviated *Inf. Soft. Tech.*; published by Elsevier.
- *Software: Practice and Experience*, abbreviated *Softw. Pract. Exp.*; published by John Wiley & Sons.
- *International Journal on Software Tools for Technology Transfer*, abbreviated *Int. J. Soft. Tools for Tech. Transfer*, or simply *STTT*; published by Springer-Verlag.
- *Software and System Modeling*, abbreviated *Soft. Syst. Modeling*, or simply *SoSyM*; published by Springer-Verlag.

A collection of computer-related failures, categorized and analyzed, appears in:

- P. G. Neumann, *Computer-Related Risks*, Addison-Wesley, 1995.

The following monthly column reports on computer-related risks:

- "Inside Risks," *Comm. Assoc. Comput. Mach.*, ACM Press.

An analysis of technology-related accidents used to outline a methodology for building safety-critical systems is:

- N. G. Leveson, *Safeware: System Safety and Computers*, Addison-Wesley, 1995.

The "executive programmers" anecdote, [p. 337] is from page 124 of:

- G. M. Weinberg, *The Psychology of Computer Programming: Silver Anniversary Edition*, Dorset House, 1998.

Extreme programming [pp. 350–1] is discussed in a number of books. The first introduction to the topic is:

- K. Beck, *Extreme Programming Explained*, Addison-Wesley, 2000.

A critical evaluation of extreme programming is:

- P. McBreen, *Questioning Extreme Programming*, Addison-Wesley, 2003.

The concept of refactoring [pp. 350–1] is introduced in:

- M. Fowler, *Refactoring: Improving the Design of Existing Code*, Addison-Wesley, 2000.

The idea of comparing refactoring to paying off debts [p. 350] is due to W. Cunningham, and is quoted on page 222 of:

- A. Cockburn, *Agile Software Development*, Addison-Wesley, 2002.

The technique of pair programming [p. 351] is discussed in depth in:

- L. Williams and R. Kessler, *Pair Programming Illuminated*, Addison-Wesley, 2003.

Psychological issues in software development [pp. 352–3] were introduced in the first edition of Weinberg's book mentioned above, which although first published in 1971 is as relevant now as it was then. Other books on the topic include:

- G. M. Weinberg, *Understanding the Professional Programmer*, Dorset House, 1988.
- T. DeMarco and T. Lister, *Peopleware: Productive Projects and Teams*, 2nd edn, Dorset House, 1999.
- L. L. Constantine, *The Peopleware Papers: Notes on the Human Side of Software*, Prentice-Hall, 2001.

The "vending machines" anecdote [p. 352] is from page 49 of:

- G. M. Weinberg, *The Psychology of Computer Programming: Silver Anniversary Edition*, Dorset House, 1998.

The philosophy behind agile methodologies [p. 352] is explained in Cockburn's book mentioned above.

A view of programmers as individual craftsmen, rather than interchangeable elements in a production line [p. 352], is:

- P. McBreen, *Software Craftsmanship: The New Imperative*, Addison-Wesley, 2000.

An early influential book on ethical aspects of programming [p. 353], written after J. Weizenbaum became dismayed by the way people anthropomorphized his ELIZA program (discussed in Chapter 15), is:

■ J. Weizenbaum, *Computer Power and Human Reason: From Judgment to Calculation*, W. H. Freeman, 1976.

An engaging yet thought-provoking introduction to professional ethics in software development, which also contains extensive further bibliographic references on this topic, is:

■ R. G. Epstein, *The Case of the Killer Robot*, John Wiley & Sons, 1997.

Chapter 14

Some of the general books on software engineering listed in the notes for Chapter 13 contain material relevant to reactive systems too. Here are some books that concentrate on the special difficulties arising in the development of such systems:

■ Z. Manna and A. Pnueli, *The Temporal Logic of Reactive and Concurrent Systems: Specification*, Springer-Verlag, 1992.

■ N. Halbwachs, *Synchronous Programming of Reactive Systems*, Kluwer Academic Publishers, 1993.

■ D. Harel and M. Politi, *Modeling Reactive Systems with Statecharts: The Statemate Approach*, McGraw-Hill, 1998.

■ R. J. Wieringa, *Design Methods for Reactive Systems: Yourdon, Statemate, and the UML*, Morgan Kaufmann, 2002.

■ K. Schneider, *Verification of Reactive Systems: Formal Methods and Algorithms*, Springer-Verlag, 2003.

The periodicals mentioned in the notes for Chapter 13 publish papers on reactive systems too.

The term "reactive system" [pp. 357–8] was first discussed in the following papers:

■ D. Harel and A. Pnueli, "On the Development of Reactive Systems," in *Logics and Models of Concurrent Systems*, K. R. Apt, ed., NATO ASI Series, vol. F-13, Springer-Verlag, pp. 477–98, 1985.

■ A. Pnueli, "Applications of Temporal Logic to the Specification and Verification of Reactive Systems: A Survey of Current Trends," in *Current Trends in Concurrency*, J. de Bakker et al., eds., Lecture Notes in Computer Science, vol. 224, Springer-Verlag, pp. 510–84, 1986.

Visual formalisms [pp. 358–9] are discussed in:

■ D. Harel, "On Visual Formalisms," *Comm. Assoc. Comput. Mach.* 31 (1988), pp. 514–30.

Petri nets [p. 359] were invented by C. A. Petri, and were first described in his influential thesis:

- C. A. Petri, *Kommunikation mit Automaten*, PhD thesis, Institut für Instrumentelle Mathematik, Bonn, 1962.

There are many books and papers about them; two of the best accounts are:

- W. Reisig, *Petri Nets: An Introduction*, Springer-Verlag, 1985.
- W. Reisig, *Elements of Distributed Algorithms: Modeling and Analysis with Petri Nets*, Springer-Verlag, 1998.

SDL diagrams [p. 359] were part of a 1976 standard originating in the International Telecommunication Union (ITU; formerly the CCITT). For an updated version, see:

- "ITU-T Recommendation Z.100: Formal Description Techniques (FDT)— Specification and Description Language (SDL)," International Telecommunication Union (ITU), Geneva, 1999.

Esterel [p. 359] was described in:

- G. Berry and G. Gonthier, "The Esterel Synchronous Programming Language: Design, Semantics, Implementation," *Sci. Comput. Program.* 19 (1992), pp. 87–152.

See also:

- G. Berry, "The Foundations of Esterel," in *Proof, Language, and Interaction: Essays in Honour of Robin Milner*, G. Plotkin, C. Stirling, and M. Tofte, eds., MIT Press, 2000, pp. 425–54.

Lustre [p. 359] is described in:

- P. Caspi, D. Pilaud, N. Halbwachs, and J. Plaice, "Lustre: A Declarative Language for Programming Synchronous Systems," *Proc. 14th Symp. on Principles of Programming Languages*, ACM Press, pp. 178–88, 1987.
- N. Halbwachs, P. Caspi, P. Raymond and D. Pilaud, "The Synchronous Dataflow Programming Language Lustre, *Proc. of the IEEE* 79 (1991), pp. 1305–20.

A detailed account can be found in Halbwach's book cited earlier.
Signal [p. 359] was described in:

- A. Benveniste and P. Le Guernic, "Hybrid Dynamical Systems Theory and the Signal Language," *IEEE Trans. on Automatic Control*, AC-35 (1990), pp. 535–46.

A good survey of it can be found in:

- P. Le Guernic, T. Gautier, M. Le Borgne, and C. Le Maire, "Programming Real-Time Applications with Signal," *Proc. of the IEEE* 79 (1991), pp. 1321–36.

An interesting account of such so-called *synchronous languages* can be found in:

- A. Benveniste, P. Caspi, S. A. Edwards, N. Halbwachs, P. Le Guernic and R. de Simone, "The Synchronous Languages Twelve Years Later," *Proc. of the IEEE* 91 (2003), pp. 64–83.

Two extremely influential approaches to specifying concurrency and interaction (which are therefore directly relevant to reactivity) are CSP and CCS. They are due, respectively, to C. A. R. Hoare and R. Milner. They are described in detail in these authors' books, listed in the notes for Chapter 10.

Statecharts [pp. 359–62] were introduced in the following paper, which also discusses the drawbacks of classical state diagrams and contains (a more intricate version of) the digital watch example [pp. 360–2]:

- D. Harel, "Statecharts: A Visual Formalism for Complex Systems," *Sci. Comput. Prog.* 8 (1987) pp. 231–74.

There are several full-fledged computerized tools that are able to execute system models based on visual formalisms and to generate running code from them [p. 359]. The earliest was released in 1987, and is described in:

- D. Harel, H. Lachover, A. Naamad, A. Pnueli, M. Politi, R. Sherman, A. Shtul-Trauring, and M. Trakhtenbrot, "STATEMATE: A Working Environment for the Development of Complex Reactive Systems," *IEEE Trans. on Software Engineering* 16 (1990), pp. 403–14.

The discussion of model execution and code generation [pp. 362–5] is adapted from:

- D. Harel, "Biting the Silver Bullet: Toward a Brighter Future for System Development," *Computer* 25:1 (1992), IEEE Press, pp. 8–20.

Verification of complex reactive behavior [pp. 364–5] is discussed in Schneider's book listed earlier. Here are a few of the many papers on the subject:

- N. Bjorner et al., "STeP: Deductive-Algorithmic Verification of Reactive and Real-time Systems," *Proc. Int. Conf. on Computer Aided Verification*, Lecture Notes in Computer Science, vol. 1102, Springer-Verlag, pp. 415–18, 1996.
- T. Bienmller, W. Damm, and H. Wittke, "The STATEMATE Verification Environment—Making it Real," *Proc. 12th Int. Conf. on Computer Aided Verification*, Lecture Notes in Computer Science, vol. 1855, Springer-Verlag, pp. 561–7, 2000.
- F. Levi, "Compositional Verification of Quantitative Properties of Statecharts," *J. of Logic and Computation* 11 (2001), pp. 829–78.

A system that records histories that include causes, and can thus help debugging systems by answering "why," "why not," and "what if" questions [p. 364], is described in:

- Y. A. Feldman and H. Schneider, "Simulating Reactive Systems by Deduction," *ACM Trans. Soft. Eng. Meth.* 2 (1993), pp. 128–75.

Object-oriented modeling, with its use of object model diagrams and statecharts [pp. 366–7], was given a significant push by the following two influential books:

- J. Rumbaugh, M. Blaha, W. Premerlani, F. Eddy, and W. Lorenson, *Object-Oriented Modeling and Design*, Prentice-Hall, 1990.

- G. Booch, *Object-Oriented Analysis and Design with Applications*, 2nd edn, Addison-Wesley, 1993.

The first tools that were able to execute object-oriented models based on visual formalisms and to generate running code from them, were ObjecTime and Rhapsody. They are described, respectively, in:

- B. Selic, G. Gullekson, and P. T. Ward, *Real-Time Object-Oriented Modeling*, John Wiley & Sons, 1994.
- D. Harel and E. Gery, "Executable Object Modeling with Statecharts," *Computer* 30:7 (1997), IEEE Press, pp. 31–42.

Message sequence charts (MSCs) [pp. 368–9] were developed as a standard by the International Telecommunication Union (ITU; formerly the CCITT). A recent report on them appears in:

- "ITU-TS Recommendation Z.120: Formal Description Techniques (FDT)—Message Sequence Chart (MSC)," International Telecommunication Union (ITU), Geneva, 1996.

Use cases are described and discussed extensively in:

- I. Jacobson, M. Christerson, P. Jonsson, and G. Övergaard, *Object-Oriented Software Engineering: A Use Case Driven Approach*, Addison-Wesley, 1992.

Live sequence charts (LSCs) [pp. 370–3] were defined in the following paper, which also discusses the drawbacks of MSCs in specifying actual system behavior:

- W. Damm and D. Harel, "LSCs: Breathing Life into Message Sequence Charts," *Formal Methods in System Design* 19 (2001), pp. 45–80.

Play-in, play-out, and the Play-Engine tool [pp. 373–5] are described in detail in:

- D. Harel and R. Marelly, *Come, Let's Play: Scenario-Based Programming Using LSCs and the Play-Engine*, Springer-Verlag, 2003.

That book also defines extensions of LSCs for dealing with symbolic instances and time [p. 374], and provides an operational semantics for the extended LSCs language.
Smart play-out [p. 374] is described in:

- D. Harel, H. Kugler, R. Marelly, and A. Pnueli, "Smart Play-Out of Behavioral Requirements," *Proc. 4th Int. Conf. on Formal Methods in Computer-Aided Design*, Lecture Notes in Computer Science, vol. 2517, Springer-Verlag, pp. 378–98, 2002.

There are many books on real-time systems [pp. 375–6]. Here are some:

- H. Kopetz, *Real-Time Systems: Design Principles for Distributed Embedded Applications*, Kluwer Academic Publishers, 1997.
- J. W. S. Liu, *Real-Time Systems*, Prentice-Hall, 2000.
- Q. Li with C. Yao, *Real-Time Concepts for Embedded Systems*, CMP Books, 2003.

The MASS specification formalism for real-time systems [pp. 375–6] is from:

- V. Gafni, A. Yehudai, and Y. A. Feldman, "Activation-Oriented Specification of Real-time Systems," *Proc. 3rd Int. School and Symposium on Formal Techniques in Real Time and Fault Tolerant Systems*, pp. 19–23, 1994.

The UML [pp. 376–7] is described in numerous books and papers, including the following:

- J. Rumbaugh, I. Jacobson, and G. Booch, *The Unified Modeling Language Reference Manual*, Addison-Wesley, 1999.
- M. Fowler with K. Scott, *UML Distilled: A Brief Guide to the Standard Object Modeling Language*, 2nd edn, Addison-Wesley, 1999.

Up-to-date versions of the UML are described in great detail on the website of the object management group (OMG):

- http://www.omg.org

Some of the many attempts at providing parts of the UML with rigorous semantics [pp. 376–7] appear in:

- R. Eshuis and R. J. Wieringa, "Requirements-Level Semantics for UML Statecharts," *Proc. 4th Int. Conf. on Formal Methods for Open Object-Based Distributed Systems*, Kluwer, pp. 121–40, 2000.
- G. Reggio, M. Cerioli, and E. Astesiano, "Towards a Rigorous Semantics of UML Supporting its Multiview Approach," *Fundamental Approaches to Software Engineering*, Lecture Notes in Computer Science, vol. 2029, Springer-Verlag, pp. 171–86, 2001.
- I. Ober, "An ASM Semantics of UML Derived from the Meta-model and Incorporating Actions," *Proc. 10th Int. Workshop on Abstract State Machines*, Lecture Notes in Computer Science, vol. 2589, Springer-Verlag, pp. 356–71, 2003.
- W. Damm, B. Josko, A. Pnueli, and A. Votintseva, "Understanding UML: A Formal Semantics of Concurrency and Communication in Real-Time UML," *Proc. Formal Methods for Components and Objects*, Lecture Notes in Computer Science, vol. 2852, Springer-Verlag, pp. 71–98, 2003.

Synthesizing state machines from rich behavioral requirements—most often from temporal logic—is a topic that has been discussed extensively in the literature. Synthesizing from LSCs [p. 377] was addressed in:

- D. Harel and H. Kugler, "Synthesizing State-Based Object Systems from LSC Specifications," *Int. J. of Foundations of Computer Science* 13 (2002), pp. 5–51.

Some of the possibilities raised by the idea of viewing biological systems as reactive systems are discussed in:

- D. Harel, "A Grand Challenge for Computing: Full Reactive Modeling of a Multi-Cellular Animal," *EATCS Bulletin*, European Association for Theoretical Computer Science, no. 81, pp. 226–35, 2003.

◼ Chapter 15

There are numerous books on artificial intelligence (AI). Here are some:

- N. J. Nilsson, *Artificial Intelligence: A New Synthesis*, Morgan Kaufmann, 1998.
- P. H. Winston, *Artificial Intelligence*, 3rd edn, Addison-Wesley, 1992.
- E. Rich and R. Knight, *Artificial Intelligence*, 2nd edn, McGraw-Hill, 1990.
- S. Russel and P. Norvig, *Artificial Intelligence: A Modern Approach*, 2nd edn, Prentice-Hall, 2002.
- E. Charniak and D. McDermott, *Introduction to Artificial Intelligence*, Addison-Wesley, 1985.
- T. Dean, J. Allen, and Y. Aloimonos, *Artificial Intelligence: Theory and Practice*, Pearson Education, 2002.

Two encyclopedic compilations of early articles on artificial intelligence are:

- *The Handbook of Artificial Intelligence*, 4 vols, A. Barr, P. R. Cohen, and E. A. Feigenbaum, eds., Addison-Wesley, 1981, 1982, 1989.
- *The Encyclopedia of Artificial Intelligence*, 2 vols, 2nd edn, S. C. Shapiro, ed., John Wiley & Sons, 1992.

A good early exposition of the subject is:

- D. L. Waltz, "Artificial Intelligence," *Scientific American* 247:4 (1982), pp. 118–33.

In addition to these, there are numerous books and papers that discuss the social, philosophical, and historical aspects of computerized intelligence. Some of the most interesting and provocative of these are:

- J. R. Lucas, "Minds, Machines, and Gödel," *Philosophy* 36 (1961), pp.112–17.
- H. Dreyfus, *What Computers Can't Do: The Limits of Artificial Intelligence*, revised edn, Harper & Row, 1979.
- H. Dreyfus, *What Computers Still Can't Do: A Critique of Artificial Reason*, MIT Press, 1992.
- Y. Wilks, "Dreyfus's Disproofs,"*British J. Philos. Sci.* 27 (1976), pp. 177–85.
- D. R. Hofstadter, *Gödel, Escher, Bach: An Eternal Golden Braid*, Basic Books, 1979.
- S. Turkle, *The Second Self: Computers and the Human Spirit*, Simon & Schuster, 1984.
- H. Gardner, *Frames of Mind: The Theory of Multiple Intelligences* , 10th edn, Basic Books, 1993.
- J. V. Grabiner, "Computers and The Nature of Man: A Historian's Perspective on Controversies about Artificial Intelligence," *Bull. Amer. Math. Soc.* 15 (1986), pp. 113–26.
- R. Penrose, *The Emperor's New Mind: Concerning Computers, Minds, and the Laws of Physics*, Penguin Books, 1999.
- J. R. Searle, *Minds, Brains, and Science*, Harvard University Press, 1984.

The following books contain some of the original papers in the field of AI, including influential papers by A. Turing, A. Newell, M. Minsky, and H. A. Simon:

- *Computers and Thought*, E. A. Feigenbaum and J. Feldman, eds., McGraw-Hill, 1961.
- *Semantic Information Processing*, M. Minsky, ed., MIT Press, 1968.
- *Readings in Artificial Intelligence*, B. L. Webber and N. J. Nilsson, eds., Morgan Kaufmann, 1994.
- *Readings in Knowledge Representation*, R. J. Brachman and H. J. Levesque, eds., Morgan Kaufmann, 1985.
- *Mind Design II: Philosophy, Psychology, and Artificial Intelligence*, J. Haugeland, ed., MIT Press, 2000.

An influential early book is:

- A. Newell and H. A. Simon, *Human Problem Solving*, Prentice-Hall, 1972.

An interesting theory of intelligence, put forward by one of the founders of the field is presented in:

- M. Minsky, *The Society of Mind*, Simon & Schuster, 1987.

An interesting account of the early history of AI is:

- P. McCorduck, *Machines Who Think*, W. H. Freeman & Co., 1979.

The following are some of the many periodicals that publish papers about AI:

- *Artificial Intelligence*, abbreviated *Artif. Intel.*; published by Elsevier.
- *Cognitive Science*, abbreviated *Cogn. Sci.*; published by the Cognitive Science Society, Inc.
- *Computational Intelligence*, abbreviated *Comput. Intel.*; published by Blackwell.
- *IEEE Transactions on Systems, Man and Cybernetics*, abbreviated *IEEE Trans. Syst., Man, Cybern.*; published by the IEEE.
- *IEEE Transactions on Pattern Analysis and Machine Intelligence*, abbreviated *IEEE Trans. Pat. Anal. Mach. Intel.*; published by the IEEE.
- *International Journal of Pattern Recognition and AI*, abbreviated *Int. J. Patt. Recog. AI*; published by World Scientific.
- *Computers and Artificial Intelligence*, abbreviated *Comput. Art. Intel.*; published by the Slovak Academy of Sciences.

In addition, the following publish short papers, anecdotes, and announcements relevant to AI:

- *ACM SIGART Newsletter*; published by ACM's Special Interest Group on Artificial Intelligence.
- *The AISB Quarterly*; published by the Society for the Study of Artificial Intelligence and the Simulation of Behaviour (SSAISB).

The aphorism relating thinking computers to swimming submarines [p. 379] is due to E. W. Dijkstra. The term artificial intelligence [p. 379] is generally believed to have been coined by J. McCarthy in 1956. The two robot stories [p. 380] were related by a member of the AI Laboratory at the Massachusetts Institute of Technology.

The following paper by Alan Turing is considered to be one of the most insightful and fundamental papers on AI. It outlines and then counters several standard arguments against AI [p. 381], and goes on to propose the Turing test [pp. 382–5]:

- A. M. Turing, "Computing Machinery and Intelligence," *Mind* 59 (1950), pp. 433–60. (Reprinted on pp. 11–35 of the aforementioned book, *Computers and Thought*).

Most of the books on AI contain discussions of the Turing test and elaborations thereof.

ELIZA [pp. 383–4] was written by J. Weizenbaum, and is described in the following influential paper:

- J. Weizenbaum, "ELIZA—A Computer Program for the Study of Natural Language Communication between Man and Machine," *Comm. Assoc. Comput. Mach.* 9 (1966), pp. 36–45.

The hypothetical exchange concerning zupchoks [pp. 384–5] was inspired by a similar one (concerning cyborgs) that appears on page 317 of:

- I. Pohl and A. Shaw, *The Nature of Computation: An Introduction to Computer Science*, Computer Science Press, 1981.

Searle's Chinese room argument [p. 385] was first presented in:

- J. Searle, "Minds, Brains, and Programs," *Behavioral and Brain Sciences* 3 (1980), pp. 417–57.

The AI books listed earlier discuss game playing and game trees [pp. 385–8] in detail. The "artificial flight" analogy [p. 386] is taken from the first of the following two books, and also appears in somewhat different form in the second:

- S. Russel and P. Norvig, *Artificial Intelligence: A Modern Approach*, 2nd edn, Prentice-Hall, 2002.
- R. A. Brooks, *Cambrian Intelligence*, MIT Press, 1999.

The following are collections of papers on game playing by computers, including papers on chess, checkers, backgammon, Go, and other games:

- *Chess, Computers, and Cognition*, T. Marsland and J. Schaeffer, eds., Springer-Verlag, 1990.
- *Computer Games*, 2 vols., D. N. L. Levy, ed., Springer-Verlag, 1988.

An interesting expository article about computerized backgammon [p. 386] is:

- H. Berliner, "Computer Backgammon," *Scientific American* 242:6 (1980), pp. 64–72.

An account of the program beating the world champion in backgammon [p. 386] appears in:

- H. Berliner, "Backgammon Computer Program Beats World Champion," *Artif. Intel.* 14 (1980), pp. 205–20.

The following extremely important early papers on computerized checkers [p. 386] describe a system that actually learns:

- A. L. Samuel, "Some Studies in Machine Learning using the Game of Checkers," *IBM J. Res. Develop.* 3 (1959), pp. 211–29. (Reprinted on pp. 71–105 of the aforementioned book, *Computers and Thought*.)
- A. L. Samuel, "Some Studies in Machine Learning using the Game of Checkers. II—Recent Progress," *IBM J. Res. Develop.* 11 (1967), pp. 601–17.

A candid account of the construction of the program Chinook and the events leading to its becoming the checkers world champion, appears in:

- J. Schaeffer, *One Jump Ahead: Challenging Human Supremacy in Checkers*, Springer-Verlag, 1997.

Good places to read about computerized chess [pp. 386–8], including the highly publicized matches between Kasparov and Deep Blue, are:

- D. Levy and M. Newborn, *How Computers Play Chess*, Computer Science Press, 1991.
- B. Pandolfini, *Kasparov and Deep Blue: The Historic Chess Match Between Man and Machine*, Fireside, 1997.
- M. Newborn, *Deep Blue: An Artificial Intelligence Milestone*, Springer-Verlag, 2003.

The story about searching for a contact lens [p. 388] was inspired by page 318 of Pohl and Shaw's book mentioned above.

Some of the early influential books on computerized vision and robotics [p. 389] are:

- D. Marr, *Vision: A Computational Investigation into the Human Representation and Processing of Visual Information*, W. H. Freeman & Co., 1982.
- B. K. P. Horn, *Robot Vision*, MIT Press, 1986.
- S. Ullman, *The Interpretation of Visual Motion*, MIT Press, 1979.
- J. J. Craig, *Introduction to Robotics: Mechanics and Control*, Addison-Wesley, 1985.
- R. P. Paul, *Robot Manipulators: Mathematics, Programming, and Control*, MIT Press, 1981.

More up-to-date books include:

- D. A. Forsyth and J. Ponce, *Computer Vision: A Modern Approach*, Prentice-Hall, 2002.
- S. Ullman, *High-Level Vision: Object Recognition and Visual Cognition*, MIT Press, 1996.
- R. Jain, R. Kasturi, and B. G. Schunck, *Machine Vision*, McGraw-Hill, 1995.
- V. S. Nalwa, *A Guided Tour of Computer Vision*, Addison-Wesley, 1993.
- O. Faugeras, *Three-Dimensional Computer Vision: A Geometric Viewpoint*, MIT Press, 1993.

- P. J. McKerrow, *Introduction to Robotics*, Addison-Wesley, 1991.
- R. C. Arkin, *Behavior-Based Robotics*, MIT Press, 1998.
- R. R. Murphy, *An Introduction to AI Robotics*, MIT Press, 2000.

There are also many periodicals devoted to vision and robotics. Some examples are:

- *International Journal of Computer Vision*, abbreviated *Int. J. Comput. Vis.*; published by Kluwer Academic Publishers.
- *Computer Vision and Image Understanding*; published by Elsevier.
- *Journal of Robotic Systems*, abbreviated *J. Robot. Syst.*; published by John Wiley & Sons.
- *International Journal of Robotics Research*, abbreviated *Int. J. Robot. Res.*; published by Sage Publications.

Virtually every textbook on AI discusses the minimax idea and its corresponding algorithm—the alpha-beta procedure [pp. 390–2]. The term "alpha-beta procedure" appears to be due to J. McCarthy, and the use of the minimax idea in searching goes back to Shannon's important paper:

- C. E. Shannon, "Programming of a Computer for Playing Chess," *Phil. Magazine* 41 (1950), pp. 256–75.

A thorough and detailed account of heuristic search procedures, including their mathematical analysis and history, is:

- J. Pearl, *Heuristics: Intelligent Search Strategies for Computer Problem Solving*, Addison-Wesley, 1984.

The collection edited by Brachman and Levesque cited above is devoted to the problem of knowledge representation [pp. 392–3], a topic discussed in many additional books and papers.

The following contain a wealth of material on expert systems [pp. 393–4]:

- R. Duda and E. Shortliffe, "Expert Systems Research," *Science* 220 (1983), pp. 261–8.
- *Building Expert Systems*, F. Hayes-Roth et al., eds., Addison-Wesley, 1983.
- D. A. Waterman, *A Guide to Expert Systems*, Addison-Wesley, 1986.
- P. Jackson, *Introduction to Expert Systems*, 3rd edn, Addison-Wesley, 1999.
- J. C. Giarratano, *Expert Systems: Principles and Programming*, 3rd edn, Brooks Cole, 1998.

The following books and collections of papers concentrate on computerized learning [pp. 394–5]:

- T. Mitchell, *Machine Learning*, McGraw-Hill, 1987.
- S. M. Weiss and C. A. Kulikowsky, *Computer Systems That Learn*, Morgan Kaufmann, 1991.
- M. J. Kearns and U. V. Vazirani, *An Introduction to Computational Learning Theory*, MIT Press, 1994.

- *Machine Learning: An Artificial Intelligence Approach*, R. S. Michalski et al., eds., Tioga Publishing Co., 1983.
- *Machine Learning: An Artificial Intelligence Approach*, vol. II, R. S. Michalski et al., eds., Morgan Kaufmann Publishers, 1986.

Two influential early papers on computerized deduction [pp. 394–5] are:

- A. Newell and H. A. Simon, "The Logic Theory Machine," *IRE Trans. Infor. Theory* IT-2 (1956), pp. 61–79.
- H. Gelernter, "Realization of a Geometry Theorem-Proving Machine," *Proc. Western Joint Computer Conf.*, WJCC, pp. 273–82, 1959.

The behavior-based approach to AI [pp. 395–6] is described in:

- R. A. Brooks, *Cambrian Intelligence*, MIT Press, 1999.
- R. A. Brooks, *Flesh and Machines: How Robots Will Change Us*, Pantheon Books, 2002.

The predictions for the future of AI [p. 397] are from:

- R. Kurzweil, *The Age of Spiritual Machines: When Computers Exceed Human Intelligence*, Penguin, 2000.

Here are some books and collections of papers that describe the problems and achievements in the computerized understanding of natural language [pp. 397–400]:

- J. Allen, *Natural Language Understanding*, 2nd edn, Addison-Wesley, 1995.
- *Natural Language Processing and Knowledge Representation: Language for Knowledge and Knowledge for Language*, L. M. Iwanska and S. C. Shapiro, eds., AAAI Press, 2000.
- R. Schank, *The Cognitive Computer: On Language, Learning, and Artificial Intelligence*, Addison-Wesley, 1984.
- J. F. Sowa, *Conceptual Structures: Information Processing in Mind and Machine*, Addison-Wesley, 1983.

Important early work on the subject is described in:

- T. Winograd, *Understanding Natural Language*, Academic Press, 1972.

Hearing the pledge of allegiance as having to do with pigeons [p. 397] is an idea used by W. Safire in one of his "On Language" columns in *The New York Times* many years ago.

The discussions with Jim's phone [pp. 399–400] are based on those appearing in the following delightful essay:

- R. W. Lucky, "The Phone Surrogate," *IEEE Spectrum* 23:5 (1986), p. 6.

It was reprinted in:

- R. W. Lucky, *Lucky Strikes . . . Again*, IEEE Press, New York, 1993.

An interesting paper relevant to the remarks about analytic AI [p. 400] is:

- A. Goldberg and I. Pohl, "Is Complexity Theory of Use to AI?" in *Artificial and Human Intelligence*, A. Elithorn and R. Banerji, eds., Elsevier Science, 1984.

A somewhat different approach to solving some of the problems raised in the chapter, dubbed *connectionism*, and related to neural networks, is described in:

- D. E. Rumelhart, J. L. McClelland, and the PDP Research Group, *Parallel Distributed Processing: Explorations in the Microstructure of Cognition, vol. 1: Foundations*, MIT Press, 1986.

An exposition of some of the ideas can be found in:

- D. W. Tank and J. J. Hopfield, "Collective Computation in Neuronlike Circuits," *Scientific American* 257:6 (1987), pp. 62–70.

Of making many books there is no end
ECCLESIASTES 12: 12

Index

For I am full of words

JOB 32: 18